Conservation of Natural Resources

A Resource Management Approach

Conservation of Natural Resources

A Resource Management Approach

David A. Castillon

Southwest Missouri State University

Book Team

Editor *Jeffrey L. Hahn*
Developmental Editor *Lynne M. Meyers*
Production Editor *Kay J. Brimeyer*
Art Editor *Carla Goldhammer*
Photo Editor *Robin Storm*
Permissions Editor *Karen L. Storlie*
Visuals Processor *Andréa Lopez-Meyer*

WCB Wm. C. Brown Publishers

President *G. Franklin Lewis*
Vice President, Publisher *George Wm. Bergquist*
Vice President, Operations and Production *Beverly Kolz*
National Sales Manager *Virginia S. Moffat*
Group Sales Manager *Vincent R. Di Blasi*
Vice President, Editor in Chief *Edward G. Jaffe*
Marketing Manager *John W. Calhoun*
Advertising Manager *Amy Schmitz*
Managing Editor, Production *Colleen A. Yonda*
Manager of Visuals and Design *Faye M. Schilling*
Production Editorial Manager *Julie A. Kennedy*
Production Editorial Manager *Ann Fuerste*
Publishing Services Manager *Karen J. Slaght*

WCB Group

President and Chief Executive Officer *Mark C. Falb*
Chairman of the Board *Wm. C. Brown*

Cover photograph: © L. Proser/Superstock, Inc.

Copyright © 1992 by Wm. C. Brown Publishers. All rights reserved

Library of Congress Catalog Card Number: 91-70378

ISBN 0-697-11229-2

No part of this publication may be reproduced, stored in a retrieval system, or transmitted, in any form or by any means, electronic, mechanical, photocopying, recording, or otherwise, without the prior written permission of the publisher.

Printed in the United States of America by Wm. C. Brown Publishers, 2460 Kerper Boulevard, Dubuque, IA 52001

10 9 8 7 6 5 4 3 2 1

Dedicated to the Memory of My Son

David Alan Castillon II
Dec. 17, 1968–Nov. 23, 1986

Shane
April 22, 1977–July 10, 1990

Contents

Preface xi
Acknowledgements xv

Part One

Physical and Biological Variables of the Natural Environment

1 Introduction to the Conservation of Natural Resources 5

Introduction 5
Brief History of Conservation 7
Natural Resources 11
    Inexhaustible Resources 11
    Renewable Resources 12
    Nonrenewable Resources 12
    Potential Resources 13
Time 13
    Geologic Time versus Biologic Time 13
    Future Time 16
The Biotic Pyramid 16
    The Laws of the Biosphere 18
        Law of Production 18
        Law of Adaptation 18
        Law of Fertility 18
        Law of Succession 20
        Law of Control 20
Summary 21

2 Lithosphere—Geology 25
Introduction 25
Composition of the Lithosphere 26
  Lithology 27
Endogenic Processes 27
  Sea Level 29
  Lithologic Circulation 31
  A Sunless Ecosystem 32
  Mount St. Helens 32
Exogenic Processes 33
  Continental Glaciation 35
Topography 37
The Biosphere through Geologic Time 38
Natural Geologic Hazards 39
Summary 41

3 Atmosphere—Climate 43
Introduction 43
Solar Energy 43
Atmosphere—Composition and Properties 47
  Atmospheric Circulation 49
Climate 50
  The Köppen System 51
  Climatic Extremes 54
  Climate Change 56
The Greenhouse Effect 57
The Ozone Problem 59
Summary 61

4 Hydrosphere—Water 63
Introduction 63
Changing States of Water 63
Hydrologic Cycle 64
Oceanic Circulation 66
Composition of the Hydrosphere 67
The Aquatic Environments 68
  Freshwater Environments 69
    Lakes 69
    Lake Zones 71
    The Acid Rain Problem 71
    Streams 74
    The Missouri River 74
  Saltwater Environments 77
    The Ocean Basins 80
    Ocean Dumping 83
  Groundwater 85
Summary 88

5 Soil 91
Introduction 91
Definition of Soil 93
  Soil Horizons 93
Soil Formation 95
  Podzolization 96
  Laterization 96
  Calcification 96

Gleization 98
Invertization 98
Soil Classification and Soil Geography 98
Soil Biota 101
Soil Erosion 102
Irrigation 104
Wetlands 106
Summary 108

6 Biosphere—Biogeography 111
Introduction 111
Energy Flow in the Biosphere 112
  Chemical Element Cycles of the Earth 113
    The Carbon Cycle 114
    The Oxygen Cycle 115
    The Nitrogen Cycle 116
    The Sedimentary Cycle 117
Biogeography of North America 117
  Natural Biotic Regions 118
  Climate as a Control in Biogeography 119
  Horizontal and Vertical Zonation of Vegetation 123
  Biologic Productivity 130
Ecoregions of North America 131
  Tropical 134
  Tropical Savanna 136
  Subtropical 138
  Hot Continental 140
  Warm Continental 142
  Subarctic 144
  Tundra 146
  Prairie 148
  Steppe 150
  Desert 152
  Marine 154
  Mediterranean 156
Summary 158

Part Two

Natural Resources Management

7 Introduction to Natural Resources Management 163
Introduction 163
The Technology of Resource Management 164
  Remote Sensing 164
    Remote Sensing of the Lithosphere 166
    Remote Sensing of the Atmosphere 168
    Remote Sensing of the Hydrosphere 171
    Remote Sensing of the Biosphere 172
  Geographic Information Systems 175
  Environmental Monitoring 176
Resource Management 177
A General Plan for Natural Resource Management 177
Summary 178

8 Forest Management 181
Introduction 181
The Forest Resource 181
Forest Fires 184
   Controlled Burning as a Forest Management Tool 185
U.S. Forest Service 185
   Sustained Yield 186
      Even-Aged Management 186
      Uneven-Aged Management 186
   Forest Service 50-Year Plans 188
Wilderness 190
National Parks 192
Forest Management Practices 194
   A Forest Management Cycle 194
   Timber Stand Improvement for Small Woodlots 195
Summary 197

9 Agricultural Management 199
Introduction 199
Pesticides 201
   Alternative Pest Controls 204
   Agricultural Chemicals in Groundwater Strategy 204
   Integrated Pest Management (IPM) 204
Farming Without Chemicals 205
The Food Security Act 209
   Conservation Reserve Program (CRP) 209
   Conservation Compliance 209
   Sodbuster 209
   Swampbuster 209
   Drought of 1988 209
   1990 Farm Bill 210
Climate as a Control in Agriculture 210
Soil Fertility 211
   Organic Matter Content—pH 211
   Nitrogen 211
   Phosphorus 211
   Potassium 213
Summary 213

10 Rangeland Management 215
Introduction 215
Brief History of Rangeland Use and Abuse 217
Public Lands 218
   Forest Service Rangeland Policy 219
   Bureau of Land Management 220
   Overgrazing 221
Rangeland Biogeography 222
Rangeland Management 226
   Feral Horses and Asses 227
Summary 229

11 Wildlife Management 231
Introduction 231
Legislation to Protect Wildlife 232
   Wildlife Restoration Act 234
   Endangered Species Act 234
Wildlife Management Techniques 235
   Whooping Crane 236
   Eastern Wild Turkey 238
   White-Tailed Deer 242
   Ring-Necked Pheasant 244
   Modern Medicine in Wildlife Management 246
Summary 247

12 Aquatic Resources Management 249
Introduction 249
Aquatic Resources Legislation 250
   State Game Laws to Protect the Fisheries Resource 252
Stream Management 252
   Stream Habitat Improvement 253
   Channelization 256
   Stocking Fish as a Management Practice 256
Pond Management 261
   Fish Farming 263
Lake Management 264
   Great Lakes 266
   Corps of Engineer Impoundments 268
Waterfowl Management 270
Summary 276

13 Energy Management 277
Introduction 277
Fossil Fuels 278
   Oil 279
      The North Slope Alaskan Oil Field 279
      The Arctic National Wildlife Refuge (ANWR) 283
      Exxon Valdez 283
      American Trader 284
   Natural Gas 286
   Coal 287
      The Surface Mining Control and Reclamation Act of 1977 289
Nuclear Energy 291
   The Shippingport Nuclear Reactor Funeral 295
Geothermal Energy 297
Solar Energy 298
   Hydropower 305
   Wind Power 306
Energy Management 307
Summary 309

14 Mineral Resources 311
Introduction 311
Metallic Minerals 311
   Abundant Metals 312
     Iron 314
     Aluminum 315
     Magnesium 316
     Titanium 317
     Manganese 317
   Scarce Metals 318
     Copper, Lead, Zinc, and Nickel 320
     Gold, Silver, and Platinoids 321
Management Strategies for Industry 323
   Underground Mining 324
Nonmetallic Minerals 325
   Building Materials 325
     Stone 325
     Sand and Gravel 326
     Cement 328
     Plaster 328
   Fertilizer and Chemical Minerals 328
     Nitrogen 329
     Phosphorus 329
     Potash (Potassium) 330
     Halite 331
     Sulfur 333
Summary 334

15 Waste Management 337
Introduction 337
Source Reduction 338
Waste-to-Energy Plants 340
Landfills 341
Hazardous Waste Management 342
   Household Hazardous Waste 343
   Industrial Waste Management 345
     Superfund 345
     RCRAs Rules 346
Wastewater Treatment 347
   Sludge as a Resource 350
Recycling 351
   Paper 352
     Paper Recycling at WCB Publishers 352
   Plastic 352
Summary 355

Part Three

People—Land Ethics—Global Sustainability

16 The Human Resource 361
Introduction 361
The Peopling of North America 362
Population Dynamics 362
Human Carrying Capacity 364
Dealing with Population Increases 366
   Birth Control 366
   Family Planning 366
Urbanization of the Human Population 367
   Urban Growth 369
   ZPG's Urban Stress Test 370
     The Environmental Index of the UST 371
   Urban Planning 371
   Land Controls 374
Sustainability 376
A Global View 378
   Biodiversity 380
Ethics 381
   Land Ethics 382
Summary 383

Appendices

A1 Periodic Chart of the Elements 385
A2 Relative Percentages of Elements in the Earth's Spheres 386
B Geologic Time and Formations 387
C Units of Measurement Metric/English Conversions 388
D Köppen Climate Classification Chart 390
E The National Wilderness Preservation System 1964–1989 391
F How to Write Your Elected Officials 403
G List of Environmental Organizations 404
H United States Government Agencies 406
I Environmental Publications 407
J Important United States Environmental Legislation 409
K Environmental Literacy Test with Answers 410
L Basic Geographic Data on Canada, Mexico, and the United States 412
M Acronyms Used in this Text 418
N Threatened and Endangered Species List for the United States 419
Index 424

Preface

Introduction

Conservation of natural resources will have new meaning in the 1990s. Almost every university in North America introduced a course into their curriculum in the 1960s, if they didn't already have one, in response to the environmental movement of that time period. Many books were written to supply these classes with material, although most books carried the pessimistic message of environmental degradation. The pessimism of the 1960s gave way to the programs of the 1970s, which began with the first Earth Day on April 22, 1970. The legislation to affect environmental improvement is in place and, in most cases, is working. The many success stories of the previous three decades have given the environmental movement an optimism it has never had before. It is in keeping with this optimism that this book is written as we move through the 1990s, **The Decade of the Environment,** and attempt to continue our successful programs in the Conservation of Natural Resources.

Wm. C. Brown Publishers is committed to improved conservation methods in their publishing business. A discussion of their recycling program is given in chapter 15. This is one of the first books published by WCB on recycled paper.

Purpose

The purpose of this book is to expose you, the reader, to the ecological processes and problems related to our physical environment, so that conservation of natural resources will have new meaning to you as an inhabitant of North

America and Planet Earth. To accomplish this purpose, the book will present material related to the conservation of natural resources so that you will:

- Understand the role of the physical variables of geology, topography, soil, water, and air in the natural environment.
- Understand the role of solar and internal heat energy as the driving force for all natural systems.
- Understand that the living world (biosphere) is a response to the interactions of the lithosphere, hydrosphere, and atmosphere with solar or internal heat energy.
- Understand the workings of ecosystems as they relate to the conservation of natural resources.
- Understand that the management and conservation of all natural resources depends on working with nature to compliment normal energy flow cycles.
- Understand the concept of *sustainability* as it relates to the management of all of our natural resources.
- Understand the individual's place in the environment in both geologic and biologic time.
- Understand that much work remains to be accomplished in the field of conservation and management of our resources and that your generation will be called on to do the work in the 21st century.
- Develop an appreciation of nature by reading excerpts form the works of authors who understand man and nature and write well to express this knowledge.
- Develop the love of the land necessary to establish for yourself a **land ethic** that makes you a part of the land community of Planet Earth.

Audience

This book is designed to be used in a one-semester (quarter) undergraduate course in Conservation of Natural Resources or Resource Management and Conservation. The vocabulary and level of discussion are appropriate for a freshman- through- junior-level college class with little or no scientific background as a prerequisite. The book could be retained as a valuable reference source after the course is completed.

Geographic Area

Throughout this book emphasis is given to the conservation of natural resources in North America. The United States, Canada, and Mexico are all included in the discussion of physical variables (Part One). Natural resources management programs of the United States are emphasized in Part Two, but mineral resources of all three countries are discussed. Part Three is devoted to the human resources of the United States. By comparing human population problems of the United States with those of Mexico, the population problems of a developing nation are highlighted. A discussion of global environmental problems, including global sustainability and biodiversity, is included in Part Three.

Organization

This book is organized into three major parts. Part One is a brief physical geography of North America with emphasis on lithologic, hydrologic, and atmospheric circulation cycles. Physical variables of rock, soil, topography, weather, climate, air, and water compose the base of a biotic pyramid. The sun provides the energy to convert these physical variables into a biosphere. Important environmental topics in Part One include acid rain, greenhouse warming, ozone depletion, irrigation problems, sunless ecosystems, ocean dumping, groundwater pollution, and wetlands conservation.

Part Two covers the management and conservation of natural resources. An introductory chapter on the "tools of the trade" for a resources manager includes a discussion of remote sensing and geographic information systems. Management chapters include forest, agriculture, rangeland, wildlife, aquatic resources, energy, minerals, and waste. These chapters can be covered in any order.

Part Three on the human resource discusses the population problem, problems of urbanization, and land-use controls. Global sustainability and biodiversity are briefly reviewed to demonstrate the need for conservation management beyond North America. The book ends with a discussion on ethics and individual land ethics.

The three major parts of the book may be presented in any order. Instructors that prefer to set the stage for environmental problems by beginning with the people problems can begin with Part Three. However, it is recommended that chapter 1 be presented first before changing the sequence of the remaining chapters, because it contains many definitions and concepts that are used throughout the book. If physical geography is a prerequisite for the course on conservation of natural resources, most of Part One, with the exception of chapter 1, could be skipped without loss of continuity. Chapter 1 and Part Two provide enough material for a course in Resources Management if appropriate outside readings are assigned.

Educational Concepts

A number of educational concepts have been applied in this book that will help to motivate the not-so-serious student. All examples that highlight important ideas have been included in the content of the text. Therefore, there are no boxed inserts or case studies separated from the text because the not-so-serious students, when pressed for reading time, tend to skip these to get through the assigned reading.

Many photographs and illustrations are included to generate and stimulate interest. A picture is worth a thousand words and is especially helpful in conveying volumes of information in a restricted amount of space.

The not-so-serious student will usually look at the photos and illustrations before he/she reads the text. Photos with captions can generate enough interest to motivate a student to read the corresponding text. If it doesn't, at least they have learned something from the illustrations.

Humor has been added occasionally to break the monotony of a serious subject. Illustrating the humorous side of an issue is an effective way to generate optimism when the outlook for improvement seems somewhat bleak.

Boldface type and italics have been used throughout the book. Boldface is used to emphasize important words or phrases and italics mark words or terms that are defined in the text.

End-of-Chapter Materials

At the end of each chapter key words and phrases used and/or defined in the chapter are listed. Also, a set of questions and discussion topics are provided for review, study, or discussion. Many of these questions attempt to motivate students to relate their own geographic area and its natural resources or conservation problems to the material in the text. Attempting to solve local problems by a method that has proved successful elsewhere is a good positive management strategy.

A list of references for further study is also given at the end of each chapter. The lists are purposely short, providing five or six choices that will extend discussion or elaborate on important ideas in the text. It should be obvious from these lists that the works of Loren Eiseley and Aldo Leopold are required reading in my classes. Leopold, in his *Sand County Almanac,* gives conservation its true meaning, and Eiseley relates humans to science and science to humans perhaps better than any other modern author.

Acknowledgements

Many people have contributed in a variety of ways to the writing of this book. The Castillon household routine was dominated by my work on the project. A special thanks to my wife Joanne who sacrificed while I did nothing around the house for three years. Thanks to my children, Cindy, Kim, Linda, Laura, Rick, and Kelly and my granddaughter Shannon for their understanding and support.

Southwest Missouri State University and the Department of Geosciences have supported me throughout this project and I am very grateful for their help and assistance. The secretaries, especially Deana Gibson, have spent many hours typing and retyping the manuscript that became this book. Doug Hemsath and Mike Klein have been my cartographers throughout this project. A special thanks to them for their work.

Obviously, the content of a book this size is the work of a large scientific community. They have shared their ideas through a vast network of publications and writings that provided me with the inspiration I needed to collect their ideas and information and present it to you in this book. To them I am grateful. I accept the responsibility for any errors that exist in this book and ask that you write to me and let me know of any that you find so that they may be corrected in later printings.

Reviewers

Miriam Helen Hill
 Indiana University Southeast
Clarence M. Head
 University of Central Florida
Eric A. Johnson
 Illinois State University
John R. Ray
 Wright State University
Robert D. Loring
 DePauw University

Conservation of Natural Resources

A Resource Management Approach

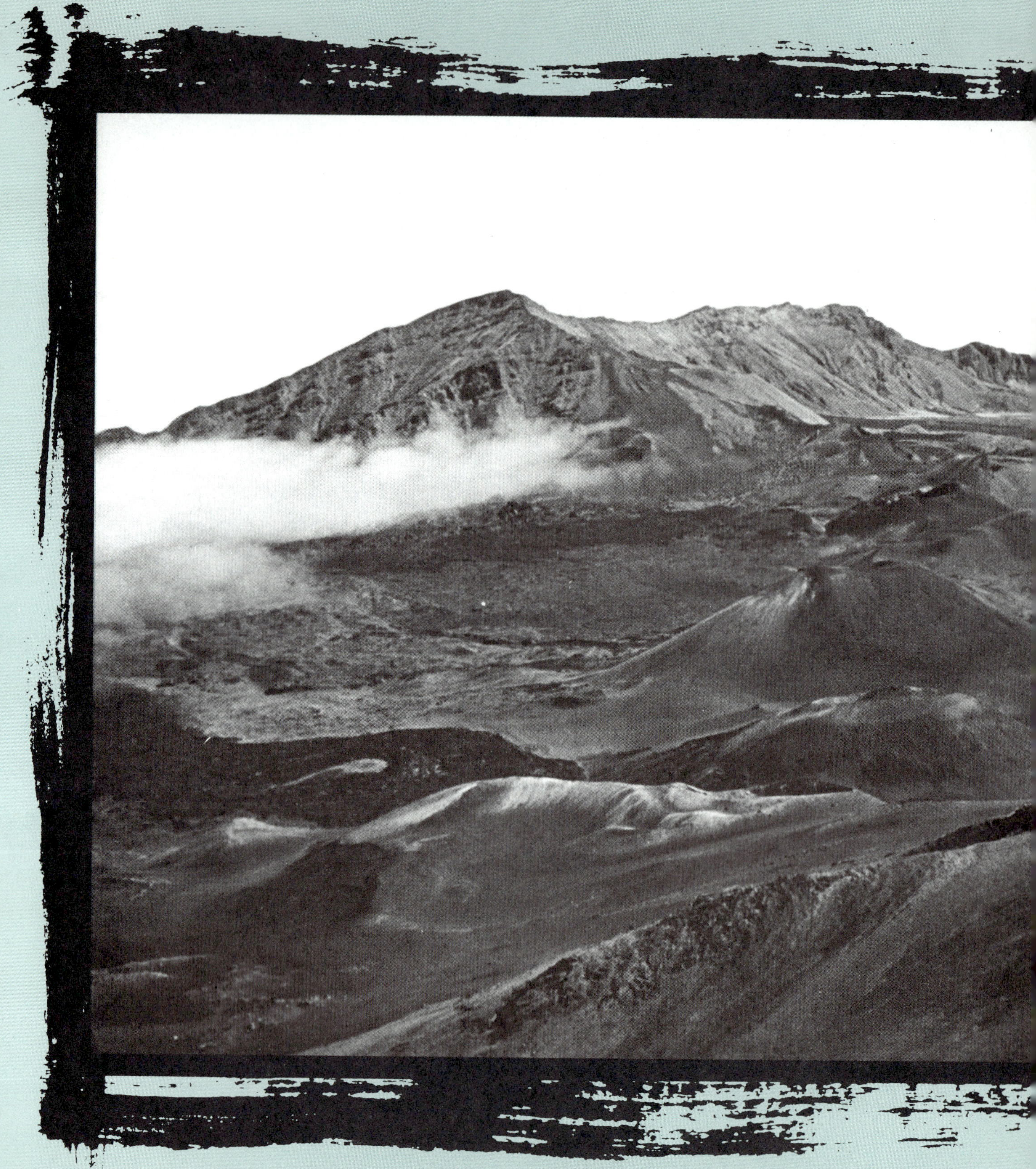

Part One

Physical and Biological Variables of the Natural Environment

Many a man, when I tell him that I have been on to a mountain, asks if I took a glass with me. It was not to see a few particular objects, as if they were near at hand, as I had been accustomed to see them, that I ascended the mountain, but to see an infinite variety far and near in their relation to each other, thus reduced to a single picture.

Henry David Thoreau, 1854

Chapter 1

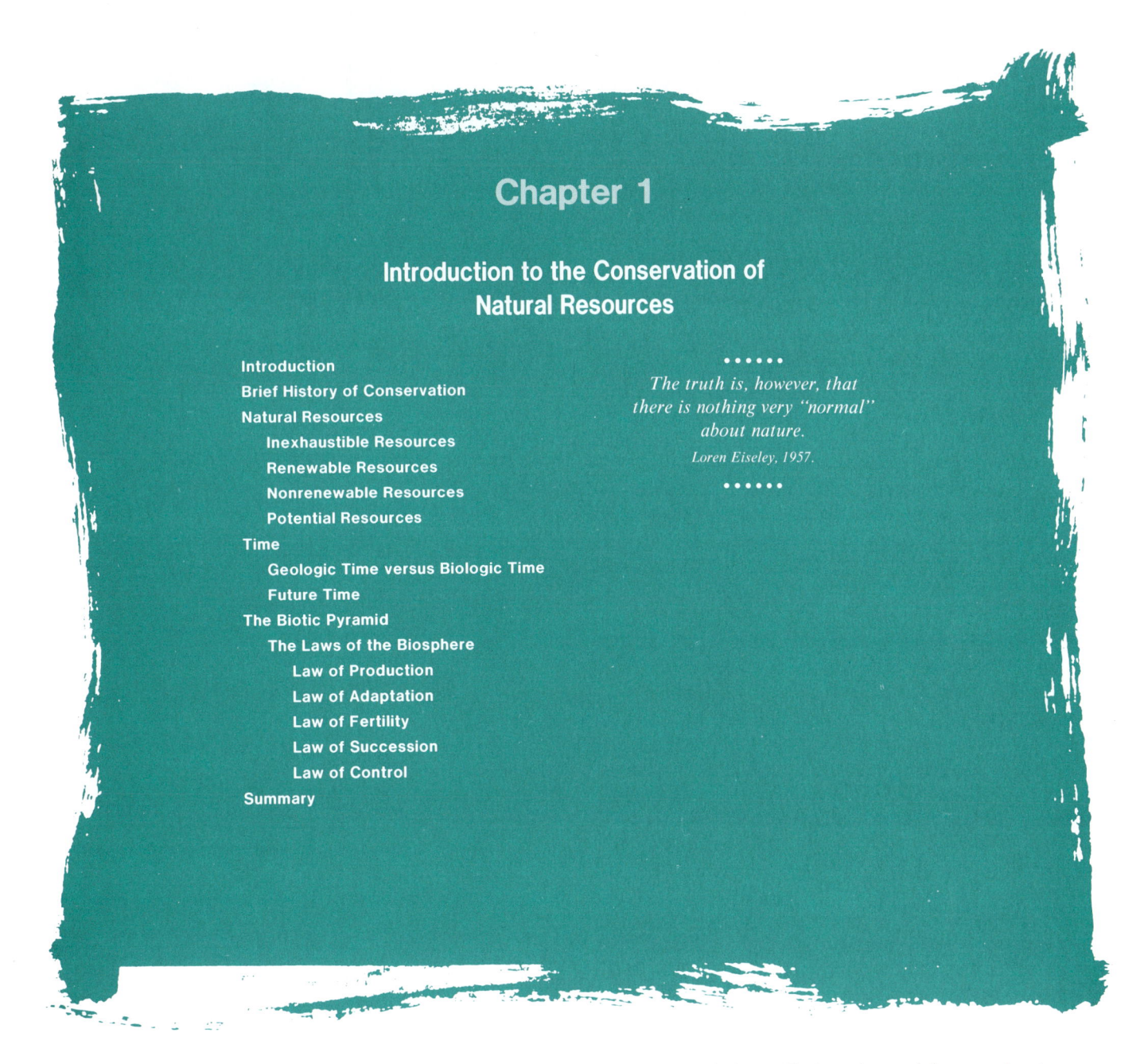

Introduction to the Conservation of Natural Resources

Introduction
Brief History of Conservation
Natural Resources
    Inexhaustible Resources
    Renewable Resources
    Nonrenewable Resources
    Potential Resources
Time
    Geologic Time versus Biologic Time
    Future Time
The Biotic Pyramid
    The Laws of the Biosphere
        Law of Production
        Law of Adaptation
        Law of Fertility
        Law of Succession
        Law of Control
Summary

The truth is, however, that there is nothing very "normal" about nature.
Loren Eiseley, 1957.

Introduction

It has been more than two decades since the first *Earth Day,* April 22, 1970, a day declared by the citizens of the United States to express concern for cleaning up the environment. In fact, so many politicians from both parties jumped at the opportunity to express their concern that Congress was forced to close down for the day. In the Gallup polls, concern over air and water pollution jumped from tenth place in the summer of 1969 to fifth place by the summer of 1970 and was perceived as more important than **race, crime,** and **teenage** problems but not as important as the perennial poll leaders, **peace** (Vietnam) and the **pocket book** issues, the dollar problems of the federal budget (taxes and expenditures). The environmental movement of the 1960s has changed from a reactionary statement by the young to an ongoing involvement by the masses. We have changed from a society that did not consider the environmental consequences of our daily actions to one that at least recognizes the environmental ramifications of our developmental projects. The *National Environmental Policy Act* (*NEPA*) of 1969 was signed by President Nixon and became law January 1, 1970. This law, for the first time in our history, made environmental concerns a national policy and priority, although we still do not always make the most environmentally sound choice in our development decisions. This act does not require that we do so however, only that we consider the action and alternatives, including the no-action alternative, before a decision can be made to proceed. We have come a long way from the days when government projects, such as building a dam, were based entirely on politics and cost benefit analyses. In light of the fact that environmental considerations have become a part of our national policy for decision making, it is important to understand as best we can the underlying principles that govern the workings of our ecosystems and the conservation of natural resources.

This text will examine the basic ingredients of all natural systems in North America. The **geology**, the **soil**, the **climate,** and the earth's **waters** are the physical variables that interact to form the natural communities making up the biosphere. The *biogeography* of a region is defined as the distribution of the plant and animal communities that occupy that region. Understanding the biogeographic community into which a proposed project is to be built will help to determine the environmental ramifications of the project, should the project be approved. The better we understand the environment, the easier it will be to manage the resources of the biotic community. The first part of this text will examine the basic physical variables of the natural environment. These include geology, climate, water, soil, and biogeography. Following the discussion of basic physical variables, Part II of the text will address the management of individual natural resources in the context of their biogeographic settings. Forest management in a region that receives 200 cm (80 in) of precipitation per year cannot and should not be the same as for a region that receives less than 76 cm (30 in) of precipitation. However, many of the decisions governing our national forests are made by representatives in Washington, D.C. who may not understand the environmental differences that should dictate separate and distinct management schemes for different natural settings. It is our duty, as environmentally concerned citizens, to keep our congressmen and women informed. We will be able to do this only if we understand the environments in which we live. Conservation and management of **water, air, forests, grasslands, agriculture, wildlife, aquatic habitats, energy, waste,** and **mineral resources** are the focus of Part II.

Part III evaluates the human resource and includes a discussion of **land ethics,** helping the reader make a conscious decision in establishing a philosophical framework for a personal *land ethic.* Aldo Leopold defined an *ethic philosophically* as a differentiation of social from antisocial conduct. An *ethic ecologically* is a limitation on freedom of action in the struggle for existence. The long-term survival of the human species depends on our ability to limit our freedom in our environmental community so that we will not cause our self-extinction.

Leopold was one of the first to propose the idea of a land ethic (figure 1.1), stating that all ethics evolved from the single premise that the individual is a member of a community of interdependent parts. Instincts prompt competition for a place in the community, but ethics motivate cooperation so there will be a place to compete for. Land ethics enlarge the boundaries of the community to include the soil, water, plants, and other animals, or collectively, **the land.**

Figure 1.1 Aldo Leopold—the father of modern-day conservation.
(*Photo:* University of Wisconsin)

A land ethic changes the role of *Homo sapien* from conqueror of the land community to member and citizen of it. It implies that each person has respect for fellow members and the community. The role of conqueror is eventually self-defeating because it is implicit in such a role that the conqueror should know what makes the community clock tick, and what and who is valuable or worthless in community life. History has shown that conquerors know neither and this is why their conquests are self-defeating.

Leopold made the observation in 1949 that the ordinary citizen assumes that science knows what makes the community clock tick; the scientist is equally sure that he does not. This observation is still true today. The more we learn, the more complex the land community becomes. The goal is still to understand our environment as best we can so we can manage it, without destroying the land community of which we are a part.

If we understand our place in the environmental community, we will be more inclined to limit our freedom in order to survive. Money is a powerful anti-force in this

Figure 1.2 Bluebird and house. Bluebird house—easy to build (5″ × 5″ × 10″ with 1½″ hole).
(*Photo:* David A. Castillon)

process. The old saying that **money talks** causes us to make economic decisions that are not in the best interests of long-term survival. If we were to survey all of the higher plants and animals of the North American continent, it is doubtful that more than 5% could be sold, fed, eaten, or put to economic use. Yet all of these members of the biotic community add stability and diversity to the land and are entitled to continuance. If we want to see an organism thrive and expand its population, we invent an economic reason to push the point. For example, instead of just saying "the environment would be a better place with more bluebirds and purple martins; therefore, everyone should put up birdhouses for them" (figure 1.2), we say "these birds will eat many insects and mosquitoes and you will save money on bug spray and electronic bug zappers." We establish economic values to justify expanding our land community.

Understanding the principles of the conservation of natural resources is a first step in the development of an ecological conscience, after which we can formulate a land ethic. A land ethic, based on an understanding of the conservation of natural resources by every member of the land community, will perpetuate survival of the human species.

Part III focuses on the human resource and the accompanying population problems. The impact of urbanization and land use controls will be addressed, along with many of the associated problems of population increases. The economic, political, and social ramifications of our actions in a global environment are also issues that must be faced in the decision-making process. Deciding how best to conserve our natural resources and, at the same time, have a high standard of living are tough choices we are all faced with. Having a land ethic to guide us will help us make the more environmentally safe choice for the future.

Brief History of Conservation

When the Europeans first came to North America they saw a much more diverse biotic community than the one they left behind. The North American forest had many more species of trees than the European forest. Appearing vast and limitless, they harbored the unknown and, therefore, were something to be conquered. The subsequent cutting, burning, and clearing for wood and agriculture continued almost unabated until about 1900. The land, the forest, and the water were all thought of as limitless commodities and were not considered resources. At the turn of the century there was evidence that some of these commodities were coming into short supply. The timber around the Great Lakes was almost gone because of logging and

Figure 1.3 Ivory-billed woodpecker—former range, southeastern United States—now extinct. Museum specimen at St. Joe Museum, MO.
(*Photo*: Jim Rathert, MDC)

Figure 1.4 President Theodore Roosevelt (top hat) with Gifford Pinchot, first Chief Forester.
(*Photo*: USDA Forest Service)

fires. Market and sport hunting, and habitat destruction had reduced large populations of some species such as wild turkeys, passenger pigeons, and ivory-billed woodpeckers to such low numbers that extinction was feared. In the case of the passenger pigeon and ivory-billed woodpecker, the fears were well founded (figure 1.3). The concern generated by the losses in the environment at this time in history was more for *preservation* than conservation. Natural and scenic places needed to be preserved for future generations and protected from human destruction.

The U.S. Forest Service was established in 1905 by President Theodore Roosevelt. He appointed Gifford Pinchot as the first Chief Forester. Pinchot was a forestry professor at Yale University and looked on the forests as natural resources that could be effectively managed and conserved as a renewable resource (figure 1.4).

Yellowstone Park in Wyoming, established in 1872, was the first national park in the United States. Stephen Mather was appointed the first National Park Service (NPS) director in 1916. He was a Sierra Club member and brought tremendous enthusiasm to the job of expanding the NPS in the face of tough opposition from anti-conservationist economic interests.

Both the U.S. Forest Service and the National Park Service brought a protectionist philosophy to the conservation movement in the United States. Canada is most like the United States in that over 90% of its commercial forest land is in federal or provincial ownership.

Another aspect of the turn-of-the-century conservation movement in the United States was the establishment of individual state departments of conservation. Forty-one departments were formed either directly or indirectly as an outgrowth of a White House conference on natural resources in 1908. Most departments were established in an attempt to reverse the decline in wildlife resources.

In the 1930s, the depression and drought in North America once again brought the conservation effort to the public's attention. This time the impetus for creating work projects to benefit the nation was the need for jobs. The depression had thrown the men out of work; the drought had accentuated the need for a conservation effort to stop erosion and replant the country. President Franklin D. Roosevelt began the **Prairie States Forest Project** in 1934. The project authorized the planting of a belt of trees along the one-hundredth meridian to stop soil erosion. The one-hundredth meridian is a North-South line of longitude through the center of North Dakota to and through the middle of Texas.

The **Soil Conservation Service** (SCS) was established in 1935. Once again the goal of the service was to show farmers proper techniques to prevent soil erosion. By the end of the 1930s, the conservation movement had taken on a new mission. Preservation of our natural resources

Figure 1.5 Tennessee Valley Authority (TVA) region with facilities.
Source: Data from Tennessee Valley Authority, Nashville, TN.

was complemented by *restoration*. Soil was recognized as a natural resource that needed to be conserved and, where possible, restored. Water was also recognized as a resource that needed management. The **Tennessee Valley Authority** (TVA) was established in 1933 to protect an entire drainage basin, including conservation of water, soil, forest, and wildlife (figure 1.5).

The **Civilian Conservation Corps** (CCC) set up 2,652 camps of two hundred men each to work on many conservation-related projects such as tree plantings, fire and pest control, and lake and stream improvements (figure 1.6).

The conservation movement of the 1930s was interrupted by World War II and the rebuilding that followed. It was 1960 before the people once again recognized the need for protecting our environment and its resources. In 1964, the **Wilderness Act** was passed by Congress. Fifty-four areas, totaling 9.14 million acres (3.7 million hectares) of land, were given the status of "wilderness" with the initial passage of the act. Once again preservation was the goal. Many more acres have been added to the system since 1964, with a total of 90.7 million acres (36.7 million hectares) included by 1990.

The conservation movement of the 1960s did not return to the preservation philosophy of the turn of the century. Instead, it had taken on a new dimension, **environmental quality**. Stewart Udall, Secretary of the Interior under President John F. Kennedy, was a key

Figure 1.6 Camp Roosevelt, Virginia—Civilian Conservation Corps (CCC) Company 322 facilities in July, 1940.
(*Photo:* National Archives Trust Fund Board)

Introduction to the Conservation of Natural Resources

Figure 1.7 Environmental Impact Statement (EIS) covers illustrating the range of topics covered by EISs.
(*Photo:* © W.C.B. Publishers; photo by Bob Coyle.)

government leader in the fight for pollution control. Scientists and university students led the way. Congress followed and passed the **Clean Air Act** in 1963, the **Federal Water Pollution Control Act** in 1964, and the **National Environmental Policy Act** in 1969. In the almost 200-year history of the United States, this was the first time that we, as a people, had declared environmental quality as a national priority.

The National Environmental Policy Act (NEPA) states that: In order to carry out the policy set forth in this Act, it is the continuing responsibility of the Federal Government to use all practicable means, consistent with other essential considerations of national policy, to improve and coordinate Federal plans, functions, programs, and resources to the end that the Nation may—

1. fulfill the responsibilities of each generation as trustee of the environment for succeeding generations;
2. assure for all Americans safe, healthful, productive, and aesthetically and culturally pleasing surroundings;
3. attain the widest range of beneficial uses of the environment without degradation, risk to health or safety, or other undesirable and unintended consequences;
4. preserve important historic, cultural, and natural aspects of our national heritage, and maintain, wherever possible, an environment which supports diversity, and variety of individual choice;
5. achieve a balance between population and resources use which will permit high standards of living and a wide sharing of life's amenities; and
6. enhance the quality of renewable resources and approach the maximum attainable recycling of depletable resources.

To assure compliance with these goals, the NEPA law requires that any federal agency must prepare an *environmental impact statement* (EIS) before it can expend federal dollars on a project. An EIS must address the environmental ramifications of each federal program or project in a prepared, written document (figure 1.7). Canada has a NEPA Law modeled after that of the United States.

The NEPA law ushered in the 1970s with an idealism that reflects the concerns of the environmental movement of the 1960s. The idealism and environmental movement was restated on April 22, 1970, the first Earth Day. This was followed by the passage of amendments to the **Clean Air Act** (1970 and 1977) and **Federal Water Pollution Control Act** (1972). The passage of the **Coastal Zone Management Act** in 1972, the **Toxic Substances Control Act** in 1975 and the **Resource Conservation and Recovery Act** of 1976. The hopes of the 1960s and 70s were dashed by the election of Ronald Reagan as President of the United States. The faltering world economy and the cost of environmental cleanup were both factors in the slowdown of the movement. In its State of Environment Report in 1982, the Conservation Foundation, a nonprofit organization dedicated to the promotion of a quality human environment, reported the negative impacts of the Reagan administration's programs on the environment:

1. The bipartisan consensus that supported federal protection of the environment for more than a decade has been broken by an Administration that has given priority to deregulation, defederalization, and defunding domestic programs.
2. Reagan Administration initiatives have polarized relations between the executive branch and conservationists in Congress and throughout the country. The polarization has disrupted the communication necessary to formulate and carry out environmental programs.
3. Without question the Reagan Administration has introduced a fundamental discontinuity into national resource and environmental policy. It has pursued its domestic goals with such single-

mindedness, so aggressively, as to allow conservationists no alternative but to protest.
4. At the Environmental Protection Agency the 1983 budget calls for a 40% reduction from the 1981 level for research and development.
5. Cuts already made have done away with the noise control program, sharply reduced efforts to deal with toxic substances, and cast doubt on the EPA's ability to fulfill its mandates under the Clean Air and Clean Water Acts.
6. At the Department of Energy, programs in energy conservation and renewable energy sources have given way to increased spending for nuclear reactor research.
7. At the Department of Interior, the emphasis has been on selling off federal land, encouraging accelerated mineral exploration and extraction; . . . the tendency has been either to neglect or exploit natural resources.

The federal government's retreat from its commitment to environmental protection throughout the 1980s left a void that state and local governments have yet to fill satisfactorily. The federal government must provide the leadership and support, both financial and political, for environmental quality improvements.

George Bush, in his Presidential Campaign of 1988, promised to be an environmental president. Some of his actions and policies are pro-environment, while others leave one doubting his promise. On the plus side of the ledger, President Bush has called a moratorium on new oil drilling off the coast of California, Florida, Washington, Oregon, and New England until the year 2000. However, one wonders why the Alaskan Coast was not included in the ban. One also wonders how long the moratorium will last in light of the Middle East situation.

Another environmental plus for the Bush administration was the addition of the northern spotted owl to the threatened species list under provisions of the **Rare and Endangered Species Act** of 1973. To add this bird to the list, knowing that protection will reduce timber cutting in the Pacific Northwest's old growth forests and cost some lumbermen their jobs, was a brave move.

On the other side of the ledger, the indecisive action taken by his administration in responding to the Exxon Valdez oil spill and cleanup efforts makes one think twice. One thing is for certain, and that is that almost anyone or anything would be an improvement, environmentally, over the Reagan administration. Time will tell.

Many federal agencies have responsibilities for protection of the environment. The NEPA law in the United States mandates that the federal agencies listed in Table 1.1 consider the ramifications of their policies and projects on the natural and human-altered environment. Conservationists hope that the present administration will reverse the trends of the 1980s and once again establish environmental protection as a top national priority. The Administration should use the federal agencies with responsibilities for environmental protection for that purpose.

Table 1.1
Federal Agencies with Major Responsibility for Environmental Policy and/or Management.

Department of Interior
National Park Service
Bureau of Land Management
Fish and Wildlife Service
Geological Survey
Mineral Management Service
Office of Surface Mining
Bureau of Mines

Department of Agriculture
Forest Service
Soil Conservation Service
Agricultural Stabilization and Conservation Service

Department of Commerce
National Oceanographic and Atmospheric Administration

Department of Defense
Army Corps of Engineers
Departments of Army, Navy, Air Force

Department of Transportation
Coast Guard

Department of Health and Human Services
Food and Drug Administration

Department of Energy
Federal Energy Regulatory Commission
National Center for Appropriate Technology
Nuclear Waste Policy Act Project Office

Executive Office of the President
Council on Environmental Quality

Independent Agencies
Environmental Protection Agency
Tennessee Valley Authority
Bonneville Power Commission
Water Resources Council
National Science Foundation/National Research Council
Nuclear Regulatory Commission
Great Lakes Basin Commission
Synthetic Fuels Corporation
Federal Emergency Management Agency

Natural Resources

Natural resources are forms of matter or energy that are considered useful in human societies. If they are not useful to humans, they are not a *resource*. If they are not the product of earth processes, they are not *natural*. Natural resources can be classified into many different categories but for our purposes, we will use only four: *inexhaustible, renewable, nonrenewable,* and *potential* (figure 1.8).

Inexhaustible Resources

Inexhaustible resources are solar energy, internal heat energy of the earth, gravity, and atomic energy. **Solar energy,** which drives atmospheric and oceanic circulation systems, also gives us **wind power** and, with gravity, **water power** (figure 1.9). Internal heat, produced by radioactive decay in the earth's interior, gives us **geothermal energy** in inexhaustible quantities. Vast quantities of fissionable

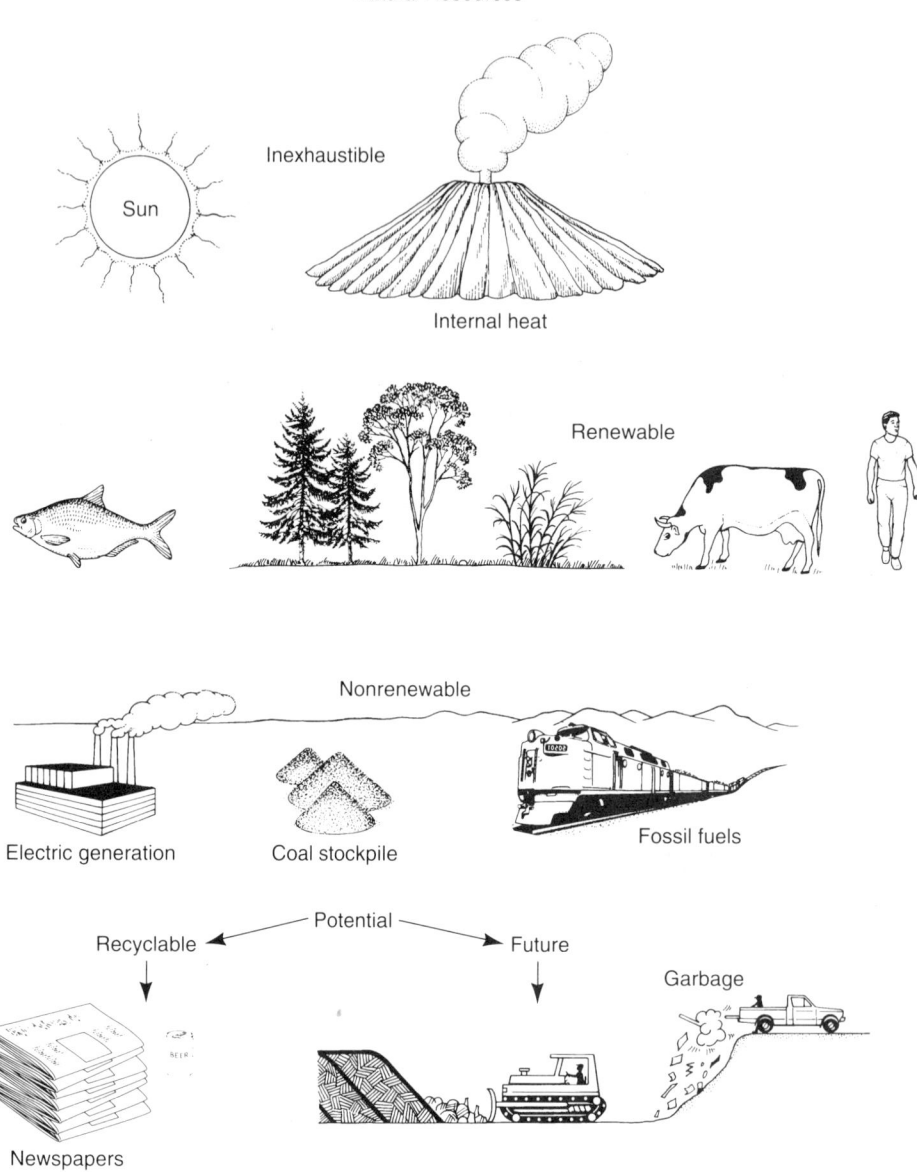

Figure 1.8 The four natural resource classifications. A resource can shift from one category to another because of changing economic or environmental conditions.

material exist at or near the earth's surface and should supply a perpetual amount of **atomic energy,** but not without its harmful side effects.

Renewable Resources

Renewable resources include **clean air, clean water, fertile soil, vegetation, wildlife,** and **humans.** All of these resources are only renewable with proper use and management. They are the focus of most conservation efforts and the resources management programs discussed in this text.

Nonrenewable Resources

Nonrenewable resources such as **coal, oil, gas,** and many mineral resources once used are not renewable in biologic time but are renewable in geologic time. Because of the vastness of geologic time, future products of geologic activity produced 1,000,000 years from now are not useful to humans today and therefore, by our definition, are not a resource. Products of past geologic activities during millions of years of time are nonrenewable resources.

Figure 1.9 Windmill—still pumping and storing water in Iowa.
(Photo: David A. Castillon)

Potential Resources

Recyclable resources best fit into the category of future or *potential resources*. Most of the **metallic mineral** elements such as iron, aluminum, copper, silver, and gold are recyclable materials. Other future resources are garbage and human waste. When the technology and cost of utilizing **garbage** for energy and **human waste** for fertilizer is realized, these will both become resources. They have the potential and in some countries are already resources.

Time

Time has many dimensions. The clock on the wall displays the time of day for all to see. If the clock displays 3:53 P.M. on the 23rd of May 1988, what does it mean? It has no meaning if you don't know geographic location, because there are an infinite number of moments with that precise description if we take time as defined by the earth-sun relationship. In most cases it would be very difficult for you, the reader, to answer the question, "What will you be doing next year at this time?" The human species has a difficult time thinking in terms of years, decades, and centuries. Time in conservation, however, is an extremely important variable. We must be trained to think in large blocks of time, because changes in natural systems require immense periods of time.

"The truth is that we are all potential fossils still carrying within our bodies the crudities of former existences, the marks of a world in which living creatures flow with little more consistency than clouds from age to age" (Loren Eiseley, 1957).

Geologic Time versus Biologic Time

During the past 200 years, the scientific community has discarded the notion that the earth is no older than 4004 BC and came to the realization that the geologic and astronomical record would indicate that the earth is approximately 4.6+ billion years old. The *geologic time* scale in Figure 1.10 gives the presently accepted scale of time that we will use in this text. A more detailed explanation of geologic time will be presented in chapter 2.

In conservation of natural resources, the names of each block of time are not as important as the immensity of time that they represent. It's hard to think in terms of millions of years when we can't remember what we did yesterday and we don't know what we're going to do tomorrow. But what happened yesterday in geologic time is very important in establishing our perspective for conservation.

Loren Eiseley, in his essay on *How Flowers Changed the World,* describes some of the important considerations of **time** that are necessary to an understanding of environmental changes (figure 1.11).

If it had been possible to observe the Earth from the far side of the solar system over the long course of geological epochs, the watchers might have been able to discern a subtle change in the light emanating from our planet. That world of long ago would, like the red desert of Mars, have reflected light from vast drifts of stone and gravel, the sands of wandering wastes, the blackness of naked basalt, the yellow dust of endlessly moving storms. Only the ceaseless marching of the clouds and the intermittent flashes from the restless surface of the sea would have told a different story, but still essentially a barren one. Then, as the millennia rolled away and age followed age, a new and greener light would, by degrees, have come to twinkle across those endless miles.

This is the only difference those far watchers, by the use of subtle instruments, might have perceived in the whole history of the planet Earth. Yet that slowly growing green twinkle would have contained the epic march of life from the tidal oozes upward across the raw and unclothed continents. Out of the vast chemical bath of the sea—not from the deeps, but from the element-rich, light-exposed

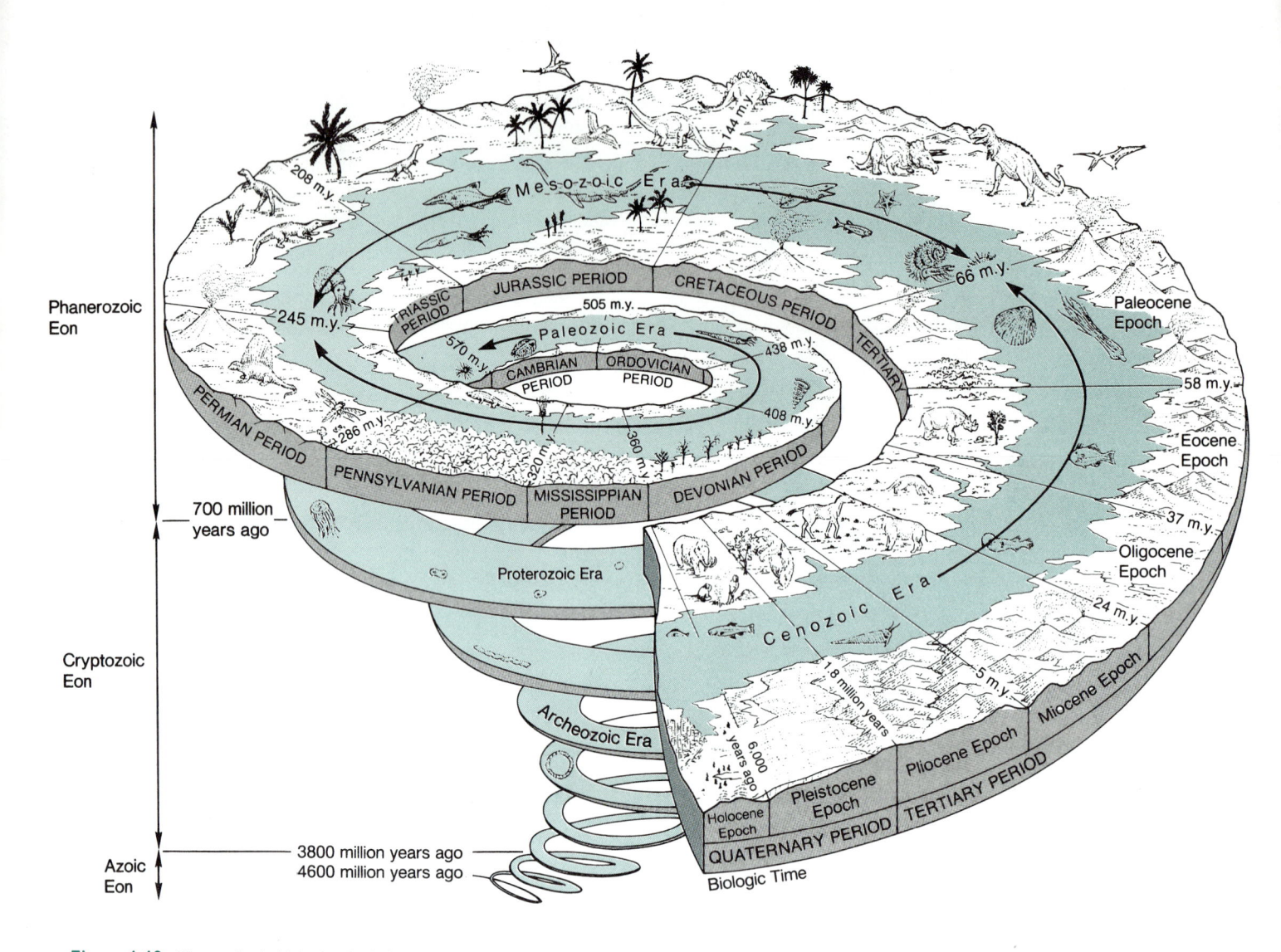

Figure 1.10 The geologic-biologic clock. Important plant and animal groups are shown where they first appear in significant numbers.
Source: "Geologic Time," U.S. Geological Survey.

platforms of the continental shelves—wandering fingers of green had crept upward along the meanderings of river systems and fringed the gravels of forgotten lakes.

In those first ages plants clung of necessity to swamps and watercourses. Their reproductive processes demanded direct access to water. Beyond the primitive ferns and mosses that enclosed the borders of swamps and streams the rocks still lay vast and bare, the sands still swirled the dust of a naked planet. The grass cover that holds our world secure in place was still millions of years in the future. The green marchers had gained a soggy foothold upon the land, but that was all. They did not reproduce by seeds but by microscopic swimming sperm that had to wriggle their way through water to fertilize the female cell. Such plants in their higher forms had clever adaptations for the use of rain water in their sexual phases, and survived with increasing success in a wet land environment. They now seem part of man's normal environment. The truth is, however, that there is nothing very "normal" about nature. Once upon a time there were no flowers at all.

A little while ago—one hundred million years, as the geologist estimates time in the history of our four-billion-year-old planet—flowers were not to be found anywhere on the five continents. Wherever one might have looked, from the poles to the equator, one would have seen only the cold dark monotonous green of a world whose plant life possessed no other color.

Somewhere, just a short time before the close of the Age of Reptiles, there occurred a soundless, violent explosion. It lasted millions of years, but it was an explosion, nevertheless. It marked the emer-

Figure 1.11 Loren Eiseley. Dr. Eiseley called Francis Bacon the man who saw through time. Loren Eiseley is the man who defined time.
(*Photo:* The University Museum, University of Pennsylvania)

gence of the angiosperms—the flowering plants. Even the great evolutionist, Charles Darwin, called them "an abominable mystery," because they appeared so suddenly and spread so fast.

Flowers changed the face of the planet. Without them, the world we know—even man himself—would never have existed. Francis Thompson, the English poet, once wrote that one could not pluck a flower without troubling a star. Intuitively he had sensed like a naturalist the enormous interlinked complexity of life. Today we know that the appearance of the flowers contained also the equally mystifying emergence of man.*

The following points are made by Eiseley:

1. There is nothing very **normal** about nature.
2. Environmental changes take millions of years.
3. There is an enormous interlinked complexity of life.

What we inhabitants of earth consider to be **normal** or **natural** has not always been that way, nor will it continue to be. The earth environment in which we live has changed continually throughout **geologic time** and is still changing. *Biologic time,* on the other hand, is defined as periods of time less than 10,000 years. The oldest living biologic organisms on the earth, trees, have maximum life expectancies of less than 6,000 years. The natural environment that surrounds each of us, and that we consider

The Immense Journey by Loren Eisely. Copyright 1946, 1950, 1951, 1953, 1956, 1957 by Loren Eisely. Reprinted by permission of Random House, Inc.

"The picture's pretty bleak, gentlemen . . . The world's climates are changing, the mammals are taking over, and we all have a brain about the size of a walnut."

Figure 1.12 It's true, but funny nonetheless.
THE FAR SIDE copyright 1985 UNIVERSAL PRESS SYNDICATE. Reprinted with permission. All Rights Reserved.

to be normal and worth preserving, is in tune with the present state of the atmosphere and its existing climatic condition. The existing climatic condition for North American locations has only been that way for the last 5,000 years. Maybe a tree could live longer than 5,000 years if the climate where it is located would persist for more years than the present record indicates it has. If the climate, where the present 5,000-year-old bristlecone pines are located does not change for the next 5,000 years, some of them probably will become 10,000 years old. Climate changes on a regular basis and the last major change for North America occurred about 6,000 years ago when the *Holocene* began.

Environmental changes take many years because climatic changes take long periods of time. As climate changes, biogeographic regions shift and/or adaptations of individuals begin to manifest themselves. The emergence of the angiosperms, which took millions of years, was one of the most spectacular natural occurrences. On the other side of the coin, the extinction of the dinosaurs also took millions of years, and their loss has to represent one of the great tragedies of the natural world's evolution (figure 1.12). Emergence of new species and extinctions of living organisms are a part of the natural world and both take a great deal of time.

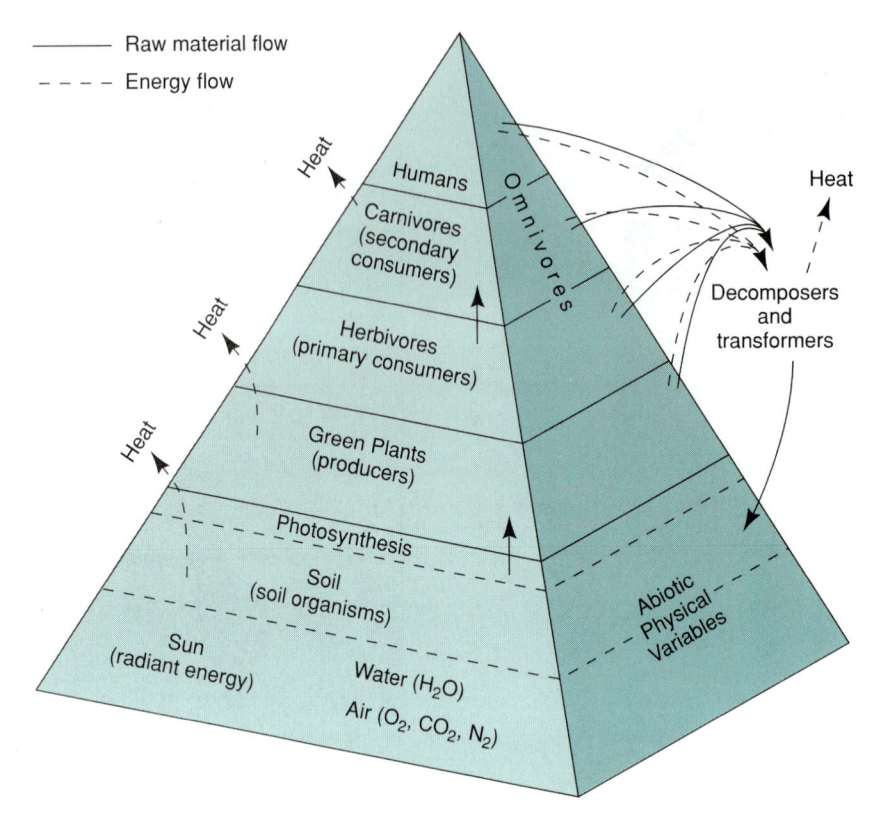

Figure 1.13 The biotic pyramid. The raw materials and energy-flow cycles of the biosphere.

In the conservation of natural resources, *human* activities have become time accelerators, the forces that have quickened the time process to such an extent that the natural evolutionary process that organisms carry within their bodies (genes), the **crudities of a former existence,** cannot keep pace with the changes introduced into the system or habitat. If an organism cannot change geographic location, then its chances of survival are limited. In the management of natural resources, time must be an environmental consideration.

Aldo Leopold said that the *outstanding scientific discovery of the twentieth century* is not television or radio but rather the **recognition of the complexity of the land** organism. Only those that know the most about the land can appreciate how little is known about it. The lifeblood of the land organism is a stream of energy that flows from the soil into the plant, then to the animal, and then back into the soil in a never-ending circuit of life.

The enormous interlinked complexity of life still has not been worked out, but we are getting closer to that goal. A major goal of this text is to gather together, in a readable format, the advances that have been made by the scientific community in understanding the complexity of the land organism. Unraveling and illustrating the complex interrelationships of the natural world should help us to manage our natural resources in an ethical and environmentally sound manner. This is the best approach to resource management until such a time as the scientific community understands more of the enormous interlinked complexity of life.

Future Time

We are all potential fossils. No one will escape that fact. What we can hope for is that when we become a fossil we will make the evolutionary difference in the survival of our human species by leaving the earth a habitable place for future *Homo sapiens*. The goal of conservation is to conserve our natural resources for future generations. This does not mean **do not use**; it means **use wisely.** Leopold defined *conservation* as the state of harmony between men and land. To arrive at the harmony he refers to requires an understanding of the land organism. Some of the complexities of the land organism can best be explained by the use of the biotic pyramid.

The Biotic Pyramid

The *biotic pyramid* illustrates the relationships between members of the biosphere and the physical environment they occupy (figure 1.13). The base of the pyramid consists of the abiotic factors of geology, soil (lithosphere), and climate (atmosphere and hydrosphere). The sun provides the energy to the system. The *photosynthetic pro-*

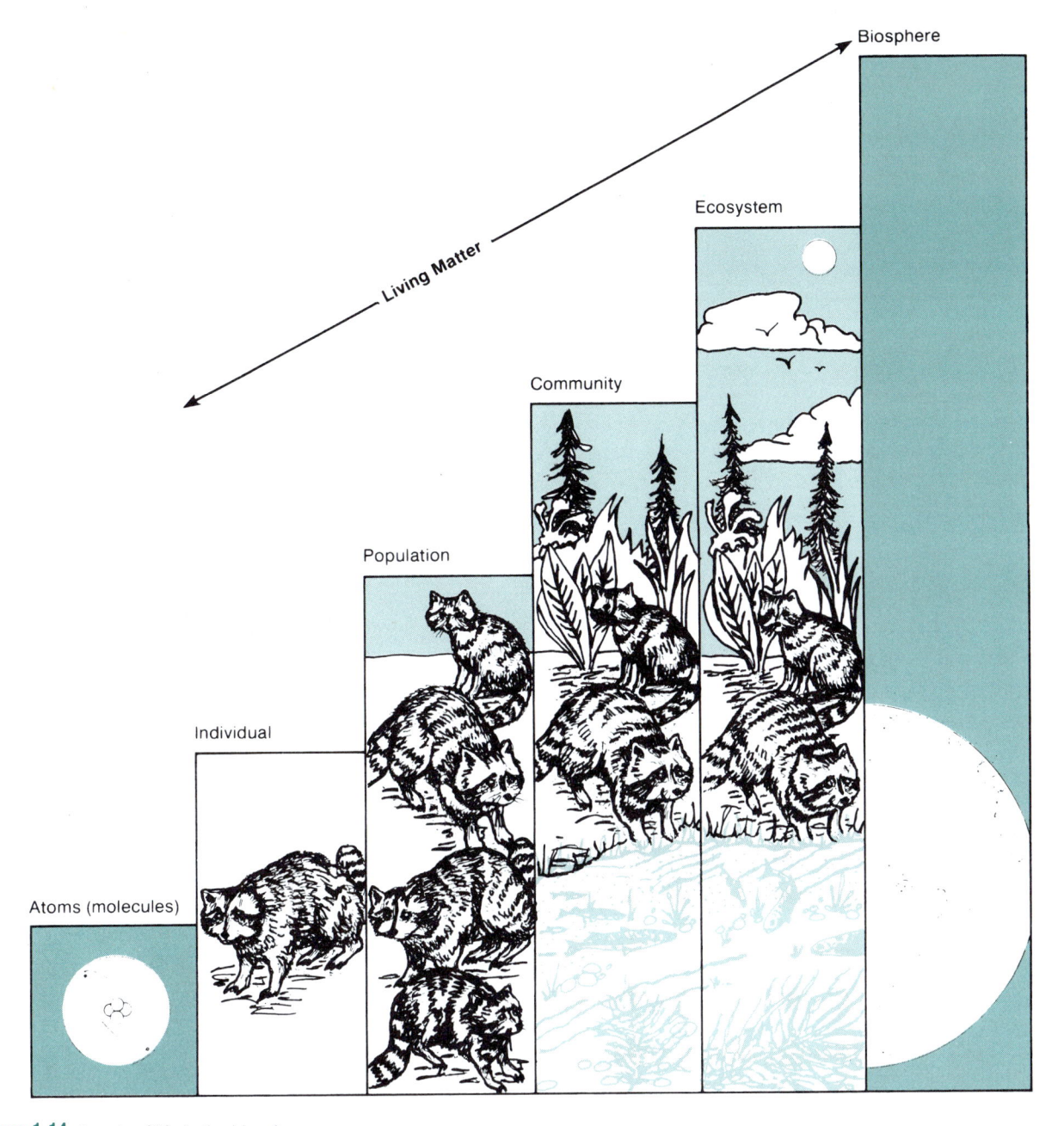

Figure 1.14 Levels of life in the biosphere.
From Eldon D. Enger, *Environmental Science*, 3d ed. Copyright © 1989 Wm. C. Brown Publishers, Dubuque, Iowa. All Rights Reserved. Reprinted by permission.

cess converts the basic materials provided by the air, soil, and water to a form useful to the living plant organisms that are the *producer* level of the biosphere. The primary and secondary *consumers* make up the next two levels of the pyramid, and humans reside on top. Humans are primary and secondary consumers. In most cases they eat both meat and vegetables (omnivores) and exercise control over the biosphere and the abiotic factors on the pyramid. It is a goal of this text to explain why humans should remove themselves from the roll of conqueror of the biotic pyramid and become both members of the biotic community and managers of the natural resources of their environment. *Homo sapien's* position on the pyramid also represents the fact that, because of their technological advancements, they are no longer the food source for any predators. In the biogeography chapter we will develop individual pyramids for each biotic region to illustrate the varying natural communities of North America.

Figure 1.14 illustrates the organization levels of life in the biosphere. An organism of a species is an *individual*. A group of individuals of a species forms a *population*. Populations of two or more species make up a *community*. Groups of communities occupying a particular geographic region are *ecosystems*. The earth habitat,

Introduction to the Conservation of Natural Resources

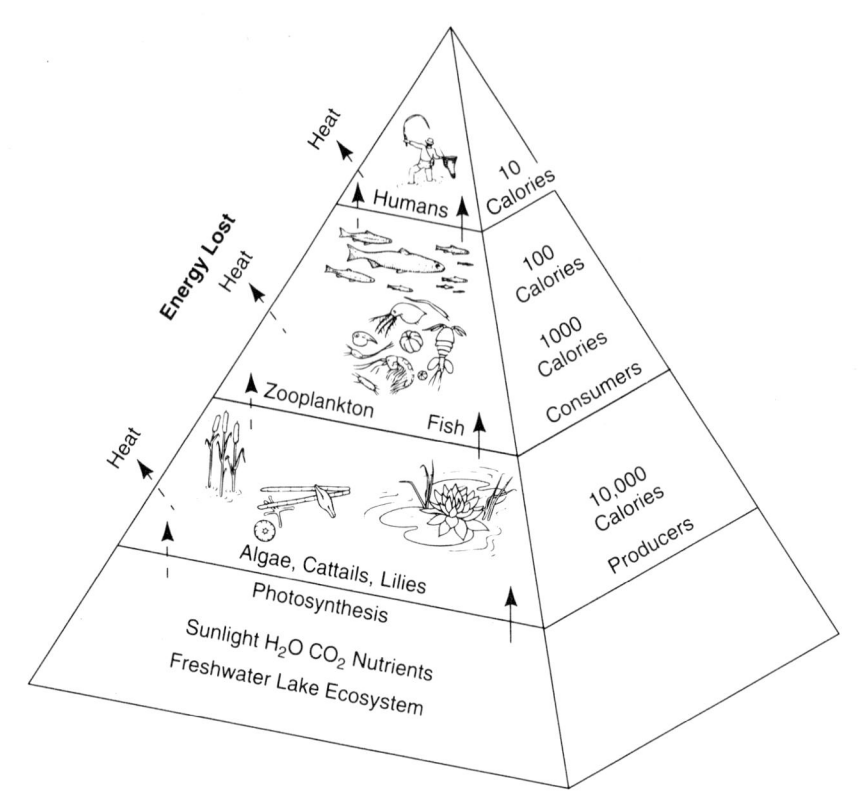

Figure 1.15 Law of production for a lake ecosystem.
Source: Data from H. T. Odum.

with all of the earth's living matter, is defined as the *biosphere*. A *species* is defined as a group of morphologically similar organisms that are capable of breeding and producing a fertile offspring.

The Laws of the Biosphere

The shape of the pyramid represents the concentration of mass and/or population of each level. The soil, air, and water contains a larger supply of necessary ingredients for the producer level than the vegetation produced by the photosynthetic process. There is a larger supply of plants and vegetation than the primary consumer level can consume, and so forth. Each higher level of complexity must have a population small enough that it will not outstrip its food supply or space. From this understanding of the relationships between members of the biosphere, there follows a series of five laws of the biosphere—**production, adaptation, fertility, succession,** and **control**.

Law of Production

The *law of production* for the biosphere states that production must always equal or exceed consumption. Another way of stating this principle is to say that each level of the pyramid has a *carrying capacity*. If the carrying capacity of any level is exceeded, the levels above it will reduce themselves by starvation or disease to bring back the pyramid shape (figure 1.15).

Law of Adaptation

The *law of adaptation,* as introduced by Charles Darwin, can be summarized as follows:

1. More are born than can survive
2. The offspring have brought with them the good and bad traits of their parents
3. These differences in individuals of any species set up a competition for food and space
4. Those with the advantages survive the competition and
5. The survivors pass the advantages for survival on to their offspring.

Albinos of any wild animal population have a slim chance of survival anywhere except in the Arctic (figure 1.16). Albinos are rare because the color trait for white is rarely passed on to offspring except as a recessive trait. A white animal is easily spotted in most natural environments by predators and removed from the population before breeding and passing on the undesirable trait.

Law of Fertility

The *law of fertility* for the biosphere states that nutrients must recycle to keep the environmental system functioning. A tree can be thought of as a nutrient pump (figure 1.17). The roots of the tree pump water and soil elements up through the plumbing of the tree cells and, by the photosynthetic process, produce leaves and branches. In a

Figure 1.16 Albino deer herd. The Argonne Laboratory in northern Illinois is home for a large herd of albino deer.
(*Photo:* David A. Castillon)

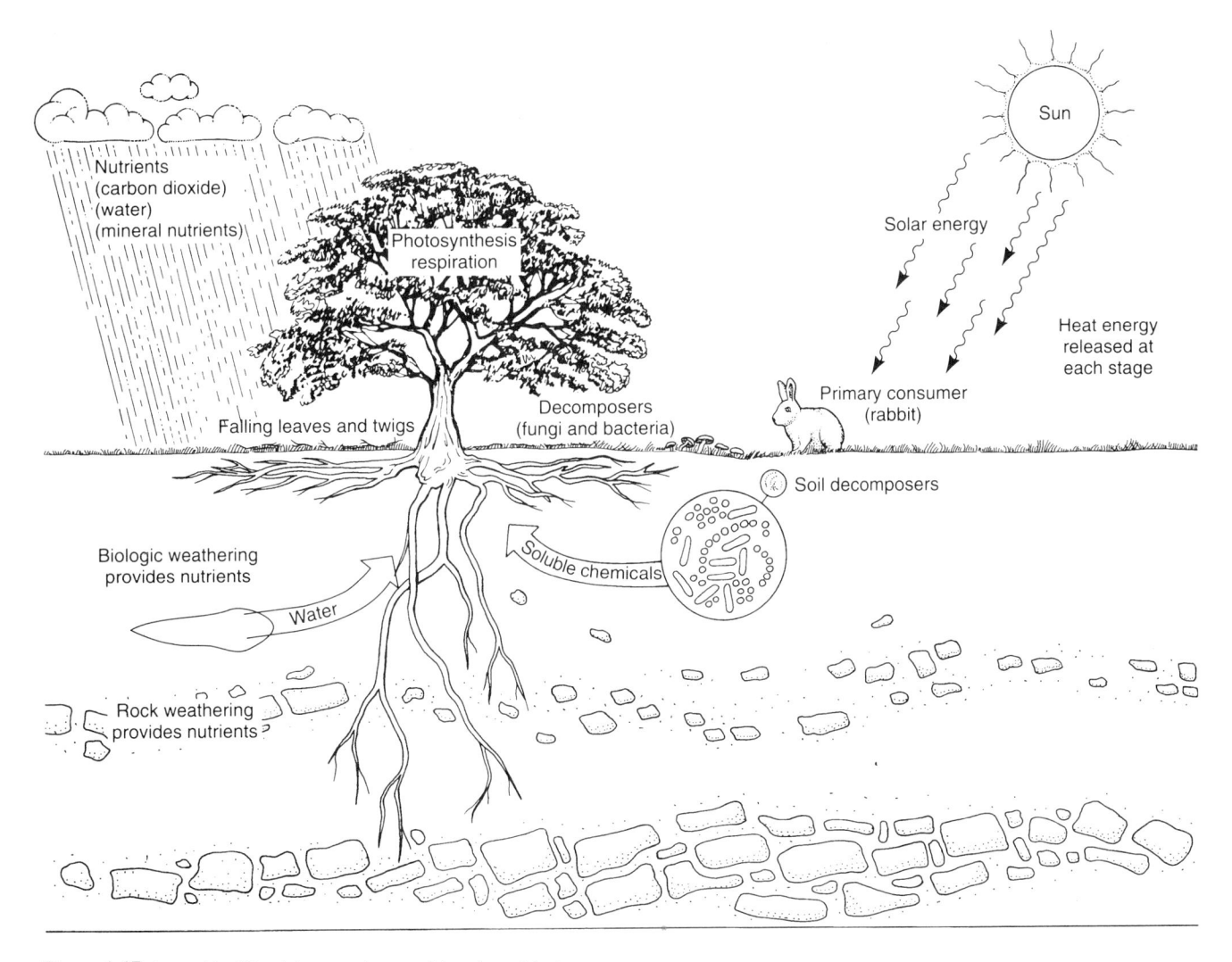

Figure 1.17 Law of fertility. A tree can be considered a nutrient pump. It extracts nutrients released by rock weathering and by biologic decomposition, then it returns these nutrients to the soil as leaf litter for recycling and maintenance of soil fertility.

Introduction to the Conservation of Natural Resources

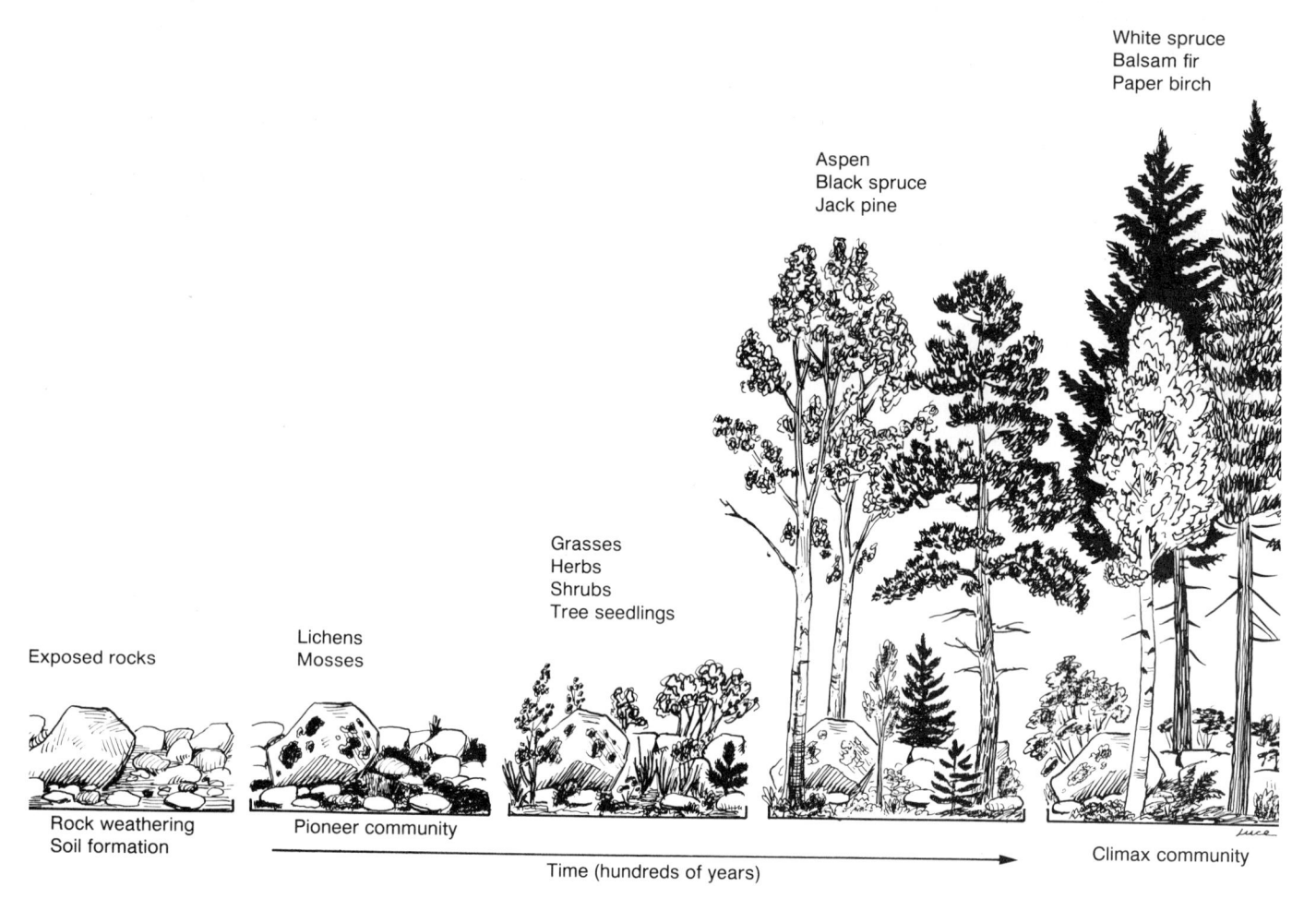

Figure 1.18 Primary succession. A new landform or rock surface evolves through a sequence of vegetative stages. A climax community forms that is adjusted to the soil and climate of the region.

From William P. Cunningham and Barbara Woodworth Saigo, *Environmental Science: A Global Concern.* Copyright © 1990 Wm. C. Brown Publishers, Dubuque, Iowa. All Rights Reserved. Reprinted by permission.

forest the leaves die and fall to the ground. The dead leaf is returned to the soil by organic decomposition, and fertility of the soil is maintained by this and the addition of elements from the atmosphere and rock weathering deeper in the soil.

Law of Succession

The *law of succession* for biotic communities states that there is an orderly sequence of plant species that will occupy a newly established landform or recently altered landscape. For example, the Kilauea volcano eruptions on Hawaii have produced an orderly sequence of vegetative growth following the deposit of new lava landforms. This is called *primary succession.* If the new landform stabilizes and no new lava flows interrupt the vegetative succession, the area will become a tropical rainforest community on the wetter, higher, windward elevations and a shrub desert at the lower, coastal, dry leeward sites.

Figure 1.18 illustrates primary succession for a North American spruce fir forest. Another example of succession that is common in North America is called *secondary succession,* the sequence of vegetation that starts after a fire. If a fire-burned forest is left to reestablish itself and there has not been serious soil erosion, it will go through an orderly sequence from pioneer species with fire-resistant seeds, to successional species, and finally to the climax vegetation that occupied the site originally. The *climax vegetation* is the association of grasses, shrubs, and/or trees that is in equilibrium with the climate and soil of the site. Many times humans will interrupt or hasten the successional process by seeding a desired species and skipping some of the earlier time-consuming successional stages.

Law of Control

The *law of control* suggests that many species of animals have population control mechanisms that govern their members. Birds like the snowy owl will change their clutch size after observing the food supply of their feeding-breeding territory (figure 1.19). They will lay only four or

Figure 1.19 Biogeography of the snowy owl. This species changes clutch size as a population control mechanism. Shaded area indicates breeding range for the snowy owl.

Redrawn by permission of the Smithsonian Institution Press from *North American Owls*, by Paul A. Johnsgard, fig. 27, p. 136; figure depicting biogeography of the Snowy Owl. © Smithsonian Institution 1988.

five eggs if the numbers of brown lemmings, which is their main food source, is low, but will lay as many as twelve to fifteen eggs during peak lemming years. The pomarine Jaeger, also an arctic nesting bird, expands its territorial size if food supply is low but always lays two eggs. This forces some potential nesting Jaegers to not breed every year. These are but two examples that illustrate animal population control mechanisms. Such population control traits are passed on through generations of these species. The control is a survival adaptation process that keeps the species from outstripping their food supply. All members of natural communities have population control mechanisms. If they didn't they would totally consume and destroy their food supply and would then starve themselves out of existence. Habitat dictates how many of each species can live in harmony with the land. The *population size* for each species is defined by the carrying capacity of the habitat for that species.

There is a maximum number of people that can be supported on earth, but exactly what this maximum population can be is yet to be decided. This number will be impossible to establish until we learn to manage wisely the natural resources of the earth. After we have established a good understanding of the workings of our environment, and have learned to manage our natural resources, we will then be able to more accurately determine the maximum number of the human species that can be supported in the areas we choose to occupy or from which we can import resources. One thing is for sure, the better we learn to manage our natural resources, the greater will be the carrying capacity of the earth for human populations.

Humans armed with the methods provided by modern technology have the ability to change the natural environment. Deserts bloom with the water from irrigation nozzles. Refrigeration allows long-term food storage. Transportation makes for easy migration. Each of these and many more human modifications of the natural environment will increase the carrying capacity of the earth and must be considered in the conservation of natural resources.

Summary

This chapter has provided an introduction, and established a format, for the text. We want to conserve our natural resources. To do this we need to understand the biotic pyramid through both geologic and biologic time. The laws that govern the biosphere apply to all environments. We must learn to adjust our thinking to act as a member of the land community. To better understand membership in the land community we need to get more geographically specific.

We will do this by developing different biotic pyramids for the different physical regions of North America. Each physical region has its own unique characteristics of soil, geology, and climate. The remaining chapters in Part I describe the physical environments of the North American continent. The geology, soils, climate, water, and biogeographic regions, will be delineated and described. For example, the relationship between climate and vegetation is illustrated in Figure 1.20.

Precipitation and temperature are both factors in the physical environment that dictate a predictable vegetative response.

In Part II we will explore the *human-land relationship,* where we play the part of land manager. Our position at the top of the biotic pyramid carries with it great responsibility as land steward. As stewards we must be responsible for the health of the land; specifically, we must respond positively to the capacity of the land for self-renewal. We must use the land and its

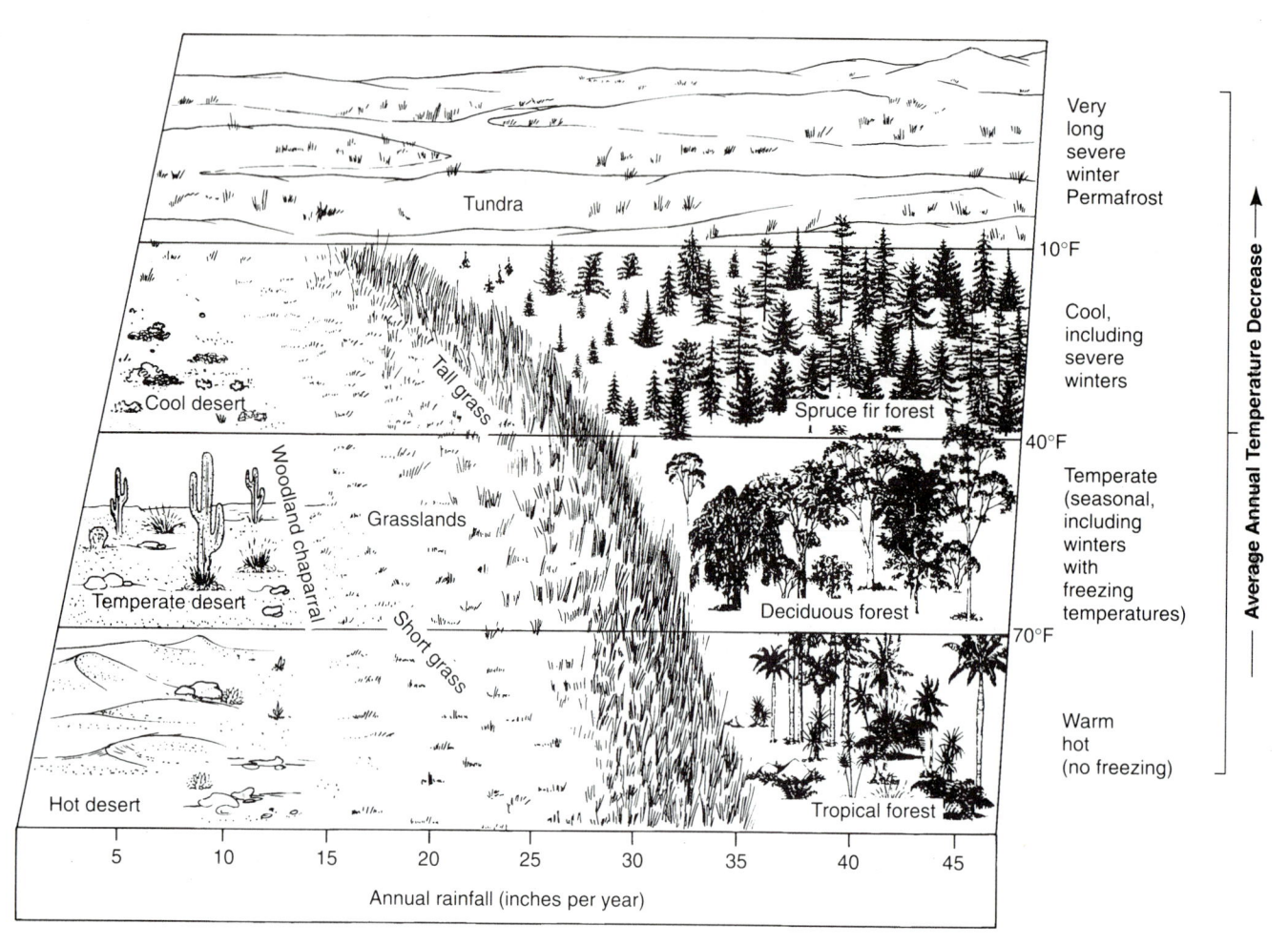

Figure 1.20 Climate-vegetation relationship. As average annual temperature decreases from hot to cold on the vertical scale, precipitation increases on the horizontal scale. The resulting vegetation associations are illustrated on the diagram.
Bernard J. Nebel, *Environmental Science: The Way the World Works*, 3/E, © 1990, p. 38. Adapted by permission of Prentice-Hall, Inc., Englewood Cliffs, NJ.

resources wisely and conserve for future generations those resources that lend themselves to conservation management. Conservation practices, both good and bad, will be discussed. Areas where additional study seem necessary for a wise management decision will be so indicated. The important thing to remember is that we must not act too hastily and remove any parts of the land organism before we understand their role in the land community.

It will be easier for each of us to establish a land ethic for ourselves that we can pass on to our offspring if we understand our place in the land community. The better we understand the land the easier it will be for us to love it, a necessary prerequisite to a land ethic.

Key Words and Phrases

Albinos
Biogeography
Biologic time
Biosphere
Biotic pyramid
Carrying capacity
Climax vegetation
Community
Conservation
Consumer
Earth Day

Ecological land ethic
Ecosystems
Environmental impact statement
Geologic time
Holocene
Homo sapien
Individual
Inexhaustible resources
Land ethic
Law of adaptation
Law of control

Law of fertility
Law of production
Law of succession
National Environmental Policy Act (NEPA)
Natural resources
Nonrenewable resources
Outstanding scientific discovery of the twentieth century
Philosophical land ethic

Photosynthetic process
Population
Potential resources
Preservation

Primary succession
Producer
Recyclable resources
Renewable resources

Resource
Restoration
Secondary succession
Species
Time

Questions and Discussion Topics

1. Preservation, restoration, and environmental quality are key ideas in the history of conservation. How do each of these ideas relate to the Conservation of Natural Resources? What role have the following agencies had in promoting these ideas: USFS, NPS, SCS, TVA, CCC, and EPA?
2. What are natural resources and how do you decide into which category a resource belongs? (Inexhaustible, Renewable, Nonrenewable, Potential)
3. Why is time important in conservation of natural resources? (Geologic, Biologic, Future)
4. Write down your name on the top of a blank biotic pyramid, then ask yourself this question: What is on each level of my own personal biotic pyramid? What is on each level of the pyramid for the natural environment of your geographic location?
5. In what ways have the laws of the biosphere affected your life? In what ways do they operate in the natural community of your geographic area? (Production, Adaptation, Fertility, Succession, Control)
6. Do you think the present governmental administrations are doing their part to promote the conservation of natural resources? What else could they do?
7. Do the environmental laws that have been passed by the government really protect the environment? (Clean Air Act, Wilderness Act, NEPA Law)
8. Do you have a personal land ethic? If yes, describe what it is? If no, why do you feel that you don't have or don't need one?

References for Further Study

Eiseley, L. 1957. *The Immense Journey.* New York: Vintage Books, Random House. An imaginative naturalist explores the mysteries of man and nature.

Fox, S. 1981. *John Muir and His Legacy: The American Conservation Movement.* Boston: Little, Brown. A good early history of conservation.

Kormondy, E. J. 1984. *Concepts of Ecology.* 3rd ed. New York: Harper and Row. A good readable ecology text.

Leopold, A. 1949. *A Sand County Almanac.* New York: Ballantine Books, Random House. A classic in conservation-required reading.

The Conservation Foundation. 1982, 1984. *State of the Environment.* Washington, D.C. Environmental updates and assessments of federal programs.

World Resources Institute. 1990. *World Resources—1990–91.* Washington D.C: Oxford University Press. Up-to-date world data on resources, published yearly. A guide to the global environment.

Chapter 2

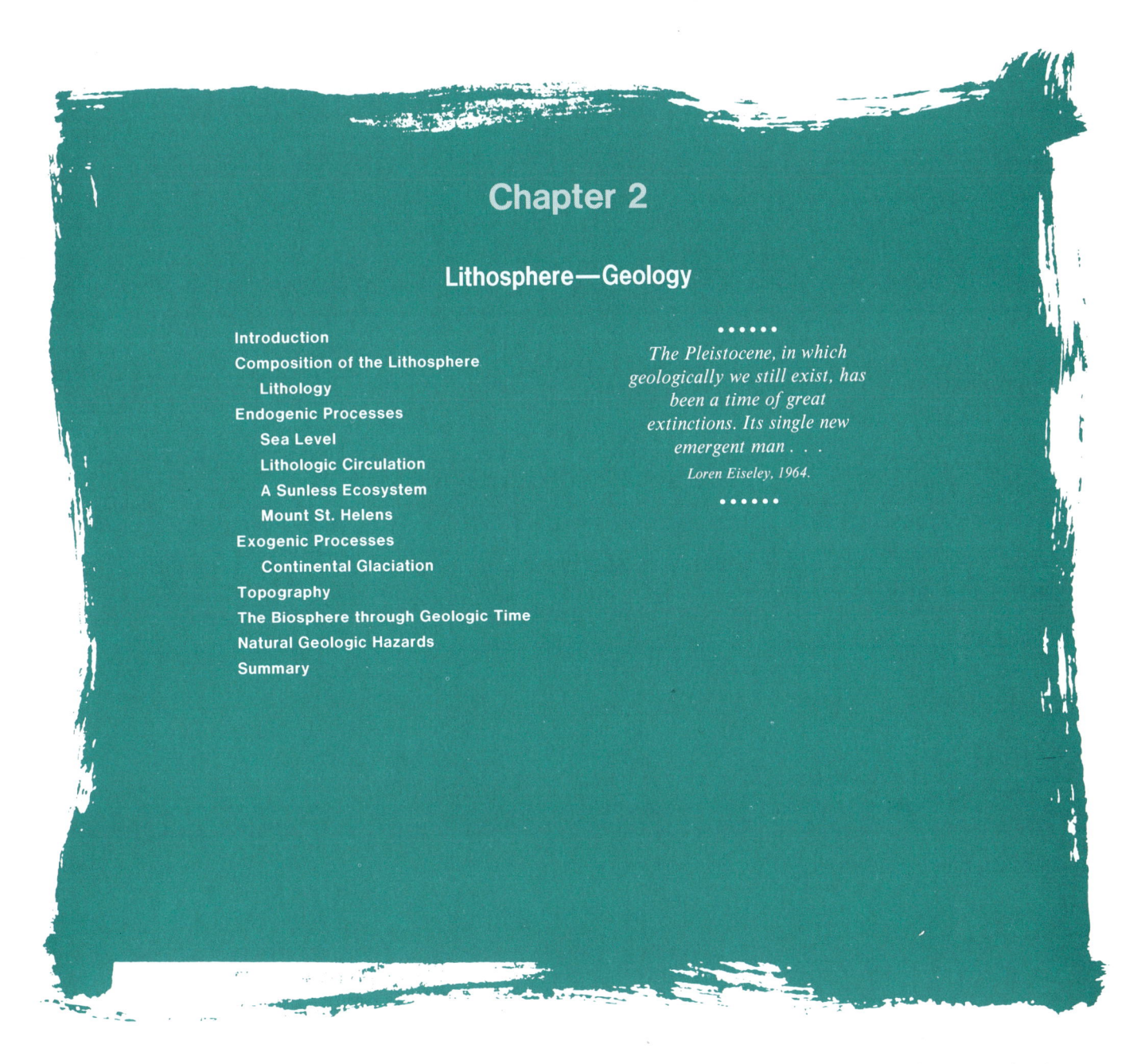

Lithosphere—Geology

Introduction
Composition of the Lithosphere
    Lithology
Endogenic Processes
    Sea Level
    Lithologic Circulation
    A Sunless Ecosystem
    Mount St. Helens
Exogenic Processes
    Continental Glaciation
Topography
The Biosphere through Geologic Time
Natural Geologic Hazards
Summary

The Pleistocene, in which geologically we still exist, has been a time of great extinctions. Its single new emergent man . . .
Loren Eiseley, 1964.

Introduction

The planet Earth has two "motors" that drive the geologic systems. The first is the **sun,** providing the energy that drives the *exogenic* (surface) systems. The land-sculpturing agents of **wind, water,** and **ice,** along with gravity, change the above-sea-level surface of the earth into diverse landforms and terrestrial habitats. The second device is the **internal heat** of the earth, generated by **radioactive decay,** which provides the energy that drives the *endogenic* (internal) systems. The distribution of internal heat and density drives the volcanism and earth movements that change the surface of the earth from within. This is especially true where the exogenic processes are not as active, such as on the ocean floor where submarine mountains and ocean basins are created. *Volcanism* is the process where *magma* (molten rock), gas, and ash are vented to the earth's surface. *Igneous rocks* are formed by the crystallization of magma as it cools.

The internal and external sources of energy have divided the North American continent into a diverse set of landscapes that can be mapped into **physiographic regions** (figure 2.1). The backbone of the continent is called the **Canadian Shield,** which is composed of rocks dated at more than 2.5 billion years. This region has been added to and eroded from by the geologic processes to form the present-day continent and the other physiographic regions. The **Appalachian Mountains** region and the **Interior Highlands** were formed during the Paleozoic Era (figure 1.10). The *Paleozoic Era* is defined by the beginning and ending of the Appalachian mountain-building episodes. The interior western basins and mountains were formed during the

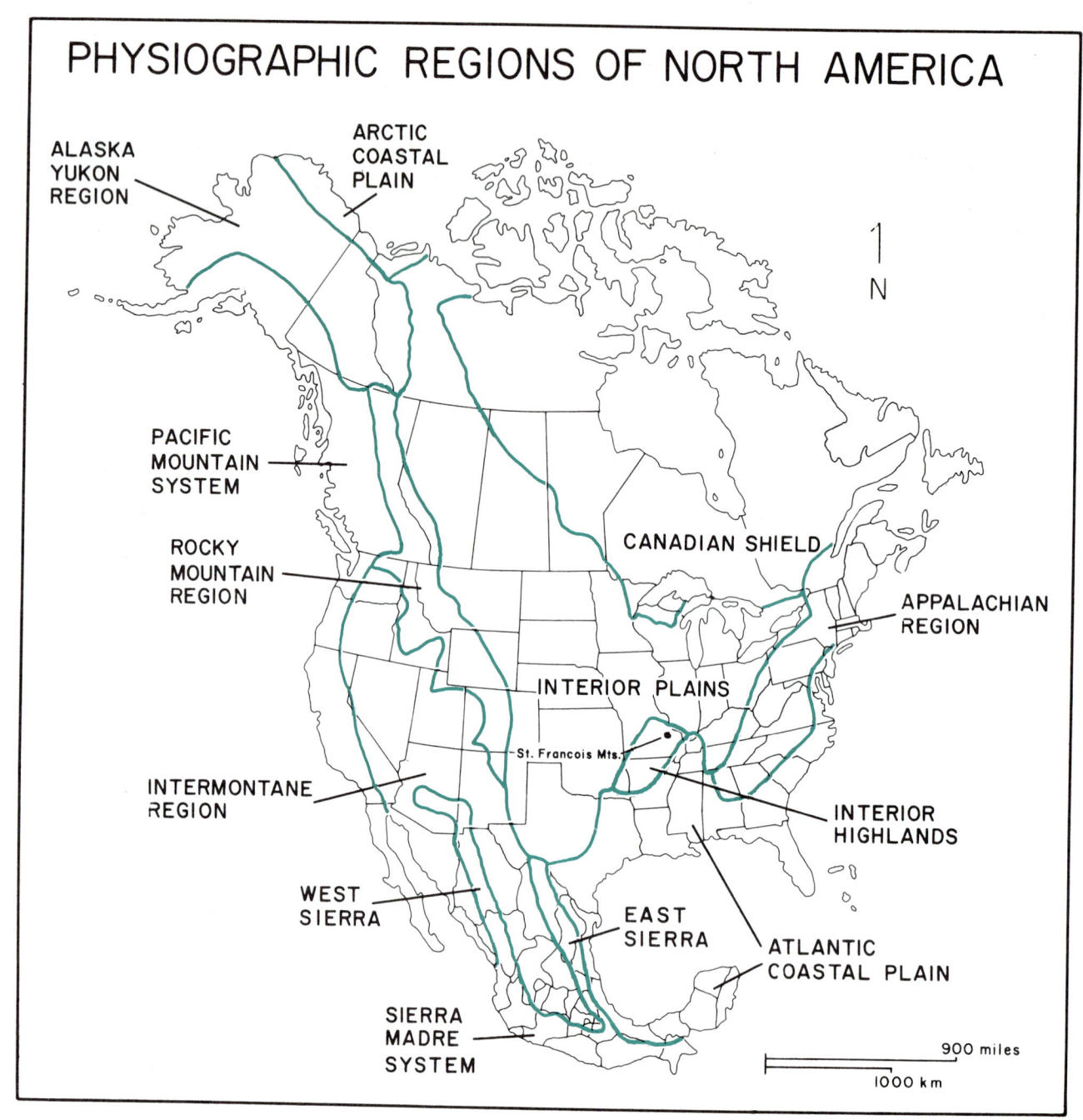

Figure 2.1 Physiographic regions of North America.
(*Cartographer:* Douglas Hemsath.)

Mesozoic Era, defined by the beginning and ending of the Rocky Mountains mountain-building episodes. The existing **Pacific Coastal** ranges are *Cenozoic Era* in age, are still forming, and define the present Era. The **Interior and Atlantic Coastal** plains consist of Paleozoic to Cenozoic-age rocks that have been uplifted at irregular intervals throughout the last 570 million years. Older Precambrian Era basement rocks protrude through the younger rocks in places to form low mountains. The *Precambrian Era* is all geologic time before the Paleozoic Era (570 my). The St. Francois Mountains in the interior highlands region is an example of a Precambrian outcrop (figure 2.2).

Composition of the Lithosphere

The *lithosphere* is defined as the near-surface solid earth (not including ice) made up mostly of *silicate rocks,* that is, rocks whose minerals have silica and oxygen as a part of their crystal structure. Silicate igneous rocks are divided into two groups, *intrusive* and *extrusive*. Igneous rocks form from the crystallization of solid earth molten material; however, intrusive rocks usually solidify slower than extrusive rocks. Table 2.1 gives the relative amount of each element in the lithosphere. Approximately 81% of the solid earth materials contain silica (Si) and oxygen

Figure 2.2 St. Francois Mts., Missouri. Precambrain granite outcrop on the eastern edge of the interior highlands. Locally known as the Elephant Rocks (exfoliation boulders).
(*Photo:* David A. Castillon)

Table 2.1

Atomic Composition of Elements in the Lithosphere in Percent

Element	Percent Composition
O	60.4
Si	20.5
Al	6.2
H	2.92
Na	2.49
Fe	1.90
Ca	1.88
Mg	1.77
K	1.37
Ti	0.27
C	0.16
P	0.08
S	0.04

(O). These numbers would appear to be in error because much of the solid earth's near-surface rocks are limestones ($CaCO_3$) and dolostones (($Mg,Ca)CO_3$), neither of which are silicates. The thin layers of *sedimentary rocks,* rocks that have been deposited by exogenic or biologic processes on the earth's surface up to thousands of feet thick, are a very small part of the lithosphere, which has a radius of almost 6,440 km (4,000 mi). The near-surface rocks of the lithosphere are more important than the deep silicates because the near surface rocks are the parent material for the soil. The soil layer, not including the soil biota, is the most important part of the lithosphere. Soil represents the interaction of climate and lithosphere, and provides the support medium and nutrients for the biosphere. The soil will be discussed in chapter 5.

Lithology

The solid earth has a rigid crust called the lithosphere. It is from 10 to 700 km (6–400 mi) thick and rides on the pliable semi-molten layer called the *asthenosphere* (figure 2.3). The plate tectonics mechanisms allow large blocks of the lithosphere, called *plates,* to move on the asthenosphere. This **lithologic circulation system** is driven by the internal heat of the earth and runs on a geological time scale.

The molten materials from the earth's interior that reach the earth's surface and then solidify are called extrusive igneous rocks. The materials that solidify below the surface are intrusive igneous rocks. Both are important lithologic materials that form the parent material for sediment and soils. Most igneous rocks are covered by a layer of *sedimentary rocks,* which are formed at near-surface temperatures by the cementation of sediments (particles of lithologic material). The top rock layers of lithologic material of the earth's terrestrial environments are mostly sedimentary. In some places sedimentary or igneous rocks have undergone marked change produced by heat or pressure (figure 2.4). These rocks are called *metamorphic.* A limestone can be changed to marble by metamorphism. Surface rocks are covered with residuum and unconsolidated materials. Residuum weathered from the rocks and unconsolidated sediments provide the parent material for the soil layer that is the surface of the terrestrial environments. Figure 2.4 is a schematic diagram illustrating the rock cycle and relationship between igneous, sedimentary, and metamorphic rocks.

Rock type and composition dictate, to a large degree, the resulting soil. Soil is a key *abiotic* (nonliving) factor on the base of the biotic pyramid. Soils are formed by physical and chemical weathering of surface rocks. *Physical weathering* of rocks occurs when they are broken down into smaller particles by physical force. Expansion and contraction from freezing and thawing is an example. *Chemical weathering* occurs when a chemical reaction changes the structure of the rock material; for example, the conversion of an igneous mineral to a clay is a chemical weathering alternation.

Endogenic Processes

The geologic time scale introduced in chapter 1 and defined in the introduction of this chapter will be used throughout this text to age the lithospheric surface of the earth, which is very old. The present surface of the earth is constantly changing and can be divided by sea level into two very different environments. The above-sea-level area is varied in character and called the terrestrial environment. Representing approximately 30% of the surface of

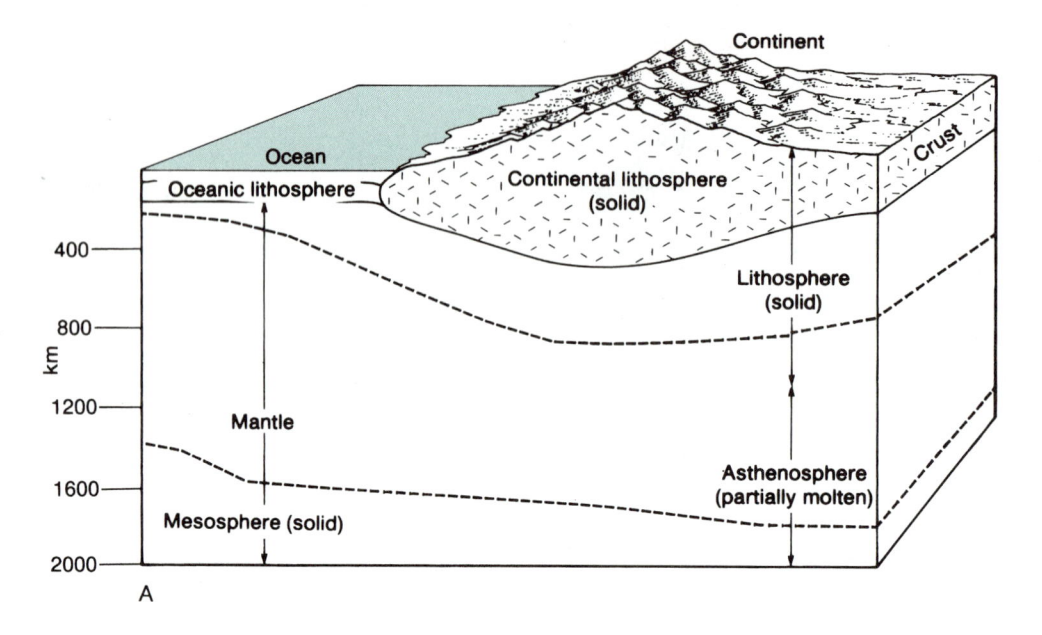

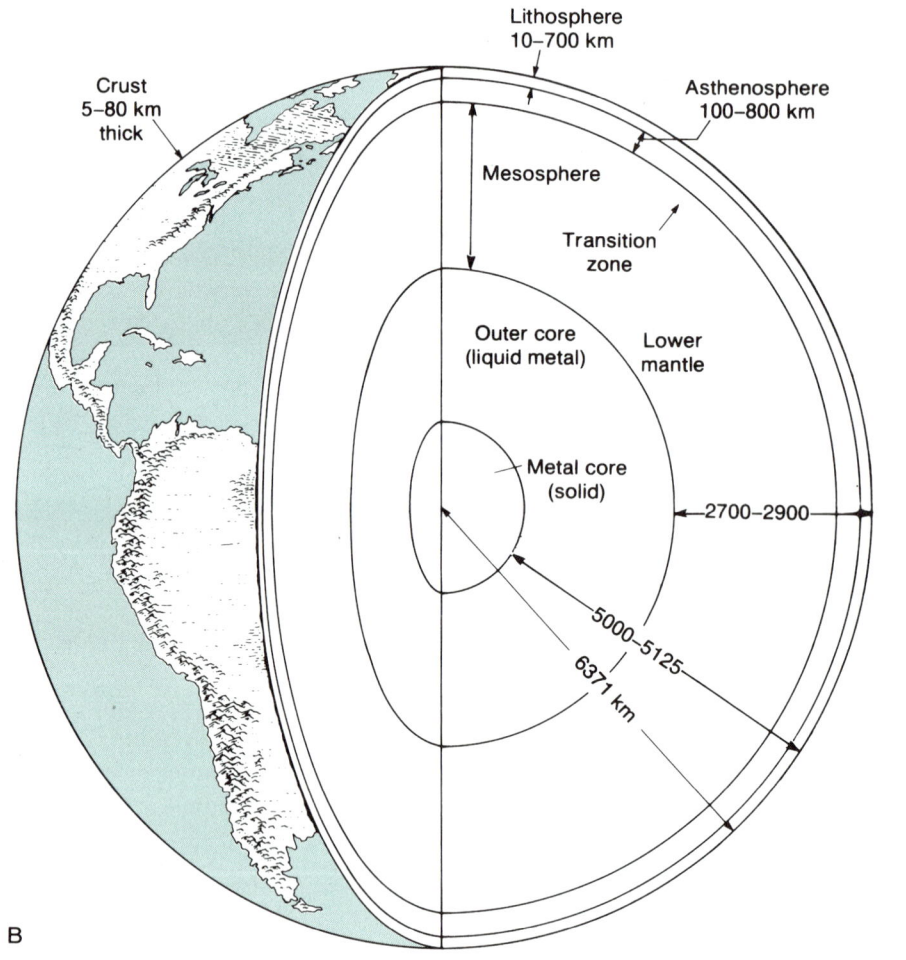

Figure 2.3 Layers of the solid earth.
From Arthur Getis, et al., *Introduction to Geography*, 3d ed. Copyright © 1991 Wm. C. Brown Publishers, Dubuque, Iowa. All Rights Reserved. Reprinted by permission.

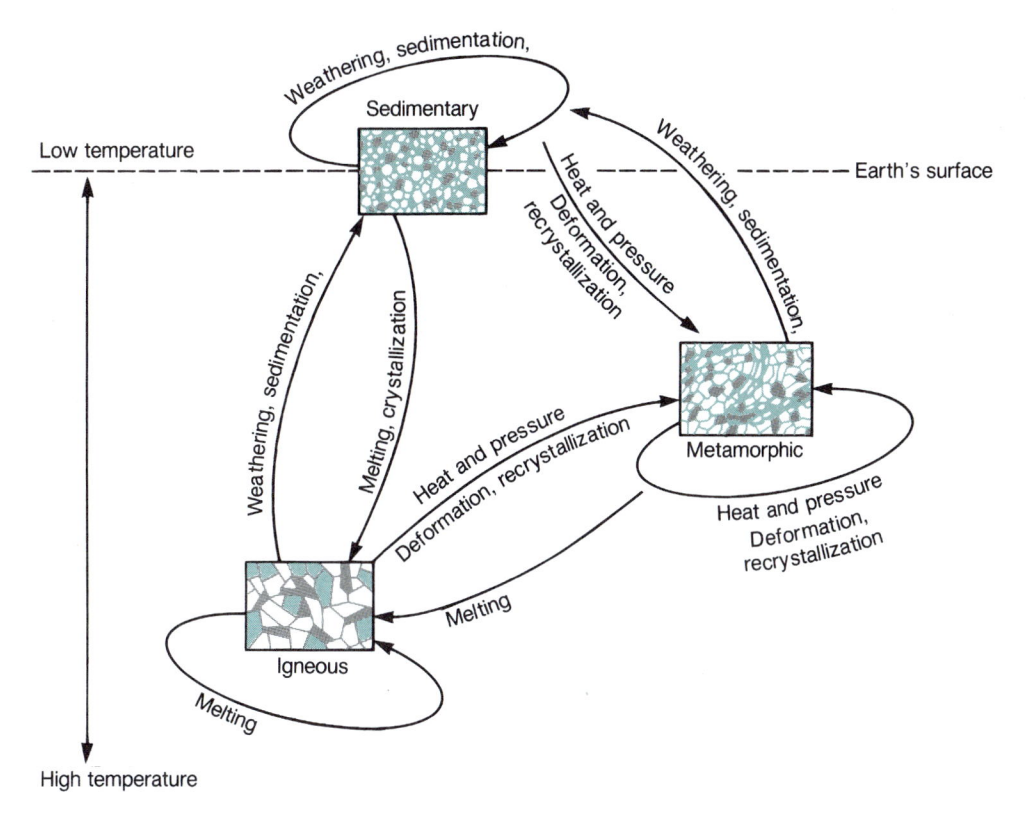

Figure 2.4 The rock cycle. Geologic processes are at work continuously forming new rocks from solid earth materials.
From Carla W. Montgomery, *Physical Geology*, 2d ed. Copyright © 1990 Wm. C. Brown Publishers, Dubuque, Iowa. All Rights Reserved. Reprinted by permission.

the earth, this terrestrial environment is dotted with and crossed by above-sea-level aquatic environments. The below-sea-level part of the earth's surface, approximately 70%, is made up of **continental shelves, slopes** and **rises, and deep ocean basins** (abyssal plains) and **trenches.** Figure 2.5 gives the defining average depths and slopes for each of these ocean floor features.

Sea Level

Sea level, which is used to separate the terrestrial from the aquatic environments, is not fixed. Sea level is constantly changing and this has profound effects on the earth's environments and the physical variables at the base of the biotic pyramid.

The present day system of oceans is believed to have begun its formation about 170 million years before present (ybp). The oldest rocks for both the Atlantic and Pacific Ocean floor basins have been dated from the Jurassic Period (figure 2.6). The Atlantic and Pacific Oceans began to alternately grow and shrink by the plate tectonic processes that build mountains and subduct ocean basins. *Plate tectonics* is the general name given to movements of the earth's surface that are caused by the venting of internal heat. The Atlantic Ocean is still growing at a rate of 1–3 cm (0.4–1.2 in) per year. The Pacific Ocean is shrinking, and continues to get smaller at a rate of from 3 to 10 cm (1.2–3.9 in) per year. The increase in the size of the Atlantic Ocean by the end of our century will not be noticeable, even to a careful observer. For conservation of natural resources, the ocean basins can be thought of as fairly stable geologic features of our environment. Even though stable, the amount of water that fills these basins is highly variable. Sea level is constantly changing and has been both hundreds of meters higher and lower than the present-day level. The latest major change occurred during the last 20,000 years. Sea level was 100 m (328 ft) lower than today during the last major ice advance over North America. Sea level continues to rise at a rate of 10 cm (4 in) per 100 years. Changing sea level has profound environmental consequences and should be taken into consideration whenever coastal areas are being examined environmentally.

Sea-level changes are the result of changing climatic conditions and changing rates of sea-floor spreading. As oceans grow, (e.g., Atlantic Ocean) new sea-floor material is extruded from the earth's interior by volcanic action building a mid-ocean ridge (*sea-floor spreading zone*). The size of the ridge is determined by the rate of flow of volcanic material up to the ocean floor. The rock material accumulates and spreads laterally, building a below-sea-level mountain called a mid-ocean ridge. The faster the rate of sea-floor spreading, the bigger the ridge. The bigger

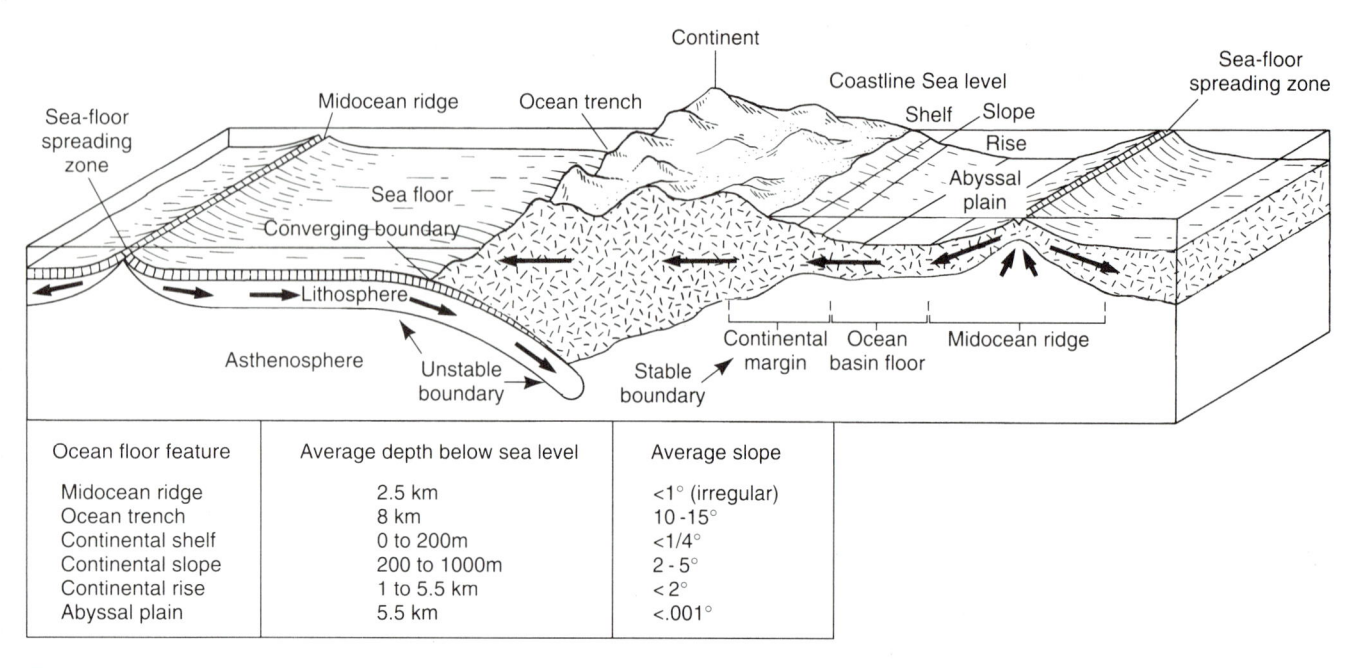

Figure 2.5 Landforms of the ocean basins. Average depths and slopes for major ocean basin features are given.

Ocean floor feature	Average depth below sea level	Average slope
Midocean ridge	2.5 km	<1° (irregular)
Ocean trench	8 km	10-15°
Continental shelf	0 to 200m	<1/4°
Continental slope	200 to 1000m	2-5°
Continental rise	1 to 5.5 km	<2°
Abyssal plain	5.5 km	<.001°

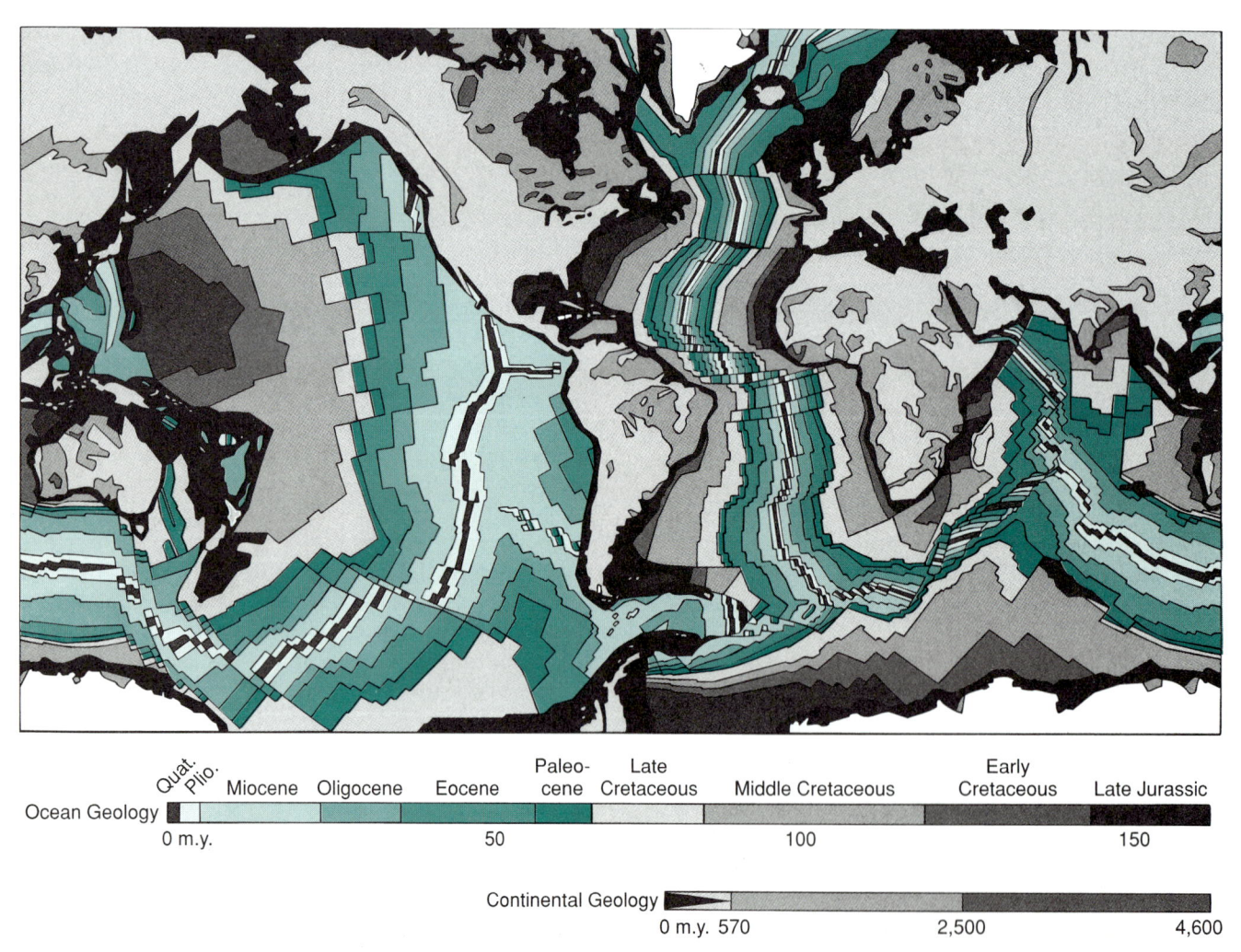

Figure 2.6 Geologic age of the floor of the ocean basins and continental backbone. Note that the youngest age ocean floor is on the mid-ocean ridge and the oldest ocean floor is at the stable continent margins.

From David Laing, *The Earth Systems*. Copyright © 1991 Wm. C. Brown Publishers, Dubuque, Iowa. All Rights Reserved. Reprinted by permission.

Physical and Biological Variables of the Natural Environment

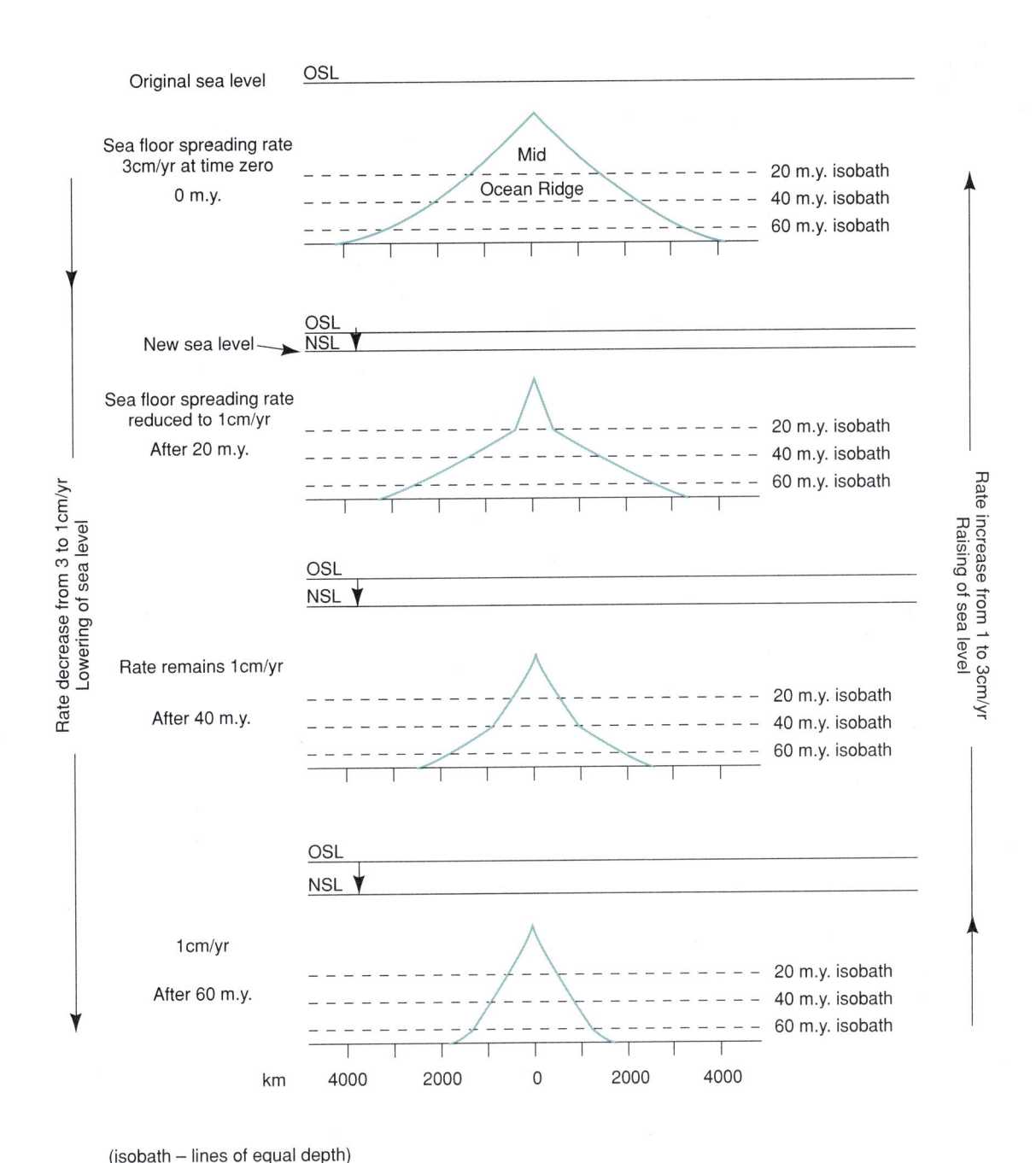

Figure 2.7 Sea-level changes in response to changing rates of sea-floor spreading. Size of the mid-ocean ridge is determined by rate of sea-floor spreading (greater the rate, the larger the ridge). A large mid-ocean ridge displaces more seawater than a small ridge. Therefore, when rate decreases, sea level drops. (20 million year (my) through 60 my cycle is illustrated).

the ridge, the more water displaced, and the higher the sea level. When rates subside, sea level goes down (figure 2.7). The rise and fall of sea level caused by changing rates of sea-floor spreading occur in geologic time frames of millions of years. However, sea-level changes that accompany climatic changes occur in shorter cycles.

Another environmental consequence of changing sea level is the changing climatic condition that accompanies reduced or increased amounts of surface water on the earth. We still do not understand the complexities of the relationships between these two variables. It is a fact that there is a relationship, and if we understood the relationship better than we do, we might be able to predict the weather accurately more than five days in advance.

Lithologic Circulation

The mechanisms of *lithologic circulation,* sometimes called **plate tectonics** or *continental drift,* are controlled by the energy emitted by radioactive decay in the interior

Lithosphere—Geology

of the earth. Motions of the lithologic plates on the asthenosphere build mountains. Figure 2.8 illustrates the movement of oceanic and continental plates along the North American coasts. The Atlantic Ocean is growing. The western half of its basin is attached to the North American continent and they move together to the west. The Pacific Ocean contact with the North American continent is one of collision and compression. The eastern half of the Pacific Ocean plate is moving east and the two are colliding along the west coast of North America. The thinner Pacific Ocean plate is being subducted under the thicker North American plate, creating a *trenching zone* (figure 2.9). The friction created by this motion is generating heat for volcanism (Mt. St. Helens, May, 1980), and shock waves called earthquakes (San Francisco-Oakland, California, October, 1989). As continents move over the face of the earth, lithologic material is cycled. Ocean basin crust is subducted, melted, and recycled in a never-ending system of lithologic circulation. Continents drifting across the face of the earth change their latitudinal position and earth-sun relationship. This causes changes in climate, which in turn changes the composition of the biosphere in geologic time.

A Sunless Ecosystem

Ocean salinity, which affects seawater density and the movement of ocean currents, is controlled to some degree by the additions of juvenile water at sea-floor spreading zones. *Juvenile water* is the hydrated brine (or salty water) released by volcanic processes as molten lava is extruded from the earth's interior. Heat is also vented in these regions and ocean temperature and density are affected. A study conducted by Robert R. Hessler and Richard A. Lutz from Scripps Institute of Oceanography aboard the submarine "Alvin" found communities of tube worms in the sunless depths of the Galápagos trench 2,400 meters (7,800 feet) below the surface (figure 2.10). Similar communities of fauna have been found as far north as the Juan de Fuca Ridge off the Oregon Coast (45°N). It is believed that hydrogen sulfide and heat from the earth's interior provide the basis for life. If life can exist and food chains develop without the aid of photosynthesis, this would mean a whole new biotic pyramid would need to be developed where the driving force is internal heat and not the sun.

Hot springs on the ocean floor that vent internal heat and magma also vent juvenile water, which reacts with ocean water to produce high concentrations of hydrogen sulfide (H_2S). **Bacteria** that derive their energy from oxidation of hydrogen sulfide are common in the hot spring ecological system. The bacteria are the primary producers at the base of this ecological pyramid (figure 2.11). The energy driving the system flows, not from the sun as in photosynthesis, but from the radioactive breakdown of long-lived isotopes of uranium, thorium, and potassium inside the solid earth. **Giant tube worms** are the primary consumers in the biotic pyramid of the deep ocean.

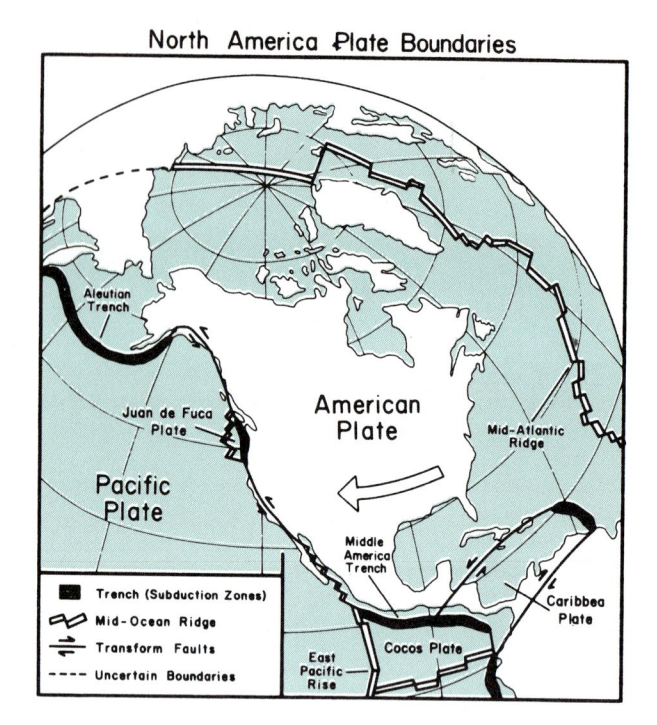

Figure 2.8 Nature of the boundaries of the north segment of the American plate. The East Coast of the North American plate is stable because it is attached to the western half of the Atlantic ocean floor. The West Coast is unstable because it is colliding with the Pacific Ocean plate.
From Colin W. Stearn, et al., *Geological Evolution of North America*, 3d ed. Copyright © John Wiley & Sons, Inc., New York, NY. Reprinted by permission of John Wiley & Sons, Inc.
(*Cartographer:* Douglas Hemsath)

The tube worms are fed upon by **eelpouts,** a scavenger vertebrate, that may be the top carnivore of the sunless ecosystem. The bacteria could be relatives of the bacteria that were the only organisms of the earth before photosynthesis and long before flowers became a part of our natural environment. We do not understand all of the complexities of the relationships that exist between the release of the internal heat of the earth and its consequences on the earth's environment and natural resources. Most of the heat vented from the earth's interior to the surface comes through the ocean floor. Because of the uncertainties surrounding the role that oceans play in overall environmental interrelationships, caution should be the guide in our use of oceans. Ocean dumping of garbage and dredging materials should be controlled since the long-term environmental consequences of such actions are not known. That is reason enough not to damage the ocean basin resource of the open seas.

Mount St. Helens

Internal heat is not always vented through the ocean floor. Volcanoes can erupt on terrestrial landscapes. An example is Mount St. Helens in Washington State, which erupted in May, 1980 (figure 2.12). Heat continues to be vented from the earth's interior to the surface of this volcano. A number of changes took place in the area of the

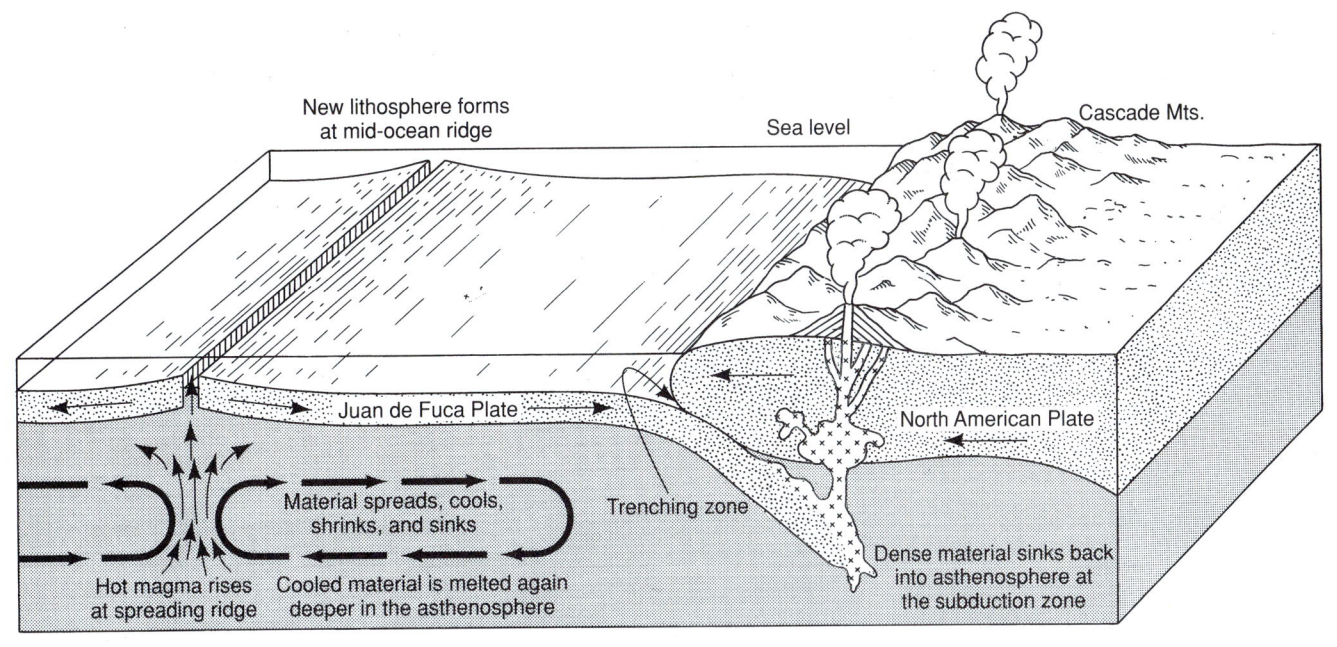

Figure 2.9 Trenching zone created from plate movements along the coast of Oregon and Washington. The Juan de Fuca plate is being subducted by the North American plate to form the Cascade Mountains, which includes Mount St. Helens.

eruption that have environmental consequences. Natural events can cause almost total environmental destruction (figure 2.13). Sulfur dioxide, ash, and other pollutants were released into the atmosphere. Snow melt and subsequent flooding was a major cause of destruction. In a day and age when humans are blamed for much environmental damage, it is somewhat reassuring to know that nature has its own way of upsetting the natural balance of our world. With a lot of time, the area of Mount St. Helens will return to normal and life will go on. But remember, there is nothing very normal about nature.

Exogenic Processes

The **sun** is the motor that runs our exogenic systems. It is the driving force that sets into motion our **atmospheric, hydrologic,** and **oceanic circulation** systems. The atmospheric circulation system will be discussed in detail in the next chapter on weather and climate. The hydrologic and oceanic circulation systems will be examined in chapter 4. These three circulation systems provide the **wind, water, ice,** and **snow** that act as agents for the exogenic processes. Water in its liquid or solid form is precipitated onto the land, where it moves by gravity down through the surface material or downhill over the surface slope. The water that sinks through the surface material continues the weathering processes of the solid earth materials, breaking them loose for transport by the *agents of erosion* (wind, water, or ice). The erosion of the surface begins the development of a new landform and a new erosional landscape. The materials being transported also create new depositional landforms (figure 2.14). The exogenic processes continually alter the landscape, creating new *erosional* and *depositional landforms* that will become terrestrial habitats for renewable natural resources.

Figure 2.10 The sunless ecosystem's organisms. Giant tube worms (*Riftia pachyptila*), mussels (*Bathymodiolis thermophilus*), crabs (*Bathograea thermydron*), and shrimp (*Alvinocaris lusca*) are the typical organisms in the Rose Garden site on the Galápagos Rift, 2,400 m below the surface.
(Photo: Dr. Robert R. Hessler, Scripps Inst. of Oceanography)

Lithosphere—Geology

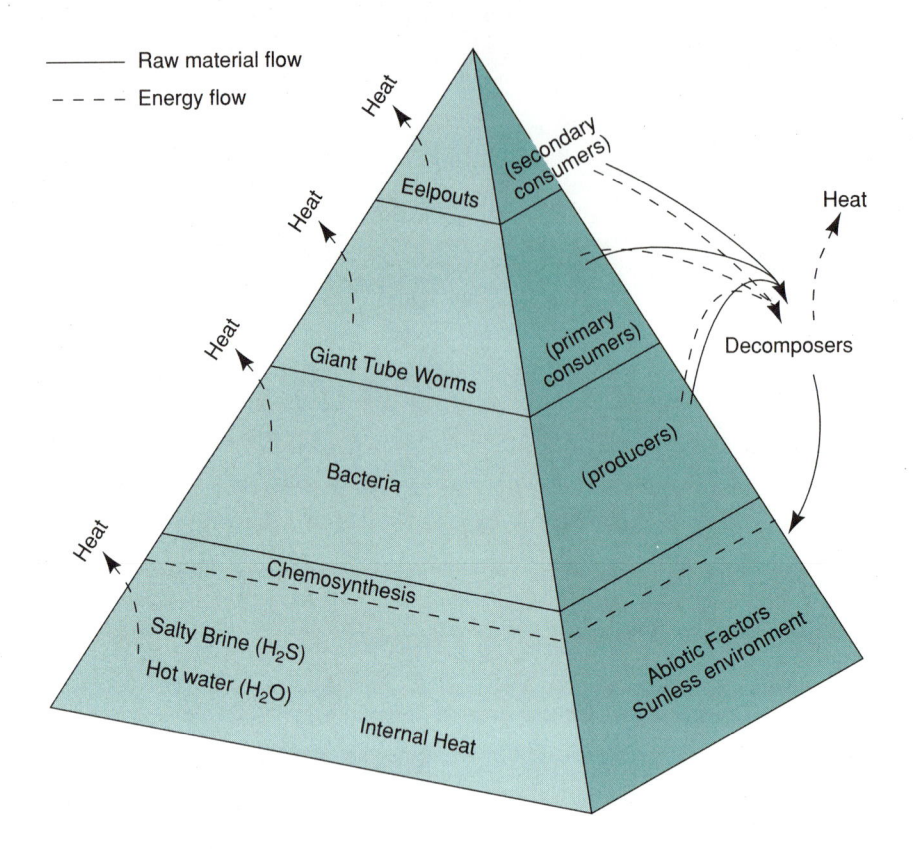

Figure 2.11 Biotic pyramid for a simple sunless food chain for hydrothermal vents.

Figure 2.12 Mount St. Helens erupts May 18, 1980. Melted snow and avalanches caused destruction along with the volcanism. (*Photo:* USGS)

Figure 2.13 The destructive force of a volcanic blast is enormous. Trees blown down and stripped by the Mount St. Helens blast of May, 1980, look like toothpicks. Loggers salvaged some of the blown-down trees for lumber. (*Photo:* USGS)

Figure 2.14 Wave action and wind have built this new depositional landform called a barrier beach. Grasses will help stabilize the sand.
(*Photo:* David A. Castillon)

Over the ocean, wind, acting by friction on the surface waters, sets waves and currents into motion. The waves strike the coasts, eroding, transporting, and depositing sediment. New landforms and new landscapes are constantly being formed and then changed again. Storm waves have a dramatic effect on coastal areas. Changing sea level caused by tidal fluctuations on their monthly and seasonal cycles have an effect on coastal landforms. Coastal areas are dynamic and unstable environments. Human attempts to stabilize coastal areas have not always been successful and many times have been met with disastrous results (figure 2.15). Coastal resources are best left in a natural state so that the natural processes can establish and maintain long-term equilibrium conditions (figure 2.15).

Natural coastlines can be classified into two categories, primary and secondary coasts. *Primary coasts* are formed by nonmarine processes such as tectonic or volcanic activity and have not been modified substantially by marine processes. *Secondary coasts* are formed or modified by marine processes such as wave erosion or deposition of sediment at the land-air-sea boundary, and their character is distinctly the result of the sea and its processes. Figure 2.16 illustrates both primary and secondary coasts.

The terrestrial environments on the earth's surface can be divided into stable and unstable regions. The stable areas are, for the most part, stable in biologic time. Tops of ridges, for example, are very stable and probably will not change much in time periods of thousands of years.

Figure 2.15 Coastal destruction from high winds and waves are a problem for coastal dwellers. Beach erosion and high winds on Sullivan Island, S.C. destroyed this home during Hurricane Hugo.
(*Photo:* Jonas Jordan, USACE)

Valleys, floodplains, and coastal regions are unstable areas and are constantly changing. With each major precipitation episode, water is sent down-slope, eroding sediment from the hillsides and valleys. This sediment is transported and deposited on an ever-changing floodplain. Each major storm generated at sea that strikes a coast changes the erosional and depositional landforms in the affected area. The stability of a landform should always be considered when an examination of the environment is undertaken for any purpose that will change the natural setting.

Continental Glaciation

Figure 2.17 shows the extent of continental glaciation in North America during the *Pleistocene Epoch* (last 1.8 million years). The existing alpine glaciers of today are all that remain after 22,500 years of melting. The most recent continental ice advance, called the *Wisconsinan*,

a. Ria coast

b. Fjord coast

c. Estuarine coast

d. Deltaic coast

e. Barrier island coast — Barrier island, Lagoon, Inlet

f. Raised platform coast

Figure 2.16 Sea-level rise following the melting of ice-age glaciers has submerged most coastlines, creating a variety of coastal types. A. Moderately embayed ria coasts have formed on stream-sculpted landscapes. B. Deeply embayed fjord coasts have formed where glaciers have deepened coastal valleys. C. Where rivers run clear, their drowned estuaries remain open. D. Deltas have filled the estuaries of muddy rivers. E. In places, uplift has outstripped sea-level rise, exposing the continental shelf and barrier islands. F. Raised wave-cut platforms on a rugged coast are a sure sign of an emergent coastline.
(A., B., C., D. are examples of primary coastlines; E. and F. are examples of secondary coasts formed by marine erosion and depositional processes.)
From David Laing, *The Earth Systems*. Copyright © 1991 Wm. C. Brown Publishers, Dubuque, Iowa. All Rights Reserved. Reprinted by permission.

Figure 2.17 The extent of continental and alpine glaciation in North America during the Pleistocene. Note location of Pomme de Terre bog site.
Source: Data from C. S. Denny, U.S. Geological Survey.
(*Cartographer:* Douglas Hemsath)

ended about 22,500 years before present (ybp). All of the continental ice had melted back into Hudson Bay about 6,000 ybp and we define the time since then as the *Holocene Epoch* (interglacial). Together the Pleistocene and Holocene make up the geologic period called the *Quaternary*. The Wisconsinan glacial period was the most recent of at least 18 glacial events that have occurred during the Pleistocene. Each glacial period was followed by an interglacial, or melting of a continental ice sheet. These geomorphic events were triggered by changing climatic conditions at the earth's surface and resulted in highly variable sea levels throughout the Quaternary.

There is much speculation about the causes of **Ice Ages.** Climate is controlled to a large extent by the earth-sun relationship. Changes in the emissivity of the sun can cause climate change. The earth wobbles on its axis as it rotates. This factor is related to the progression of the North Star (Polestar) in the northern heavens, which had to be tracked by navigators for accurate positioning. (One wobble takes about 40,000 years). This could cause climate changes. A single, massive volcanic eruption or a series of eruptions could put enough ash into the atmosphere to block the sun and cause climatic change. The exact cause of climate change is yet to be determined. Much geomorphic evidence, including sea level fluctuations of 100 m (328 ft) or more, indicates that it has changed repeatedly during the Pleistocene. These changes have had a profound effect on the biosphere.

An examination of the pollen and fossils in bogs in the interior plains of Missouri shows that as the climate of North America changed following the last glacial event, the vegetation and fauna also changed. The plant growth along the Pomme de Terre River in Missouri during the Wisconsinan glacial maximum (22,500 to 12,500 ybp) was a spruce-fir forest, and the associated fauna included mastodon, giant beaver, and sloth (figure 2.18a & b). As the ice began to melt, the climate warmed and evapotranspiration increased. The vegetation changed to an open pine parkland. This, in turn, gave way to drier, almost desert-like conditions before prairie grasses took over, which were then replaced by oaks and hickories about 5,000 ybp. A combination of oak-hickory and long bluestem prairie occupies the site of these bogs at present. Thick deposits of *loess,* a wind-blown silt, in this area is evidence to support extended dry periods during this interglacial event.

Continental glaciation of North America has been a blessing to some areas of the continent and a scourge to others. Most of the agricultural soils of the corn belt were formed from glacial material deposited by ice or ice meltwater. This material was scraped off of other areas that have been left pockmarked with ice-scoured lake depressions, bare rock surfaces, or surfaces with little or no topsoil. Much of east-central Canada was scraped by the ice of recent glacial events.

Topography

The solid earth and the atmosphere above the surface are arranged according to **density.** The rocks of the high mountains are less dense than the rocks of the ocean floor. Lithologic circulation and plate tectonic mechanisms arrange and rearrange lithologic materials according to density, just as atmospheric circulation rearranges the air according to density. When solid lithospheric materials are not arranged according to density, a disequilibrium exists and tectonic mechanisms rearrange materials to get them back into order. Uplift and subsidence occur on a regular basis at or near the earth's surface in an attempt to reestablish equilibrium. Sometimes these movements are rapid and disastrous. On July 16, 1990, a strong earthquake jolted the Philippine island of Luzon, causing much destruction and loss of life. It was one of nature's minor adjustments to disequilibrium and stress—just a faint ripple in the plate movements.

The adjustments of the solid earth by tectonic mechanisms create landforms and relief on the surface. *Topography,* as an abiotic factor, is an important variable in conservation. Elevation, along with slope and aspect, represent the landform or geomorphic condition. Elevation is usually measured above and below sea level. We already know that sea level is not fixed, so this probably is not a good reference to use, but it is standard practice. Because sea level is changing very slowly, however, there should not be a real problem in elevation determination.

Figure 2.18A Layer of fossil bones in the Boney Spring bone bed of the Pomme de Terre Missouri site.
(*Photo:* Illinois State Museum)

Figure 2.18B Painting depicting western Missouri 14,000 ybp showing American mastodons in a bog forest—Robert G. Larson, artist. The Boney Spring bone bed fossil and pollen assemblages were used to make this painting as realistic as possible for 14,000 ybp.
(*Photo:* Illinois State Museum)

Elevation is defined as the number of meters or feet above or below sea level of a point on a landform. *Aspect* is defined as the direction the landform is facing. South-facing landforms in North America receive more sunlight and are usually drier than north-facing ones. In North America, west-facing landforms usually receive more precipitation than those that face east.

Slope is the angle that a landform makes with a horizontal plane. The position on a landform is also important. The top of a hill *(summit)* is different from the side or the bottom of a hill. Figure 2.19 illustrates a hill and its defined parts. The top of a hill or landform is its most stable part. Some geomorphologists call it the **belt of no erosion** (BNE) because it does not change noticeably in short periods of geologic time.

The *backslope* of a landform is the least stable (erosional) part of a hillslope. The steeper the slope, the less stable the backslope. The Soil Conservation Service (SCS) recommends that any backslope steeper than 15% not be developed without engineering modifications to insure its stability. Slopes between 8% and 15% can have stability problems if the hillslope material is weak. The *footslope* and *toeslope* of a hill are less stable than the summit, but more stable than the backslope. The footslope and toeslope are the depositional apron for the colluvial material eroded from the backslope. The *floodplain* of a landscape is also unstable because of its flooding potential.

The Biosphere through Geologic Time

The Earth's initial life forms were simple structures dependent on the lithosphere for their nutrient supply. The free oxygen supply of the atmosphere was zero. Therefore, organisms had to originate in an *anoxic* (oxygenless) environment. Fossil cells, or the structures they produced by their activity, give us our initial evidence for life on the earth. The oldest evidence comes from Australia. Rocks about 3.5 billion years old contain biogenic sedimentary structures called **stromatolites,** and rocks about 2.8 billion years old contain fossil **paleomicrobiota.** The oldest evidence from North America is found in two-billion-year-old chert from the Lake Superior region. *Chert* is a very fine-grained secondary silicate (SiO_2). These cherts contain contemporaneous microbial fossils that compare favorably with the richest modern microfloras. Such fossils show a clear differentiation of biota into more than one type of cell. The fossils resemble blue-green algae and budding bacteria. Their presence together implies a continuity of biological function from two billion years ago to today.

The chronology of the high points in life form developments of the biosphere through geologic time parallel the increase in available oxygen in the atmosphere. The initial activities in the biosphere, which were a result of interactions of the lithosphere with the atmosphere and hydrosphere, produced profound changes in the composition of the atmosphere. Free oxygen (O_2) began to in-

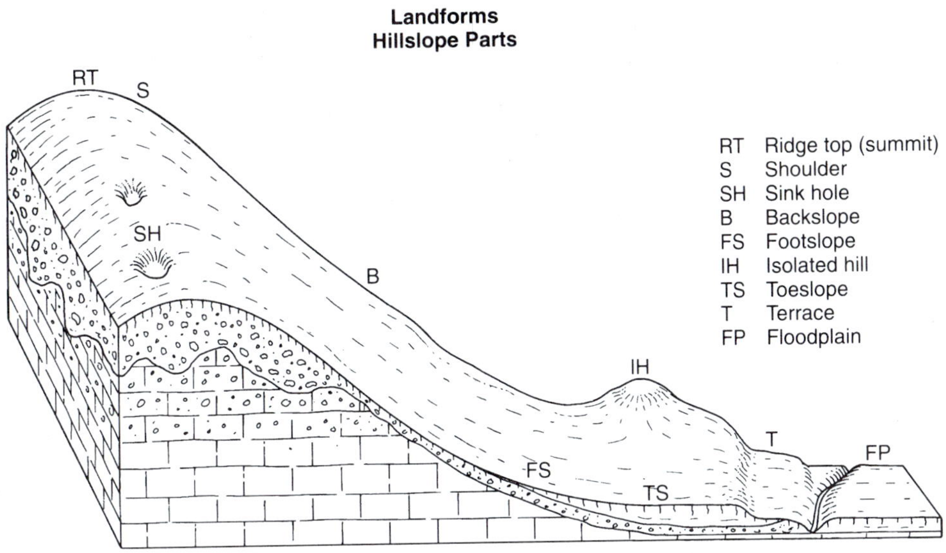

**Landforms
Hillslope Parts**

RT	Ridge top (summit)
S	Shoulder
SH	Sink hole
B	Backslope
FS	Footslope
IH	Isolated hill
TS	Toeslope
T	Terrace
FP	Floodplain

Figure 2.19 The defined parts of a hillslope.

crease in the atmosphere as a result of the life processes of the early organisms. As free oxygen increased, the biosphere diversified and became more complex (figure 2.20). The chert from the Lake Superior region is the first evidence in North America that oxygen was escaping from a previously anoxic hydrosphere into the anoxic atmosphere. About two billion years ago the atmospheric composition of free oxygen was only about one percent of its present day amount. The appearance of chlorophyll as a mediator for photosynthesis, and the appearance of cells capable of mitotic cell division are very important events in the evolution of the biosphere. These events occurred more than 1.4 billion years ago. Between 1.4 billion and 0.7 billion years ago the fossil cellular remains of organisms increased dramatically, but the fossil record contains no remains of marine organisms. The oldest soft-bodied marine organism fossils appeared in sedimentary rocks dated between 670 and 550 million years old. Most of the early marine fossils are open sea drifters such as jellyfish. Worms are also common. These organisms began their existence at a time when free oxygen was less than 10% of present-day levels. The biosphere reached its present-day levels of oxygen about 400 million years ago. Flowering plants arrived 300 million years later.

Biologists estimate that over four million species of plants and animals make up the biosphere. New species, mostly insects, are being catalogued at the rate of 10,000 per year. Organisms sometimes evolve rapidly. The Hawaiian Islands are less than six million years old. In that brief span of geologic time, the honeycreepers, ancestors of the finches, have evolved into two dozen different species of birds. Both climate and geographic isolation were factors involved in the evolutionary changes that took place in the family. On a grander scale, the extinction of the dinosaurs at the close of the Mesozoic Era was an evolutionary change produced by a changing climate and the earth's lithospheric circulation system of plate movements.

Natural Geologic Hazards

Volcanism, earthquakes, flooding, and landslides are all geologic hazards. In conservation of natural resources, humans must live in harmony with their natural environment to reap the largest benefit from this association. The earth's surface provides a diverse set of landscapes. Some of these are stable and some are not. If stable environments were selected for habitation by humans and less stable areas left to other uses, humans and their world would be better off (figure 2.21).

The historical record and the archaeological record both indicate that humans have inhabited floodplains throughout time. It was important for a person to live on the land that he also used to grow his food. Most people in North America living on a floodplain today buy their food in a grocery store. They don't need to live there. As soon as a flood comes along and destroys their home, they want federal disaster assistance so that they can rebuild in the exact same place and wait for the next flood. Not too smart!

With an understanding of natural systems and some planning, we can occupy fairly safe environments and lessen the risk of natural geologic disasters.

A worst-case analysis should be used on high-risk areas to determine the potential for destruction. And even in hazardous locations, there are areas with less potential for danger. For example, in the Alaskan Earthquake of 1964, some areas very close to the epicenter of the quake received only minor damage because of the rock unit they were built on. The areas with the greatest destruction were built on an unstable shale layer that gave way because of the vibrations following the quake.

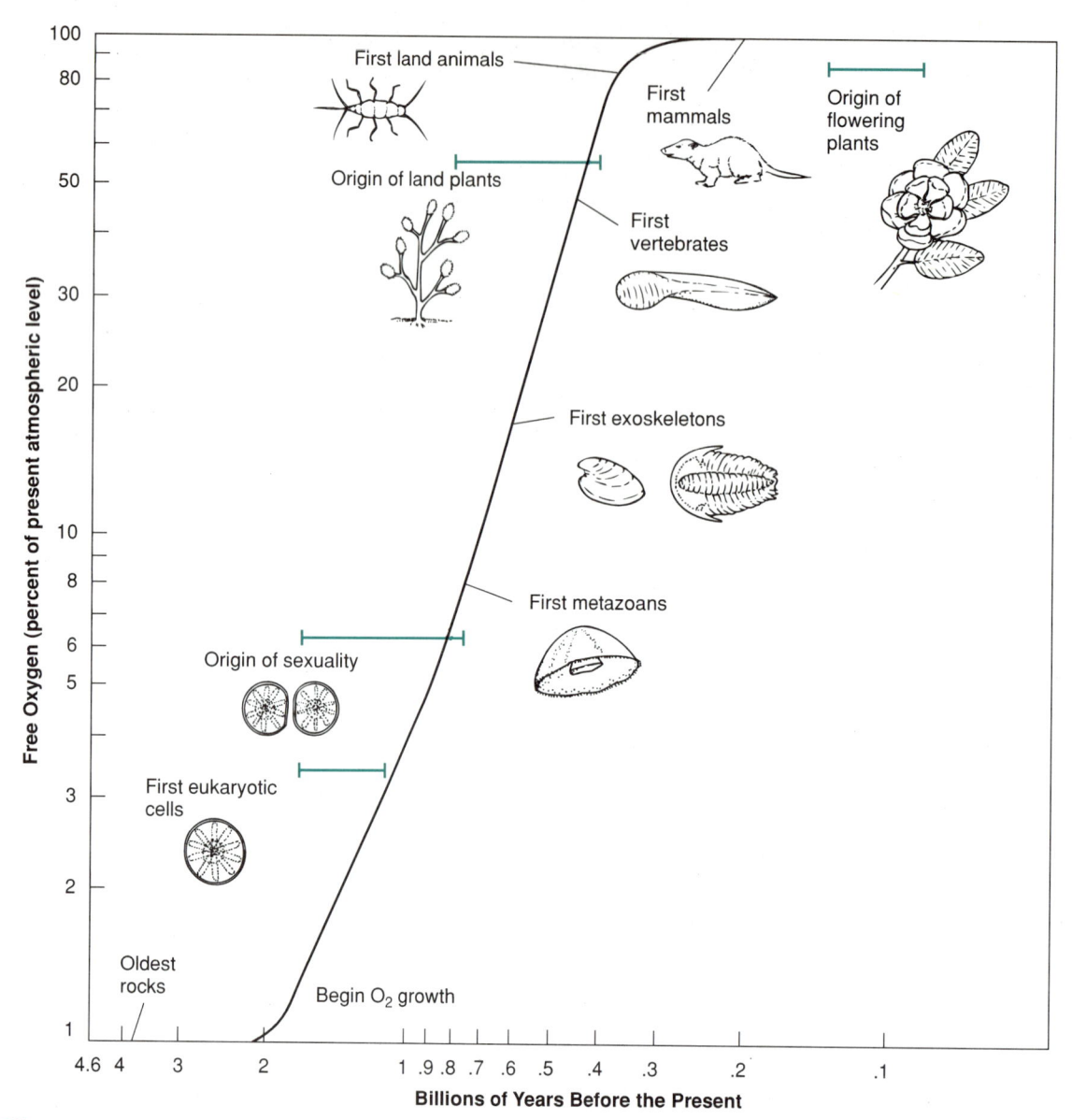

Figure 2.20 The oxygenation of the atmosphere through geologic time. Enrichment in oxygen of the earth's originally anoxic atmosphere is traced on this double logarithmic graph. The abscissa measures billions of years before the present; the ordinate shows the estimated increase of molecular oxygen from about 1% of its present level to what it is today. Leaders indicate the timing of key events in the evolution of the biosphere as they relate to the evolution of the atmosphere. In the case of events where there is uncertainty about the time of origin, a range bar indicates the possible limits. For example, microbial land plants of the simplest kind might have appeared at or before the beginning of the Phanerozoic eon, but spores that have been interpreted as being those of true vascular plants did not appear until the late Ordovician, some 440 to 430 million years ago. In turn, the oldest organisms generally accepted as being land plants in the modern sense are of late Silurian age, perhaps 420 to 415 million years old. Scorpionlike arachnids of about the same age are known. Primitive insects do not appear until the Middle Devonian, some 380 million years ago.

From "The Biosphere," by Preston Cloud. Copyright © 1983 by Scientific American, Inc. All Rights Reserved.

Figure 2.21 Missouri River in flood near Jefferson City, Missouri. A river floodplain is no place for humans.
(*Photo:* Jim Rathert, MDC)

Summary

The solid earth is a very important physical variable at the base of the biotic pyramid. It is the solid matter that weathers into soil, releasing elements into the biosphere to maintain growth. It provides energy in the form of heat to drive the lithologic circulation system we call plate tectonics. Since we do not totally understand the role that the geologic systems play in relation to other natural systems, we must proceed with caution in our use of the earth's resources.

Later in this text we will look at energy minerals and metallic and nonmetallic materials that have become natural resources. To manage these resources effectively will require an understanding of the geologic processes that have produced these minerals and materials. This understanding will allow for better methods of conservation and management.

Key Words and Phrases

Abiotic
Agents of erosion
Anoxic
Aspect
Asthenosphere
Backslope
Cenozoic Era
Chemical weathering
Chert
Continental drift
Elevation
Endogenic systems
Exogenic systems
Floodplain
Footslope
Holocene Epoch

Igneous rocks
  extrusive
  intrusive
Juvenile water
Landforms
  depositional
  erosional
Lithologic circulation
Lithosphere
Loess
Magma
Mesozoic Era
Metamorphic rocks
Paleozoic Era
Physical weathering
Plate tectonics

Plates
Pleistocene Epoch
Precambrian Era
Primary coasts
Quaternary Period
Sea-floor spreading zone
Secondary coasts
Sedimentary rocks
Silicate rocks
Slope
Summit
Toeslope
Topography
Trenching zone
Volcanism
Wisconsinan glaciation

Questions and Discussion Topics

1. What factors in lithologic circulation are of greatest importance in the conservation of natural resources?
2. What factors in lithologic circulation have the greatest potential to create geologic hazards for humans?
3. What problems could be created for humans if sea level rose 10 m (33 ft)? What if it dropped 10 m (33 ft)?
4. Would it be possible for a sunless environment to evolve into a complex system like our solar environment? Do you think a sunless environment based on bacteria could exist in a deep oxygenated zone of the terrestrial lithosphere?
5. Do you think a strong earthquake or a volcanic eruption will occur during the academic term you are reading this text. If yes, where geographically? Will it, or could it affect your life?
6. Why do humans live on floodplains? Are agricultural or recreational uses of floodplains a good idea?

References for Further Study

Cloud, P. 1983. The Biosphere. *The Dynamic Earth*. New York: W. H. Freeman. Excellent article on the history of the biosphere through geologic time.

Eiseley, L. 1964. *The Unexpected Universe*. New York: Harcourt Brace Jovanovich. A naturalist's response to the unexpected aspects of the natural world.

Marsh, W. M. 1987. *Earthscape: A Physical Geography*. New York: John Wiley and Sons Inc. A good introductory text in physical geography.

Montgomery, C. W. 1989. *Fundamentals of Geology*. Dubuque, Ia.: Wm. C. Brown. A good introductory book on geology.

Saunders, J. J. 1977. *Late Pleistocene Vertebrates of the Western Ozark Highlands, Missouri*. Springfield, Il. Illinois State Museum Report of Investigation No. 33. The paleoecology of the central United States during and following the last Ice Age.

Chapter 3

Atmosphere—Climate

Introduction
Solar Energy
Atmosphere—Composition and Properties
    Atmospheric Circulation
Climate
    The Köppen System
    Climatic Extremes
    Climate Change
The Greenhouse Effect
The Ozone Problem
Summary

······

Man has lost the memory of that huge snowfall from whose depths he has emerged blinking.
Loren Eiseley, 1964.

······

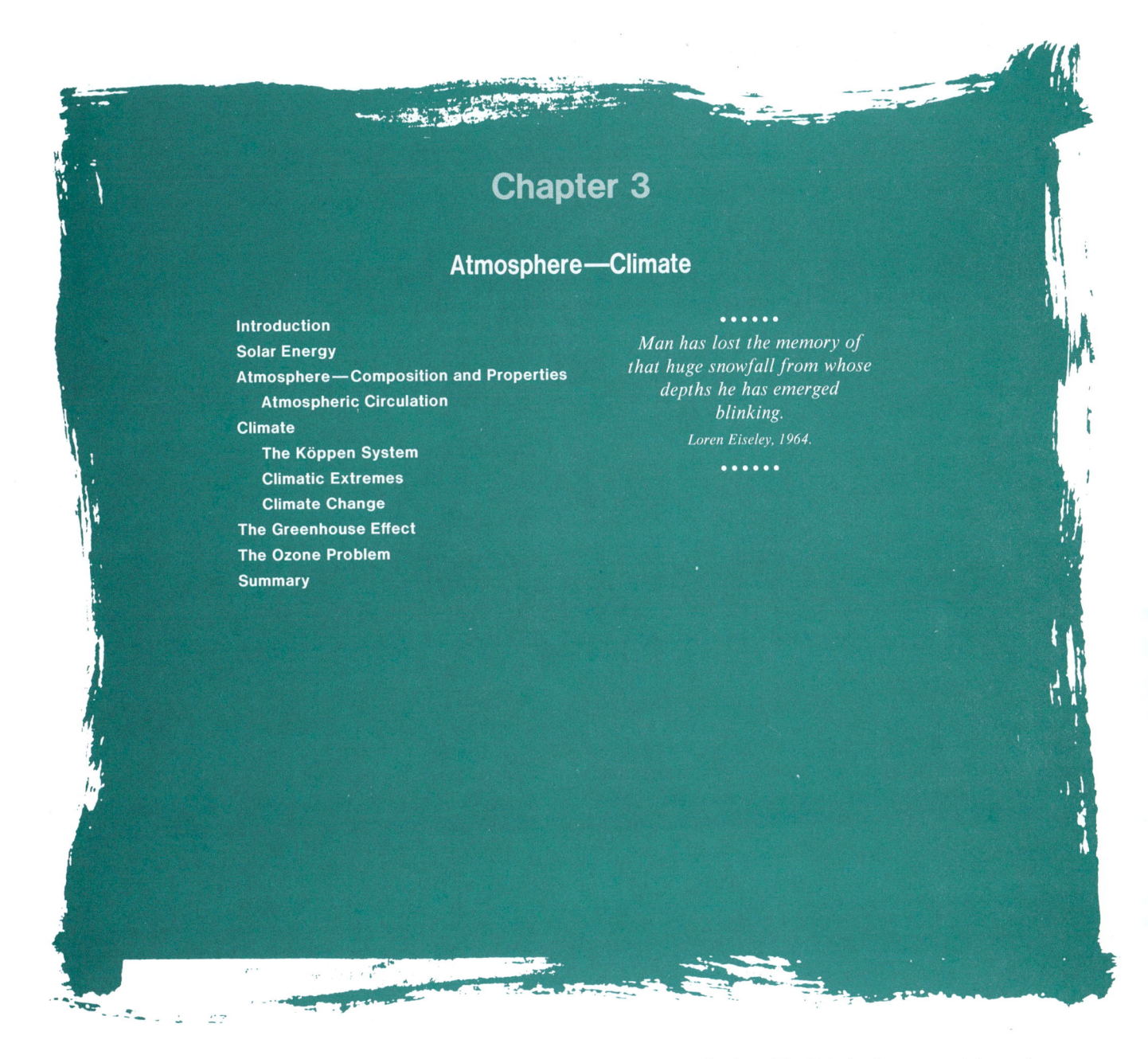

Introduction

The sun is the earth's external motor, just as radioactive decay in the interior of the earth is the earth's internal motor. The energy from the sun drives the atmospheric, oceanic, and hydrologic circulation systems. Internal heat, as you recall from chapter 2, drives the lithologic circulation system that we call plate tectonics. The mechanisms are very similar. All of these systems are driven by heat. In each system, heat creates changes in density, conduction, and convective motion. The big difference in the system driven by internal heat versus those driven by the sun's energy is time. The lithologic system ticks to the tune of a geologic clock, whereas the exogenic systems tick to a clock in biologic time. In this chapter, we will examine the workings of the atmosphere and the climatic conditions produced on the earth's surface.

Solar Energy

Most life processes at or near the earth's surface use the sun as their source of energy. Even though in chapter 2 we examined some systems in the deep ocean that utilized

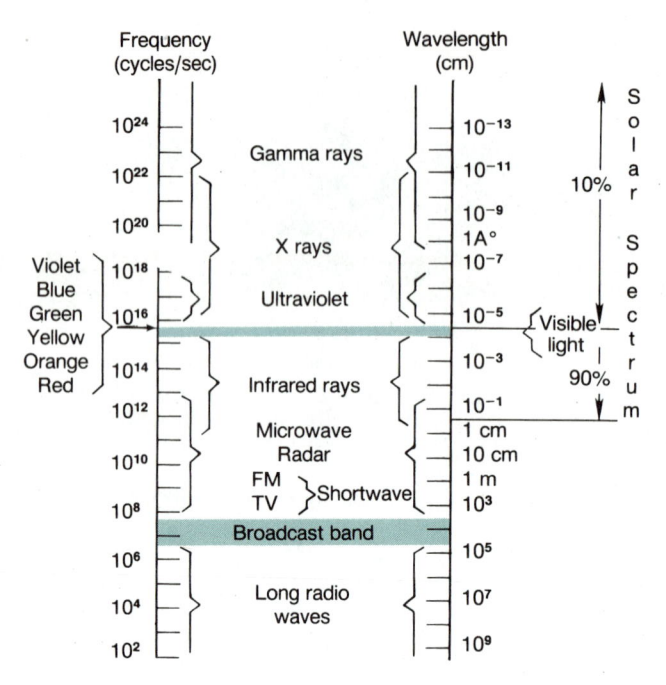

Figure 3.1 The electromagnetic spectrum. Ranges of wavelengths and the corresponding frequencies for various kinds of electromagnetic radiation.
From Alyn C. Duxbury and Alison B. Duxbury, *Introduction to the World's Oceans*, 3d ed. Copyright © 1991 Wm. C. Brown Publishers, Dubuque, Iowa. All Rights Reserved. Reprinted by permission.

internal heat, they are a very small part of the total biosphere. The earth intercepts a tremendous amount of energy from the sun (one and one half quadrillion megawatt hours per year), about 28,000 times as much as humans consume each year. The flow of energy from the sun to the earth, and the many transformations of that energy, represent a very complex system. Solar energy is transformed, stored, and transported as it moves through the system. Examination of the system reveals that it, like all other systems operating at or near the earth's surface, is in a state of long-term equilibrium. The concept of a *radiation balance* states that the energy absorbed by the earth is matched by the planetary output of energy into space.

The *sun* is a star of about average size and temperature. It emits short-wave electromagnetic radiation from its surface radially outward. This radiation requires about 8.3 minutes to reach the earth's surface (150 million km-93 million mi). The earth intercepts about one two-billionth of the sun's total energy output at the top of the atmosphere. The amount of energy received, called the *solar constant,* is about 1.9 cal/sq cm/min. In English units, this is equivalent to 430 BTUs/sq ft/hr (1372 w/m²). The sun's energy spectrum ranges from the shortest wavelengths (gamma, X rays, and ultraviolet) through the visible and infrared spectrum (figure 3.1). More than 90% of the sun's energy to the earth comes from the visible and infrared wavelengths, with infrared accounting for 50% of the total.

Only a small part of the energy from the sun is intercepted by the earth. The amount of energy received at any point on the earth's surface is determined by the angle at which the sun's rays strike the surface and the length of exposure. Direct interception of sunlight delivers the greatest amount of energy. Variations in incoming solar energy also occur because of the relative motions of the earth with respect to the sun. The earth *rotates* on its axis, creating a day-night cycle and *revolves* around the sun, creating a seasonal cycle. These motions change the angle of incidence of the sun's rays and the length of exposure for all points on the earth's surface through both cycles, because the earth's axis is tilted at an angle of 23½° to the *plane of the ecliptic,* the plane in which the earth revolves around the sun while rotating on its axis (figure 3.2). The amount of energy reaching the surface governs the thermal environment of the life layer. This environment

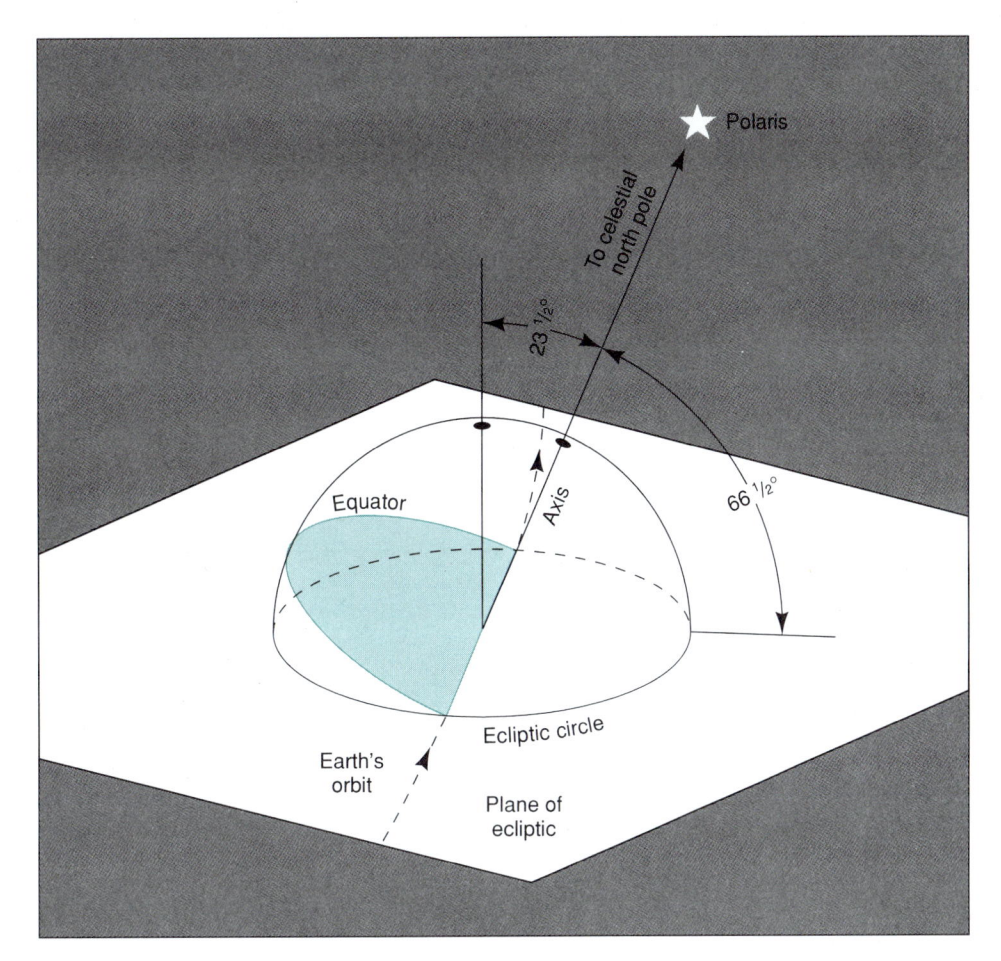

Figure 3.2 The plane of the ecliptic is the plane in which the earth revolves around the sun. The earth's axis is tilted at an angle of 66 1/2° to the plane of the ecliptic.
From A. N. Strahler and A. H. Strahler, *Modern Physical Geography*. Copyright © John Wiley & Sons, Inc. New York, N.Y. Reprinted by permission of John Wiley & Sons, Inc.

at or near the surface can be divided into zones, with the region receiving maximum solar radiation being a zone of heat excess extending around the earth and centered on the equator. Regions receiving little or no solar radiation for half the year are the zones of heat deficit, centered over the two poles and extending equatorially. The *global heat balance latitude* is located approximately 38° north and south of the equator. At this latitude, the amount of incoming solar radiation equals the amount of radiation loss into outer space.

The equatorial regions (tropics) would burn up and the polar regions would be totally locked in ice if there were not some mechanism to transfer, transform, and/or store the solar energy received. This incoming energy is constant but not equally distributed over the earth's surface.

The sun's radiation contains almost all of the energy at 150 km (93 mi) above the earth's surface. Between 150 and 88 km (93 and 55 mi) above the earth, almost all of the X rays and some of the ultraviolet (UV) have been absorbed. Between 88 km and 20 km (55 and 12 mi) above the earth, almost all of the UV is absorbed, most of this captured by the ozone layer (20 to 40 km—12 to 25 mi) (figure 3.3). As the sun's energy penetrates atmospheric space above the earth, further reductions in energy occur because of **scattering, diffuse reflection,** and **absorption.** Carbon dioxide and water vapor absorb infrared radiation, but this is accompanied by a rise in air temperature. On a clear day about 80% of the incoming solar radiation intercepted at the top of the earth's atmosphere reaches the ground. On a cloudy day, however, from 10% to 50% of this solar radiation can be reflected from the top of the

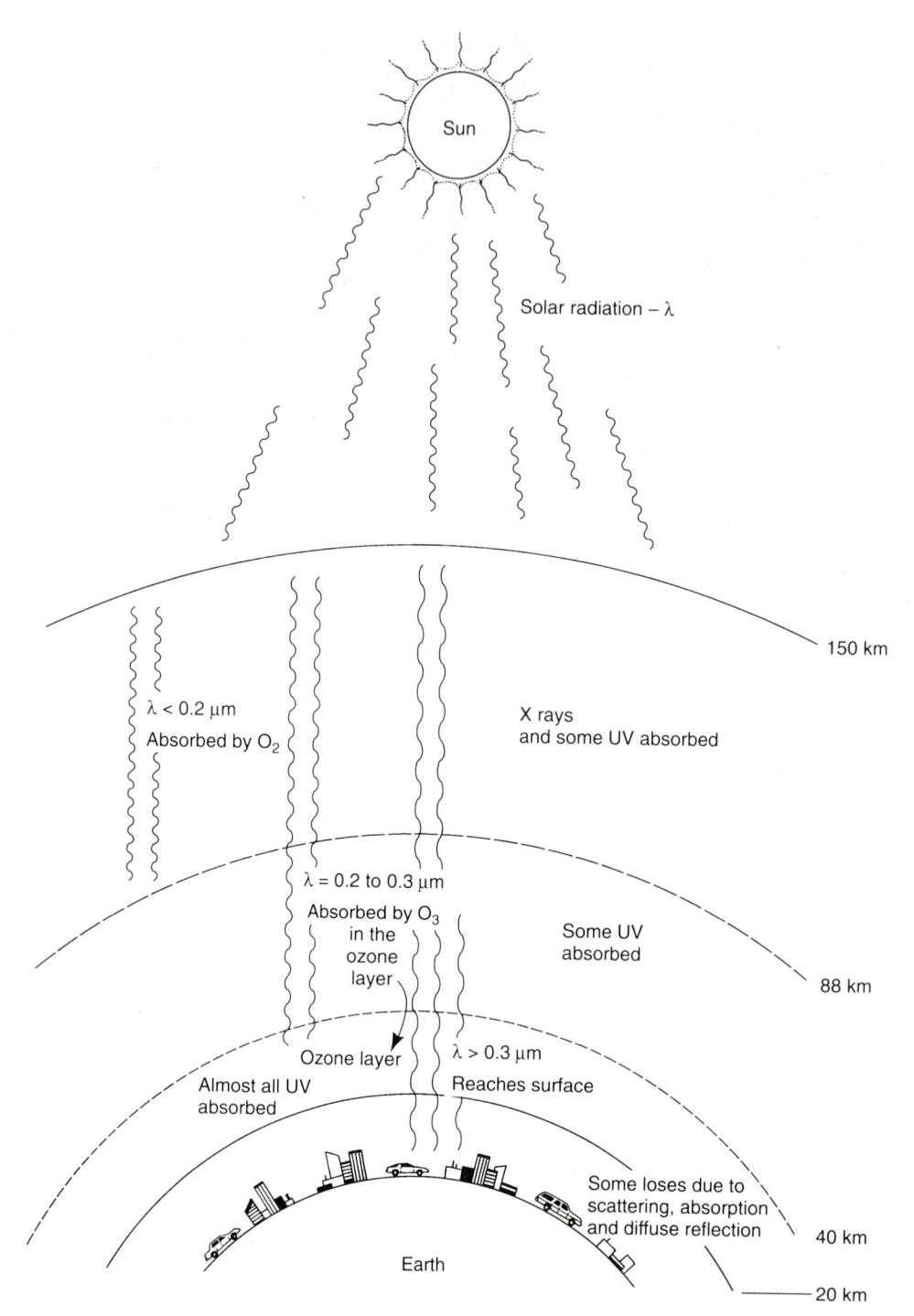

Figure 3.3 Regions above the earth's surface that absorb incoming solar radiation.

Labels in figure:
- Sun
- Solar radiation – λ
- 150 km
- $\lambda < 0.2$ μm Absorbed by O_2
- X rays and some UV absorbed
- $\lambda = 0.2$ to 0.3 μm Absorbed by O_3 in the ozone layer
- Some UV absorbed
- 88 km
- Ozone layer
- $\lambda > 0.3$ μm Reaches surface
- Almost all UV absorbed
- Some loses due to scattering, absorption and diffuse reflection
- 40 km
- 20 km
- Earth

Physical and Biological Variables of the Natural Environment

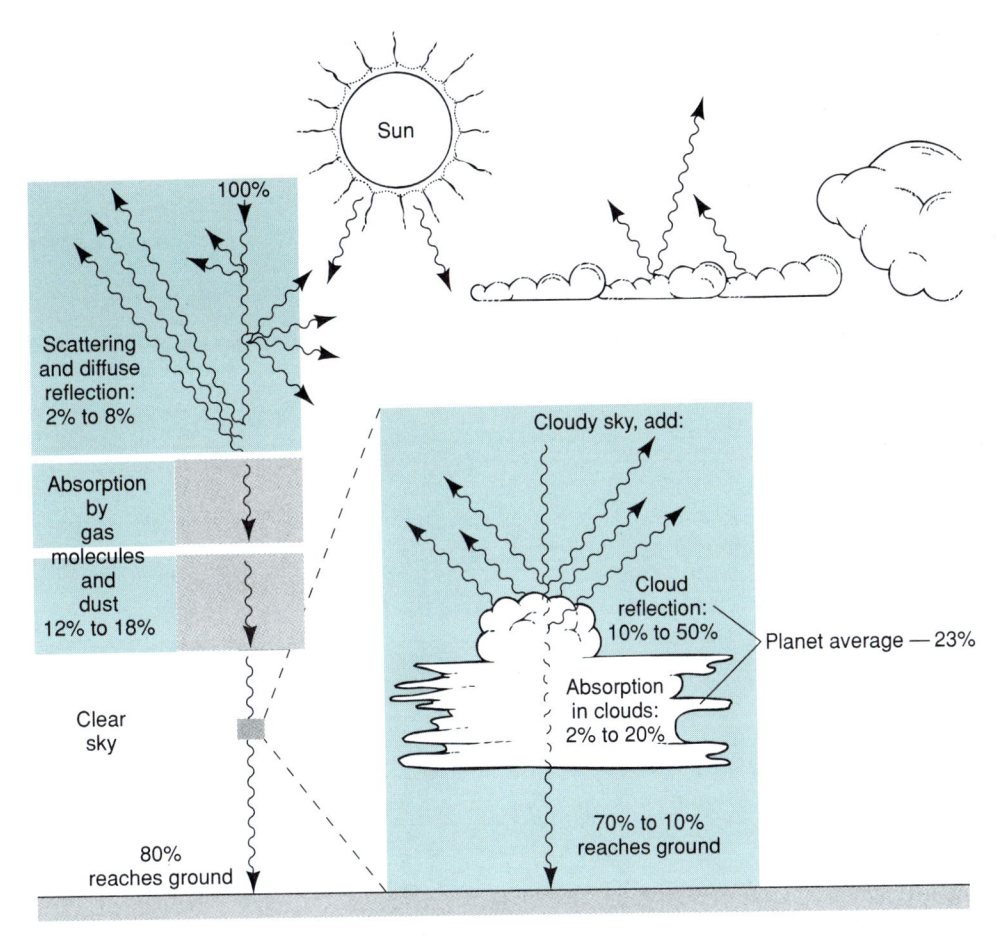

Figure 3.4 Global solar energy budget comparisons for a clear versus cloudy sky.

clouds and another 2% to 20% absorbed by the clouds. A planet average for cloud reflection and absorption is 23%, with reflection representing 20% of the total. Figure 3.4 illustrates the global energy budget for average daily solar and terrestrial radiation.

Atmosphere—Composition and Properties

The atmospheric space above the earth's surface, like the solid earth (lithosphere), is layered according to density and pressure. The atmosphere is mostly **nitrogen** (78%-N_2) and **oxygen** (21%-O_2). The important gases in the remaining one percent are **argon** (0.93%) and **carbon dioxide** (.033%). Carbon dioxide is a necessary ingredient for the growth and health of all plants that utilize the photosynthetic-respiration process. It is also an important gas in heating the atmosphere. Table 3.1 contains a list of other gases included in the atmosphere. Water vapor ($H_2O\uparrow$), not included in the list because it is considered part of the hydrosphere, exists in the atmosphere in varying amounts from time to time and place to place. Ranging from 0 to 4% and averaging about 1%, it replaces some of

Table 3.1
Composition of the Atmosphere

Element	Gas	Molecular %	% Mass
Nitrogen (N)	N_2	78.08	75.51
Oxygen (O)	O_2	20.95	23.1
Argon (A)	A	0.93	1.28
Carbon (C)	CO_2 (carbon dioxide)	0.0325	0.049
Neon (Ne)	Ne	0.0018	0.0012
Oxygen (O)	O_3 (Ozone)	0.0006	0.0010
Helium (He)	He	0.0005	0.0001
Krypton (Kr)	Kr	0.0001	0.0003
Hydrogen (H)	H	0.00005	0.000002

the other gases where it exists. Almost all (97%) of the gases that make up the atmosphere are trapped by gravity within a layer extending 30 km (18 miles) above the earth's surface. The weight of these gases that make up the atmosphere averages about 14.7 lbs/sq in (1013 mb), and this is known as *standard atmospheric pressure*. Figure 3.5 illustrates the layers of the atmosphere and the important thermal properties within each layer or zone.

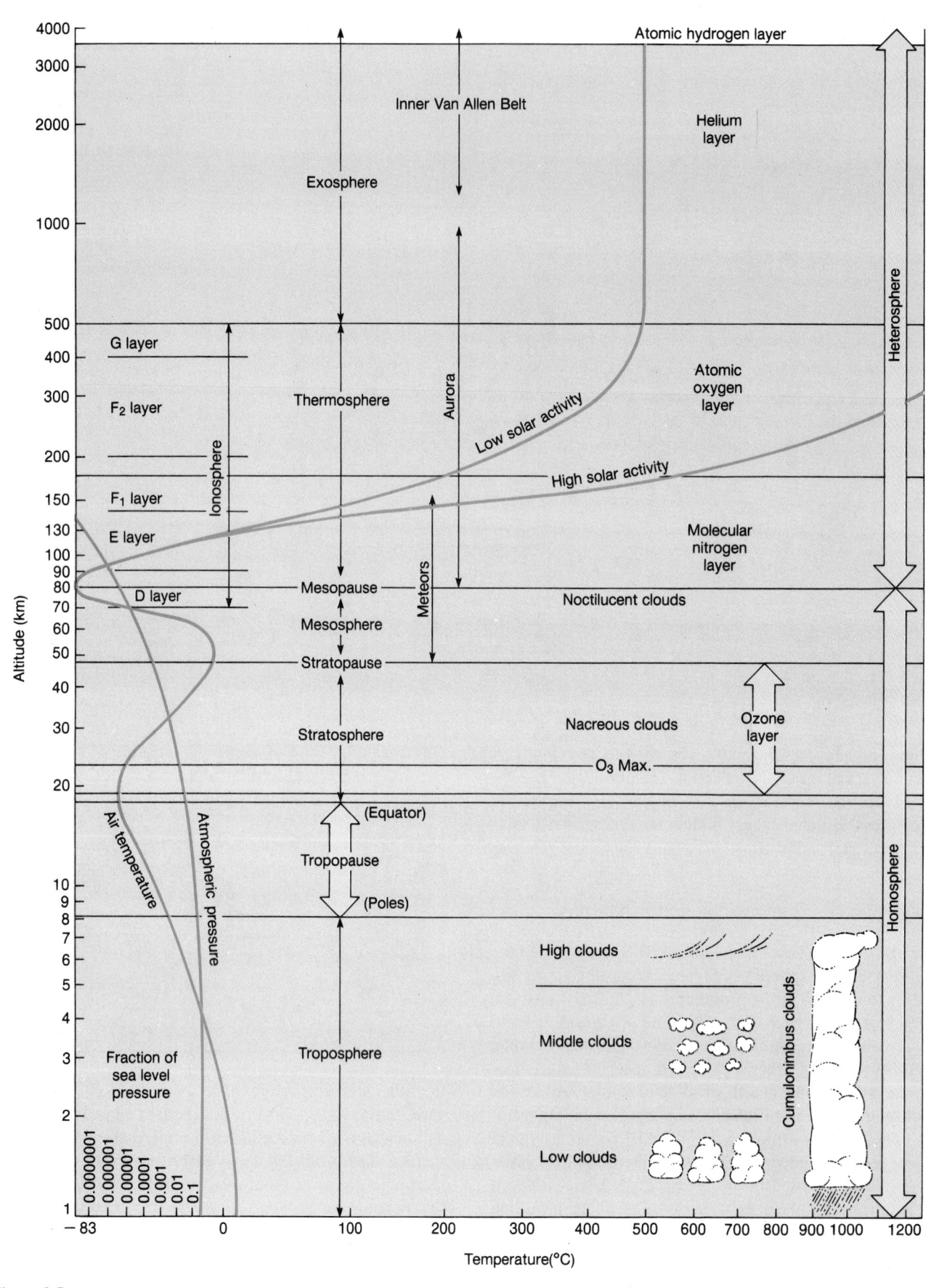

Figure 3.5 A vertical profile through Earth's atmosphere. Its main divisions are given at the far right, and left of center. Curves of temperature and pressure are at the left. Compositional layers and various atmospheric phenomena, including cloud types, ozone, meteors, auroras, ionospheric layers, and a Van Allen belt, are also shown. All scales are logarithmic.

From David Laing, *The Earth Systems*. Copyright © 1991 Wm. C. Brown Publishers, Dubuque, Iowa. All Rights Reserved. Reprinted by permission.

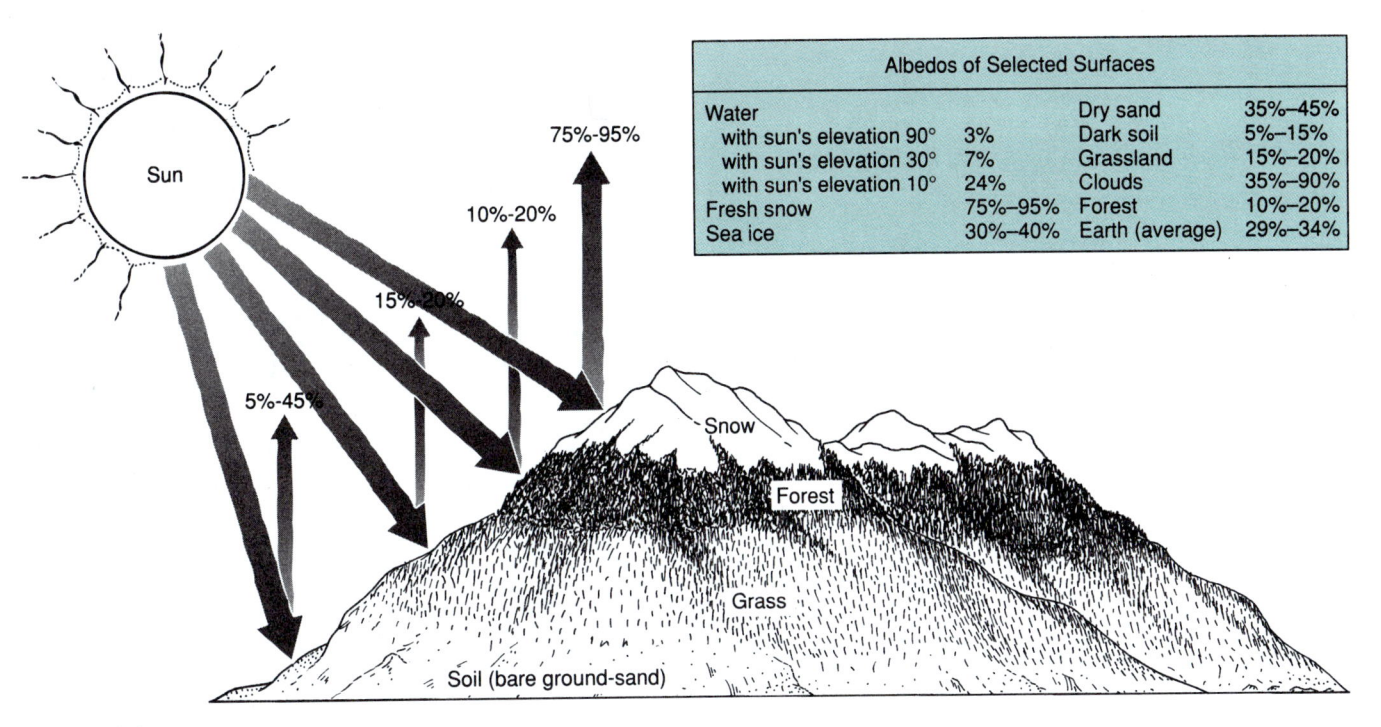

Figure 3.6 Albedos for selected earth's surfaces.
From Marsh, *Earthscape: A Physical Geography.* Copyright © 1987 John Wiley & Sons, Inc., New York, NY. Reprinted by permission of John Wiley & Sons, Inc.

Albedos of Selected Surfaces			
Water		Dry sand	35%–45%
with sun's elevation 90°	3%	Dark soil	5%–15%
with sun's elevation 30°	7%	Grassland	15%–20%
with sun's elevation 10°	24%	Clouds	35%–90%
Fresh snow	75%–95%	Forest	10%–20%
Sea ice	30%–40%	Earth (average)	29%–34%

The energy to drive atmospheric circulation is provided by the short-wave solar radiation that reaches the earth's surface. The surface of the earth is highly variable, but 70% of it is water. The *albedo* of a surface is the percent of the radiant energy reflected back into space by that surface. Satellite data indicate that the earth's average albedo is between 29 and 34. This compares with an albedo for the moon of 7; Mars, 16; Mercury, 6; and Venus, 76. This makes the earth unique in our solar system. The albedo for specific earth surfaces ranges from a low of 3 for vertical rays of the sun intercepted by water to as high as 95 for vertical rays intercepted by snow-covered land surfaces. Bare rock, forests, grasslands, and other terrestrial surfaces have highly variable albedos that depend on the season of the year and angle of the sun (figure 3.6). The remaining short-wave solar energy not lost by one of the processes just described is absorbed by the earth's surface. The absorbed short-wave energy is converted to long-wave radiation and reradiated to warm the atmosphere (**sensible heat**). The evaporation-condensation cycle provides additional energy (**latent heat**), and both sensible and latent heat provide energy to run biological systems. The atmospheric circulation system uses a lot of solar energy, but the sun provides the earth with a tremendous amount of additional unused energy. Potential uses for some of the additional unused solar energy will be discussed in chapter 13 on Energy Management.

Atmospheric Circulation

Solar short-wave energy received at the earth's surface in the equatorial region is absorbed by ocean waters and tropical forests. Short-wave energy is converted to *sensible heat* (long-wave energy) and reradiated to warm the air above the surface. The warmed air becomes less dense and begins to rise (*convection*) in an attempt to reestablish an equilibrium with its environment. The rising air sets up a low pressure cell into which air is drawn. Because the earth is rotating on its axis, the air drawn into the low pressure cell is deflected to the right of its direction of movement in the northern hemisphere and to the left in the southern hemisphere. This deflection is referred to as the *Coriolis effect*. The rising air continues to rise to the top of the **troposphere,** where it turns to the north and the south and descends back to the earth's surface in the latitude zone from 20° to 30° north or south of the equator. This region of descending air creates a high pressure zone known as the **subtropical high pressure belt.** Descending air reaching the earth's surface will diverge out from the center of this region of high pressure and be deflected by the Coriolis effect. This sets up a clockwise spiral of air in the northern hemisphere subtropical high pressure belt and a counter-clockwise flow in the southern hemisphere (figure 3.7).

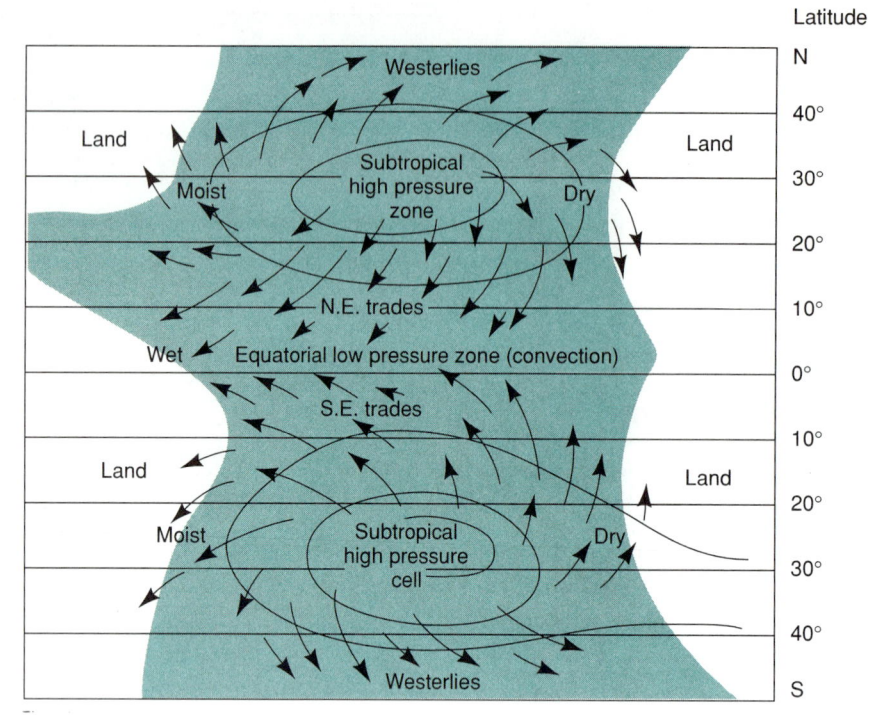

Figure 3.7 Relationship between latitude and pressure zones in the earth's atmosphere. Surface winds and deflection by the Coriolis effect set the initial atmospheric circulation conditions.
Copyright © 1973 by Arthur N. Strahler. Reproduced by permission.

Wind is air in horizontal motion and is named for the direction from which it blows. Wind results from variations in atmospheric pressure created dynamically or thermally by differences in air temperature. Air in regions of high pressure will move toward regions of lower pressure. The subtropical high pressure cells in the northern hemisphere, with their clockwise movement of air, set into motion the **northeast trades** and the northern hemisphere **westerlies** at the earth's surface. At the surface in the southern hemisphere, the **southeast trades** and southern hemisphere **westerlies** are created.

The cold polar regions of dense air are weak, and variable high pressure regions and descending air move along the surface to the south in the northern hemisphere and to the north in the southern hemisphere. The Coriolis force deflects these winds to form the surface wind systems we call the **polar easterlies.** In the upper atmosphere, where the polar easterlies meet the westerlies, the **polar front jet** occurs. Likewise the **subtropical jet** occurs in the upper atmosphere above the surface region between the northeast trades and the westerlies. Figure 3.8 is a schematic diagram of global surface and upper air winds around the earth. The diagram disregards the disrupting effect of the topography and mountain systems on large northern hemisphere continents.

The wind systems on the earth's surface are important for three reasons: (1) They represent heat transfer mechanisms that move heated air from the tropics to the north and south well beyond the global heat balance latitudes. (2) Winds create a frictional drag on the surface of the oceans, which produce surface ocean currents. The warm ocean waters are moved north and south along with the winds. Deflection of the ocean waters at the continental margins enhance the transfer of warm water out of the zone of heat excess and into the zone of heat deficit. These heat transfer mechanisms transfer both sensible heat and latent heat present in water vapor. (3) Winds transport moisture from zones of evaporation over the ocean waters to the continents. Some of the moisture falls in the form of precipitation (rain, snow, sleet, hail) onto the land, creating a net increase in moisture for terrestrial environments. Movement of moisture, and therefore energy, by the wind systems creates climatic regions on the earth's surface. Climate is the most important physical variable in determining the productivity of biotic communities.

Climate

Weather is the state of the atmosphere at a particular place and time. For example, the noon weather conditions for St. Louis, Missouri, on February 10, 1989 were: temperature, 0° C (32° F); relative humidity, 58%; winds out of the southwest at 10 mph; skies clear; one inch (2.54 cm) of snow on the ground. One hour before these readings

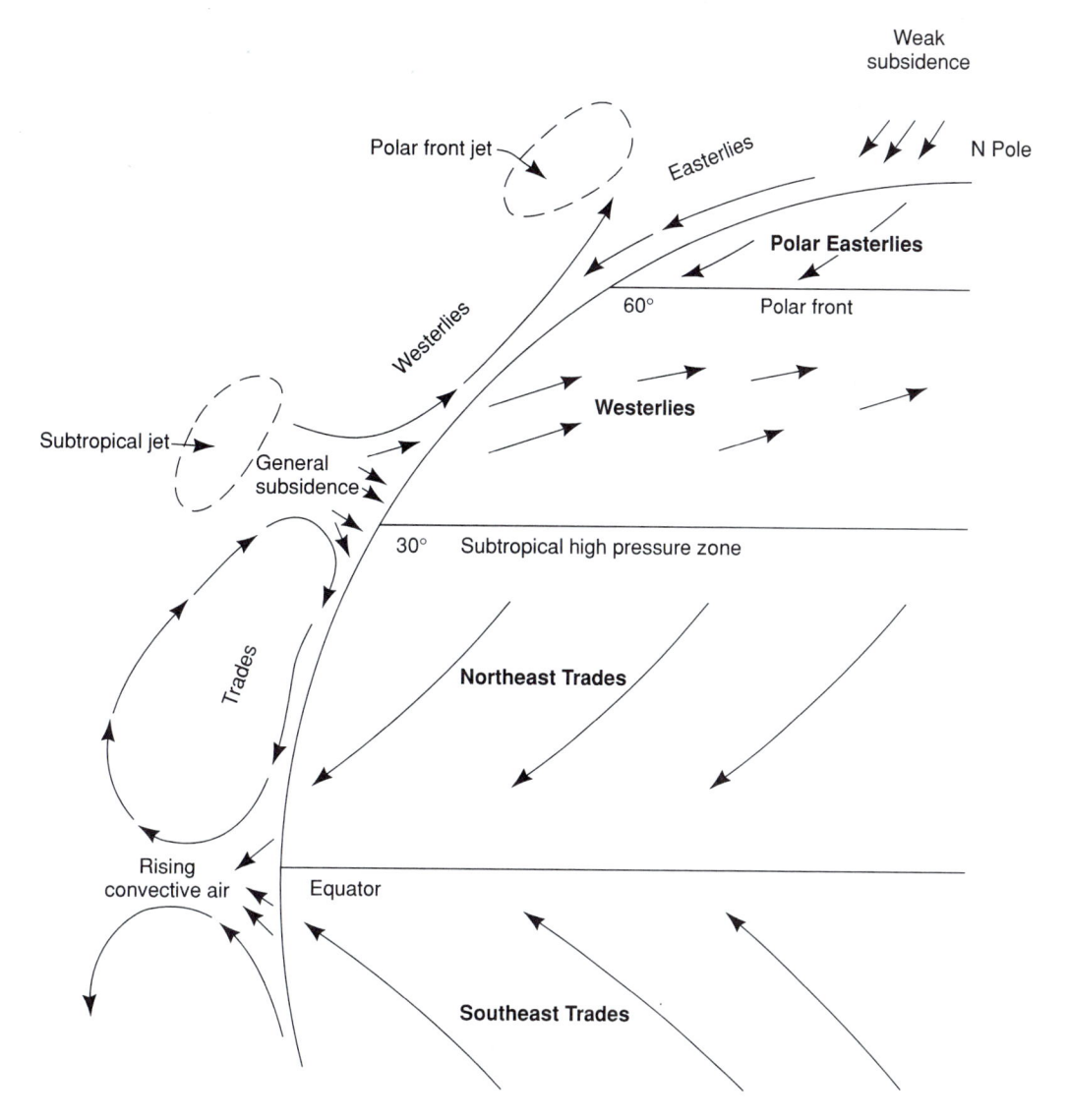

Figure 3.8 General atmospheric circulation system for the Northern hemisphere.

and one hour after these readings, the conditions were different. Thus, exact numerical observation of weather conditions, except for extremes, have short-term usefulness in climatology.

If all of the weather data collected at St. Louis were averaged over a long period of time, then the resulting averages would represent the climate for that weather station and its surrounding region. *Climate,* then, is the average weather condition for a region over an extended period of time (usually 30 years or more). For conservation of natural resources planning, climatic data are a necessity.

Many different schemes have been devised to define climates. In this text, the *Köppen-Geiger-Pohl* system of climatic classification will be used, but it will be referred to simply as the Köppen system. Köppen was a climatologist and biogeographer; therefore, his primary interest in climatic boundaries was generated by mapped climatic-vegetative boundaries. His system was empirical, not subjective, which appealed to many, especially geographers and biologists.

The Köppen System

The **Köppen** system defines each climate on the basis of annual or monthly values of temperature and precipitation. A weather station can be assigned to a climatic classification group on the basis of temperature and precipitation records. The U.S. Weather Service uses 30-year averages to provide stability to the averages. Unfortunately, extreme variations in weather conditions, which occur from time to time, are masked when averaged over this length of time. The Köppen system uses letters to designate major climatic groups and subgroups. Table 3.2 gives the defining properties for each letter in the system.

Table 3.2

Primary Letter Designations for Climatic Groups

A Tropical rainy climates. Average temperature of every month is above 18° C (64.4° F). These climates have no winter season. Annual rainfall exceeds annual evapotranspiration.

B Dry climates. Evaporation exceeds precipitation on the average throughout the year. There is no water surplus; hence no permanent surface streams originate in B climate zones.

C Mild, humid (mesothermal) climates. Coldest month has an average temperature under 18° C (64.4° F), but above −3° C (26.6° F); at least one month has an average temperature above 10° C (50° F). The C climates have both a summer and a winter season.

D Snowy-forest (microthermal) climates. Coldest month average temperature is under −3° C (26.6° F). Average temperature of the warmest month is above 10° C (50° F), that *isotherm* (a line of equal temperature) coinciding approximately with the southern limit of permafrost.

E Polar climates. Average temperature of the warmest month is below 10° C (50° F). These climates have no true summer and permanently frozen soil or subsoil.

Note that four of these five groups (A, C, D, and E) are defined by temperature averages, whereas one (B) is defined by a precipitation-to-evaporation ratio. Groups A, C, and D have sufficient heat and precipitation for the growth of forest and woodland vegetation. Figure 3.9 shows the boundaries of the five major climate groups in North America.

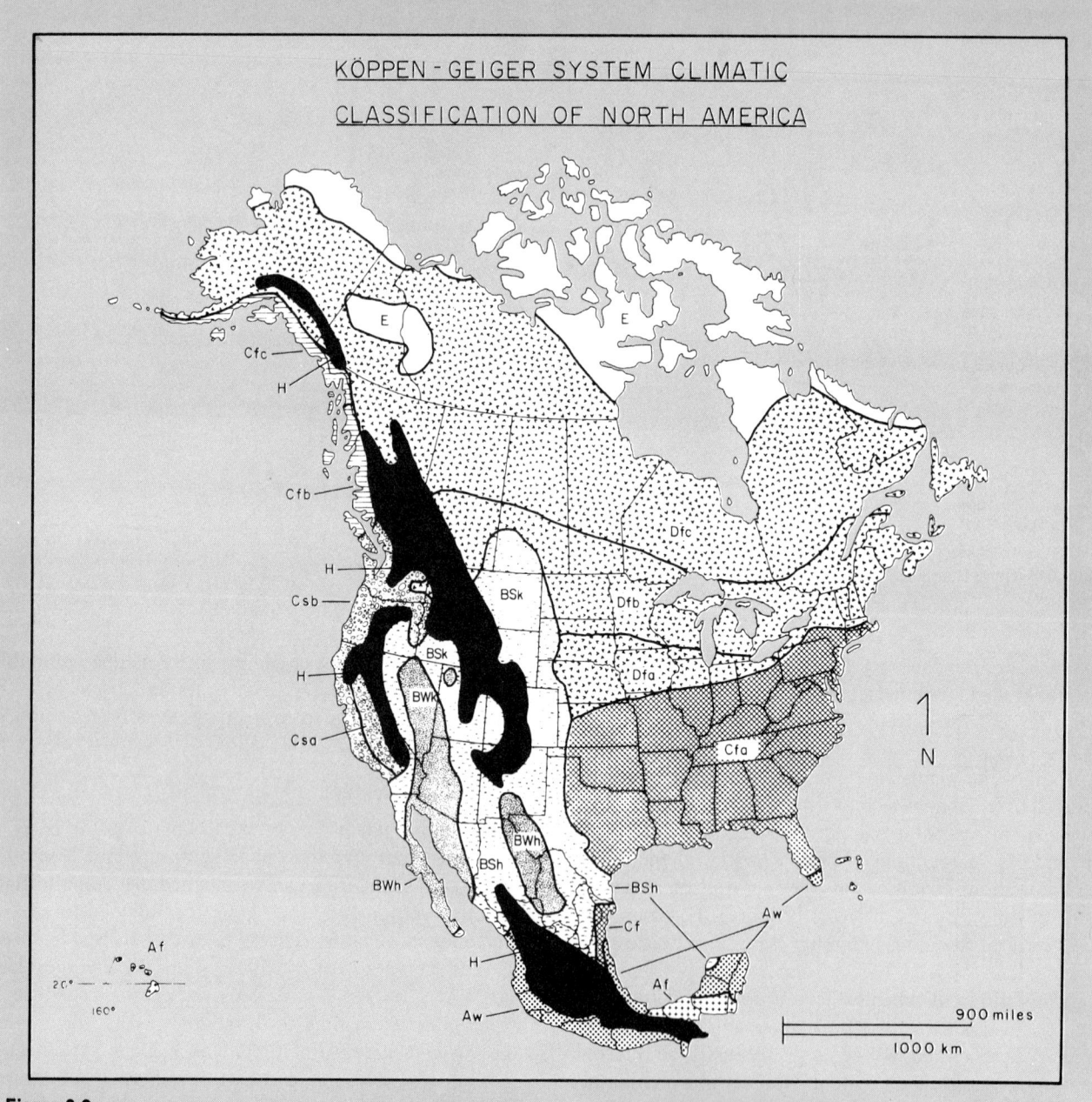

Figure 3.9 Köppen system climatic classification for North America.
(*Cartographer:* Douglas Hemsath)

Table 3.2
Continued

H Highlands. Climate changes with elevation and aspect.

Subgroups within the five major groups are designated by a second letter, according to the following code.

S Semiarid (steppe).

W Arid (desert).
(The capital letters S and W are applied only to the dry B climates.)

f Moist. There is adequate precipitation in all months and no dry season. This modifier is applied to A, C, and D groups.

w Dry season in winter (low sun) of the respective hemisphere.

s Dry season in summer (high sun) of the respective hemisphere.

m Rainforest climate despite short, dry season in monsoon type of precipitation cycle. This applies only to A climates.

T Tundra (permafrost)

F Ice Cap (permanent snow or ice cover)
(The capital letters T and F are applied only to the cold E climates.)

From combinations of the two letter groups, 12 distinct climates emerge:

Af Tropical rainforest climate. Rainfall of the driest month is 6 cm (2.4 in) or more.

Am Monsoon variety of Af. Rainfall of the driest month is less than 6 cm (2.4 in). The dry season is not strongly developed.

Aw Tropical savanna climate. At least one month has rainfall less than 6 cm (2.4 in). The dry season is strongly developed.

Figure 3.10 shows the boundaries between Af, Am, and Aw climates as determined by both annual rainfall and rainfall of the driest month.

BS Steppe climate. A semiarid climate characterized by grasslands. It occupies an intermediate position between the desert climate (BW) and the more humid climates of the A, C, and D groups. Boundaries are determined by formulas given in figure 3.11.

BW Desert climate. An arid climate with annual precipitation usually less than 40 cm (15 in). The boundary with the adjacent steppe climate (BS) is determined by formulas given in figure 3.11.

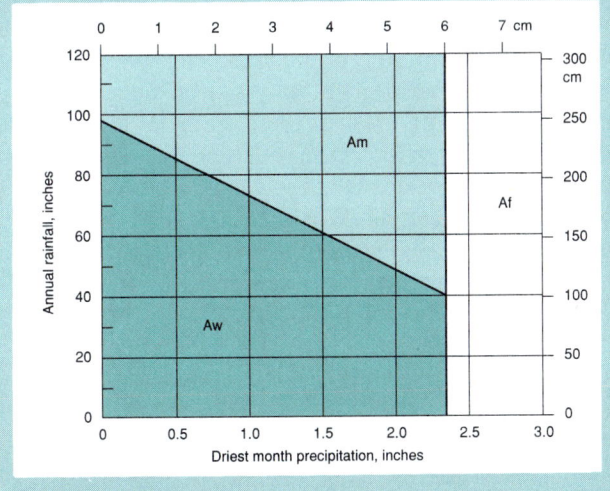

Figure 3.10 The climatic boundaries of the A climate.
Copyright © 1973 by Arthur N. Strahler. Reproduced by permission.

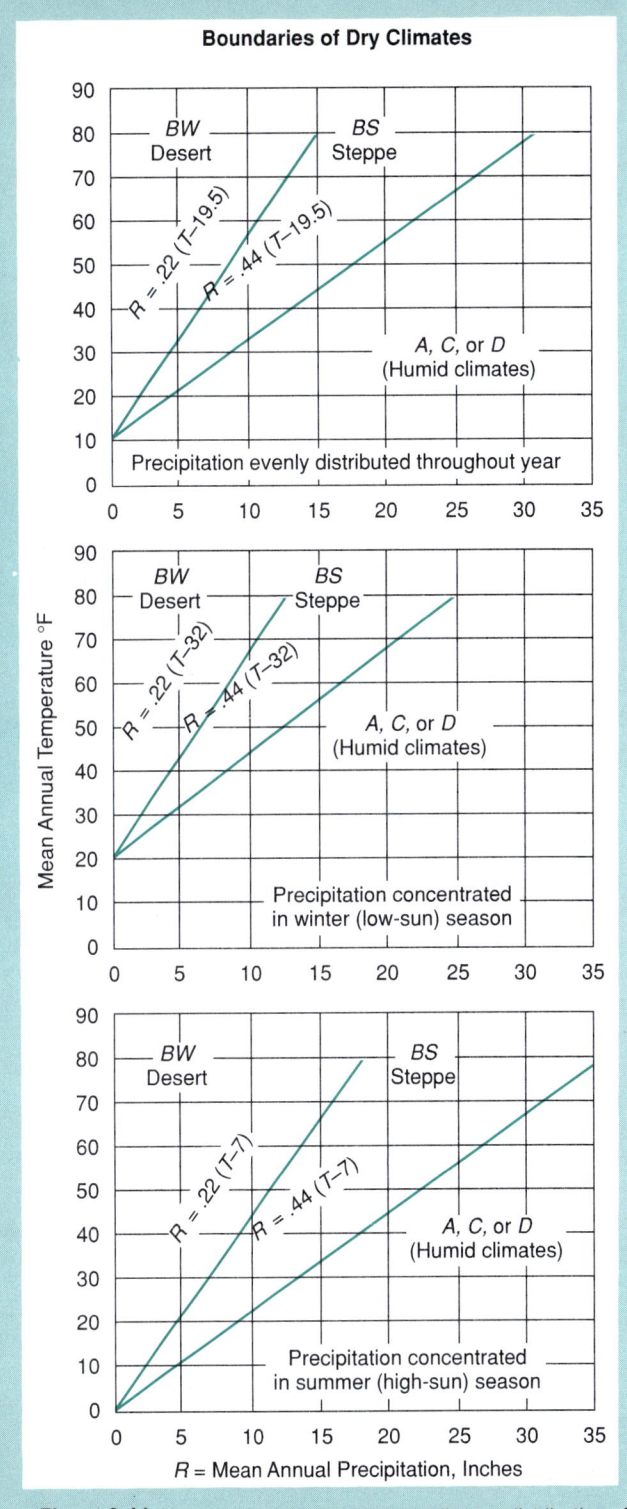

Figure 3.11 Dry climate boundaries depending on distribution of precipitation throughout the year.
Copyright © 1973 by Arthur N. Strahler. Reproduced by permission.

Table 3.2
Continued

Cf	Mild humid climate with no dry season. Precipitation of the driest month averages more than 3 cm (1.2 in).
Cw	Mild humid climate with a dry winter. The wettest month of summer has at least 10 times the precipitation of the driest month of winter. (Alternate definition: Seventy percent or more of the mean annual precipitation falls in the warmer six months.)
Cs	Mild humid climate with a dry summer. Precipitation of the driest month of summer is less than 3 cm (1.2 in). Precipitation of the wettest month of winter is at least three times as much as the driest month of summer. (Alternate definition: Seventy percent or more of the mean annual precipitation falls in the six months of winter.)
Df	Snowy-forest climate with a moist winter. No dry season.
Dw	Snowy-forest climate with a dry winter. Dry low sun season.
ET	Tundra climate. Mean temperature of the warmest month is above 0° C (32° F) but below 10° C (50° F).
EF	Perpetual frost climate. Ice-sheet climate. Mean monthly temperatures of all months are below 0° C (32° F).

To denote further variations in climate, Köppen added tertiary third letters to the code group. Meanings are as follows:

C and D climates:

a	With hot summer; warmest month is over 22° C (71.6° F).
b	With warm summer; warmest month is below 22° C (71.6° F).
c	With cool, short summer; less than four months are over 10° C (50° F).
d	With very cold winter; coldest month is below −38° C (−36.4° F); (D climates only).

B climates:

h	Dry-hot; mean annual temperature is over 18° C (64.4° F).
k	Dry-cold; mean annual temperature is under 18° C (64.4° F).

Examples of complete Köppen climate codes, BWk, refers to a cool desert climate; and Dfc, refers to a cold, snowy forest climate with cool, short summers (see Appendix D for a flow diagram for complete climatic classification, using the Köppen System).

Temperature values used by Köppen to separate his climatic regions have a biologic significance. The 18° C (64.4° F) isotherm separates the tropics from the nontropics on the basis of coral growth. **Coral** growth requires an average monthly temperature above 18° C (64.4° F). Regions with monthly temperatures less than 64.4° F have no coral in their marine environments. The −3° C (26.6° F) isotherm is the average freezing temperature of ocean salt water. Since about 70% of the earth's surface is salt water, it makes sense to use 26.6° F rather than 32° F (0° C), which is the freezing temperature of fresh water. The 10° C (50° F) isotherm has a double significance in the physical environment. If every month of the year has an average temperature less than 50° F, then frost does not leave the ground and the area is called a *permafrost* region. The 50° F isotherm marks the poleward limit of tree growth and thus is also called the **tree line**, because if every month of the year averages below 50° F, then trees can't grow because the roots can't penetrate the permafrost. The separation of climate by precipitation amounts is made on the basis of the difference between precipitation (P) and potential evapotranspiration (PE). *Potential evapotranspiration* is the conversion of liquid water to water vapor by evaporation and plant transpiration. When P is greater than PE (P>PE), the region or area is moist; when P is less than PE (P<PE), a deficit occurs and the region or area is defined as dry. Moist versus dry conditions affect the soil moisture and available moisture for potential vegetation. Vegetative regions are defined to a large extent on the basis of available moisture in the soil.

Climatic Extremes

The Köppen system of climatic classification is a very useful way to generalize about climates. It is not without its limitations, however. In the real (physical) world, temperature and precipitation averages are not what happens on a daily basis. Remember what Eiseley said, "There is nothing very normal about nature." During northern hemisphere midwest winters, two weeks of severe cold followed by two weeks of above average temperatures will be entered in the climatological record as a normal month. A twenty-four hour period for this same geographic location with 10 cm (4in) of precipitation on August 1, followed by 30 days of drought, shows up on the record books as a normal month. Both of these examples illustrate the great variability of the weather that produces our average weather, our climate. Weather conditions create periods of stress for vegetation. When climatic stress exceeds the limits of a vegetative species, then it dies out of the region temporarily or permanently, depending on future conditions.

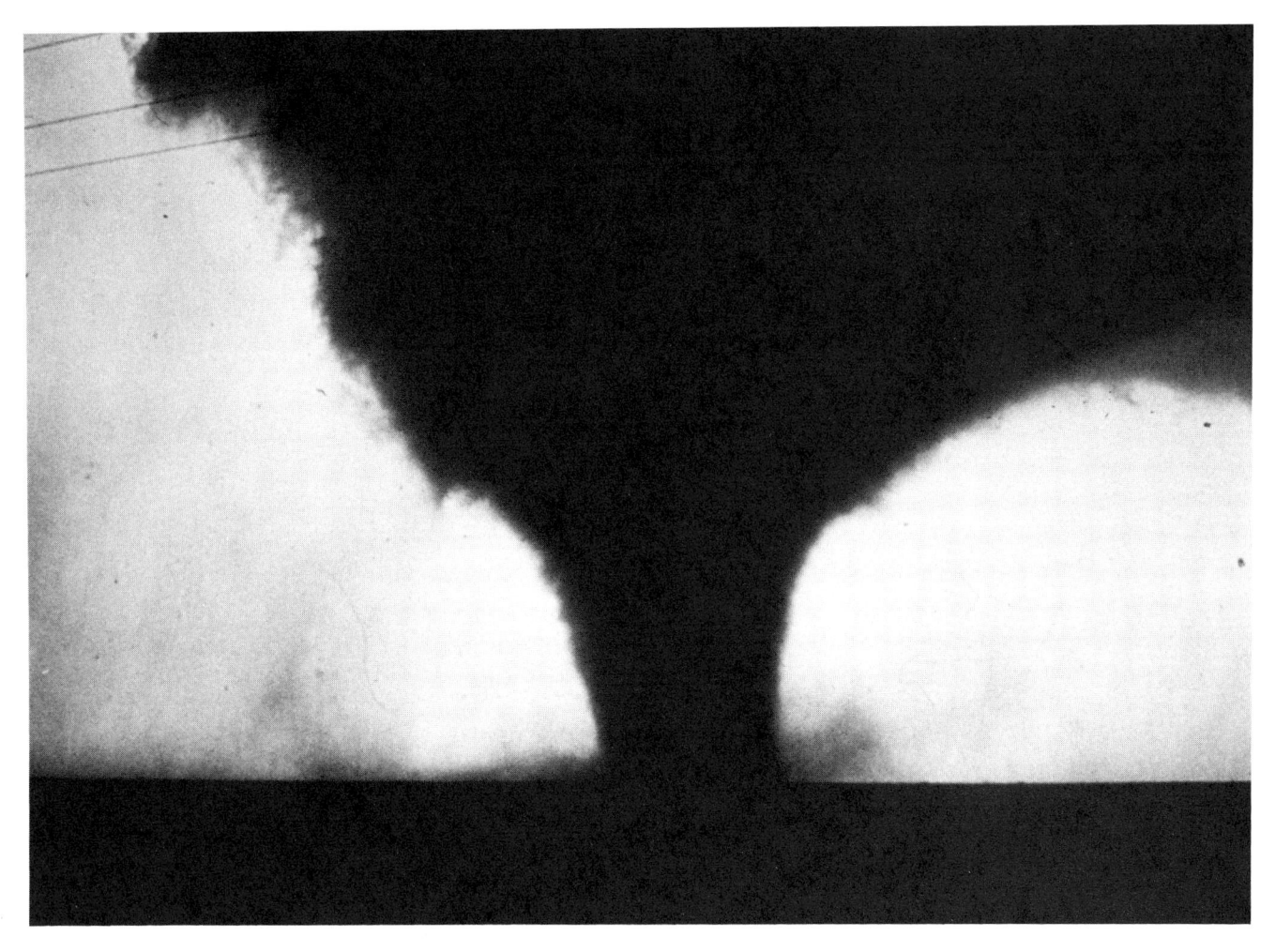

Figure 3.12 Tornadoes in the United States are the most destructive weather condition that can occur inland from the oceans.
(Photo: NOAA)

In the conservation of natural resources, climate is one of the most important, if not the most important, physical variable. Its importance cannot be underestimated. Consideration of climate must also include consideration of the climatic extremes. Temperature maximums and minimums, first and last days of killing frost, greatest amount of precipitation in a 24-hour period, greatest number of days with no precipitation, and depth of frost penetration of the soil layer are but a few of the **climatic extremes** that must be taken into consideration when analyzing the climatic variable in resource management.

Severe weather can also be considered a climatic extreme. Tornadoes, hurricanes, tidal waves, flash floods, ice storms, large hail, and heavy thunderstorms are all severe weather conditions that can have damaging effects on the natural environment (figure 3.12). While most severe weather conditions are not predictable as to exact time of occurrence, they are statistically predictable geographically. There are known storm tracks and paths for tornadoes and hurricanes for each season of the year.

In resources management, a detailed understanding of the climatic condition is a prerequisite to management of any resource of a region or geographic area. In many cases, present climate and weather conditions would be sufficient to manage a resource, but the long-term climatic condition for North America has not been fixed and has changed on a semi-regular basis throughout the Quaternary Period.

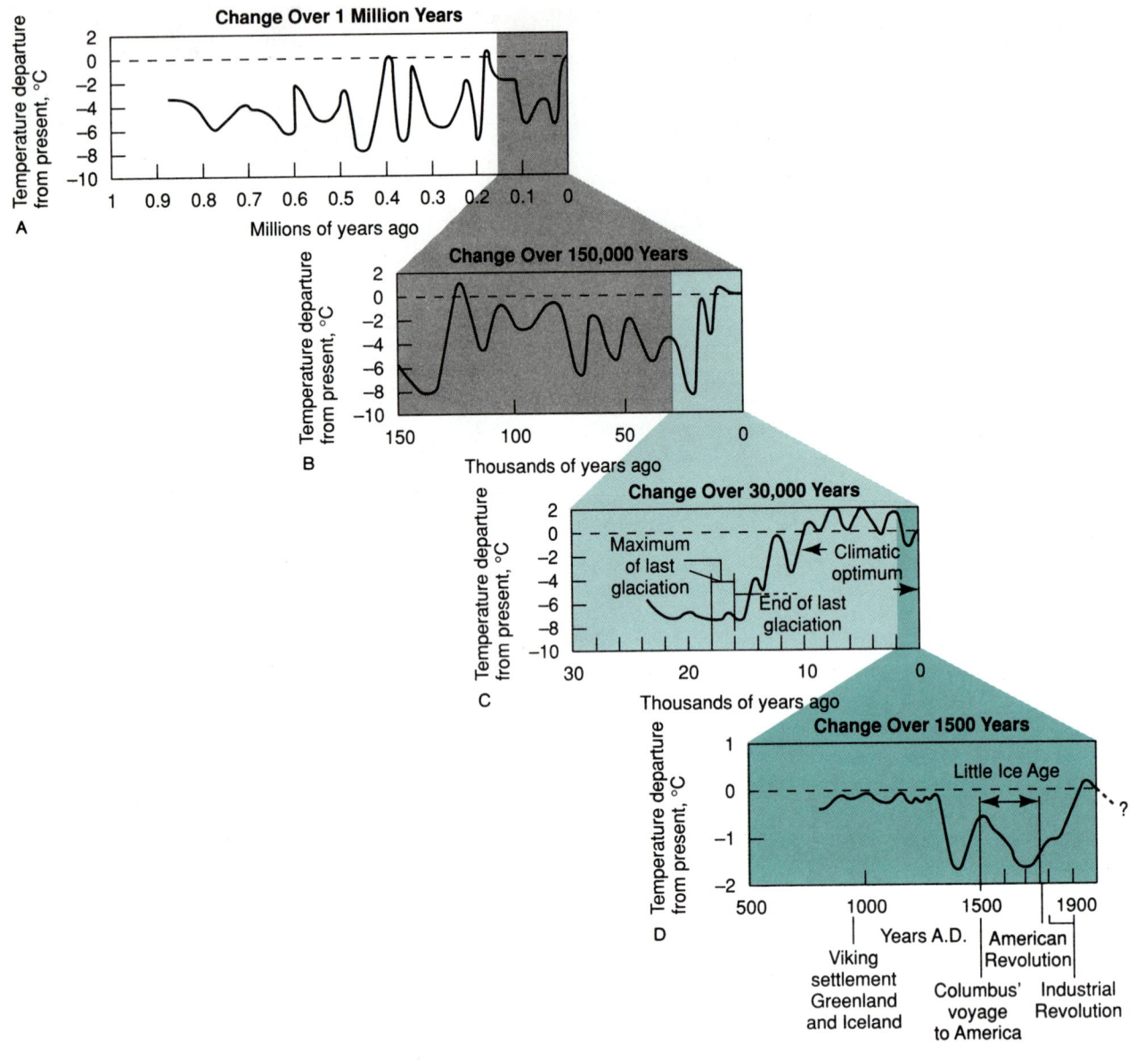

Figure 3.13 Climate change during recent geologic time.
From Marsh, *Earthscape: A Physical Geography*. Copyright © 1987 John Wiley & Sons, Inc., New York, NY. Reprinted by permission of John Wiley & Sons, Inc.

Variation in temperature over different periods of time:
(a) 1 million years; (b) 150,000 years; (c) 30,000 years; (d) 1500 years.

Climate Change

The climatic conditions in North America have changed many times (figure 3.13), with alternating periods of continental glaciation and warmer interglacial periods. Many lines of evidence suggest that as many as 18 glacial and interglacial periods have occurred during the last 1.8 million years. The most recent of these glacial periods has been named the **Wisconsinan** glacial period. It began about 35,000 ybp, reached its glacial maximum about 22,500 ybp, and melted off the continent completely about 6,000 ybp. We are presently in the interglacial period called the Holocene Epoch. The Wisconsinan glacial episode has had a profound influence on the natural resources. First, because of the climate change, the hydrologic regime was altered. The major drainageways that carried away meltwater were permanently enlarged, especially the Mississippi River system. Second, the soil layer of much of the midwestern and eastern states and Canada was permanently changed. Canada lost much of its topsoil and the north central and eastern states of the United States were the recipients. And third, the vegetative boundaries between biogeographic regions were altered drastically.

DROWNED RIVER VALLEYS

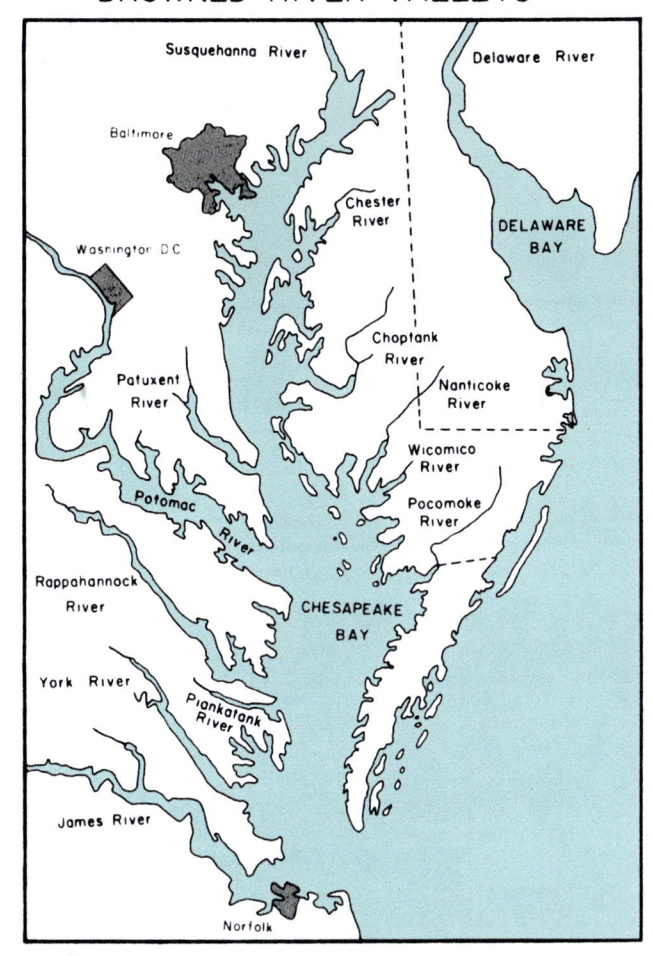

Figure 3.14 Chesapeake Bay, Delaware Bay, and their tributaries are drowned river valleys that were carved by running water when the sea level was much lower during the glacial periods of the Pleistocene.
(*Cartographer:* Douglas Hemsath)

These same observations are true of our mountainous western regions in the United States and Canada but to a lesser degree, depending on the history of alpine glacial systems and elevations in these mountains.

Recognition of the fact that climate is a variable and that it changes through time is important in understanding and managing environmental systems. Many preglacial and glacial niches still exist in North America. A *niche* in this sense refers to a habitat supplying the factors necessary for the existence of an organism or species. The mixed *mesophytic* (mesophytic = medium or average moisture conditions) hardwood coves of the Smoky Mountains in Tennessee are an example of a vegetative community that has survived the climate changes of the several glacial and interglacial periods of the Pleistocene Epoch. Many colder climate plants remain and represent remnants of vegetation of past colder periods that have found a protected niche (habitat) for survival.

Climatic changes are accompanied by sea-level changes. Continental ice accumulations during glacial periods caused sea levels 100 m (300 ft) lower than today. New coastal environments are created, destroyed, and/or relocated by these changes. Rising seas following the melting of the last ice sheet have drowned many of the river valleys on the east coast of North America, producing a variety of shapes and sizes of inlets, bays, and estuaries (figure 3.14). Many of the aquatic habitats created along our coasts are important to our fisheries resource.

The Greenhouse Effect

The *greenhouse effect* is the name given to the physical process whereby short-wave (high frequency) energy from the sun passes relatively freely through the atmosphere, while heat (long-wave energy) radiating from the earth is partially absorbed, then reradiated, by certain *triatomic gases* (gases with three atoms per molecule such as CO_2) in the atmosphere (figure 3.15). The difference in wavelength is explained by the fact that our sun is warmer than the earth, causing its energy to be radiated at a shorter wavelength (higher frequency) than the long-wave energy radiated by a cooler earth. Short-wave sun energy is not absorbed well by the triatomic gases. However, these gases are effective absorbers of the lower frequency (longer wave) energy radiated by the earth. Although these gases represent only a small portion of the total atmospheric gases, they are very important factors in climatic control at the earth's surface. In general, the energy absorbed by different gases can be calculated. As the concentration of triatomic atmospheric trace gases increases, the energy being absorbed also increases and warms the air. If, for example, a doubling of the concentration of CO_2 in the atmosphere were to occur, it would lead to a global air temperature increase of 1.2° C or about 2.2° F, assuming no other changes occurred in the climatic system.

The current numerical computer models of the earth's climate predict that the warming due to the increase in CO_2 will lead to more evaporation of water vapor from the oceans. Water vapor itself (H_2O) is a greenhouse (triatomic) gas, so, as its concentration increases in the atmosphere, the planet will warm even further. With rising temperatures, there will be less snow and ice to reflect solar energy. (Snow has a high albedo.) This promotes further warming as more of the sun's heat is retained by the earth. Increased cloud cover predicted by the model could also enhance atmospheric warming, but there are major uncertainties about the overall effects of cloud cover changes.

The result of all of the positive feedback mechanisms in the computer model indicates a tripling of the warming caused by a doubling of the CO_2 levels. This would produce a total global warming of about 4° C (7° F). Global warming would also cause the sea level to rise due to thermal expansion of the oceans. Sea-level rise would be further enhanced by glacial melting from Greenland and Antarctica and from mountain summits on the continents.

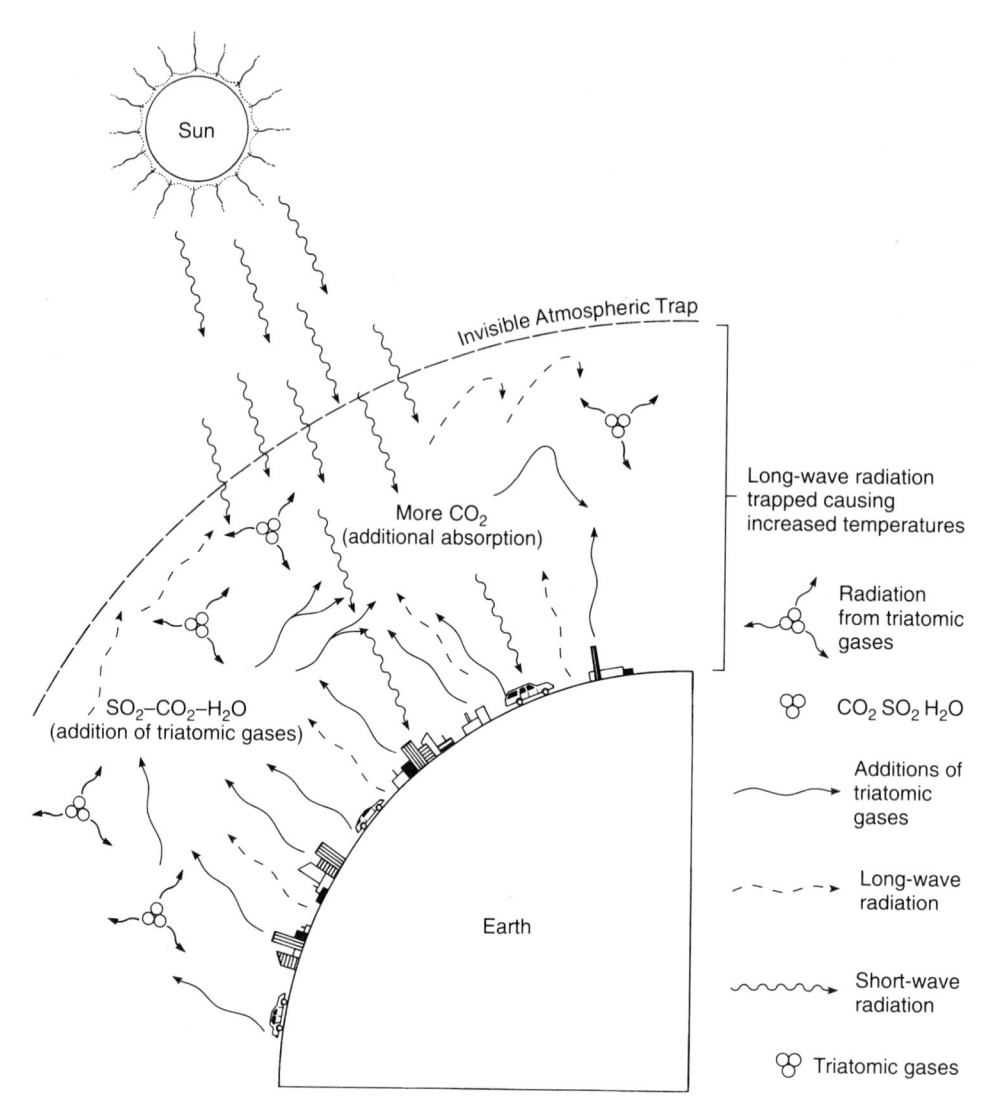

Figure 3.15 The greenhouse effect can cause global warming by trapping long-wave radiation in the lower atmosphere.

Estimates of sea-level rise in the next century because of global warming are for a 1.8 to 2.1 m (6 to 7 ft) total rise in the sea surface.

In 1958, a system for atmospheric monitoring was established at Mauna Loa Observatory in Hawaii. Since that time, CO_2 levels in the atmosphere have increased from 315 to 350 parts per million (ppm). Studies of air trapped in glacial ice on Antarctica and Greenland indicate that the CO_2 levels up to the time of the industrial revolution had not exceeded 280 ppm. The rising CO_2 concentrations are believed to be associated with the burning of fossil fuels, industrial processes, and the denudation of the world's tropical rain forests. Also contributing to the greenhouse effect are the additions of chlorofluorocarbons (CFCs) and other trace gases to the atmosphere. Figure 3.16 illustrates the contribution of gases from human activities to the atmosphere that have enhanced the greenhouse effect.

It is estimated that the average surface air temperature has increased globally about 0.6° C (1° F) in the past 100 years. The overall warming for the past century is the right order of magnitude for the expected greenhouse effect. The five warmest years, globally, during the past century were all in the 1980s. The Goddard Institute of Space Studies (GISS) forecasts changes of 2° C (3.6° F) by the year 2020, which would make the earth warmer than it is thought to have been at any point in historical time. Estimates for summer temperatures in the doubled CO_2 climate indicate that Washington, D.C., which currently experiences 36 days per year of temperatures above 32° C (90° F), would have 87 such days; Dallas, Texas would go from 100 days with temperatures above 32° C (90° F) to 162 days, and Los Angeles would increase from 5 days per year above 32° C (90° F) to 27 days. There are models other than the GISS System that forecast lesser and greater changes in climate caused by

Man-Made Contributions to the Greenhouse Effect

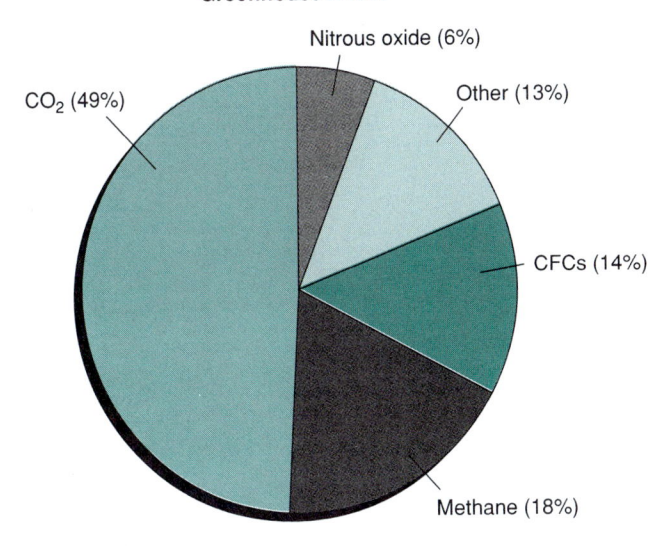

- CO_2 (49%)
- Nitrous oxide (6%)
- Other (13%)
- CFCs (14%)
- Methane (18%)

Figure 3.16 Man-made contributions to the greenhouse effect.
Source: Environmental Protection Agency Journal, Vol. 15, No. 1, January/February 1989.

the greenhouse effect. Climate has always been a physical **variable** of the natural environment.

The climate is being altered by the release of greenhouse gases, which are inherent in our current civilization. It may be possible to limit specific trace gases such as CFCs and slow down the rate of CO_2 increase through energy conservation practices. But it is likely that the additions of the past 50 years have already built considerable warming into the system because of the slow warming response of the oceans. With this in mind, it is worthwhile for us to factor climatic change into decision-making processes related to our future management of natural resources.

The Ozone Problem

Ozone is the key atmospheric gas that shields us against damaging solar ultraviolet (UV) radiation (figures 3.1 and 3.3). Extensive measurements by both ground- and satellite-based instruments indicate very large decreases in ozone during the months of September through November that have occurred above Antarctica over the past decade. There is no doubt that the gases released from certain human activities are threatening the integrity of the protective ozone layer.

Unlike the abundant atmospheric gases, oxygen O_2 (21%) and nitrogen N_2 (78%), ozone (O_3) represents only a tiny fraction of the total atmosphere, with an average global concentration of about 300 parts per billion in volume (ppbv). If all of the ozone were compressed to surface pressure it would form a layer around the earth only 3 mm (0.1 in) thick. As discussed earlier, the sun gives off radiation across a broad spectrum (figure 3.1). Wavelengths from the visible spectrum, 0.4 to 0.7 μm (micrometers) can be tolerated by biological species at the earth's surface. In contrast, the adjacent wavelengths in the ultraviolet spectrum (0.3–0.4 μm) have been shown to be biologically damaging. Fortunately, most of this radiation is absorbed by ozone high in the earth's atmosphere (figure 3.17).

Complex natural forces are continually at work creating and destroying ozone in the atmosphere. This dynamic equilibrium first involves the breakdown of individual molecules of oxygen (O_2) into atomic oxygen (O_2 + UV (sunlight) $\rightarrow$ O + O) through its absorption of ultraviolet radiation. In turn, each atom of oxygen combines with an oxygen (O_2) molecule to form ozone (O_3) (O + O_2 $\rightarrow$ O_3). Destruction of ozone can be caused by the occasional recombination of ozone with atomic oxygen to form two molecules of diatomic oxygen. As long as the earth's sunlit atmosphere contains molecular oxygen, as it has for more than two billion years, ozone will be maintained in this dynamic balance between formation and destruction. This balance can be upset by the introduction of ozone-destroying chemicals into the atmosphere.

In the 1930s, General Motors, while searching for a substitute for ammonia, discovered a family of chemicals known as **chlorofluorocarbons** (CFCs). They proved to have many uses in refrigeration, air conditioning, packaging, insulation, cleaning solvent use, and as an aerosol propellant. CFCs appeared to be environmentally safe because they were chemically inert, nontoxic, and easily liquified.

It is the absence of chemical reactivity that makes CFCs so dangerous to the ozone layer. Unlike less inert compounds, CFCs are not destroyed or removed in the lower atmosphere by rainout, oxidation, or sunlight. Instead, being lighter than many other atmospheric gases, they drift into the upper atmosphere where their **chlorine** components are released into the atmosphere. There, under the effects of ultraviolet radiation, these chlorine components encounter and destroy ozone. Almost all of these freed chlorine atoms find and react with the ozone in one to two seconds, creating chlorine oxide (ClO) as a by-product. In a subsequent reaction, the chlorine oxide releases its oxygen atom to form molecular oxygen, and the chlorine atom is freed once again to repeat the process of destroying ozone. Through this continuing cycle of reactions, each chlorine atom acts as a catalyst, destroying about 100,000 molecules of ozone before the chain reaction is permanently ended. The atmospheric lifetimes for the most commonly used CFC compounds (CFC-11, CFC-12, and CFC-13) have been estimated to be from 75 to 110 years.

Widespread use of CFCs by industry and consumers began in the 1970s. Releases of CFCs worldwide have been nearly one million tons per year. The natural level of chlorine in the atmosphere before 1900 is believed to have been

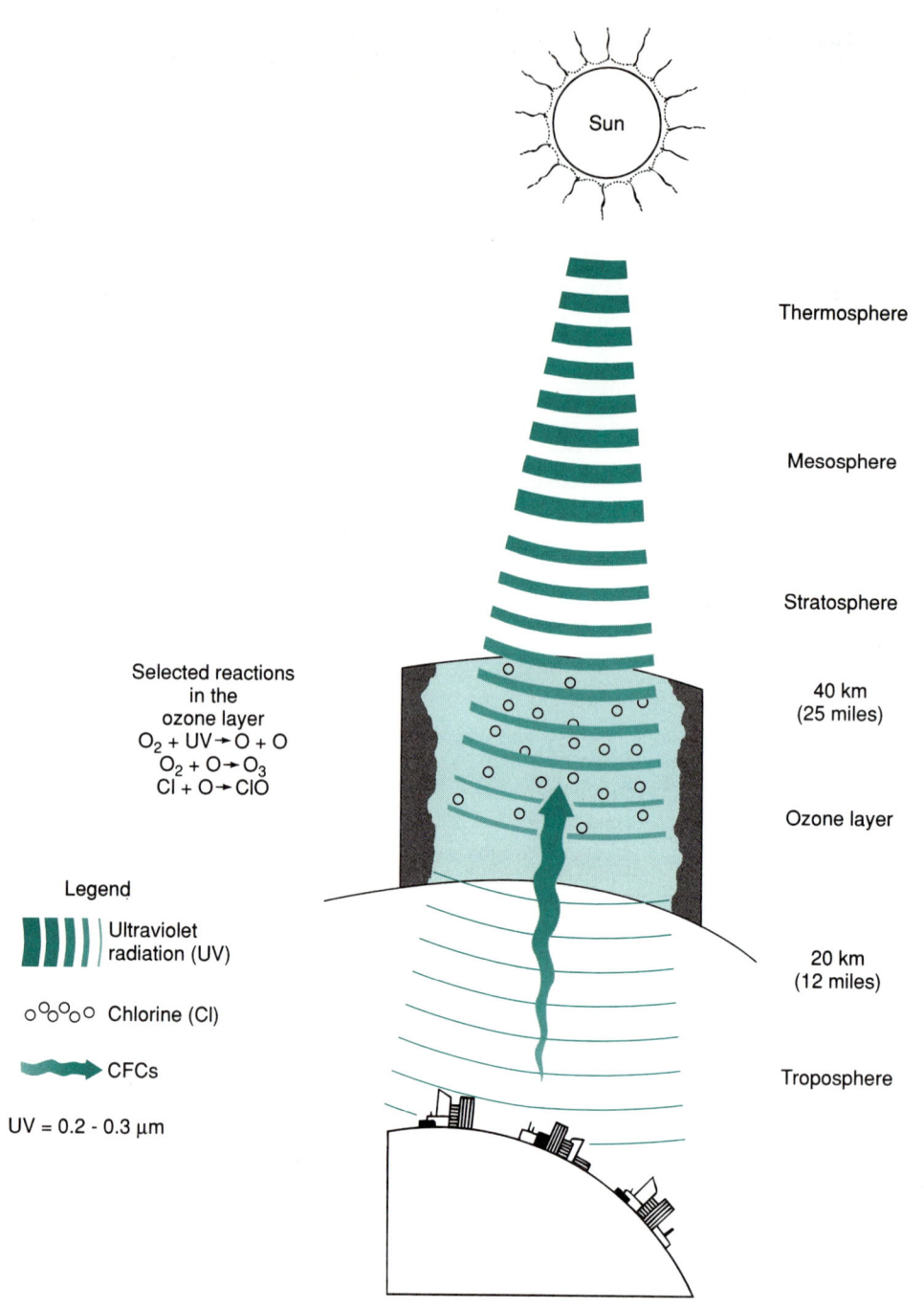

Figure 3.17 Selected reactions in the ozone layer.
Source: Environmental Protection Agency Journal, Vol. 12, No. 10, December 1986.

Selected reactions in the ozone layer
$$O_2 + UV \rightarrow O + O$$
$$O_2 + O \rightarrow O_3$$
$$Cl + O \rightarrow ClO$$

Legend:
- Ultraviolet radiation (UV)
- Chlorine (Cl)
- CFCs

$UV = 0.2 - 0.3 \ \mu m$

about 0.6 ppbv, derived almost entirely from methylchloride. The present chlorine level is about 3.5 ppbv and is increasing by more than 1.0 ppbv per decade. The excellent correlation between the increase in atmospheric chlorine and ozone losses during the Antarctic spring provide strong circumstantial evidence that CFCs are involved in the process.

The risks from ozone depletion since 1976 have been described by the National Academy of Sciences, and include not only the increased UV effect on humans in the form of skin cancer, but also UV attack on many other biological systems (figure 3.18). Despite the growing scientific record against CFCs, world use continues to increase. A possible solution to the ozone depletion problem is the development of alternative chemicals to replace the present CFCs. Industry's search for less harmful chemicals has produced a hydrogen-containing **CFC-22** that has been in use for home air conditioners and represents a much reduced threat to the ozone layer because the molecule is strongly susceptible toward oxidation in the lower

The Kansas City Star, Friday, March 25, 1988

"I MISS THE OZONE LAYER...."

Figure 3.18 Going to the beach just wouldn't be the same without the ozone layer to protect us.
Copyright, 1988, Los Angeles Times Syndicate. Reprinted with permission.

atmosphere. Another alternative chemical is **fluorocarbon-134a,** which has many of the same industrial properties found in CFC-12. This compound has a negligible potential for ozone depletion because it does not contain chlorine.

Industries must begin to design closed industrial processes with recycling, which could dramatically reduce emissions by using these potentially harmful chemicals more efficiently. Because of the very long atmospheric lifetimes of CFCs, any damage done to the atmosphere will persist throughout the entire 21st century. The costs of expeditiously moving away from these suspect chemicals is a very small price compared to the potential damages if we fail to act now. Fifty countries including the United States, Canada, and Mexico have signed the **1987 Montreal Protocol,** which calls for a reduction by 50% of all CFC use by the year 2000. The United States, with the passage of the 1990 amendments to the Clean Air Act, will completely ban CFC use by the end of the century.

Summary

The composition of the atmosphere has been changing throughout geologic time. The changes because of interactions among the earth's spheres (atmosphere, biosphere, hydrosphere, and lithosphere) have been a part of the system. Oxygen content in the atmosphere has increased because of the life processes of the biosphere. Changes continue to occur but the rates of change have become alarming. Carbon dioxide increases and ozone decreases are occurring at rates too great for organisms to adapt. Evolutionary changes cannot keep pace with the climatic changes predicted for the early 21st century. Global warming and the accompanying rise in sea level threatens all coastal environments and habitats. Ozone depletion promises to bring with it thousands of additional cases of skin cancer for the human population.

The composition of the atmosphere and its climatic condition is the most important abiotic physical variable at the base of the biotic pyramid. Climate dictates the distribution of plant organisms or the biogeography of the producer level. The vegetation and climate then determine the primary consumers (herbivores). The herbivores and climate determine the omnivores and carnivores. In the final analysis, climate controls the biosphere and human activities.

Key Words and Phrases

Albedo
Chlorofluorocarbons
Climate
Convection
Coriolis effect
Global heat balance latitude
Greenhouse effect
Isotherm
Köppen-Geiger-Pohl system
Latent heat
Mesophytic
Niche
Ozone
Permafrost
Plane of the ecliptic
Potential evapotranspiration
Radiation balance
Revolves
Rotates
Sensible heat
Solar constant
Standard atmospheric pressure
Sun
Triatomic gases
Weather
Wind

Questions and Discussion Topics

1. In what ways does atmospheric circulation affect the weather in your geographic location?
2. What is the climate in your geographic location?
3. Compare the average temperature and precipitation figures for your local area with the record highs, record lows, and greatest amounts of precipitation. What climate category would your geographic area be in if your monthly average temperature were the record low for the month?

4. What effect would a drop of 25 cm (10 in) per year in precipitation have on your local natural vegetation?

5. What is the greenhouse effect? How will it effect your local area in the next 50 years?

6. What is the ozone problem? How can we as economic consumers help to slow down the increase in CFCs in the atmosphere?

References for Further Study

Eiseley, L. 1964. The Angry Winter (chapter 5). *Unexpected Universe*. New York: Harcourt Brace Jovanovich.

(Four excellent issues of the EPA Journal on the problems of the atmosphere follow.)

Environmental Protection Agency. Dec., 1986. Our Fragile Atmosphere: The Greenhouse Effect and Ozone Depletion. *EPA Journal*. 12: No. 10.

Environmental Protection Agency. Oct., 1987. The Challenge of Ozone Pollution. *EPA Journal*. 13: No. 8.

Environmental Protection Agency. Jan. Feb., 1989. The Greenhouse Effect: How It Can Change Our Lives. *EPA Journal*. 15: No. 1.

Environmental Protection Agency. Mar. Apr., 1990. The Greenhouse Effect: What Can We Do About It? *EPA Journal*. 16: No. 2.

Mather, J. R. 1974. *Climatology: Fundamentals and Applications*. New York: McGraw Hill. A good climatology textbook.

Moran, J. M. and M. D. Morgan. 1989. *Meteorology: The Atmosphere and the Science of Weather*. 2nd ed. New York: MacMillan. A good meteorology textbook.

Neiburger, M., J. G. Edinger, and W. D. Bonner. 1982. *Understanding Our Atmospheric Environment*. 2nd. ed. San Francisco: W. H. Freeman. A good atmospheric science textbook.

Strahler, A. N. and A. H. Strahler. 1976. *Elements of Physical Geography*. New York: John Wiley & Sons. A good discussion of the atmosphere and climate in a physical geography textbook.

Chapter 4

Hydrosphere—Water

Introduction
Changing States of Water
Hydrologic Cycle
Oceanic Circulation
Composition of the Hydrosphere
The Aquatic Environments
    Freshwater Environments
        Lakes
        Lake Zones
        The Acid Rain Problem
        Streams
        The Missouri River
    Saltwater Environments
        The Ocean Basins
        Ocean Dumping
    Groundwater
Summary

There are other things brewing and growing in the ocean vat. . . . There are things down there still coming ashore. Never make the mistake of thinking life is now adjusted for eternity.
Loren Eiseley, 1957.

Introduction

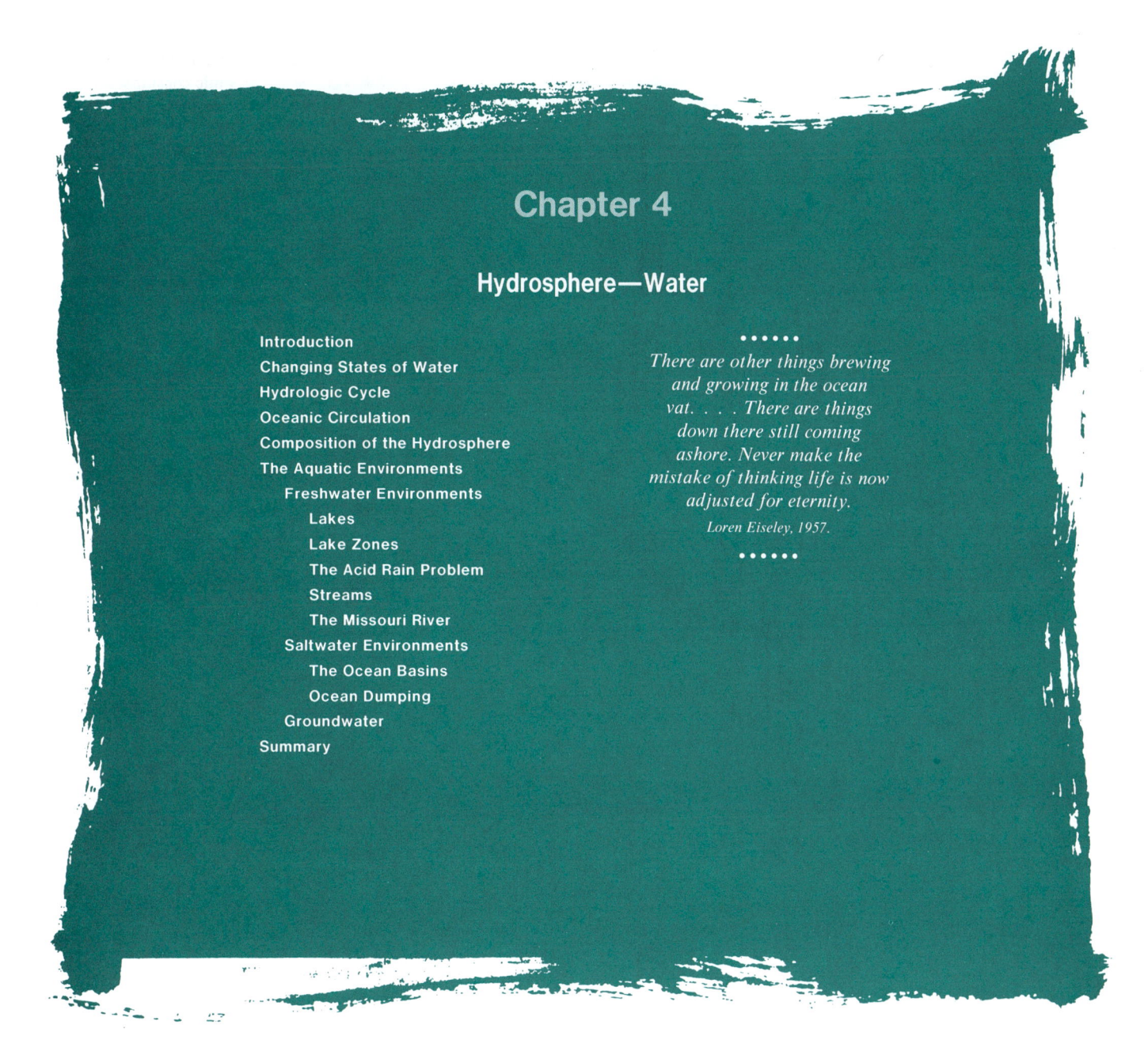

The hydrosphere is very complex, representing all the earth's waters. The surface waters, the oceans, rivers, lakes, streams, ponds, estuaries, lagoons, and bays, make up the majority of the earth's surface. Less obvious, but also large and spectacular, are the continental glaciers of Antarctica and Greenland. Alpine glacial ice is also a part of the hydrosphere. Least obvious, but also very important in the environment, are the subsurface waters of the soil water zone and the many aquifers contained in the rocks of the lithosphere. Table 4.1 gives the distribution of waters on the earth. Most of the earth's waters are locked in the lithosphere and do not circulate in biologic time, but rather in geologic time. However, the water contained in the atmosphere as water vapor and cloud droplets does circulate rapidly in a process called the hydrologic cycle.

Changing States of Water

Water is a remarkable chemical compound (H_2O). It is present in the earth environment as a liquid, a gas, and a solid. To change water from one form to another requires a transfer of heat. Heat is required to **evaporate** water, to **melt** ice, and to **sublimate** ice to water vapor. Heat is given

Table 4.1
Distribution of Waters on the Earth

Location	Volume in Cubic Miles	Volume in Cubic KM	Percentage of Total
Oceans	317,000,000	1,320,600,000	97.217
Glaciers and ice caps	7,000,000	29,200,000	2.147
Groundwater	2,000,000	8,330,000	0.613
Saltwater lakes and inland seas	25,000	104,150	0.008
Freshwater lakes	30,000	125,000	0.009
Soil water	16,000	66,660	<0.001
Atmosphere	3,100	12,900	<0.001
Steambeds	300	1,250	≤0.001
Total	326,074,400	1,358,439,960	99.997
Lithosphere*	328,000,000	1,366,448,000	

*Water bound chemically or physically in the rocks of the lithosphere and released very slowly as juvenile water by endogenic processes (chapter 2).
Source: U.S. Geological Survey

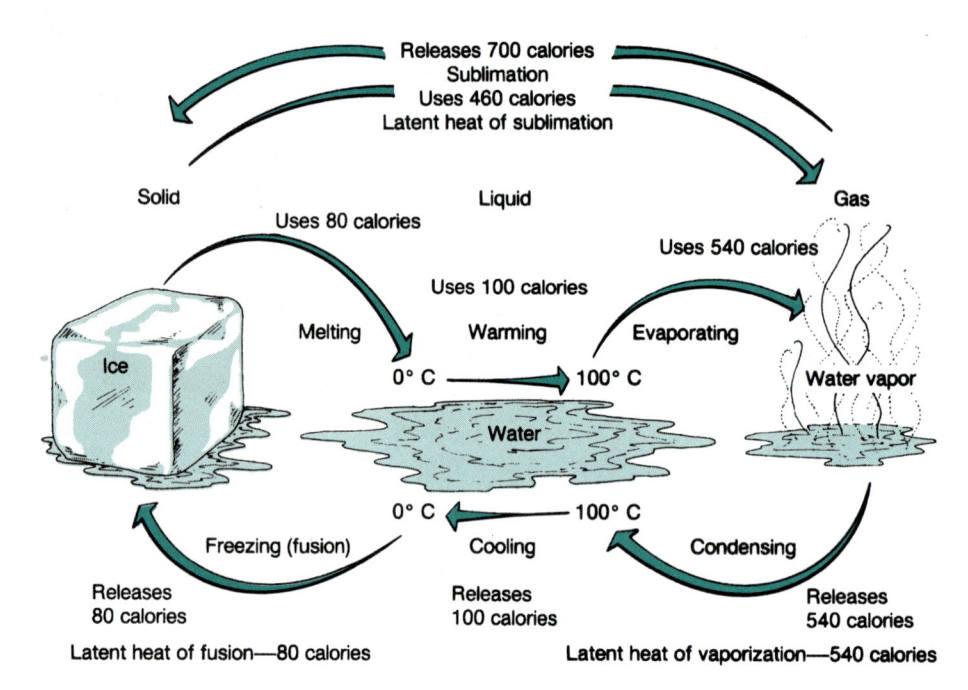

Figure 4.1 The changing states of water. Heat energy required to change one gram of water from liquid↔gas↔ice↔liquid. Using and releasing heat energy from the atmosphere for the changing states of water is a very important thermal regulator for earth environments.
From Alyn C. Duxbury and Alison B. Duxbury, *Introduction to the World's Oceans*, 3d ed. Copyright © 1991 Wm. C. Brown Publishers, Dubuque, Iowa. All Rights Reserved. Reprinted by permission.

off to **freeze** liquid to ice, to **condense** water vapor to liquid, and to **sublimate** water vapor to ice. Figure 4.1 illustrates the changing states of water and gives the amount of energy required or given off to make these changes. Water is our **thermal regulator.** It keeps us from icing over and/or burning up by changing its state to either use excess heat or give off needed heat.

Hydrologic Cycle

The *hydrologic cycle* is the movement of water through the earth's spheres. Water from the oceans is changed from a liquid to a gas (water vapor) by *evaporation*. Eighty-nine percent of the incoming solar radiation from the sun is used to evaporate water. Evaporation requires a great

The Hydrologic Cycle

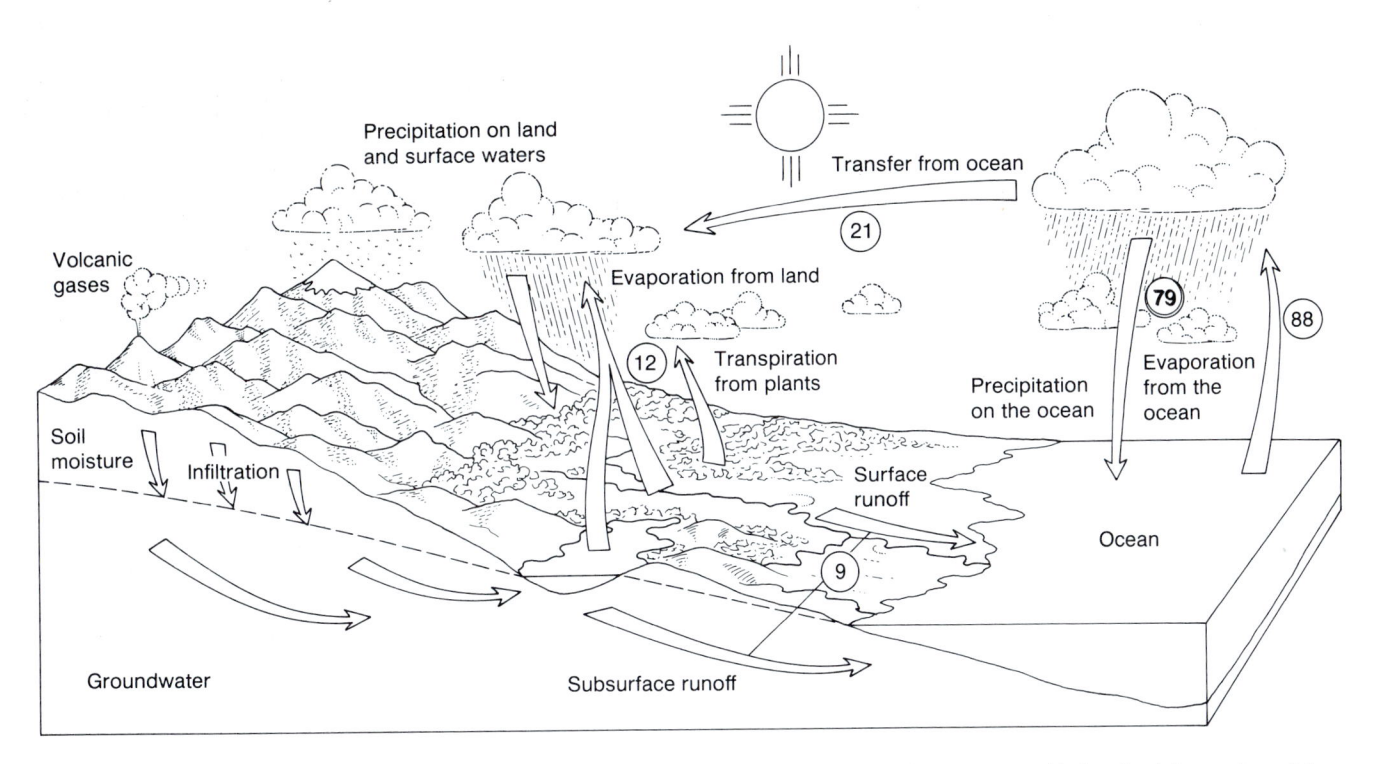

Figure 4.2 Powered by solar energy, the water cycle is an endless interaction of ice, water, and water vapor with the circulation system of the atmosphere and with gravity. Arrows show major pathways. Circled numbers indicate percentages of the total amount of water evaporated or transferred annually. Note that water losses from the land (12 + 9 = 21) are compensated by transfers from the ocean (21), and that runoff from land plus precipitation on the ocean (9 + 79 = 88) balance evaporation from the ocean (88).
From Arthur Getis, et al., *Introduction to Geography*, 3d ed. Copyright © 1991 Wm. C. Brown Publishers, Dubuque, Iowa. All Rights Reserved. Reprinted by permission.

amount of energy, and the utilization of solar energy to evaporate water is one of the thermal regulators that keeps the tropics from burning up. Most tropical regions have a mean monthly and annual temperature of approximately 27° C (80° F). This temperature would be much higher if there were no evaporation. Convection of the moisture-laden air, which rises and cools at the **dry adiabatic rate** of 1° C/100 m (5.6° F/1,000 ft), condenses when the temperature drops to the dew point and clouds form. Condensation gives off heat and, as the air continues to rise, it cools at the reduced **wet adiabatic rate** of approximately 0.5° C/100 m (2.8° F/1,000 ft), because the air is being heated as it cools by the addition of energy added in the condensation process. Precipitation that occurs over the oceans represents a very short hydrologic cycle. Atmospheric circulation also moves some of the clouds over land, creating a more complex pathway for water in the hydrologic cycle (figure 4.2).

Water precipitated on land can fall onto a soil or rock surface, a water surface, or be intercepted by vegetation. Depending on the condition of the surface, the water will either soak in or **run off.** The part that soaks in first restores any moisture deficiencies in the soil water zone and then, if sufficient in volume, replenishes the groundwater supply. The part that runs off is, in most cases, on its way back to the ocean by way of a surface drainage system. However, there are some places on the earth's surface that are not integrated by a surface drainage system. The Great Salt Lake is an example where runoff to the lake has no moisture outlet other than evaporation from the lake by the sun and transfer of this moisture by the winds. Vegetation in the biosphere can intercept water in the hydrologic cycle from the soil water zone, from raindrops, or from water vapor in the atmosphere. Water utilized by vegetation in the growth processes and evaporated from the foliage, and water evaporated from the land, are collectively referred to as *evapotranspiration*.

The evapotranspiration pathway of the hydrologic cycle is very complex. This pathway serves as the nutrient transfer route for soluble and nonsoluble elements needed by vegetation for growth and development. Water in the soil water zone dissolves solubles and picks up *colloids*

Table 4.2
Renewal Time for Water in the Hydrologic Cycle

	Location of Reservoir	Total Water Supply (in %)	Renewal Time
On the land	Ice caps	2.225	10,000 to 37,000 years
	Glaciers	.015	1 to 16,000 years*
	Freshwater lakes	.009	1 to 100 years*
	Saltwater lakes	.007	10 to 1000 years*
	Rivers	.0001	10 to 30 days
Subsurface	Soil moisture	.003	14 to 365 days
	Groundwater		
	To half-mile depth	.303	1 day to 1000 years
	Beyond half-mile depth	.303	4,600 years+
	Lithosphere	(not a supply)	1,000,000 years+
Other	Atmosphere	.001	1–12 days
	Biosphere	.0001	1–5000 days
	World's oceans	97.134	3,000 to 37,000 years*
Total		100.000	

*Varies with depth and other environmental factors.
Source: U.S. Geological Survey

(particles less than 2 microns in size) of organic and inorganic materials, and these nutrients are taken up, along with the water by the roots of vegetation, producing growth. Some of these nutrients are returned to the soil during the yearly cycles of growth and dormancy. This natural cycling of nutrients in the environment is referred to as the **law of fertility.**

The time frame for the hydrologic cycle can be very short. For example, evaporation takes water from the ocean in the morning and that same moisture may be returned to the ocean in the afternoon as precipitation. Water vapor from the Gulf of Mexico transferred by the wind system over midwestern United States may take days, months, or years to return, depending on the pathway the water follows on its return. If the precipitation falls into the Mississippi River, it will take days to return to the Gulf. If the water soaks into the soil, continues into the groundwater supply, and surfaces as a spring, it could take months. If the precipitation soaks into the soil and is picked up by the roots of a tree, it could be in storage in the tree for years. In general, the time water spends in the hydrologic cycle depends on the pathway and the plumbing of the drainage system. Some systems are very direct and fast while others are very slow (table 4.2).

The *soil water zone* is the zone of water available to plants. A **zone of aeration** exists between the soil water zone and the top groundwater zone. The top of the *groundwater zone* is called the **water table,** which fluctuates with the climatic condition. It is higher in wet years and lower in dry years. Many groundwater zones can exist below the surface at any one location. The number and extent of these zones is controlled by the local geology. Permeable rock layers separated by impermeable layers of rock (*aquicludes*) are ideal geologic conditions for trapping water and forming an *aquifer*. **Sandstone** is an ideal host rock for water, provided the layer is not broken by geologic faults that can act as conduits to lower levels. **Shale** that is not fractured by faults is the ideal aquiclude (figure 4.3).

Oceanic Circulation

Movements of the surface waters of the earth's oceans are called *ocean surface currents*. These currents follow the wind systems except where the waters are deflected by land masses. The atmosphere exerts an average pressure (standard sea-level pressure) on the oceans of 14.7lb/sq in (1013 mb). The weight of the atmosphere sets up a frictional drag on the water as the winds blow across the ocean surface.

Figure 4.4 is a map of the major ocean surface currents of the world. The map illustrates the movement of warm tropical water (**North Equatorial Current**) from the equatorial region of the Atlantic Ocean by the Northeast trade winds. This warm water continues north as the **Gulf Stream** and **North Atlantic Drift.** A significant amount of warm water, representing stored solar energy, is transferred from an area of heat excess in the tropics to an area of heat deficit in the North Atlantic. This is one of the most important thermal regulator systems of the earth's environment. It moderates the temperature extremes of the tropics and the arctic.

The **Labrador, California,** and **Alaskan** currents are also very important currents for the North American continent. The *Labrador current* is a cold current that moves arctic water south. It mixes with the warm waters of the Gulf Stream and North Atlantic Drift, creating a very important fisheries habitat in the Atlantic Ocean. The *California current,* a cool current, and the *Alaskan current,* a warm current, act as climatic modifiers for the west coast of North America. These currents shift north and

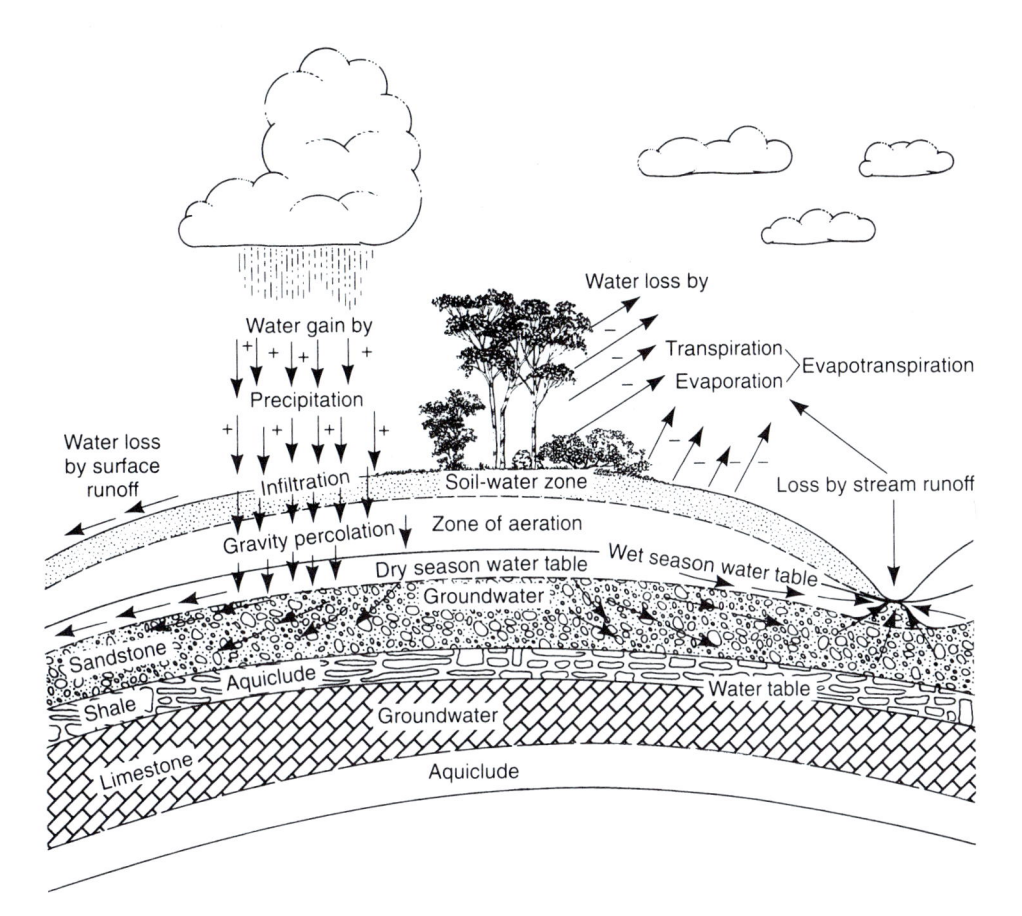

Figure 4.3 Subsurface water zones.
From A. N. Strahler and A. H. Strahler, *Modern Physical Geography*. Copyright © John Wiley & Sons, Inc., New York, NY. Reprinted by permission of John Wiley & Sons, Inc.

south with the seasonal movement of the northern hemisphere westerlies, creating a dry summer (Mediterranean) climate for the California coast of the United States. California averages less than 5 cm (2 in) of precipitation during the month of June.

Composition of the Hydrosphere

The dominant chemical elements of the **hydrosphere** are hydrogen and oxygen (H_2O). The oceans are salty, about 34 to 35 parts per thousand (ppt) salt. Fresh water, in general, has a salt content of about 2 ppt salt.

Table 4.3 gives the relative amounts of each chemical element in the hydrosphere. Major constituents in the salt content of the oceans are sodium chloride (NaCl) 23 ppt, magnesium chloride ($MgCl_2$) 5 ppt, and potassium chloride (KCl) 1 ppt. Another important compound in water is carbon dioxide (CO_2). Carbon dioxide is a necessary ingredient for photosynthesis. The photosynthetic-respiration processes in the phytoplankton of the oceans helps to maintain the oxygen supply of the atmosphere. Marine organisms extract carbon (C) from CO_2 for their skeletal parts ($CaCO_3$) and give off $O_2\uparrow$ to the water and

Table 4.3A
Major Ionic Components of Seawater

Element	PPT Seawater	Hydrosphere Atomic %
Hydrogen (H^+)	643.650	66.4
Oxygen (O^-)	320.440	33.0
Chloride (Cl^-)	19.345	0.33
Sodium (Na^+)	10.752	0.28
Sulfate ($SO_4^=$)	2.701	0.017
Magnesium (Mg^{++})	1.295	0.034
Calcium (Ca^{++})	0.416	0.006
Potassium (K^+)	0.390	0.006
Bicarbonate (HCO_3^-)	0.145	0.0014
Bromide (Br^-)	0.066	0.0002
Total	999.200	

Table 4.3B
Comparison of Important Gas Concentrations in the Atmosphere and Hydrosphere

Gas	Atmospheric Concentration	Saturation in Water
Oxygen O_2	210 cc./l. (21%)	7 cc./l. (32.9%)
Nitrogen N_2	780 cc./l. (78%)	14 cc./l. (65.7%)
Carbon Dioxide CO_2	0.3 cc./l. (0.03%)	0.3 cc./l. (1.4%)

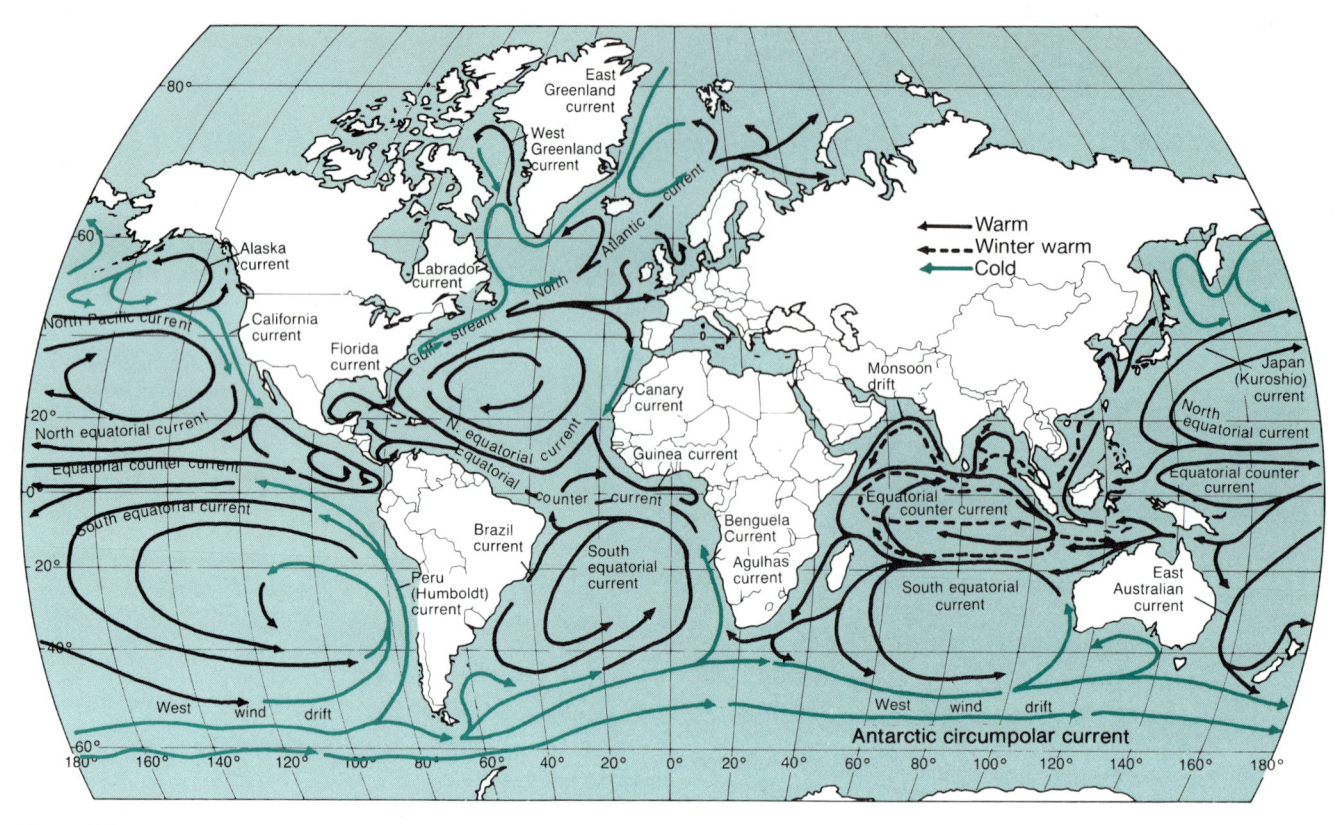

Figure 4.4 Major ocean surface currents of the world.
From Arthur Getis, et al., *Introduction to Geography,* 3d ed. Copyright © 1991 Wm. C. Brown Publishers, Dubuque, Iowa. All Rights Reserved. Reprinted by permission.

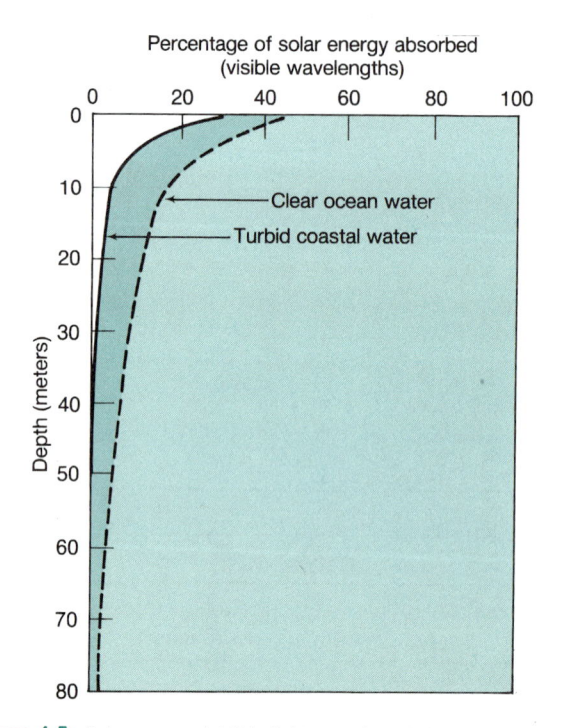

Figure 4.5 Solar energy (visible light wavelengths) penetration for clear and turbid ocean salt water as a function of depth.
From Alyn C. Duxbury and Alison B. Duxbury, *Introduction to the World's Oceans,* 3d ed. Copyright © 1991 Wm. C. Brown Publishers, Dubuque, Iowa. All Rights Reserved. Reprinted by permission.

atmosphere. Since 70% of the earth's surface is water, and the lighted regions of the oceans absorb sunlight in the photosynthesis of phytoplankton, a tremendous amount of carbon and oxygen is transferred from hydrosphere to biosphere to atmosphere. Maintenance of a 21% oxygen (O_2) level in the atmosphere is believed to be, in large part, a product of this exchange in the lighted zone of the oceans (figure 4.5).

The Aquatic Environments

The aquatic environments can be divided into two major categories, **fresh water** and **salt water.** The freshwater regions can be further subdivided into moving water systems and impoundments. *Moving water systems* can range from rushing mountain streams to sluggish silty rivers. An *impoundment* can be a small farm pond or one of the Great Lakes. Other freshwater environments can be as diverse as glacial ice or a subsurface aquifer. Saltwater environments include not only the water in ocean basins, but also evaporation basin impoundments such as the Great Salt Lake and saline aquifers.

Some of these environments have limited biota. Deep groundwater aquifers can sustain a population of bacteria far below the surface if conditions are right. Glacial ice

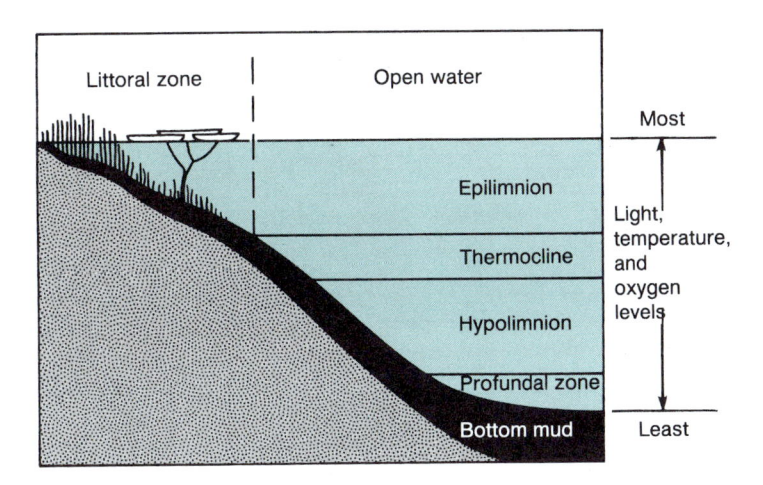

Figure 4.6 Deep lake stratification in the summer for a temperate climate (Cf, Df) environment.
From William P. Cunningham and Barbara Woodworth Saigo, *Environmental Science: A Global Concern.* Copyright © 1990 Wm. C. Brown Publishers, Dubuque, Iowa. All Rights Reserved. Reprinted by permission.

has been found to contain microorganisms in pockets of liquid salty brine at temperatures as cold as −10°C (14°F). Aquatic environments of greatest concern to conservationists include freshwater lakes and streams, saltwater ocean basins, and groundwater aquifers. These aquatic environments will be examined as habitats for the fisheries resource.

Freshwater Environments

The fresh water of the hydrosphere is essential for life on the earth's terrestrial environments. Fresh water occurs in **lakes, rivers, ponds,** in the **soil water zone,** and in the **groundwater zone.** All of these freshwater regions are temporary storage locations for the water that moves by way of the hydrologic cycle through the earth's spheres. The amount of storage time varies with the many factors that control rate of entry into each storage, and climatic factors such as rate of precipitation and rate of evaporation. Rates of movement and the medium through which water passes are important environmental factors because they determine, to a large degree, the amount of filtration and purification to which the water is subjected. Examination of each of earth's water regions reveals unique aquatic habitats.

Lakes

Freshwater lakes are standing bodies of water with a very low dissolved salt content. They may have more than one inlet, but usually one outlet. Lakes in temperate climates with no outlet usually have a dissolved salt content too high to contain fresh water. Deep lakes are thermally stratified. Pure water reaches its maximum density of one at 3.94° C (39.1° F); all fresh water at any other temperature in the earth's environment is less dense. Therefore, fresh water at any other temperature will float on 3.94° C water unless some other force, such as the wind, is acting to mix the waters. A stratified lake is divided into three layers: the *epilimnion,* the top layer warmed by the sun and mixed by the wind and other currents; the *hypolimnion,* the deepest layer, not heated or mixed; and the *thermocline* (also called the *metalimnion*), which separates the other two layers. (figure 4.6).

Seasonal temperature variations in temperate climates produce a very warm epilimnion in the summer. As fall progresses and temperatures decline, heat is lost from the surface waters to the atmosphere faster than it is absorbed. When the epilimnion reaches the same temperatures as the hypolimnion, the thermocline ceases to exist and mixing can take place from top to bottom. This period of total lake circulation is called the *overturn*. In the winter, a thermocline redevelops, with a cold epilimnion overlying a warmer hypolimnion. Winter stratification is less well defined than summer because ice forms on the surface and mixing by wind will cease. Spring melting and warming produces a second overturn. Lakes with two overturns per year are called *dimictic* (figure 4.7). Lakes with one overturn per year are called *monomictic.*

Thermal stratification of standing fresh water can be a basis for classification of lakes. Table 4.4 gives the defining properties for first-, second-, and third-class lakes, all of which can also be classified as oligotrophic or eutrophic. *Oligotrophic lakes* are clear, cold, high in oxygen, and low in nutrients. They are usually found at higher elevations and are fed by snow melt. They have a rocky bottom with limited amounts of rooted vegetation. *Plankton* (microscopic plant and animal life) are usually not abundant because of the low nutrient supply, but fishermen pursue large sport fish such as **trout, pike,** and **muskellunge** from these lakes. Most first-class lakes are oligotrophic.

Hydrosphere—Water 69

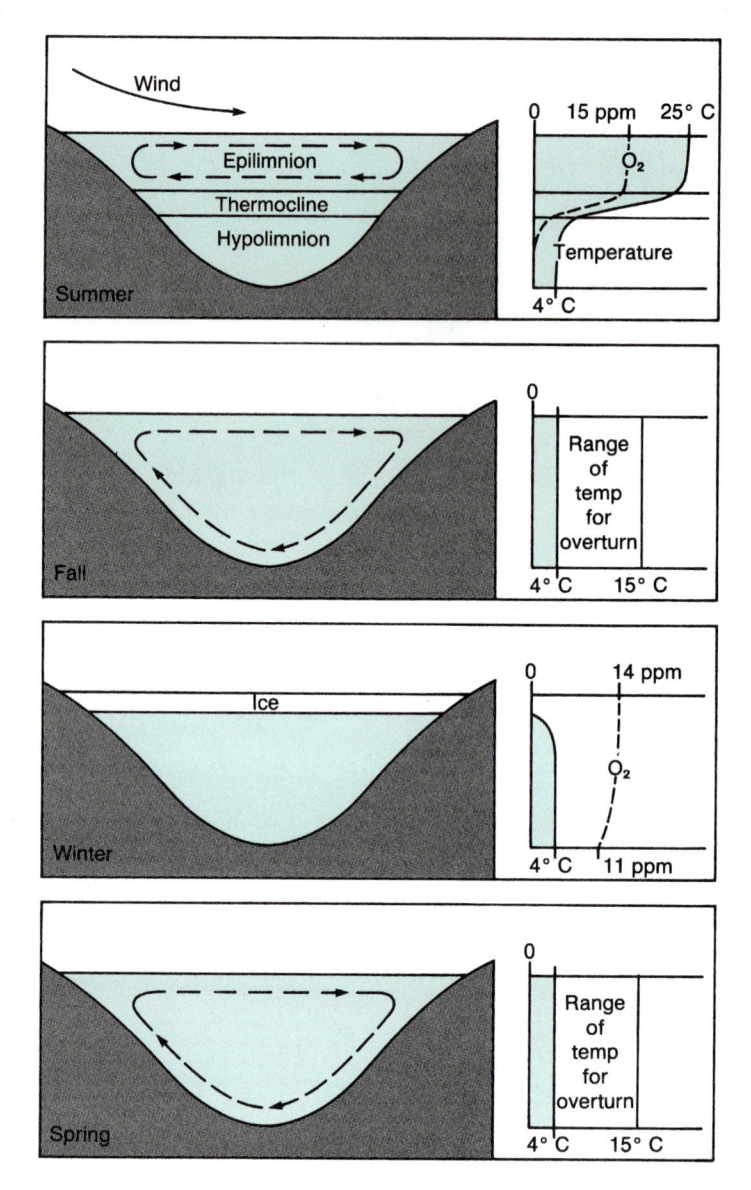

Figure 4.7 Lakes tend to have annual cycles based mainly on changes in water temperature and density. Many lakes experience a fall and spring overturn as cool, dense water (densest at 4° C) sinks. Nutrient upwelling, which enriches surface waters, results. Range of temperatures for fall and spring overturns are controlled by climate of the region.
From William P. Cunningham and Barbara Woodworth Saigo, *Environmental Science: A Global Concern*. Copyright © 1990 Wm. C. Brown Publishers, Dubuque, Iowa. All Rights Reserved. Reprinted by permission.

Table 4.4

Classification of Lakes

First class lakes	Very deep lakes where the hypolimnion remains at 3.94° C (39° F) all year. Overturns take place when the epilmnion reaches 3.94° C and these overturns are of short duration.
Second class lakes	Deep lakes where heat is absorbed by the hypolimnion and epilimnion in summer and the hypolimnion temperature in the summer is about 10° C (50° F).
Third class lakes	Lakes too shallow to stratify because of mixing from top to bottom by wind or other outside forces.

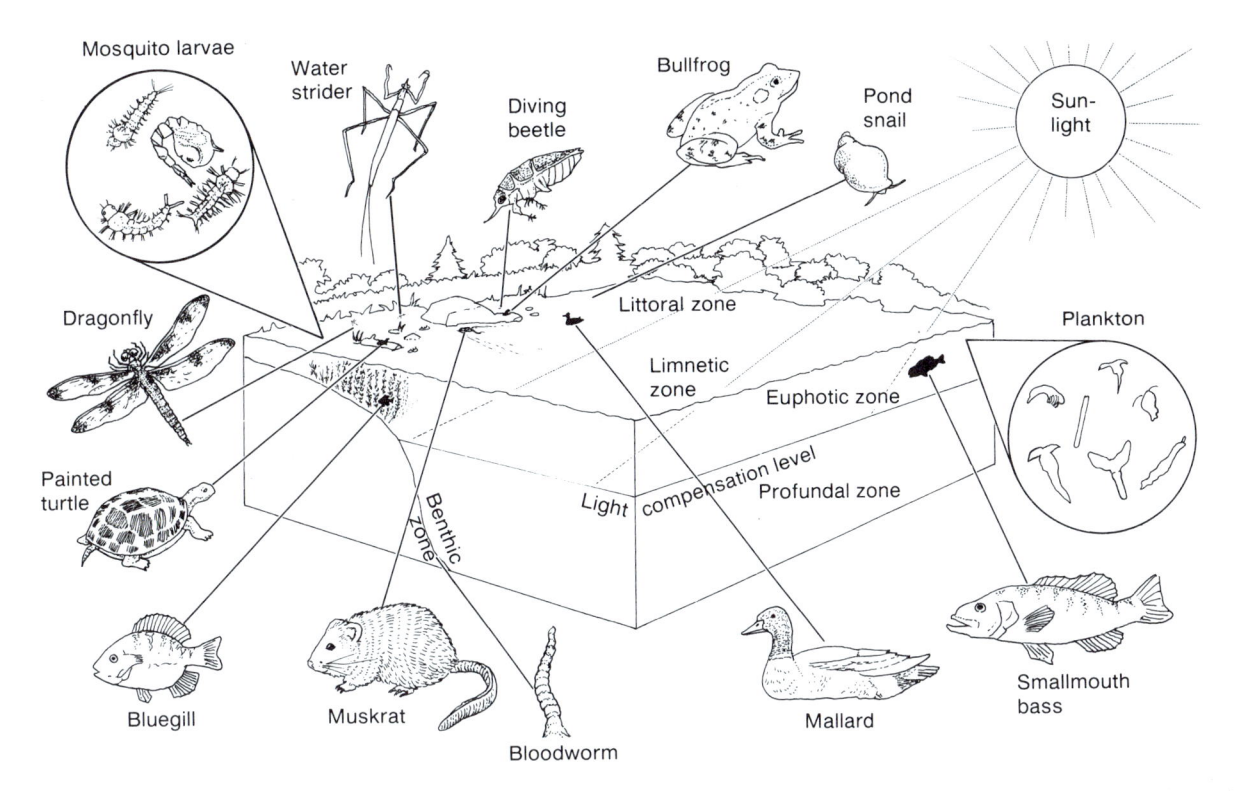

Figure 4.8 Life zones in a freshwater temperate environment. The light compensation level is variable and depends on sediment and organism concentrations in the water.
From Eldon D. Enger, *Environmental Science*, 3d ed. Copyright © 1989 Wm. C. Brown Publishers, Dubuque, Iowa. All Rights Reserved. Reprinted by permission.

Eutrophic lakes, on the other hand, are warmer, more turbid, lower in oxygen, and higher in nutrients. Living organisms are abundant. Plankton, invertebrates, amphibians, reptiles, and fish are abundant. Rooted vegetation occupies the gently sloping shoreline both above and below water level. The lake bottom sediment is fine-grained and vegetation roots easily. Most second class lakes are eutrophic.

All lakes are geologically short-lived. The processes of erosion and deposition will cause an oligotrophic lake to evolve into an eutrophic lake as sediment accumulates in the lake basin. Man also has contributed to the eutrophication of lakes by the additions of nutrients (especially fertilizers) to such an extent that the aquatic environment of the lake basin becomes suitable only for blue-green algae and/or anaerobic bacteria.

Lake Zones

Figure 4.8 illustrates the major environmental zones of a freshwater lake. The *limnetic zone* is the lighted zone of open water where there is sufficient sunlight for photosynthesis to take place. The shallow water zone where sunlight can penetrate to the bottom and rooted vegetation can grow is called the *littoral zone*. When the light intensity in the water reaches 1% of full sunlight and photosynthesis balances respiration, the *compensation depth* has been reached. The compensation level separates the limnetic zone from the *profundal zone*. The bottom of the lake in the unlighted region is called the *benthic zone*, occupied by large numbers of bacteria and fungi in the bottom sediment. These organisms are very active in decomposition of organic material that accumulates on the bottom of a lake.

The most productive zone of the lake environment is the littoral zone. The littoral zone provides food, cover, and breeding sites for a large variety of vertebrates and invertebrates. A small pond environment is entirely littoral. Rooted plants are absent in the limnetic zone, but the photosynthetic niche of the open water is characterized by an abundance of phytoplankton (mostly algae). The high oxygen supply of the limnetic zone in the summer comes from both the atmosphere and the photosynthesis-respiration process of the phytoplankton. The profundal zone contains little or no green plant life. Oxygen is a limiting factor for this deep water zone and many fish migrate into and out of this zone.

The Acid Rain Problem

Acid rain is nothing new. Robert Angus Smith coined the term "acid rain" in 1872 in a book entitled *Air and Rain: The Beginnings of a Chemical Climatology,* where he recognized the damaging effect of acid rain on plants and materials. All rainfall is naturally acidic because the atmosphere contains many naturally occurring acidic chemicals. Volcanic eruptions and decomposing organic matter are two common sources of atmospheric acidic chemicals. The principal factor in the formation of acid rainfall, however, is carbon dioxide in the atmosphere. It combines with atmospheric moisture to form a slightly acidic (pH 5.6) rainfall (table 4.5).

[Chemically $H_2O + CO_2 \rightarrow H_2CO_3$]

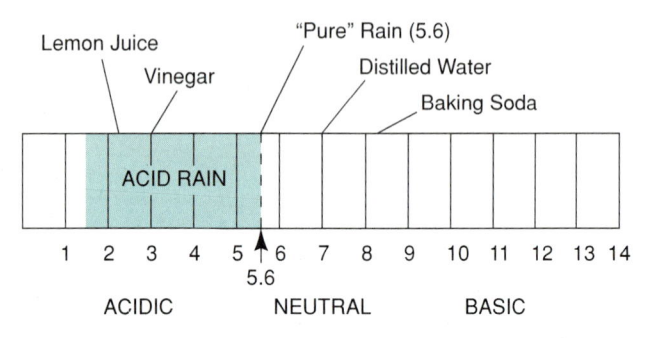

Acid rain is defined as rainfall with a pH less than 5.6. Table 4.5 explains the pH scale for acid rain in relation to some known chemical substances.

Acid rain has become a very serious problem for the northeastern United States and southeastern Canada. Figure 4.9 shows the geographic extent of the acid rain problem. In the northeastern United States, the average pH of rainfall is 4.6 and it is not unusual to have rainfall

Source: Environmental Protection Agency Journal, Vol. 12, No. 5, June/July 1986.

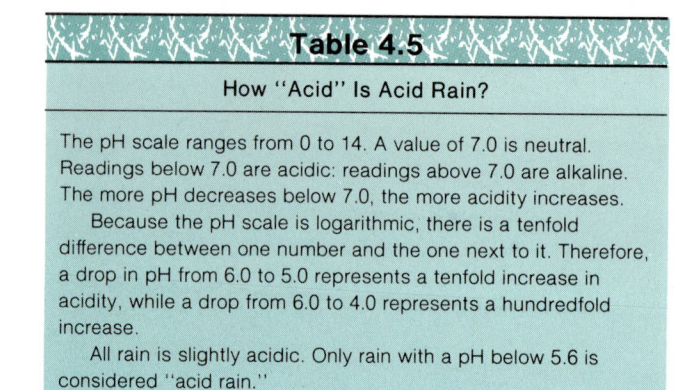

Table 4.5
How "Acid" Is Acid Rain?

The pH scale ranges from 0 to 14. A value of 7.0 is neutral. Readings below 7.0 are acidic: readings above 7.0 are alkaline. The more pH decreases below 7.0, the more acidity increases.

Because the pH scale is logarithmic, there is a tenfold difference between one number and the one next to it. Therefore, a drop in pH from 6.0 to 5.0 represents a tenfold increase in acidity, while a drop from 6.0 to 4.0 represents a hundredfold increase.

All rain is slightly acidic. Only rain with a pH below 5.6 is considered "acid rain."

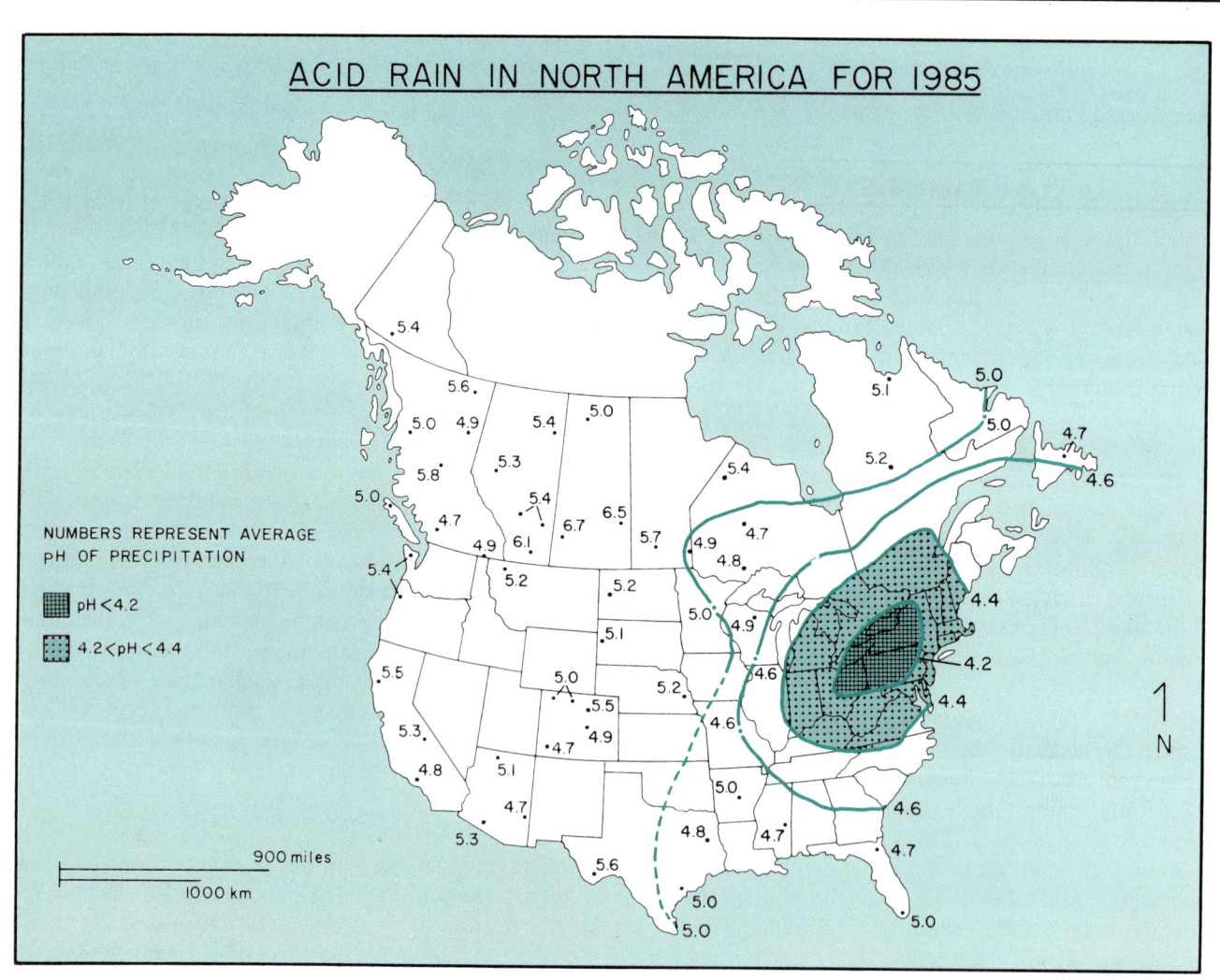

Figure 4.9 Acid precipitation in North America for 1985.
Source: Environmental Protection Agency.
(*Cartographer:* Douglas Hemsath)

with a pH of 4.0. Precipitation in the western states is less acidic than in the east, but incidents of fog with a pH less than 3.0 have been documented in southern California. There is little doubt that human-generated pollutants, in particular **sulfur dioxide** (SO_2) and **nitrogen oxides** (NO_x), have accelerated the acidification of rainfall.

The passage of the Clean Air Act in 1970 helped to slow down SO_2 and NO_x emissions in the United States. Table 4.6 gives the emissions of SO_2 and NO_x in millions of tons from 1940 to 1984. The reduction in emissions from 1970 to 1980 was a direct result of restrictions placed on industry by the Clean Air Act. These reductions occurred, even though the combustion of fossil fuels grew substantially over the same period. As a result of the 1990 amendments to the Clean Air Act, which requires further reductions in the gaseous emissions of electric generating and other industrial plants in the United States, air quality should improve throughout the 1990s.

Acid-forming gaseous emissions come mainly from ten states in the central and upper Midwest. Missouri, Illinois, Indiana, Tennessee, Kentucky, Michigan, Ohio, Pennsylvania, New York, and West Virginia produce 53% of the total sulfur dioxide and 30% of the total nitrogen oxides emissions. Table 4.7 lists the top ten states for SO_2 and NO_x emissions. Sulfur dioxide emissions are concentrated in the Ohio River Valley. Nitrogen oxide emissions are more evenly distributed, but once again there is a concentration of emissions in the Ohio River Valley. This valley and the states adjacent to this area lead the United States as a source region for both major components of acid rain.

The current pattern of acid rain deposition shows a strong correlation between the source region for SO_2 and NO_x emissions. Data collected on the pH of rainfall indicate that acid rain occurs downwind and to the northeast of the Ohio River Valley source region for SO_2 and NO_x emissions. Figure 4.10 illustrates how the Ohio Valley sends its acid rain to the northeast by winds from the southwest.

The environmental effects of acid rain can be classified into four categories: **aquatic, terrestrial, materials,** and **human health.** How acid rain affects an area depends on the total acidity deposited and on the sensitivity of the receiving region. If the receiving region has acid-

Table 4.6
SO_2 and NO_x Emissions of the U.S.
(In Millions of Tons)

	1940	1950	1969	1970	1980	1984
SO_2	19.8	22.4	22.0	31.1	25.6	23.6
NO_x	7.5	10.3	14.1	20.0	22.5	21.7

Source: Environmental Protection Agency.

Table 4.7
Top Ten SO_2 and NO_x Producing States in 1984
(In Millions of Tons)

	SO_2		NO_x
1. Ohio	2.58	Texas	3.25
2. Indiana	1.67	California	1.17
3. Pennsylvania	1.60	Ohio	1.14
4. Illinois	1.38	Illinois	0.99
5. Texas	1.24	Pennsylvania	0.92
6. Missouri	1.18	Indiana	0.83
7. West Virginia	1.02	Florida	0.70
8. Florida	0.99	Michigan	0.69
9. Georgia	0.93	Louisiana	0.68
10. Tennessee	0.92	New York	0.62

Source: Environmental Protection Agency.

Acid Rain Precursers

Nitrogen Oxides (NO_x) — 19.7 million metric tons NO_x
- Transportation: 44%
- Electrical utilities: 34%
- Industrial processes and fuel combustion: 18%
- Commercial/industrial/residential: 3%
- Other: 1%

Sulfer dioxide (SO_2) — 21.4 million metric tons SO_2
- Transportation: 4%
- Electrical utilities: 68%
- Industrial processes and fuel combustion: 25%
- Commercial/industrial/residential: 3%

Acid Rain Sources in the Ohio River Valley

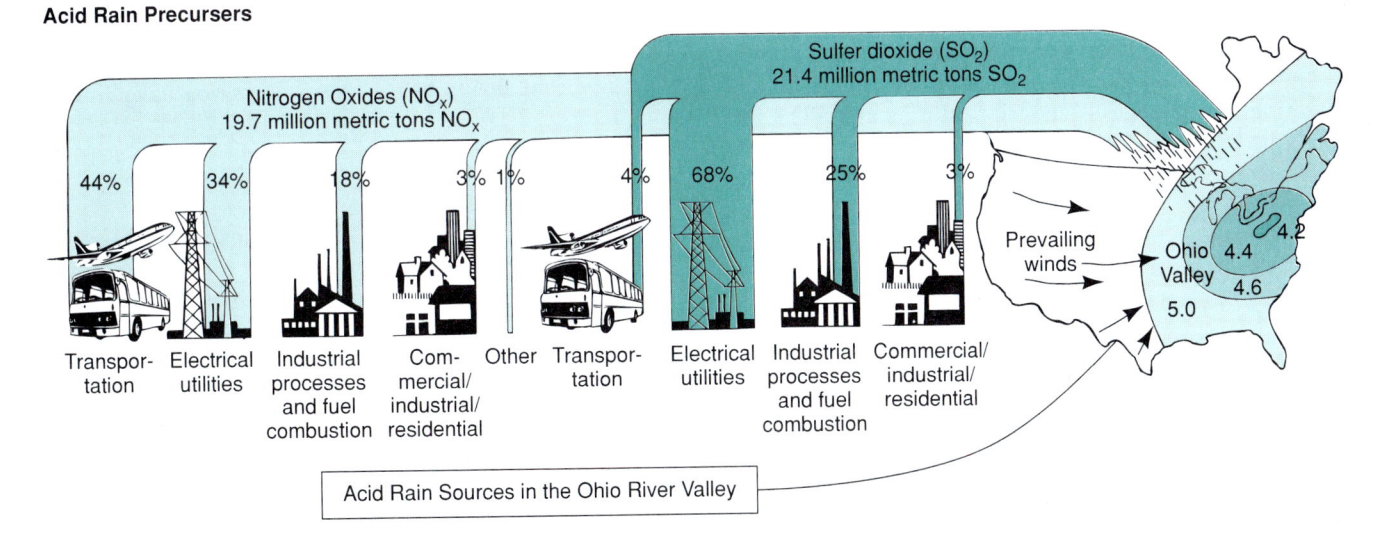

Ohio Valley pH values: 4.2, 4.4, 4.6, 5.0 — Prevailing winds

Figure 4.10 The industrial Ohio River Valley is the source area for much of the acid rain that falls on the northeastern United States and the southeastern Canadian region.
Source: Environmental Protection Agency, Vol. 12, No. 5, June/July 1986.

neutralizing compounds in the soil, (e.g., the glacial soils of the Midwest), then years of acid deposition can occur without substantial damage. However, the thin rocky soils of the northeastern United States and southeastern Canadian mountain region have little or no acid-buffering capacity, making them very susceptible to acid rainfall damage.

Obvious signs that acid rain was becoming a serious problem were **forest dieback** and **forest lake sterility** in the New England area. The **terrestrial effects** of acid rain on the forest environment include leaching of soil nutrients, inhibiting of photosynthesis, killing of essential microorganisms in the soil, and the mobilizing of toxic metal ions in the soil. One or all of these could produce a forest dieback, but direct evidence to prove that acid rain is the cause of dieback does not exist. Some scientists believe that acid rainfall is beneficial to some species of pine (pitch pine) and spruce (red spruce). Experiments have shown better growth for these species when treated with acidic water and/or exposure to acid rain mist.

The **aquatic effects** of acid rain are easier to substantiate than the terrestrial effects. Female fish, frogs, and salamanders, when exposed to acidic water, may either fail to produce eggs or produce eggs that do not develop. A major damaging aquatic effect is really a continuation of a terrestrial effect. Acid rain moving through the soil mobilizes toxic metals such as aluminum, manganese, and mercury. These toxic metals are transported through the hydrologic subsystem of the watershed and accumulate in the lakes. Lakes with a low buffering capacity have been found to be highly acidic and lifeless, while other lakes in sensitive areas have not suffered the same fate. Time and other environmental factors play a part in the death of a lake.

The **material effects** of acid rain can be documented by observing the loss of details and features on a stone statue exposed to acid rain for many years (figure 4.11). Loss of features and shape, along with general deterioration, occurs. Degradation is accelerated by acid rain. In a New York study, scientists developed a formula for calculating the damage to materials in that area. The formula is: 10mm (0.4 in) of fine grain marble will be worn away every century for every part per million of SO_2 in the air.

The **human health effects** of direct contact with acid rain are not known, but inhaling acidic moisture in acid fog can't be good for a person. Neither can drinking water from a fountain where lead has been leached from the pipe solder by acidic water. But to date no direct evidence to link acid rain with damage to human health has been proven. More research is needed to confirm the human health effect of acid rain.

Figure 4.11 Material effect of acid rain.
(Photo: © John D. Cunningham/Visuals Unlimited)

Streams

Moving water environments such as streams, rivers, and springs are characterized by motion. Rate of flow and discharge are important variables of the system. Regular and smooth water flow is called *laminar,* whereas irregular nonparallel flow is termed *turbulent.* Turbulent flow is more erosive and oxygen content is higher than for laminar or near laminar flow. These factors are of great importance to the stream community. The Missouri River will be used as an example to study a stream environment and its different habitats through various climatic and geomorphic conditions. Most of the large rivers and streams that flow south in North America have similar habitats.

The Missouri River

John G. Neihardt provides a description of the Missouri River through the seasons in his book *The River and I.* His description serves as a good introduction to the Missouri River.

> I have come to look upon the Missouri as something more than a stream of muddy water. It gave me my first big boy dreams. It was my ocean. I remember well the first time I looked upon my turbulent friend,

who has since become as a brother to me. It was from a bluff at Kansas City. I know I must have been a very little boy, for the terror I felt made me reach up to the saving forefinger of my father, lest this insane devil-thing before me should suddenly develop an unreasoning hunger for little boys. My father seemed as tall as Alexander—and quite as courageous. He seemed to fear it almost not at all. And I should have felt little surprise had he taken me in his arms and stepped easily over that mile or so of liquid madness. He talked calmly about it— quite calmly. He explained at what angle one should hold one's body in the current, and how one should conduct one's legs and arms in the whirlpools, providing one should swim across.

Swim across! Why, it took a giant even to talk that way! For the summer had smitten the distant mountains, and the June floods ran. Far across the yellow swirl that spread out into the wooded bottom-lands, we watched the demolition of a little town. The siege had reached the proper stage for a sally, and the attacking forces were howling over the walls. The sacking was in progress. Shacks, stores, out-houses suddenly developed a frantic desire to go to St. Louis. It was a weird retreat in very bad order. A cottage with a garret window that glared like the eye of a Cyclops, trembled, rocked with the athletic lift of the flood, made a panicky plunge into a convenient tree; groaned, dodged, and took off through the brush like a scared cottontail. I felt a boy's pity and sympathy for those houses that got up and took to their legs across the yellow waste. It did not seem fair. I have since experienced the same feeling for a jack-rabbit with the hounds a-yelp at its heels.

But—to *swim* this thing! To fight this cruel, in-vulnerable, resistless giant that went roaring down the world with a huge uprooted oak tree in its mouth for a toothpick! This yellow, sinuous beast with hell-broth slavering from its jaws! This dare-devil boy-god that sauntered along with a town in its pocket, and a steepled church under its arm for a moment's toy! Swim this?

For days I marvelled at the magnificence of being a fullgrown man, unafraid of big rivers.

But the first sight of the Missouri River was not enough for me. There was a dreadful fascination about it—the fascination of all huge and irresistible things. I had caught my first wee glimpse into the infinite; I was six years old.

Many a lazy Sunday stroll took us back to the river; and little by little the dread became less, and the wonder grew—and a little love crept in. In my boy heart I condoned its treachery and its giant sins. For, after all, it sinned through excess of strength, not through weakness. And that is the eternal way of virile things. We watched the steamboats loading for what seemed to me far distant ports. (How the world shrinks!) A double stream of "roosters" coming and going at a dog-trot rushed the freight aboard; and at the foot of the gang-plank the mate swore masterfully while the perspiration dripped from the point of his nose.

And then—the raucous whistles blew. They reminded me of the lions roaring at the circus. The gang-plank went up, the hawsers went in. The snub nose of the steamer swung out with a quiet majesty. Now she feels the urge of the flood, and yields herself to it, already dwindled to half her size. The pilot turns his wheel—he looks very big and quiet and masterful up there. The boat veers round; bells jangle. And now the engine wakens in earnest. She breathes with spurts of vapor!

Breathed? No, it was sighing; for about it all clung an inexplicable sadness for me—the sadness that clings about all strong and beautiful things that must leave their moorings and go very, very far away. (I have since heard it said that river boats are not beautiful!) My throat felt as though it had smoke in it. I felt that this queenly thing really wanted to stay; for far down the muddy swirl where she dwindled, dwindled, I heard her sobbing hoarsely.

Off on the perilous flood for "faerie lands forlorn"! It made the world seem almost empty and very lonesome.

And then the dog-days came, and I saw my river tawny, sinewy, gaunt—a half-starved lion. The long dry bars were like the protruding ribs of the beast when the prey is scarce, and the ropy main current was like the lean, terrible muscles of its back.

In the spring it had roared; now it only purred. But all the while I felt in it a dreadful economy of force, just as I have since felt it in the presence of a great lean jungle-cat at the zoo. Here was a thing that crouched and purred—a mewing but terrific thing. Give it an obstacle to overcome—fling it something to devour; and lo! the crushing impact of its leap!

And then again I saw it lying very quietly in the clutch of a bitter winter—an awful hush upon it, and the white cerement of the snow flung across its face. And yet, this did not seem like death; for still one felt in it the subtle influence of a tremendous personality. It slept, but sleeping it was still a giant. It seemed that at any moment the sleeper might turn over, toss the white cover aside and, yawning, saunter down the valley with its thunderous seven-league boots. And still, back and forth across this heavy sleeper went the pigmy wagons of the farmers taking corn to market!

But one day in March the far-flung arrows of the geese went over. Honk! honk! A vague, prophetic sense crept into the world out of nowhere—part sound, part scent, and yet too vague for either. Sap seeped from the maples. Weird mist-things went moaning through the night. And then, for the first time, I saw my big brother win a fight!

For days, strange premonitory noises had run across the shivering surface of the ice. Through the foggy nights, a muffled intermittent booming went on under the wild scurrying stars. Now and then a staccato crackling ran up the icy reaches of the river, like the sequent bickering of Krags down a firing line. Long seams opened in the disturbed surface, and from them came a harsh sibilance as of a line of cavalry unsheathing sabres.

But all the while, no show of violence—only the awful quietness with deluge potential in it. The lion was crouching for the leap.

Then one day under the warm sun a booming as of distant big guns began. Faster and louder came the dull shaking thunders, and passed swiftly up and down, drawling into the distance. Fissures yawned, and the sound of the grumbling black water beneath came up. Here and there the surface lifted—bent—broke with shriekings, groanings, thunderings. And then—The giant turned over, yawned and got to his feet, flinging his arms about him! Barriers formed before him. Confidently he set his massive shoulders against them—smashed them into little blocks, and went on singing, shouting, toward the sea. It was a glorious victory. It made me very proud of my big brother. And yet all the while I dreaded him—just as I dread the caged tiger that I long to caress because he is so strong and beautiful.

Since then I have changed somewhat, though I am hardly as tall, and certainly not so courageous as Alexander. But I have felt the sinews of the old yellow giant tighten about my naked body. I have been bent upon his hip. I have presumed to throw against his Titan strength the craft of man. I have often swum in what seemed liquid madness to my boyhood. And we have become acquainted through battle. No friends like fair foes reconciled!

And I have been panting on his bars, while all about me went the lisping laughter of my brother. For he has the strength of a god, the headlong temper of a comet; but along with these he has the glad, mad, irresponsible spirit of a boy. Thus ever are the epic things.

The Missouri is unique among rivers. I think God wished to teach the beauty of a virile soul fighting its way toward peace—and His precept was the Missouri. To me, the Amazon is a basking alligator; the Tiber is a dream of dead glory; the Rhine is a fantastic fairy-tale; the Nile a mummy, periodically resurrected; the Mississippi, a convenient geographical boundary line; the Hudson, an epicurean philosopher.

But the Missouri—my brother—is the eternal Fighting Man!*

The days of fury on the Missouri River, described by John Neihardt, are separated by months of normalcy. It is the normal river, with its aquatic habitat, that we will examine, keeping in mind that the fury is just a storm away.

The Missouri River begins in the Rocky Mountains as a small, cold, fast-moving stream. Its flow is turbulent and it actively erodes its channel. The streambed is composed of large boulders smoothed and rounded by corrosion and corrasion. *Corrasion* is the physical weathering of these boulders by abrasion, whereas *corrosion* is the chemical weathering that smooths the rocks of the streambed. The turbulent flow oxygenates the water, making it an ideal environment for **trout.** Before the river leaves the mountains, it is joined by many snow-melt tributaries that tremendously increase its flow discharge (figure 4.12).

Coming out of the Rockies the gradient is reduced, giving the stream a **concave-up longitudinal profile** (figure 4.13). As the topography flattens in the high plains, the energy of the stream that had been used for downcutting is shifted to the task of *lateral erosion* (stream-bank cutting) and the stream begins to meander. Along with the change in river dynamics comes a change in aquatic habitats. The stream is actively eroding the banks on the outside of the meander loops and depositing sediment on the inside of the loops as **gravel bars** (*lateral accreation deposits*). The stream bottom has changed from boulders to gravel. The channel alternates between riffles and pools. The water isn't as clear, its temperature is higher, and the oxygen content is reduced. This environment is now the preferred habitat for the **bass.** Along with the change in the river, the climate has changed downstream. The river started in an ET or EF climate zone, went through a Dfb and Dfa region, passed through a BSk dry zone, and is headed for a Cfa climate in Missouri and on to the Gulf of Mexico by way of the Mississippi River (figure 3.9). In the Kansas-Missouri area, the Missouri River has flattened its gradient to such an extent that it flows almost entirely in its own sediment of silt and sand. The flow is slow, the sediment load is high, and the water is no longer clear and cold. The oxygen level is low, and the environment is now the preferred habitat for **catfish** and **carp.**

---

*From John G. Neihardt, *The River and I.* Copyright © Macmillan Publishing Company, New York, N.Y.

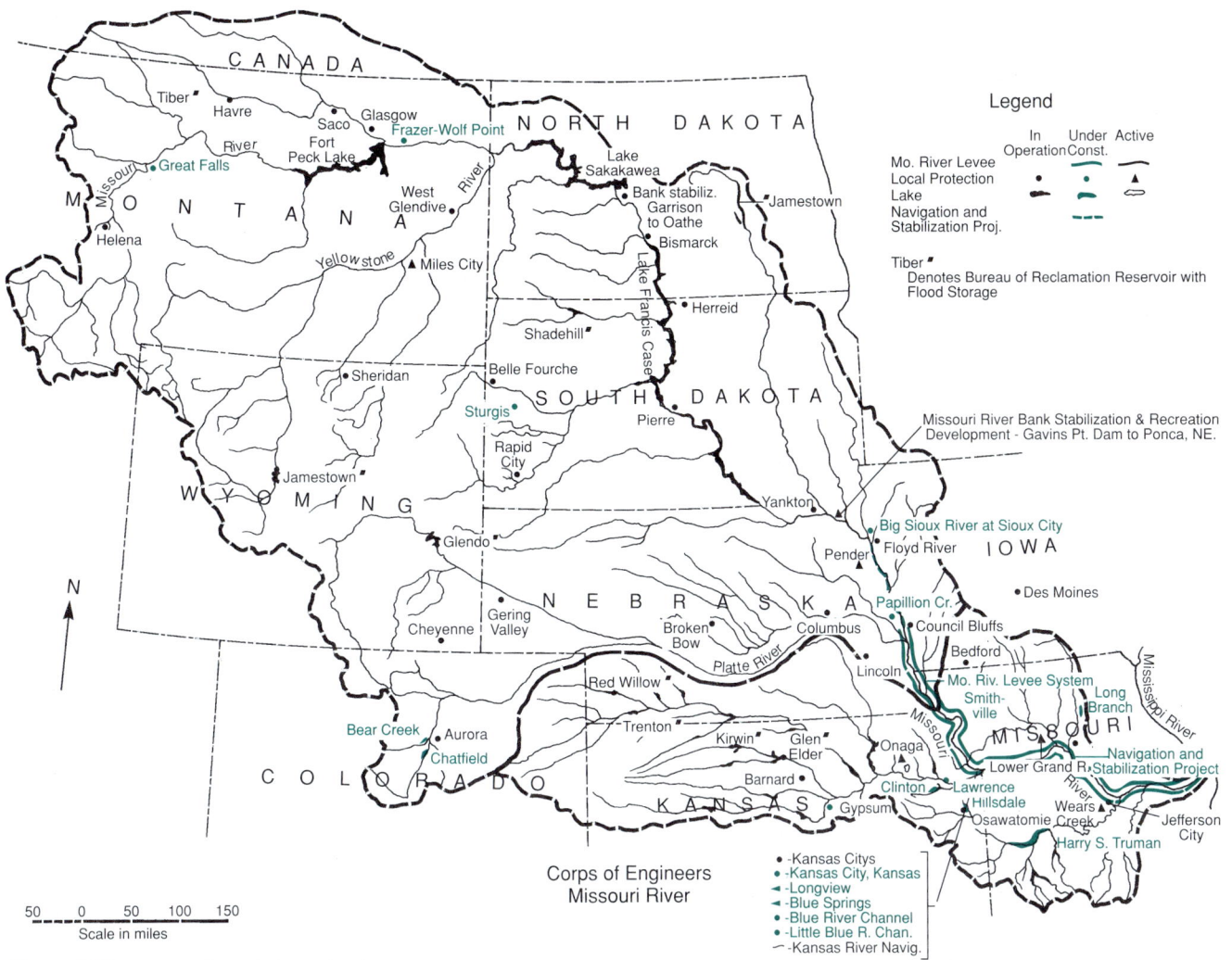

Figure 4.12 Missouri River drainage basin.
Source: U.S. Army Corps of Engineers, Kansas City District, *Missouri River Corridor Inventory*, February 1981.

The Missouri River and most of the other meandering rivers in North America have an underground ecosystem. The gravel bars on the surface usually cover buried gravel bars and gravels of former channel beds. These *alluvial deposits* form a highly permeable, slowly flowing, water-saturated region called the *hyporheic zone* (figure 4.14). This zone is as wide as the floodplain of the river and can be as much as 9 m (30 ft) below the bottom of the river. The unlighted subterranean hyporheic zone is home for many species of worms, bacteria, algae, and insects and is a major breeding ground for the larval stage of insects that feed the surface stream's fish.

The Missouri River, like most streams, changes with time and distance from its source. Six major dams interrupt the normal flow and geomorphic processes of the Missouri River. The geomorphic changes, however, continue to occur on the geologic clock. The environmental changes as described by Neihardt are on a seasonal and biological clock. River flooding and ice jams are both common occurrences, in spite of the Corps of Engineers' attempts to control them. It is one river with many different aquatic environments, many different climate zones, and many different political boundaries to cross—one river with many different variables to consider for effective environmental management. Aquatic management must take into consideration all of the different habitats of a stream.

Saltwater Environments

Seventy percent of the earth's surface is covered with water and most of it is salty. The ocean basins and gulfs that adjoin the North American continent include the Atlantic, Pacific, and Arctic Oceans, the Gulf of Mexico, and the Gulf of California. The moving freshwater environments previously discussed empty into the saltwater basins. The transition zone between most rivers and the sea are called *estuaries*. They are partially enclosed coastal bodies of water freely connected to the open sea, and salty seawater is diluted by the fresh water from the rivers. The connection to the sea in an estuary is free enough to allow

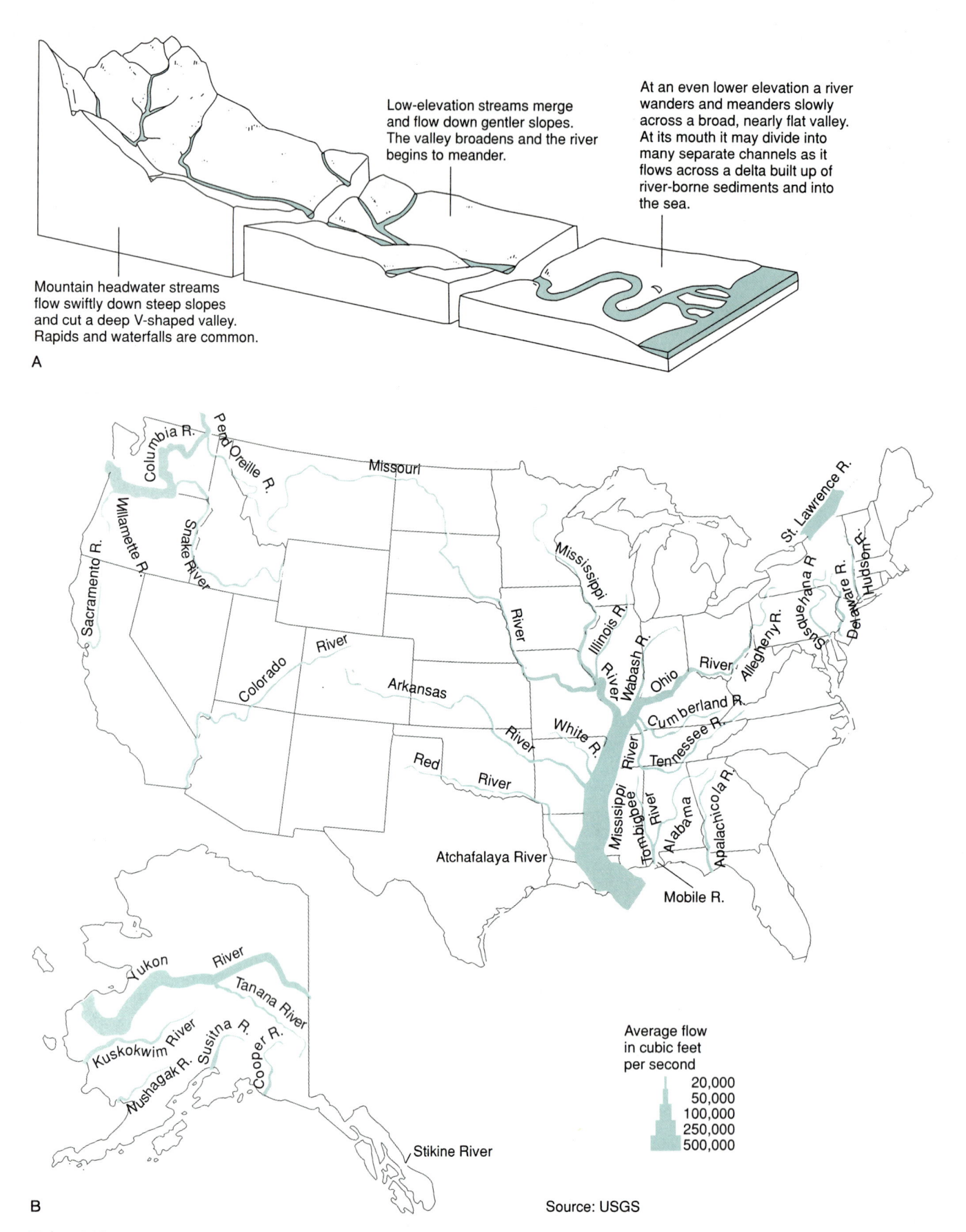

Figure 4.13 (a) Concave-up longitudinal profile of a natural river. (b) Major drainage discharges for the United States.

(a) From *Resource Conservation and Management* by G. Tyler Miller, Jr. © 1990 by Wadsworth, Inc. Reprinted by permission of the publisher. (b) *Source:* U.S. Geological Survey.

78 Physical and Biological Variables of the Natural Environment

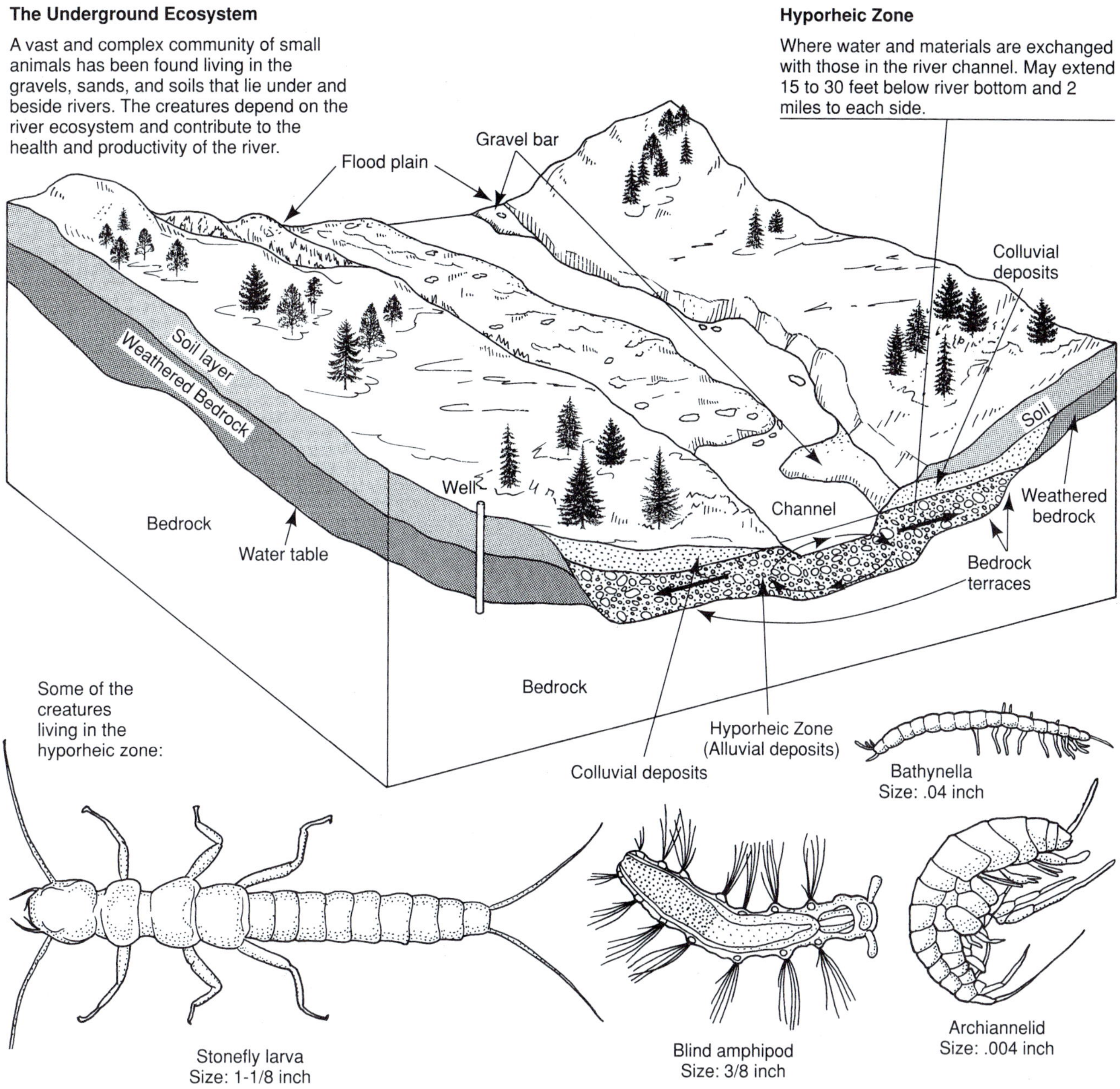

The Underground Ecosystem

A vast and complex community of small animals has been found living in the gravels, sands, and soils that lie under and beside rivers. The creatures depend on the river ecosystem and contribute to the health and productivity of the river.

Hyporheic Zone

Where water and materials are exchanged with those in the river channel. May extend 15 to 30 feet below river bottom and 2 miles to each side.

Some of the creatures living in the hyporheic zone:

Stonefly larva
Size: 1-1/8 inch

Blind amphipod
Size: 3/8 inch

Bathynella
Size: .04 inch

Archiannelid
Size: .004 inch

Figure 4.14 The hyporheic zone of a mature river valley. The hyporheic zone harbors an underground ecosystem. The surface stream cycles water and nutrients into the complex hyporheic community. Larva from many terrestrial insects such as the stonefly and the mayfly need this ecosystem for survival. The hyporheic can be many miles wide in a mature river valley and as deep as the top of the bedrock surface below the valley floor.

Copyright © 1989 The Washington Post. Reprinted with permission.

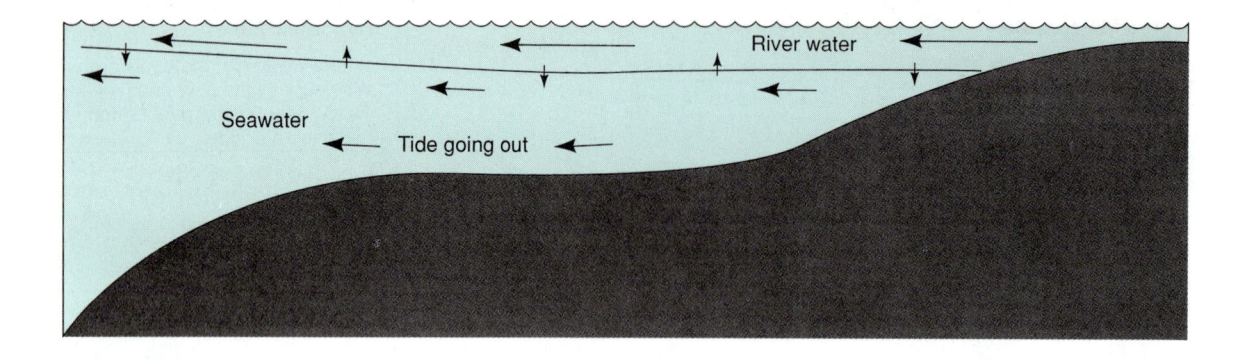

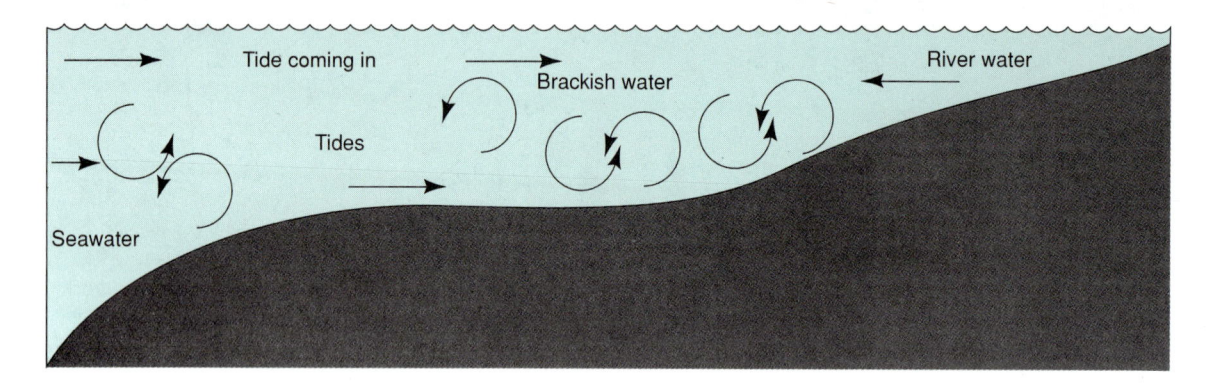

Figure 4.15 (a) Less dense river water will flow on the surface above the salty seawater when tidal influence is not a factor, or when the tide is going out. (b) When the tide is coming in, mixing of salt water and fresh water, along with agitation of the bottom sediments, creates a brackish water environment.
Reprinted with permission of Macmillan Publishing Company from *Natural Ecosystems* by W. B. Clapham. Copyright © 1983 by Macmillan Publishing Company.

for a tidal influence. The tidal currents act as a plunger to flush the estuary and mix the salt and fresh water (figure 4.15). The estuarian environment is highly variable. Water level, salinity, flow, and turbidity change with the tides. Biomass productivity in the estuarian zone is exceeded only by that found in coral reef communities. Productivity is high because the habitat provides the essential materials for life. **Dissolved oxygen** is high because water is shallow and turbulent. **Nutrients** from the river and the sea are concentrated in this zone and kept there by back-and-forth tidal movements. Thus the estuary acts as a trap for nutrients and high-energy organic materials that wash in from upstream. The best known estuarian organisms are detritus-feeding **oysters, clams, crabs,** and **lobsters.** Figure 4.16 is an insider's look at life in an estuary.

The Ocean Basins

The three ocean basins and two gulfs that surround the continent all have similar aquatic environmental zones. These zones are similar to the life zones of a lake but are much deeper and more complex. Figure 4.17 is a general diagrammatic cross section of an ocean basin adjacent to a continent. Each of the topographic regions identified has a life zone associated with it. Typical organisms associated with each zone are also illustrated. The *littoral zone* is the zone on the continental shelf between high and low tide levels. Rooted vegetation in this zone provides food and cover for fish and other saltwater organisms. The *sublittoral zone* extends from low tide level to the edge of the continental shelf. The open water from the shore to the edge of the continental shelf is called the *neritic zone* and the rest of the ocean is the *pelagic zone*. The neritic zone is the region where most of the commercial fishing takes place. The water above the light compensation level is called the *photic zone* and below the compensation level is called the *aphotic zone*. The photic zone can extend up to 150 m (492 ft) below the surface in the clearest parts of the open sea. The deep-water aphotic zones of the ocean basins are the *bathyal zone* above the continental slopes, the *abyssal zone* above the abyssal plains, and the *hadal zone* in the deep-ocean trenches. The bathyal and abyssal zone organisms are fed by food from the photic zone above. The hadal zone is the habitat for the sunless ecosystem of bacteria and tube worms discussed in chapter 2.

Marine life is exceedingly diverse. One of the most important organisms of the sea environments is **pelagic plankton.** Phytoplankton, mostly **diatoms** and **dinoflagellates,** produce most of the organic carbon in the sea and most of the free oxygen in the atmosphere in their photosynthetic-respiration processes.

Figure 4.16 Life in an estuary.
Source: *Environmental Protection Agency Journal*, Vol. 13, No. 6, July/August 1987.

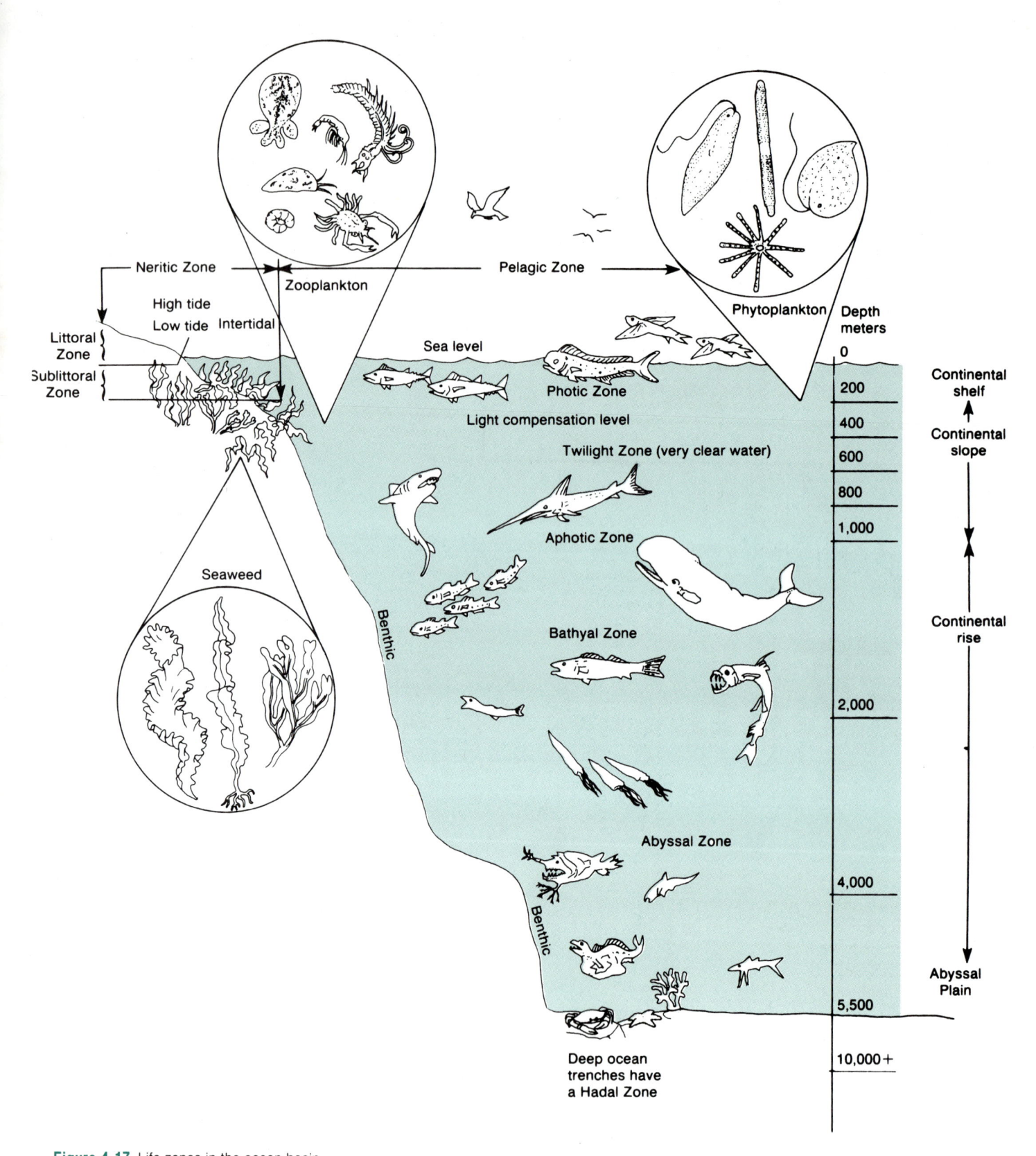

Figure 4.17 Life zones in the ocean basin.
From Eldon D. Enger, *Environmental Science*, 3d ed. Copyright © 1989 Wm. C. Brown Publishers, Dubuque, Iowa. All Rights Reserved. Reprinted by permission.

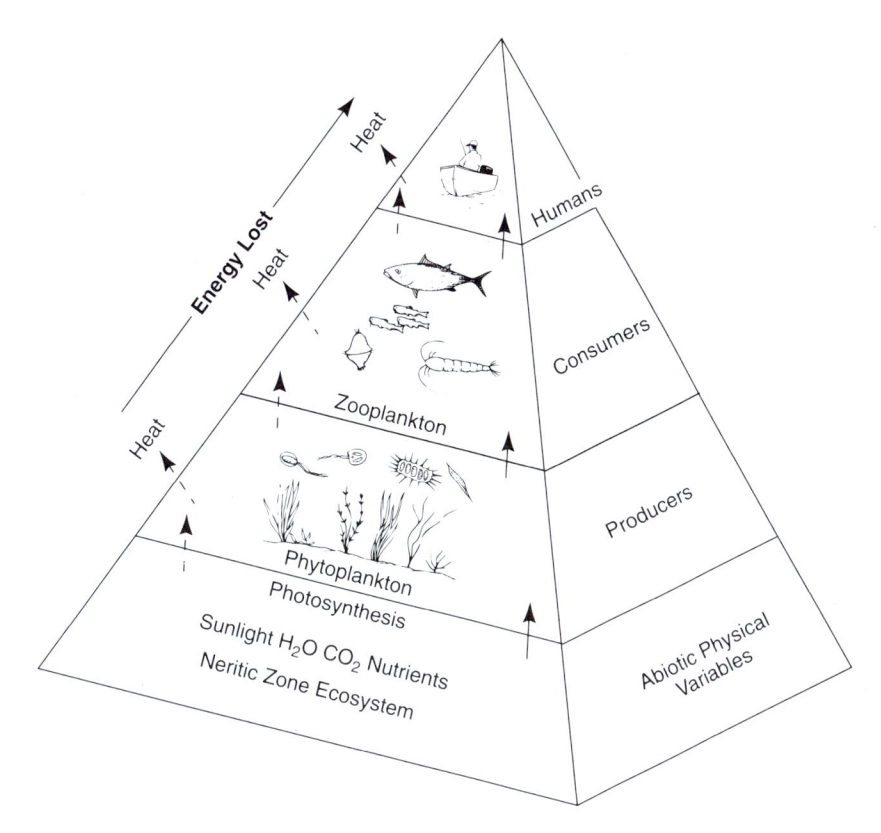

Figure 4.18 The food chain of the neritic zone. The seafood supply of the American people depends on maintenance of a healthy neritic ecosystem.

The marine environment is famous for its large fish. More than 90% of the fish and other seafood harvested by American fishermen comes from the neritic zone (figure 4.18). Approximately 65% of the harvested fish spend some time in the fish nurseries of the estuaries. A prime consideration in estuaries management is protection of these nurseries.

Ocean Dumping

The scientific community knows more about outer space than the oceans because the NASA space program has answered many questions about our solar systems. If we had a NASA-type program to study the deep oceans, we could manage our ocean environment more effectively. Without hard scientific data about deep-ocean ecosystems, it is difficult to speculate on the damage caused by ocean dumping. A case in point is the dumping of sewage sludge into the ocean by New York and New Jersey.

There is an active debate on the detrimental effect to marine environments by sludge disposal. *Sewage sludge* is human waste and other sewage treated and produced in the form of a semi-solid residue from sanitary waste treatment facilities. In 1977, Congress voted to end all ocean dumping by 1981 by amending the **Marine Protection, Research, and Sanctuaries Act** (Ocean Dumping Act). The amendments to the Ocean Dumping Act were successfully challenged in court by New York City in 1981. The court ruled that sewage sludge could continue to be dumped into the sea beyond 1981 unless the EPA could prove that sludge would unreasonably degrade the marine environment. As a result, nine sewage districts in New York and New Jersey are continuing to discharge sewage sludge into the ocean 106 miles east of Cape May, New Jersey (figure 4.19).

Many environmentalists and some members of Congress have demanded an end to all ocean dumping, which includes not only sewage sludge, but tons of garbage as well. Edward I. Koch, former New York City mayor, and others have argued that ocean disposal of sludge is both safe and environmentally sound and the best method available for New York City. New Jersey is to end its ocean dumping in the early 1990s and is formulating a land-based sludge management plan. However, landfill dumping is not without its problems and many argue that it is worse than the ocean-dumping alternative. A successful alternative for sludge is to treat it with bacterial digestion to

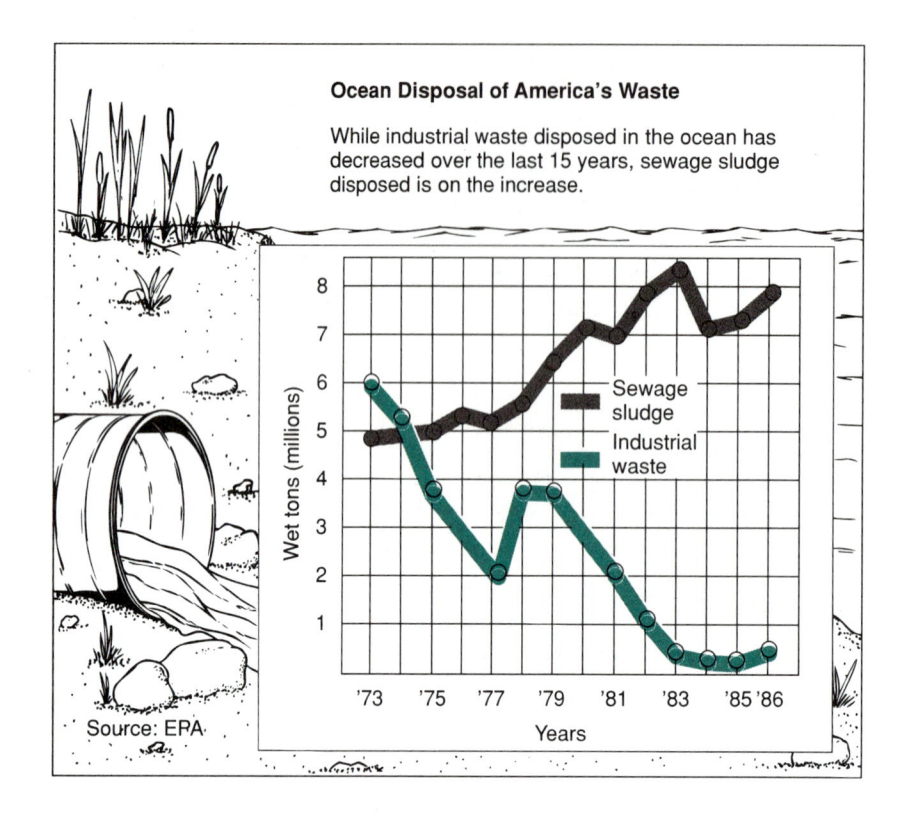

Figure 4.19 (a) Ocean disposal of sewage sludge leaves a trail of pollution for the ocean ecosystem to absorb. How long can our oceans tolerate this abuse? (b) Ocean disposal of America's waste.
(a) Reprinted with permission of U.S. Water News, Inc. (b) Photo: Greenpeace.

Physical and Biological Variables of the Natural Environment

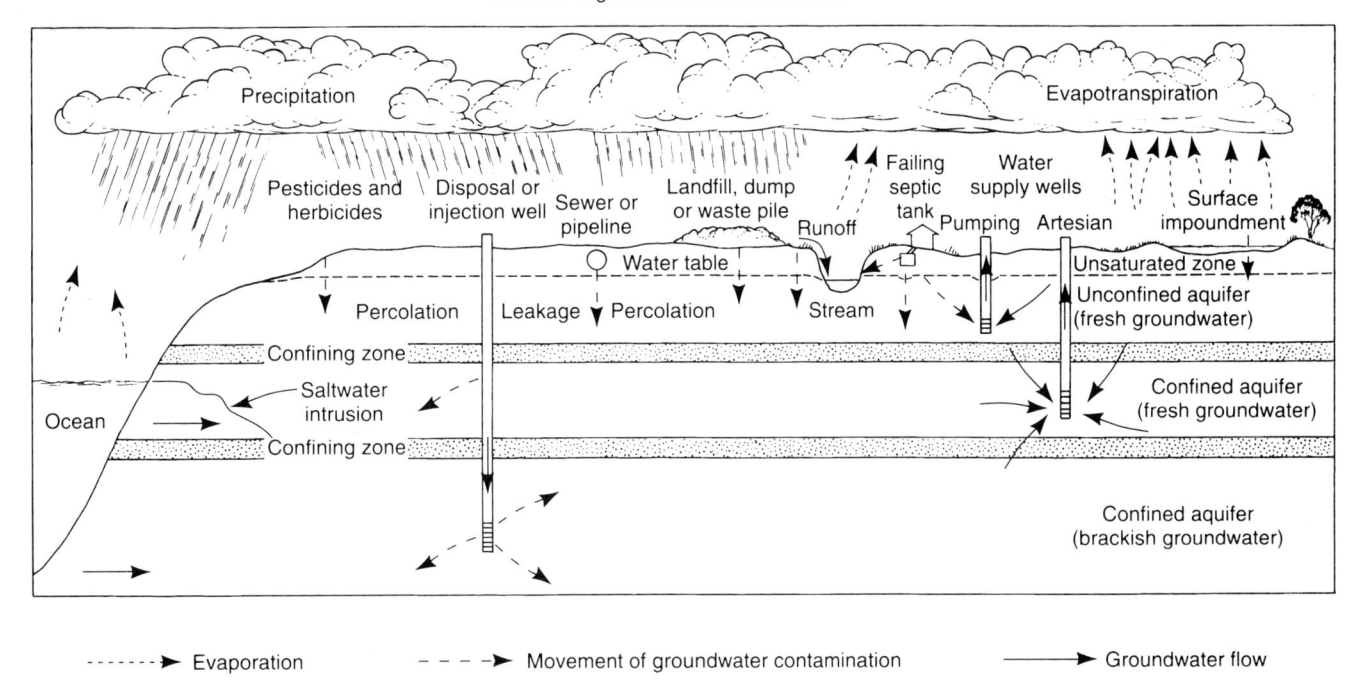

Figure 4.20 The groundwater reservoir has many potential sources of pollution.
Source: Environmental Protection Agency, *Environmental Trends.*

remove the odor and health hazard potential and then use it as a liquid fertilizer. Chicago, Illinois is successfully applying this technique. If the government spent as much money on understanding the deep-ocean environment as it spends on its space program, some of the questions concerning ocean dumping would have answers.

Groundwater

Groundwater is underground water, below the water table, that fills the pore spaces of saturated rock (figure 4.20). The North American groundwater resource includes this liquid and the rocks that enclose the liquid. During the past 100 years the American population has increased more than 200% and the per capita consumption of water has increased from 500 to 800%. Consumption of fresh water is about 7,580 liters (2,000 gal) of water per person per day. Americans withdraw approximately 279 billion liters (bl) (100 billion gallons (bg)) of water per day from the groundwater supplies. Approximately 50% of all Americans obtain all or part of their drinking water from groundwater sources. Figure 4.21a is a map of the United States showing the location of groundwater regions. Mining (removing water that is not returned by the hydrologic cycle) of groundwater is occurring at an alarming rate. Areas of water-table decline and groundwater mining are illustrated in figure 4.21b.

Much of the North American groundwater supply is contained in major aquifers. An *aquifer* is a body of permeable saturated rock material capable of conducting groundwater and yielding economically significant quantities of fresh water to **wells** and/or **springs**. The **Ogallala aquifer** is the largest single American aquifer in terms of geographic area (figure 4.22). As indicated in Table 4.1, only 0.6% of the hydrosphere is in the groundwater supply, but it is becoming an increasingly important part of our water supply. According to the U.S. Water Resources Council, Americans are withdrawing 80 bl (21 bg) per day from the groundwater storage that is not being returned by the normal workings of the hydrologic cycle (figure 4.23). Most of this deficit is being created by agriculture. The water from the Ogallala aquifer is used for crop irrigation in the Great Plains. The water used to irrigate crops exported to foreign countries is lost forever to the hydrologic system of the North American continent. A very high percentage of all irrigation water is lost through evaporation and evapotranspiration.

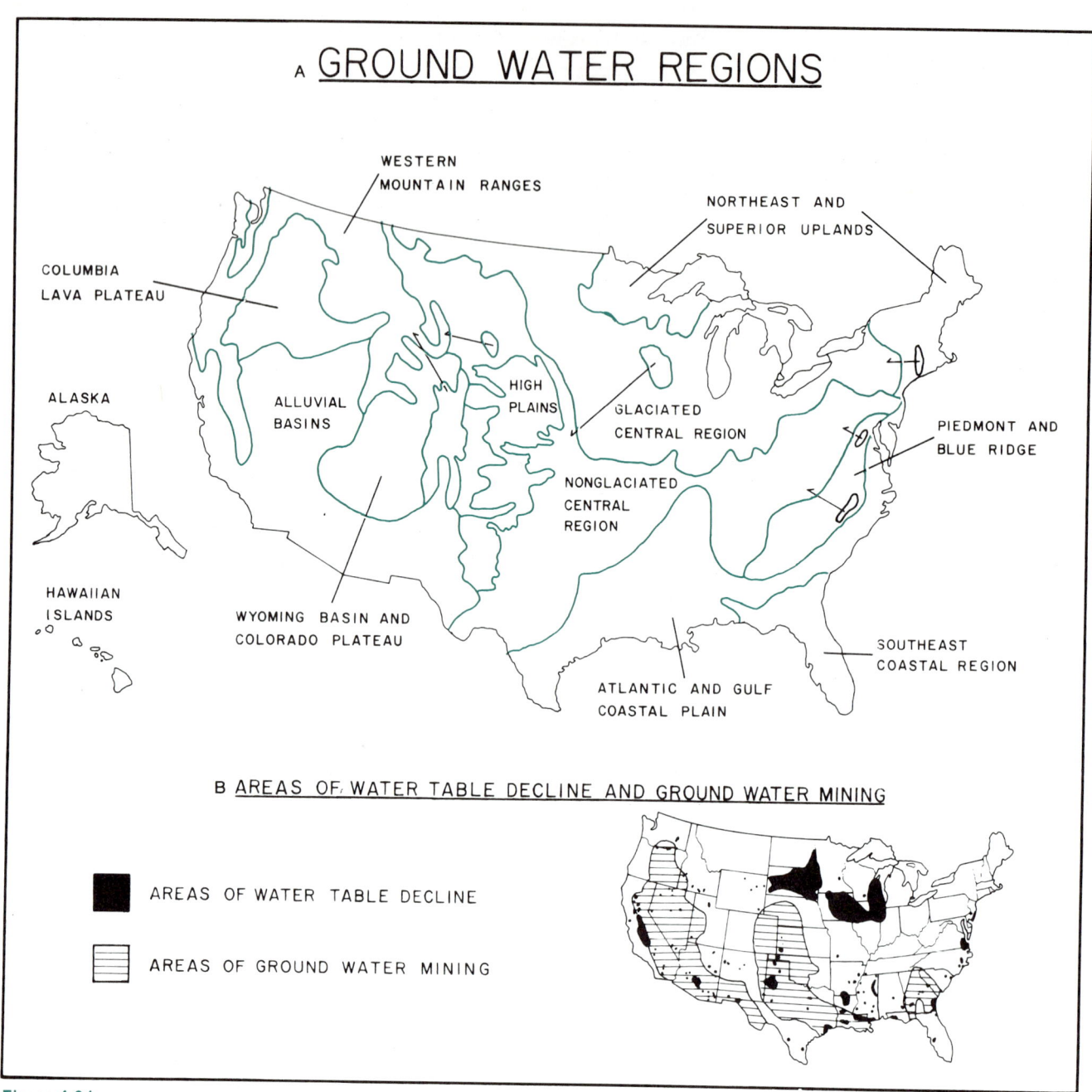

Figure 4.21 (a) Groundwater regions in the United States. The High Plains groundwater region contains the Ogallala aquifer. (b) Areas of water-table decline and groundwater mining.
Source: Environmental Protection Agency, *Environmental Trends*.
(Cartographer: Douglas Hemsath)

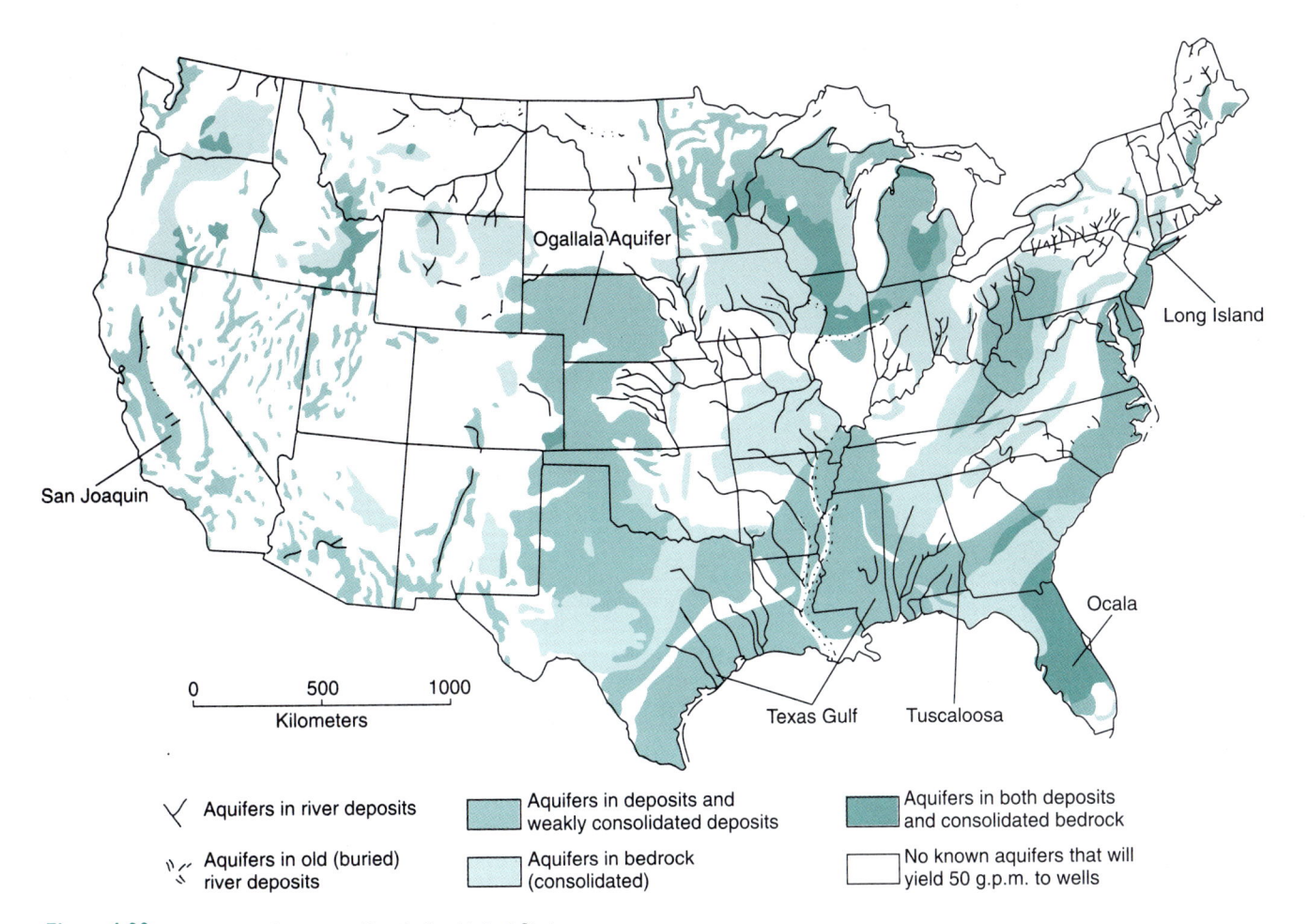

Figure 4.22 Major groundwater aquifers in the United States.
From Marsh, *Earthscape: A Physical Geography.* Copyright © 1987 John Wiley & Sons, Inc., New York, NY. Reprinted by permission of John Wiley & Sons, Inc.

Hydrosphere—Water

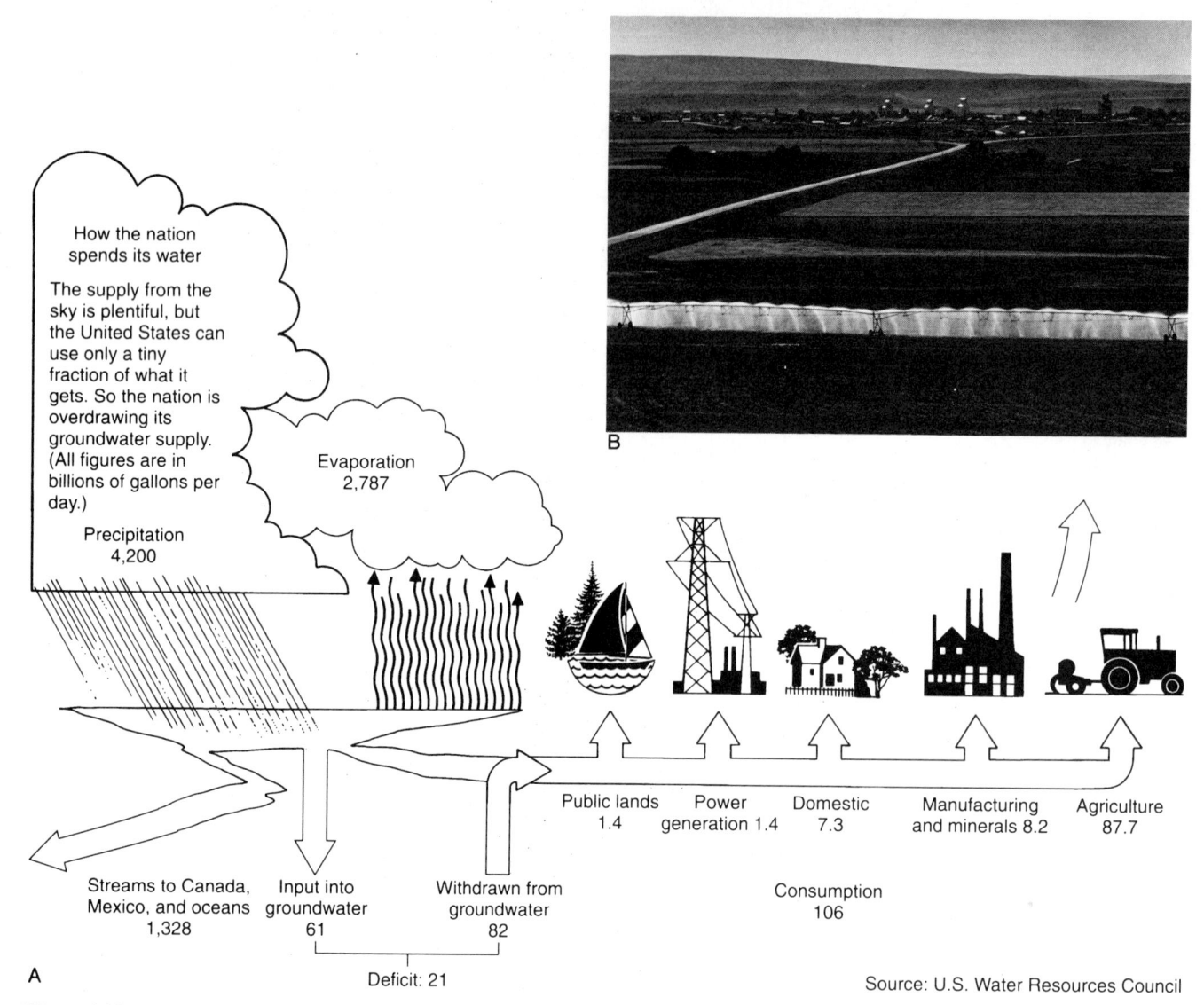

Figure 4.23 The mining of the nation's groundwater resources is due in large part to agricultural irrigation.
Source: U.S. Water Resources Council
(Photo: USDA—SCS)

How the nation spends its water

The supply from the sky is plentiful, but the United States can use only a tiny fraction of what it gets. So the nation is overdrawing its groundwater supply. (All figures are in billions of gallons per day.)

Precipitation 4,200
Evaporation 2,787
Streams to Canada, Mexico, and oceans 1,328
Input into groundwater 61
Withdrawn from groundwater 82
Deficit: 21

Public lands 1.4
Power generation 1.4
Domestic 7.3
Manufacturing and minerals 8.2
Agriculture 87.7
Consumption 106

Source: U.S. Water Resources Council

Summary

Water has been described as our most precious resource. It certainly is our most important ingredient in sustaining life on the earth's surface. In examining the lunar surface we have found that the missing ingredient for life is water. Bacteria that stowed away on the unmanned Surveyor 3 spacecraft in 1967 spent two years on the lunar surface. When Apollo astronauts brought pieces of the spacecraft back to earth, it took only four days to revive the bacteria. The missing ingredient for the continuation of their life on the moon was moisture in the atmosphere.

All life forms in the biosphere of the earth require water. We cannot build a biotic pyramid without water as one of the abiotic variables on the bottom of the pyramid. We have found that we can build a biotic community without sunlight (chapter 2). We can produce an anaerobic community without air (oxygen). We can have aquatic vegetation that doesn't need soil. But we must have water.

Key Words and Phrases

Abyssal zone
Acid rain
Alaskan current
Alluvial deposits
Aphotic zone
Aquicludes
Aquifer
Bathyal zone
Benthic zone
California current
Colloids
Corrasion
Corrosion
Dimictic
Epilimnion
Estuaries
Eutrophic lakes

Evaporation
Evapotranspiration
Freshwater lakes
Groundwater
Groundwater zone
Hadal zone
Hydrologic cycle
Hypolimnion
Hyporheic zone
Impoundment
Labrador current
Laminar flow
Lateral accreation deposits
Lateral erosion
Limnetic zone
Littoral zone
Metalimnion

Monomictic
Moving water systems
Neritic zone
Ocean surface currents
Oligotrophic lakes
Overturn
Pelagic zone
Photic zone
Plankton
Profundal
Sewage sludge
Soil water zone
Sublittoral zone
Thermocline
Turbulent flow
Water

Questions and Discussion Topics

1. In what ways do the changing states of water act as thermal regulators for the natural environment?
2. Explain the hydrologic cycle for a 10 cm (4 in) rainfall for your geographic location.
3. How do ocean currents act as thermal regulators for earth?
4. What is the acid rain problem? How does it affect forests? lakes?
5. Explain the similarities and differences between the most productive freshwater environments and the most productive saltwater environments.
6. Would you swim across the Missouri River? Why? or why not?
7. Do you feel that the oceans are big enough that they can serve as dumping grounds for waste?
8. Where does your local drinking water come from? How does it get there through the hydrologic cycle? How long does the water you flush take to get back to your faucet?

References for Further Study

Davis, R. A. Jr. 1987. *Oceanography: An Introduction to the Marine Environment.* Dubuque, Ia.: Wm. C. Brown. A good introductory oceanography text.

Duxbury, A. C. and A. B. Duxbury. 1989. *An Introduction to the World's Oceans,* 2nd ed. Dubuque, Ia.: Wm. C. Brown. A physical geography of the world's oceans.

Eiseley, L. 1957. *The Immense Journey.* New York: Vintage Books, Random House Inc. Chapter 4, The Snout, in particular is appropriate for the hydrosphere.

EPA Journal. Articles on problems in the hydrosphere follow.

Environmental Protection Agency. 1986. *Acid Rain: Looking Ahead.* Washington, D.C.: EPA Journal, (June July), 12: No. 5.

Environmental Protection Agency. 1987. *Protecting Our Estuaries.* Washington, D.C.: EPA Journal. (July August), 13: No. 6.

Environmental Protection Agency. 1988. *The Marine Environment.* Washington, D.C.

Kansas City District U.S. Army Corps of Engineers. 1981. *Missouri River Corridor Inventory.* Kansas City. Inventory of the Missouri River with emphasis on the section through Missouri.

Neihardt, J. G. 1927. *The River and I.* New York: The MacMillan Co. A poetic account of the Missouri River written at the turn of the century.

Roth, P. et. al. 1985. *The American West's Acid Rain Test.* Holmes, Pa.: World Resources Institute. Research Report No. 1. Testing for acid rain effects in the western United States.

Chapter 5

Soil

- Introduction
- Definition of Soil
  - Soil Horizons
- Soil Formation
  - Podzolization
  - Laterization
  - Calcification
  - Gleization
  - Invertization
- Soil Classification and Soil Geography
- Soil Biota
- Soil Erosion
- Irrigation
- Wetlands
- Summary

••••••
If we are to protect our margin of life, we must restore the soil from which it comes.
Gene Poirot, 1978.
••••••

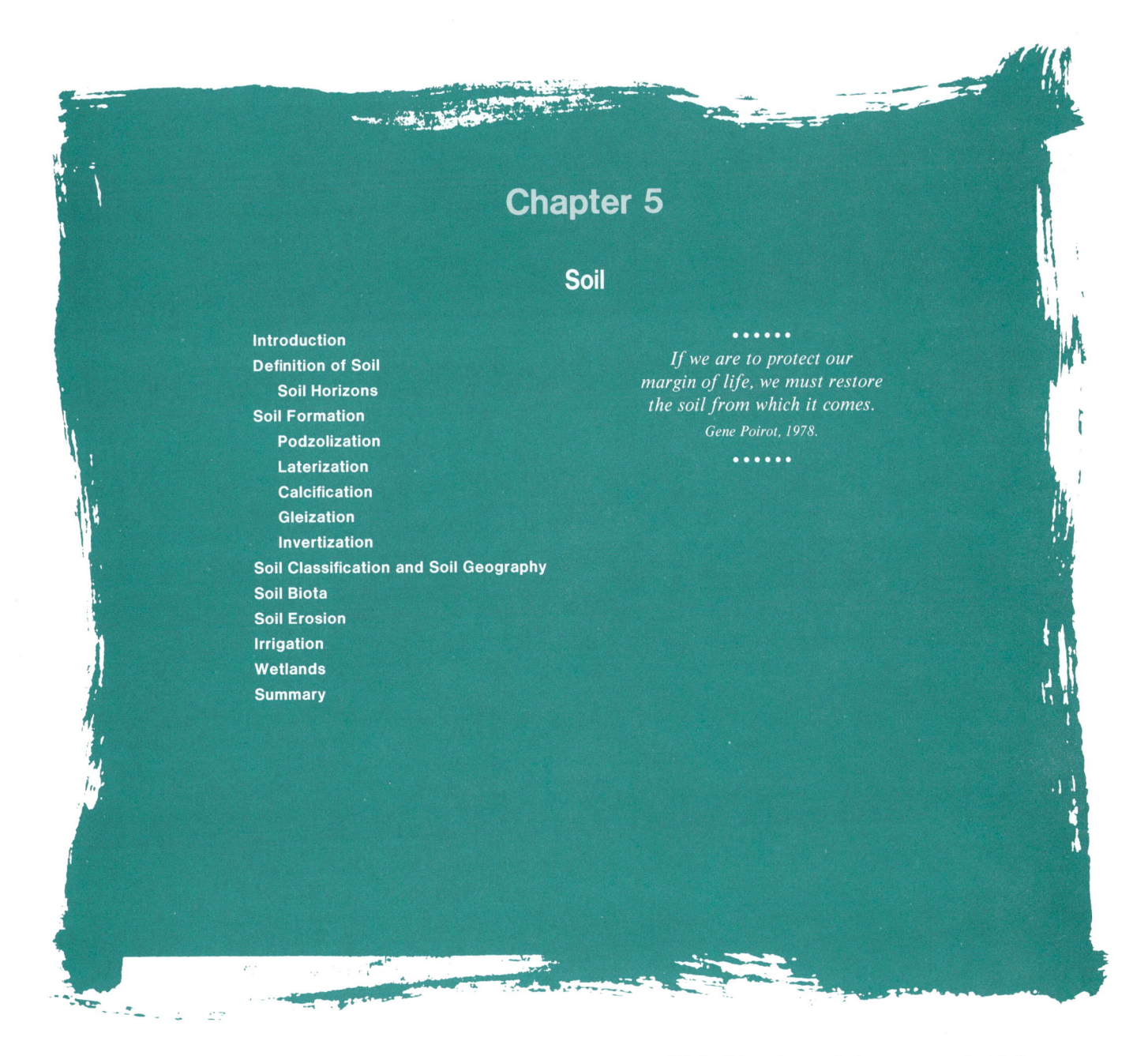

Introduction

Peter Steinhart (1985) in his essay entitled *Soil: The Miracle We Take For Granted* provides a good introduction for a chapter on soil in a conservation text.

> Of all the Earth's resources, the one we take the most for granted is soil. It is everywhere around us, brown and prosaic, so easily found and so easily wasted. Perhaps that's why many of us think of soil only in the abstract—as something farmers use to feed us.
>
> Those of us who live in cities are aware of soil only when it becomes dirt, smudged onto our clothes after a picnic or carried into the house on our shoes. Then it is considered matter out of place and something to get rid of.
>
> We bulldoze it out of the way to make highways and to erect shopping centers. We ignore its fragility when we cut timber or build houses on hillsides. And then it comes back to haunt us when it clogs our drains, clouds our drinking water, causes floods or simply falls away beneath the footings of our home.
>
> The truth is that soil is a resource of astonishing balance, complexity, beauty, and frailty. If we could narrow our vision down to microscopic scale and tunnel into the top few inches of earth, we would be dumbstruck with its mystery and vitality.
>
> There is enormous variety to soil. Experts say there are some 15,000 different soil types in the United States, and perhaps hundreds of thousands worldwide. They differ on the basis of the kind of rock that weathered into clay and sand to form the

soil, the mix of organic matter inside it, the amount of water, the texture, and the age. There are rust red soils of the tropics, from which most of the soluble aluminum and iron has been leached. There are dark brown loams in the U.S. Midwest that are made of materials scoured off the top crust of Canada and pushed southward by ancient glaciers. There are North American soils built largely from ancient silts, blown here from Asia on prehistoric winds. There are places where the soil is 200 feet deep and places it is but a thin film on top of rock.

Living soil is full of air passages that let oxygen, carbon dioxide, and nitrogen circulate. A well-aerated soil may be almost half airspace by volume. There are acres of surface area on the particles of sand and clay. Films of moisture cling to those surfaces, forming peds and atmospheres that nurture a vast array of bacteria, fungi, viruses, and protozoans. A cubic inch of soil can contain literally billions of creatures.

We know many of these organisms because they cause or cure disease. The bacterium Clostridium tetani for instance, causes tetanus, while another, Clostridium botulinum, causes botulism. Some fungi have given us penicillin. Actinomycetes, which are responsible for the sweet aroma of freshly turned earth, provide such useful antibiotics as streptomycin.

But the teeming life of the soil has far more powerful significance than disease or medicine. For it is the bacteria and fungi in the soil that break down the complex molecules of dead organic matter, the cellulose and lignin of wood and leaf, into molecules that plants can use for food. Only the microbes can take the salts out of soil minerals and make them available to plants. Only bacteria can oxidize ammonia into nitrite.

There are other soil creatures with which we are more familiar. Moles and earthworms, burrowing crickets and insect larvae, all tunnel through the soil, moving vast amounts of dirt, rearranging it, compacting it here and opening up air and water passages there. Their digging continually changes the habitat for microbes. One day there may be billions of one kind of bacteria, and the next day they may be replaced by an entirely different species. Waterlogging may choke out those that depend on air and favor those that thrive without it. There may be thousands of species lying dormant, waiting for the right conditions. Thus, an activity like plowing can cause the number of organisms to proliferate thirtyfold in a few days.

There is an enormous commerce in chemicals going on in the ground. Microbes and fungi make nutrients available to plants. Some also attack plants and cause them to wilt and die. Some use up essential minerals and thus retard plant growth. Other microbes boost plant growth by liberating more nitrogen or phosphorus or potassium. And there are bacteria that provide plants with growth hormones.

Soil microbes also dispose of sewage and some kinds of trash. In laboratories, we see that the right sequence of bacteria can break down oil. And studies in the field have shown that some soil microbes can consume up to 99 percent of the DDT sprayed on them within a few weeks. But it doesn't always work. Other soil microbes will refuse to "digest" a pesticide as adamantly as a child may refuse to eat spinach. And too often toxic chemicals get into groundwater before any bacteria can get to them.

Healthy soil has millions of possibilities: decomposers, benefactors, curatives, tiny chemical factories. But so complex and minute is the life of soil, and so remote are its inhabitants from our eyes, that we do not think of it as a living world. Rather, we think of it as a manufactured commodity. Plow it right, water it right, add a little nitrogen here and a little phosphorus there and, we think, things will grow.

Unfortunately, we are finding out that it doesn't always work that way. Much of our technology turns out to be bad for soil. When we take away the vegetative cover by using a plow, we leave the soil open to the forces of wind and rain.

We are now losing topsoil at a rate of about six billion tons a year in the United States, and more worldwide. The causes are varied. Too many farmers plow up and down hillsides, leaving furrows that turn to gullies when it rains. Too many speculators are plowing up dry lands or steep lands that should not be farmed. Too many farmers are abandoning traditional crop rotations that once rebuilt overworked soils. Too many developers are careless with bulldozers.

The consequences of such actions could be enormous in the years ahead. Ours is already a hungry world. If, as the experts believe, one-third of the Earth's cropland is eroding faster than nature can replace the soil, we are losing productivity. We may cultivate the same number of acres, but as the soil gets thinner, we will harvest less food from it. And we will see more streams silting, more fish species vanishing, more sediment filling our lakes.

If we are to turn things around, we are going to have to make some choices. And to make those choices, we will have to understand that soil is not a commodity but a habitat. And we are going to have to conserve it much the way we go about conserving other habitats—by thinking of it as part of the immense and complex variety of life.*

---

*Copyright 1985 by the National Wildlife Federation. Reprinted from the February/March 1985 issue of National Wildlife Magazine.

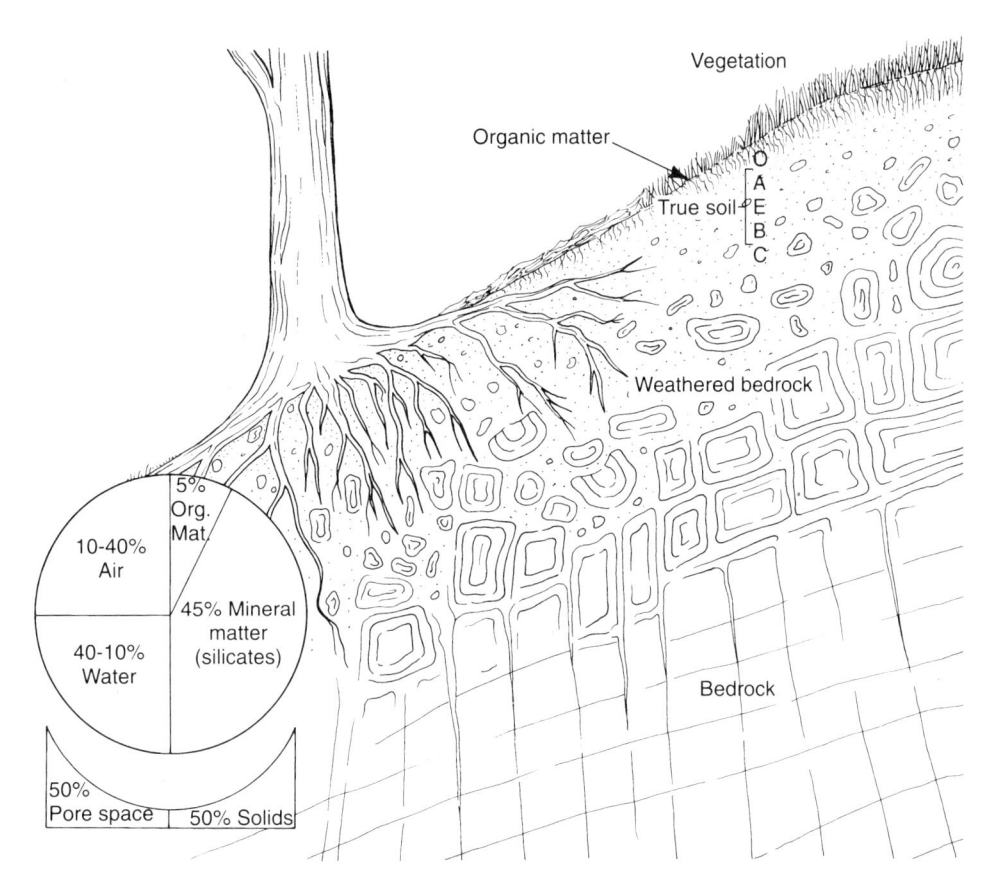

Figure 5.1 The soil layer of the earth's surface.
Copyright © 1973 by Arthur N. Strahler. Reproduced by permission.

Definition of Soil

Soil is a natural part of the earth's surface, characterized by layers parallel to the surface, that have resulted from the modification of parent material by physical, chemical, and biological processes, operating under varying conditions of climate and topography, through varying periods of time. The soil is a product of biogeochemical weathering of rock, called parent material, that provides the primary and secondary inorganic minerals for the soil medium. The soil biota and vegetation on the surface, along with their roots, provides the organic material. The climatic condition adds air for oxidation and water for hydration to aid in the weathering process. The layers, called **horizons,** that make up the soil develop as a result of the interaction of lithosphere (rocks or sediment), with the climatic condition of the atmosphere, which also provides the water (hydrosphere), and the organisms of the biosphere. The interactions between lithosphere, atmosphere, hydrosphere, and biosphere that produce one meter (3 ft) of soil on the earth's surface require thousands of years of time. Typically, soil is about 45% inorganic mineral material, 5% organic material, and 50% pore space. The pore space alternates between wet and dry, according to changes in the weather (figure 5.1). The inorganic mineral material is mostly silica (Si), oxygen (O), iron (Fe), and aluminum (Al).

Soil Horizons

The soil layers that develop in response to weathering of the parent material because of physical, chemical, and biological processes are called *horizons*. True soil consists of three of the top four layers (horizons) (figure 5.2). These horizons are identified by the use of symbols (letters). The A and E horizons are called the *zone of eluviation* because they lose material downward as water percolates through the profile. The B horizon is called the *zone of illuviation* because it accumulates some of the materials that have been removed from the A and E horizons. The B horizon can accumulate any material small enough to be carried by water through the pore spaces in the profile. **Humus** and **clay** have a particle size less than two microns and can accumulate in the B horizon. The soluble bases (Ca, Na, and K) and metals (Fe, Al, and Mg) that are dissolved or chemically altered by water can also move into the B horizon, but in moist climates many of these stay in solution and are washed out of the soil water zone and into

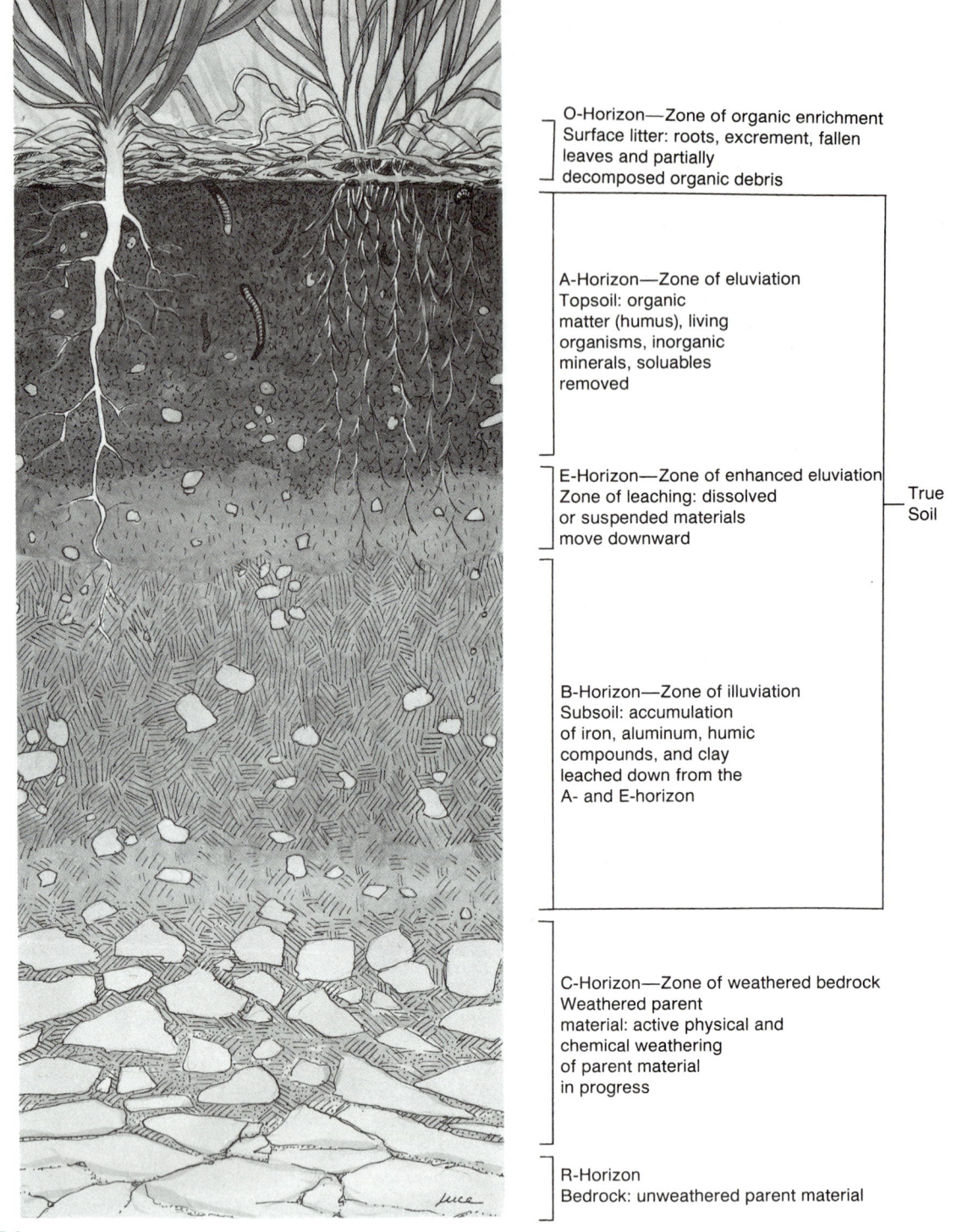

Figure 5.2 Soil horizons.

O-Horizon—Zone of organic enrichment
Surface litter: roots, excrement, fallen leaves and partially decomposed organic debris

A-Horizon—Zone of eluviation
Topsoil: organic matter (humus), living organisms, inorganic minerals, soluables removed

E-Horizon—Zone of enhanced eluviation
Zone of leaching: dissolved or suspended materials move downward

B-Horizon—Zone of illuviation
Subsoil: accumulation of iron, aluminum, humic compounds, and clay leached down from the A- and E-horizon

True Soil

C-Horizon—Zone of weathered bedrock
Weathered parent material: active physical and chemical weathering of parent material in progress

R-Horizon
Bedrock: unweathered parent material

From William P. Cunningham and Barbara Woodworth Saigo, *Environmental Science: A Global Concern.* Copyright © 1990 Wm. C. Brown Publishers, Dubuque, Iowa. All Rights Reserved. Reprinted by permission.

Table 5.1 A

Soil Horizon Symbols and Subscripts
(Nomenclature of Soil Horizons.)

Horizon[a]	Characteristics
O	Upper layers dominated by organic material above mineral soil horizons. Must have > 30% organic content if mineral fraction contains > 50% clay minerals, or > 20% organics if no clay minerals.
A	Mineral horizons formed at the surface or below the O horizon. Contains humic organic material mixed with mineral fraction. Properties may result from cultivation or other similar disturbances.
E	Mineral horizons in which main characteristic is loss of silicate clay, iron, or aluminum, leaving a concentration of sand and silt particles of resistant minerals. A deeply eluviated A horizon.
B	Dominated by obliteration of original rock structure and by illuvial concentration of various materials including clay minerals, carbonates, sesquioxides of iron and aluminum. Often has distinct color and soil structure.
C	Horizons, excluding hard bedrock, that are less affected by pedogenesis and lack properties of O, A, E, and B horizons. Material may be either like or unlike that from which the solum presumably formed.
R	Hard unweathered bedrock underlying a soil.

Source: Data adapted from Soil Survey Staff 1960, 1975, 1981.
[a]Horizons can be divided into subhorizons indicated by Arabic numbers such as B_1, A_2, B_{12}, etc.

the groundwater zone by hydrologic circulation. The process of element removal by chemical solution is called *leaching*.

Other horizons of importance are the O and Ap layers. The O horizon is a zone of **organic enrichment** at the top of the profile. This layer accumulates leaves, twigs, roots, animal feces, and organics from insects and other organisms. The Ap horizon is a **plow zone** caused by mixing soil materials in the top 7 or more inches (18 cm) of a profile by cultivation. The C horizon is a zone of partially weathered parent material below the true soil but above the bedrock, which is designated the R horizon. The slow release of nutrients by physical and chemical weathering of the bedrock is most active in the C horizon, and this activity is an important part of the law of fertility. Subscripts can be added to horizon symbols to indicate accumulated material or significant characteristics. Table 5.1 gives major horizon designations and some of the common subscripts used to designate soil conditions in a particular horizon.

The soil is the material upon which we build houses, plant gardens, spray insecticides, herbicides, and fertilizers, cover with concrete, and generally take for granted. Soil horizon classification is necessary to understanding soil formation and the limitations for soil use.

Table 5.1 B

Some Common Descriptive Symbols to be Used in Conjunction with Major Soil Horizons.

Symbol[a]	Meaning
b	buried soil horizon
g	strong gleying
h	illuvial humus
s	illuvial iron
k	accumulation of carbonates, commonly $CaCO_3$ (K replaces Ca)
m	strong cementation
p	mixed by plow
t	illuvial clay
x	fragipan character

Source: Data adapted from Soil Survey Staff, 1975, 1981.
[a]Symbols used with other profile designations. For example: B_{21}, B_{1h}, Ck

Soil Formation

The rocks of the lithosphere, the parent material for the inorganic component of the soil, in most cases formed at a temperature and pressure different from that found on the surface of the earth. Therefore, most rocks and their associated minerals are unstable near the earth's surface. The climatic condition to which the parent material is exposed at the earth's surface provides the weathering environment that breaks down the rocks into smaller particles and in some cases changes their composition to secondary minerals (clays). Climate also controls, to a large degree, the vegetation and soil biota for biologic weathering. All of the decomposition (chemical) and physical breakdown of rock material to form soil particles is collectively referred to as *biogeochemical weathering*. Biogeochemical weathering includes physical weathering such as expansion and contraction from **freeze-thaw** or **thermal expansion,** chemical weathering such as **solution** or **oxidation,** and biologic weathering such as **root expansion.**

Soil-formation processes can be divided into five soil-forming regimes on the basis of biogeochemical weathering activity. Three of these are **bioclimatic** and two are **hydroclimatic.** Podzoliation (spodsolization), laterization (oxisolation), and calcification (salinization) are bioclimatic and are associated with a particular climatic-

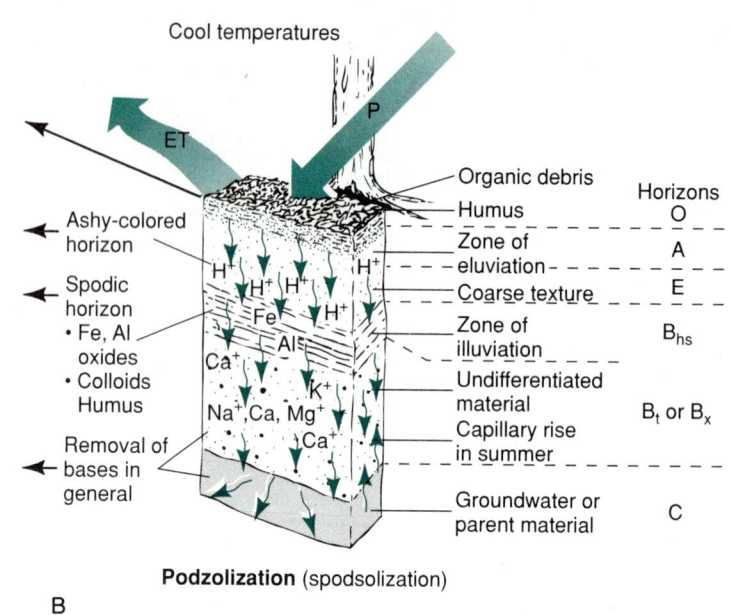

Figure 5.3 The podzolization (spodsolization) process in cool, humid climates (Cf, Df).
(*Photo:* David A. Castillon)
(b) From Marsh, *Earthscape: A Physical Geography.* Copyright © 1987 John Wiley & Sons, Inc., New York, NY. Reprinted by permission of John Wiley & Sons, Inc.

vegetative regime. Gleization and invertization are hydroclimatic processes because they require water along with a variable climatic condition.

Podzolization

Podzolization (spodsolization) (figure 5.3) is the soil-formation process where iron (Fe) and aluminum (Al) are leached from the A and E horizons and are concentrated in the B horizon of the soil profile. This process occurs in moist climates with a seasonal variation in temperatures (Cf and Df climates; figure 3.9). The winter season with cool to cold temperatures slows down the organic decomposition of the surface and root zone organic debris. The moisture surplus filters through the A and E horizons (zone of eluviation), dissolving soluble elements and carrying colloidal size (< 2 microns) particles down through the pore spaces in the soil. Thus the A and E horizons are usually coarser textured than the B horizon. Some iron (Fe) and aluminum (Al) oxides, along with the clays and humus colloids, accumulate in the B horizon (zone of illuviation), giving it a very clayey texture (B_t or B_{hs}). The soluble bases, sodium (Na), calcium (Ca), magnesium (Mg), and potassium (K) leave the soil water zone by way of the groundwater system. Removal of these bases (leaching) creates an acid soil water condition. The podzolization soil formation process occurs in the eastern part of the North American continent to the east of the 100th meridian and in Canada north of the 50th parallel to the permafrost line. Podzolization also occurs on selected site-specific locations (places where the climate, elevation, and geology are right) throughout the western regions of North America. The deciduous and coniferous forests of the United States and Canada are the dominant natural vegetations of the podzol soil.

Laterization

Laterization (oxisolation) (figure 5.4) is the soil-formation process where iron (Fe) and aluminum (Al) are oxidized to rock-hard brick-red nodules, called laterites, in the B horizon of the soil profile. This process is dominant in the tropical climates (Am, Af; figure 3.9). Warm moist climates, with the associated wetting and drying of the soil, are ideal for the **oxidation** of metal ions ($2Fe + 3O + H_2O \rightarrow Fe_2O_3 \cdot H_2O$). The soil takes on the deep red color of iron oxides and the B horizon accumulates sesquioxides of both iron and aluminum (Fe_2O_3 and Al_2O_3). Clay also accumulates in the B horizon (B_t). The abundant moisture of the Af and Am climates remove Na, Ca, Mg, K, and Si in solution to the groundwater zone and out of the reach of plant roots. This leaves an abundance of free hydrogen ions (H^+) in the soil water zone, making lateritic soils very acid. Tropical rainforest vegetation in Mexico and Hawaii is the dominant biotic response on the lateritic soils in North America.

Calcification

Calcification (salinization) (figure 5.5) is the soil-formation process where bases are kept near the top of the soil profile by evaporation of water from the surface. This process occurs where there is a moisture deficit in the

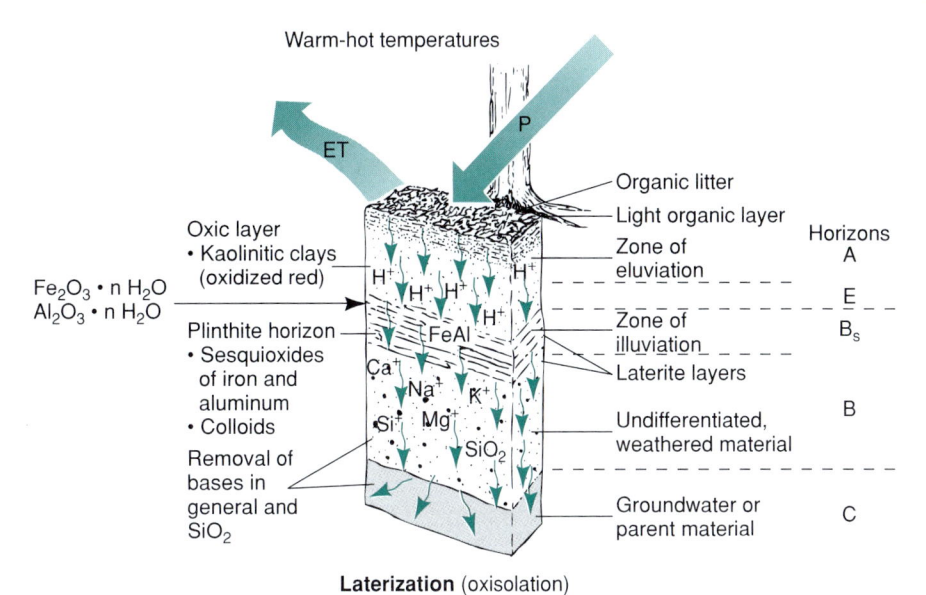

Figure 5.4 The laterization (oxisolation) process in warm, wet climates (Af, Am).
From Marsh, *Earthscape: A Physical Geography.* Copyright © 1987 John Wiley & Sons, Inc., New York, NY. Reprinted by permission of John Wiley & Sons, Inc.

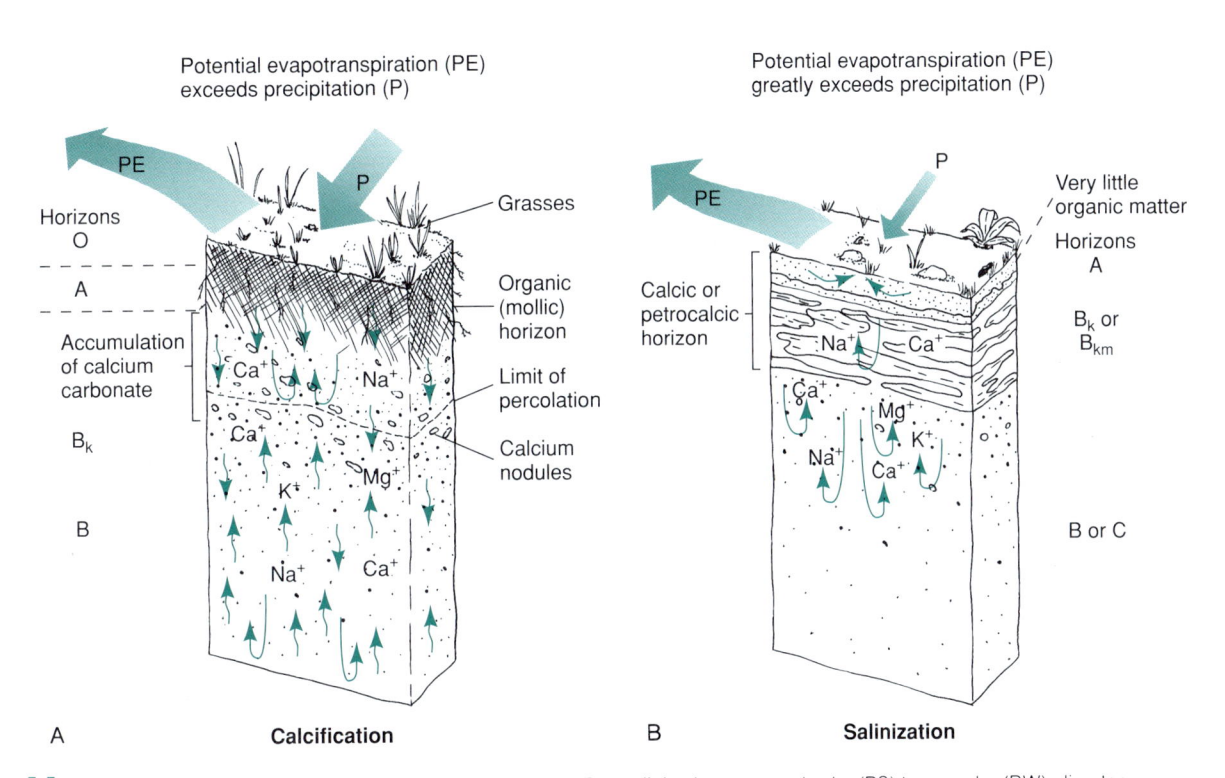

Figure 5.5 (a) The calcification process in semiarid BS climates. (b) The salinization process in dry (BS) to very dry (BW) climates.
From Marsh, *Earthscape: A Physical Geography.* Copyright © 1987 John Wiley & Sons, Inc., New York, NY. Reprinted by permission of John Wiley & Sons, Inc.

yearly water budget. The desert (BW) and steppe (BS) climates of the North American continent are the regions for this soil-formation process (figure 3.9). The precipitation that falls in the dry regions is not sufficient to leach the bases (Ca, Na, Mg, K) out of the soil water zone. They go into solution after a precipitation episode, but are drawn by capillarity back toward the surface by evaporation. The repetition of the process allows calcium carbonate ($CaCO_3$) nodules to accumulate in the B horizon of the soil (B_k). The drier the climate the closer to the surface the salts accumulate, and calcification progresses to **salinization** in areas of extreme aridity. Calcified soils are usually near neutral to basic (pH 6.5 to 8.0) and, because of the high nutrient supply (bases), are very productive when irrigated. Saline soils, on the other hand, will only support halophytic (salt-tolerant) vegetation.

Soil 97

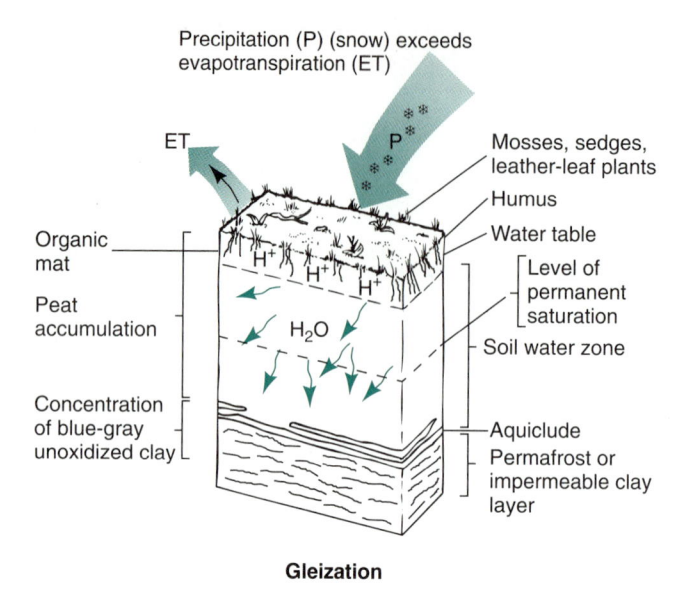

Figure 5.6 The gleization process in cold, wet (ET) climates.
From Marsh, *Earthscape: A Physical Geography.* Copyright © 1987 John Wiley & Sons, Inc., New York, NY. Reprinted by permission of John Wiley & Sons, Inc.

Gleization

Gleization (figure 5.6) is the soil-formation process where a sticky, blue-gray accumulation of clay and humus, called gley, forms in the B horizon of the soil profile. This process is hydroclimatic because it requires standing water, and the Tundra climate (ET; figure 3.9) provides the ideal conditions for the process. Gleization also occurs in other climates if water is perched in the B or C horizon of the soil for extended periods of time throughout the year. This can happen when the geologic condition ponds water or when a strong clayey B horizon (B_t) becomes an aquiclude to water percolation through the soil. The coastal wetlands and swamps of the southeastern United States are suitable locations for the gleization soil-formation process to occur. The tundra climate, however, is also ideal for the process of gleization because of the permafrost layer in the subsoil. In the spring, the surface of the soil thaws and water becomes ponded above the permafrost, which acts as an aquiclude. The ponded water retards oxidation and the soil takes on a characteristic blue-gray color indicative of poor drainage and no oxidation. The treeless environment of the tundra supports a vegetation of mosses, sedges, and leather-leaf plants. As microorganisms convert this vegetation to humus, the soil water becomes acid (humic acid). The organic breakdown is not complete and peat accumulates as an organic soil layer (O horizon).

Invertization

Invertization (figure 5.7) is the soil-formation process that produces an inverted soil profile. The process requires a highly expandable clay content near the surface. It is a hydroclimatic process, because water is required from precipitation, along with extended periods of drying. Precipitation wets the soil, causing the clays to swell. An extended period of evaporation will dry the clays, causing them to shrink and crack. Surface activity allows some of the topsoil (O and A horizon) material to fall into the deep cracks that extend into the B horizon zone. Repetition of this process over thousands of years gives the soil an inverted profile. It appears to have the A horizon below the B horizon, or at least a dark organic layer out of place in the profile. Figure 5.8 illustrates the layered structure of clays that allows them to expand and contract as they wet and dry. Soils formed by the invertization process are called *vertisols*. Vertisols are usually good agricultural soils but they have the disadvantage of becoming sticky when wet.

Soil Classification and Soil Geography

The U.S. Comprehensive Soil Classification System was developed to standardize soil nomenclature throughout the world. Soils are divided into ten soil orders and further subdivided into suborders and groups.

Table 5.2 gives the ten soil orders and their defining properties. Figure 5.9 is a map showing the distribution of the ten soil orders in North America. In mountainous regions, soils thin as elevation increases and most mountain slopes have a very thin soil layer or no soil.

Alfisols, spodosols, and ultisols are formed by the podzolization (spodsolization) process. They are acid soils leached of their bases by a wet climactic condition. **Ultisols** are formed in the warmer Cfa (figure 3.9) climates of the southeastern United States. The **alfisols** and **spodosols** are typically soils of the Df climates (figure 3.9) but can form in the Cf climates when conditions are right.

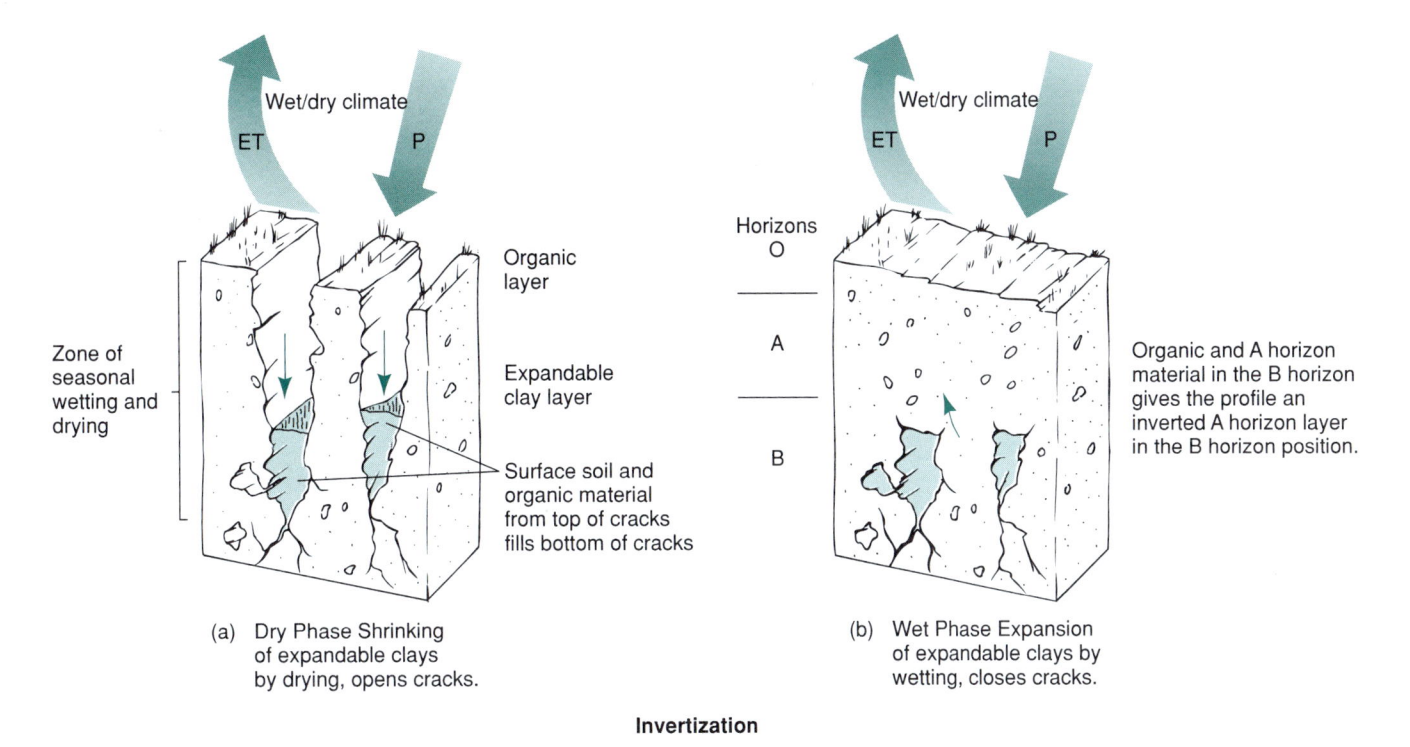

Figure 5.7 The invertization process occurs in an alternating wet/dry environment, where the soil layers contain a large percentage of expandable clays close to the surface.
From Marsh, *Earthscape: A Physical Geography.* Copyright © 1987 John Wiley & Sons, Inc., New York, NY. Reprinted by permission of John Wiley & Sons, Inc.

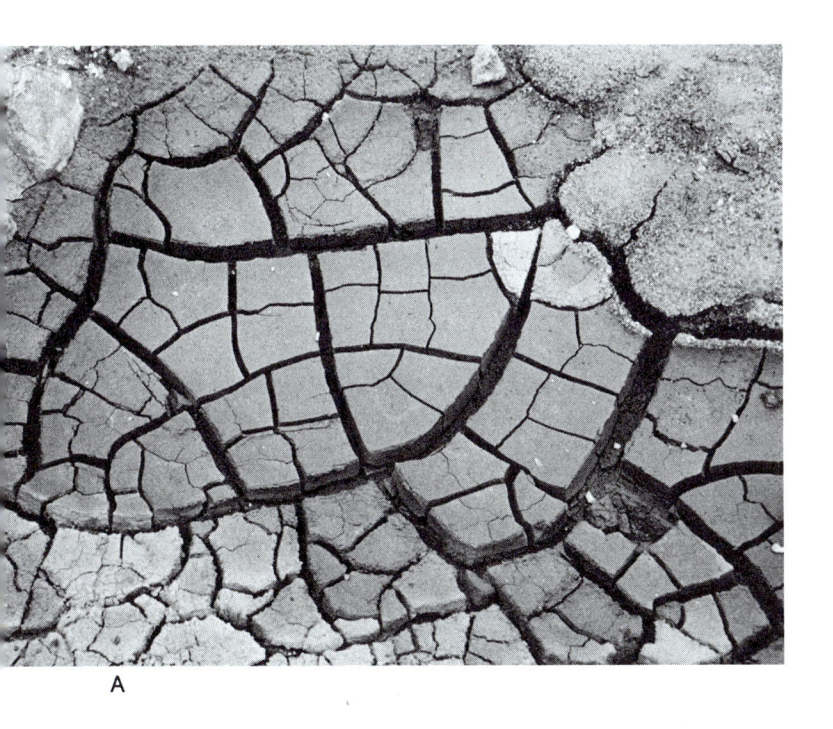

Figure 5.8 (a) Mud cracks in dry soil material (expandable clays). (b) Expansion and contraction on expandable clays from wetting and drying is a physical weathering process in soil formation.
(*Photo:* David A. Castillon)
From Costa and Borcer, *Surficial Geology.* Copyright © John Wiley & Sons, Inc., New York, NY. Reprinted by permission of John Wiley & Sons, Inc.

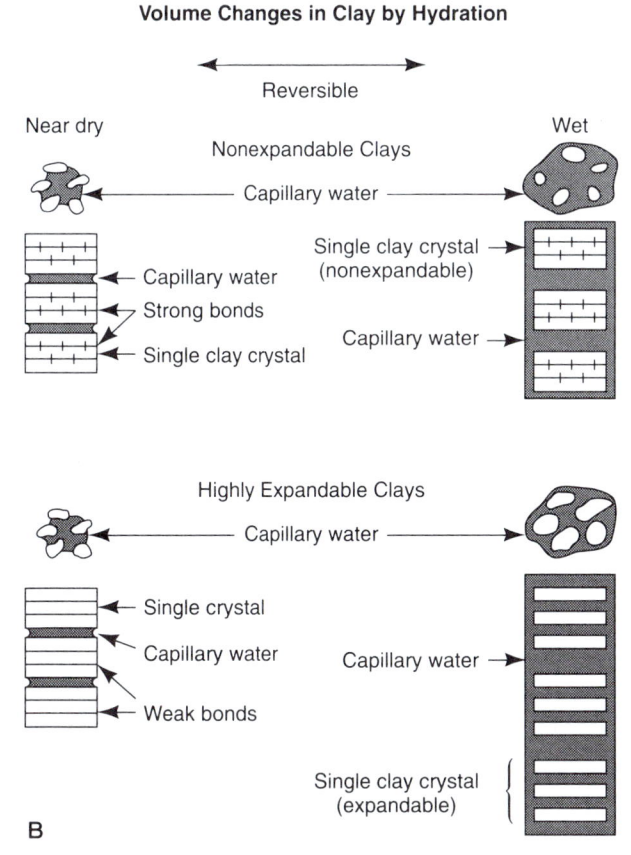

Soil 99

Table 5.2
Major Soil Orders

Name	Soil Characteristics
Alfisol	Mineral soils formed by the podzolization process with light or dark surface layers, but with low base saturations (leached) and a distinct clay horizon.
Aridisol	Mineral soils with a light-colored surface horizon that have formed by the calcification or salinization process.
Entisol	A mineral soil having no distinct horizons within 100 cm (40 in) of the soil surface. Soil-formation processes just beginning or obscured by erosion.
Histosol	Highly organic soils, many of which are formed by the gleization process.
Inceptisol	Mineral soils with at least one horizon in which minerals other than carbonates and silica have been altered. Podzolization in a youthful stage of soil development or retarded by erosion.
Mollisol	Mineral soils with a dark surface layer that contains at least 0.58% organic carbon. These soils exhibit properties of both podzolization and calcification and may be the product of climate change in the Holocene Epoch.
Oxisol	A mineral soil containing a horizon at least 53 cm (21 in) thick that has no weatherable primary minerals. Mainly found in tropical climates and formed by the laterization process.
Spodosol	Mineral soils that often have a light ashy-colored leached (acid) E horizon. These soils were formed by the spodsolization process.
Ultisol	Mineral soils with a distinct clay horizon and with a base saturation of less than 35% deeply leached and weathered podzolization soils.
Vertisol	Mineral-clay-dominated soils that develop cracks when dry because of their expandable clay content. These soils formed by the invertization process.

Source: Data from Soil Conservation Service, U.S. Department of the Interior, 1981.

They have not been leached of their bases as completely as the ultisols. Part of the reason for the differences is related to parent material and part of the reason is time. The parent material for ultisols is weathered bedrock residuum, but for most of the alfisol and spodosol regions the parent material is unconsolidated glacial deposits or loess. The time since the last glacial episode is less than 20,000 years, whereas most of the bedrock parent material from which the ultisols have formed has been exposed to the biogeochemical weathering environment for millions of years. Agriculturally the alfisols are the best soils of the three because they are less acidic than the spodosols and need less fertilization than the ultisols.

Oxisols have been formed by the laterization (oxisolation) process. They are the tropical climate (Af) soils, and are not found extensively in North America because the only tropical climates are in Florida, Hawaii, and Mexico (figure 3.9). The oxisols are poor, clayey, acid soils with limited redeeming features. The rainforest vegetation of the tropics, however, finds them an excellent medium in which to grow. The destruction of these forests is an environmental disaster for the oxisols as well as for the rest of the planet.

Aridisols are the product of the calcification (salinization) process. As the name implies, they are the soils of the arid regions of North America. They are very good soils when it comes to nutrient supply, because evaporation has kept the bases and salts in the root zone and available for vegetation. Some of the aridisols that accumulate the wrong kind of salts (NaCl) in the upper layers of the soil profile become a medium for only salt-tolerant vegetation (halophytes).

The best soil, agriculturally, is the **mollisol**. It has formed along the margins of the wet and the dry climates and in the floodplains of North America. Forming along the margins of the wet (Cf and Df) and dry (BS) climate region, it retains the good attributes of the calcification process (bases not removed), and the deep thick A horizons are a product of the podzolization process. The vegetation (prairie grasses) has helped to produce the thick dark A horizons, containing humus, that are characteristic of mollisols. The mollisols of the floodplains and terraces of the river valleys are the product of organic-rich sediment accumulation in these low-lying areas.

Histosols are bog soils. They are made up of thick accumulations of organic material. Areal extent of these soils is limited. In most cases, the histosols were formed by the gleization process.

Vertisols were formed by the invertization process. They are of limited extent, with the only major area of these soils occurring in Texas. The expandable clays in these soils are very sticky when wet, creating a major problem for tractors during cultivation because the soil sticks to the tractor tires to such an extent that they lose their mobility.

The **entisols** and **inceptisols** are beginning soils with a limited horizon development. Climate, topography, and/or time are factors that have limited soil development to

GENERALIZED NORTH AMERICA SOILS MAP

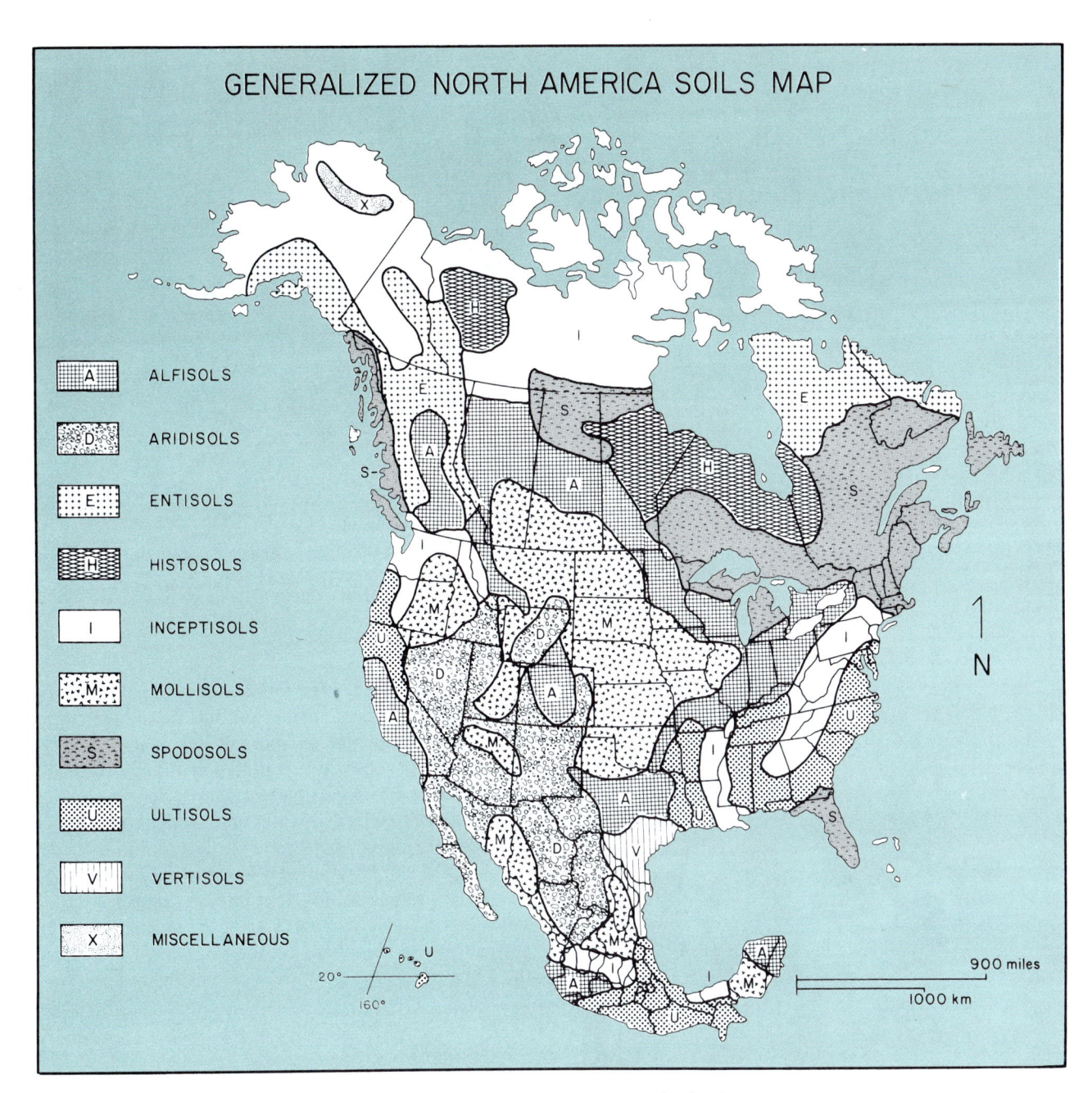

A	ALFISOLS
D	ARIDISOLS
E	ENTISOLS
H	HISTOSOLS
I	INCEPTISOLS
M	MOLLISOLS
S	SPODOSOLS
U	ULTISOLS
V	VERTISOLS
X	MISCELLANEOUS

Figure 5.9 Generalized North America soils map showing the probable occurrence of soil orders.
Source: Data from the U.S. Department of Agriculture—SCS.
(Cartographer: Douglas Hemsath)

the extent that a recognizable B horizon has not formed. In most cases, these soils are forming by the gleization or podzolization processes. Many of the gleyed soils of the permafrost region in Alaska and northern Canada are entisols. Many of the soils in the Mexican Highlands and in the Appalachian and Rocky Mountain regions are inceptisols. The steep slopes erode faster than soil development can take place and limited horizon development occurs.

Soil Biota

Soil is more than just the inorganic and organic (humus) material we call dirt. It is the miracle we take for granted. An integral part of each soil-forming process involves the soil organism and vegetation (**soil biota**) whose roots use the soil as a medium for support (figure 5.10). The dark

Figure 5.10A Soil biota aid in soil development and maintenance of soil fertility and are a necessary part of a healthy soil.
From William P. Cunningham and Barbara Woodworth Saigo, *Environmental Science: A Global Concern.* Copyright © 1990 Wm. C. Brown Publishers, Dubuque, Iowa. All Rights Reserved. Reprinted by permission.

Figure 5.10B Fungi and bacteria are the principal organisms for breakdown of organic material to humus.
(*Photo:* David A. Castillon)

humus-rich A horizon of a soil contains billions of organisms. The obvious ones are worms, ants, moles, mites, nematodes, beetles, snails, and many terrestrial insect larvae. These organisms **mix, aerate,** and **fertilize** the soil with their activity, excrement, and decay. But microorganisms such as bacteria and fungi are far more important to soil development. They provide the chemicals needed to continue the biogeochemical weathering that maintains soil fertility. All of these organisms continue their soil-forming work in the B horizon of the soil, but to a lesser degree. How deep do the soil microorganisms operate? Microbiologists have generally considered anything deeper than 7.6 m (25 ft) a biological desert. New evidence indicates that life exists as deep as water and nutrients can provide the necessary ingredients for life. To date, the bottom depth of life in the soil has not been found.

Soil conservation must take into consideration that the soil is a living environment. Use of fertilizers, herbicides, pesticides, and chemicals on the soil should not destroy the living organisms that are a part of the soil.

Soil Erosion

Soil erosion is a natural geomorphic process. Wind and rainwater, with the help of gravity, move the earth's surface materials from high places to low places. In a completely natural setting, the vegetation will hold most soil in place and what little is moved by wind or rain will be replaced by biogeochemical weathering of the rock below the surface to maintain a balance in the soil. Human activity has removed much of the native vegetation in North America, and agriculture has cleared over 170 million hectares (420 million acres) in the United States (figure 5.11). Almost 40% of this now-productive farmland is losing soil by water and wind erosion faster than it is being replaced by soil-forming processes. As soil washes or blows away its biological potential and productivity is reduced. Figure 5.12 shows soil loss per acre per year for the United States. Soil loss is a very serious problem in the United

Figure 5.11A Severe water erosion has created many acres of nonproductive land on this Iowa farm.
(*Photo:* USDA—SCS)

Figure 5.11B In Kansas, severe wind erosion has buried this farmer's fence with topsoil.
(*Photo:* David A. Castillon)

SOIL LOSS PER ACRE PER YEAR
IN THE UNITED STATES

WIND EROSION
w 1-5 TONS
Ⓦ 10 TONS OR MORE

WATER EROSION
0-5 TONS
5-10 TONS
10 TONS OR MORE

Figure 5.12 Soil loss in the United States caused by wind and water erosion on poorly managed agricultural land.
Source: Data from *National Wildlife Magazine*, February/March 1985.
(*Cartographer:* Douglas Hemsath)

Soil

Figure 5.13A No-till corn planted in wheat stubble in Illinois reduces soil erosion and helps to conserve soil moisture.
(Photo: USDA—SCS)

Figure 5.13B Conservation tillage of barley stubble, disked one to four inches (10 cm), leaving about 2,200 lbs. per acre (2500 kg per hectare) of crop residue in a North Dakota field.
(Photo: USDA—SCS)

States. Experts from the Department of Agriculture estimate that almost 10% of our cropland is easily erodable land and should not be cultivated (figure 5.12).

Two soil conservation practices in use to stop soil erosion are conservation tillage and no-till cultivation (figure 5.13). *Conservation tillage* uses a plow that does not turn the soil over, leaving 30% of the ground cover in place after planting and harvesting. *No-till cultivation* does not use a plow, but rather a special planter that either slices a slot or punches a hole in the sod cover for the crop seeds. To control the ground cover not removed in either conservation practice requires the use of pesticides and herbicides. The herbicide stunts the growth of the ground cover not removed and gives the growth advantage to the planted crop. The U.S. Department of Agriculture estimates that 90% of the American farmers will be using a conservation tillage program by the year 2010 (figure 5.14). Many environmentalists believe the environmental advantages of reduced soil erosion from conservation tillage will be offset by the environmental degradation caused by the increased use of herbicides and pesticides. No one can say what will happen to the soil biota from extensive use of pesticides and herbicides. If the soil biota is killed, have we really gained anything by saving the soil?

Irrigation

Irrigation in the wheat belt of North America is a soil-and-water conservation problem. It's a soil problem because the composition of the soil is changing and its fertility is reduced. It's a water problem because the water being used for irrigation is creating a deficit in the hydrologic circulation system recharge of groundwater storage. Water quality is also affected, because salt content in freshwater supplies is increasing.

Irrigation in the wheat belt uses water primarily from the Ogallala aquifer (figure 4.22). Water is pumped from the groundwater zone and spread on the surface by a pivot irrigation system (figure 5.15). The soil in the region being irrigated was formed in a dry climate by the calcification process. Most of the salts and bases are near the surface in these soils. The continued addition of irrigation water puts the salts and bases into solution, changing the soil-forming process from calcification to podzolization. The salts and bases are leached through the system and into the groundwater zone. This leaves the soil acidic and nutrient poor. Where this salty water seeps to the surface, evaporation releases the salt and the soil becomes useless because of its salt content.

The salts that are put into solution by irrigation water resurface in the waters of the surface drainage system or move into the groundwater zone. Many of the surface streams that drain the Great Plains are carrying water too salty to be classified as fresh water. The salinity of the Colorado River draining into Mexico is so high that the water is not usable. Therefore, the American government has built a desalinization plant to remove the salt. The water is then returned to the river to continue its journey to Mexico.

The major water problem with irrigation is the drawdown of our major aquifers. Every year farmers withdraw more water from the Ogallala than the entire flow of the

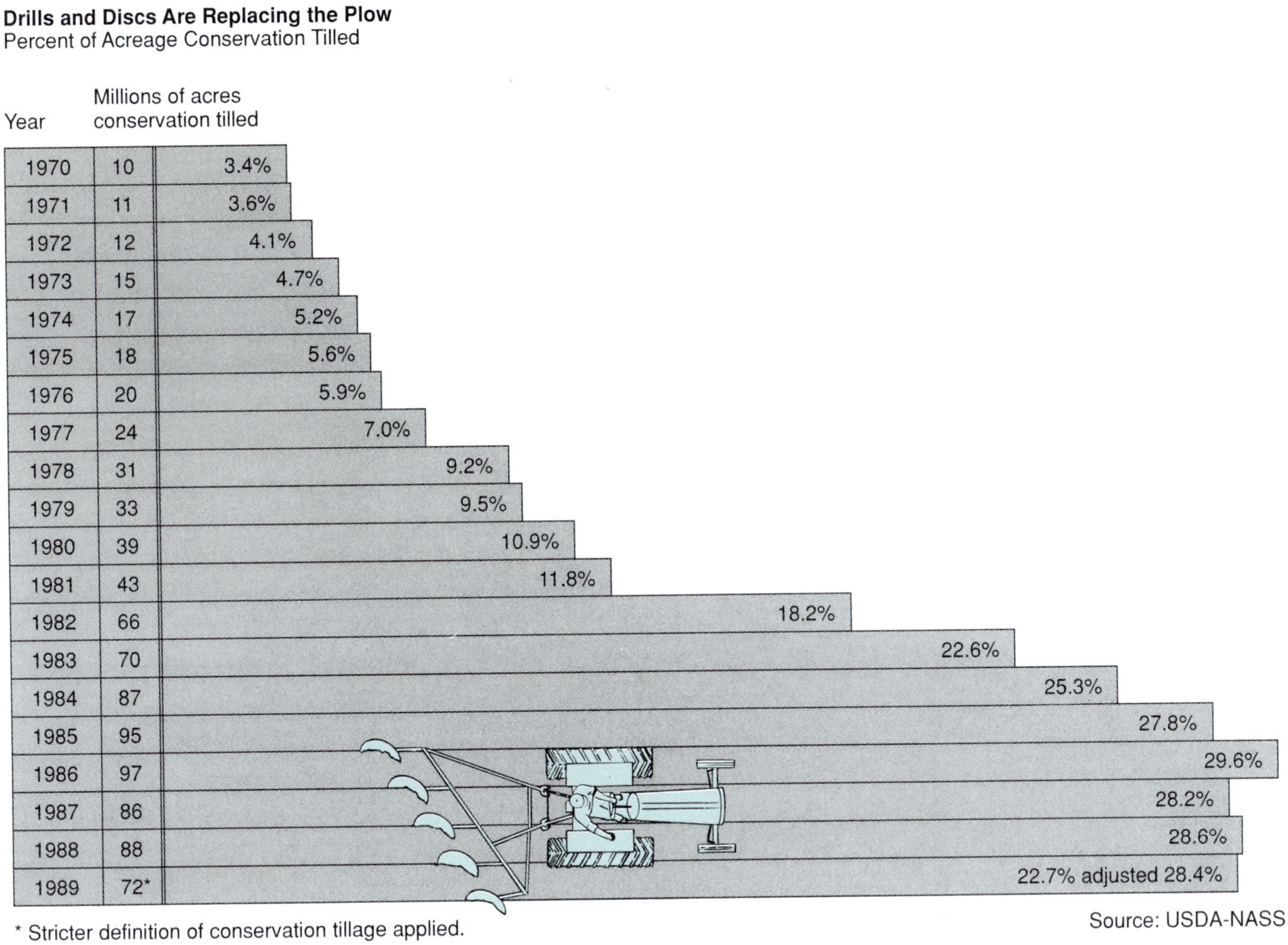

Drills and Discs Are Replacing the Plow
Percent of Acreage Conservation Tilled

Year	Millions of acres conservation tilled	Percent
1970	10	3.4%
1971	11	3.6%
1972	12	4.1%
1973	15	4.7%
1974	17	5.2%
1975	18	5.6%
1976	20	5.9%
1977	24	7.0%
1978	31	9.2%
1979	33	9.5%
1980	39	10.9%
1981	43	11.8%
1982	66	18.2%
1983	70	22.6%
1984	87	25.3%
1985	95	27.8%
1986	97	29.6%
1987	86	28.2%
1988	88	28.6%
1989	72*	22.7% adjusted 28.4%

* Stricter definition of conservation tillage applied.

Source: USDA-NASS

Figure 5.14 Conservation tillage and no-till agriculture are resulting in reduced soil erosion and saving the farmer money by reducing energy consumption for farm implements. However, increased use of herbicides to control vegetation is causing environmental damage.
Source: Data from the U.S. Department of Agriculture—NASS.

A

Figure 5.15A Aerial view of irrigated circle in eastern Colorado.
(Photo: David A. Castillon)

B

Figure 5.15B Center-pivot self-propelled sprinkler irrigation system.
(Photo: USDA—SCS)

Figure 5.16 Saltwater intrusion is causing freshwater pollution (salt) problems in many of the aquifers along the coasts of North America. Fresh water is consumed faster than the hydrologic cycle can replenish the aquifer.
From Carla W. Montgomery, *Physical Geology*. Copyright © 1987 Wm. C. Brown Publishers, Dubuque, Iowa. All Rights Reserved. Reprinted by permission.

Colorado River. The water table of the Ogallala is dropping from 15 cm (6 in) to 0.9 m (3 ft) per year. If this rate continues, it will be dry in 40 years. In coastal areas of Texas, drawdown in aquifers has created a problem of saltwater intrusion from the Gulf of Mexico, with salt water replacing fresh water in the Texas Gulf aquifer (figure 5.16).

Another major problem caused by irrigation is land subsidence. As water is withdrawn in large quantities from the groundwater zone, the land settles or subsides. The surface in the San Joaquin Valley has subsided more than 10 m (30 feet) since 1925, primarily because of groundwater withdrawals for irrigation (figure 5.17).

Wetlands

The U.S. Fish and Wildlife Service defines *wetlands* as those areas where saturation with water is the dominant factor determining the nature of soil development and the types of plant and animal communities living in the soil and on the surface. The single feature that most wetlands share is soil or substrate that is at least periodically saturated with, or covered by, water. Wetlands include, but are not limited to, **coastal** or **inland marshes** or **estuaries,** rivers and their associated **water saturated areas, inland lakes, potholes, bogs, mudflats,** and **bottomland hardwood forests.** These areas are vital to the survival of fish and wildlife, the maintenance of water quality, groundwater recharge, and flood control (figure 5.18).

Wetlands were originally believed to cover 87 million hectares (215 million acres) in the United States. Today

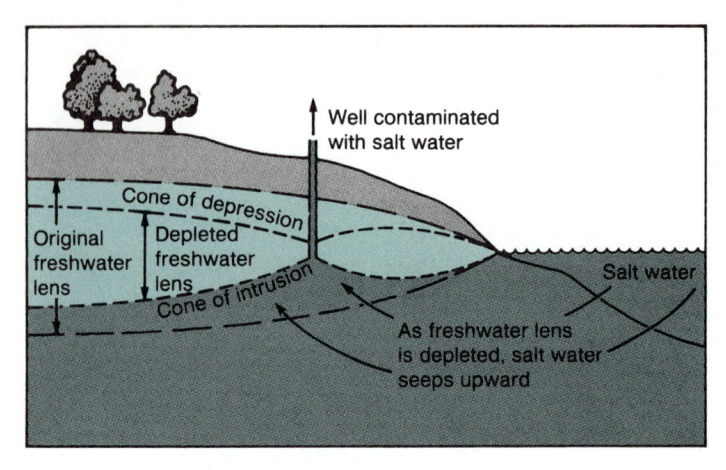

Figure 5.17 Land subsidence of more than half a foot (15 cm) per year is occurring in the San Joaquin Valley, California, because of drawdown of the San Joaquin aquifer for agricultural irrigation.

Physical and Biological Variables of the Natural Environment

Figure 5.18 Wetlands are an important resource. Survival of fish and waterfowl depend on these areas. Maintenance of good quality water, groundwater recharge, and flood control all depend on good wetlands management.
(*Photo:* Don Wooldridge, MDC)

we have less than 40 million hectares (100 million acres) and the decline continues at the rate of a 0.20 million hectares (0.5 million acres) per year. Wetlands are important as waterfowl breeding grounds, nurseries for many commercial and recreational fish species, and as purification systems for freshwater recharge of groundwater. For years they have been considered wastelands. They have been and still are being drained, filled, and converted to other uses. Government money has paid to drain wetlands for flood control, navigation, and agricultural development.

Most environments do not fit neatly into one niche. Wetland conservation really belongs with both water and soil conservation. Water is a part of every environment. Wetlands and soil conservation fit best together when we look at the wetlands as a soil layer that works as a water filter. Wetlands are natural sponges, collecting water and slowly releasing it to the subsurface groundwater zone. In the process, sediment and many pollutants are filtered out. Wildwood, Florida, (population 2,500) has treated its sewage in a 200-hectare (500-acre) cypress-gum swamp for more than 20 years. It seems to have worked very well for them but there is a limit to how much a wetland area can handle before it becomes polluted. Learning the limits and capabilities of our natural systems should be a continuing goal of conservation.

Summary

Many consider soil to be on the bottom of the biotic pyramid and one of the abiotic physical variables. But if you consider the soil's biota, it becomes a living entity. Soil does not fit neatly on the pyramid, but it is an important basic ingredient for terrestrial life on the earth's surface. A product of interactions between the lithosphere, atmosphere, hydrosphere, and biosphere, it should be placed just above the atmosphere, hydrosphere, and lithosphere and just below terrestrial species in land environments. An understanding of soil as a complex living entity on the biotic pyramid is a necessity for every aspect of conservation management programs in the biosphere.

Soil provides support for rooted vegetation. It stores the water necessary for growth, and releases nutrients to plant life in the proper amounts by complex biogeochemical weathering to maintain a balance with climate for plant associations. Soil acts as a filter for water moving down to the groundwater zone. Soil organisms break down organic material to maintain an equilibrium in the natural systems of the biosphere. These actions and processes reflect the law of fertility in nature. The complex living surface of the earth we call soil has many functions in the natural world. Conservation must strive to better understand the role of the soil layer in all of its management programs since this recognition is a prerequisite for good conservation. Figures 5.19 and 5.20, although created to be humorous, provide a message that suggests current or impending tragedy.

"They're not full of grain. They're full of topsoil. I'm gonna sell it for $1000 a bushel when nobody has any!"

Figure 5.19 Soil is a nonrenewable natural resource.
© Bruce Cochran—*National Wildlife Magazine*. Reprinted by permission.

"Hey Dad. What's erosion?"

Figure 5.20 Soil erosion is a very serious problem for the resource manager.
© Bruce Cochran—*National Wildlife Magazine*. Reprinted by permission.

Key Words and Phrases

Biogeochemical weathering
Calcification
Conservation tillage
Gleization
Horizons
Invertization
Irrigation
Laterization
Leaching
No-till cultivation
Podzolization
Soil
Vertisols
Wetlands
Zone of eluviation
Zone of illuviation

Questions and Discussion Topics

1. What aspects of Peter Steinhart's description of soil were most enlightening to you?
2. Do you think the material that supports a potted plant in your house qualifies as soil? What parts of the definition of soil are not included?
3. What is the soil-formation process of your geographic area? Could any of the other processes also occur in your locale?
4. Compare the Soils Map of North America (figure 5.9) with the climate map of North America (figure 3.9). The highest degree of correlation occurs between which soils and which climates?
5. What soil organisms (soil biota) would be seriously impacted by the use of pesticides?
6. Why is the soil erosion problem not as serious in the eastern part of the United States as it is in the west?
7. Why is irrigation in the Great Plains such a serious environmental problem?
8. How do wetland soils work as water filters?

References for Further Study

Brady, N. C. 1974. *The Nature and Properties of Soils.* 8th ed. New York: MacMillan. A good soils textbook.

Environmental Protection Agency. Oct., 1983. Saving Our Nation's Wetlands. *EPA Journal* 9: No. 2. EPA's wetlands concerns.

Environmental Protection Agency. July, Aug. 1984. Protecting Ground Water: The Hidden Resource. *EPA Journal* 10: No. 6. Good articles on wetlands and the problems of irrigation.

National Wildlife Federation. Feb./Mar. 1985. Soil, the Miracle We Take for Granted. *National Wildlife.* 23: No. 2. Good article on soil.

National Wildlife Federation. June/July. 1989. Opening the Door to the Unknown. *National Wildlife.* 17: No. 4. Good article on the deep soil.

Poirot, E. M. 1978. *Our Margin of Life.* Raytown, Mo.: Acres U.S.A. Pioneer work in promotion of soil protection and restoration.

Soil Conservation Service. 1981. *Soil Survey Manual.* Washington, D.C.: Superintendent of Documents. The soil scientist bible.

Chapter 6

Biosphere—Biogeography

Introduction
Energy Flow in the Biosphere
    Chemical Element Cycles of the Earth
        The Carbon Cycle
        The Oxygen Cycle
        The Nitrogen Cycle
        The Sedimentary Cycle
Biogeography of North America
    Natural Biotic Regions
    Climate as a Control in Biogeography
    Horizontal and Vertical Zonation of Vegetation
    Biologic Productivity
Ecoregions of North America
    Tropical
    Tropical Savanna
    Subtropical
    Hot Continental
    Warm Continental
    Subarctic
    Tundra
    Prairie
    Steppe
    Desert
    Marine
    Mediterranean
Summary

> *The outstanding scientific discovery of the twentieth century is not television, or radio, but rather the complexity of the land organism.*
> Aldo Leopold, 1949.

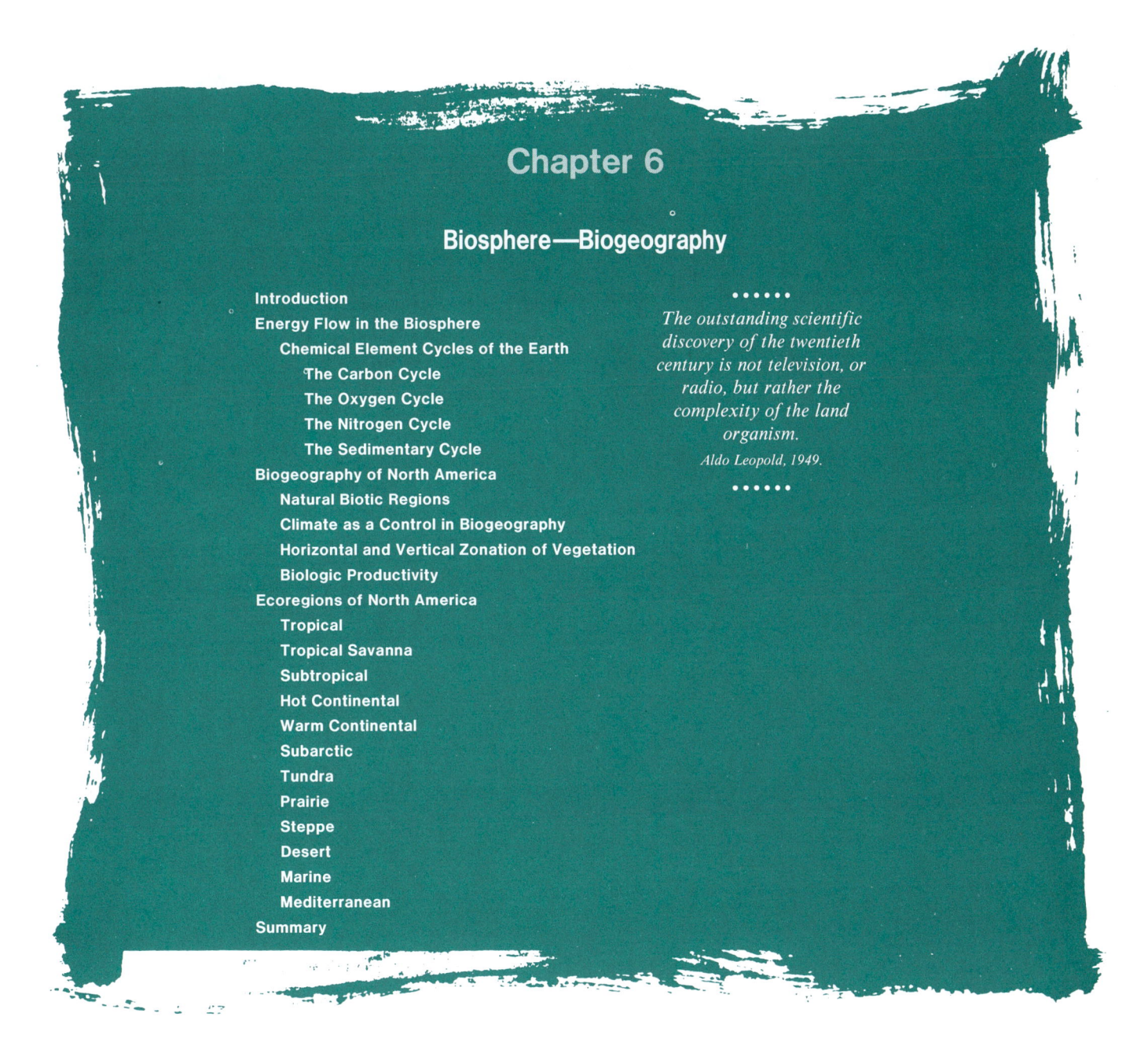

Introduction

The *biosphere* contains all of the living organisms of the earth. The sun is the earth's motor. It drives the atmospheric and hydrologic circulation systems and provides the energy for life in the biosphere. The one exception, the sunless environment in the ocean trenches that receives its energy from the internal heat of the earth, is probably not the only exception. Other sunless environments in the deep soil are under investigation at the present time. The bacteria of the deep soil could get their energy from the organic material above them or from the heat energy below. Many questions about the biosphere remain unanswered. Attention here will be directed toward the environments in the biosphere that use solar energy.

The sun provides the energy. The atmosphere provides the carbon dioxide (CO_2), nitrogen (N_2), and oxygen (O_2). The hydrosphere provides the water (H_2O). The soil, in most cases, provides the nutrients and physical support. The process of *photosynthesis* takes the abiotic ingredients and brings them to life in the biosphere. The *respiration* process maintains life and cycles necessary elements for both processes.

Photosynthesis = $H_2O + CO_2$ + solar energy → HCOH * + $O_2 \uparrow$
*{HCOH is the general chemical form for carbohydrates of the biosphere; carbohydrates are long chains of sugar molecules.}
Respiration = HCOH + O_2 → $CO_2 + H_2O$ + chemical energy

The long-term climatic and topographic condition for a region, along with the evolutionary history of the plant species, establishes a plant association and an animal community. The study of geographic distribution patterns of the plant and animal associations, and the processes that

Figure 6.1 A food chain in an ecosystem is a sequence of organisms that feed on or become the food for another organism. For example, producers (grass) feed primary consumers (rabbits), who feed secondary consumers (foxes) is a food chain. When food chains interconnect, a food web is formed.

From William P. Cunningham and Barbara Woodworth Saigo, *Environmental Science: A Global Concern.* Copyright © 1990 Wm. C. Brown Publishers, Dubuque, Iowa. All Rights Reserved. Reprinted by permission.

produce these patterns, is *biogeography.* The floral and faunal associations indicate the adaptability of resident plants and animals to the physical variables of the region. The collection of physical variables (air, water, topography, soil), along with the sun, provide the climate. **Climate** dictates the vegetation. The vegetation, along with water supply, dictates the consumers (animals, insects). The biogeographic associations then persist until the climate changes or humans alter the environment. Much of North America is a man-altered environment.

The **biosphere** reflects the collective response of the natural earth's processes to the formation of a living world. The natural environment and its living, natural resources can be managed if we understand how the system works. Explaining how the earth's natural system works is our goal. From an understanding of the workings of an ecosystem, conservation of natural resources through resource management is a possibility.

Energy Flow in the Biosphere

Energy transformation in any ecosystem occurs in a **food chain** or **food web** (figure 6.1). Organisms that store energy by engaging in the photosynthetic process form the base of the food chain or web and are called *producers.* Organisms that use the producers for food, called **herbivores,** occupy the next higher level in the food chain. These organisms are called *primary consumers.* The next higher level of the food chain is occupied by the *secondary consumers* that feed on the primary consumers and producers. Most of the secondary consumers are **omnivores** but some are **carnivores.** Dead or decaying organic matter from all levels of the food chain are fed upon by microorganisms and bacteria. These organisms are called *decomposers.* The difference between a food chain and a food web is that the path of energy transfer in a food web is not as direct and as easy to trace as in the food chain. The web, as the name implies, branches in many directions.

The *food chain* is an energy flow system. It traces the path of solar energy, which is initially stored in the producers as chemical energy, through the ecosystem. At each level of the chain some of the initial energy is stored, some is used, some is lost, and some is transferred to the next higher level. **Respiration** is the process organisms use to burn up some of their food and continue operating. The energy expelled on respiration cannot be stored for use by other organisms higher up the food chain. As each transformation of energy takes place, energy is lost as waste

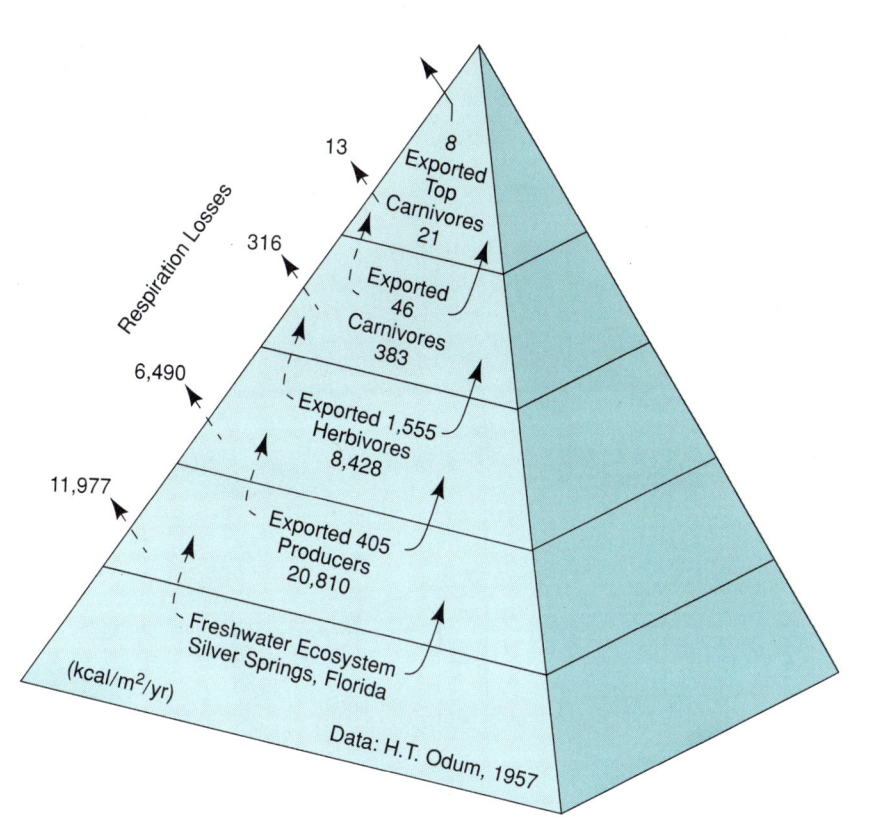

Figure 6.2 Energy lost and transferred through a freshwater food chain in Silver Springs, Florida.
Source: Data from H. T. Odum, "Trophic Structure and Productivity of Silver Springs, Florida" in *Ecology Monographs*, Vol. 27, 1957.

Table 6.1
Laws of Thermodynamics

First Law of Thermodynamics (Law of Conservation of Energy)
In any transformation between heat and other forms of energy, any increase in heat energy is accompanied by an equal decrease in some other form of energy and vice versa.

Second Law of Thermodynamics
There is no natural process the only result of which is to cool a heat reservoir and do external work—i.e., heat can be made to go from a body at lower temperature to one at higher temperature only if external work is done.

Table 6.2
Atomic Composition of Earth's Living Matter Biosphere

	Element	Percent
Basic	Hydrogen (H)	49.8
Carbohydrates	Carbon (C)	24.9
	Oxygen (O)	<u>24.9</u>
		99.6
Other		
Nutrients	Nitrogen (N)	0.272
	Calcium (Ca)	0.073
	Potassium (K)	0.046
	Silicon (Si)	0.033
	Magnesium (Mg)	0.031
	Phosphorus (P)	0.030
	Sulfur (S)	0.017
	Aluminum (Al)	0.016
	Chlorine (Cl)	0.011
	Sodium (Na)	0.006
	Iron (Fe)	0.005
	Manganese (Mn)	0.003

heat. Because of the losses of energy, both the number of organisms and the amount of biomass decrease considerably up the food chain (figure 6.2).

The **first and second laws of thermodynamics** govern the flow of energy in ecosystems (Table 6.1). The first law, simply stated, says that energy cannot be created or destroyed but can be transformed. The second law states that in any transformation of energy, some of the energy is converted to thermal energy (heat) and is lost.

The food chains of the biosphere represent the living parts of the biotic pyramid introduced in chapter 1. The biotic pyramid (figure 1.13) places the abiotic variables at the bottom of the food chain and humans at the top. The laws of the biosphere exercise control over food chains in the biosphere. Here our task is to examine the carbon, oxygen, nitrogen, and sedimentary cycles. These cycles cause the flow of chemical elements from atmosphere, to hydrosphere, to lithosphere, to biosphere, and tie together the workings of the natural world.

Chemical Element Cycles of the Earth

The chemical composition of the biosphere is given in Table 6.2. Most of the biosphere is carbon and water. The hydrologic cycle, discussed earlier, is an extremely important cycle to the food chain because it serves as the pathway to bring nutrients into the biosphere. Soluble chemical elements and compounds go into solution in the soil water zone and are taken up, along with water, by plant roots. Rooted vegetation acts as a nutrient pump to cycle most of the chemical elements listed as other nutrients in Table 6.2.

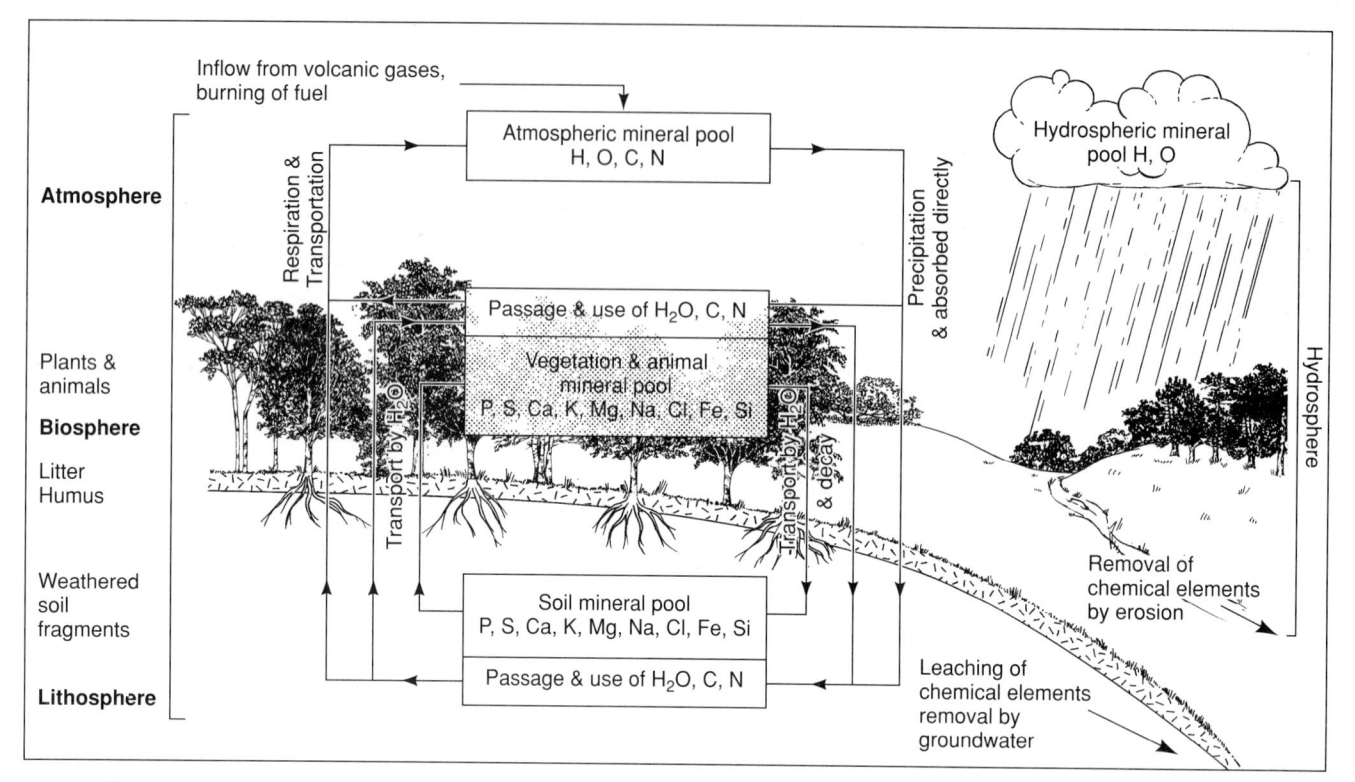

Figure 6.3 Biogeochemical cycles are pathways for chemical elements through the spheres at or near the earth's surface. The sun provides the energy to drive the cycles. Evaporation, transpiration, photosynthesis respiration, condensation, oxidation, nitrification, fermentation, precipitation, and decomposition are the processes that alter the chemical state of an element and set it up for movement in a cycle. Many elements follow the flow of water in the hydrologic cycle.
Source: From D. Watts, *Principles of Biogeography,* Modified from A. I. Perel'man, *Geochemistry of Epigenesis.*

A general flow diagram to illustrate the path of carbon, oxygen, hydrogen, and other chemical elements from abiotic to biotic is given in Figure 6.3. The processes of photosynthesis, respiration, and decomposition create a continuous cycle for carbon, oxygen, and hydrogen. If the additions of these major elements and other trace elements to the system by rock weathering equals the amount stored in the plant tissues of the biosphere, the ecosystem is in equilibrium with its physical environment. The cycle begins in the spring of the year with the intake of water and nutrients from the soil water zone. As the plants resume activity after winter dormancy, water travels through the living tissue and green leaves are produced. Sunlight provides energy for photosynthesis, and carbon dioxide (CO_2) is provided by the atmosphere. The process produces hydrocarbons for the plant and gives off oxygen (O_2) to the atmosphere. Respiration alternates with photosynthesis to create short atmospheric and hydrologic cycles of carbon dioxide (CO_2), water (H_2O), and oxygen (O_2). The transfer of oxygen (O_2) from atmosphere to biosphere by the respiration process and the return of O_2 to the atmosphere by photosynthesis helps maintain the oxygen supply of the atmosphere (21%). The short cycle of carbon dioxide (CO_2) by the same but reverse processes is an important part of the carbon cycle. Carbon, oxygen, water, and its dissolved nutrients all cycle through the detrital cycle. The *detrital cycle* is the decomposition cycle where microorganisms convert organic matter to humus and gases. Decomposers break down the dead organic material, completing the fertility cycle. This is a closed system, that is, all of the elements stay in the system and cycle. None of the matter is lost but some is stored.

The Carbon Cycle

Most life is composed of carbon compounds. The great storehouses of carbon are marine sediments called **limestone** ($CaCO_3$) or **dolostone** $(Ca, Mg)CO_3$. Carbon from the weathering of these rocks is released very slowly to the atmosphere and is not readily available for cycling. The atmospheric composition of carbon dioxide is only about 0.033% but represents the major available supply of carbon for the vegetative processes of the biosphere.

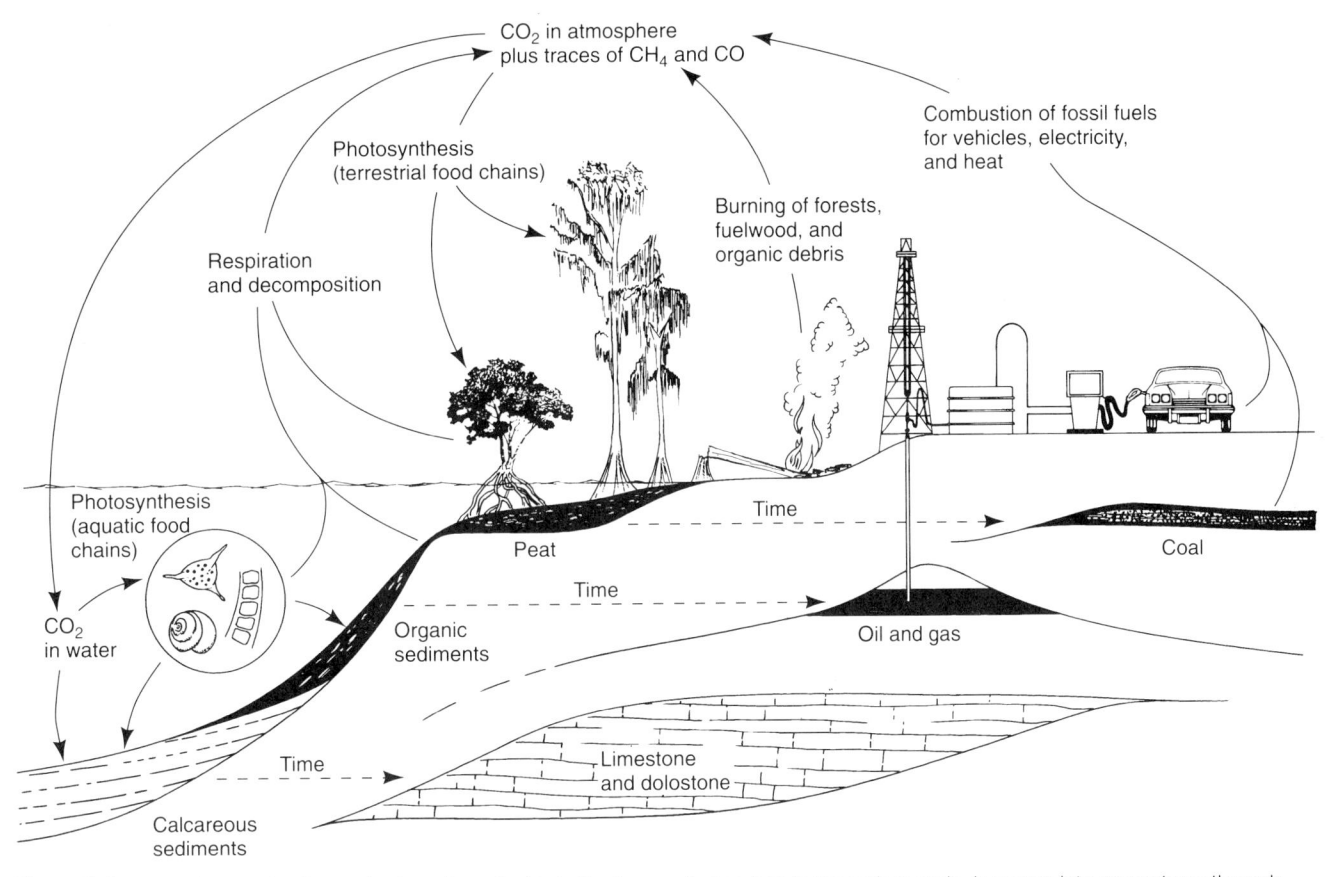

Figure 6.4 The carbon cycle. Atmospheric carbon dioxide is the "source" of carbon in the carbon cycle. It passes into ecosystems through photosynthesis and is captured in the bodies and products of living organisms. It is released into the atmosphere mainly by respiration and combustion. Carbon may be locked up for long periods in both organic and inorganic geological formations.
From William P. Cunningham and Barbara Woodworth Saigo, *Environmental Science: A Global Concern.* Copyright © 1990 Wm. C. Brown Publishers, Dubuque, Iowa. All Rights Reserved. Reprinted by permission.

In the atmosphere, carbon moves as a free gas as the compound carbon dioxide (CO_2) (figure 6.4). It can also move as a dissolved gas in both fresh and salt water. In the soil layer, carbon resides as carbohydrate molecules of organic matter. The lithosphere stores carbon as calcium carbonate, coal, and petroleum. New carbon is added to the atmospheric supply each year by rock weathering, volcanism, and the burning of fossil fuels. The large additions of carbon as carbon monoxide (CO) and carbon dioxide (CO_2) from human activities has the potential of upsetting the balance of the **carbon cycle** (The Greenhouse Effect; chapter 3).

About 2% of the active carbon dioxide (CO_2) is contained in the atmosphere. It supplies the biosphere with the CO_2 needed for photosynthesis and the biosphere returns much of it to the atmosphere by respiration. Most of the earth's surface is water, so a major portion of the photosynthesis-respiration cycle of carbon is performed by the **phytoplankton** of the oceans. They are the primary producers of the marine food chain. Phytoplankton have calcium carbonate ($CaCO_3$) skeletal structures and when these organisms die they either settle to the floor of the ocean and become part of a new rock layer of the lithosphere or they dissolve in the ocean water to be recycled.

The Oxygen Cycle

Oxygen is cycled as O_2, H_2O, and CO_2. Because the cycling of oxygen as water and carbon dioxide has already been discussed, the cycling of gaseous oxygen (O_2) demands consideration (figure 6.5). Free oxygen represents 21% of the total atmospheric composition of gases by volume. Photosynthesis releases O_2 to the atmosphere and, as with the carbon cycle, phytoplankton plays the major role. New oxygen that had been stored in the rocks of the lithosphere is added each year by volcanism. Some oxygen is taken out of circulation by mineral oxidation. Use of

Biosphere—Biogeography

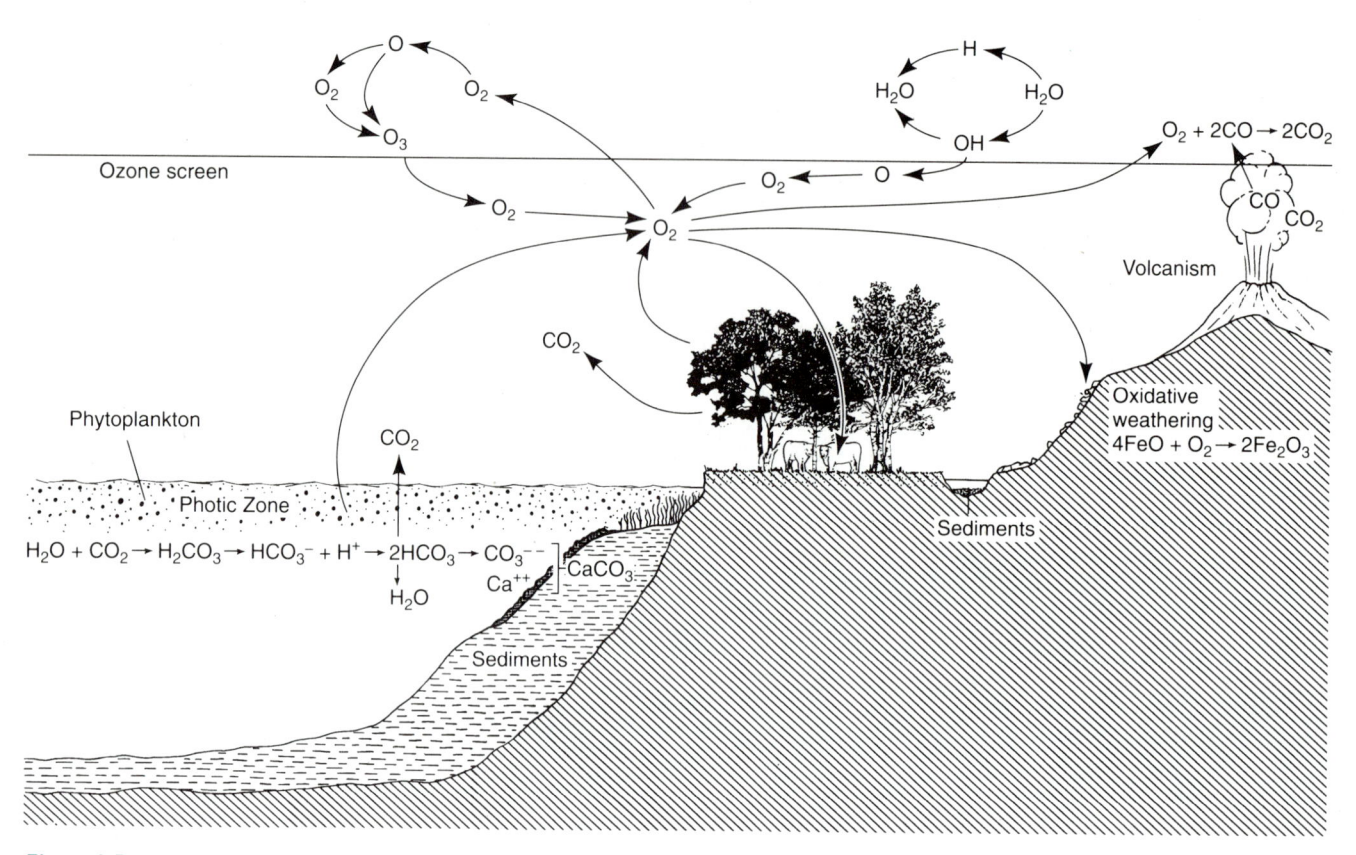

Figure 6.5 The oxygen cycle. The great storehouse of oxygen is the atmosphere, but the cycle is complicated because oxygen appears in so many chemical forms and combinations, primarily as molecular oxygen (O_2), in water, and other organic and inorganic compounds.
From A. N. Strahler and A. H. Strahler, *Modern Physical Geography*. Copyright © John Wiley & Sons, Inc., New York, N.Y. Reprinted by permission of John Wiley & Sons, Inc.

oxygen (O_2) for respiration of both plants and animals represents the greatest use of atmospheric oxygen (O_2). Human use of oxygen has increased steadily and takes many forms. The burning of fossil fuels uses oxygen. Any activity that reduces vegetative cover, such as clearing for agriculture, urban development, or lumbering, decreases photosynthesis and reduces the amount of oxygen being supplied to the atmosphere. However, the storehouse of atmospheric oxygen is so large that human activities seem to have had little effect on the supply.

The Nitrogen Cycle

The big storehouse for nitrogen (N_2) in the nitrogen cycle is the atmosphere (figure 6.6). Seventy-eight percent of the volume of the atmosphere is nitrogen. The gaseous form of nitrogen (N_2) cannot be assimilated directly by either plants or animals. Soil microorganisms and some blue-green algae are the only organisms known to be able to fix, or change, atmospheric nitrogen into an available form for plant use. The soil organisms that **fix nitrogen** can be free-living soil bacteria or bacteria of the genus Rhizobium. The **Rhizobium bacteria** infect the roots of plants and act symbiotically with the plant to fix nitrogen. Bacteria, acting in nodules on the host plant roots, supply the nitrogen to the plant through nitrogen fixation. The plant, in turn, supplies nutrients and organic compounds to the bacteria. This symbiotic relationship is common in members of the legume family. Agricultural legumes such as clover, alfalfa, soybeans, and cowpeas are used as rotational crops to fix nitrogen in the soil and improve fertility.

Denitrification is a process whereby usable nitrogen is converted back to N_2 and released to the atmosphere. Bacteria in the soil biota complete the organic phase of the nitrogen cycle by the denitrification process.

Human activities have created a large imbalance in the nitrogen cycle. Nitrogen fixation far exceeds denitrification and the excess nitrogen is accumulating in the

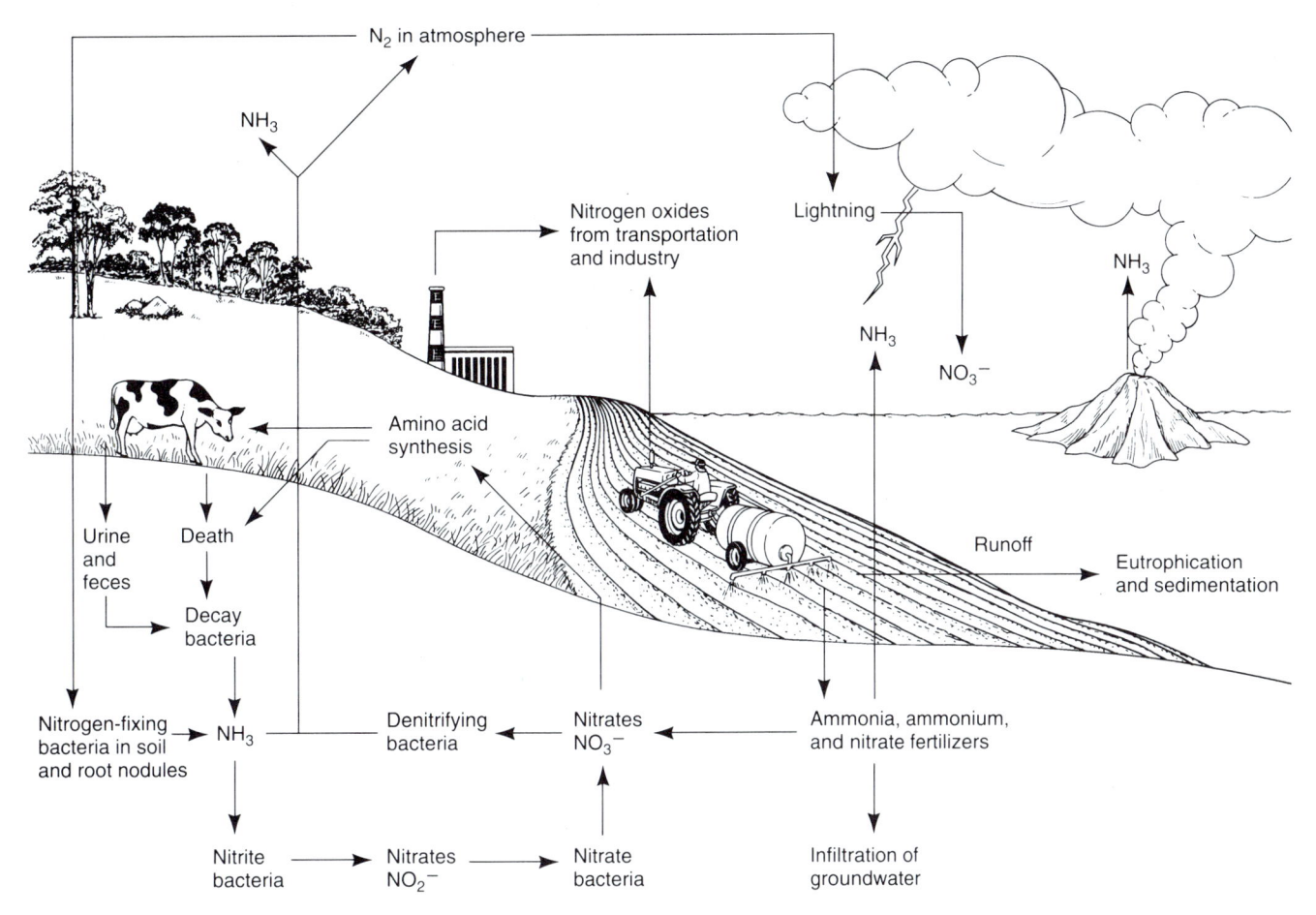

Figure 6.6 The nitrogen cycle. Nitrogen is incorporated into ecosystems when plants and bacteria use it to build their own amino acids and is released from ecosystems by bacterial decomposition. Natural and human interactions with the nitrogen cycle are depicted here also.
From William P. Cunningham and Barbara Woodworth Saigo, *Environmental Science: A Global Concern.* Copyright © 1990 Wm. C. Brown Publishers, Dubuque, Iowa. All Rights Reserved. Reprinted by permission.

biosphere. The manufacture of nitrogen fertilizer and the oxidation of nitrogen in the burning of fossil fuels are the major contributors of additions to the cycle. Nitrous oxide is a major contributor to the acid rain problem (chapter 4). The excess nitrogen in the soil layer is washed into streams, lakes, and rivers and eventually reaches the ocean. Water pollution problems are accelerating because the excess nitrogen enhances algae growth at the expense of more desirable aquatic species. Small pond and lake systems can become **eutrophicated** (degraded; disorganized) rapidly because of the additions of agricultural nitrogen.

The Sedimentary Cycle

The *sedimentary* (sulfur) *cycle* represents generally how nongaseous nutrients move through the earth's spheres (figure 6.7). The storehouse for the **macronutrients** calcium (Ca), iron (Fe), magnesium (Mg), potassium (K), sodium (Na), and phosphorus (P) is the soil. Seawater is the storehouse for sulfur (S) and chlorine (Cl). These soluble and colloidal-sized particles are held in the soil and taken up, with soil water, by plants through their root system. The macronutrients in the sedimentary cycle have almost no atmospheric phase. They can be blown into the air as dust and become **condensation nuclei** in raindrops, but, for the most part, they remain in the soil or water in the active phase of the cycle. They are deposited as sediment by geomorphic processes and remain in storage for release later on a geologic time scale.

Biogeography of North America

Biogeographic communities of North America can be separated into two categories, natural climax communities and human-altered communities. The *natural climax communities* are those associations of plants and animals that occupy a region as a response to the natural abiotic variables and the earth-sun relationship for that area

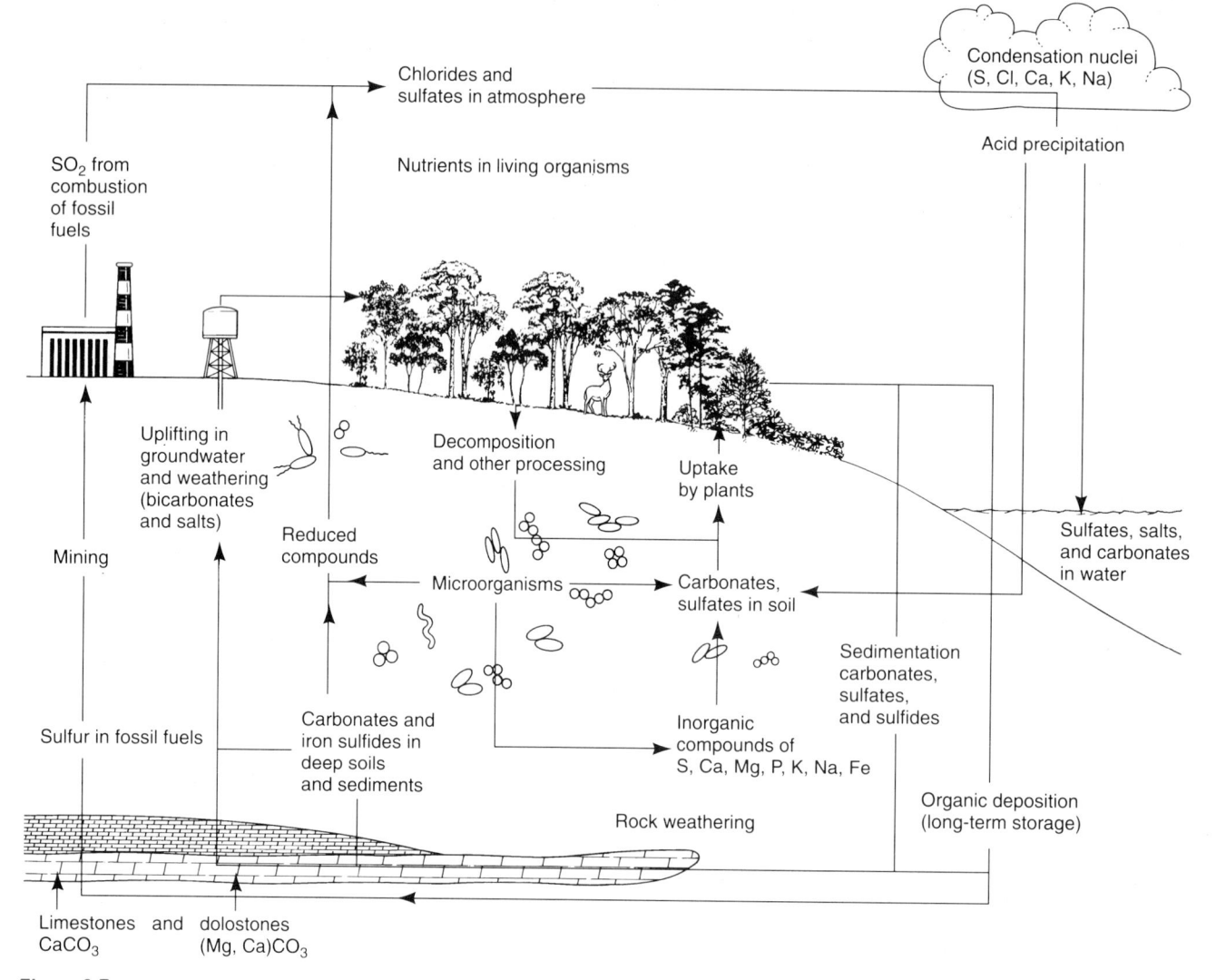

Figure 6.7 The sedimentary (sulfur) cycle. Macronutrients calcium, iron, sulfur, magnesium, potassium, sodium, and phosphorus are soluble and cycle through the soil into the biosphere and back to the soil.

without interruptions in the evolutionary process by humans and their machines. *Human-altered environments* are those regions that have had the natural climax communities removed by human activities. Most human-altered communities are agricultural communities or disturbed environments resulting from urban development, lumbering, mining, or dam building. A map of North America (figure 6.8) shows the natural vegetative regions that are the natural climax associations. Many of the areas we call natural climax areas today are the result of regrowth following lumbering and/or human-induced fires at the turn of the century or before. Very little of North America can truly be called pristine (figure 6.9).

Natural Biotic Regions

The natural biotic regions of the coterminous United States were separated into 116 different potential natural vegetation associations by Küchler. His definition of *po-*

tential natural vegetation is the vegetation that would exist today if humans were removed from the scene and the resulting plant successions were telescoped into a single moment in the future without any climate change. The effects of earlier human activities, such as the introduction of new species from the European continent, are permitted to stand. This differs from *real vegetation,* defined as the vegetation present at the time of observation (wheat fields, fescue pastures, etc.). The natural vegetation of North America is difficult to define because it has changed drastically in the last 25,000 years. Ice sheets have melted and the climates have changed. Along with these changes in the physical world, the plant and animal communities have changed also. As was pointed out earlier, there is nothing very natural or normal about nature. For now, the **natural vegetation** and **animal communities** of North America will be defined as the plant and animal complexes that came into existence in the Holocene Epoch. They are the naturally evolving plant and animal associ-

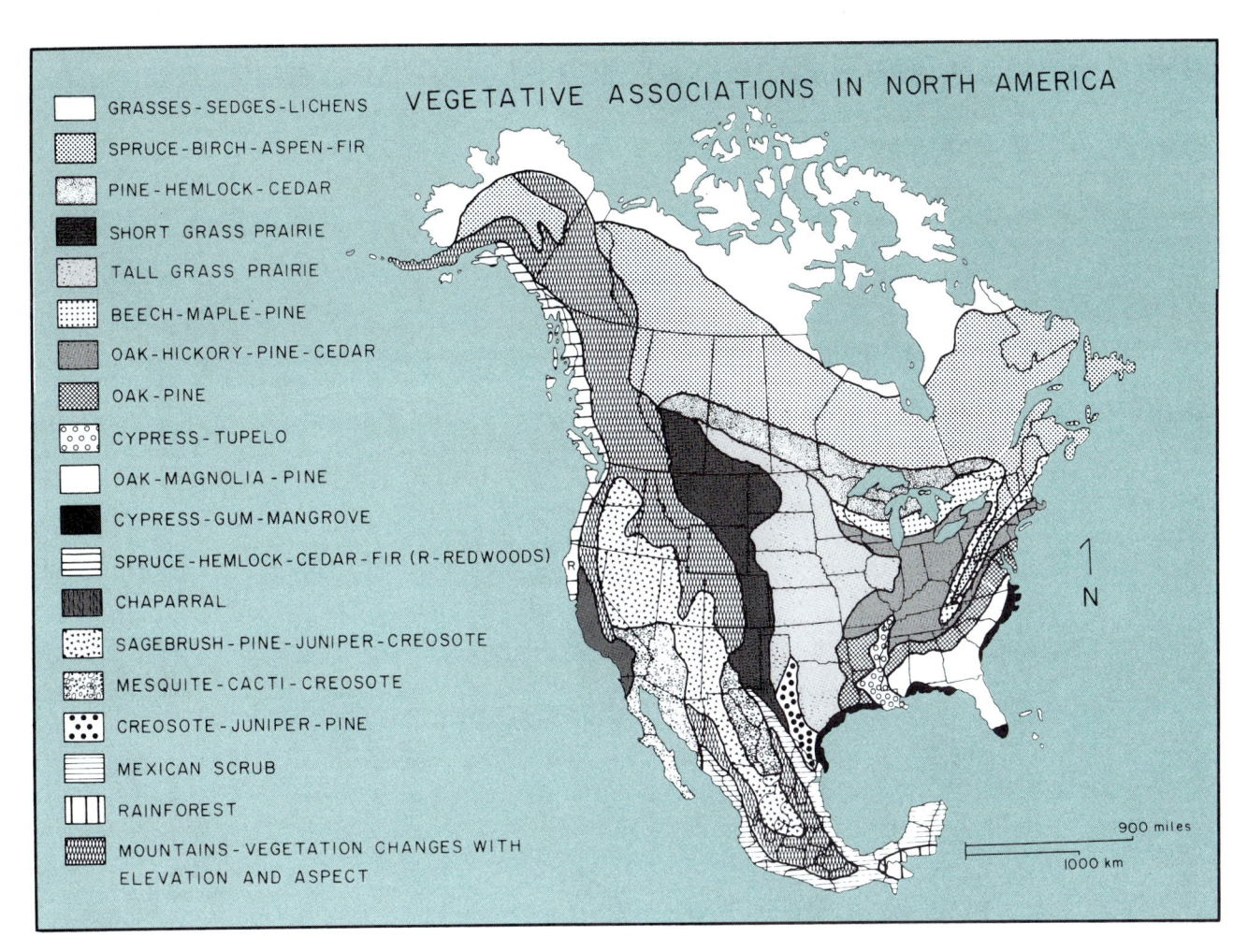

Figure 6.8 Vegetative associations in North America.
Source: Data from Robert G. Bailey, *Ecoregions of the United States*, May 1978.
(*Cartographer:* Douglas Hemsath)

ations of the interglacial period that began with the disappearance of the Wisconsinan ice sheet from the North American continent. The plant and animal species that have acclimatized and managed to survive and spread on their own after being helped across the ocean by man are considered part of the natural environment.

Climate as a Control in Biogeography

Seasonal and latitudinal patterns of solar energy that control temperature, precipitation, and wind, dictate the distribution of plant and animal life on the earth's surface to a large degree. There are dry areas in wet climatic regions and wet places in dry climatic areas. An overhanging cliff can produce a very dry niche in a wet tropical environment. A spring can bubble up in a desert and produce an oasis. Availability of water is the most important factor in determining the distribution of plants and animals. Evolution has caused plants and animals to become adapted to excesses or deficiencies in water availability. Figure 6.10 gives the tolerance ranges of some trees, shrubs, and grasses to water availability in the United States.

Figure 6.9 Old-age forests such as this pristine stand of sequoias in the Sequoia National Forest are dwindling at an alarming rate.
(*Photo:* Roy Murphy, USFS)

Biosphere—Biogeography

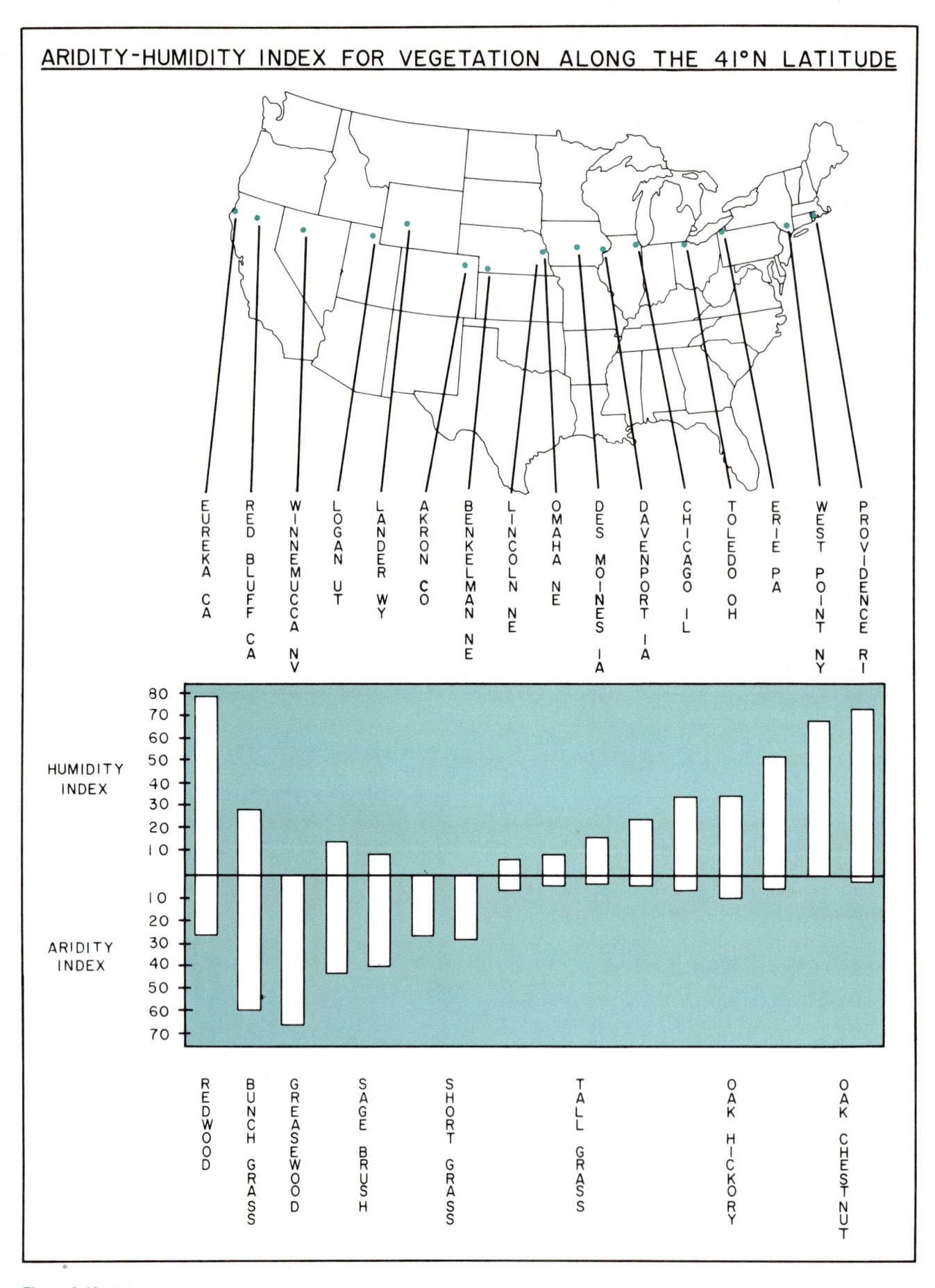

Figure 6.10 Tolerance ranges of selected trees, shrubs, and grasses to water surpluses and deficit supplies along the 41°N. latitude.
Source: Data from Thornthwaite and Mather, *Publications in Climatology*, Vol. 8, No. 1, 1955.
(*Cartographer:* Douglas Hemsath)

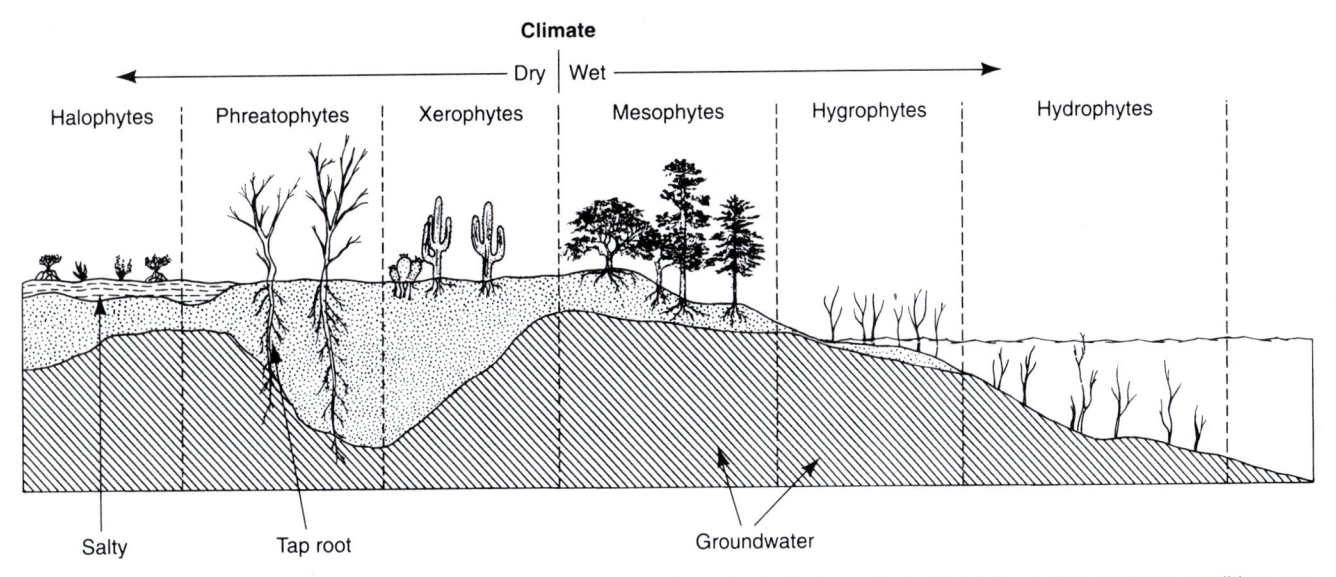

Figure 6.11 Plant classification based on their moisture environment. *Tropophytes* that are adapted to highly variable moisture conditions are not illustrated.
From Marsh, *Earthscape: A Physical Geography.* Copyright © 1987 John Wiley & Sons, Inc., New York, NY. Reprinted by permission of John Wiley & Sons, Inc.

Scientists classify some plants according to their water needs. Figure 6.11 illustrates the water needs of groups of plants. *Xerophytes* are plants that grow in dry habitats. If the soil is salty, the plants are *halophytes*. *Hygrophytes* grow in water-saturated soil and *hydrophytes* grow in water. *Mesophytes* are intermediate-wetness plants that require a somewhat uniform soil moisture availability. Plants with a deep taproot that can draw water from the deep water zone are *phreatophytes*. Plants that have adapted to highly variable fluctuations in seasonal moisture (frozen soil, water, long dry season) are called *tropophytes*.

Air and soil temperature are also important factors in biogeography because they influence the rates of physiological activity (table 6.3). Each plant has temperature limits and an optimum yearly temperature for growth, development, and reproduction. The colder the climate, the fewer the species capable of surviving. Cold-blooded animals, whose body temperatures mirror their environment, become inactive in cold weather and **hibernate** to conserve energy. Warm-blooded animals have adaptations for survival in the cold season. **Feathers, hair, winter fat,** and other biologic attributes minimize heat loss and protect the animal during winter.

Light availability is also an important factor in biologic communities. Most vegetative associations are layered. The uppermost layer, called the *canopy*, receives ten times the solar radiation as the understory in a temperate deciduous forest in summer after full leafing (figure 6.12). The utilization of incoming solar energy in a temperate forest is very inefficient. Only about one to two percent of the solar energy received by the vegetation is utilized for photosynthesis (figure 6.13). Light helps to structure the forest community into layers (figure 6.14). The canopy receives maximum solar radiation and intercepts precipitation. The *understory*, also a tree layer, receives maximum sunlight before the canopy is in full leaf in a

Table 6.3
Critical Biological Temperatures

Air Temperature		Effect of Critical Temperatures
C°	F°	
−25	−13	Frost damages many cold resistant plants
−18	0	
−10	18	
0	32	Limit of survival for many plant species
10	50	Lower limit of significant metabolic activity in many plants
20	68	
25	77	
30	86	Optimum temperature for maximum photosynthesis and respiration
35	95	
40	104	Too hot for most plants

Figure 6.12 The top of the canopy in a temperate deciduous forest receives ten times more solar energy than the understory trees after full leafing. Vegetation and animal life are stratified by the amount of solar energy penetration.

Reprinted with permission of Macmillan Publishing Company from *Communities and Ecosystems* by Robert H. Whittaker. Copyright © 1975 by Robert H. Whittaker.

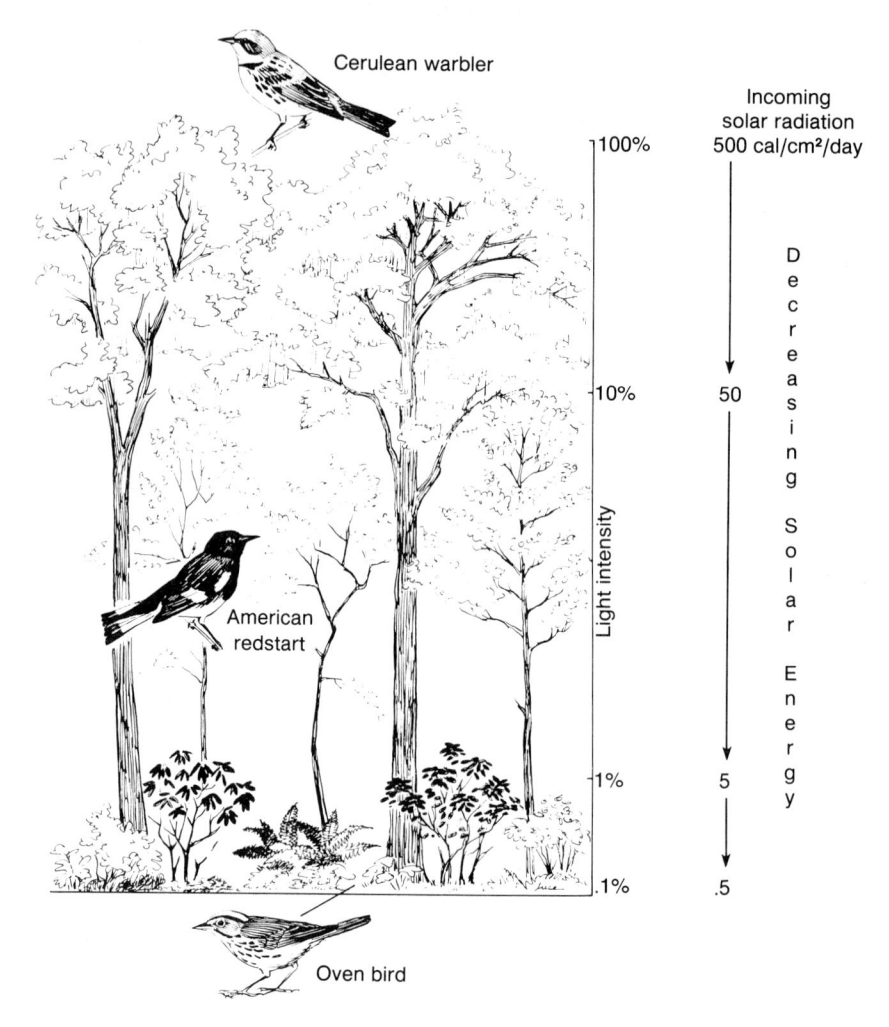

deciduous forest, and little or no direct sunlight thereafter. The shrub layer and ground cover also receive reduced amounts of sunlight in a deciduous forest and very little or no direct sunlight in a tropical (evergreen) or coniferous forest. *Shrubs* are defined as woody plants with several stems branching near the ground. *Trees* are woody plants with a single trunk. The *ground cover* includes herbs and mosses. *Herbs* have no woody stems and include forbs (broad-leaved plants) and grasses.

Plants that do not fit into the four-layered structure of the forest above ground level include the epiphytes and thallophytes. The *epiphytes* are plants that use other plants for support and live above the ground. They could occupy any or all of the layers above the ground. Spanish moss is a common example of an **air plant** (epiphyte) in the southeastern United States. The *thallophytes,* including bacteria, algae, molds, and fungi, all lack true roots, stems, and leaves. **Lichens,** which are a partnership of **algae** and **fungi,** are *bryoids,* a common ground cover of the arctic-alpine region. The **algae** provides the food and color for the lichen and the **fungi** provides the support and water. They remain alive through the winter season. **Thallophytes** are common organisms of the sunless soil biota zone.

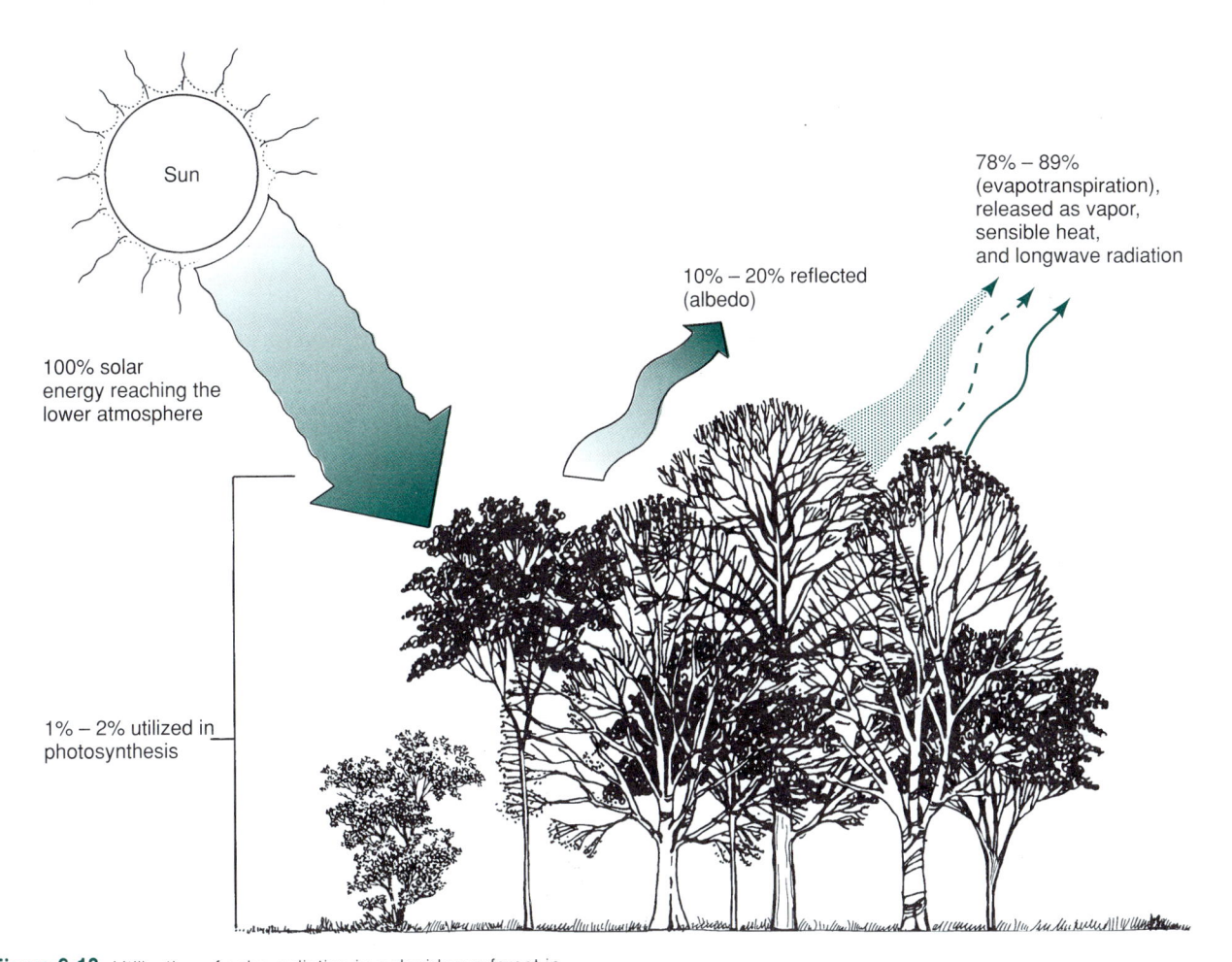

Figure 6.13 Utilization of solar radiation in a deciduous forest in summer.
From Marsh, *Earthscape: A Physical Geography*. Copyright © 1987 John Wiley & Sons, Inc., New York, NY. Reprinted by permission of John Wiley & Sons, Inc.

Horizontal and Vertical Zonation of Vegetation

Latitude, elevation, and **aspect** are important factors in determining the vegetative association of a region. Plant associations are distributed horizontally north and south from the equator to the poles. Plants are also distributed according to elevation and aspect. Climate changes from equator to pole and also from sea level to the top of a mountain. Figure 6.15 illustrates the horizontal zonation of life zones in North America. The *tropical life zone* is defined as the zone warm enough for coral to grow in the aquatic saltwater environments. North of the tropical zone are the **Lower Austral, Upper Austral, Transition, Canadian, Hudsonian,** and **Arctic** zones. A transect from the Gulf of Mexico to the Hudson Bay illustrates the changes in vegetative composition through these life zones (figure 6.16). Each life zone has its dominant vegetative species and these general categories do not include the unusual. Neither do they take into consideration the changes in vegetation that would occur if the transect crossed the Smoky, Appalachian, or Adirondack Mountains. All of these ranges have elevations high enough to reach the spruce-fir vegetative zone.

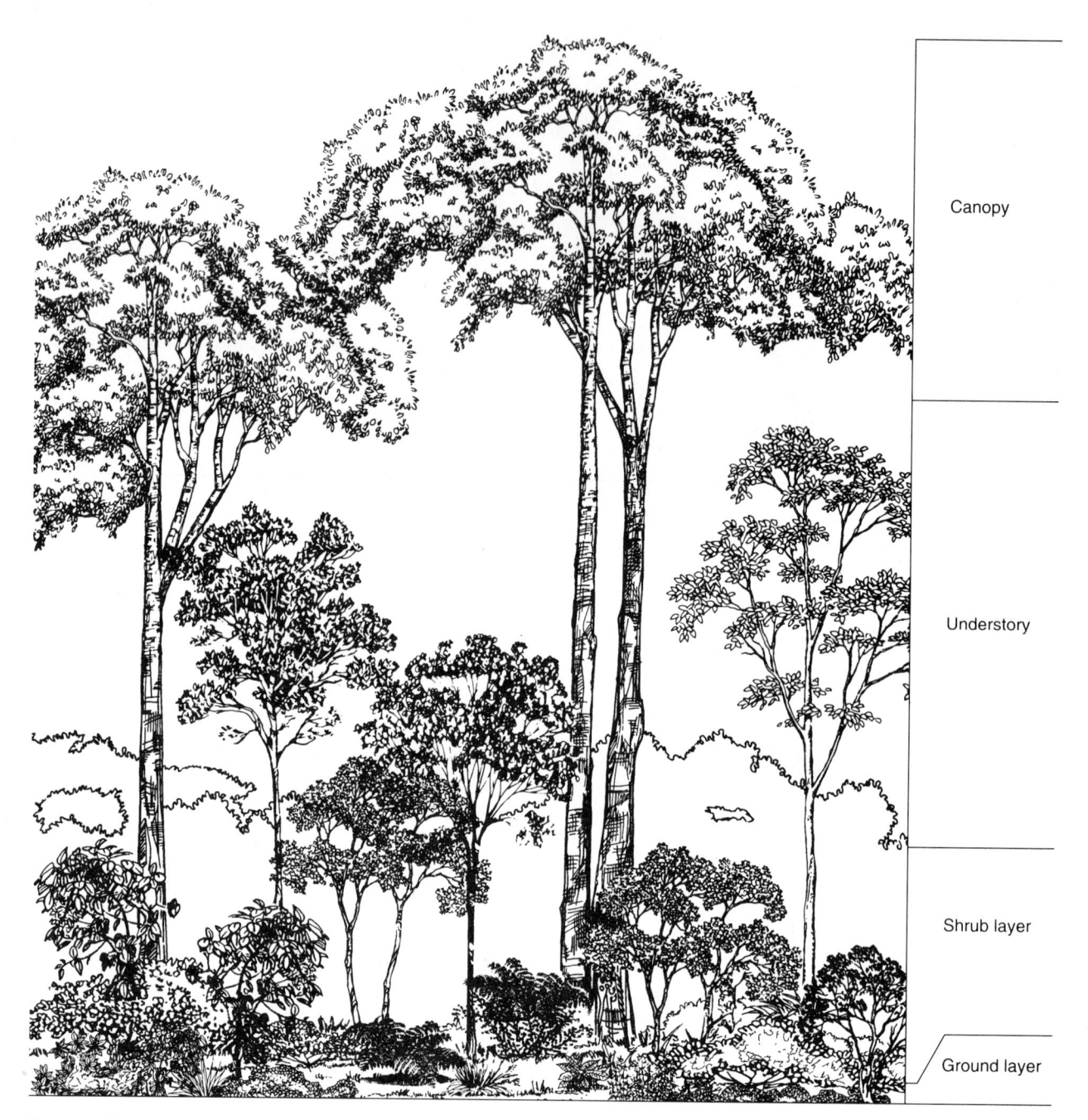

Figure 6.14 The four layers in a forest community are stratified by light intensities and create different habitats for plants and animals in an Eastern deciduous forest.

124 Physical and Biological Variables of the Natural Environment

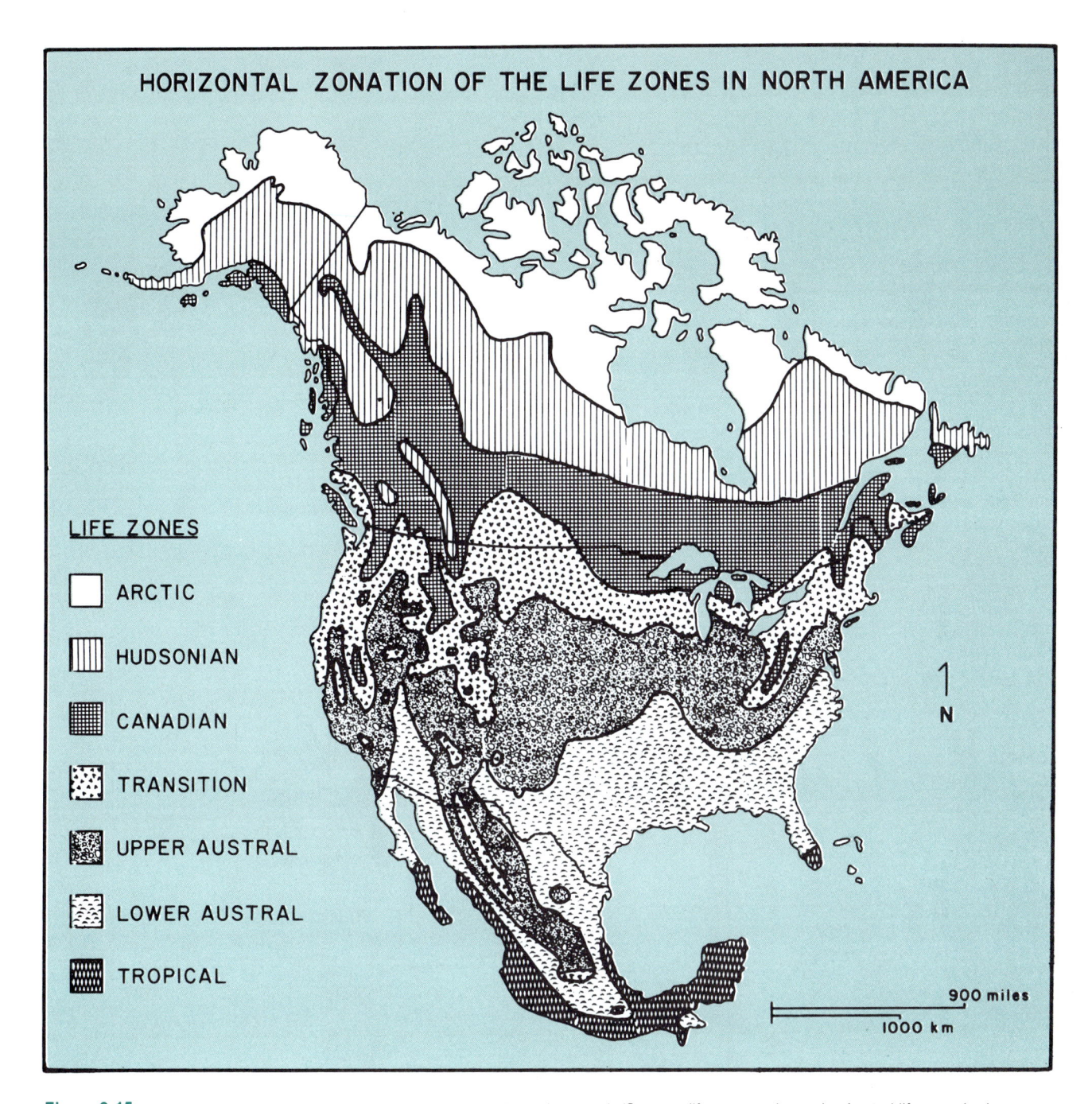

Figure 6.15 Horizontal zonation of life zones in North America (latitude zones). (Sonoran life zone replaces the Austral life zone in dry climates.)

From *Natural Resources of the United States and Canada*. By Charles B. Hunt. Copyright © 1967, 1972 by W. H. Freeman and Company. Reprinted by permission. (*Cartographer:* Douglas Hemsath)

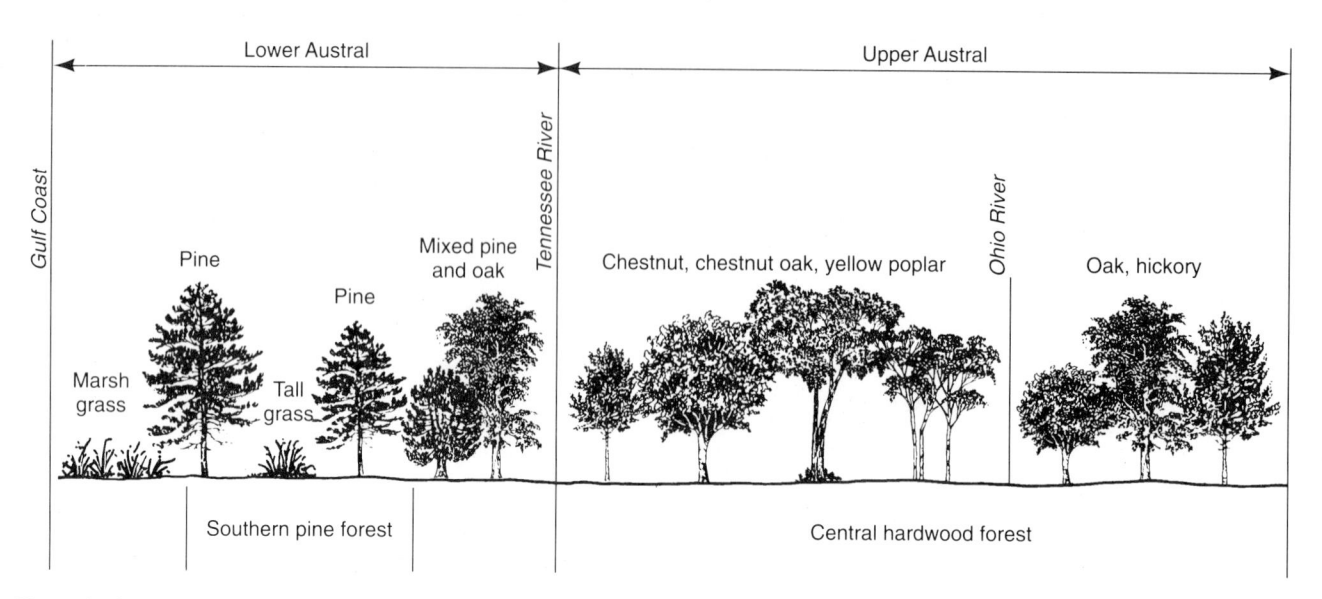

Figure 6.16 Transect from the Gulf of Mexico to Hudson Bay showing the principal vegetative composition of each life zone.
From *Natural Resources of the United States and Canada*. By Charles B. Hunt. Copyright © 1967, 1972 by W. H. Freeman and Company. Reprinted by permission.

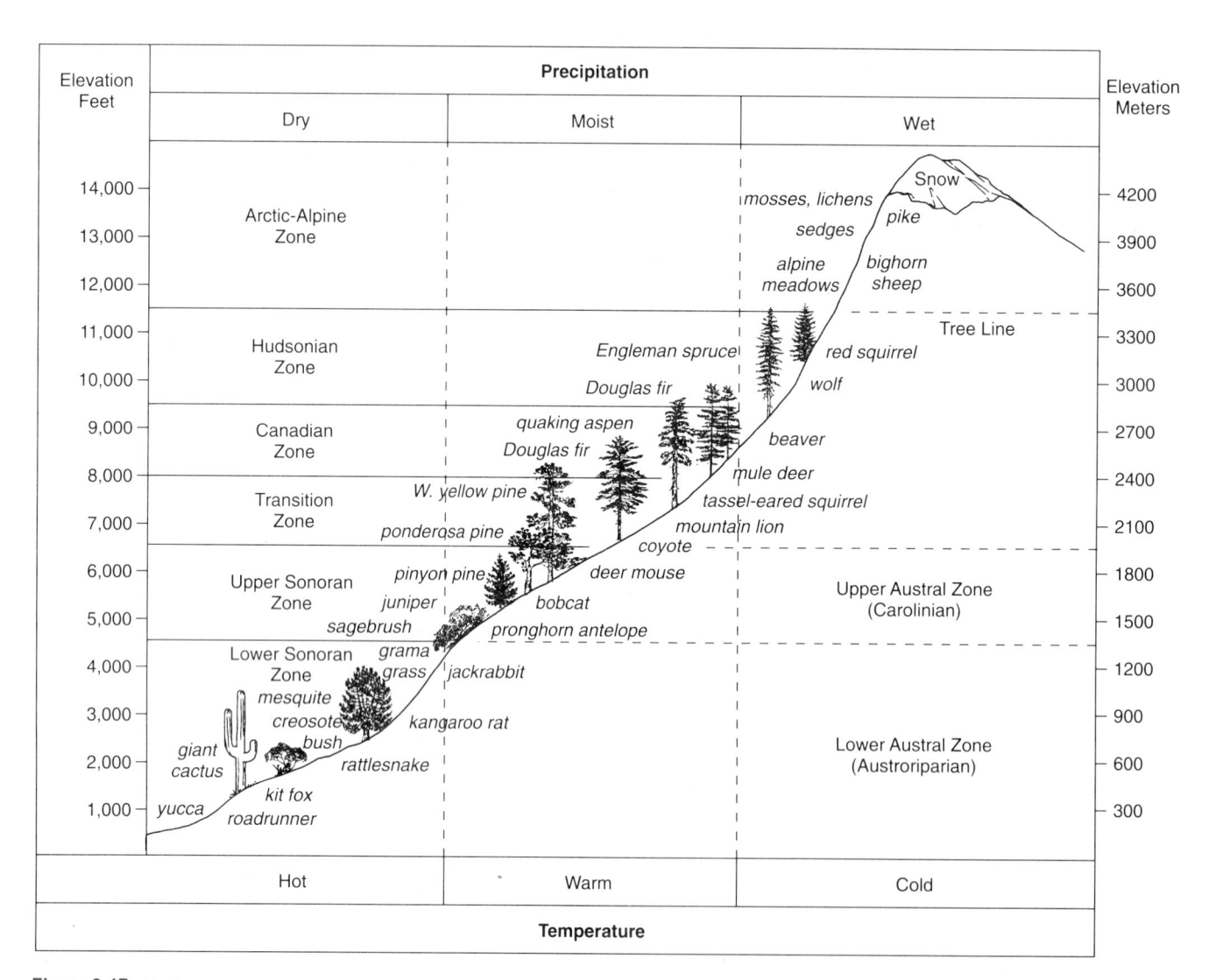

Figure 6.17 Vertical zonation of life zones in the southwestern United States (elevation zones).
Illustration from, *Mammals of the Southwest Mountains and Mesas*, by George Olin. Courtesy Southwest Parks and Monuments Association, Tucson, AZ.

[Figure 6.16 shows horizontal zonation from Transition through Canadian, Hudsonian, to Arctic zones, with Northern hardwood forest (Birch, beech, maple, hemlock), Straits of Mackinac, Northern pine forest (Pine), Spruce-fir forest (Spruce, fir), Taiga (Spruce, lichens), Hudson Bay, and Tundra (Lichens).]

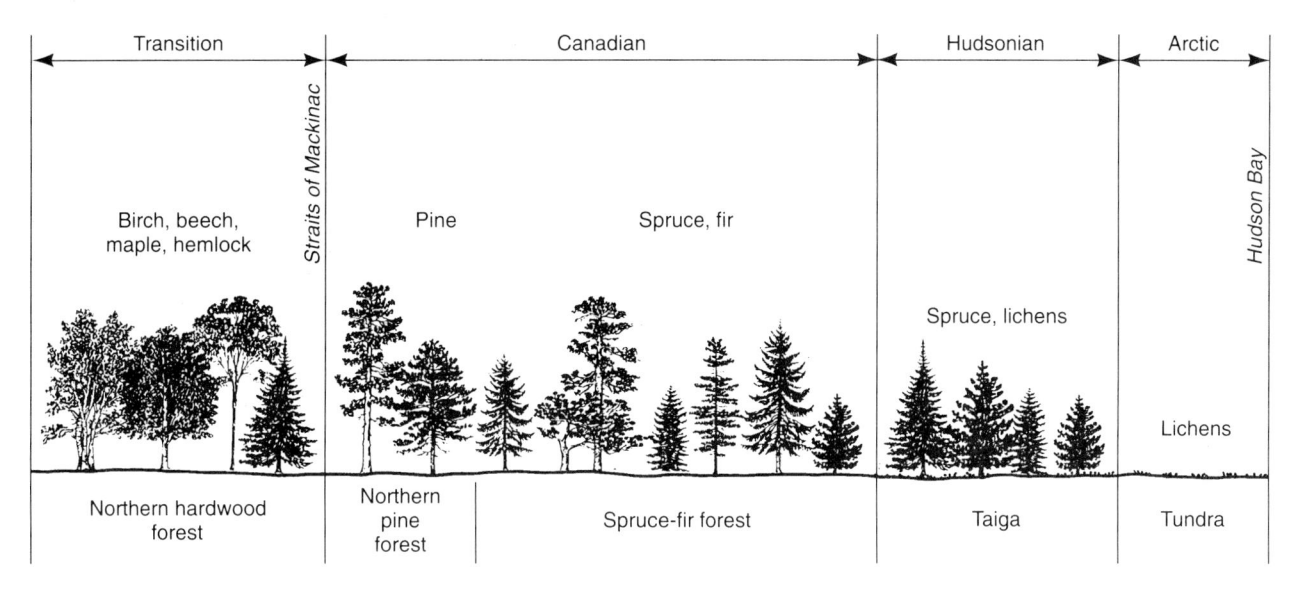

Figure 6.16 Continued.

Changes in vegetation associated with changes in elevation produce a vertical zonation of plant associations. Figure 6.17 presents a cross section of a typical mountain in the southwestern United States. The **Lower and Upper Sonoran zones** are the dry-climate equivalent of the Lower and Upper Austral zones of the humid eastern United States. At the elevation where the water balance becomes positive, the transition zone is reached, and the life zones above this elevation are the same as the life zones on the horizontal zonation scheme. Also, the life zone lines are higher on the east side of a mountain than they are on the west side in North America (figure 6.18). The tree line 10° C (50° F) warmest month average is the line of demarcation between the Hudsonian and Arctic-Alpine zones. In the southwestern United States, the tree line has an elevation of approximately 3,500 m (11,500 ft). This tree line drops to an elevation of approximately 2,000 m (6,500 ft) at the United States/Canada border, and to about 760 m (2,500 ft) in central Alaska. Elevations of the other life zones drop accordingly in a polar direction.

Moisture-bearing winds are from the west in North America and the lee side of mountains is usually drier. *Aspect* is the direction a slope faces. South-facing slopes in North America receive more direct sunlight and have a poorer moisture balance than north-facing slopes in the same geographic area. South-facing is defined as slopes facing compass directions from 120° through 330°. North-facing slopes extend from compass directions 330° through 120°. Figure 6.19 illustrates a major vegetative difference related to aspect. This example from the Ozark Plateau region shows an aspect contrast in vegetation. Pines occupy the upper southwest-facing slopes, whereas oaks and hickories are on the northeast-facing slopes. Cedars dominate the lower south-facing slopes. Ferns are more abundant in this forest on north slopes than south slopes.

The geomorphology (landforms) of a region defines changes in topography and parent material of the soil, derived from the geologic complex that affects the vegetation of a region. Figure 6.20 illustrates the modifications in vegetation in the Connecticut River Valley in response to changes in glacial parent material. Parent material differences create changes in water availability and moisture balance, and vegetation responds to these differences.

Active sand dune development in the Great Lakes area creates desert-like environments where the sand is actively being eroded. These areas, called **blowouts,** are not stable enough for vegetation to gain a foothold and they appear as a sandy desert. The **area of encroachment,** where

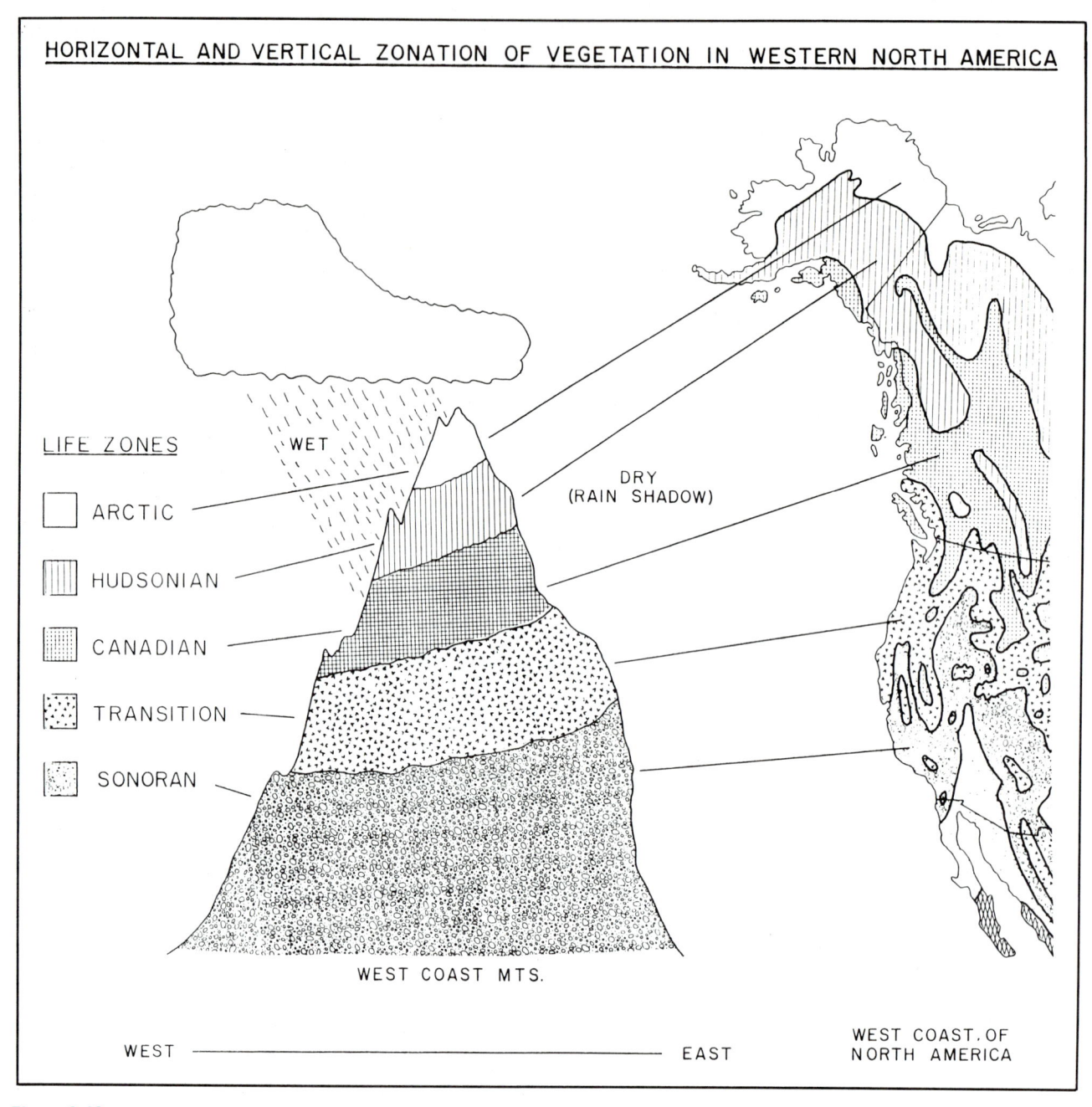

Figure 6.18 Relationship between horizontal and vertical zonation of vegetation on mountains in western North America. The east side of mountains in the westerly wind belt have a rain-shadow effect on the eastern slopes.
(*Cartographer:* Douglas Hemsath)

Figure 6.19 Aspect affects vegetation. Southwest-facing slopes that are drier, because of enhanced evapotranspiration, contain Shortleaf Pine and Eastern Red Cedar, whereas northeast-facing slopes contain Oak-Hickory in the Ozarks.
(*Photo:* David A. Castillon)

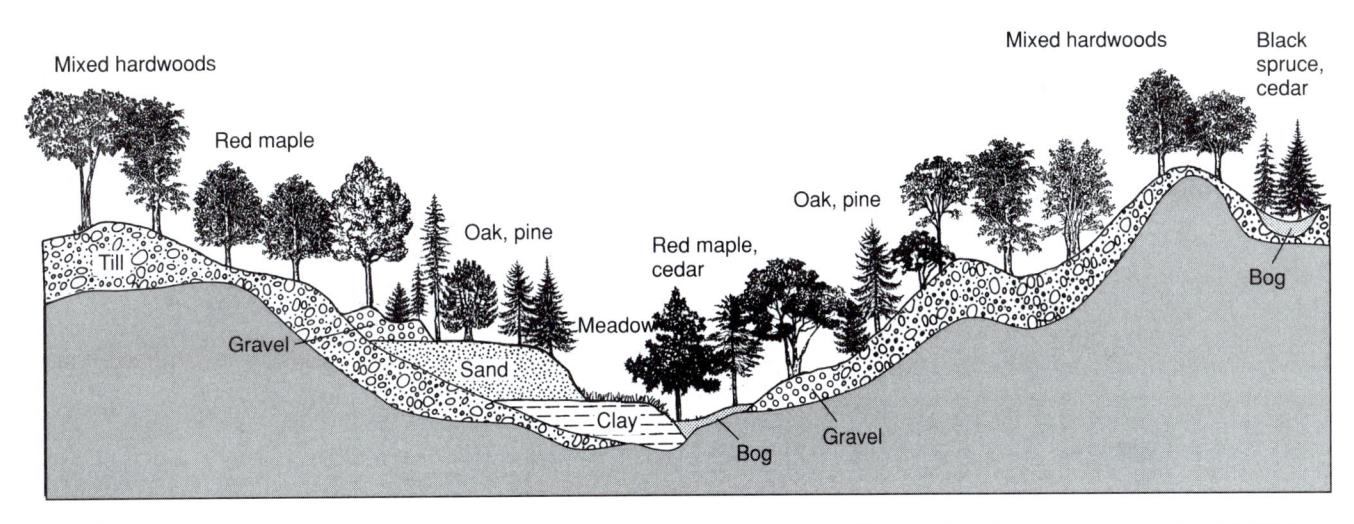

Figure 6.20 Relationship between vegetation and glacial parent material in the Connecticut River Valley. Parent material determines moisture retention, which in turn determines vegetation.
The Connecticut Agricultural Experiment Station, New Haven, CT. Reprinted by permission.

Biosphere—Biogeography

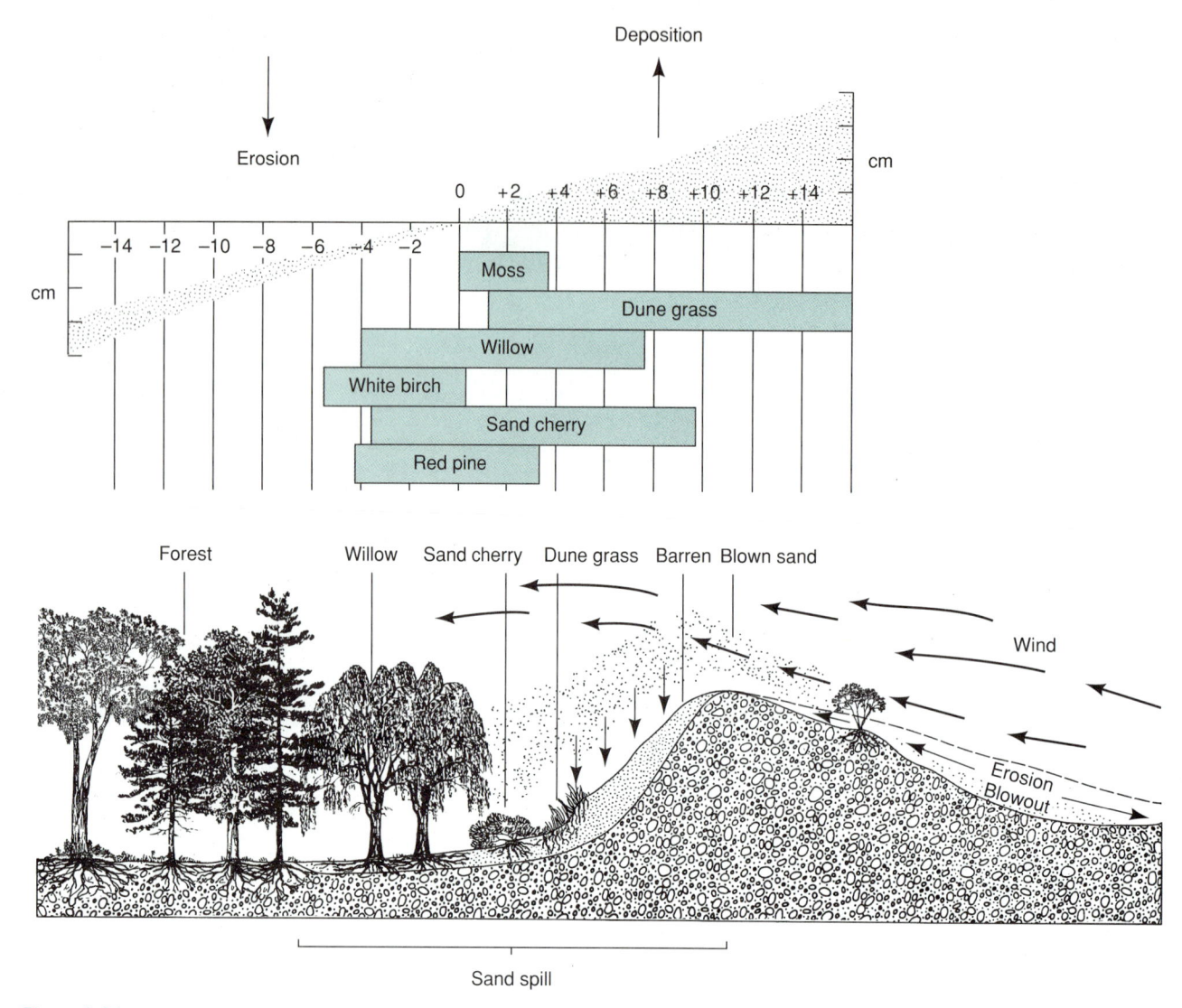

Figure 6.21 Tolerance ranges for selected vegetation to sand erosion and deposition in the dune fields of the Great Lakes region.
From Marsh, *Earthscape: A Physical Geography.* Copyright © 1987 John Wiley & Sons, Inc., New York, NY. Reprinted by permission of John Wiley & Sons, Inc.

the sand is being deposited, develops a moisture deficit and living vegetation is choked. Figure 6.21 is a cross section of a dune illustrating the tolerance ranges of plants to sand erosion and deposition.

Figure 6.22 illustrates a cross section of habitats found within three adjacent microenvironments. Researchers have recognized the relationship between parent material, topography, climate, drainage, and the vegetation of forest communities. Topography and soil affect water availability, which in turn produces vegetative changes.

Biologic Productivity

Biologic productivity begins with photosynthesis. Photosynthesis begins with the absorption of light particles (**photons**) by the green parts of plants (**chloroplasts**). The rate of photochemical activity depends, to a great extent, on the wavelength of the solar radiation and the **photoperiod.** Shortwave solar radiation intensity increases and decreases with sun angle and season, and photosynthesis mirrors the solar radiation curve on its daily and seasonal cycle in terrestrial environments. The strong positive correlation between solar radiation and photosynthesis in terrestrial environments does not exist in aquatic

130 Physical and Biological Variables of the Natural Environment

Parent material

- Clayey residue
- Limestone
- Sandy residue
- Sandstone

a.

Climate and topography

- Precipitation
- Low infiltration
- Water table
- Shaded, cool, and moist
- Shadow
- Sunny, warm, and dry
- Wet
- Precipitation
- High infiltration

b.

Vegetation

- Broadleaf trees
- Ca, P, N
- Conifers
- Mixed shrubs and herbs

c.

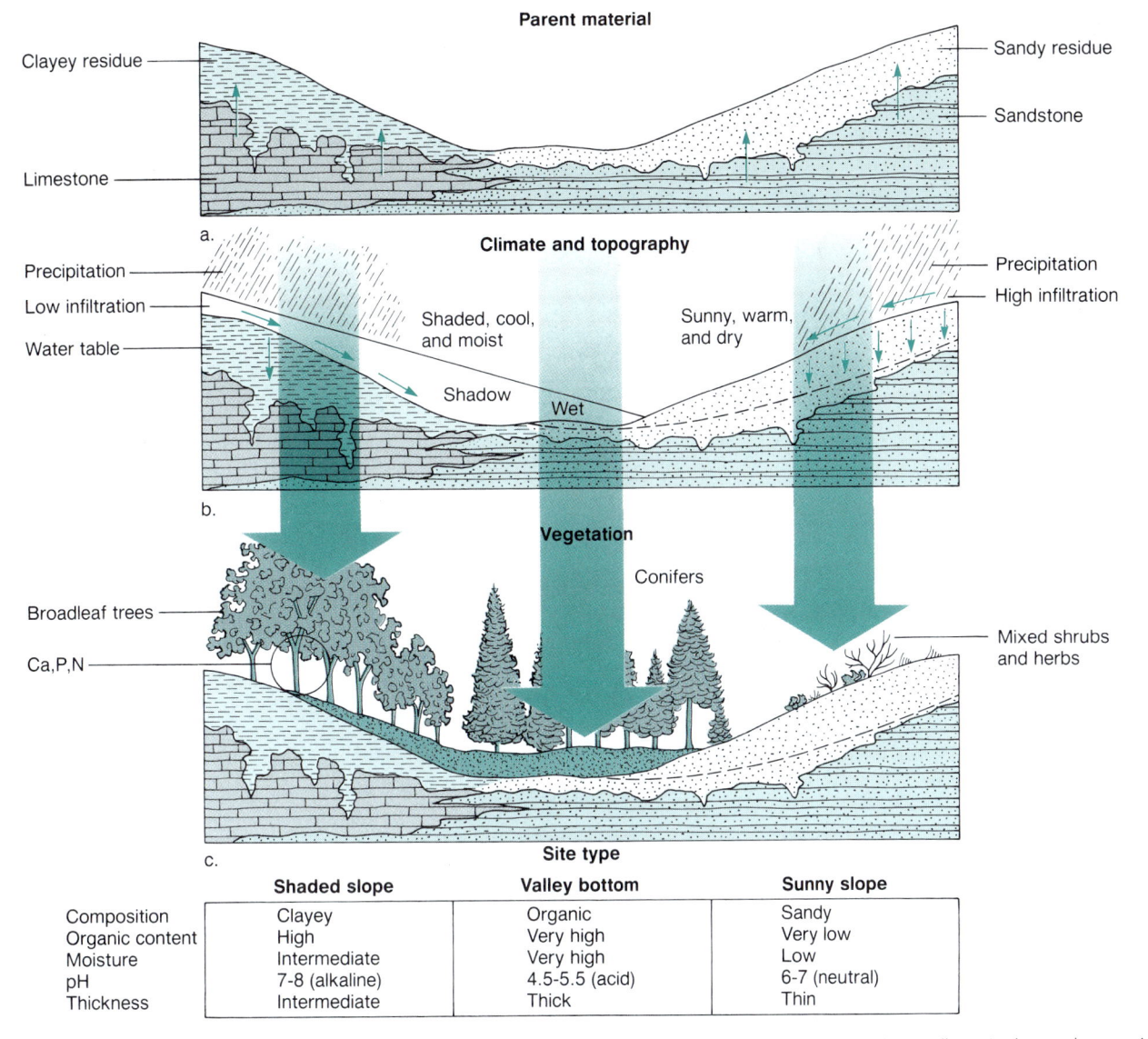

Site type	Shaded slope	Valley bottom	Sunny slope
Composition	Clayey	Organic	Sandy
Organic content	High	Very high	Very low
Moisture	Intermediate	Very high	Low
pH	7-8 (alkaline)	4.5-5.5 (acid)	6-7 (neutral)
Thickness	Intermediate	Thick	Thin

Figure 6.22 The effects of parent material, climate and topography, and drainage on forest development in three adjacent microenvironments. From W. M. Marsh and J. Dozier, *Landscape: An Introduction to Physical Geography.* Copyright © John Wiley & Sons, Inc., New York, NY. Reprinted by permission of John Wiley & Sons, Inc.

environments. Marine phytoplankton achieve a maximum productivity at 25% of full solar radiation.

Figure 6.23 illustrates the biologic productivity of North American life zones. The most productive biologic regions are the coastal wetlands (e.g., marshlands = 4,000 to 6,000 grams/m² (95–140 lb/ft²)). For comparison, the biomass productivity in grams of dry matter per square meter per year for most agriculture ranges from 1,000 to 4,000 grams/m²/yr. (24–95 lb/ft²/yr). The importance of these wetlands as nursery regions for a great variety of life forms cannot be overemphasized. Productivity of the mountains varies with elevation and life zone.

Ecoregions of North America

The biogeographic distribution of plants and animals in North America are presented as the natural response to the interactions of the physical environment. The geology, landforms, soil, climate, available water, and human activity dictate the flora and fauna of a region. Figure 6.24 is an ecoregions map of North America. Regions on this map define vegetative and faunal associations based on the interactions of the abiotic variables. Each region is defined by its physical variables and the resulting biologic response.

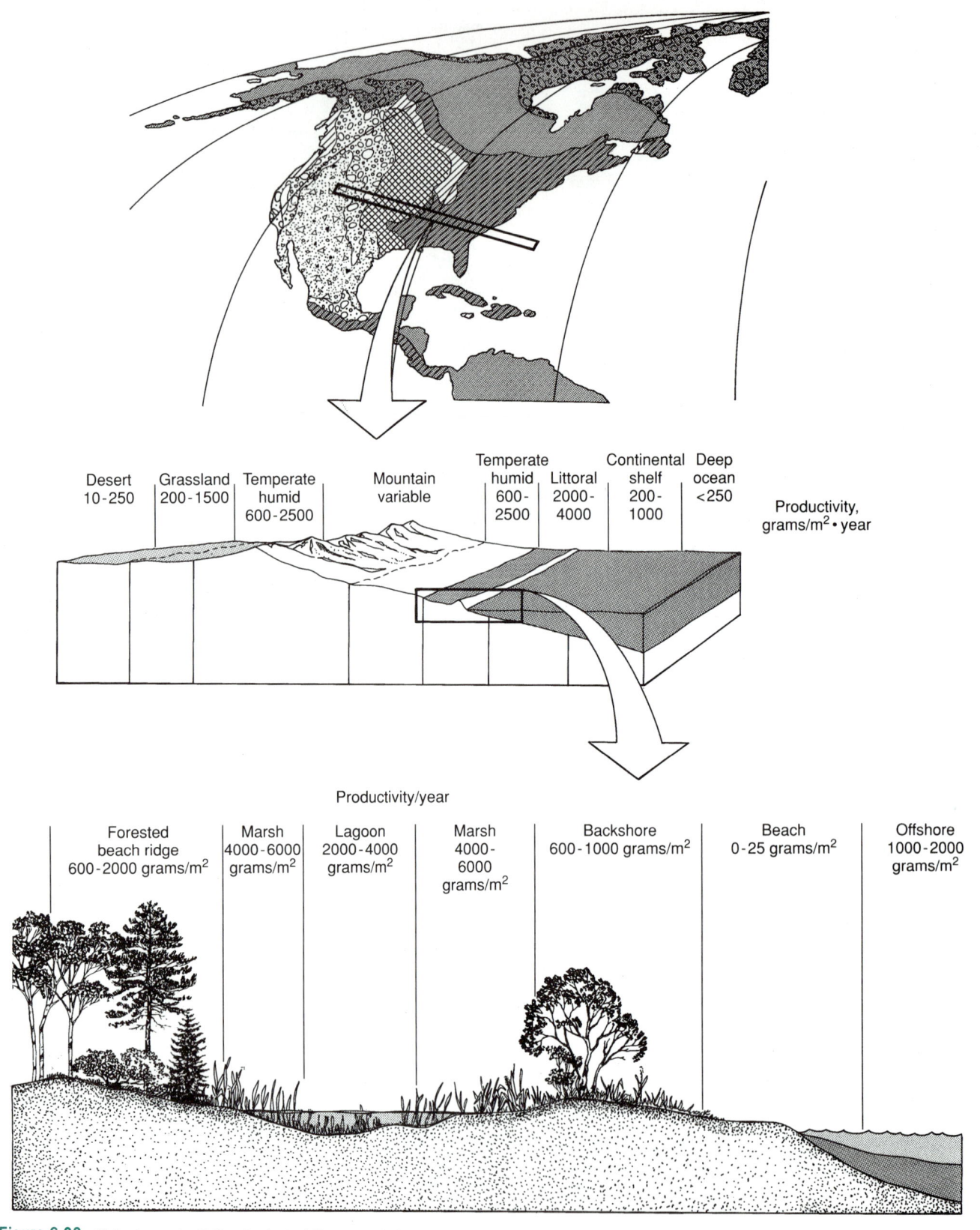

Figure 6.23 Biologic productivity of selected life zones in North America.
From Marsh, *Earthscape: A Physical Geography*. Copyright © 1987 John Wiley & Sons, Inc., New York, NY. Reprinted by permission of John Wiley & Sons, Inc.

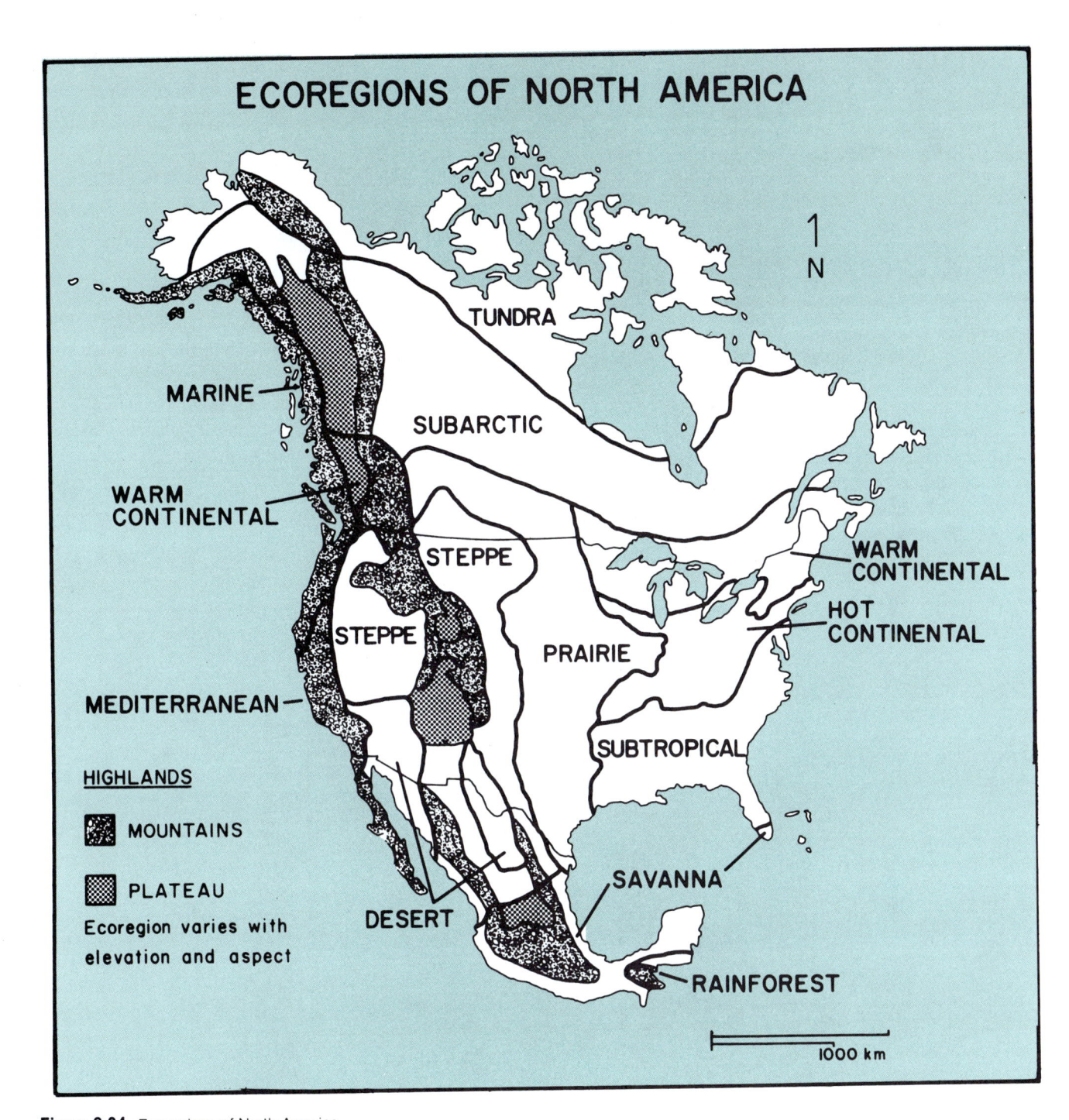

Figure 6.24 Ecoregions of North America.
Source: Data from Bailey, U.S. Department of Agriculture Forest Service.
(Cartographer: Douglas Hemsath)

Tropical (Tropical Life Zone)

Geographic Location: Hawaii (Mexico)

Landforms: Volcanic-mountainous to hilly. Peaks greater than 3,900m (13,000 ft). Seventy-five percent of the land area has an elevation less than 198 m (2,000 ft).

Climate: Af: Mean annual temperature 23° C (74° F)
January mean 21° C (70° F)
July mean 24° C (75° F)
Frost has never occurred below 760 m (2,500 ft). Precipitation is concentrated on the windward side of volcanoes and can exceed 5,000 mm (200 in). Leeward slopes are semiarid and average about 500 mm (30 in) of precipitation per year.

Soils: Process: laterization, Ultisols and Oxisols dominate, but Entisols and Inceptisols occur on the rocky slopes.

Flora: Tropical forests grow from sea level to 2,900 m (9,500 ft) on the wet windward side of the volcanoes and above 760 m (2,500 ft) on the dry lee side. The dry side is characterized by a shrub forest below 670 m (2,500 ft). Mosses and lichens are the dominant vegetation above tree line.

Fauna: Waterbirds such as terns, boobies, and petrels are common. Snakes are absent. Introduced mammals include wild boar, axis deer, feral sheep, and goats.

Note: Parts of southern Mexico have a similar climate but a different tropical vegetation and fauna.

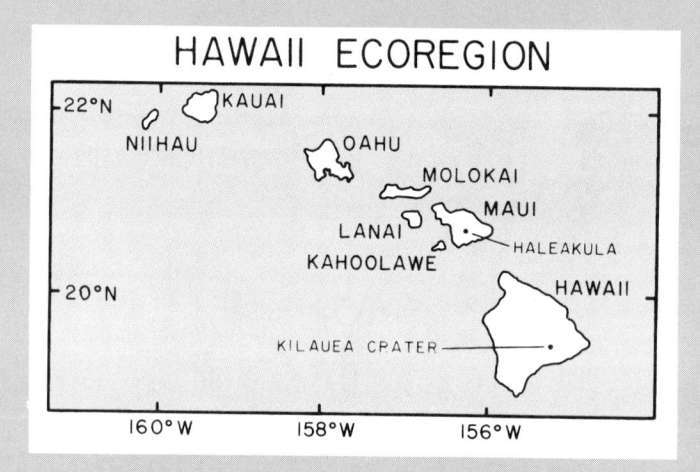

Figure 6.25A Map of Hawaii ecoregion.
(*Cartographer*: Douglas Hemsath)

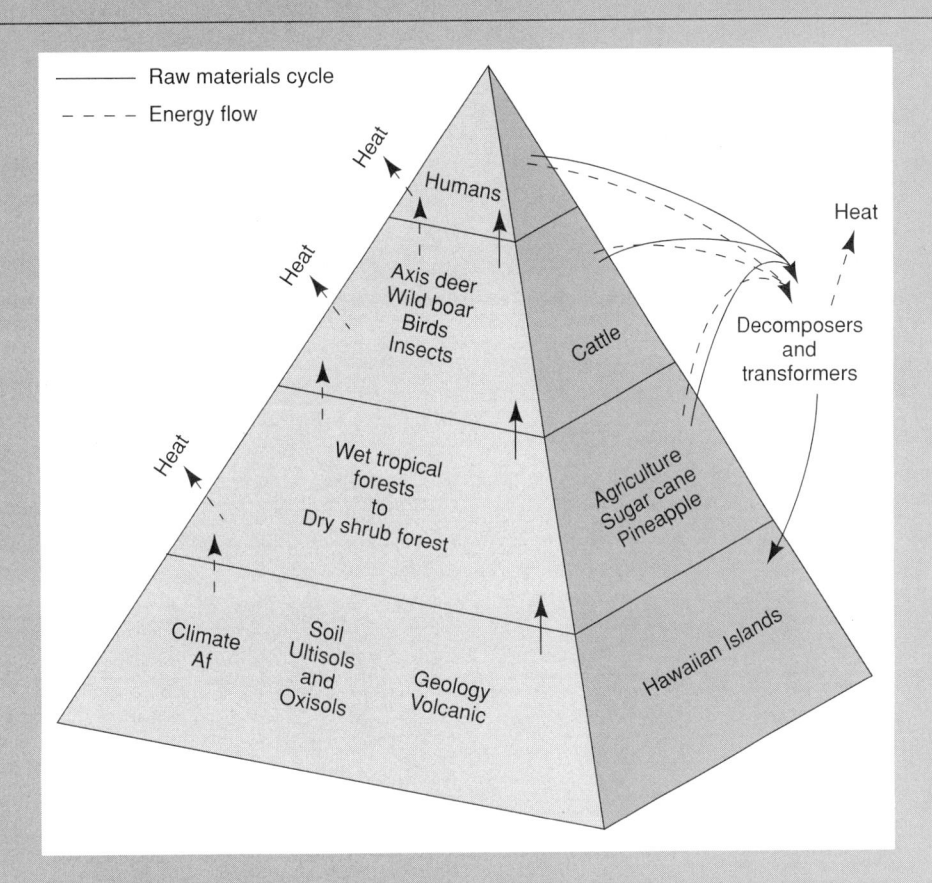

Figure 6.25B Biotic pyramid for the Hawaiian ecoregion;

Figure 6.25C Haleakala Crater, 10,025 ft, on the island of Maui.
(*Photo:* David A. Castillon)

Biosphere—Biogeography

Tropical Savanna (Tropical Life Zone)

Geographic Location: Southern Tip of Florida (Mexico)

Landforms: Relatively flat with elevations from sea level to 7.6 m (25 ft). Swamps, marshes, and poorly defined drainageways.

Climate: Aw: Mean annual temperature 21–24° C (70–75° F)
January mean 19° C (66° F)
July mean 26°C (81° F)
Mean total precipitation 1,270 to 1,650 mm (50 to 65 in). Concentration spring through mid-autumn.

Soils: Histosols are the dominant soil. Inceptisols occur where the soil is less wet.

Flora: Tropical moist hardwood forest with cypress forest as the dominant association. Mangrove swamp forests are also extensive. Open marsh filled with aquatic herbaceous plants are common. Raised areas called **hammocks** contain mahogany, red bay, and palmettos.

Fauna: White-tailed deer, black bear, raccoon, bobcat, opossum, skunk, marsh and swamp rabbit, cotton rat, and fox squirrel are some of the common mammals. Key deer and Florida panther are both on the rare and endangered species list and their numbers are dwindling. Many birds, including herons, egrets, kites, and ducks make this habitat their home. The American alligator and the Florida coral snake are year-long residents.

Figure 6.26A Map of Tropical Savanna ecoregion.
(*Cartographer:* Douglas Hemsath)

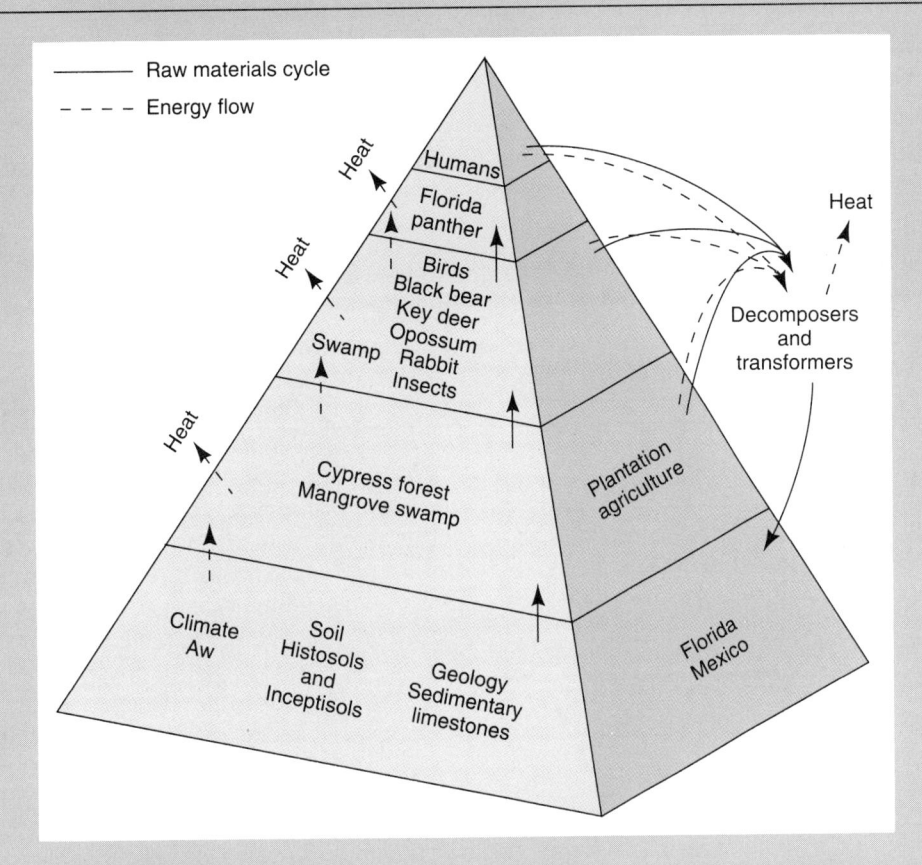

Figure 6.26B Biotic pyramid for the southern tip of Florida;

Figure 6.26C Key deer, which are on the endangered species list.
(*Photo:* Gerald Ludwig, USFWS)

Figure 6.26D Florida panther, also on the endangered species list.
(*Photo:* USFWS)

Biosphere—Biogeography 137

Subtropical (Lower Austral Life Zone)

Geographic Location: Southeastern United States, including most of the states of Florida, Georgia, Alabama, Mississippi, Louisiana, South Carolina, North Carolina, Virginia, West Virginia, Delaware, New Jersey, and Arkansas.

Landforms: Elevations range from sea level to 610 m (2,000 ft). Most of the area has gentle slopes but relief can be as great as 300 m (1,000 ft) in the Piedmont. Streams are sluggish and marshes, lakes, and swamps are numerous.

Climate: Cfa: Average annual temperatures range from 15° to 21° C (60° to 70° F). Precipitation ranges from 1,000 to 1,525 mm (40 to 60 in) per year.

Soil: The process of soil formation is podzolization and the dominant soil order is Ultisol. Vertisols, Spodosols, Inceptisols, and Entisols are locally conspicuous. Most soils are wet, acidic, and low in nutrients.

Flora: Temperate rain forest or temperate evergreen forest are the common names given to the dominant vegetation of this region. Evergreens, oaks, magnolia, gums, and cypress are the dominant climax species of the coastal plain. Uplands are forested with stands of loblolly pine, yellow pine, shortleaf pine, oaks, hickories, gums, red maple, and winged elm. Understory trees and shrubs include dogwood, viburnum, haw, blueberry, and youpon. Grasses include bluestem, panicums, and longleaf uniola.

Fauna: White-tailed deer, raccoons, opossums, squirrels, rabbits, rodents, bobwhite quail, wild turkey, American alligator, ducks, fox, mourning dove, pine warbler, cardinal, summer tanager, Carolina wren, ruby-throated hummingbird, warbler, towhee, and tufted titmouse are all common. Cottonmouth, copperhead, rough green snake, rat snake, coachwhip, and king snake are all residents of this region.

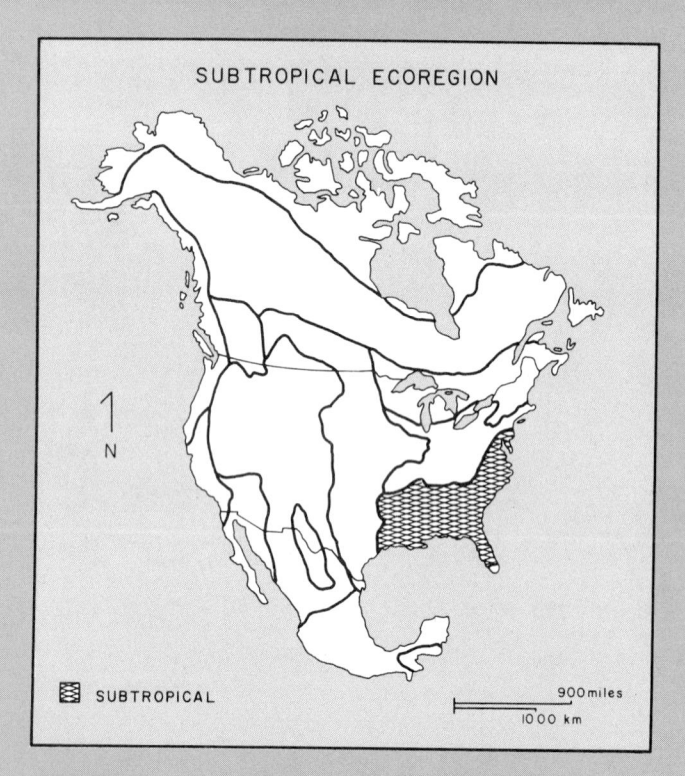

Figure 6.27A Map of Subtropical ecoregion.
(*Cartographer:* Douglas Hemsath)

Figure 6.27B Eastern deciduous forest (Oak-Hickory).
(*Photo:* David A. Castillon)

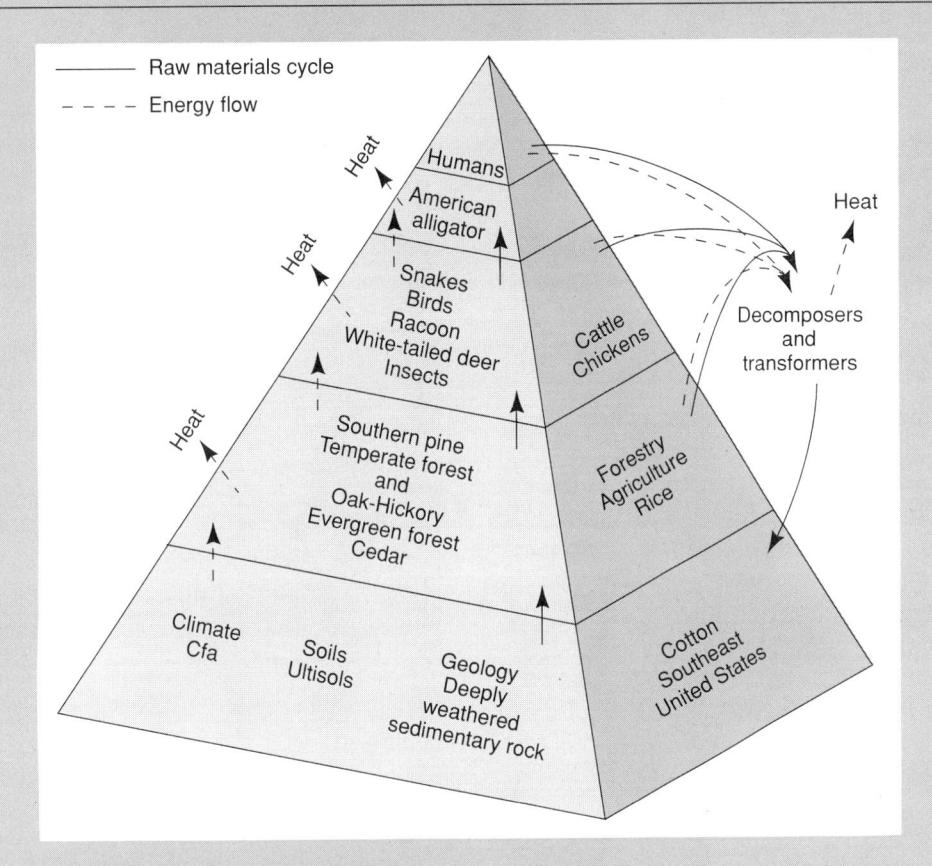

Figure 6.27C Biotic pyramid for the southeastern United States.

Figure 6.27D Cypress tupelo forest along the Gulf Coast.
(*Photo*: David A. Castillon)

Figure 6.27E American alligator.
(*Photo*: David Gache, USFWS)

Biosphere—Biogeography 139

Hot Continental (Upper Austral Life Zone)

Geographic Location: Central Eastern United States including parts of Arkansas, Missouri, Tennessee, Kentucky, West Virginia, Illinois, Indiana, Ohio, Pennsylvania, New Jersey, Massachusetts, Rhode Island, Connecticut, Wisconsin, Michigan, Minnesota, and small parts of many of the adjoining states.

Landforms: This region is rolling to hilly, with general elevations below 760 m (2,500 ft) and a few peaks reach above 1,370 m (4,500 ft). Relief can be as great as 900 m (3,000 ft) in the Appalachian Mountains.

Climate: Cfa to Dfa: Average annual temperatures range from 4° to 15° C (40° to 60° F). Average annual precipitation ranges from 900 to 1,500 mm (35 to 60 in). With a summer concentration, soil water is usually available all year. August can be dry.

Soils: Podzolization is the dominant soil-formation process of the region and the soils are Ultisols in the south and Alfisols in the north.

Flora: Winter deciduous forest, also called temperate deciduous forests, are dominated by tall broadleaf trees. Common trees include: oak, beech, birch, hickory, walnut, maple, basswood, elm, ash, cedar, poplar, chestnut, and hornbean on the uplands and alder, willow, sycamore, ash, and elm in the lowlands.

Fauna: Mammals include the white-tailed deer, black bear, bobcat, fox, raccoon, squirrel, chipmunk, white-footed mice, pine vole, short-tailed shrew, and cotton mice. Wild turkey, ruffed grouse, bobwhite quail, mourning dove, cardinal, tufted titmouse, wood thrush, summer tanager, red-eyed vireo, blue-grey gnatcatcher, hooded warbler, and Carolina wren are common birds of this region. Box turtles, garter snakes, and rattlesnakes are characteristic reptiles.

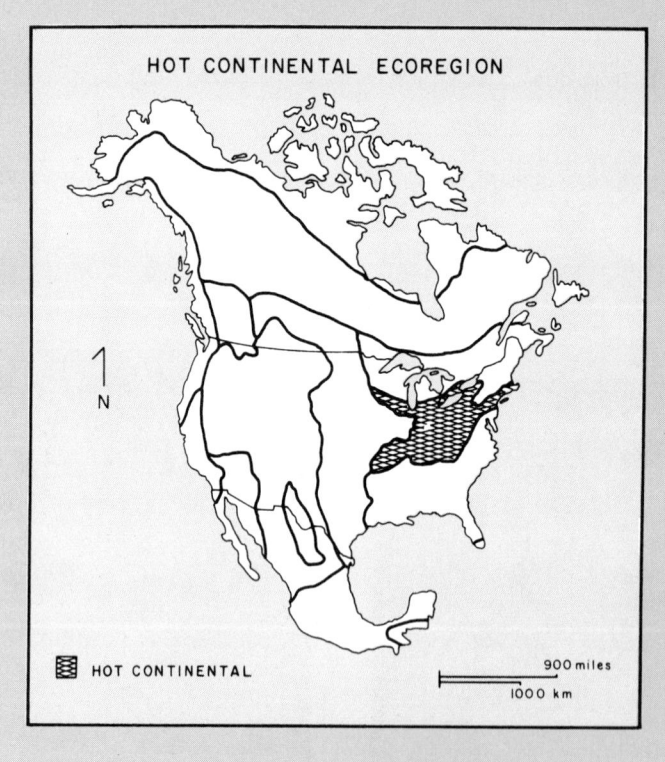

Figure 6.28A Map of the Hot Continental ecoregion.
(*Cartographer:* Douglas Hemsath)

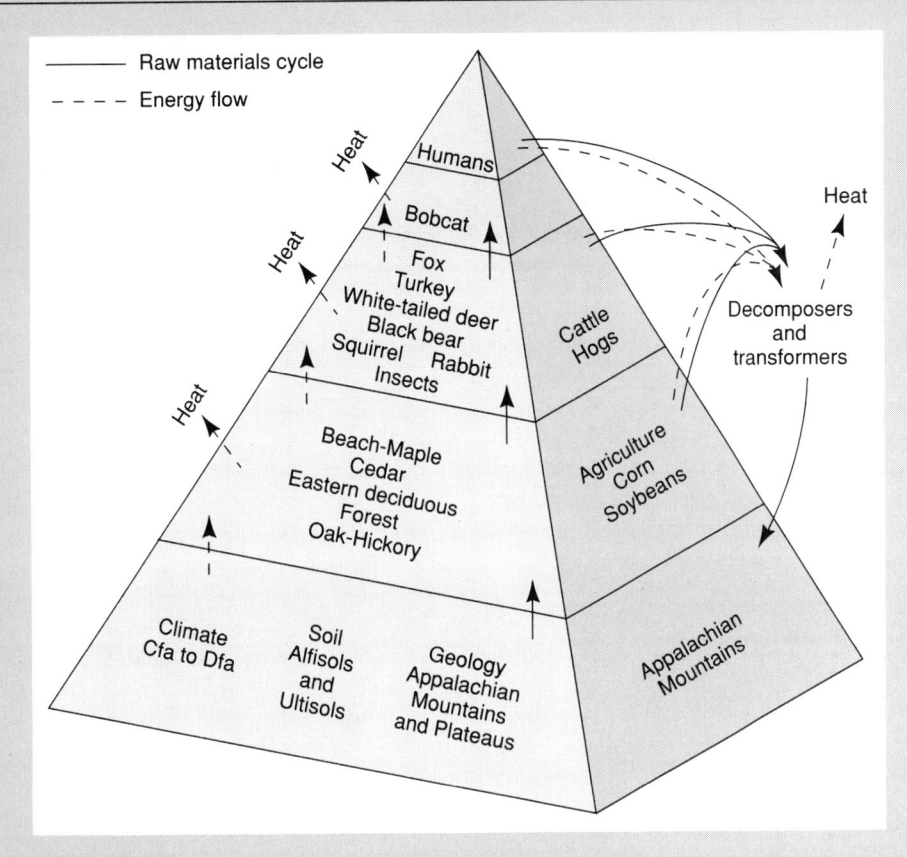

Figure 6.28B Biotic pyramid for the east-central United States;

Figure 6.28C Deciduous forest of the Appalachian Mountains region;
(*Photo:* David A. Castillon)

Figure 6.28D Black bear.
(*Photo:* S. C. Armstrup, USFWS).

Warm Continental (Transition and Canadian Life Zones)

Geographic Location: The Great Lakes States, southeastern Canada and the Columbia Plateau. States include parts of Idaho, Montana, Washington, Minnesota, Wisconsin, Michigan, Pennsylvania, New York, Connecticut, New Hampshire, Vermont, and Maine in the United States and parts of Ontario, Quebec, and New Brunswick in Canada. Also included in this ecoregion are the highlands and mountains with elevations great enough for vertical zonation.

Landforms: Most of the area in the warm continental ecoregion has been glaciated. Low rolling hills and low mountains are the terrain features of the Great Lakes section, but high mountains rising to over 2,700 m (9,000 ft) occur in the Columbia Plateau section in the west. Local relief can be as great as 900 m (3,000 ft) in this section.

Climate: Dfb: Winters are moderately long and somewhat severe but the frost-free period is more than 100 days per year. Average annual temperatures range from 2° to 10°C (35° to 50° F). Snow can persist for long periods of time in the winter. Precipitation ranges from 500 to 1,150 mm (20 to 45 in) with a summer concentration in the east and winter concentrations in the west.

Soils: In the Great Lakes region, Spodosols and Alfisols are dominant but in the Columbia Plateau section Inceptisols are formed by the podzolization process.

Flora: The southern part of the warm continental region in the east and the lower elevations of this region in the west are pine forests (Transitional Life Zone). In the Great Lakes states, white pine is dominant; in the west, ponderosa pine is the transitional species. Above the pine in the west Western red cedar, hemlock, and Douglas fir forests are major vegetative associations. In the east, pines give way to the spruce and fir forests in the southern Canadian provinces (Canadian Life Zone).

Fauna: In winter the ptarmigan and snowshoe hare turn white. The black bear, skunk, marmot, chipmunk, badger, ground squirrel, beaver, and muskrat are joined in the west by deer, elk, mountain lion, and bobcat as important mammals of this region. Familiar birds that don't migrate out of the region include hawks, jays, and owls.

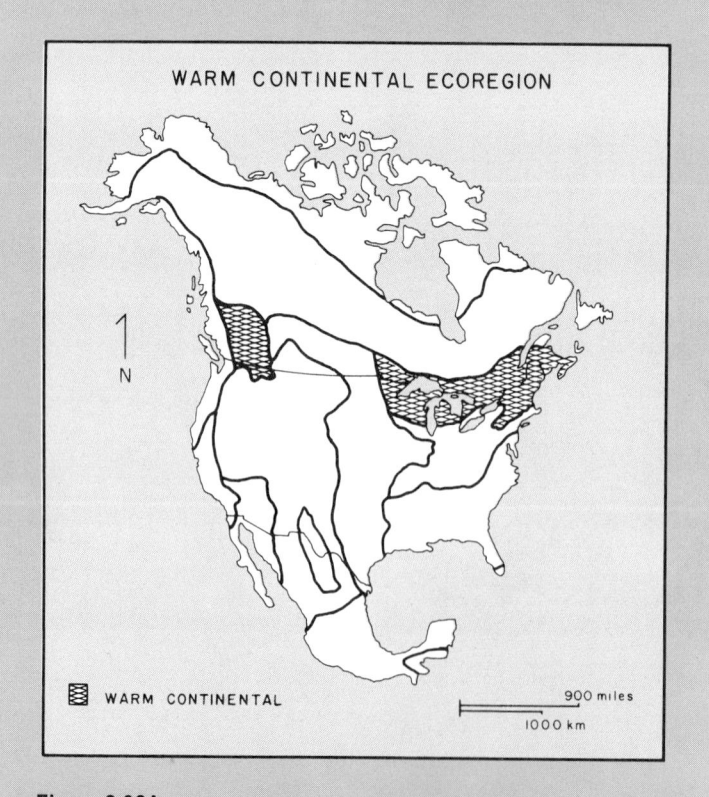

Figure 6.29A Map of the Warm Continental ecoregion.
(*Cartographer:* Douglas Hemsath)

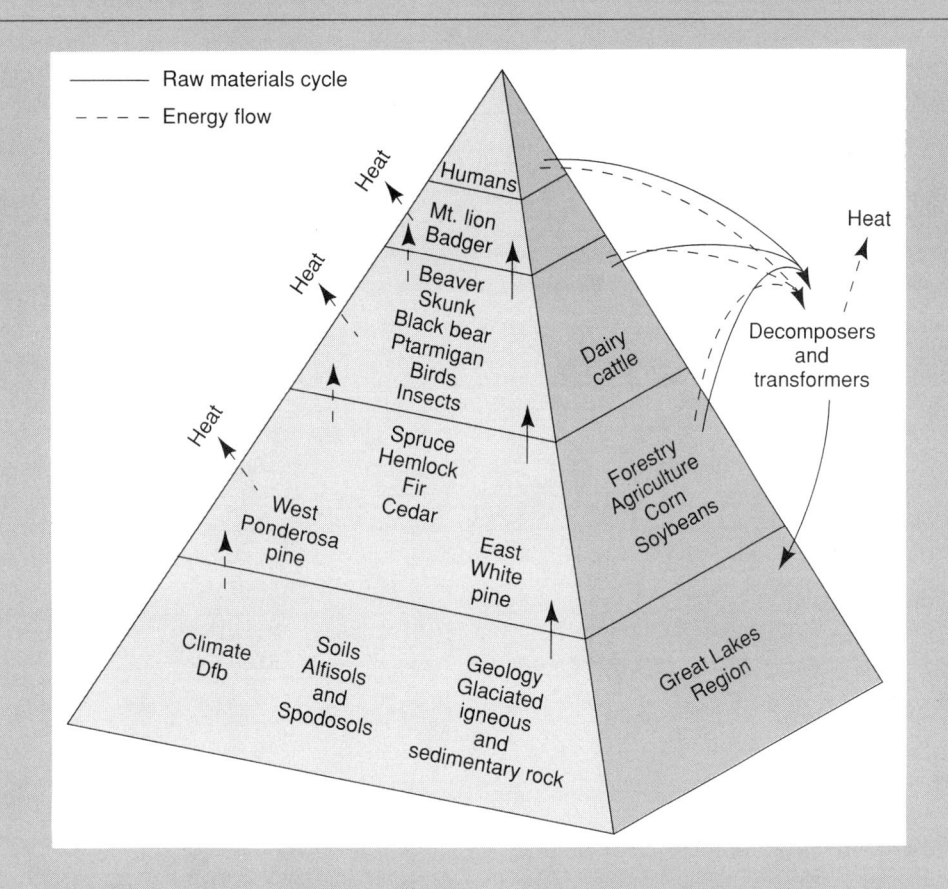

Figure 6.29B Biotic pyramid for the Great Lakes region of the United States;

Figure 6.29C Ponderosa Pine is a transition zone species in the West;
(*Photo:* David A. Castillon);

Figure 6.29D The badger is a resident of the warm continental ecoregion.
(*Photo:* USFWS).

Subarctic (Hudsonian Life Zone)

Geographic Location: The subarctic zone stretches across Canada and Alaska from the Atlantic to the Pacific Ocean. This region also includes mountains in the United States, Mexico, and Canada, with high enough elevation to have a Hudsonian zone from vertical zonation.

Landforms: This region is dominated by broad valleys, dissected uplands, and poorly drained lowland basins. The area was recently deglaciated and drainage is poorly integrated.

Climate: Dfc: Temperatures are extreme. Summers are short, less than 100 days, and hot, up to 38° C (100° F). Winters are long and cold, with temperatures to −60° C (−75° F). Average annual precipitation is only 430 mm (17 in). Permafrost is present on north-facing slopes and on the higher elevations in the region.

Soils: The dominant soils of the ecoregion are Inceptisols. Many poorly drained lowlands and bogs have Histosols.

Flora: Forests cover the area below 900 m (3,000 ft) with black and white spruce as the dominant species (Spruce hardwood forest region). Cottonwood, poplar, alder, willow, birch, and aspen are all common trees. Most prefer the lowland areas. The bogs are choked with mosses, mainly sphagnum, and sedges.

Fauna: The spruce hardwoods are excellent habitat for furbearers. Wolf, wolverine, fox, mink, beaver, muskrat, weasel, otter, and both black and brown bears are present. Caribou and moose also frequent the Hudsonian zone. Birds include osprey, hawks, sharptail, spruce and ruffed grouse, ptarmigan, and peregrine falcons.

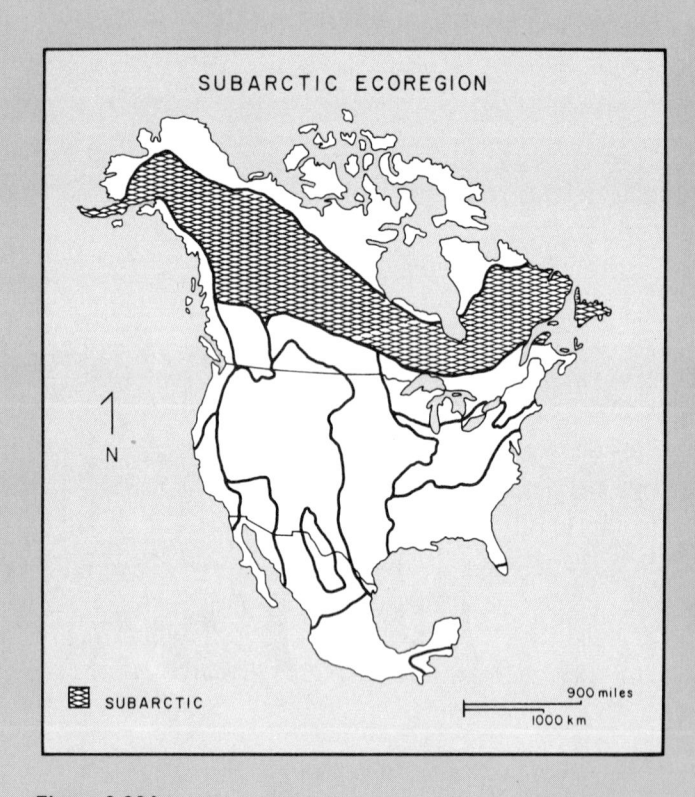

Figure 6.30A Map of the Subarctic ecoregion.
(*Cartographer:* Douglas Hemsath)

Figure 6.30B Aspen-Spruce-Fir association.
(*Photo:* David A. Castillon)

144 Physical and Biological Variables of the Natural Environment

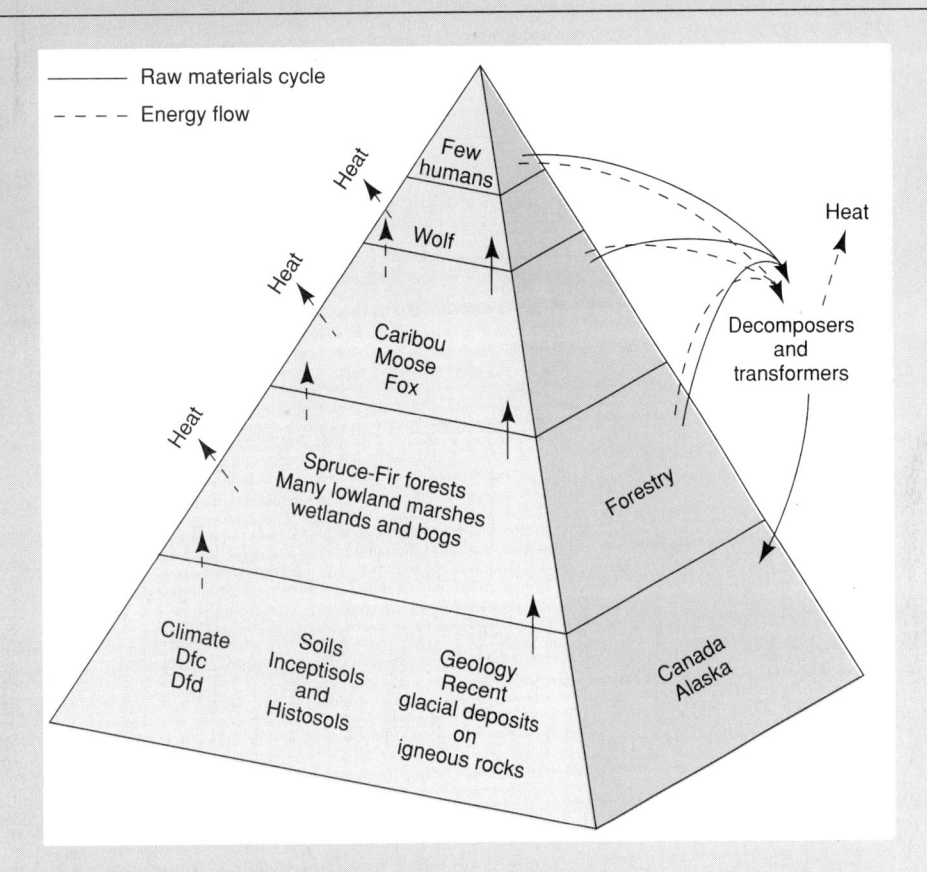

Figure 6.30C Biotic pyramid for the subarctic region of Canada and Alaska.

Figure 6.30D Caribou.
(*Photo:* Steve Kaufman, USFWS).

Biosphere—Biogeography

Tundra (Arctic Life Zone)

Geographic Location: The tundra stretches from the Atlantic to the Pacific and borders the Arctic Circle on the south and the Arctic Ocean on the north. Alaska, the Yukon, and Northwest Territories in Canada, along with mountain peaks above the tree line in the United States, Mexico, and Hawaii are included in the tundra ecoregion.

Landforms: The north coast of the tundra ecoregion is a relatively level plain with elevations less than 300 m (1,000 ft). Elevations and relief increase toward the mountain ranges, which can reach above 2,200 m (9,000 ft). Broad U-shaped valleys and morainal topography are evidence of the recent glaciation.

Climate: ET: The tundra is the climate of permafrost. Permanently frozen subsoil requires every month of the year to have an average temperature of less than 10° C (50° F). Average annual temperature is approximately −12° C (10° F), and ranges from 32° C (90° F) to −60° C (−75° F). Precipitation is sparse, ranging from 180 mm (7 in) to about 430 mm (17 in). Evapotranspiration rates are low and moisture deficits only occur in late summer. Sunlight is highly variable. Summers can have as many as 85 days of total sunlight with an average angle of incidence of 41° and as many as 67 days of total darkness. Growing season averages 2 weeks per year.

Soils: The dominant soils are wet cold Inceptisols and Histosols that have formed by the gleization process.

Flora: Trees with roots can't grow in permafrost. The frozen ground is also impermeable and extensive marshes and lakes form in the summer season. Cottongrass-tussock vegetative association contains sedges, dwarf shrubs, lichens, mosses, dwarf birch, Labrador-tea, and cinquefoil.

Fauna: Animals of the tundra include brown bear, wolf, wolverine, caribou, Arctic hare, mink, weasel, and lemming. Migratory birds include ptarmigans, ravens, hawks, and owls. Migratory waterfowl (ducks and geese) use the many lakes for summer nesting. Polar bears, walrus, and Arctic fox are year-round residents near the pack ice.

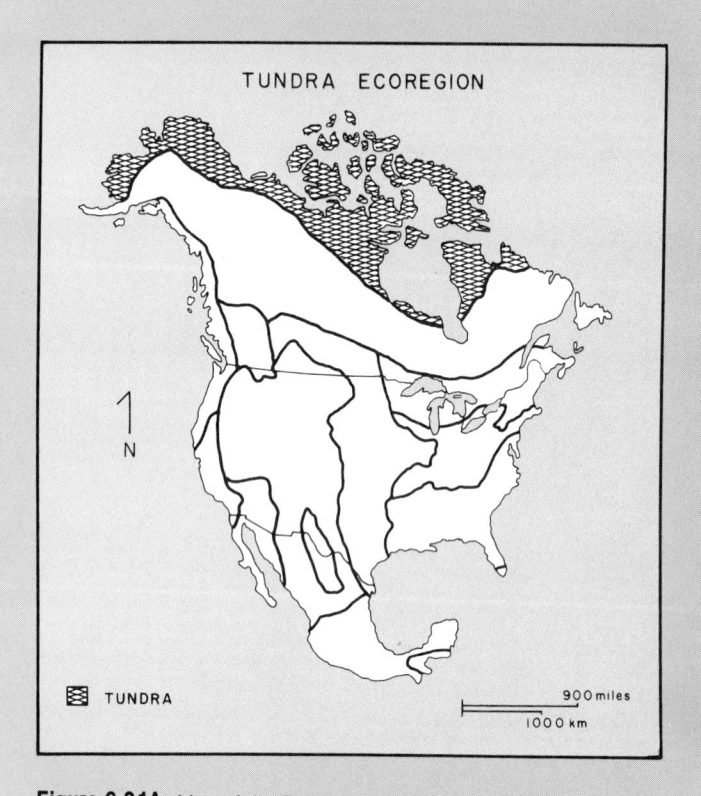

Figure 6.31A Map of the Tundra ecoregion.
(*Cartographer:* Douglas Hemsath)

Figure 6.31B Arctic alpine zone at the tree line in Colorado.
(*Photo:* David A. Castillon)

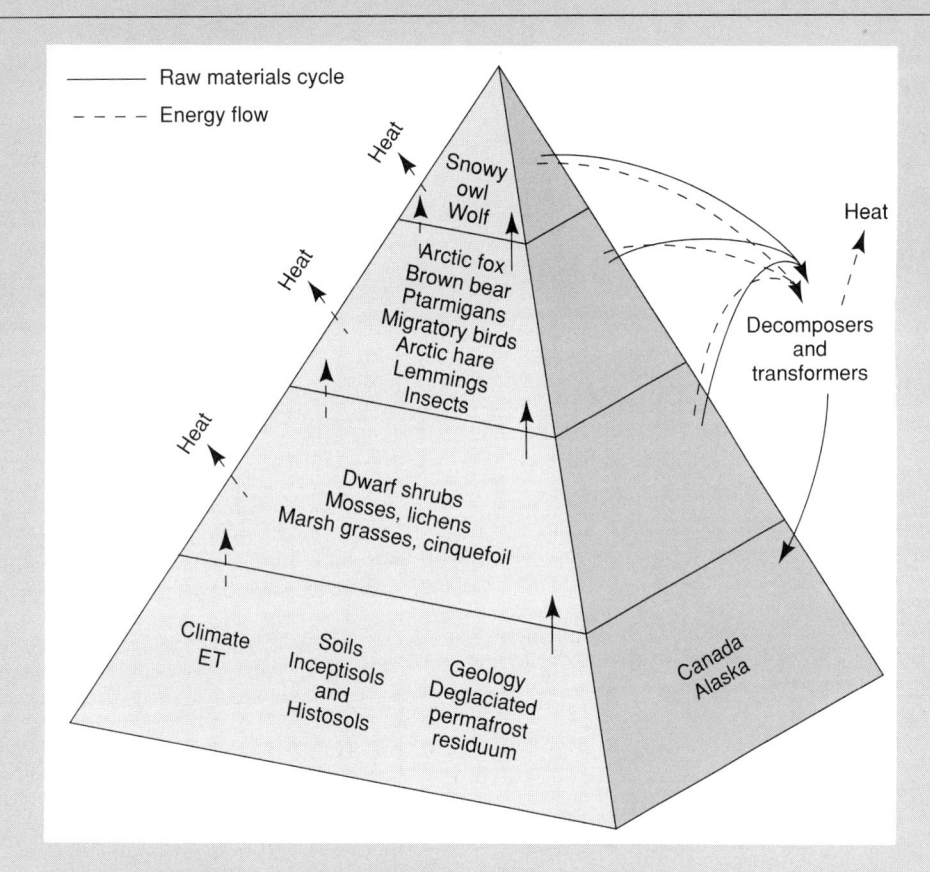

Figure 6.31C Biotic pyramid for the tundra.

Figure 6.31D Arctic alpine zone on the White Mountains of New Hampshire;
(*Photo:* David A. Castillon)

Figure 6.31E Arctic fox.
(*Photo:* Brian O'Donnell, USFWS).

Biosphere—Biogeography 147

Prairie (Mosaic of Many Life Zones)

Geographic Location: The Prairie and the Great Plains are almost synonymous. The tall grass prairie is called **prairie** and the short grass prairie is called **steppe**. States in this ecoregion include parts of Missouri, Iowa, Illinois, Minnesota, Texas, Oklahoma, Kansas, Nebraska, South and North Dakota, and parts of the Canadian provinces of Manitoba, Saskatchewan, and Alberta.

Landforms: Gently rolling to hilly topography dominates, but near stream valleys steep bluffs are common. Elevations range from sea level to 1,100 m (3,600 ft). Topography is more rugged on the west and in the south. The northern part of the ecoregion has been glaciated.

Climate: Cf, Df border with BS: Temperatures average below 4° C (40° F) in the Canadian provinces to over 21° C (70° F) in Texas. The frost-free season is over 300 days per year in Texas and less than 100 days per year in Canada, where the ecoregion borders the subarctic. Precipitation ranges from 500 to 1000 mm (20 to 40 in), with amounts decreasing from south to north.

Soils: The entire region is dominated by Mollisols that have formed from a combination podzolization-calcification process. Alfisols and vertisols are common in Texas and decrease in area to the north. Entisols are found throughout the region.

Flora: Vegetation changes from north to south in the Prairie region. Arid grasslands of xerophytic grasses such as bluestem, grama, and buffalograss are mixed with mesquite and are common in the south. Oaks and junipers are often mixed with the grasses. Forest-steppe is characterized by the intermingling of prairie and groves or strips of deciduous trees in the south, but give way to long-grass prairie with cottonwood along the streams in the north. Oak-hickory is the dominant association of upland forest in the south but elm, sycamore, cottonwood, hackberry, redbud, and buckeye are found in the lowlands. Dominant grasses in the long-grass prairie are bluestem, grama, wheatgrass, junegrass, prairie dropseed, porcupine grass, panic grass, and sedge.

Fauna: This was once the home range for the bison. Antelope and jackrabbits are still common along with cottontail rabbits, prairie dogs, pocket gophers, and badger. In the south, white-tailed deer, wild turkey, and armadillo become more numerous. The northern part of the region is an important breeding ground for migrating ducks and geese. Mourning doves, sharp-tailed grouse, bobwhite quail, and greater prairie chickens are upland game species of the region.

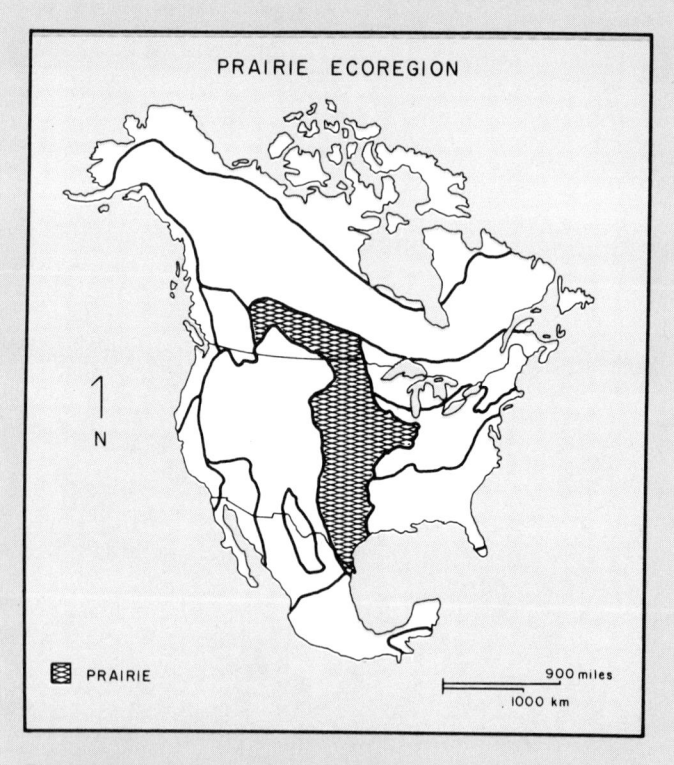

Figure 6.32A Map of the Prairie ecoregion.
(*Cartographer:* Douglas Hemsath)

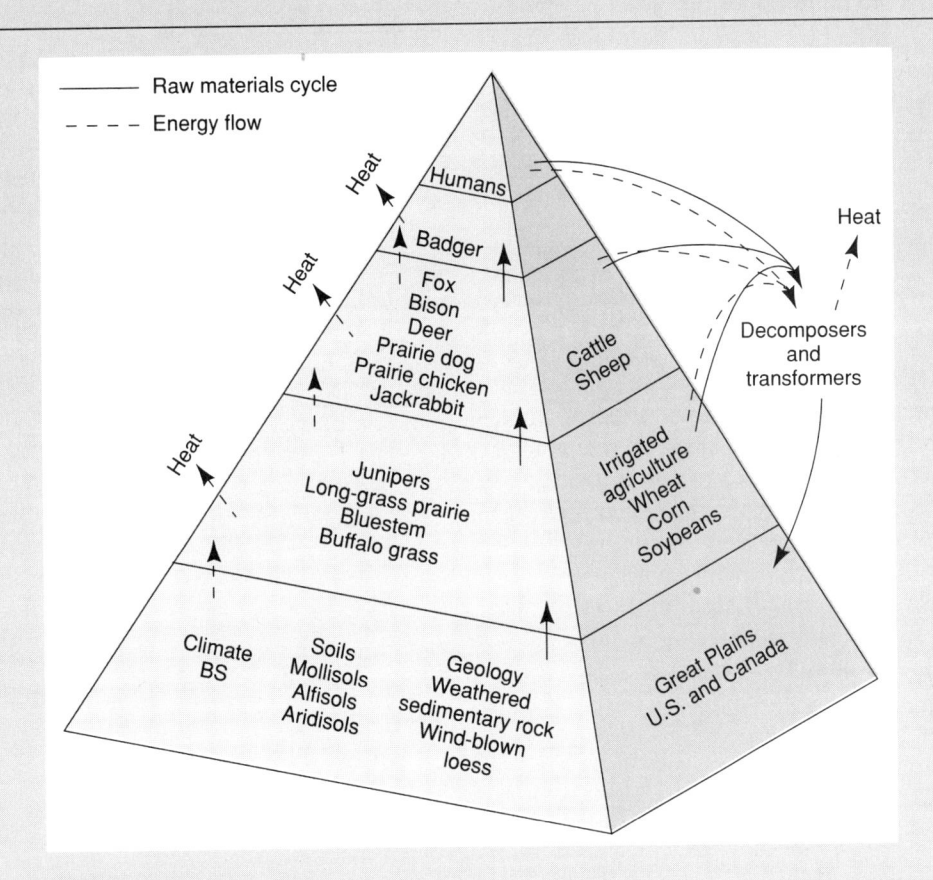

Figure 6.32B Biotic pyramid for the prairie.

Figure 6.32C Long-grass prairie.
(*Photo:* Jim Rathert, MDC).

Figure 6.32D Male prairie chicken.
(*Photo:* Jim Rathert, MDC).

Biosphere—Biogeography

Steppe (Upper Sonoran Life Zone)

Geographic Location: The Steppe ecoregion is scattered throughout the western continent of North America from Mexico to Canada. All of the states and provinces west of the 100th meridian have some steppe vegetation.

Landforms: Landforms of this ecoregion are highly variable. The steppe vegetation occurs on western slopes below 1,950 m (6,500 ft), but are higher on the drier eastern slope.

Climate: BSk: The steppe ecoregion, more than any other, is defined by climate. Lack of precipitation and high evapotranspiration rates create a scattered semiarid region in western North America that is produced, to a large degree, by the rain-shadow effect of the western mountains and the prevailing westerly winds. Annual temperature averages are from 4° to 15° C (40° to 60° F). Precipitation ranges from 250 to 500 mm (10 to 20 in).

Soil: The dominant soils are Aridisols formed by the calcification process, however Mollisols are common on the higher elevations and in the Palouse of Washington.

Flora: The vegetation and the physical variables are very diverse. The vegetative associations can be short-grass prairie, sagebrush, pinion pine-juniper (PJ) or mesquite, yuccas, and choya cactus. The diversity makes it difficult to generalize.

Fauna: Common species include: jackrabbit, deer, pronghorn antelopes, many burrowing mammals, coyote, bobcat, and cottontail rabbits. Sage grouse, prairie chickens, doves, owls, hawks, and eagles are common birds.

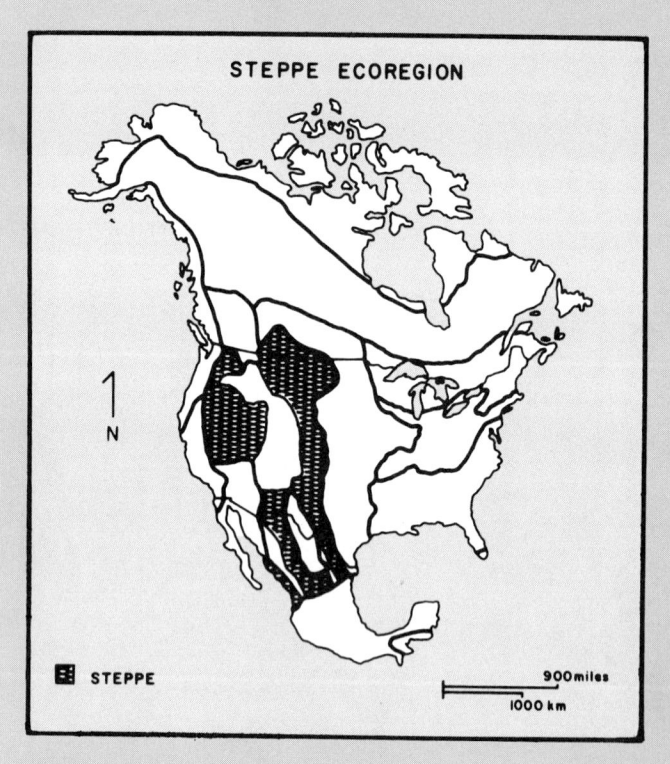

Figure 6.33A Map of the Steppe ecoregion.
(*Cartographer:* Douglas Hemsath)

Figure 6.33B Cattle on open range in the dry steppe.
(*Photo:* David A. Castillon)

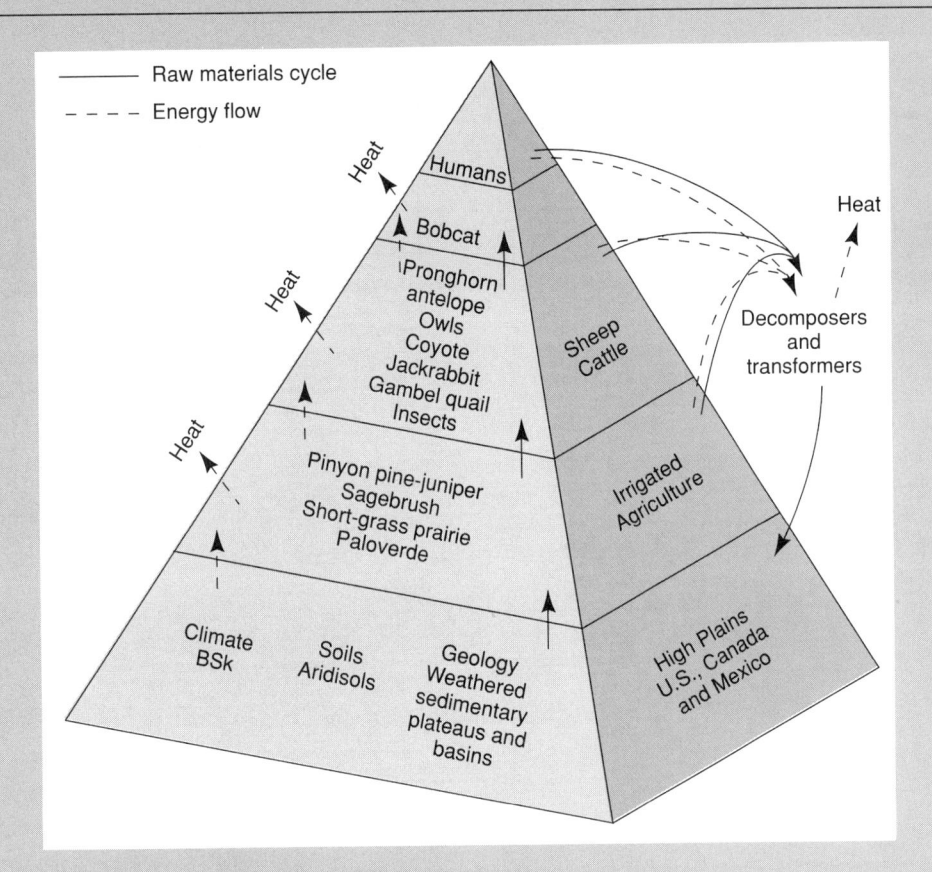

Figure 6.33C Biotic pyramid for the Steppe ecoregion.

Figure 6.33D Prairie dog;
(*Photo*: W. H. Sontag, USFWS);

Figure 6.33E Bobcat.
(*Photo*: Ken Timothy, USFS).

Biosphere—Biogeography

Desert (Lower Sonoran Life Zone)

Geographic Location: The true desert is restricted to parts of Texas, New Mexico, Arizona, California, and Nevada in the United States and continues on into Mexico.

Landforms: The desert vegetative zone is found on slopes and plains below 1,350 m (4,500 ft). The topography is highly variable and very few streams cross the region. Dry streambeds called **arroyos** are common.

Climate: BW: The desert has less than 250 mm (10 in) of precipitation per year. Evapotranspiration rates are extremely high because of the extremes of temperature. The highest temperature ever recorded in North America occurred in Death Valley in 1913, 57° C (134° F).

Soils: The lack of precipitation has allowed the calcification (salinization) process to blanket the region with Aridisols. However, on the stony ground Entisols are common.

Flora: The characteristic vegetation of the desert is thorny shrubs. Creosote bush and cacti are widely spaced and much of this region is bare ground.

Fauna: Nocturnal burrowers are at home in the desert. Kangaroo rats and pocket mice are common. The kit fox is an endangered species, but coyote, peccary, and jackrabbit are common animals. Birds include quail, hawks, owls, eagles, and roadrunners. Reptiles include the Gila monster and many snakes and lizards.

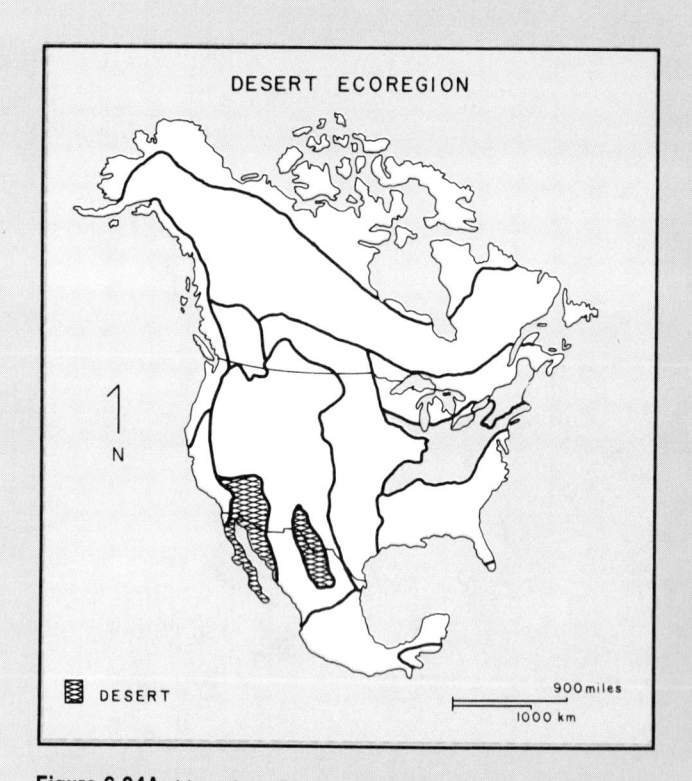

Figure 6.34A Map of the Desert ecoregion.
(*Cartographer:* Douglas Hemsath)

Figure 6.34B Desert bighorn sheep.
(*Photo:* Bill Hutchinson, USFWS).

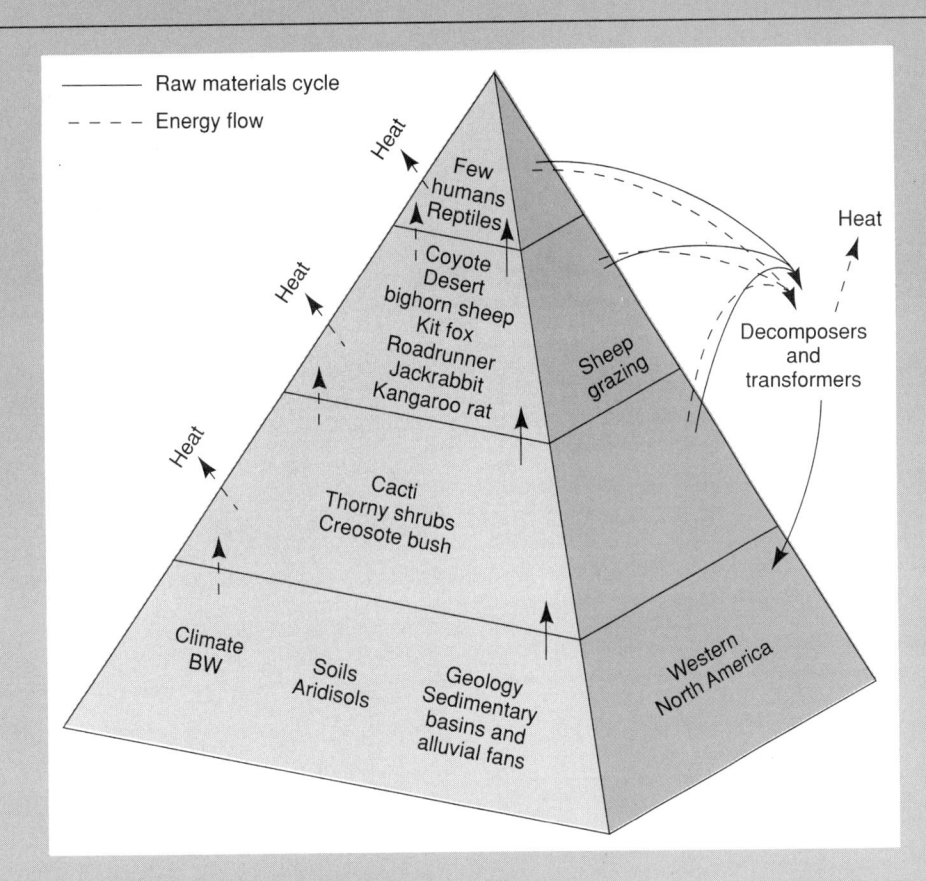

Figure 6.34C Biotic pyramid of the Desert ecoregion.

Figure 6.34D Desert vegetation in Arizona and New Mexico.
(*Photo:* David A. Castillon)

Biosphere—Biogeography

Marine (Transition Life Zone)

Geographic Location: The west coast of North America from California to Alaska is in the Marine ecoregion.

Landforms: Elevations range from sea level up to the Canadian Life Zone on the mountains.

Climate: Cfb-c: The principal climatic factor of the region is the moderating effect of the westerly winds and the moisture they bring off of the Pacific Ocean. Average annual temperatures range from 2° to 13° C (35° to 55° F). Precipitation averages 750 to 1,525 mm (30 to 60 in), but can be as high as 150 inches (3,800 mm). Precipitation is concentrated in winter.

Soils: Soils are highly variable and range from Entisol, to Inceptisol, Alfisol, and Ultisol. The podzolization process is enhanced and accelerated in this ecoregion by excessive precipitation.

Flora: The western spruce-fir-cedar-hemlock forest is the dominant association. Western red cedar, Western hemlock, Douglas fir and Sitka spruce are all common trees.

Fauna: Elk, deer, bear, mountain lion, bobcat, and moose live in this ecoregion. Smaller animals include mice, squirrel, chipmunk, rabbit, and martens. Common birds are chickadees, nuthatch, and both gray and Stellers jays.

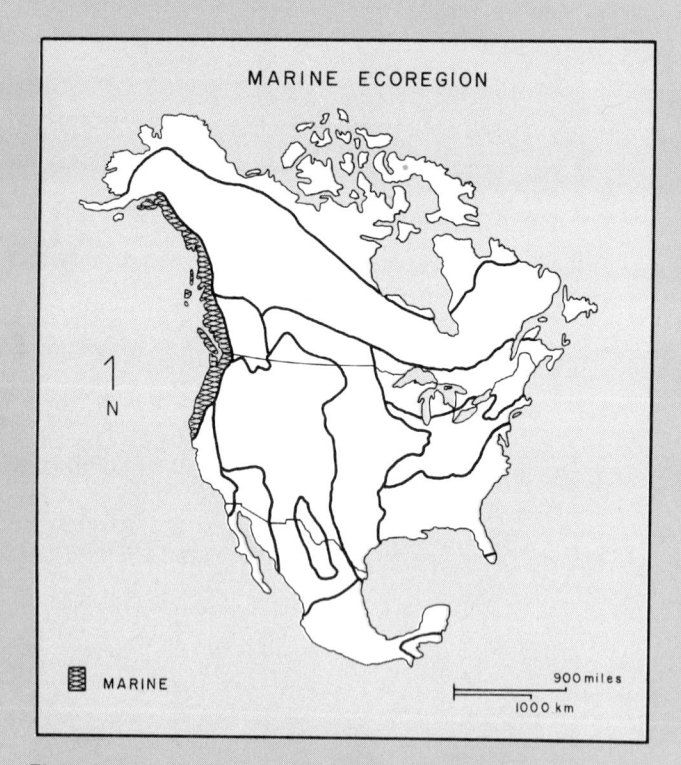

Figure 6.35A Map of the Marine West Coast ecoregion.
(Cartographer: Douglas Hemsath)

Figure 6.35B Oregon coast.
(Photo: David A. Castillon)

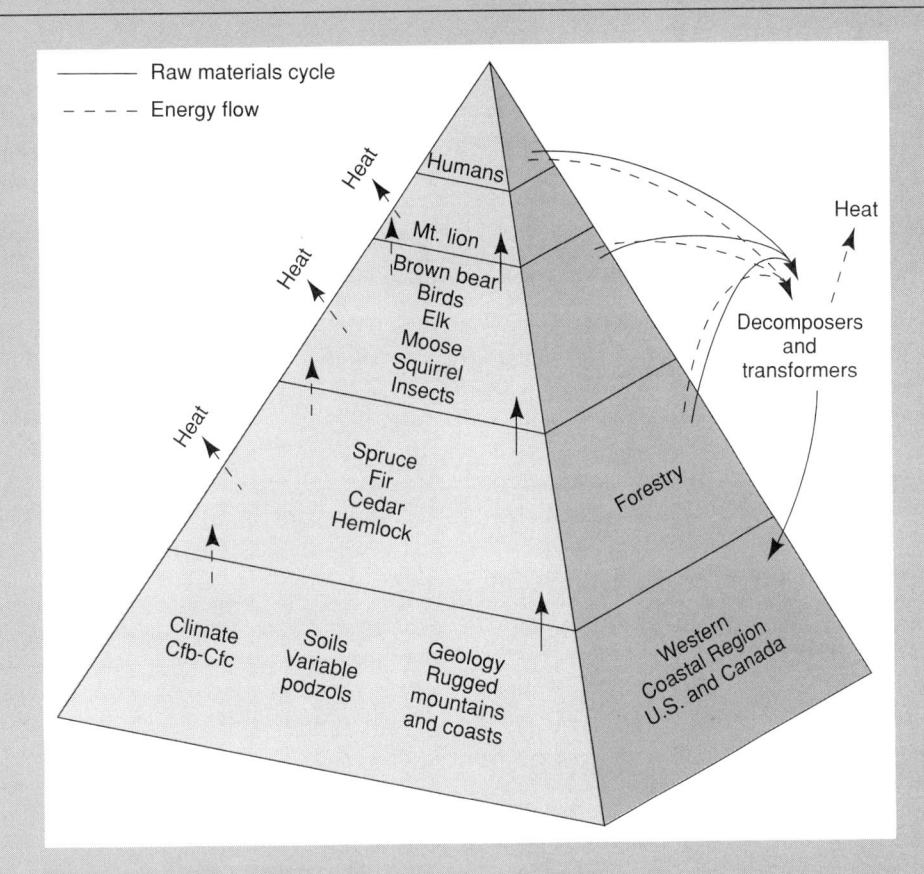

Figure 6.35C Biotic pyramid for the Marine West Coast ecoregion.

Figure 6.35D Brown bear;
(*Photo:* Jon Nickles, USFWS);

Figure 6.35E Mountain lion.
(*Photo:* Shirer, USFWS).

Biosphere—Biogeography

Mediterranean (Upper Sonoran Life Zone)

Geographic location: The west coast of California and into Mexico is the location of this ecoregion. It is the smallest region in areal extent.

Landforms: Elevation ranges from sea level up to where vertical zonation takes over in the Sierra Nevada's and changes the vegetation to a Transition Life Zone. Topography is level to steeply sloping.

Climate: Csa: The Mediterranean ecoregion has a Mediterranean climate, which is a temperate rainy climate with hot, dry summers. Precipitation ranges from 150 to 750 mm (6 to 30 in) and is concentrated in the winter months. Summers are extremely dry and two to four rainless months can occur. Annual temperatures average from 13° C (55° F) in the north to 19° C (67° F) in the south.

Soil: Entisols and Alfisols are the dominant soils of the ecoregion. Podzolization is the dominant process.

Flora: The natural vegetation of the lowlands was needlegrass prairies but this has been replaced by introduced annual grasses like fescue, avena, brome, and barley. The higher elevations are covered with an evergreen scrub association called **chaparral.** Buckbrush, manzanita, and several oaks are the dominant species.

Fauna: Common mammals include squirrels, rabbits, mice, rats, coyotes, and chipmunks. Birds include quail, warbler, pine siskin, chickadee, hawks, and owls.

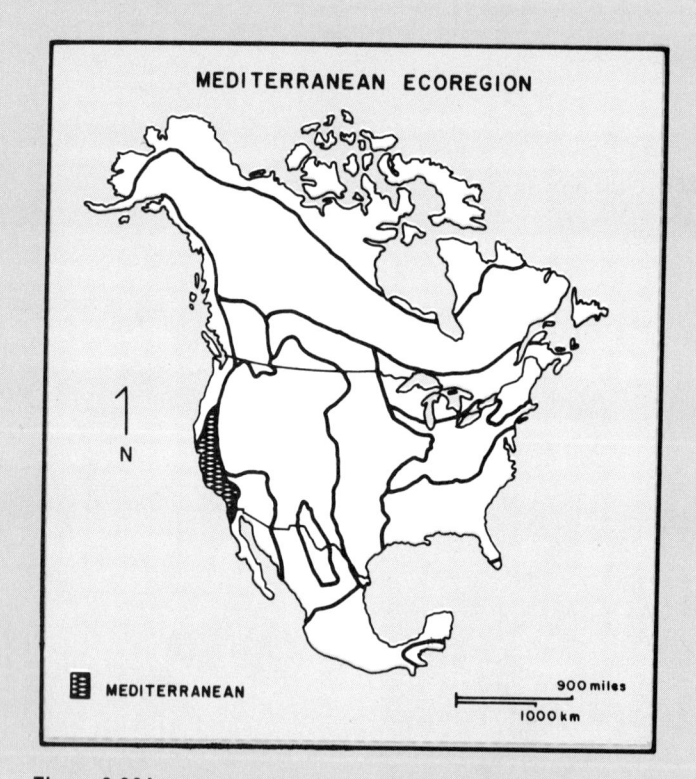

Figure 6.36A Map of the Mediterranean ecoregion.
(*Cartographer:* Douglas Hemsath)

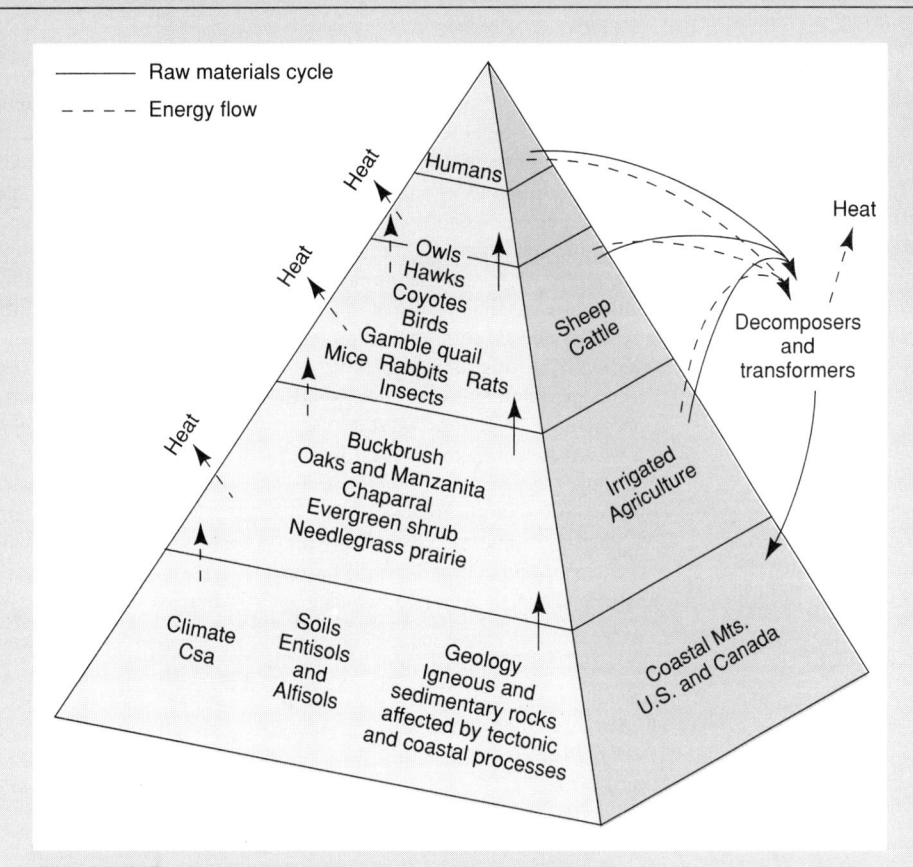

Figure 6.36B Biotic pyramid for the Mediterranean ecoregion;

Figure 6.36C Gambel's quail.
(*Photo:* Tom Smylie, USFWS).

Summary

The organisms of the **biosphere** represent the living response, the interactions of the physical variables of the lithosphere, atmosphere, and hydrosphere, to the utilization of solar energy. Food chains develop and the basic elements of all of the spheres are cycled in a continuous flow of energy and matter. The climatic condition, more than any other physical constraint, controls the climax association and equilibrium in natural cycles. A change in climate can cause changes in species composition and/or changes in biogeography.

Throughout Part I of this text the emphasis was to define and classify. The classification was geographic in nature.

Given a blank map of North America, you should now be able to describe the physical environment and the resulting natural vegetation at any point on that map. The geologic condition, the geomorphic condition, the soil and soil-formation process, and the climatic condition are all the necessary ingredients needed to predict the biotic condition. Knowing what should be there biogeographically can help you to either manage or change what is there in a way that will have the least impact on the environment, should you ever be called upon for such responsibility!

Part II of this text emphasizes the management and conservation of natural resources in North America, which requires either an understanding of the bottom of the biotic pyramid for each geographic area, or knowledge of where the resource fits on the pyramid. Questioning the irrigation of a desert makes sense if you understand the calcification soil-formation process. Knowing **what** and **where** the "B" climates are gives you a map of calcified soils and arid landscapes. Rangeland management, agricultural management, and minerals management all require that you know soils, climate, and vegetative classification. The potential for effective resource management increases tremendously when the resource manager understands the bottom of the biotic pyramid.

Key Words and Phrases

Aspect
Biogeography
Biosphere
Bryoids
Canopy
Decomposers
Denitrification
Detrital cycle
Epiphytes
Food chain
Ground cover
Halophytes
Herbs
Human-altered environments
Hydrophytes
Hygrophytes
Mesophytes
Natural climax communities
Photosynthesis
Phreatophytes
Potential natural vegetation
Primary consumers
Producers
Real vegetation
Respiration
Secondary consumers
Sedimentary (sulfur) cycle
Shrubs
Thallophytes
Trees
Tropical life zone
Trophophytes
Understory
Xerophytes

Questions and Discussion Topics

1. What are the similarities and differences in the chemical element cycles of the biosphere? (carbon vs. oxygen.) (oxygen vs. nitrogen) etc.
2. Why does the vegetation change up the side of a mountain?
3. What would the differences be on the west versus east side of a mountain in the state of Oregon? Why?
4. Take a blank map of North America and fill in each region on the map with its soil, climate, and vegetation. Discuss the possible differences that could occur in each region because of local variations in geology or topography.
5. What are the defining characteristics of each of the eleven ecoregions in North America? (Give geographic location, landforms, climate, soils, plants, and animals)

References for Further Study

Bailey, R. G. 1978. *Ecoregions of the United States.* Ogden, Utah: USDA Forest Service. The North American ecoregions are defined.

Clapham, W.B. Jr. 1973. *Natural EcoSystems.* New York: MacMillan. A good little book on the workings of ecosystems.

Küchler, A.W. 1964. *Potential Natural Vegetation of the Conterminous United States.* New York: American Geographical Society. Special Pub. No. 36. Wall map and text.

Leopold, A. 1949. *Sand County Almanac.* New York: Ballantine Books, Random House Inc. Part II, The Quality of Landscape, contains good descriptions of U.S. biogeography.

Marsh, W. M. 1987. *Earthscape: A Physical Geography.* New York: John Wiley and Sons Inc. Excellent chapters on ecosystems and biologic processes.

Omernik, J. M. March, 1987. *Ecoregions of the Conterminous United States.* Washington, D.C.: Annals of the Association of American Geographers. 77: No. 1. Excellent map supplement of U.S. biogeography (ecoregions).

Scientific American Book. 1970. *The Biosphere.* San Francisco: W. H. Freeman and Co. The cycles of the biosphere are explained in detail.

Tivy, J. 1982. *Biogeography: A Study of Plants in the Ecosphere.* 2nd ed. New York: Longman. A good introductory biogeography text.

Watts, D. 1971. *Principles of Biogeography.* New York: McGraw-Hill Book Co. Another good, but a little older, introductory biogeography text.

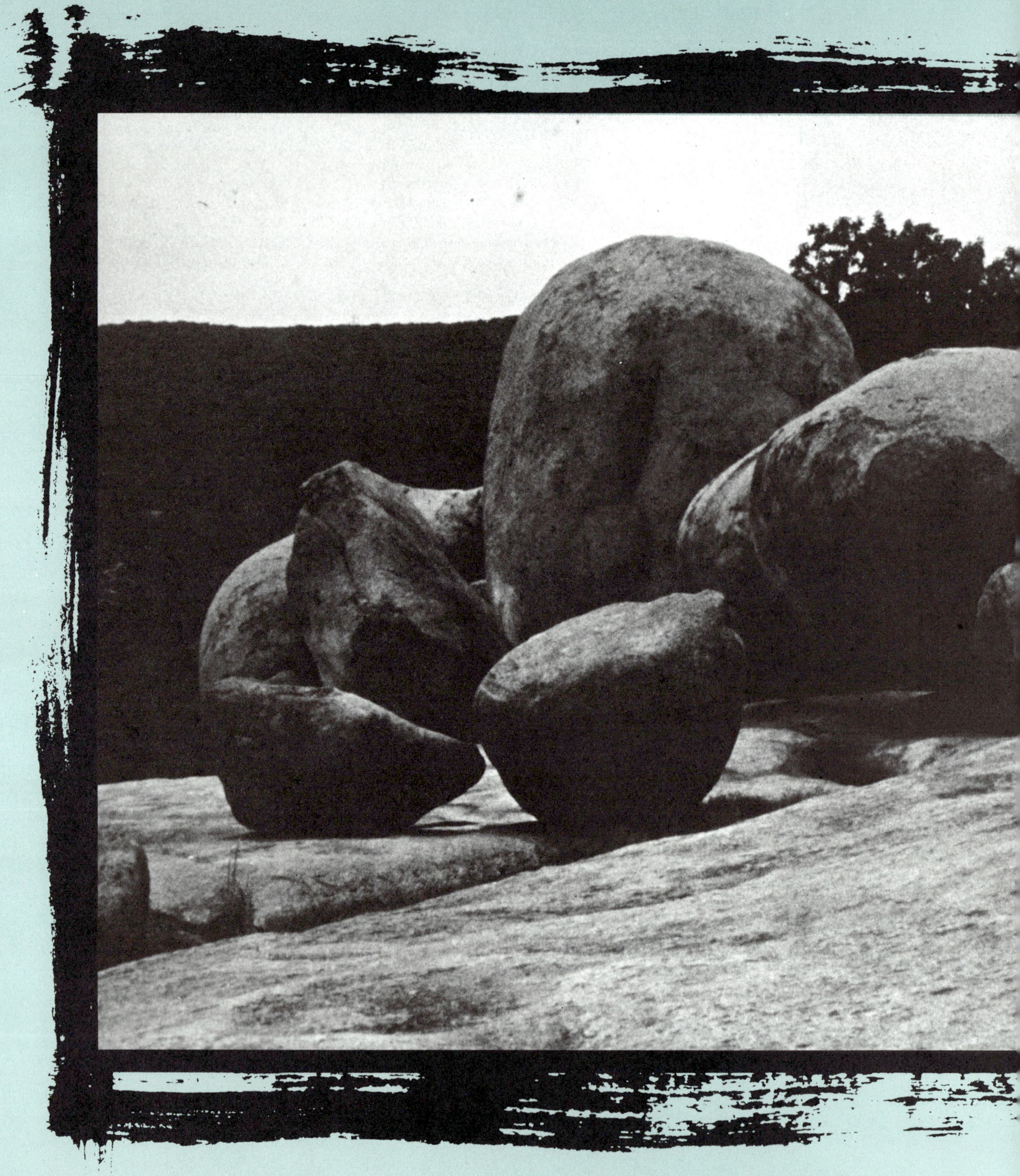

Part Two

Natural Resources Management

. . . when a man must be afraid to drink freely from his country's rivers and streams that country is no longer fit to live in. Time then to move on, to find another country or—in the name of Jefferson—to make another country.

Edward Abbey, 1968

Chapter 7

Introduction to Natural Resources Management

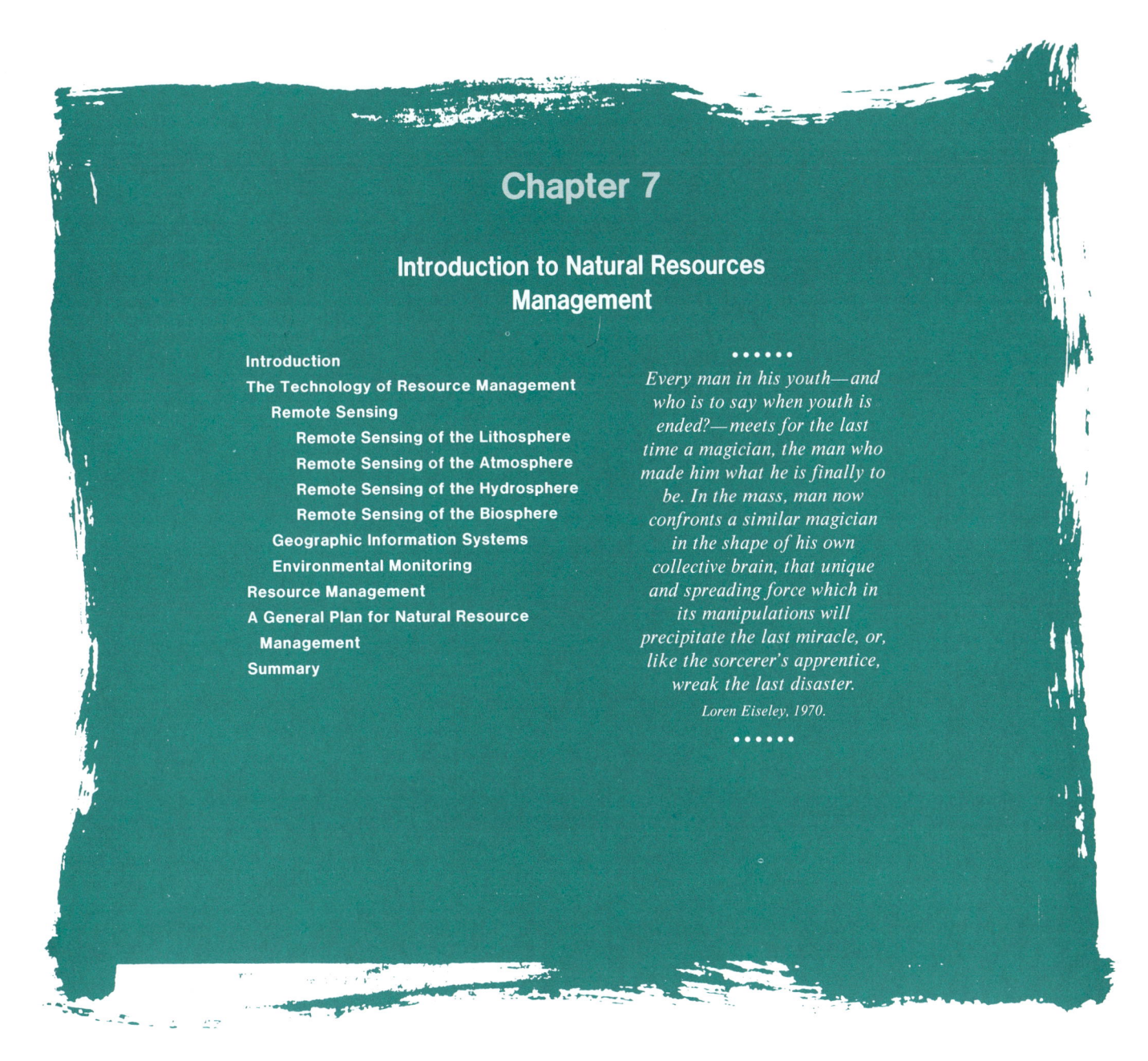

Introduction
The Technology of Resource Management
   Remote Sensing
      Remote Sensing of the Lithosphere
      Remote Sensing of the Atmosphere
      Remote Sensing of the Hydrosphere
      Remote Sensing of the Biosphere
   Geographic Information Systems
   Environmental Monitoring
Resource Management
A General Plan for Natural Resource Management
Summary

•••••

Every man in his youth—and who is to say when youth is ended?—meets for the last time a magician, the man who made him what he is finally to be. In the mass, man now confronts a similar magician in the shape of his own collective brain, that unique and spreading force which in its manipulations will precipitate the last miracle, or, like the sorcerer's apprentice, wreak the last disaster.

Loren Eiseley, 1970.

•••••

Introduction

The conservation goal of North America must be the development and protection of a quality sustainable environment which takes into consideration both the demands of nature for an ecological balance and the demands of humans for social and psychological balance.

Technology has enhanced our natural resource potential in many areas: it has increased our ability to grow food through the use of fertilizers; it has turned some of our deserts green by effectively using irrigation systems; it has reduced, with painkillers, the headaches of a crowded people; it has extended our life expectancy through medical science. But it has not provided us with one more square centimeter of new land.

We live in a closed system. The land, water, air, and soil we have are all we're going to get. Therefore, we must take care of this environment we call earth, our home, by managing our natural resources. To do this properly we need to consider two factors: the first is **the quality of human life we want to establish;** second, is what **combination of environmental ingredients will give us this quality.**

To clarify the quality life we desire, a value system needs to be established, where we identify those attributes we consider desirable and undesirable. Acceptable characteristics to most people would be beauty, serenity, diversity, and cleanliness. Unacceptable characteristics would include noise, congestion, pollution, and filth. After listing all of the desirable and undesirable attributes, answering the question of where our environment is on the scale between the extremes will give us a starting point. For example, we have all seen pictures of crystal clear drinking water. We have also seen pictures of water polluted with dead fish and sewage. What do we desire on the scale somewhere between these two extremes? What standard of water purity do we require? Do all waters have to be clean enough to drink? To answer these questions requires a value system to measure water quality and define desirables in terms of these measurements.

After quality is defined for each environmental factor, priorities must be established. The total environmental approach to resources management requires that all side effects be evaluated before a decision to proceed with a project is considered. A farmer wants to add 65 hectares (160 acres) to the productive land of the farm, but to do so requires draining a prairie pothole. Is he willing to sacrifice the reduction in diversity of landscape that will result? Will the ducks and fish that live there be lost forever? Does he really need the additional income generated by the new cropland? In answering these questions he is setting his priorities. Each of us sets our own environmental priorities with each new project we accomplish or approve.

Technology is our tool. How we use its power will have lasting environmental effects. Our increased capacity to induce change requires a matching capacity to control change. Resource management requires **programmed technology.** Conservation needs informed, knowledgeable individuals who can translate knowledge and technology into **effective, environmentally sound social action.**

The Technology of Resource Management

Remote Sensing

Technology has produced many of the environmental problems we are faced with today. Technology also provides the instrumentation necessary to help solve many environmental problems and also to monitor and manage the natural resources of our North American environment. Remote sensing, Geographic Information Systems (GIS), and the environmental monitoring programs of the EPA are the technologies available to the resource manager. Each of these tools will be examined for their benefits to conservation of natural resources.

Remote sensing is the examination of distant or concealed objects by sound waves, electronic signals, or other means. Aircraft and satellites are the vehicles that provide the panoramic perspective of our environment needed for resource management. **Radar** and **sonar** are eyes below the surface of land and sea, resulting in computer-enhanced imagery that accentuates environmental factors for analysis. All of this technology has provided the resource manager with many of the tools needed to **inventory, monitor,** and **manage** our natural resources.

Figure 7.1 illustrates the electromagnetic spectrum in relation to the remote sensing equipment used to record data. Normal color photographs record only the visible spectrum of light. Multispectral Scanners (MSS), Infrared Scanners (IR), and Thematic Mapper (TM) sensors record data in parts of the visible and infrared spectrum. Radar images such as the SIR-A and B and Seasat systems record reflected signals from microwaves. Gases such as water vapor, carbon dioxide, and ozone that affect signals by absorption are also shown as the spectral transmittance of the atmosphere. Wavelengths in the electromagnetic spectrum that allow maximum signal return without atmospheric gas interference are called *windows*. Table 7.1 gives the wavelengths of the principal windows used in each wavelength region. Wavelengths are given in nanometers, micrometers, and centimeters. A *nanometer* is one billionth of a meter and a *micrometer* is one millionth of a meter.

Aerial photography has been used since the 1930s to map soil data. Black-and-white air photos were the original form of remotely sensed data. Aerial photography was also used to discover many oil and mineral deposits. These successes, using visible wavelengths of light, suggested that possibly other wavelengths could be used to enhance features not visible to the naked eye. In the 1960s especially, manned and unmanned satellites provided a vantage point that never existed before for earth images. The old saying to "stand way back and take a good look" never meant more than when the first satellite pictures rolled off of the photo printers. To scientists, the tool to inventory and monitor the atmosphere, hydrosphere, and lithosphere had been created.

The National Aeronautics and Space Administration (NASA) and the Department of Interior (USGS-US Geological Survey), in a joint venture, launched the first Earth Resources Technology Satellite (ERTS) (later called Landsat 1) on July 23, 1972. The satellite could capture 34,225 sq km (13,225 sq mi) of the Earth's surface in a single image. The principal sensor on Landsat 1, 2, and 3 was a Multispectral Scanner (MSS) that imaged

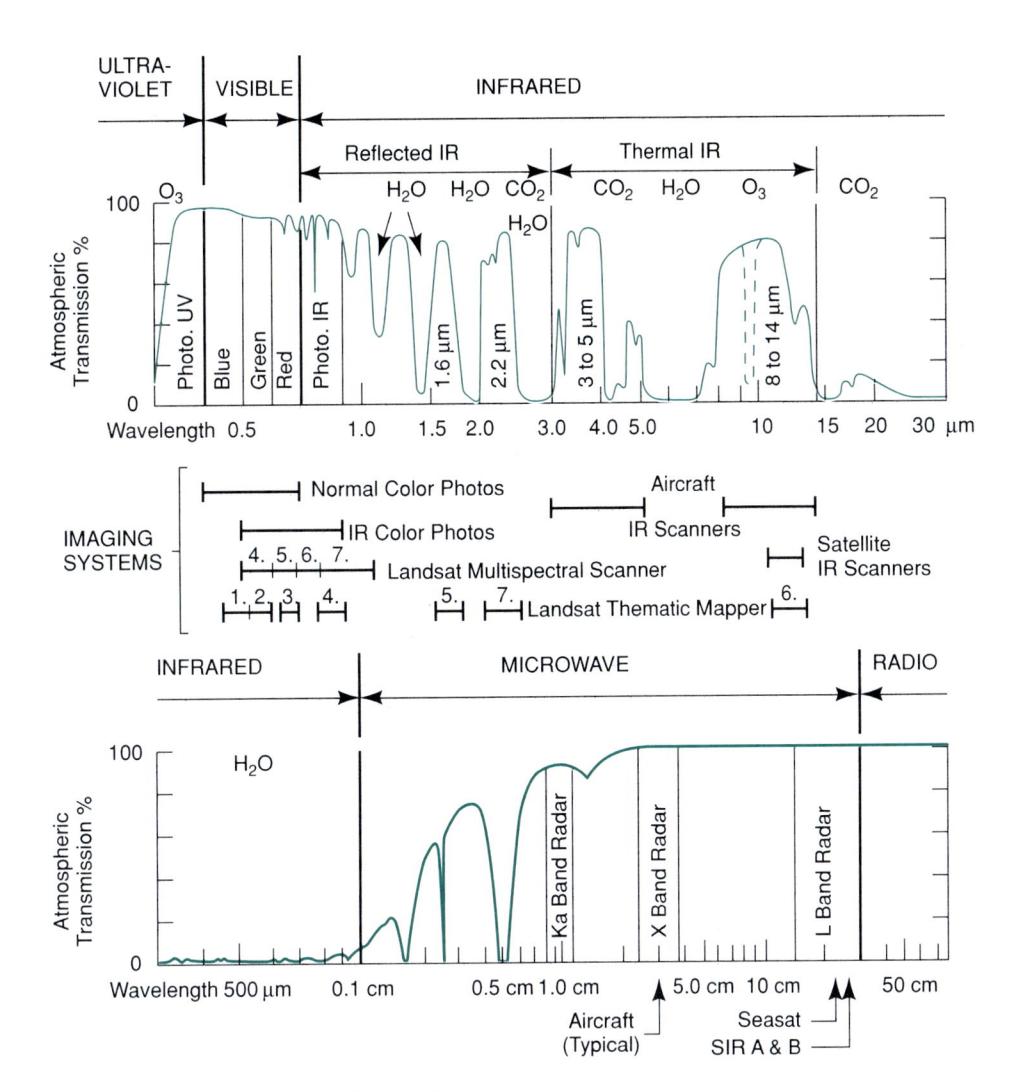

Figure 7.1 Expanded diagrams of the visible and infrared regions (upper) and the microwave region (lower) showing atmospheric windows. Wavelength bands of commonly used remote sensing systems are indicated. Gases responsible for atmospheric absorption are shown.

the Earth in four spectral bands (figure 7.1). Each band had a ground resolution of 80 m (260 ft).

Figure 7.2 illustrates the history of Landsat satellites. Landsat 4 and 5, which were launched under the National Oceanic and Atmospheric Administration (NOAA), added a single-sensor Thematic Mapper (TM) system to compliment the MSS data.

On September 27, 1985, Earth Observation Satellite Company, (EOSAT) a private business, was awarded a 10-year contract to sell Landsat data. Before that time satellite data and images were sold by the U.S. Government through EROS Data Center in Sioux Falls, South Dakota. The U.S. Government retains ownership of all satellites, and the data they generate, with the intent to continue funding the operations of Landsat 4 and 5 through their lifetimes. The future of the satellite program through the 1990s, and Landsats 6 and 7, are in the hands of the National Space Council headed by the Vice President of the United States.

Table 7.1
Spectral Regions of the Electromagnetic Spectrum

Band	Wavelength	Remarks
Gamma ray	<0.03 nm	Incoming radiation from the sun is completely absorbed by the upper atmosphere, and is not available for remote sensing. Gamma radiation from radioactive minerals is detected by low-flying aircraft as a prospecting method.
X ray	0.03 to 3 nm	Incoming radiation is completely absorbed by atmosphere. Not employed in remote sensing.
Ultraviolet, UV	0.03 to 0.4 μm	Incoming UV radiation at wavelengths < 0.3 μm is completely absorbed by ozone in the upper atmosphere.
Photographic UV	0.3 to 0.4 μm	Transmitted through the atmosphere. Detectable with film and photodetectors, but atmospheric scattering is severe.
Visible	0.4 to 0.7 μm	Detected with film and photodetectors. Includes earth reflectance peak at about 0.5 μm.
Infrared, IR	0.7 to 100 μm	Interaction with matter varies with wavelength. Atmospheric transmission windows are separated by absorption bands.
Reflected IR	0.7 to 3 μm	This is primarily reflected solar radiation and contains no information about thermal properties of materials. Radiation from 0.7 to 0.9 μm is detectable with film and is called photographic IR radiation.
Thermal IR	3 to 5 μm 8 to 14 μm	These are the principal atmospheric windows in the thermal region. Imagery at these wavelengths is acquired through the use of optical-mechanical scanners, not by film.
Microwave	0.1 to 30 cm	These longer wavelengths can penetrate clouds and fog. Imagery may be acquired in the active or passive mode.
Radar	0.1 to 30 cm	Active form of microwave remote sensing.
Radio	> 30 cm	Longest wavelength portion of electromagnetic spectrum. Some classified radars with very long wavelengths operate in this region.

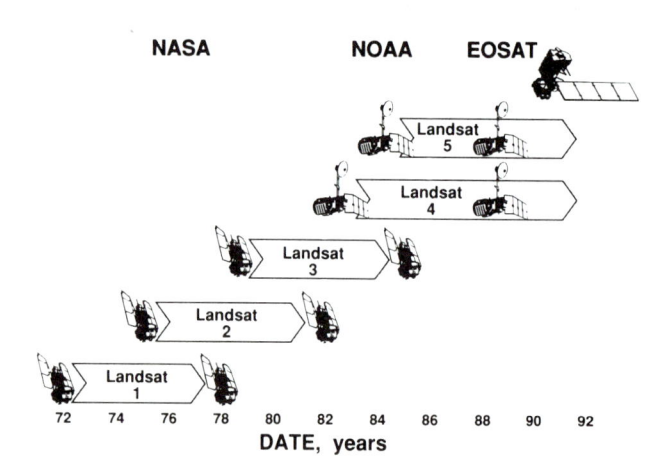

Figure 7.2 History of Landsat.
Earth Observation Satellite Company, Lanham, MD, USA. Reprinted by permission.

Remote Sensing of the Lithosphere

During the almost 20 years of the Landsat program, many significant events occurring in the lithosphere have been recorded. In 1973, the major flooding of the Mississippi-Missouri River Basin was recorded. In 1980, the Mount St. Helen's eruption and aftermath were documented. In 1985, the historic high water level for the Great Salt Lake was recorded. And in 1986, a thematic mapper image of the Augustine volcanic eruption in Cook Inlet near Anchorage, Alaska was captured within a few hours after the eruption. Landsat's real legacy, however, lies in the record of subtle but continuous changes on the earth's surface that have been recorded and preserved by these satellites.

Landsat is not the only remote sensing tool for lithospheric studies. Radar images can penetrate the earth's surface materials and record hidden subsurface geologic features. A radar image of the eastern Egyptian desert reveals an ancient drainageway that is buried by rock and sand (figure 7.3). Figure 7.4 shows the rocky eolian landscape in the vicinity of the drainageway that has no surface expression. The radar sensor penetrates the moisture-free surface materials and channel deposits and records the underground channel shown in Figure 7.3. The channel filling is less dense than the sandstone into which it was carved.

The technology to locate subsurface lithologic features is a tremendous tool for the resource manager. Locating buried channels in a dry environment could provide a source of water for irrigation. Locating geologic structures in the subsurface can help to pinpoint the location of mineral and energy resources. Locating subsurface geologic structures that serve as conduits to groundwater supplies would help avoid water contamination problems in the siting of waste-disposal facilities. Resource managers need remote sensing tools to effectively manage the environment.

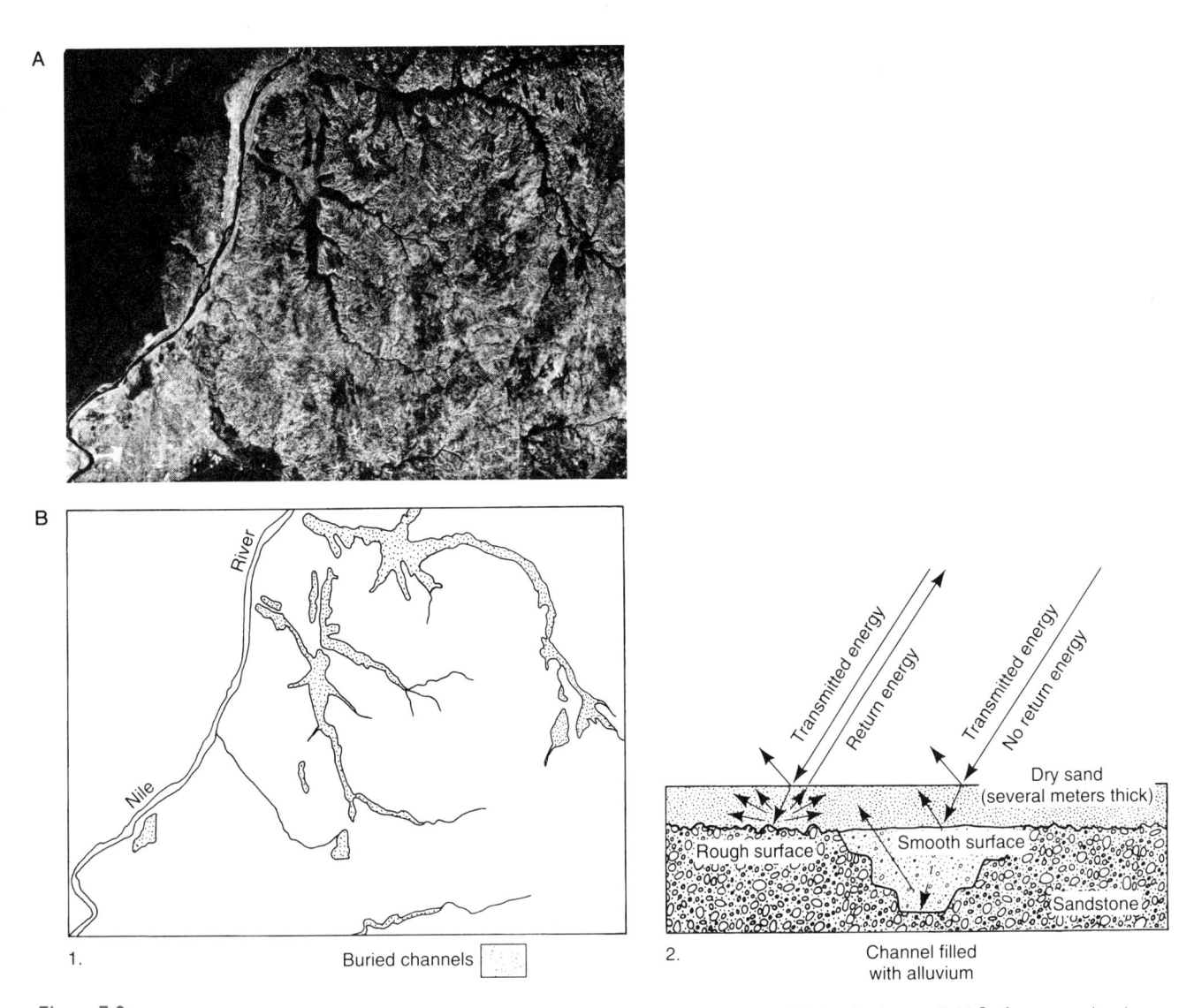

Figure 7.3 Buried river channels detected by SIR-A radar in the eastern Egyptian desert. (a) SIR-A radar image; (b1.) Surface map showing buried channels; (b2.) Cross section of a buried channel.
(*Cartographer:* Mike Klein)

Figure 7.4 Eastern Egyptian desert landscape—dry rocky surface conceals buried channels.
(*Photo:* David A. Castillon)

Introduction to Natural Resources Management 167

Figure 7.5 Satellite image of a line of severe thunderstorms over eastern Texas and southern Louisiana.
(*Photo:* NOAA)

Remote Sensing of the Atmosphere

The public is exposed daily to satellite photos of the clouds or a radar image of precipitation as a part of the daily weather report and forecast (figure 7.5). A look at the atmosphere from a space platform tells us much about our present and future weather. Remotely sensed data on the atmosphere were first obtained in the 1930s by a radiosonde, a small package equipped with a radio transmitter and carried aloft by a helium-filled balloon. Data on the atmosphere are still collected by radiosonde, but the upper limit for readings is about 30 km (19 mi). Weather satellites have become our eyes in the sky, with data on cloud patterns, winds, temperature, humidity, and radiation collected on a regular basis.

Weather radar is a valuable tool for detecting and monitoring severe weather. Tornadoes are too small to be detected by the widely spaced network of weather-observing satellite instrumentation, but hurricanes are studied from formation to dissipation. Conventional weather radar transmitters emit short pulses of microwaves in the 5–10 cm (2–4 in) wavelength range. These waves can see through the clouds, but are scattered by precipitation and return an echo off of rain or snow. Radar is an ideal tool to pick up individual thunderstorm cells and, in some cases, a hook echo is formed, indicating the presence of a tornado. Doppler radar has the added capacity to detect motion in the targeted precipitation and is replacing conventional radar. Color plate number 1 is a Nexrad radar printout of a severe storm in Oklahoma on March 3, 1990, at 5:43 P.M. CDT. Color reveals storm intensity.

Figure 7.6 is a satellite image of Hurricane Hugo as it came on land in Charleston, South Carolina on September 22, 1989. Predictions of the hurricane's arrival and the force of the winds were made possible by satellite images. Property damage was tremendous but loss of life was minimized by the accurate forecast (figure 7.7). Data from remote sensing of storm tracks and individual hurricanes, like Hugo, are digitized and put into computer models. These models generate risk-potential maps such as the one illustrated in Figure 7.8. These risk maps become important input information sources for resource managers.

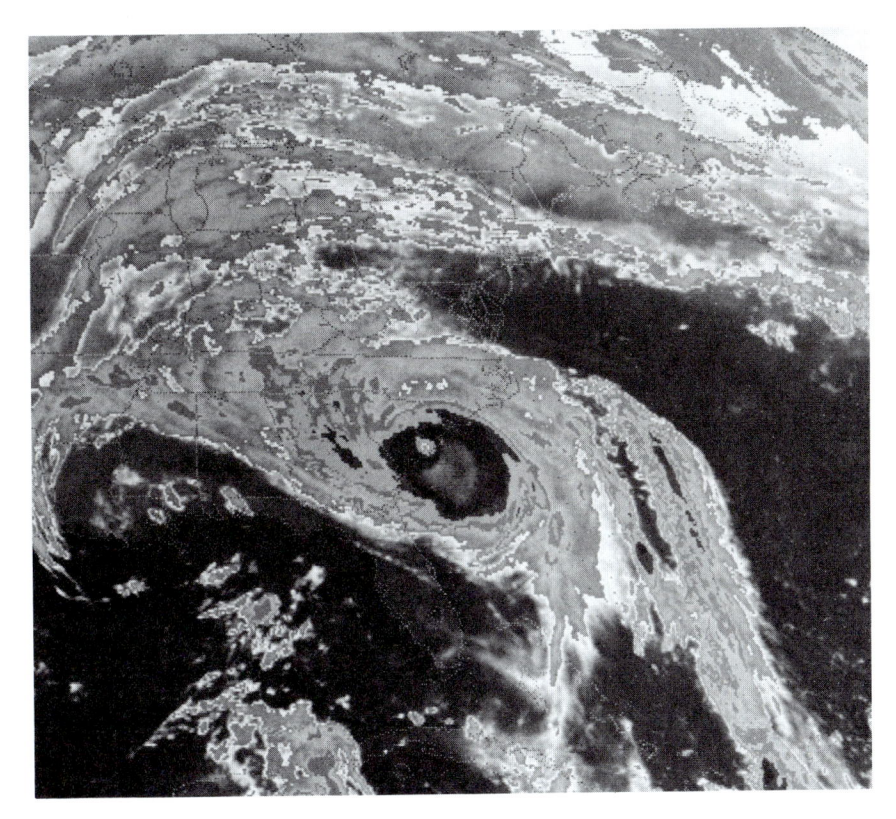

Figure 7.6 Satellite image of Hurricane Hugo coming ashore in South Carolina on September 22, 1989.
(*Photo:* NOAA)

Figure 7.7 Damage from Hurricane Hugo was extensive. Homes were damaged, beaches were eroded, and boats were tossed around like toys.
(*Photo:* Jonas Jordan, USACE)

Introduction to Natural Resources Management

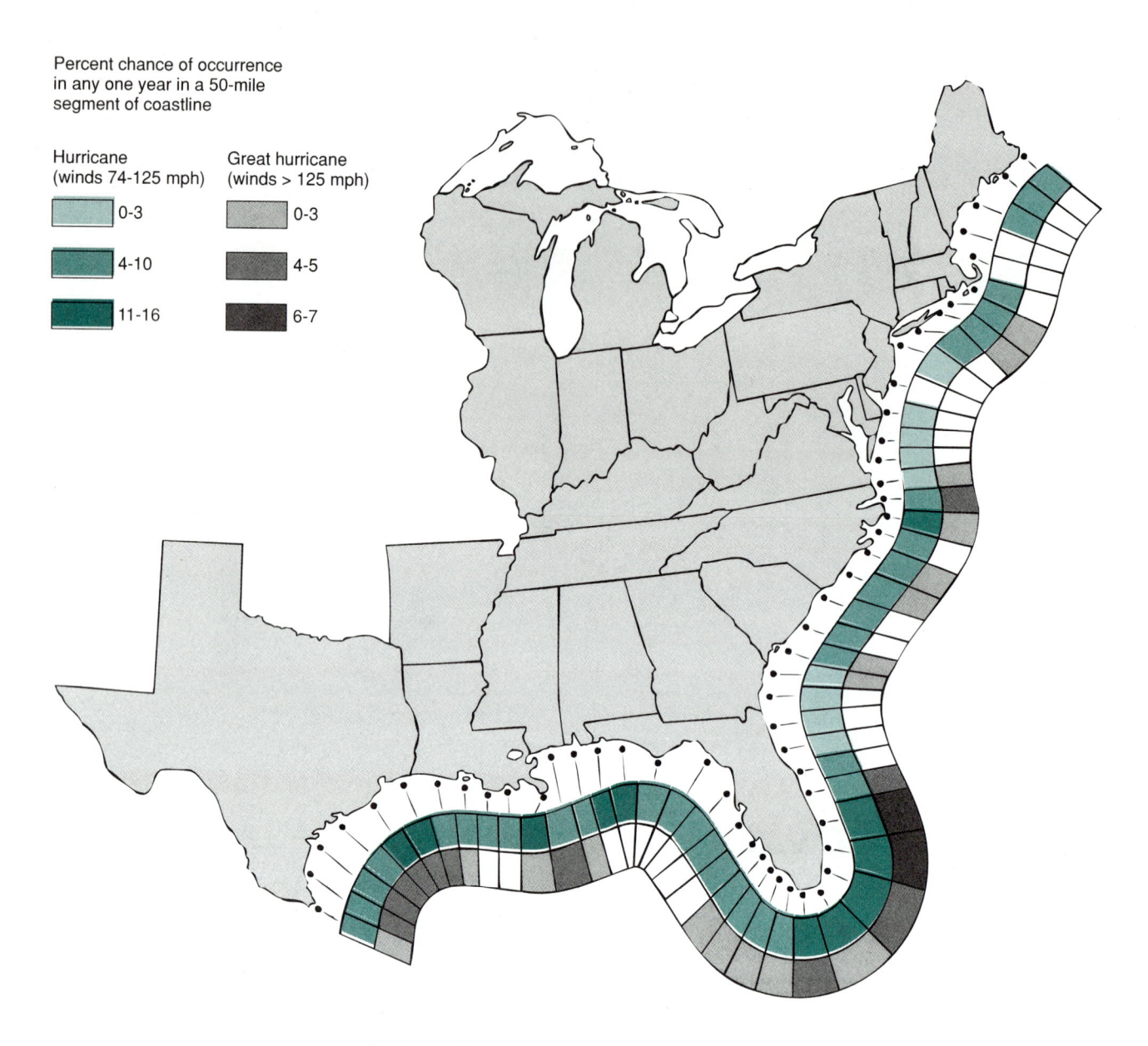

Hurricane Risk along the Gulf and Atlantic Coasts

Figure 7.8 Hurricane risk along the Gulf and Atlantic coasts.
Source: Environmental Protection Agency, *Environmental Trends*, 1989.

Weather observations from satellites have become commonplace. But these are not the only uses for remotely sensed data of the atmosphere. Air pollution and dust storms have both been recorded by sensors on satellites. Gaseous pollutants of the atmosphere can be detected and concentrations determined, but individual signatures for each pollutant cannot be identified at this time. Sulphur dioxide (SO_2) cannot be separated from NO_2 or CH_4, for example. Satellite images have provided valuable information about the source region and depositional area for dust storms. Another use for satellite images has been snow and ice surveys. Mapping the extent of snow cover can be valuable information for flood prediction before the spring melt. Landsat images also recorded the extent of ice coverage in Chesapeake Bay during the coldest recorded winter (1977) in that area. These and many other uses of satellite data have become the information base for environmental monitoring and resource management.

Another example of the use of remotely sensed data that affects both the atmosphere and lithosphere is the distribution of ash after a volcanic eruption. The violent eruption of Mount St. Helens in May 1980 (figure 2.12) was not particularly large on a geologic scale. Nonetheless, it put 1.25 km^3 (0.3 mi^3) of ash into the atmosphere for distribution downwind. Figures 7.9a, b, and c illustrate a three-day sequence of ash distribution across North America. Some of the ash was transported by the upper atmospheric jet stream and circled the globe in 17 days, but most was deposited a short distance downwind from the volcano. Large eruptions can put enough ash into the upper atmosphere to block out the sun's energy and change climate.

Remote Sensing of the Hydrosphere

Observations of the ocean in a panoramic view were not possible before humans took to the air. Satellites have given us that platform in the sky needed to study the oceans. Satellite infrared (IR) data can be mapped as sea-surface temperatures over a vast ocean in less than a day. Oceanographic ships could only map 40 km^2 (15 mi^2) in a day. By the time they finished a survey, ocean temperatures had changed where the survey began. The movement of currents and tides can be displayed on a single image for an entire ocean (Color Plate No. 2a). The spring bloom of phytoplankton in the oceans can be studied as it relates to water temperature and mixing. Even the depth of the ocean can be determined from satellite data (Color Plate No. 2b).

Remote sensing of our two major ice sheets in Greenland and Antarctica have given new insights into the fresh water contained in them. Radio-echo-sounding (RES) has provided a rapid and accurate method for measuring ice thickness. It has also provided information on internal structure, dynamics, and thermodynamic properties of the ice. The harsh glacial environments and the remoteness of these areas lend themselves well to the data-collection techniques provided by unmanned satellites. Remotely sensed data aided in the discovery of the hole in the ozone layer over Antarctica. Extrapolation of the findings from the data from these two ice sheets have applicability in studies of the alpine glaciers in North America. Sea-level fluctuations are controlled by the amount of ice in glaciers. Being able to predict sea level accurately is very important to coastal communities.

Satellite data and remotely sensed images have many applications in studying the hydrosphere. Surface-water inventories have been conducted. Water-quality studies have detected source regions for pollution. Side-looking radar signals have the ability to penetrate the surface of a desert and detect underground channels and water-saturated sediment. The list of uses for remotely sensed data for studying the hydrosphere seems almost endless.

Figure 7.9 Ash distribution by upper-level winds following the Mount St. Helens eruption on May 18, 1980. Ash highlights the west-to-east movement (in approximately 6 hours) of air in the Polar Front jet stream (7.9c)
(*Photo*: U.S. Weather Bureau)

Managers of aquatic environments must have the data provided by remote sensing to effectively manage these ecosystems.

The U.S. Fish and Wildlife Service (USFWS) was concerned with the impact of agricultural development adjacent to the Loxahatchee National Wildlife Refuge wetlands in Florida (Color Plate No. 3a). A detailed, up-to-date map of the wetlands vegetation was needed for an inventory and baseline assessment monitoring program. A single SPOT image could cover the entire area ($3,600$ km^2–$1,400$ mi^2) and provide the data needed to map the four basic land cover classes of slough, wet prairie, saw grass, and tree islands into 18 vegetative classes (Color Plate No. 3b). Mapping was accomplished in 600 m^2 (1/40 acre) units. This wetlands vegetation map is an essential data component in the Geographic Information System (GIS) established to analyze and monitor the Loxahatchee NWR, which has been classified by the USFWS as one of the 10 most threatened refuges in the United States.

SPOT images taken on a yearly cycle or images taken following a drought or flooding episode could be used to detect environmental impacts on the refuge. Monitoring the impact of the agricultural development to the west and northwest of the refuge will be an ongoing endeavor of the USFWS resource managers. Changes in the land use of the agricultural areas adjacent to the NWR should be easily detected on later images.

Remote Sensing of the Biosphere

Photographs of the earth's surface from an aircraft or satellite are pictures of the tops of vegetation on the surface being recorded. Remote sensing in wavelengths of the nonvisible spectrum has produced images that see through the foliage, but, in studying the biosphere, it is the vegetation we usually want to capture on the image. Satellite images have been used extensively to map the biogeography of North America. The biogeographic maps produced have then been used for crop inventory, forest inventory, wildlife habitat assessment, grazing management, fire damage assessment, disease detection, and mapping land-use change. The list of potential uses for remotely sensed data is only limited by the imagination of the investigator.

The USGS Professional Paper 964 (1976) developed a land-use and land-cover classification system for use with remote sensing data. The system separates land uses into nine Level I categories and further subdivides Level I into Level II and III categories (table 7.2). This system of land-use categories has been widely accepted for mapping from satellite images. Expansion and extension of categories have been common practices in research directed at a particular land-use category. For example, in studying a wilderness area in a Midwestern deciduous forest, the entire area would be mapped as a Level II 41 or 43. Close examination of low-altitude aerial photographs or *ground truthing* (the examination of an area by foot or vehicle) would dictate separate regions of Oak-Hickory, Oak-Pine, Cedar Glade, and Riparian Zone Vegetation. A Level IV classification can be added, which takes into consideration individual project goals and objectives. Vegetative associations would be the appropriate level of biogeographic mapping for wilderness research. Table 7.3 gives the terrain and vegetation signatures on normal color film and on color IR film that are used for land-use mapping.

The Pacific Northwest is being clear-cut at an alarming rate. Satellite images can be used to effectively monitor the removal of forest cover. SPOT Quad Maps™ present the forester with up-to-date, detailed information on a USGS 7.5 minute format (Maps with a RF 1:24,000 scale).

Oakridge, Oregon is under siege by loggers. Color Plate No. 4 is a SPOT Quad Map™ of the Oakridge area showing the extent of logging in two time periods. Areas cut between 1982 and 1986 are shown in red. Areas cut between 1986 and June 1989 are shown in yellow. As you can see, almost all of the southwest quarter of the image area has been logged. The image also illustrates the problems created by cloud cover for this type of project. Images collected in the future can be used to monitor environmental changes caused by clear cutting the Pacific Northwest, and other forests.

These uses of remotely sensed data are designed to expose the reader to the field of remote sensing. It is the tool of the resource planner, but a word of caution is in order. Like any tool, it has its limitations. For example, the cool radiant temperatures of an oil film on ocean water can have the identical signature of a cold ocean current on a thermal IR image. Experienced interpreters understand the capabilities and limitations of the imaging system and the characteristics of the features being interpreted. If the imaging data have been processed, the interpreter must understand the processing that has converted the original data. There is no substitute in remote sensing for experience. Anyone interested in a career in conservation or resource management should take a college-level course in remote sensing and aerial photo interpretation. They are the tools of the trade.

The future for remotely sensed data to remain readily available as a research tool in conservation and resource management looks bright. Plans by the world community to launch additional satellites into orbit are proceeding. European countries and Japan have satellite launch programs that run through the 1990s. Figure 7.10 illustrates the time frame for NASA and internationally-approved-and-planned resource observation programs. In addition, the shuttle missions are flying again and are using a Large-Format Camera (LFC) capable of taking high-resolution stereo photographs from space. The shuttle program has

Table 7.2

A Land-Use and Land-Cover Classification System for Use with Remote Sensor Data

Classification level	Typical data characteristics
I	SPOT or LANDSAT (formerly ERTS) type of data.
II	High-altitude data at 40,000 ft (12,400 m) or above (less than 1:80,000 scale).
III	Medium-altitude data taken between 10,000 and 40,000 ft (3,100 and 12,400 m) (1:20,000 to 1:80,000 scale).
IV	Low-altitude data taken below 10,000 ft (3,100 m) (more than 1:20,000 scale).

Level I		Level II		Level III	
1	Urban or Built-up Land	11	Residential.	111	Single-family Units.
		12	Commercial and Services.	112	Multi-family Units.
		13	Industrial.	113	Group Quarters.
		14	Transportation, Communications, and Utilities.	114	Residential Hotels.
		15	Industrial and Commercial Complexes.	115	Mobile Home Parks.
		16	Mixed Urban or Built-up Land.	116	Transient Lodgings.
		17	Other Urban or Built-up Land.	117	Other.
2	Agriculture Land	21	Cropland and Pasture.		
		22	Orchards, Groves, Vineyards, Nurseries, and Ornamental Horticultural Areas.		
		23	Confined Feeding Operations.		
		24	Other Agricultural Land.		
3	Rangeland	31	Herbaceous Rangeland.		
		32	Shrub and Brush Rangeland.		
		33	Mixed Rangeland.		
4	Forest Land	41	Deciduous Forest Land.		
		42	Evergreen Forest Land.		
		43	Mixed Forest Land.		
5	Water	51	Streams and Canals.		
		52	Lakes.		
		53	Reservoirs.		
		54	Bays and Estuaries.		
6	Wetland	61	Forested Wetland.		
		62	Nonforested Wetland.		
7	Barren Land	71	Dry Salt Flats.		
		72	Beaches.		
		73	Sandy Areas other than Beaches.		
		74	Bare Exposed Rock.		
		75	Strip Mines, Quarries, and Gravel Pits.		
		76	Transitional Areas.		
		77	Mixed Barren Land.		
8	Tundra	81	Shrub and Brush Tundra.		
		82	Herbaceous Tundra.		
		83	Bare Ground Tundra.		
		84	Wet Tundra.		
		85	Mixed Tundra.		
9	Perennial Snow or Ice	91	Perennial Snowfields.		
		92	Glaciers.		

Source: U.S. Geographical Survey Professional Paper 964, 1976.

Table 7.3

Terrain and Vegetation Signatures on Normal Color Film and IR Color Film

Subject	Normal color film	IR color film
Healthy vegetation:		
Broadleaf type	Green	Red to magenta
Needle-leaf type	Green	Reddish brown to purple
Stressed vegetation:		
Previsual stage	Green	Pink to blue
Visual stage	Yellowish green	Cyan
Autumn leaves	Red to yellow	Yellow to white
Clear water	Blue-green	Dark blue to black
Silty water	Light green	Light blue
Damp ground	Slightly darker	Distinct dark tones
Shadows	Blue with details visible	Black with few details visible
Water penetration	Good	Green and red bands: same IR band: poor
Contacts between land and water	Poor to fair discrimination	Excellent discrimination
Red bed outcrops	Red	Yellow

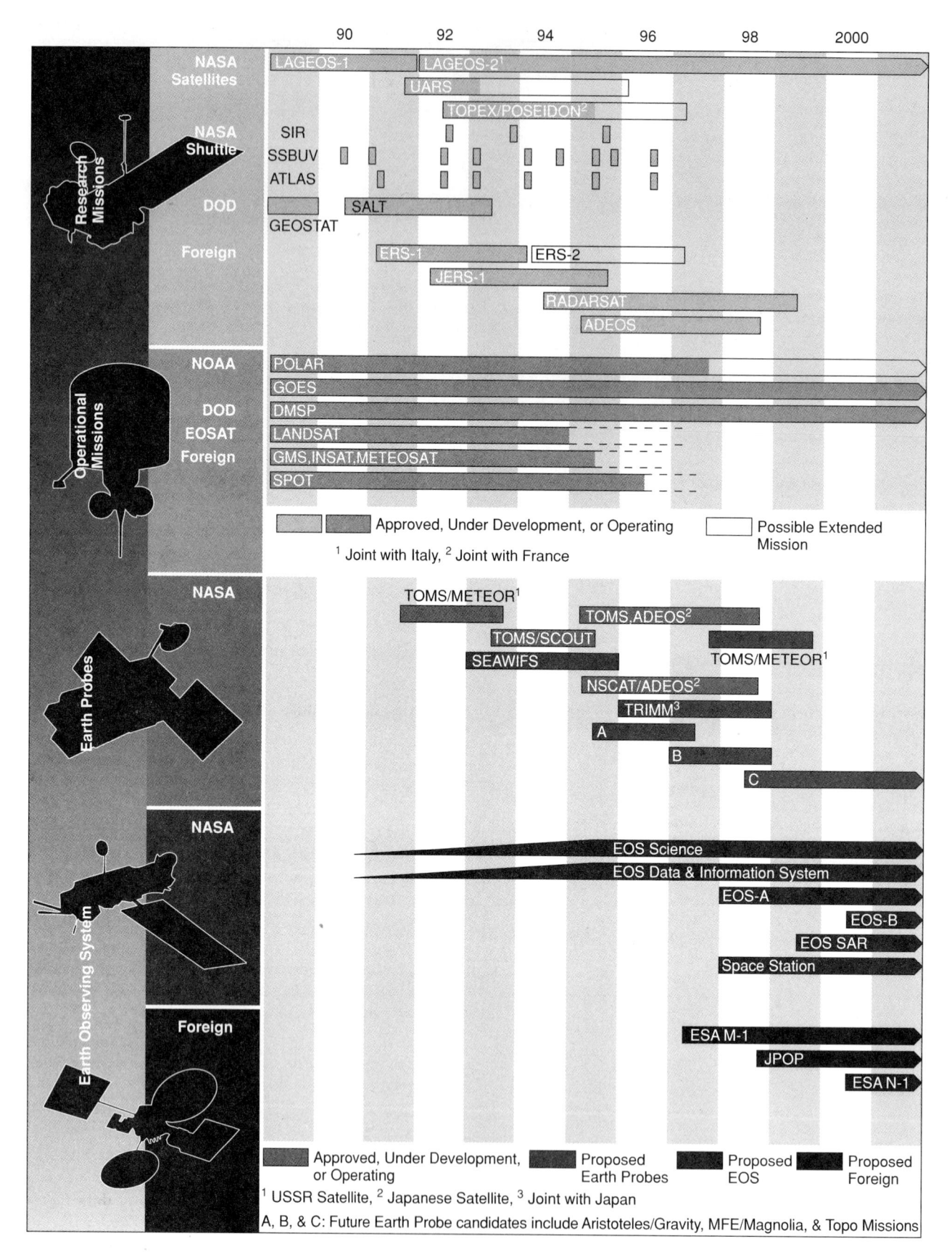

Figure 7.10 International remote sensing systems—past, present, and future.
Source: NASA.

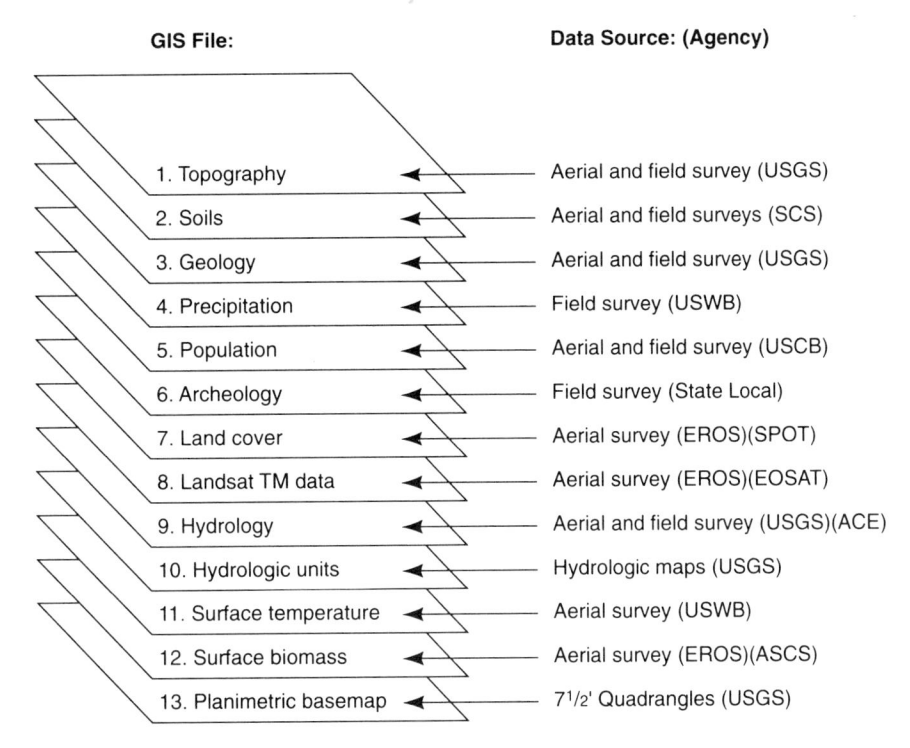

GIS File:	Data Source: (Agency)
1. Topography	Aerial and field survey (USGS)
2. Soils	Aerial and field surveys (SCS)
3. Geology	Aerial and field survey (USGS)
4. Precipitation	Field survey (USWB)
5. Population	Aerial and field survey (USCB)
6. Archeology	Field survey (State Local)
7. Land cover	Aerial survey (EROS)(SPOT)
8. Landsat TM data	Aerial survey (EROS)(EOSAT)
9. Hydrology	Aerial and field survey (USGS)(ACE)
10. Hydrologic units	Hydrologic maps (USGS)
11. Surface temperature	Aerial survey (USWB)
12. Surface biomass	Aerial survey (EROS)(ASCS)
13. Planimetric basemap	7½' Quadrangles (USGS)

Figure 7.11 A geographic information system (GIS), consisting of biophysical and cultural files geometrically registered to a planimetric basemap. The information contained in the GIS is derived from a number of sources.
Source: William J. Ripple (ed.), *Fundamentals of Geographic Information Systems*. Copyright © 1989 American Society of Photogrammetry, Falls Church, VA.

successfully launched the Hubble Space telescope into orbit. This remote sensing device will become our eyes in the universe after a focusing problem with the mirrors is corrected. The future of remote sensing, however, has economic and political constraints. Only time will tell how long governments will be willing to finance these much-needed space programs that provide the resource manager with the increasingly necessary tools of his trade.

Geographic Information Systems

A *Geographic Information System* (GIS) is defined as an integrated network of hardware (computers), software (programs), and personnel designed to capture, store, manage, analyze, and display large volumes of digital data base information of a geographic nature. There are a variety of information systems, each with its own specific purpose and data base. An information system designed to use global data would find little utility in analyzing or solving a local problem. If the global system has the software to handle the local project, the data base and scale would have to be changed. A natural resource manager with a well-defined set of management goals can find a suitable GIS network that will enhance the resource management capabilities of any project with a large data base.

A GIS network is the ideal technology to analyze natural resource management problems, since it is designed to accept large volumes of spatially distributed data from a variety of sources (figure 7.11). To illustrate the GIS methodology, a program designed by Jensen and Christensen, and described in an article entitled, "Solid and Hazardous Waste Disposal Site Selection Using Digital Geographic Information System Techniques," will be used as an example. Their goal was to select future industrial hazardous waste-disposal sites so that their impact on the environment and public was minimized. Accomplishing this goal required the collection, storage, and analysis of volumes of multidisciplinary information, integrating a variety of economic and environmental constraints. Data were collected on wetlands, land cover, transportation network, sensitive areas, existing waste sites, and topography. Industrial location constraint criteria included elevation, proximity to wetlands, sensitive areas, existing waste sites, and road access.

The methodology for industrial waste site selection includes: 1) Identification of industrial location constraint criteria (ILCC); 2) Specifying the environmental and cultural information required to address the ILCC; 3) Collecting the required information in a digital data format using remote sensing techniques or field data; 4) Transferring all data to the same scale as the basemap; 5) Digitizing the thematic data on the base map to an acceptable

Introduction to Natural Resources Management

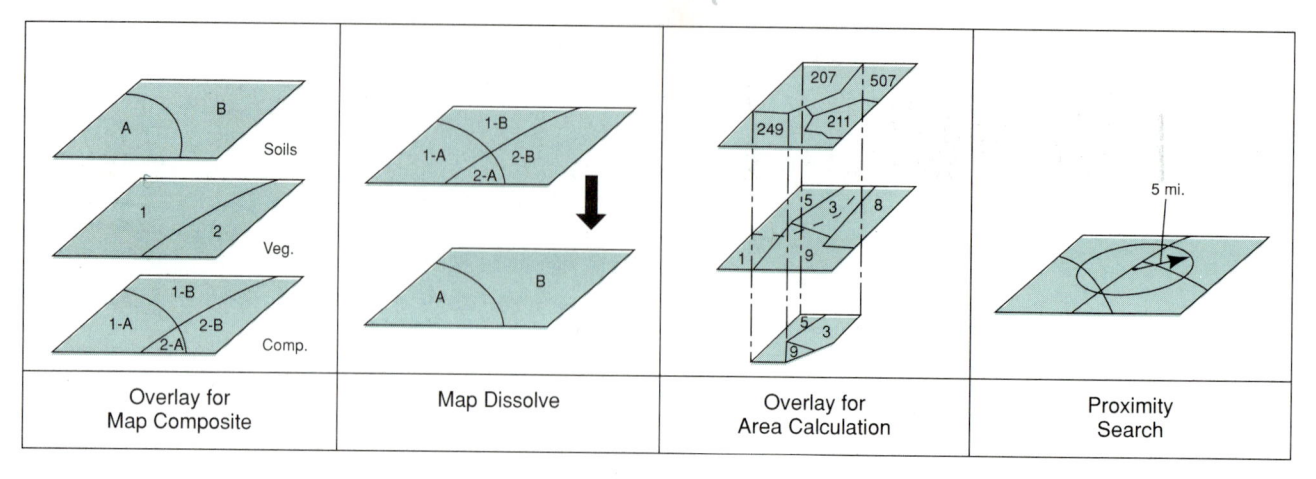

Figure 7.12 Diagrammatic examples of map overlay, map dissolve, area calculation logic, and proximity search using a polygon (vector) based geographic information system.
Source: William J. Ripple (ed.), *Fundamentals of Geographic Information Systems.* Copyright © 1989 American Society of Photogrammetry, Falls Church, VA.

coordinate system suitable for a grid-based analysis; 6) Analyzing the thematic data using GIS techniques; and 7) Statistically analyzing and mapping the geographic areas suitable for hazardous waste disposal.

Federal regulations require that hazardous waste disposal sites meet the following guidelines. These guidelines become the ILCC rules for this project. Sites for disposal cannot be located in or near environmentally sensitive areas that include; **wetlands, 100–year floodplains, permafrost areas, endangered species habitats** or **recharge zones of sole source aquifers.** Safe distances from environmentally sensitive areas range from 100 to 200m (320 to 656 ft). In addition to the environmental constraints placed by federal regulations, biophysical constraints of geology, soil water and groundwater, topography, and climate must be considered. Cultural constraints include location of cities and roads, location of archeological and historical sites, and land-use and land-cover constraints.

Data collection for input into the GIS depends on the scale of the project. Most natural resource management projects require data to be collected from field work, existing maps, aerial photography, and other remote sensing images. These data are then transferred to basemap scale and digitized. (Use caution to insure that remotely sensed data are not geometrically distorted.) The digitized data are then integrated into a grid-based cartographic format using a suitable coordinate system. Cartesian coordinates (x,y) are usually the preferred system for data location.

To produce meaningful information from a GIS data base requires that the analyst ask logical questions. The analyst must have the capability to browse within the digital data base and **window** in on a region of interest. After an area has been selected, the researcher can analyze the region by performing map overlay and map dissolve functions, proximity searches, and area calculations (figure 7.12). The data manipulation should result in the identification of only those points (areas) on the map that are suitable hazardous waste site locations. These sites were determined by the initial criterion, the data collection, and the data analysis. **GIGO** (garbage in-garbage out) concept applies here, in that if the resource manager sets good criteria, collects accurate data, and performs meaningful analyses, the sites will be acceptable. If not, the sites will be unacceptable.

The GIS for hazardous waste disposal site location has many other applications in resource management. Modification in the initial user-specified constraints will result in a different data base. But the methodology would remain essentially the same. If the proper information is placed in the GIS and appropriate analyses applied, then suitable site selection for any desired purpose can be achieved. GIS technology is particularly well suited to analyzing large volumes of diverse multidisciplinary data and managing natural resources.

Environmental Monitoring

There is no substitute in the geosciences for **field data.** The collection of raw data by an experienced researcher can provide necessary baseline information for many resource management projects. The technology exists to monitor almost all of the physical variables that make up the earth environment. We can collect water quality data, air quality data, data on noise pollution, data on soil chemistry, and so on. The list is endless. The major problem is interpretation of the data collected. How many DDTs

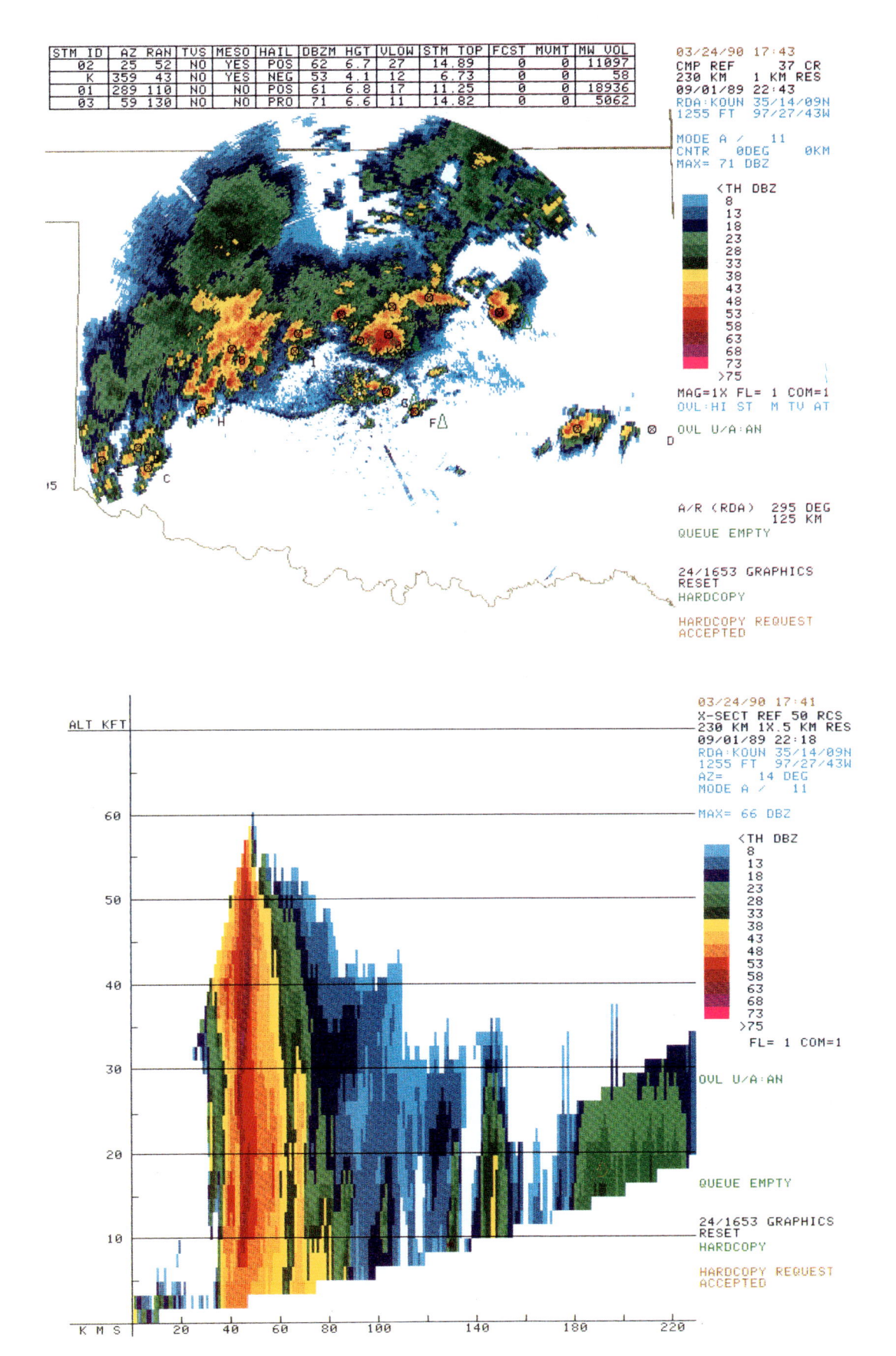

Color Plate 1 Nexrad radar printouts of a severe storm in Oklahoma on 3-4-90 at 5:43 P.M. CDT. Intensity ranges from blue (low) < 8, to red, max 66 dbz. Maximum intensity reached by this storm was between 61 and 77 dbz.

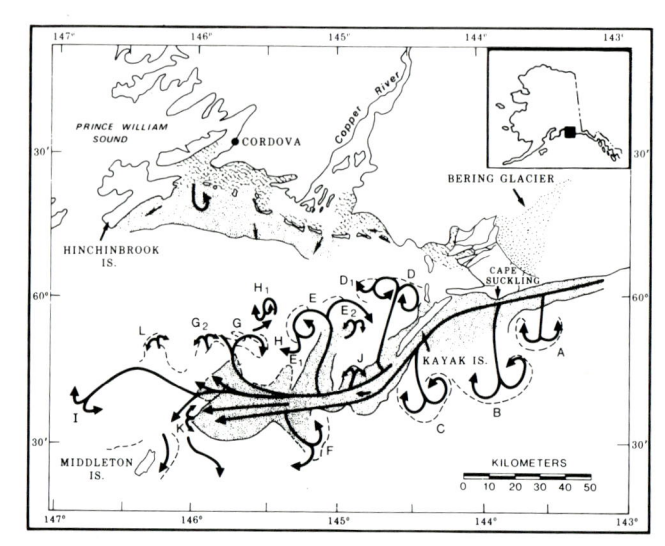

Color Plate 2A Visible bands of the Landsat Thematic Mapper (TM) data have revealed unusual flow patterns within the Alaska Current during April of 1985.
Landsat data by the Earth Observation Satellite Company, Lanham, Maryland. (right) Reproduced from Ahlnäs Royer and George 1987, Fig. 2. "Multiple Dipole Eddies in the Alaska Coastal Current Detected with Landsat Thematic Mapper Data." *Journal of Geophysical Research*, Vol. 92: 13,041–13,047, 1987.

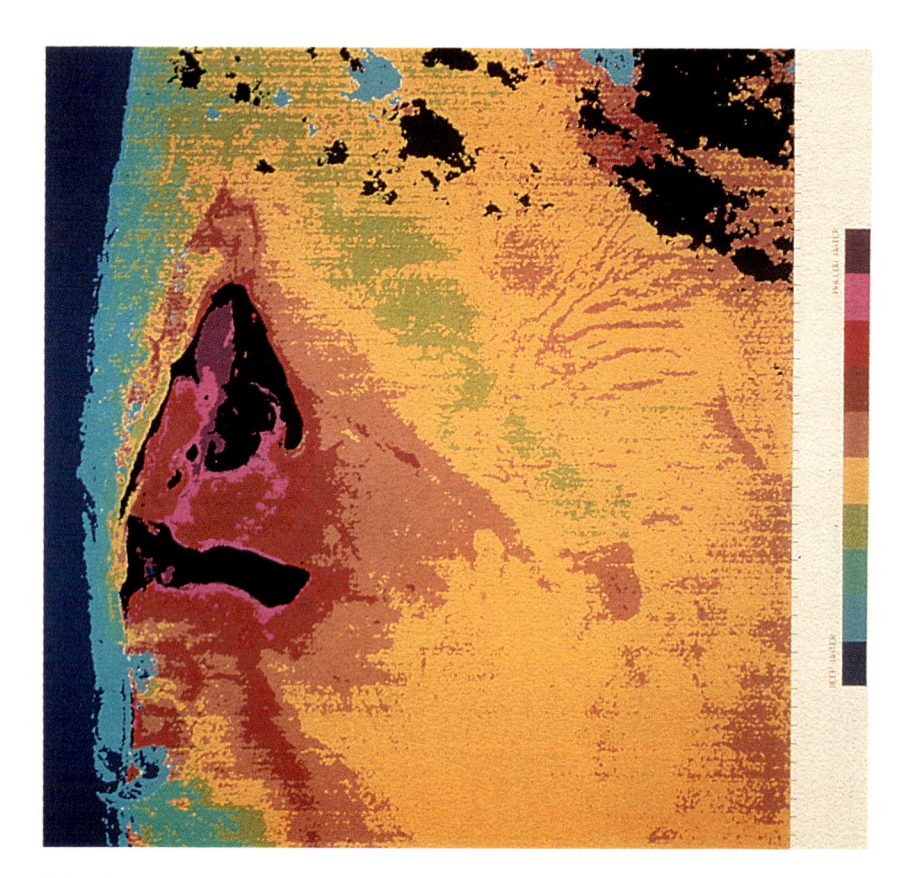

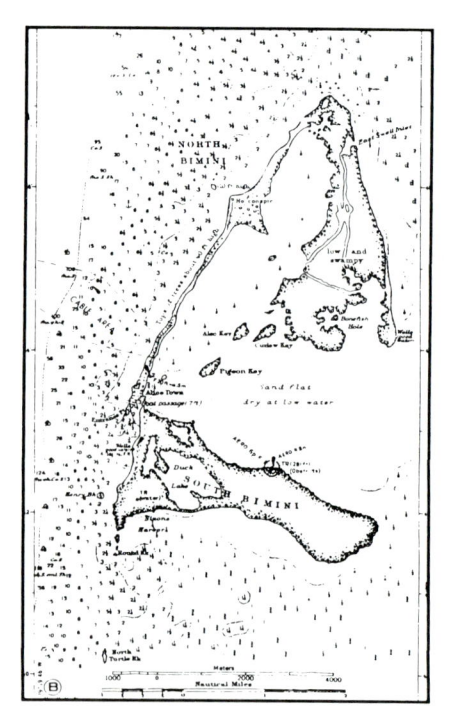

Color Plate 2B Bathymetric profile of the Atlantic Ocean off of the Florida coast near Bimini.
Landsat data by the Earth Observation Satellite Company, Lanham, Maryland.

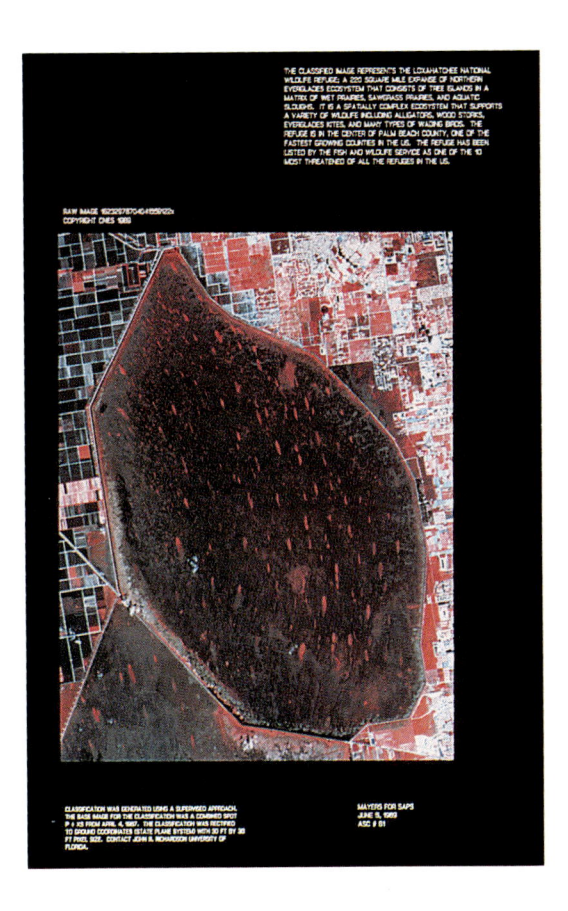

Color Plate 3A Loxahatchee National Wildlife Refuge (NWR) and adjacent developed land in Florida. A SPOT image covers 1400 sq mi (3626 sq km). Separation of the four basic land-cover classes (slough, wet prairie, saw grass, and tree island) are possible on this image.
(© 1990 CNES. Provided by SPOT Image Corporation.)

Color Plate 3B Color-enhanced SPOT image of the Loxahatchee NWR. Vegetation is mapped into 18 classes (1/40-acre units) based on density, species composition, and other factors.
(© 1990 CNES. Provided by SPOT Image Corporation.)

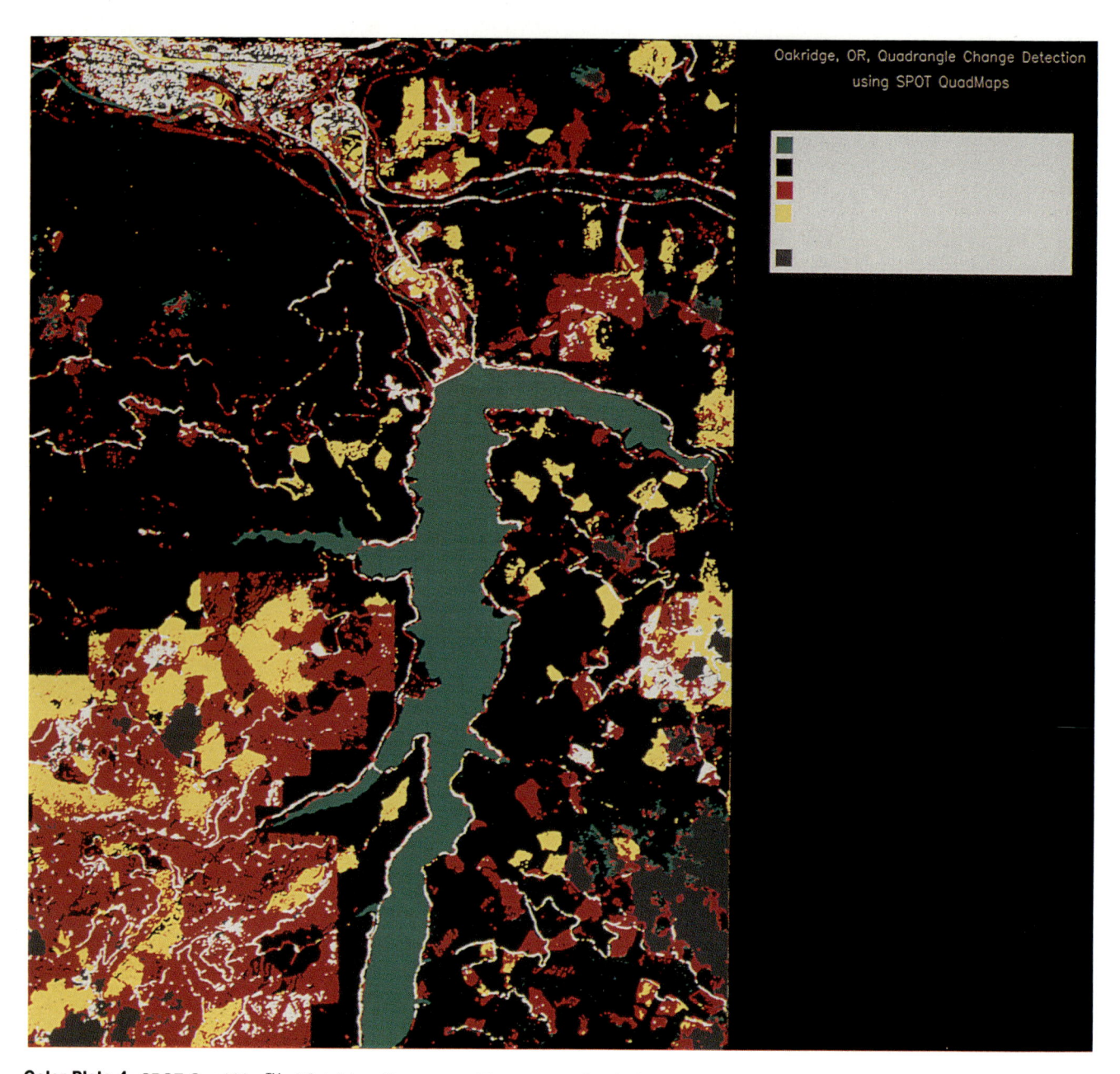

Color Plate 4 SPOT Quad Map™ of Oakridge, Oregon, provides an up-to-date look at clearcut forest areas. Regular monitoring of environmental changes are possible with SPOT images.
(© 1990 CNES. Provided by SPOT Image Corporation.)

does it take to kill a fish? How many dioxines does it take to kill a person? We don't have answers to these and many other environmental questions, but a need exists to collect environmental data so that some day we can answer them.

The Council on Environmental Quality (CEQ) is required by the NEPA law to report on the status and condition of the environment each year. To answer this charge, the EPA has established environmental monitoring stations across the United States to monitor the physical variables by collecting field data. The collected data fills volumes and, in most cases, is available to the resource manager. This valuable source of information should not be overlooked when an environmental problem or project is undertaken. The Environmental Quality Report, issued yearly by the President, is a readily available government publication.

Resource Management

Resource management is the controlled use of resources for the benefit of both the environment and humans. Included in this definition is the extension of the life of the resource for as long as possible. Prerequisite to controlled use and management of a resource is the need to inventory and evaluate the resource and make objective decisions about the resource. Long-range planning and conservation will follow.

The planning process begins with the establishment of goals. These should be as specific as possible. A comprehensive analysis of the resource management issue should be made and all aspects of the issue analyzed. Alternatives for achieving the specified management goals should be established and evaluated, including the no-action alternative. One of these alternatives should be selected as the desired course of action. A procedure for implementation of the selected alternative, along with mitigation of its side effects, should be designed in detail. A plan for **safe failure** or a **worst-case scenario** for hazardous projects should always be included in the implementation procedure. Within the socio-economic system in which we live, the most environmentally sound alternative is not always possible. A plan for **safe failure** can help the environment, should something go wrong.

Everyone knows the environmental hazards of shipping oil in supertankers. If Exxon had devised a **safe failure** plan before the Valdez hit a reef in March, 1989, and spilled 42 million liters (11 million gallons) of crude oil off of the Alaskan coast, maybe the environmental consequences wouldn't have been so disastrous. The time delay between the crash and decisive clean-up action multiplied the environmental destruction a hundredfold.

Environmental decisions can be public or private. Public decisions usually take the form of a law passed by elected officials of local, state, or federal governments. As an example of a public environmental decision, consider the Clean Air Act passed by Congress in 1970. The wording of the act spells out specific goals for maintenance of clean air. The Environmental Protection Agency (EPA) was assigned the responsibility to analyze and evaluate the air resource. Data were gathered to define clean air by setting emission limits for known atmospheric pollutants. These are called **clean air standards.** The EPA is also responsible for monitoring the condition of the air and enforcing the standards. When violations occur, citations are issued and fines assessed. The Clean Air Act is continually under public scrutiny and the law has been amended a number of times since its original passage. The 1990 amendments to the Act are the most stringent air quality standards ever imposed by a government on industry.

Private environmental decisions are made on a daily basis by consumers. Do we consider the environmental consequences of buying an energy-efficient refrigerator or air conditioner? Or is our main concern the price of the appliance? Both models contain CFCs in their refrigeration units. We could live without the air conditioner, but a refrigerator is a necessity. A small car saves fuel but the large model is more comfortable. Does economics dictate our decision or do we give the environmental consequences of our choice any consideration? As a consumer, we should consider the environment before we purchase. The ozone layer of the future depends on it. The carbon dioxide level of the atmosphere and global warming are affected by our decision. The private decisions of the public are an important part of the conservation of natural resources.

A General Plan for Natural Resource Management

The first step in management of a natural resource is to accumulate as much background information as possible on the natural environmental setting of the geographic area of the resource. Another way of stating this is to say that a complete inventory of the base of the biotic pyramid is required. What are the abiotic factors that control the environmental setting of the natural resource we propose to manage? The following questions need to be answered:

1. What is the underlying geology of the region?
2. Are there any geologic hazards in the area that need to be considered (earthquakes, volcanoes, landslides)?
3. What is the topographic setting and condition?
4. What are the geomorphic considerations (stable ridge top, erodable backslope, floodable valley floor)?
5. What are the soils characteristics for the region (claypan, perched water table, high acidity)?

6. What is the climate for the area (temperature extremes, precipitation extremes—both drought and deluge, frost-free period)?
7. What is the hydrologic regime for the locale (water cycle, groundwater zones, water quality, surface and subsurface drainage)?
8. What is the condition of the atmosphere (acid rain, high concentrations of CO_2 and SO_2, heat island effect)? (A *heat island* is a higher temperature microclimate produced by the heat of a city or industrial park.)
9. What is the dominant land use of the area?
10. What effect does the present land use have on the local environment?
11. What are the animal and human populations of the area (rare and endangered species present)?
12. What are the political and economic constraints on the region?

The answers to these 12 questions will provide the background inventory to proceed with the natural resource management program. The extent and detail required for the answers will also be dictated by the program goals under consideration. In almost every case air photos and a set of remotely sensed data will be required to complete the inventory of the region under consideration. If the complete inventory of an area has already been prepared, a set of maps and remotely sensed data should be available along with the inventory. Suspect the quality of the inventory if this information is not included. The background inventory, in the form of the answers to the 12 questions, should alert the resource manager to potential constraints that can include both environmental hazards and political or economic policy. The management objectives and goals should be consistent with these known constraints.

A natural resource manager must formulate his management policy to conform with the management objective of a private or public sector of society. Management objectives for the public sector usually come from legislation dictated by politicians. For example, forest management objectives are directed by the **Forest Resource Management Act** of 1976. Wetlands are managed under the dictates of the **Coastal Zone Management Act** of 1977 and the **Food Security Act** of 1985 and 1990 amendments to the Farm Bill. In the private sector, forest management is dictated, for the most part, by the profit motives of the company that owns the land. Each management program should require an abiotic inventory as a prerequisite.

Summary

Barry Commoner (1971), in his discussion of the ecosphere, presented four laws of ecology. These laws are most appropriate for the natural resource manager to consider as he develops his natural resource management objectives.

Law No. 1 Everything is connected to everything else.

Law No. 2 Everything must go somewhere.

Law No. 3 Nature knows best.

Law No. 4 There is no such thing as a free lunch.

Key Terms and Phrases

Geographic Information System
Ground truthing
Heat island

Micrometer
Nanometer
Remote sensing

Resource management
Windows

Questions and Discussion Topics

1. Remote sensing as a "tool of the trade" for resource managers and conservationists is in the news on a regular basis. What are some of the projects in your local area or in the news that use satellite data?
Lithosphere Projects?
Atmosphere Projects?
Hydrosphere Projects?
Biosphere Projects?

2. Why are Geographic Information Systems (GIS) so important to resource managers?

3. Why is it so difficult to answer the questions about safe levels of chemicals? For example, why can't we answer the question "How many dioxines does it take to kill a person?"

4. Select an area of the country or your own geographic area and answer the required 12 questions of a general plan for natural resource management for a project. The project can be designing a park, protecting an endangered species, or managing a cattle feedlot.

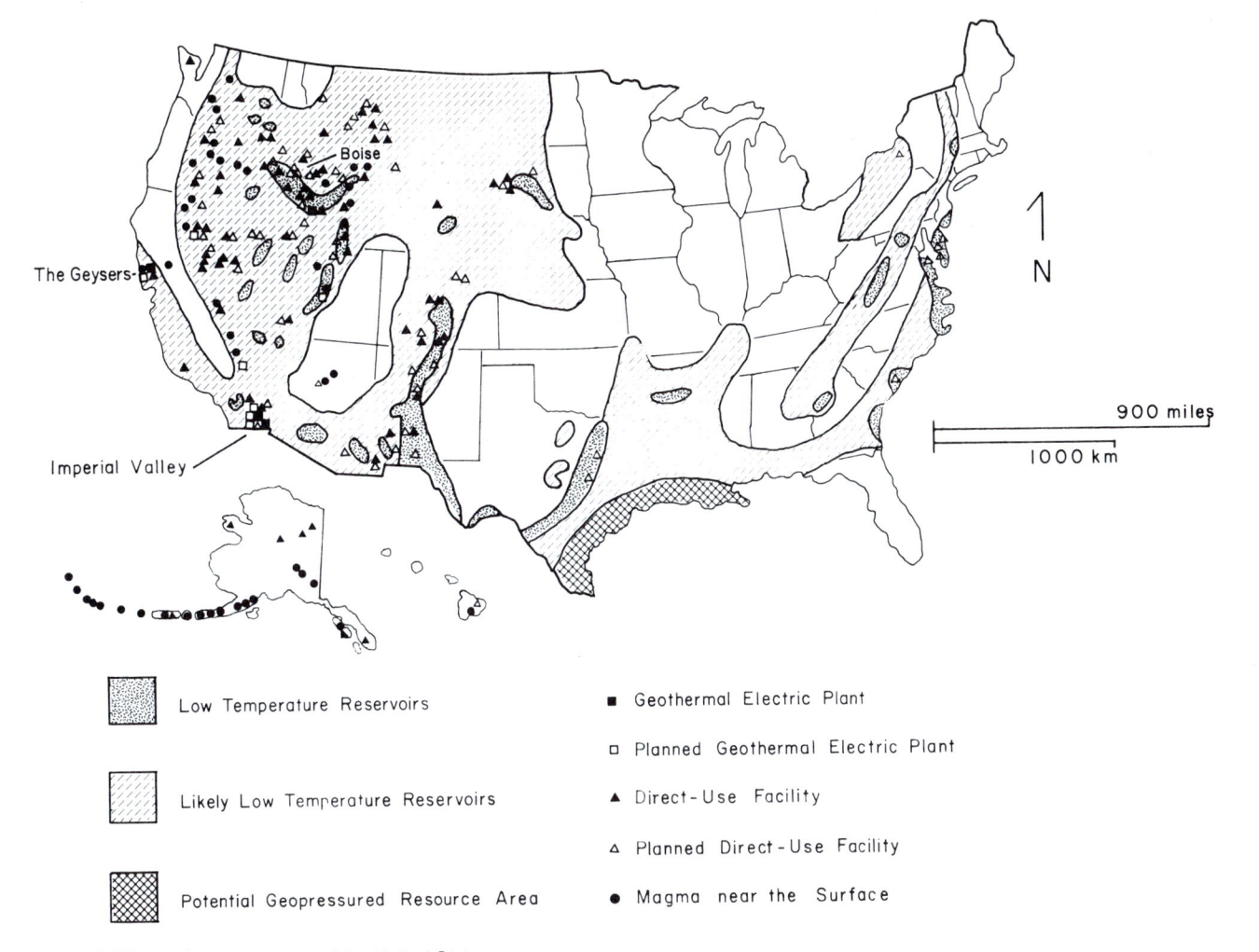

Figure 13.23 Geothermal regions of the United States.
Source: Data from "Special Report on Energy" in *National Geographic*, February, 1981.
(*Cartographer:* Douglas Hemsath)

issue of nuclear waste disposal has been "ducked" by those responsible for so many years that we have a serious problem today. The third alternative of breaking the reactor up into small pieces and storing the pieces in an underground storage facility will only hide the problem temporarily. An economically safe method for nuclear waste disposal does not exist at this time.

Geothermal Energy

Radioactive decay in the interior of the earth generates heat that has great potential as an energy resource. Scientists estimate that the potentially recoverable supply of energy from *geothermal* sources could meet United States energy needs at 1990 rates of consumption for 600 to 700 years. One of the major problems with the potential geothermal resource is location. The greatest amounts of accessible heat are located in the western mountains of North America. Figure 13.23 is a map of geothermal regions in the United States.

Four types of geothermal energy sources are recognized. These are dry-steam and wet-steam deposits, hot-water deposits, and hot dry-rock deposits. Dry-steam deposits are the best geothermal energy resource but they are also the rarest. The Geysers geothermal electric generating plant 90 miles (145 km) north of San Francisco, California is a dry-steam deposit (figure 13.24). It has been in operation since 1960, and now generates 6% of northern California's electricity. More than 100 wells have been drilled into the dry-steam deposit. The deepest hole penetrates to a depth of more than 2,440 m (8,000 ft). Temperatures in the underground reservoir are about 225°C (480°F). The source of the heat is a large (100 to 500 square mile) area three to five miles below the surface. Electricity is generated at less than half the cost of a new coal-fired generating plant.

Wet-steam deposits are more common but it is more expensive to generate electricity from these sources. Demonstration plants built in the United States since 1980 are not economically competitive with conventional coal power

Figure 13.24 The Geysers geothermal complex provides electrical power to about one million residential customers in the northern and central California area.
(*Photo:* Pacific Gas & Electric Co.)

electric generating plants. In contrast, hot-water deposits for noncommercial uses have been used to heat homes in Boise, Idaho since 1890. A hot-water deposit in Imperial Valley, California went on-line in 1984. The major problem has been that the salty, hot-water brine is corroding and clogging the pipes. Efforts are under way to solve these problems by underground recycling of the water with the wastewater from the facility.

The major advantage of geothermal energy is its long-term supply for areas geographically near the deposits. The cost of producing electricity from geothermal sources appears to be less than half of the cost for coal-fired plants and as little as one-fourth the cost of a nuclear power electric generating plant.

Geothermal is not without its environmental problems. The steam emitted from the Geysers plant contains hydrogen sulfide (rotten-eggs smell), methane, and ammonia. The wastewater from geothermal plants is high in dissolved salts and can contain toxic compounds. Noise, odor, and polluted water runoff are all environmental problems associated with geothermal energy, but they seem somewhat insignificant compared to the problems of nuclear waste disposal.

Solar Energy

The sun is the earth's exogenic motor. It drives the atmospheric and hydrologic circulation systems that give us **wind power** and **hydropower.** The energy in fossil fuels is stored solar energy over geologic time. Solar energy drives all of the biologic systems on the earth's surface and in the shallow seas, and the sun is the ultimate source of energy for humankind.

The amount of solar energy received by the earth's surface on a cloud-free day is almost 100,000 times greater than the world's total electric power capacity. Most of the sun's radiant energy is lost (99%) as heat energy. How do we harness more of this lost energy?

Figure 13.25 is a potential solar energy map for North America. It shows that the greatest potential for solar energy utilization exists in the arid regions of the southwestern United States. A major part of this potential is the number of cloud-free days. Table 13.3 shows individual states and their number of cloud-free days per year. New technologies for solar heating, photovoltaic cells, solar electricity, and satellite solar power stations (SSPS) are all in our energy future.

298 Natural Resources Management

SOLAR ENERGY POTENTIAL FOR NORTH AMERICA

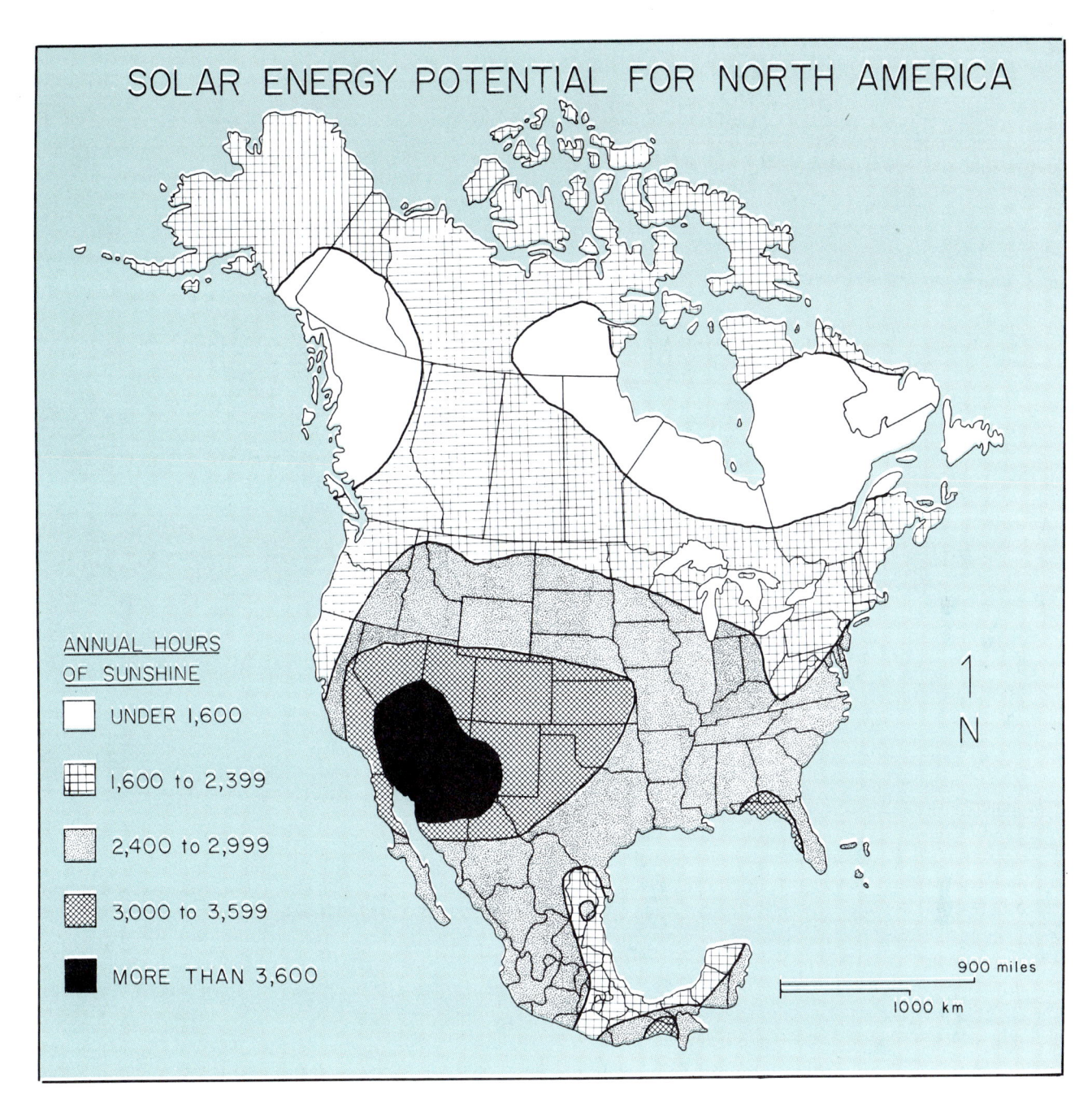

ANNUAL HOURS OF SUNSHINE
- UNDER 1,600
- 1,600 to 2,399
- 2,400 to 2,999
- 3,000 to 3,599
- MORE THAN 3,600

Figure 13.25 Solar energy potential for North America.
Source: U.S. Department of Energy.
(Cartographer: Douglas Hemsath)

Solar heating is becoming more popular in North America. But even in the Southwest it must be supplemented with a fossil fuel system. The average household uses a little over 55,000 kilojoules (52,200 BTUs) of energy daily to heat water for a family of four. The Washington, D.C. sun will provide about one-half of that amount in winter. Figure 13.26 illustrates a mobile/modular solar home that could be marketed for less than $30,000.

Figure 13.27 gives two general solar space-heating designs that can be built relatively inexpensively. Depending on the location in North America, these designs can provide from 25% to 50% of a home's heating needs.

Photovoltaic cells convert solar energy directly to electricity. These cells are a valuable by-product of the U.S. space program. Figure 13.28 is a photovoltaic building on the campus of Georgetown University in

Energy Management

Table 13.3

The Number of Cloud-Free Days by Month for the United States. These Numbers Can be Used to Judge Solar Energy Potential for Each State.[1]

Name of State[2]	Jan.	Feb.	Mar.	Apr.	May	June	July	Aug.	Sept.	Oct.	Nov.	Dec.	Total per year
						Number of days							
Alabama	6.4	6.4	6.9	6.5	6.2	4.1	2.4	2.9	5.9	11.4	9.7	6.3	75.1
Arizona	15.3	13.2	15.7	18.3	22.0	23.7	15.8	15.8	20.2	21.5	18.3	16.2	216.0
Arkansas	7.0	6.9	6.6	6.5	5.6	5.8	5.7	7.2	9.1	11.8	9.0	7.8	89.0
California	7.4	6.7	8.4	9.3	9.7	11.5	12.7	12.8	13.3	13.1	10.8	8.6	124.3
Colorado	7.5	5.8	5.7	4.6	4.6	7.0	5.5	5.4	10.3	11.3	9.4	8.4	85.5
Connecticut	6.1	7.1	7.6	6.4	6.8	5.2	5.4	6.4	6.7	9.1	6.1	6.6	79.5
Delaware	5.5	5.7	5.6	5.2	5.5	4.0	4.5	4.7	6.6	9.2	6.4	5.5	68.4
Florida	5.9	6.7	7.4	6.7	5.0	2.7	1.4	1.5	2.8	6.0	7.7	6.3	60.1
Georgia	6.8	7.1	7.9	7.3	6.6	4.1	2.4	3.0	5.6	10.8	10.6	7.3	79.5
Idaho	2.7	3.7	4.3	4.6	5.5	8.8	13.3	18.4	12.5	9.8	5.7	3.5	92.8
Illinois	4.9	4.7	4.8	5.1	5.1	4.5	6.3	6.5	7.9	9.0	6.4	5.1	70.3
Indiana	4.2	3.8	4.2	4.5	4.4	3.7	4.9	5.4	7.1	9.2	6.2	4.4	62.0
Iowa	5.8	5.4	4.8	5.3	5.0	4.8	7.2	6.6	7.8	8.9	5.9	5.4	72.9
Kansas	8.5	7.3	6.7	5.8	5.6	6.2	8.7	8.2	9.6	10.7	9.6	8.4	95.3
Kentucky	4.8	4.8	5.2	5.4	6.1	5.8	7.2	6.3	8.4	10.7	7.2	4.9	76.8
Louisiana	6.9	6.3	6.6	6.9	6.2	5.7	3.9	4.7	7.3	11.3	9.6	6.8	82.2
Maine	5.6	6.3	5.8	4.8	3.8	3.4	3.4	4.6	5.8	6.8	4.0	5.3	59.6
Maryland	5.2	5.5	5.4	5.0	5.0	3.8	4.1	4.3	6.3	8.9	6.0	5.4	64.9
Massachusetts	3.6	4.2	4.5	4.0	3.5	2.5	2.2	3.6	4.2	5.1	3.5	3.4	44.3
Michigan	2.2	3.1	4.1	5.0	4.8	4.6	5.4	4.6	4.6	4.3	1.9	1.9	46.5
Minnesota	5.4	5.8	5.2	5.8	5.6	4.9	7.1	6.8	6.2	6.3	4.2	5.1	68.4
Mississippi	6.3	5.8	6.8	6.3	5.7	5.5	3.2	3.8	6.6	11.8	9.4	6.2	77.4
Missouri	7.4	7.1	6.8	6.8	6.8	6.8	9.2	8.9	9.9	11.6	9.2	7.3	97.8
Montana	3.5	3.7	3.5	4.1	3.8	4.2	9.9	9.0	7.3	6.9	4.3	4.0	64.2
Nebraska	6.9	5.7	5.3	4.9	4.7	5.5	8.4	7.4	8.9	10.2	7.1	6.9	81.9
Nevada	6.7	6.2	7.5	8.4	8.7	13.8	18.6	18.8	16.9	14.2	10.1	7.4	137.3
New Hampshire	3.3	3.8	4.1	3.7	3.2	2.2	2.0	3.0	3.8	4.4	2.8	2.9	39.2
New Jersey	6.1	6.2	6.1	5.6	6.5	4.5	5.3	5.6	7.1	9.9	7.3	5.9	76.1
New Mexico	10.5	8.4	8.7	8.3	8.1	10.5	5.4	5.3	10.2	14.0	12.7	12.3	114.4
New York	2.3	2.9	4.1	4.9	5.5	4.8	4.8	4.7	5.5	5.1	2.5	2.0	49.1
North Carolina	6.8	6.8	7.3	7.1	6.7	4.2	3.6	3.9	6.1	11.1	10.1	7.4	81.1
North Dakota	5.0	4.9	4.4	5.3	5.1	4.3	7.5	7.2	6.7	6.6	4.3	5.3	66.6
Ohio	3.5	3.1	4.1	4.8	5.8	5.1	6.2	6.2	7.3	7.1	4.3	2.9	60.4
Oklahoma	8.0	6.7	6.5	5.8	5.4	6.7	7.6	8.7	9.5	10.8	10.3	8.3	94.3
Oregon	2.0	2.6	3.0	4.7	5.0	6.8	13.4	13.2	9.5	6.2	2.9	2.1	71.4
Pennsylvania	3.0	3.2	3.9	4.2	4.9	3.7	3.9	4.2	5.8	6.4	3.4	2.5	49.1
Rhode Island	4.9	5.3	6.6	5.8	5.9	4.0	5.1	6.1	6.6	7.8	5.3	4.4	67.8
South Carolina	6.4	7.0	7.1	7.0	6.0	3.3	2.3	2.9	5.0	10.1	10.3	7.2	74.6
South Dakota	5.9	5.4	4.9	4.8	4.5	5.0	8.2	8.3	8.6	8.9	6.4	6.7	77.6
Tennessee	5.3	5.5	6.2	5.4	5.7	4.5	4.2	5.1	7.1	11.2	8.8	5.9	74.9
Texas	7.8	6.3	7.2	7.1	6.4	7.4	5.7	6.7	7.6	11.1	8.9	7.9	90.1
Utah	7.1	5.8	7.0	7.1	7.8	12.6	11.0	11.3	14.2	13.7	10.4	7.6	115.6
Vermont	2.9	2.9	3.3	3.1	2.7	1.7	1.6	2.0	3.2	3.2	1.5	1.8	29.9
Virginia	5.4	5.6	5.6	6.1	5.9	4.1	4.3	4.4	6.0	9.2	7.1	5.6	69.3
Washington	1.3	2.1	2.6	3.7	3.8	5.1	11.6	11.1	7.5	4.9	1.6	1.2	56.5
West Virginia	2.3	2.2	3.6	3.8	4.2	3.0	3.2	3.0	4.0	4.7	3.2	2.0	39.2
Wisconsin	4.9	5.3	4.6	5.1	5.4	4.6	7.0	6.5	6.4	7.2	4.4	4.7	66.1
Wyoming	4.7	4.5	4.3	3.8	3.2	4.8	6.9	6.7	8.2	7.9	5.7	5.5	66.2

[1]Compiled from U.S. Weather Bureau Records. Figures shown represent the number of days per month with 10 percent cloud cover or less. Averages should be used with discretion, as wide variations may occur from one part of a state to another.
[2]Data unavailable for Alaska and Hawaii, but cloud cover would be similar to the Pacific Northwest states of Washington and Oregon.

Figure 13.26 Active solar mobile/modular home containing 1,000 square feet plus of solar living space for about $25,000, if mass produced.
(*Photo:* DOE)

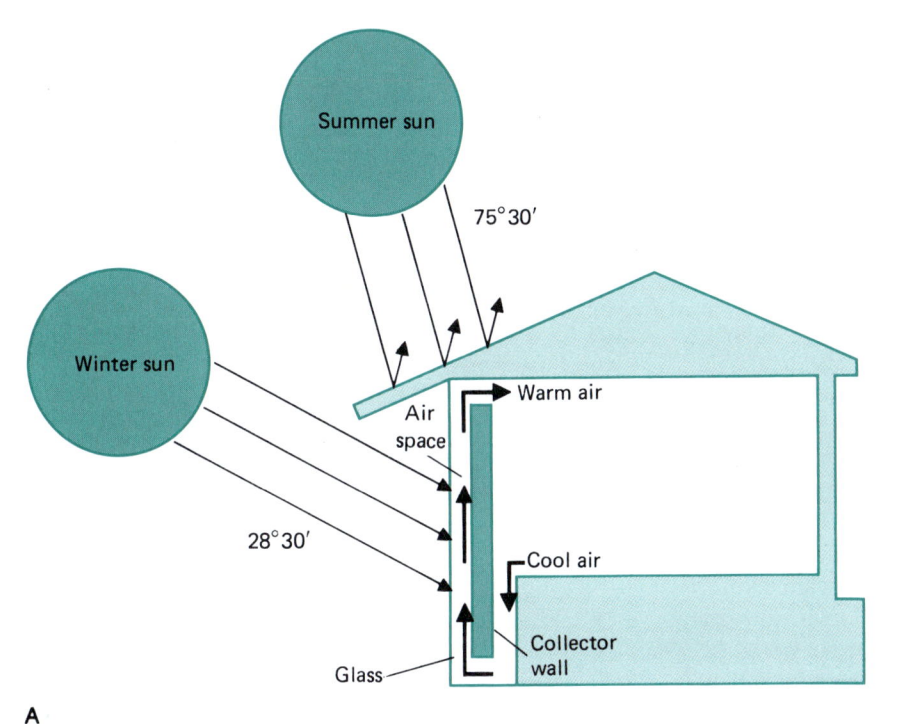

Figure 13.27 (a) Passive solar room design for a house at 38° N latitude. The length of overhang in this home is designed for solar heating at the latitude of St. Louis, MO (38° N). In this design, a wall 30–40 cm (16 in) thick is used to collect and store heat. The collecting wall is located behind a glass wall and faces south. During a midwinter day when the sun's angle is 28°, light energy is collected by the wall and stored as heat. At night, the heat stored in the wall is used to warm the house. Natural convection causes the air to circulate past the wall and the house is heated. During a mid-summer day when the sun's angle is 75°, the overhang shades the collector from the sun. (b) Active solar hot water heater design for a school. Angles of solar collectors are adjusted to the altitude of the noonday sun.
From Eldon D. Enger, *Environmental Science*, 3d ed. Copyright © 1989 Wm. C. Brown Publishers, Dubuque, Iowa. All Rights Reserved. Reprinted by permission.

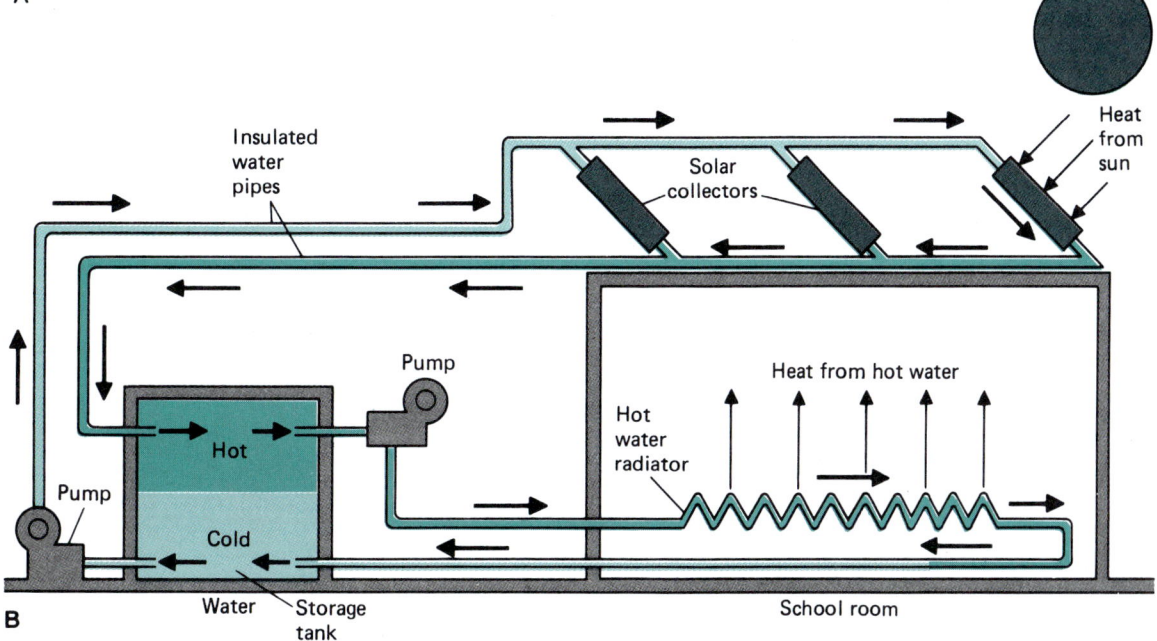

Energy Management

Figure 13.28 Georgetown University's intercultural center. The roof supports a 300 kw photovoltaic power system.
(*Photo:* DOE)

Washington D.C. that houses the intercultural student center. The south-facing roof supports a 300 kw photovoltaic power system. The conversion of inexhaustible supplies of solar energy directly to electricity is the most attractive energy alternative environmentally. No atmospheric pollution is produced. No disruptions in free-flowing streams will result. There is no mined land to reclaim, and no nuclear waste is generated. The problem is economic. It costs about $15,000 (1990 dollars) to produce a photovoltaic cell that can produce one kilowatt of electricity, compared with a cost of $1,000 per kilowatt from conventional coal-fired power plants. (It would be interesting to compare the cost per kilowatt hour for energy from the Shippingport Nuclear Reactor Plant with this figure, after the cost of construction, the cost of the funeral, the disposal of the nuclear waste pellets, and after the government subsidies are totaled.) We have the technology for solar power but the economic incentives are not a reality at this time.

Satellite Solar Power Stations (SSPS) would have the major advantage of eliminating cloud cover and the day-night cycle (figure 13.29). This would provide eight times more solar energy availability than a solar power station on the earth's surface. Solar energy would be converted to electrical energy, which would then be converted to microwaves (figure 7.1). The microwaves would be beamed to a receiver on earth and reconverted to electricity. A 5,000 megawatt SSPS would be enormous in size (8 miles long, (13 km) 3 miles wide (5 km), and weigh 20,000 tons (18,180 metric tons)). It would cost billions and take at least 20 years to build. However, it would not be the panacea to solve our energy problem. Some of the environmental problems would include*:

1. Microwaves could cook birds that fly through the beams (like a microwave oven cooks food).
2. Microwaves could cause human injuries such as eye cataracts, and nervous and genetic disorders.
3. Hydrochloric acid would be released into the atmosphere during the building and maintenance of the satellite.
4. Communication could be disrupted by the satellite.

Sunrayce USA was a solar-powered car race that began in Lake Buena Vista, Florida on July 9, 1990 and ended in Warren, Michigan on July 19, 1990 (figure 13.30 and Table 13.4a). The 1,641 mile (2,642 km) race was run in 11 one-day segments, with 32 solar cars entered (figure 13.31). Each solar car was powered by photovoltaic cells and storage batteries. The Sunrunner from the University of Michigan won the race, with an average speed of about 37 kmph (23 mph). Table 13.4b gives the top eight finishers and their times. The race proves that we have the technical capabilities to utilize solar energy and replace fossil fuel, even in our transportation system, when the economics of the situation presents itself.

---

*The telephone companies have beamed microwaves from their towers for years and have not experienced these difficulties. Maybe these claims are just hype, but they should be considered as potential environmental problems.

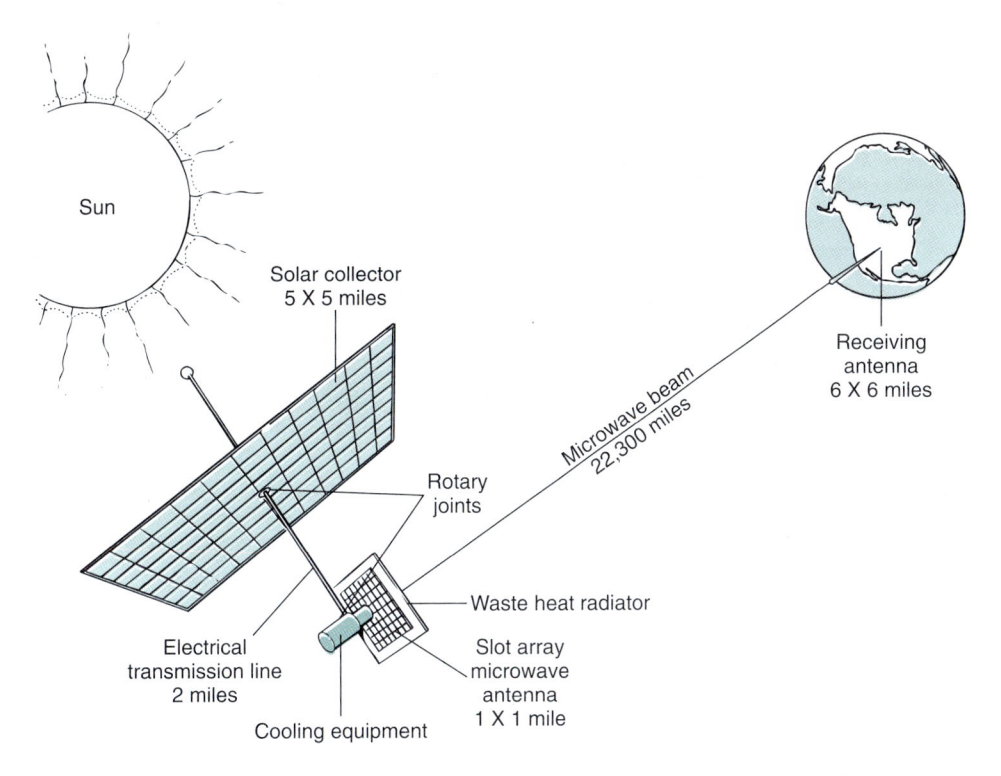

Approximately 60 satellite solar power stations needed to meet one-half the projected U.S. power needs by the year 2000.

Figure 13.29 Satellite solar power station (SSPS) design by NASA. High cost of such a project would not make it feasible at the present time.
Source: NASA.

Figure 13.30 The route of Sunrayce USA. Thirty-two colleges and universities competed for a free trip to a solar race in Australia.
(*Cartographer:* Douglas Hemsath)

Energy Management 303

Table 13.4a
Colleges and Universities Competing in GM Sunrayce USA

Arizona State University Tempe, Ariz.	University of Michigan Ann Arbor, Mich.
Auburn University Auburn, Ala.	University of North Texas Denton, Texas
California State Polytechnic University, Pomona Pomona, Calif.	University of Ottawa, Ont. Ottawa, Ontario, Canada
California Polytechnic State University, San Luis Obispo San Luis Obispo, Calif.	University of Pennsylvania Philadelphia, Pa.
California State University, Los Angeles Los Angeles, Calif.	University of Puerto Rico, Mayaguez Campus Mayaguez, Puerto Rico
California State University, Northridge Northridge, Calif.	Rochester Institute of Technology Rochester, N.Y.
Clarkson University Potsdam, N.Y.	Rose-Hulman Institute of Technology Terre Haute, Ind.
Colorado State University Fort Collins, Colo.	Stanford University Stanford, Calif.
Crowder College Neosho, Mo.	Stark Technical College Canton, Ohio
Dartmouth College Hanover, N.H.	University of Texas, at Austin Austin, Texas
Drexel University Philadelphia, Pa.	Villanova University Villanova, Pa.
Florida Institute of Technology Melbourne, Fla.	Virginia Polytechnic Institute & State University Blacksburg, Va.
Iowa State University Ames, Iowa	University of Waterloo, Ont. Waterloo, Ontario, Canada
Mankato State University Mankato, Minn.	Western Michigan University/Jordan College Kalamazoo/Grand Rapids, Mich.
University of Maryland College Park, Md.	Western Washington University Bellingham, Wash.
Massachusetts Institute of Technology Cambridge, Mass.	Worcester Polytechnic Institute Worcester, Mass.

Source: Data from Crowder College, Neosho, MO.

Figure 13.31 Star II, the solar-powered car from Crowder College in Neosho, Missouri, finished fifth.
(*Photo:* Crowder College)

Table 13.4b
Top Eight Finishers in 1990 GM Sunrayce USA

Place	School	Car Name	Time hr:min:sec
1st	Univ. of Michigan	Sunrunner	72:50:47
2nd	Western Washington Univ.	Viking xx	74:10:06
3rd	Univ. of Maryland	Pride of Maryland	80:10:55
4th	Calif. State. Univ. Los Angeles	Solar Eagle	81:03:44
5th	Crowder College, Mo.	Star II	81:06:18
6th	Massachusetts Inst. Tech.	Galaxy	84:17:37
7th	Stanford Univ. Calif.	SUn SUrfer	93:56:53
8th	Western Mich. Univ.-Jordan College	Sunseeker	96:55:20

Source: Data from Crowder College, Neosho, MO.

The future for solar power is tremendous. It is our only true inexhaustible source of energy. All other energy resources are only temporary. More dollars should be spent on solar research now, while the cost of fossil fuels is still a bargain. The technology exists today to provide, from photovoltaic cells, all of the electrical power needed by the United States. Twelve thousand square kilometers (4,680 sq mi) of solar cells would do the job, and the space required would be no greater than the space now occupied by existing buildings. Rooftop solar cells would provide the electricity but not the heat. Space requirements for solar cells to provide heat are too great near locations where they are needed. A possible solution would be solar power towers. A 15-story solar power tower could generate enough electricity to provide for the needs of a town of 3,000 people. Figure 13.32 is an artist's concept of a solar thermal electric power station in Barstow, California that could provide electricity equivalent to a solar power tower. The future for solar energy is undeniable. **Solar energy** is the only permanent solution for our future energy needs.

Hydropower

Water moving downslope by gravity (*hydropower*) has always been a source of energy with great potential. The amount of water available for hydropower in a region is a function of the climatic condition and hydrologic cycle for that area and both are controlled by solar energy.

Hydropower has been used in North America to run grinding mills and sawmills since early in the nineteenth century. Large- and small-scale hydroelectric power plants have been a small part of the energy pie since the turn of the century. Today more than 1,500 hydropower sites in the United States (the world's largest producer of electricity from hydropower) supply about 4% of our energy needs.

Figure 13.32 Artist's concept of the solar power plant built near Barstow, California. A 72-acre field of more than 1800 heliostats (mirrors), each about 20 sq ft, surrounds the central receiver on the high tower.
(*Photo:* DOE)

Figure 13.33 Hydroelectric dam on the Tennessee River provides electricity and recreation in a cost-effective manner for the TVA area.
(*Photo:* David A. Castillon)

Figure 13.34 The wind turbine at Clayton, New Mexico, with an old rural windmill in the foreground.
(*Photo:* DOE)

The main environmental advantage of hydropower is that it is relatively pollution free. Hydroelectric power generating facilities do not emit carbon dioxide or other pollutant's into the atmosphere. The major economic advantage of hydropower is that it is relatively inexpensive. Hydroelectricity is cheaper because it is more efficient than coal or nuclear energy. Energy efficiency for hydroelectricity ranges from 83% to 93%, compared with 65% efficiency for coal-fired electric plants and 60% for nuclear powered electric facilities. Another reason hydroelectric power is cheaper is because many of the hydroelectric facilities were built, without tax dollars, when construction costs were lower. Once a hydroelectric dam is built, it is cheaper to operate and maintain (figure 13.33). They rarely need to be shut down and have a longer life span than either coal or nuclear facilities. A final, and probably the most important, advantage for hydropower is that it is as perpetual as sunlight. The climatic condition provides a predictable amount of precipitation, and water is going to flow downslope with tremendous potential energy.

The disadvantages of hydropower are mostly economic. Large hydroelectric power plants are expensive to build, especially with no federal dollar incentives. Construction costs, along with the low price of oil ($20 a barrel), make them noncompetitive in the 1990s marketplace. Reservoir sedimentation is also a major drawback for hydroelectric dams. In areas of dry climates (BS, BW), erosion and sedimentation rates are so high that a dam may not last 20 years. Mono Dam at Santa Barbara, California was filled with sediment in less than 20 years, resulting from poor watershed management.

The major environmental objection to hydropower is the destruction of the natural beauty provided by a free-flowing stream and the forest and wildlife habitat the waters inundate behind the dam. The reservoir can alter the ecological balance both upstream and downstream from the dam. Spoonbills, salmon, and other migrating species of fish are particularly affected. According to the National Research Council, more ecological damage is caused for each unit of energy produced by hydropower than by any other source of energy. The only reason they can make that statement is that they haven't witnessed the ecological destruction yet to come from nuclear power waste!

Wind Power

Windmills were a part of the landscape on almost every farm before 1930. They were used to pump water, run electric generators, and grind flour (figure 13.34). Rural electrification brought an end to the need for wind power on the farm. As energy becomes increasingly expensive, and the search for cheaper alternatives continues, wind once again becomes a viable source of power.

The Department of Energy (DOE) is studying wind power. Wind is a solar energy by-product created by atmospheric circulation. The DOE has built a 200-kilowatt

Figure 13.35 Wind turbines at Goodnoe Hills, Washington, can each generate 2.5 mw of electricity if the wind is at least 14 mph. (Photo: DOE)

wind machine at Clayton, New Mexico (figure 13.34). The experimental windmill, with 40-foot blades, is connected to conventional power lines and is used to supply electricity to the existing network for the town. Successful wind-powered electric generation systems are also operating in California and Washington state (figure 13.35). Environmental problems include the unattractive appearance of wind machines, interference with bird movements, and wind velocity alterations both up- and downwind from the machines.

Energy Management

The standard of living enjoyed by the United States, Canada, and other industrialized nations results in large part from readily accessible and relatively cheap energy. The gross national product (GNP) in the United States grew by 40% between 1973 and 1985, while energy consumption remained nearly constant. On the other hand, Mexico and other developing countries need more energy to raise their standard of living. Energy consumption grew by 22% in developing countries between 1980 and 1985.

As the knowledge increases of how the burning of fossil fuels threatens our global environment, so also does the demand for energy. Coal and oil combustion produces sulphur dioxide (SO_2), which produces acid rain. Acid rain damages our lakes and forests. Nuclear fission produces radioactive wastes that have no place to go. Cars and light trucks consume more than one out of every three barrels of oil and contribute about 10% of the carbon dioxide emissions to the atmosphere in the United States. Carbon dioxide (CO_2) is the major triatomic gas that contributes to the greenhouse effect. Humankind has a pretty good idea about the global environmental problem. The question is: What can be done about the problem while the standard of living remains high?

Technological ingenuity (energy conservation) can reduce the amount of energy required to provide for the present standard of living and at the same time reduce the harmful effects on the global environment produced by energy consumption. Energy efficiency appears to be the best energy management strategy for the 1990s.

The average home owner has many opportunities for energy efficiency. Figure 13.36 illustrates some of the ways in which the individual can participate in energy savings. As an energy-conscious consumer, the buyer should demand the most energy efficient model affordable when purchasing a home, car, or major appliance. In most cases, energy savings of as much as 50% can be obtained by selecting the best model over the average model.

If a choice of home heating fuels exists, it is best to choose natural gas. Burning gas produces fewer pollutants than burning oil or coal. Natural gas releases 14 kilograms (31 lbs) of carbon dioxide for every billion joules produced (a *joule* is the amount of work done by one newton acting through a distance of one meter. One joule equals ten million ergs); whereas oil releases 20 kg (44 lbs) and coal releases 24 kg (48 lbs) of carbon dioxide into the atmosphere. Coal gasification, the conversion of coal to natural gas, could be a way to convert "dirty coal" to cleaner-burning gas, but the technology for this economically is in the future.

Solar energy research must continue. A one-cent tax on every gallon of gas put into a motor vehicle could be levied and earmarked for solar energy research. It's the only truly long-range energy alternative. We don't have the million years it takes to produce new deposits of oil, gas, or coal. Nuclear energy, at the present state of technology, is not an alternative. Nuclear waste disposal is an unsolvable problem in today's economic, political, social, and technological environment. One or all of these environments must change to make it solvable.

Energy management should be directed toward energy efficiency in the 1990s. Technology has the potential to push automobile fuel economy to over 65 mpg (400 kmpl). The price paid for energy should include the costs for economic, environmental, and geopolitical considerations. The cost of a gallon of gas in the United States does not include the cost of defense of the Middle East, where more and more of our oil comes from. Nor does it include the millions of dollars the United States spends on air pollution (smog) produced by auto exhaust. The cost does not include the cost of the trade imbalance caused by ever-increasing oil imports. Gasoline should be at least $3 per

Opportunities for Energy Efficiency in the Home

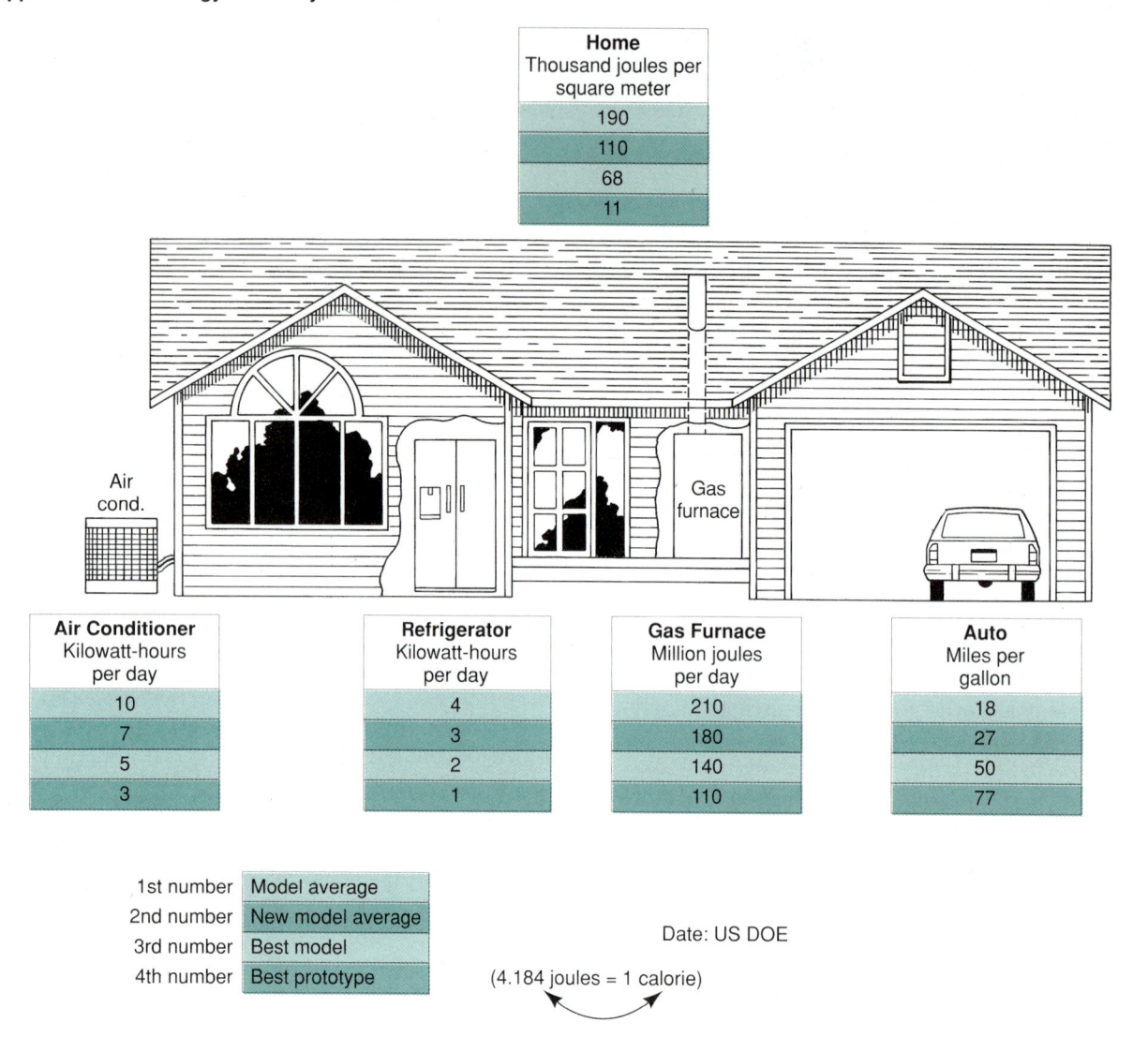

Home
Thousand joules per square meter

190
110
68
11

Air Conditioner
Kilowatt-hours per day

10
7
5
3

Refrigerator
Kilowatt-hours per day

4
3
2
1

Gas Furnace
Million joules per day

210
180
140
110

Auto
Miles per gallon

18
27
50
77

1st number	Model average
2nd number	New model average
3rd number	Best model
4th number	Best prototype

Date: US DOE

(4.184 joules = 1 calorie)

Figure 13.36 Each person can practice energy conservation through energy efficiency. Buying energy efficient homes, autos, and appliances can save many energy dollars and conserve nonrenewable energy resources.
Source: Data from the U.S. Department of Energy.

gallon. Then Americans would demand more efficient cars and as, a fringe benefit, the environment would reap the benefits of cleaner air.

Energy efficiency is also technologically feasible in the building industry. New and better insulation, energy efficient windows and doors, new energy-efficient condensing furnaces, greater utilization of sunlight, better indoor and outdoor temperature sensors and controls, and more efficient appliances could reduce the need for energy in every North American home, office, and business. Superinsulated homes in Minnesota have realized a 68% reduction in heat energy requirements.

Electric companies are very energy-inefficient industries. A typical steam boiler electric generation facility converts only about one-third of the steam heat it produces to electricity. Two-thirds is lost as waste heat. Cogeneration, which combines the production of electricity and steam heat, can considerably improve energy efficiency. The energy remaining in the steam heat after electric generation can be used for other industrial processes.

Summary

Energy management for long-term sustainability is an attainable goal. It will require many years of improved energy efficiency as the technology for long-term sustainability becomes a reality. The only long-term sources of energy are from the sun and the earth's internal heat. Money for research to investigate and tap these two energy sources should be a very high priority for the governments of each North American country. A livable global environment requires that we begin to make the sacrifices necessary to achieve energy sustainability by the year 2050.

Key Words and Phrases

Anthracite
Bioremediation
Bituminous
Coal
Coke
Crude oil
Geothermal energy
Hydropower
Joule
Lignite
Natural gas
Nuclear power
Peat
Subbituminous
Sunrayce USA
Synfuel

Questions and Discussion Topics

1. Why are fossil fuels considered a nonrenewable energy resource?
2. How can we protect the ocean resource with billions of gallons of oil floating in tankers on its surface?
3. What are the environmental consequences of shifting from oil to coal as our number one energy resource?
4. Do you feel nuclear energy has been given a "bum rap" by the American people? What are the advantages of nuclear power over fossil fuel energy? What should we do with nuclear waste?
5. Is geothermal energy a potential resource in your geographic area? Where is the closest place to your locale that you could get geothermal power?
6. How long do you feel it will take for solar energy to become 25% of our energy pie? Do you feel solar cars are a potential reality for your generation?
7. What can you do individually to conserve energy? Are you willing to make the sacrifices necessary to reduce energy waste and help solve the environmental problems created by excess consumption?

References for Further Study

Brocoum, S. et.al. Jan, 1989. Yucca Mountain: Geoscientists help make 10,000 year decisions. *Geotimes*. 34: No. 1. Underground nuclear storage facility plan.

Eiseley, L. 1960. *The Firmament of Time*. New York: Atheneum Publishers. An original exploration of the changes in man's vision of nature and himself.

Goldenberg, J. et.al. 1987. *Energy for a Sustainable World*. Washington, D.C.: World Resource Institute. The energy problem and alternative energy solutions.

Hill, G. June/July, 1974. Waiting for the Pipeline. *National Wildlife* 12: No. 4. The story before the Alaskan pipeline.

Johnson, Carl and Peter Hummel. August, 1991. Yucca Mountain, Nevada. *Geotimes*. 36: No. 8. Is Yucca Mountain fit for nuclear waste, or does it have mineral resource potential.

Michel, J. May 1990. The Exxon Valdez Oil Spill: Status of the Shoreline. *Geotimes*. 35: No. 5. NOAA evaluation of the Valdez oil spill.

Miller, G. T. Jr. 1990. *Resource Conservation and Management*. Belmont, Calif.: Wadsworth Publishing Company. Good chapters on energy conservation and management.

National Geographic. Feb., 1981. *Energy: Facing Up to the Problem, Getting Down to Solutions*. A special issue on energy.

Scientific American. 1980. *Energy and Environment*. San Francisco, Calif.: W. H. Freeman and Company. A collection of excellent articles on energy.

Shulman, S. Oct., 1989. When a Nuclear Reactor Dies, $98 Million is a Cheap Funeral. *Smithsonian Magazine*. 20: No. 7. The Shippingport Nuclear Reactor Funeral.

Chapter 14

Mineral Resources

Introduction
Metallic Minerals
   Abundant Metals
      Iron
      Aluminum
      Magnesium
      Titanium
      Manganese
   Scarce Metals
      Copper, Lead, Zinc, and Nickel
      Gold, Silver, and Platinoids
Management Strategies for Industry
   Underground Mining
Nonmetallic Minerals
   Building Materials
      Stone
      Sand and Gravel
      Cement
      Plaster
   Fertilizer and Chemical Minerals
      Nitrogen
      Phosphorus
      Potash (Potassium)
      Halite
      Sulfur
Summary

......

*This petrified branch with the
harsh look whose mineralized
splinters are needle-sharp
was living a hundred million
years ago,
bent to invisible wind, put out
leaves on the mountain. Today
the mountain is gone and this
fragment
lies on my desk imperishable
and waits for me in turn to be
gone.
Living once it has taken to
minerals for survival.*
   Loren Eiseley, 1977.

......

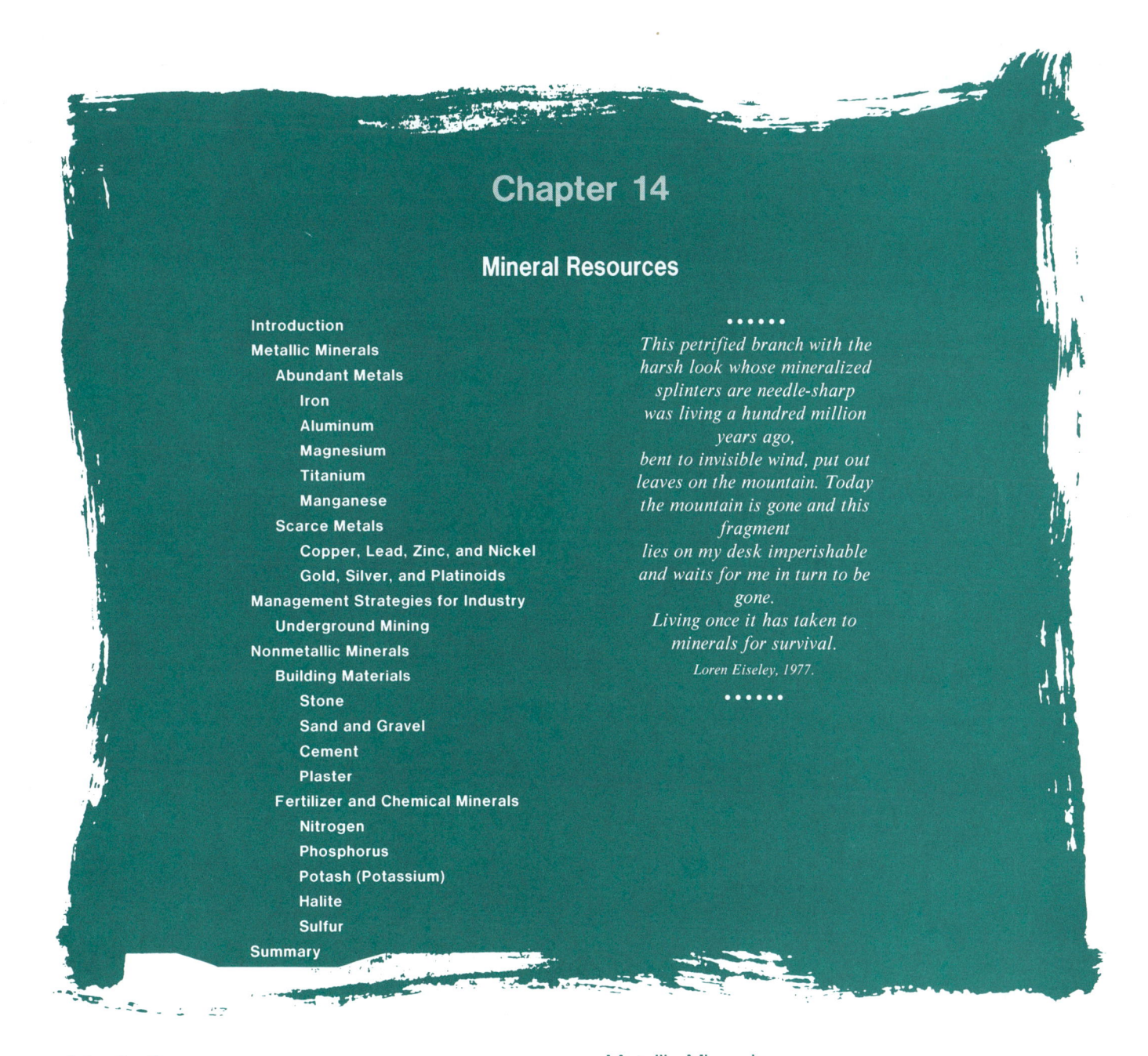

Introduction

A *mineral* is an **inorganic** substance occurring naturally in the earth, having a consistent and distinctive set of physical properties, and a composition that can be expressed by a chemical formula. According to this definition, coal and petroleum are not minerals because they are **organic** substances. In this section, the discussion of mineral resources will concentrate on the commodities of industry. Table 14.1 classifies minerals into two categories: metallic and nonmetallic. It further separates the metallics into abundant and scarce metals. The nonmetallics are separated into materials for building and mineral elements for fertilizers or chemicals.

Metallic Minerals

The lithosphere of the earth contains some of all 92 natural elements of the periodic table (Appendix A). But 99% of its total mass is made up of only ten elements. Table 14.2 gives the relative abundance of these ten common elements.

Most minerals occur in their natural state as compounds of two or more chemical elements. The metal element, lead (Pb), is extracted from the mineral, galena (PbS), by removing the sulfur. A few minerals such as silver, gold, and diamonds occur as free elements. Concentrations of minerals as deposits occur as a result of rock cycles. Igneous minerals can concentrate in deposits as a

Table 14.1
Classification of Mineral Resources

Metallic Minerals	Nonmetallic Minerals
Abundant Metals Minerals (greater than 0.1 percent of the crust)	Building Materials Stone Sand and Gravel Cement Gypsum (Plaster)
Iron Aluminum Magnesium Titanium Manganese	
Scarce Metals (less than 0.1 percent of the crust)	Fertilizer and Chemical Minerals Nitrogen Phosphorus Potash (Potassium) Halite Sulfur
Copper Lead Zinc Nickel Gold Silver Platinoids	
Platinum Palladium Rhodium Iridium Ruthenium Osmium	

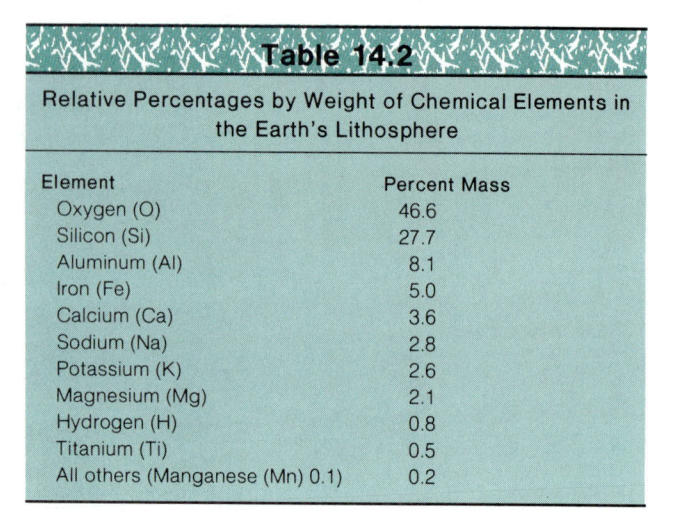

Table 14.2
Relative Percentages by Weight of Chemical Elements in the Earth's Lithosphere

Element	Percent Mass
Oxygen (O)	46.6
Silicon (Si)	27.7
Aluminum (Al)	8.1
Iron (Fe)	5.0
Calcium (Ca)	3.6
Sodium (Na)	2.8
Potassium (K)	2.6
Magnesium (Mg)	2.1
Hydrogen (H)	0.8
Titanium (Ti)	0.5
All others (Manganese (Mn) 0.1)	0.2

Table 14.3
U.S. Reserves and Potential Resources, 1980

Mineral (units)	Reserves	Potential Resources
Iron (MMT)	3,628.0	17,777.0
Aluminum (MMT)	9.1	45.4
Magnesium (MMT)	9.1	unlimited
Titanium (KMT)	16,326.0	94,872.2
Manganese (KMT)	0.0	66,755.2

Source: Mineral Facts and Problems 1980–USDI Bureau of Mines.

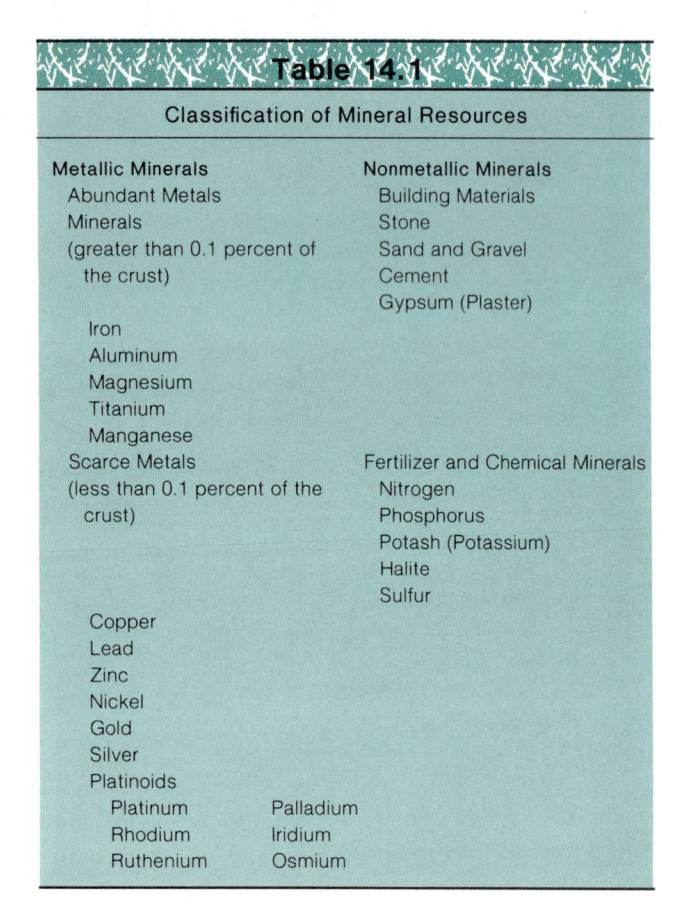

result of cooling rate, where elements will separate and crystallize at different temperatures. Mineral deposits of marble are the result of the metamorphosis of limestone. The deep trenches at plate boundaries and the mid-ocean ridges between plates are both places where there is sufficient heat to produce hydrothermal deposits of metallic ores. Rock weathering and percolation of water through the cracks and crevasses of fractured rocks can concentrate minerals by solution and recrystallization as deposits. Many of the geologic processes (vulcanism, metamorphism) operating at the earth's surface have the potential for concentrating minerals into deposits suitable for extraction and use.

Geologic processes have concentrated minerals into deposits throughout geologic time. Because of the large expanse of time required to replace mineral deposits, these resources are considered nonrenewable. Understanding the geology of an area gives a clue to the potential for mineral concentration sufficient for exploration. Remote sensing techniques can reveal geologic structure and potential locations of economically viable mineral deposits. Initial investigations of the mineral potential of an area may warrant detailed exploration by drilling. In most cases an environmental assessment must precede this stage of development and, if any federal permits are required or any federal monies are to be spent, a complete Environmental Impact Statement (EIS) must be completed to satisfy the requirement of the NEPA law. Should exploratory drilling indicate that a deposit suitable for extraction exists, a method of mining must be selected. Mining would be followed by processing, and that would be followed by delivery of the metal to the manufacturer. Reclamation of the affected area is required by law.

Metallic mineral recycling has become as important to industry as primary production. Aluminum, iron, steel, copper, and most other metals are recyclable and this process is cost effective when compared with primary processing. The topic of recycling will be covered later in this chapter and also in the next chapter.

Abundant Metals

The abundant metals, including **aluminum, iron, manganese, titanium,** and **magnesium,** are abundant for two reasons:

1. They are among the ten most common elements of the lithosphere (Table 14.2) with one exception, manganese (manganese is 0.1% of the lithosphere, but not in the top ten); and
2. They are economically extractable from identified accessible ore bodies called reserves. Table 14.3 gives the economically proven reserves and the potential resources for each abundant metal in the United States in million metric tons (MMT) or thousand metric tons (KMT).

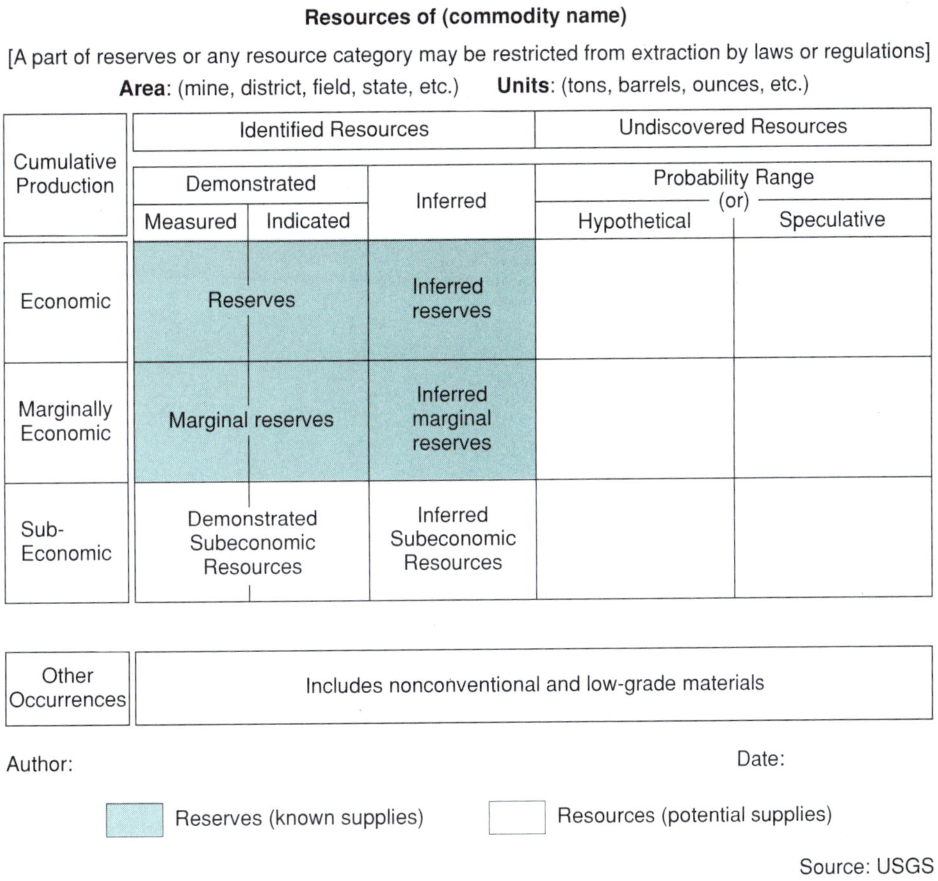

Resources of (commodity name)

[A part of reserves or any resource category may be restricted from extraction by laws or regulations]

Area: (mine, district, field, state, etc.)   **Units**: (tons, barrels, ounces, etc.)

Cumulative Production	Identified Resources			Undiscovered Resources	
	Demonstrated		Inferred	Probability Range (or)	
	Measured	Indicated		Hypothetical	Speculative
Economic	Reserves		Inferred reserves		
Marginally Economic	Marginal reserves		Inferred marginal reserves		
Sub-Economic	Demonstrated Subeconomic Resources		Inferred Subeconomic Resources		

Other Occurrences	Includes nonconventional and low-grade materials

Author: Date:

▢ Reserves (known supplies)   ▢ Resources (potential supplies)

Source: USGS

Figure 14.1 Resources can become reserves if the price of the resource increases or the cost of mining decreases. Exploration and discovery of new deposits can also expand the reserves of a company or country.
Source: U.S. Geological Survey.

Table 14.4
1980s Metal Prices in the United States

Year	¢/lb Aluminum	¢/lb Copper	$/tr. oz. Gold	¢/lb Lead	$/tr. oz. Platinum	$/gt Steel Scrap	$/tr. oz. Silver	$/lb Titanium	¢/lb Zinc
1980	71.6	102.2	612.5	42.5	437.0	86.7	20.63	7.02	37.4
1981	76.0	85.6	459.6	36.5	475.0	91.8	10.48	7.65	44.6
1982	76.0	74.6	375.9	25.5	328.0	57.8	7.95	5.55	38.5
1983	77.8	78.3	423.8	21.7	423.0	72.4	11.44	5.55	41.4
1984	81.0	68.8	360.2	25.6	359.0	83.1	8.14	5.55	48.6
1985	81.0	68.9	317.3	19.1	291.0	72.9	6.14	3.75	40.4
1986	55.9	67.9	367.7	22.0	464.0	73.5	5.47	4.10	40.8
1987	72.3	84.8	446.4	35.9	555.0	87.2	7.01	4.10	44.4
1988	101.0	114.5	436.9	37.1	531.0	113.5	6.53	4.50	62.1
1989	101.0	136.9	381.4	40.0	510.0	108.3	5.50	5.00	83.0

gt = gross ton = 2240 lbs.
Source: Data from *CRB Commodity Yearbook*, 1990.

Figure 14.1 is a diagram that shows the relationship between reserves and potential resources. Potential resources can become reserves if the price of the metal increases enough to allow for mining or if new technologies or discoveries provide incentives for extraction. The price of metals fluctuates regularly on the world market, and reserve supplies shift with the economy. Table 14.4 shows the price changes of common metals through a ten-year cycle. Reserves of aluminum would have been highest in 1988 and 1989 and lowest in 1986 based on market price in the United States for this ten-year period.

The **boom-and-bust cycles** of the minerals industry are apparent in the economic cycles of the minerals listed in Table 14.4. Silver is a good example of a scarce metal that

Mineral Resources

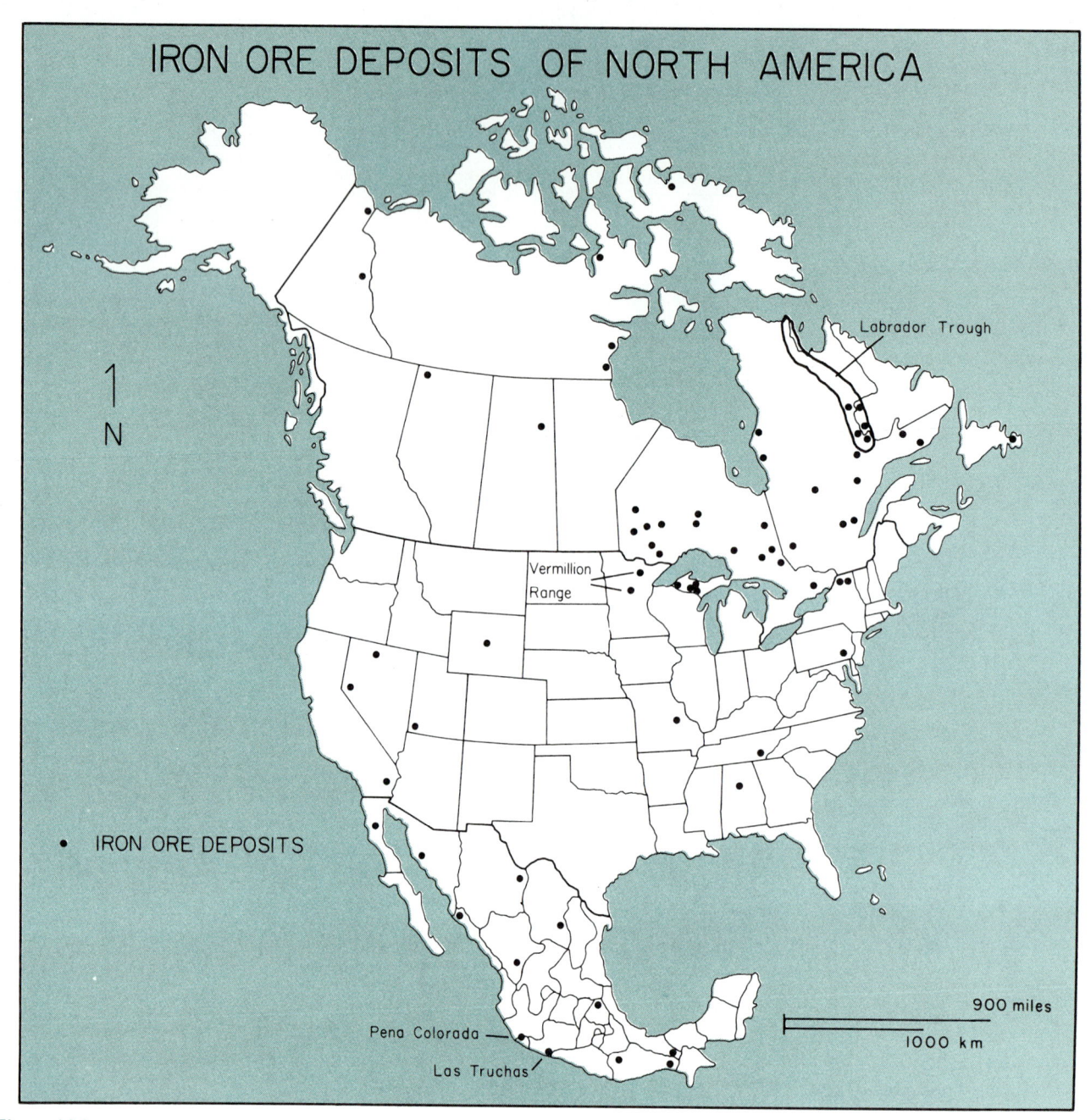

Figure 14.2 Iron ore deposits of North America.
Source: U.S. Geological Survey.
(*Cartographer:* Douglas Hemsath)

has dropped in economic value almost 200% in ten years. Aluminum, copper, and zinc, on the other hand, finished the decade of the 1980s at record highs. Resource management of mineral reserves that fluctuate widely in value is a very difficult task.

Iron

Iron is the fourth most abundant mineral and rock-forming element of the lithosphere. Iron is spatially ubiquitous, but concentrations of this metal into deposits are widely spaced. Figure 14.2 is a map of North American iron ore deposits. The map shows that mineral concentrations of iron ore are widely spaced but readily available (figure 14.3).

Iron is the basic ingredient of **steel,** the dominant metal of industry. Iron, when alloyed with other metals, is strong and relatively inexpensive. Aluminum was seven times more expensive per ton than iron in 1989. A significant proportion of the nickel, chromium, molybdenum, tungsten, vanadium, cobalt, and manganese are mined to be added to iron to produce steel. Each of these additives improves the strength or resistance to corrosion of the iron

Figure 14.3 Pea Ridge Iron Mine in Missouri. Magnetite and hematite are mined 2,000+ ft (610 m) below the surface.
(*Photo:* David A. Castillon)

alloy. They also increase the price of the steel, making aluminum more competitive economically.

Iron ore consists of iron oxides, iron carbonates, or iron sulfides. Magnetite (Fe_3O_4), hematite (Fe_2O_3), and geothite (limonite) $FeO(OH)$ are common iron oxides. Siderite ($FeCO_3$) is an iron carbonate and pyrite (FeS_2) (fool's gold) is an iron sulfide. Major concentrations of iron oxides in a host rock that is 50% to 60% iron ore are mined in the Lake Superior region and from the Vermillion range in Minnesota. The iron ore reserves of the Labrador Trough deposit in Canada are of the same type Precambrian bonded iron formation as in the Lake Superior district. Mexico enters the 1990s with iron ore resources of 580 million tons (527 MMT), giving them self-sufficiency for the immediate future. The mines at Peña Colorado and Las Truchas are major producers of magnetite from Jurassic or younger igneous deposits.

Aluminum

Aluminum is the most abundant metallic element in the lithosphere. Its utilization by industry and its growth as a product have been unparalleled by any other metal. Figure 14.4 is a map of North American metallic mineral deposits. *Bauxite* is the mineral name for hydroxides of aluminum. Aluminum is second to iron in both quantity and value in North America. It is lightweight, resistant to corrosion, and, when alloyed with copper, manganese, or magnesium, is as strong as steel. Its major disadvantage is the cost of production.

Bauxite forms from chemical weathering of aluminum-rich rocks such as syenite or nepheline. Warm, wet, tropical weathering conditions in relatively flat topography allow the percolation of acidic precipitation and soil water through the weathered zone of the aluminum-rich bedrock. The bases such as calcium (Ca), sodium (Na), potassium (K), and magnesium (Mg), and the silica (Si) are removed in solution and the hydrous aluminum gibbsite (H_3AlO_3) or diaspore ($HAlO_2$) remains. The gibbsite can further weather to a kaolinite clay ($Al_2Si_2O_5(OH)_4$), which has a lower aluminum content. Figure 14.5 illustrates the weathering process and alteration of aluminum-rich bedrock to a bauxite deposit, which contain the hydrous aluminum minerals of gibbsite or diaspore.

The smelting of aluminum requires large expenditures of electricity. Each ton of aluminum requires the electrical energy produced by seven tons (6,363 kg) of coal. Bauxite is mined, crushed, washed, and dried at the mine. (Then the bauxite is given a hydrochemical bath to extract the hydrated alumina oxide. The alumina produced is then processed in a fused fluorine salt electrolysis bath to extract the aluminum metal. The electrolysis process requires around 3.6 kwh per kg of aluminum and is about 70% of the metal production costs.) New energy-efficient smelters in South Carolina have reduced the electrolysis process to 2.8 kwh of electricity per kg of aluminum produced. Recycled aluminum metal requires only 5% of the energy input of primary production.

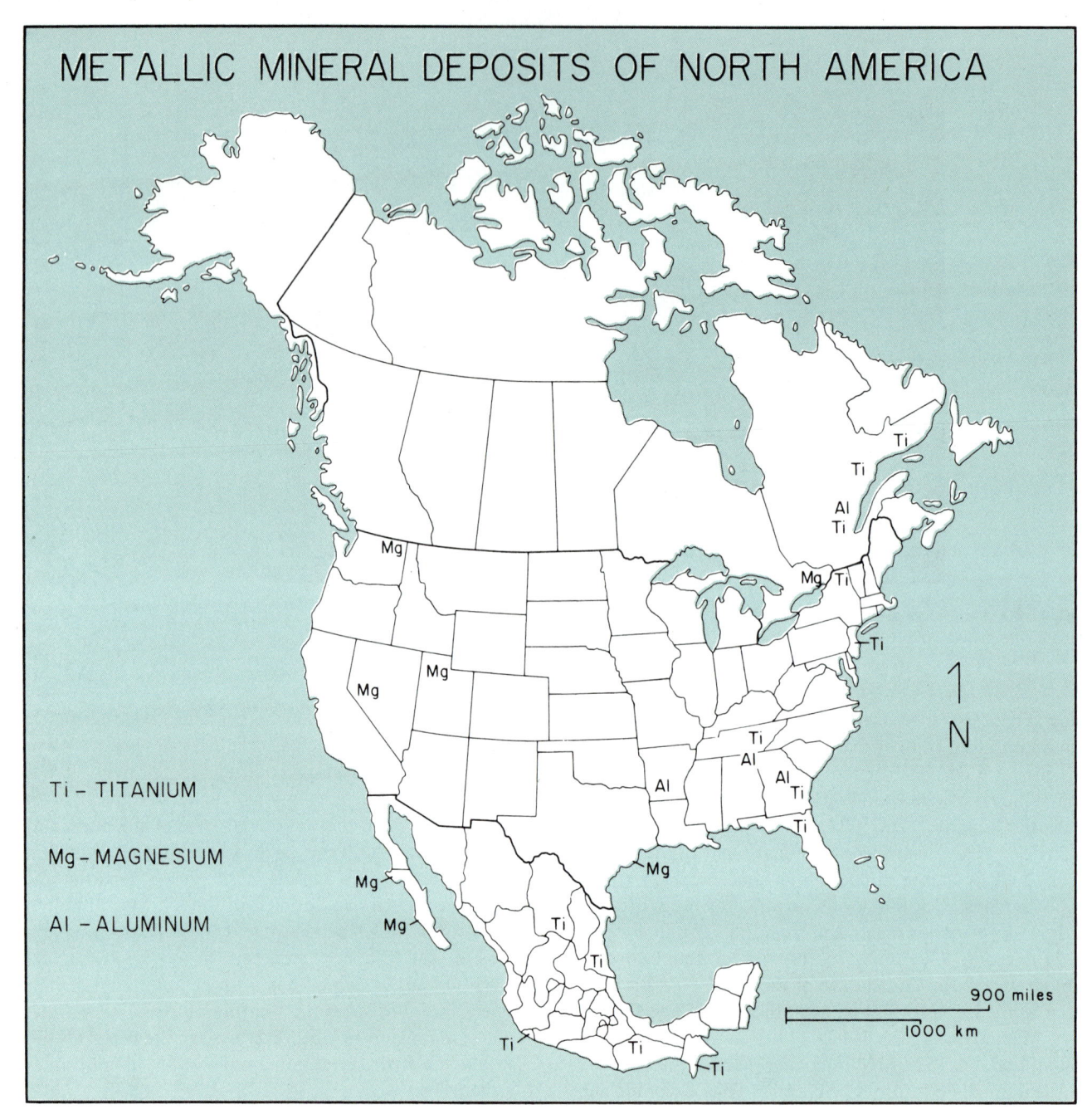

Figure 14.4 Metallic mineral deposits of North America, including aluminum (bauxite), magnesium, and titanium.
Source: U.S. Geological Survey.
(*Cartographer:* Douglas Hemsath)

The infrastructure to effectively recycle most aluminum products is in place in North America. The tremendous savings in energy costs have allowed the cost of recycling aluminum to remain high enough that most consumers will make the effort to save aluminum cans. Recycled aluminum cans brought 40 to 45 cents per pound in 1990, so more cans were recycled than were discarded. More and more metallic mineral resources will need to join aluminum as recyclable resources in the 1990s.

Magnesium

Magnesium in its metallic form is the lightest abundant and stable metal. It is strong and corrosion-resistant when alloyed with aluminum. However, it is even more expensive to produce than aluminum because of the great amount of electrical energy required for the electrolytic smelting process. Magnesium requires 3.6 to 4.0 kwh per kg of metal fabricated. A new silicothermic smelting process that uses much less energy and reduces environmental pollution is replacing the old electrolytic process.

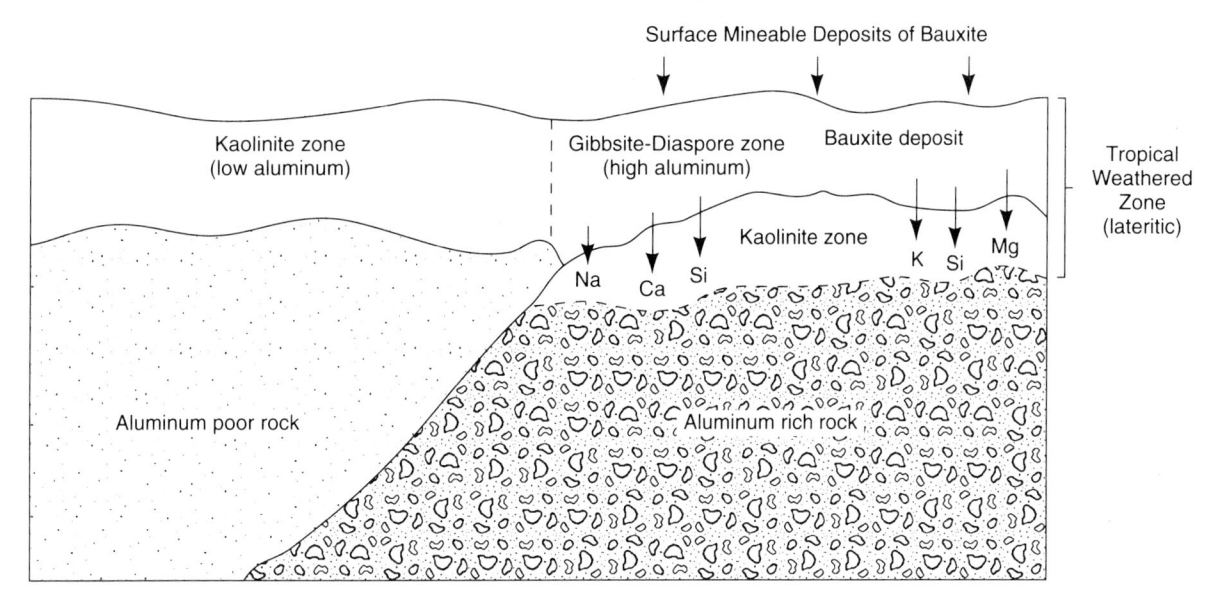

Figure 14.5 Weathering of aluminum-rich rocks such as syenite or nepheline to gibbsite or diaspore in a tropical weathering environment. Leaching of the most soluble components, such as Si, Na, Ca, K, and Mg, during chemical weathering leaves a lateritic capping (gibbsite-diaspore zone) in which the less soluble aluminum and iron hydroxides are concentrated. When aluminum hydroxides predominate, the laterite is called a bauxite deposit.
Reprinted with permission of Merrill, an imprint of Macmillan Publishing Company, from *Earth Resources* by Douglas G. Brookins. Copyright © 1981 by Bell & Howell Company.

Magnesium has many industrial uses because of its desirable thermal and electrical insulating properties. It is used in its oxide form in metallurgical furnace refractories, as a vulcanizing agent in rubber, and for air-cooled car engines in its alloyed form.

Figure 14.4 shows the location of North American magnesium reserves. Deposits in Utah and Texas in the United States, and in Ontario, Canada, are important sources. Magnesite ($MgCO_3$) and dolomite ($CaMg(CO_3)_2$) are important mineral sources for magnesium. The oceans of the world contain an inexhaustible supply of magnesium. Seawater contains about 34 ppt salt and magnesium is about 3.68% of the salt content. Future prospects for the sustainability of magnesium are very good. As new technology to reduce the smelting cost by energy savings continues to develop, magnesium will remain a valuable and vital metal of industry in North America.

Titanium

Titanium, combining light weight with high strength and corrosion resistance even at very high temperatures, is the metal desired by the airline and space industry. Heat shields on spacecrafts are 85% titanium alloys. However, the major use for titanium is as an oxide (TiO_2), which is used as a white pigment in paint.

Ilmenite ($FeTiO_3$) is the main ore mineral for titanium. The largest known deposits of ilmenite are at Allard Lake in Quebec, Canada. Similar deposits of titanium ore can be found at Sanford Lake in the Adirondack Mountains of New York State. Figure 14.4 shows the location of titanium ore deposits in North America. Rutile (TiO_2), a second titanium ore mineral, has not been concentrated by geologic processes into minable deposits. It is, however, quarried from beach sands off the Atlantic Coast of Florida, along with some ilmenite. Reserves and potential resources of titanium for North America are more than adequate through the 21st century.

Manganese

Manganese is essential as an alloy for steel because it protects the steel from oxygen and sulfur corrosion. As much as 7 kg (15 lb) of manganese are required for every ton (909 kg) of steel produced and no satisfactory manganese substitute has been discovered. The metallurgical industry used about 95% of the total manganese output for metal alloys.

Reserves of manganese are almost nonexistent in North America. The largest reserves of manganese are in the Soviet Union, at Chiaturi in the Republic of Georgia. Pyrolusite (MnO_2) is a chemical sedimentary manganese ore. Another important residual manganese ore mineral is psilomelane ($Mn_2O_3 2H_2O$). These terrestrial deposits were mined during World War II from fracture-filled veins in igneous rocks in Missouri, but they were sparse when compared with the vast deposits of manganese nodules found on the ocean floor. These nodules are mixtures of manganese, iron oxides, and hydroxides (figure 14.6). The

Figure 14.6 A manganese nodule from the floor of the Pacific Ocean also contains iron, nickel, copper, and cobalt. Dimensions: (180 × 160 × 45 mm) (7.0 × 6.4 × 1.8 in).
(*Photo:* David A. Castillon)

nodules appear to grow very slowly (less than a mm per 1,000 years). Some nodules contain copper, nickel, cobalt, and other scarce metals. A multinational consortia of countries joined together to locate and extract the vast manganese deposits on the ocean floor. But the problems of mining by vacuuming were too great to overcome. What effects vacuuming the ocean floor for these nodules would have on the ocean environment is an unanswerable question. We should proceed with caution in this unknown field.

Scarce Metals

Scarce metals are defined as those metallic elements that are less than 0.1% of the lithospheric mass. Deposits and reserves of scarce metals are geochemically rare and pose the most serious challenge to technology and resource managers. Common commodities of industry are in the list of scarce metals; which include copper, lead, zinc, and nickel, along with silver, gold, and the platinoid metals. Cost of recovery of each metal determines the concentration in an ore body necessary for economical extraction and use. Figure 14.7 illustrates the concentrations in the host rock necessary for economic recovery. The percentages in parentheses are the minimum metal content an ore must have to be mined economically (1980s prices). As the price of a metal goes up, the concentration needed for recovery goes down.

Figure 14.8 is a map of North American scarce metal deposits. Copper, lead, zinc, nickel, gold, silver, and platinum deposits are indicated on this map. Other rare metallics such as molybdenum, tin, antimony, mercury, cadmium, and lithium are not included because their industrial uses are limited. Limited, however, should not be construed as unimportant.

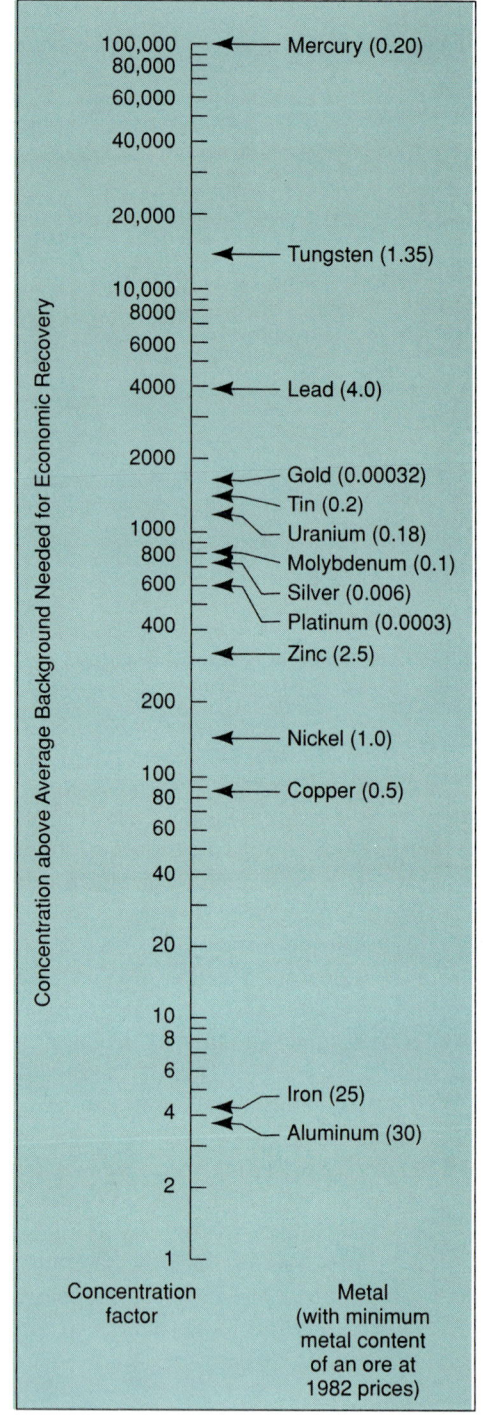

Figure 14.7 Economically recoverable reserves of scarce metals depend on the concentration of the metal in the host rock and the price of the metal. The crustal abundances of geochemically scarce metals are so low that large concentrations above background average are needed before deposits can be profitably mined. The abundant metals require lower concentration factors to produce rich ores. The bracketed percentages are the minimum metal contents an ore must have before it can be mined under the most favorable circumstances with present day technology. As the price of a metal goes up or down, its position will change. Between 1969 and 1982, for example, the concentration factor needed for a viable gold deposit dropped from about 4,000 to 1,600, largely as a result of the rising price of gold. Gold was about $400 an ounce in 1982. (See Table 14.4 for the 1982 value of other metals.)

Brian J. Skinner, *Earth Resources*, 3d ed., © 1986, p. 97. Reprinted by permission of Prentice-Hall, Inc., Englewood Cliffs, NJ.

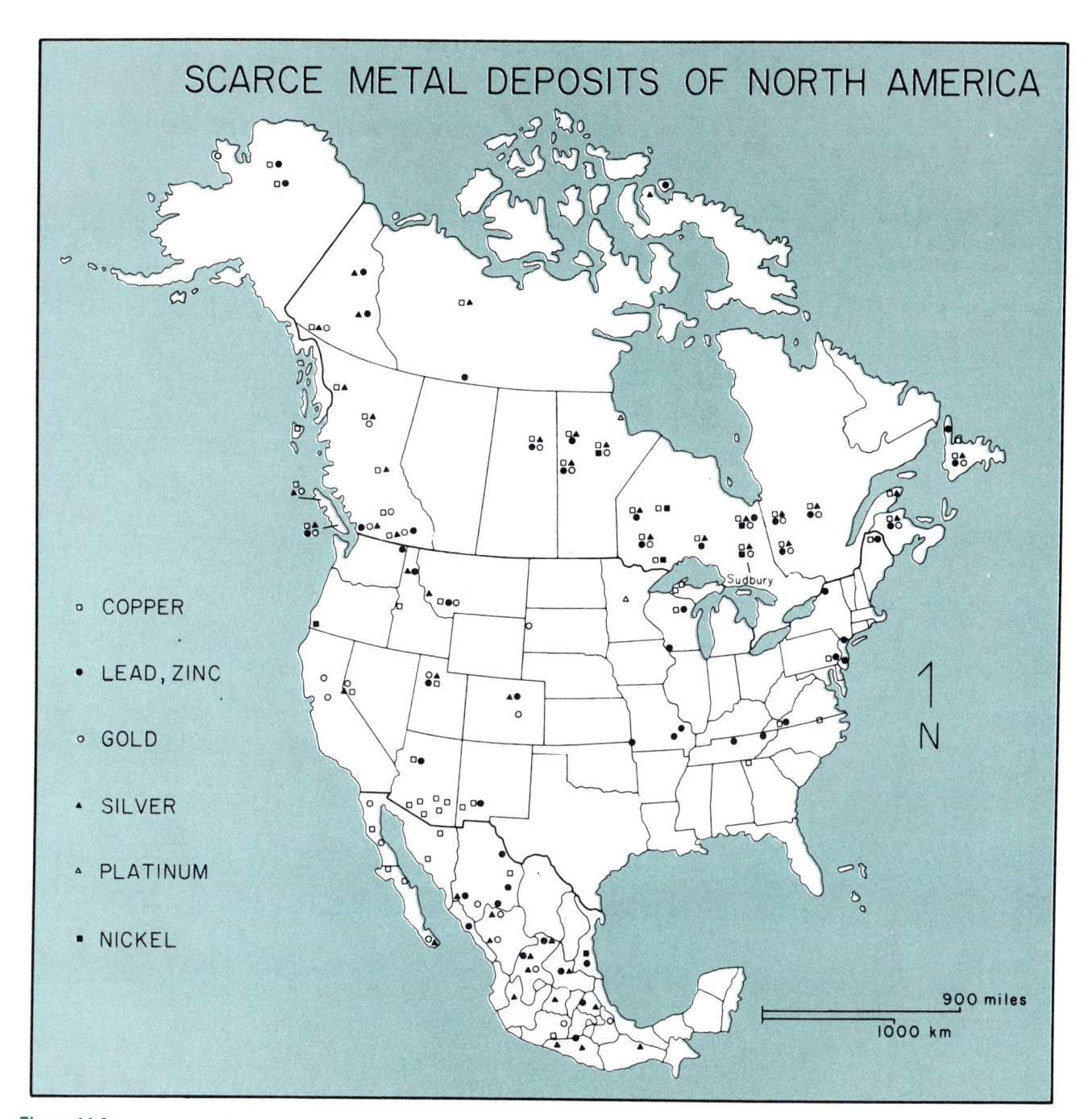

Figure 14.8 Scarce metal deposits of North America (copper, lead, zinc, nickel, gold, silver, and platinum).
Source: U.S. Geological Survey.
(Cartographer: Douglas Hemsath)

Mineral Resources 319

Copper, Lead, Zinc, and Nickel

Copper, lead, zinc, and nickel are grouped together for two reasons:

1. All of these metals occur in deposits primarily as sulfides.
2. All of these metals have important historical and industrial significance to the North American population.

North American exploration was initiated by Europeans looking for new sources of scarce metals. Spanish land grants and land controlled by the French were given to settlers of the Mine La Motte area about 100 miles (161 km) south of St. Louis, Missouri, to work the lead and zinc deposits discovered in the late 1700s.

Copper is mined from low-grade hydrothermal deposits of chalcocite (Cu_2S) and chalcopyrite ($CuFeS_2$). These deposits are typically associated with igneous porphyritic rocks (figure 14.9). The largest U.S. copper producer is the Bingham Mine in Utah, (figure 14.10) but

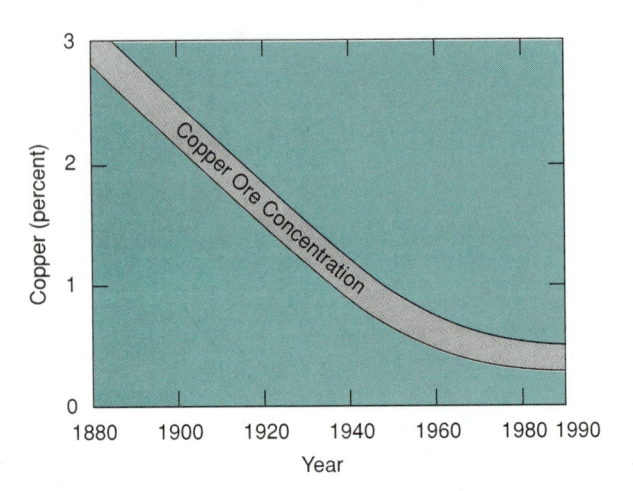

Figure 14.9 Copper ore rock with less than a half percent copper is mineable with today's technology. Three percent copper ore rock was needed in 1880. This trend does not apply to all metals, but has been observed in metals that can be mined by mass mining methods.
Source: Data from the U.S. Bureau of Mines.

Figure 14.10 Bingham Canyon copper mine in Utah. Daily charge to break up the rock is being released in this scene.
(*Photo:* David A. Castillon)

large deposits of copper are also mined in Arizona and in Nova Scotia, Canada. Potential resources of copper are difficult to evaluate but the outlook for copper is very good through the year 2015 and possibly longer. Both rising prices and recycling are hopes for the future sustainability of copper. Technology has discovered many ways to substitute aluminum for copper, particularly in the electrical industry, because aluminum is a good conductor of electrical currents. But corrosion problems and the tendency for it to produce electrical fires has increased the demand for copper.

Lead and *zinc* commonly form together geologically. Lead sulfide called galena (PbS) and zinc sulfide called sphalerite (ZnS) account for most of the world's production of these metals. Missouri is a world leader in lead and zinc production (figure 14.11). Lead, zinc, and copper are extracted from underground mines 300–600 m (1,000 to 2,000 ft) below the surface. Cambrian- and Ordovician-age dolomites are the main host rocks, with concentrations as high as 10% metal ore. Lead is used mainly for storage batteries. A giant lead-acid battery at an electrical substation in Chino, California is used for "load leveling" during peak electrical use periods. The Japanese have begun using lead in building foundations to absorb earthquake shock. Lead tetraethyl, the antiknock additive in gasoline, had been a major use of lead for many years, but government regulations and the switch to unleaded gasoline have considerably decreased the need for lead. Many health hazards are caused by lead in the environment. Lead poisoning is a major cause of mortality for many species of wildlife. Lead shotgun pellets ingested by bottom-feeding waterfowl and birds accumulates in the blood and will eventually poison the organism. Human health hazards created by lead in paint, lead in pipe solder, and lead in gasoline are diminishing because these uses have been banned. These environmental hazards, along with low prices, caused a depressed lead market in the mid-1980s, but the early 1990s indicate a revitalized lead industry as technology creates new, safer uses for lead.

Zinc is used mainly as an alloy for die-cast metal products and as an anticorrosion additive for steel. Zinc mixes chemically into iron and will not spall (break off). Therefore, it is an excellent metal for iron galvanizing to prevent rust and corrosion. Zinc is also used to alloy brass and in the production of paint. Zinc ranks fourth after iron, aluminum, and copper as a metal for industry. Sustainability for both lead and zinc appears to be very good.

Nickel is extracted from the mineral pentlandite [$(FeNi)_9S_8$] contained in the host rock norite (similar to gabbro). The United States must import almost all of its nickel from the Sudbury deposit in Canada, which contains both nickel and copper ore. Almost 65% of the imported nickel is used to alloy steel. Canadian reserves of nickel appear to be sustainable for the North American continent for the near future, but technology should look for a nickel substitute as a steel alloy.

Gold, Silver, and Platinoids

Gold, silver, and the platinoid metals are scarce precious metals. They are precious because of their physical properties. Each of these metals can be found in its native state and are dense enough to collect as placer deposits. Figure 14.12 illustrates some of the possible locations placer deposits can be found in various geologic settings. However,

Figure 14.11A Fletcher mine is a St. Joe Minerals lead-zinc mine in the southeast Missouri lead belt.
(*Photo:* David A. Castillon)

Figure 14.11B ASARCO lead smelter in southeast Missouri produces 99.99% pure lead bars for the world market.
(*Photo:* David A. Castillon)

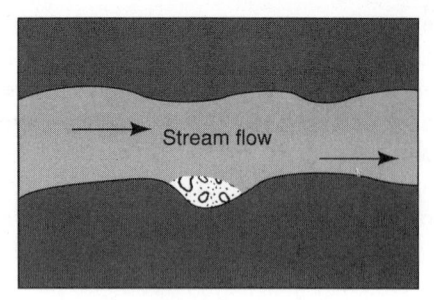

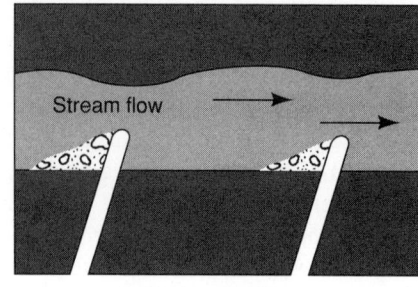

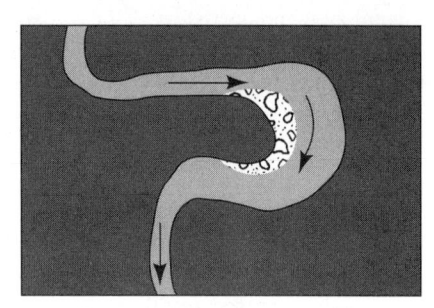

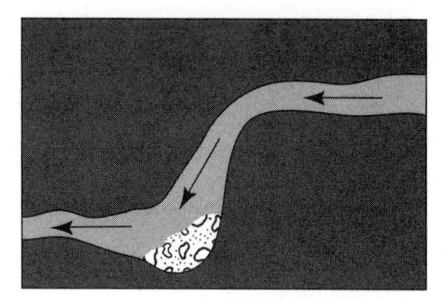

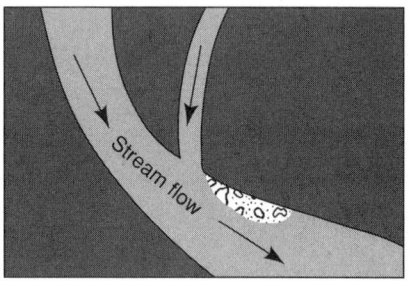

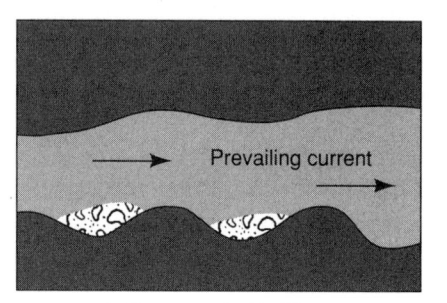

Figure 14.12 Typical sites for placer deposits in moving water environments.
Brian J. Skinner, *Earth Resources*, 3d ed., © 1986, p. 121. Reprinted by permission of Prentice-Hall, Inc., Englewood Cliffs, NJ.

much of the gold and silver extracted by mining results from extraction of these precious metals as a by-product of copper, lead, or zinc mining operations.

Gold, as a monetary base for international trade, is justified by its scarcity. It is a metal that has almost no rivals or substitutes. South Africa has more than 50% of the world's gold reserves. The United States imports roughly 75% of the gold it needs; however, recent discoveries of large gold deposits in Nevada may reduce the amount of imports in the near future.

Silver is more abundant and therefore less expensive than gold. It is more common as a sulfide than gold or the platinoids, and is extracted, along with lead and zinc, as a by-product of those mining and milling operations. Silver's main market is in the photographic industry, but large amounts of silver are also used by electrical industries. Silver on photographic and X-ray film is recyclable and many small recycling plants have been set up to recover it from hospital X-ray and film processing laboratories. Silver is also important in the electronics industry because of its use on computer chips and boards. The increased demand for silver in the 1990s may create a short supply.

Platinoid metals include platinum, palladium, rhodium, iridium, ruthenium, and osmium. These are rare earth metals because they exist in the earth's lithosphere at levels less than 0.0000005%. The platinoids all occur in their native state in igneous mantle magmas. They are mined as valuable by-products of nickel and copper sulfide mining and milling operations. However, they are heavy metals that are essentially unaffected by chemical weathering and can be found in placer deposits as well as among the sulfides. Potential resources are uncertain but low-grade deposits exist in Montana and Minnesota in the United States, and active mines in Ontario and Manitoba in Canada produce platinoids as by-products of other mining operations.

Platinoids are critical to specific high-tech uses in the aerospace industry. As precious metals, they have considerable value in the jewelry industry because of their strength and workability. The platinoids play an indispensable role in modern industry because of their chemical inertness over wide temperature ranges. In the chemical industry, platinoids are used as catalysts in making pharmaceuticals. Their chemical inertness and thermal stability make them the only metal that can be used in some electrical and electronic devices. The catalytic converter for automobiles, which reduces exhaust emissions, is the major use of platinoid metals today. Recycling of catalytic converters to recover the platinoids is becoming a major industry of the 1990s. Each automobile catalytic converter contains about $35 worth of recoverable platinoids at 1990s platinum prices of $500 per troy ounce.

Management Strategies for Industry

Examination of the abundant and scarce metals of industry indicates that most of the important metallic resources have reserves and potential resource supplies sufficient to last well into the 21st century. But sustainability of these metallic resources for industry requires a new management strategy. The old model of industry required that the manufacturer take in the raw metallic mineral, expend tremendous amounts of cheap energy, and generate a product with a limited life span. In the process of manufacturing, waste was generated and disposed of almost casually. For economic and environmental reasons, the old system has to go if sustainability is the goal.

Beginning with the mining process, environmental protection laws require that the structure of the mining processes be modified to reduce the number of operations at the mine site. Such changes will be extremely expensive and the cost passed on to industry, driving up the price of the metallic mineral needed for manufacturing. The cost of energy in its various forms is much higher than it was in the pre-1970s era and these costs will continue to climb as energy resources are diminished. Energy conservation must become a part of the new strategy for industry. Waste, especially hazardous waste, must be reduced or eliminated, because the environmental costs of waste disposal will not be tolerated by the American public. Consumers are demanding longer-lasting products because of the initial cost and because of the waste-disposal problems they are facing. Recycling and waste reduction must become a part of the new industrial system.

This new system must take on the workings of the biosphere. Raw materials would enter the system at the bottom of the pyramid. Within the pyramid, the manufacturing process takes the place of photosynthesis and converts the raw materials to products. The products are consumed (used) by the human population. Figure 14.13 illustrates the operation of the industrial systems pyramid. The basic laws of the system are: 1) conservation of energy, 2) minimum waste, 3) alternate paths for by-products, and 4) recyclable waste and end products.

The industrial systems pyramid is an ideal that may never be attained, but both industry and the consumer must change their habits for it to be a possibility. To build a sustainable world that contains limited nonrenewable resources requires that we move in the direction of an industrial systems pyramid. The only losses would be energy and these could be kept to a minimum with maximum energy conservation.

Corporate, government, and public attitudes must change in the direction of the industrial systems pyramid. Government regulations must move in a direction that favors waste minimization and recycling. Waste-generating industries can sell their materials to buyers who, in turn, need the materials for their manufacturing processes. Waste-exchange operations are becoming a part of the by-product alternative path of the industrial systems pyramid in the United States and Canada. Instead of paying to dispose of its wastes, the selling industry must determine how it can profit from the use of its waste. This might include processing the waste into a saleable product or selling it to another processor. The buying industry would probably pay less for the waste as a raw material from the selling industry than from a primary source. The environment would then benefit because of the reduction in materials sent to a landfill.

Many economists promote financial incentives to reduce pollution and promote energy efficiency. They would like to see investment in research credits, tax relief, or fees or taxes on manufactured hazardous waste by-products. Environmentalists who want wastes eliminated or reduced at the source claim that such fees or taxes are

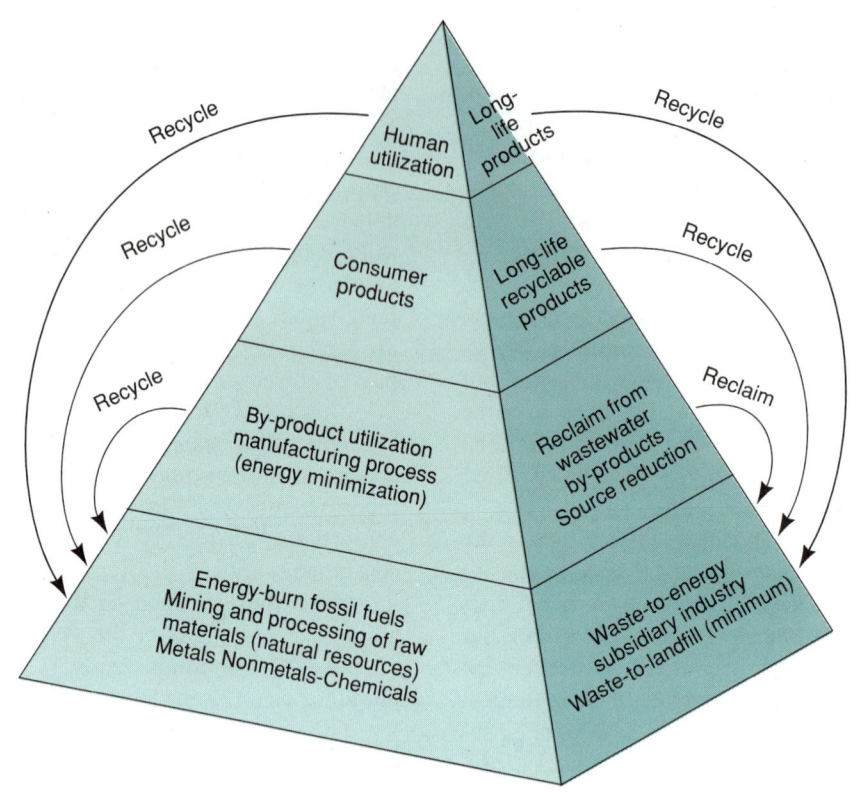

Figure 14.13 Industrial systems pyramid.

"licenses to pollute," whereas, government officials claim they would be incentives to reduce hazardous waste. Government, industry, and environmentalists must abandon their adversarial relationships and begin to work together toward an industrial systems pyramid approach. It's the only acceptable direction for a sustainable industrial earth.

Underground Mining

Underground mining is chosen as the mining method if the ore deposits are too deep for openpit mining and the ore mineral cannot be removed by solution mining. The underground method is used for many layered, vein, or lode-type ore deposits. Gold, silver, lead, zinc, copper, salt, coal, and uranium are all mined underground.

After locating a buried ore body, a shaft is sunk to contact the ore deposits (figure 14.14). Drifts (tunnels) off the main shaft are then excavated, removing the ore as the drift is extended. In most underground mines, the shaft and drifts intersect groundwater zones and water must be pumped continually to keep the mine dry. Contamination of groundwater is an environmental problem that must be constantly monitored during the mining operation. In underground coal mines, explosive gases like methane can accumulate. Radioactive radon gas is also a problem in some underground mines. It is chemically inert, and not explosive, but radioactively unstable. A sophisticated ventilation system, usually requiring a second shaft, must be installed in most underground mines to remove these gases and provide fresh air.

Mining laws that govern safety and afford environmental protection have improved both aspects of underground mining during the past 25 years but accidents still occur. Uranium mines have one of the best underground mining safety records because the mines are less extensive and because radiation and safety regulations are rigidly enforced. But the hazards of working underground in an uranium mine take a long time to manifest themselves, and miners that have worked in these mines have developed various forms of cancer from long-term exposure. The potash, salt, and limestone underground mines also have a very good safety record but the underground coal mines, even though they are better than they used to be, are very hazardous working environments. These mines are a significant environmental danger, especially to the groundwater and surface water systems in the mined area.

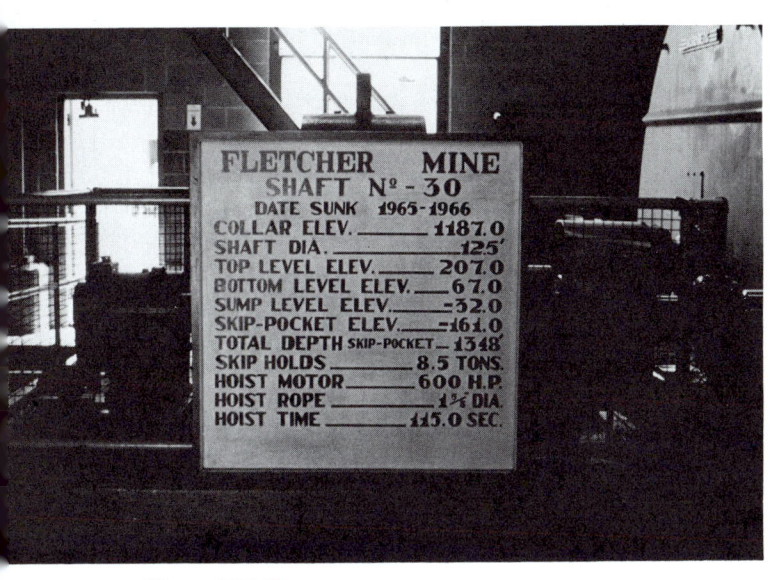

Figure 14.14A Fletcher mine shaft no. 30—lead-zinc mine of St. Joe Minerals, southeast Missouri.
(Photo: David A. Castillon)

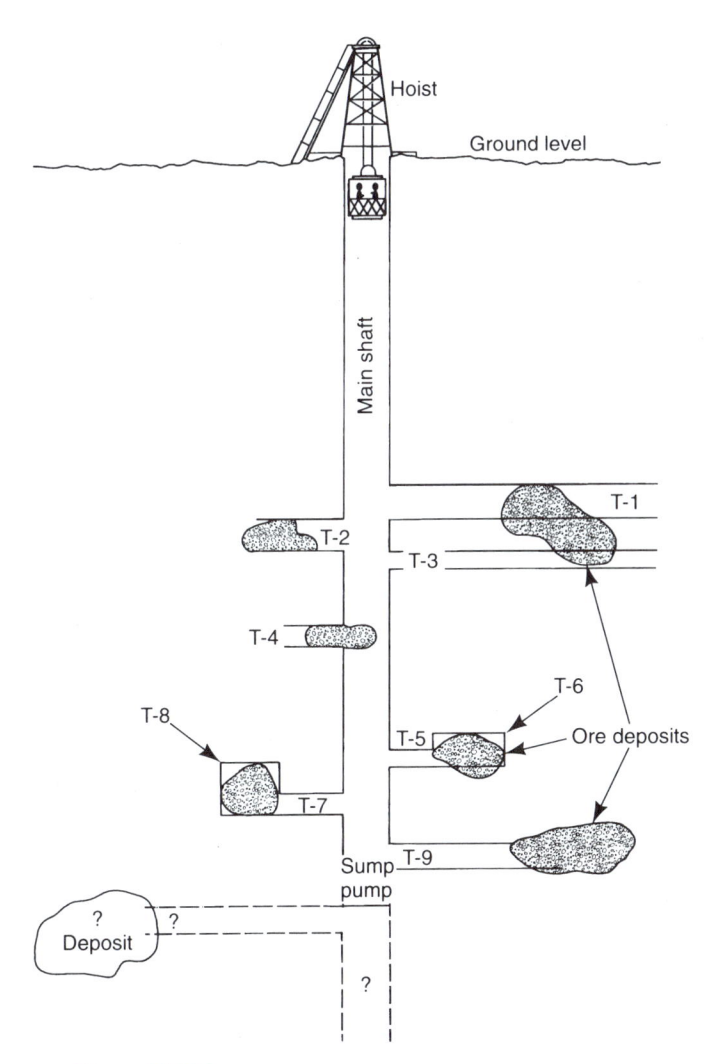

Figure 14.14B Diagram of an underground mine.

Nonmetallic Minerals

Nonmetallic mineral resources represent the natural resources used in greatest volume. Natural building materials such as stone, and sand and gravel have been the base of the construction industry for many years and this trend will continue into the future. The reserves of these materials would appear to be almost limitless. The bulk of the costs involved in the utilization of natural building materials is in energy use for transportation. This forces the use of local sources of stone, and sand and gravel, causing quarrying of these materials to occur in everyone's backyard. Processed nonmetallic minerals converted into building products continue to capture a larger share of the construction materials market. Calcium and magnesium carbonate (limestone ($CaCO_3$) and dolostone ($MgCO_3$)) are processed into cement, and gypsum ($CaSO_4 \cdot 2H_2O$) is converted into plasterboard.

Nonmetallic minerals used for fertilizer and by the chemical industries include lime, nitrogen, phosphorus, potash, sulfur, and salt. Although other nonmetallic minerals are utilized, this list represents the minerals used in greatest volume by industry.

Building Materials

Stone and lumber have been and still are the two most important building materials in North America. But in lumber-poor countries like Japan, substitute products, particularly metals and petroleum (plastic) products, are widely accepted as building materials. The construction industry in North America has reduced its dependence on wood in commercial and industrial buildings. Stone, sand and gravel, cement, and plaster are the leading nonmetallic mineral building materials for the construction industry.

Stone

Rocks, such as limestone, marble, sandstone, slate, and granite, quarried or mined for industrial use without changing their chemical or physical characteristics except for sizing and shaping, are called *stone*. Cut-and-shaped building stone has been almost completely replaced by cement as a building material (figure 14.15). Crushed rock, on the other hand, is used in ever-increasing quantities by the construction industry.

Crushed rock is usually quarried by open pit techniques that require drilling and blasting of a rock face. The broken stone is then transferred to a crusher and size-sorted on vibrating screens. Most crushed stone is limestone or dolostone that has a multitude of uses. The finest

Mineral Resources 325

Figure 14.15A Cut stone blocks on the floor of a limestone mine in Ste. Genevieve County, Missouri.
(*Photo:* James E. Vandike, MDNR)

Figure 14.15B Crushed rock of all sizes for the building industry is in constant demand.
(*Photo:* David A. Castillon)

crushed limestone, almost a powder, is used for agricultural purposes to adjust the pH of the soil and is called *lime*. Pulverized limestone is the primary ingredient for cement. Crushed limestone is also used for metallurgical flux by the iron and steel industry. More than 85% of the crushed stone in the United States is used by the construction industry to build roads and buildings and to make cement. There is no substitute for limestone in the manufacture of cement, but sand and gravel can usually be substituted for crushed stone to reduce transportation costs when it is locally available.

Underground limestone mines in urban areas have been transformed into storage and commercial space for industry. The use of underground mines is well suited to large refrigerated storage warehouses. The rock, once cooled, retains the reduced temperatures with tremendous savings in energy costs. Kansas City, Missouri has a vast network of underground storage and industrial space occupying former limestone mines. Recreational activities such as tennis and ice skating are also well suited to these underground locations (figure 14.16).

Sand and Gravel

Size-sorted deposits of sand and gravel are a product of moving water. The velocity of running water or the periodicity of wave activity dictate the size of the material being deposited. Composition of the material is dictated by the geology of the drainage area supplying the material. Vast quantities of washed, size-sorted sands and gravels were deposited in North America and Europe by glacial meltwaters. These materials, along with river-deposited sands and gravels and coastal deposits, are the raw materials of the sand and gravel industry.

Particle size is used to define unconsolidated depositional materials. Figure 14.17 is a chart that gives the defining size ranges used by industry to separate materials. *Sand* is defined by highway engineers as particles between 0.74 and 2.0 mm, whereas *gravel* is any material larger than 2.0 mm but less than 75 mm. Materials larger than 75 mm (3 in) are called *boulders* or *cobbles*.

Sand and gravel, like limestone, are widely distributed throughout North America. Some regions, like the coastal region of the Gulf of Mexico, have vast quantities of sand but little or no gravel. The streams feeding this region are too slow to move gravel. Sand and gravel collection from streambeds and beaches creates major disruptions in the aquatic ecosystems affected. Just as there is a closed fishing season during spawning, there should also be a closed season on sand and gravel removal during the spring spawning season.

Sustainability of the sand and gravel resource should not be a problem for North America. The high cost of

Figure 14.16 Underground space in the limestone mines of Missouri. (a) Outside entrance to underground space; (b) Office space; (c) Tennis courts; (d) Ice-skating rink.
(*Photos:* James E. Vandike, MDNR)

energy to transport these materials is, however, a limiting factor for the industry. Shorter travel distances to haul the raw material could put a quarry in every neighborhood. With proper design and management, a well-designed quarry could become an attractive park after use. Crushed stone is a suitable substitute for gravel for most construction purposes.

Glass is an important product of high silica sand and/or sandstone. It has challenged many older, more established structural materials in the building industry and use and consumption is rising rapidly. Glass is manufactured by melting high silica sand with other minerals, then quenching them so rapidly that crystals do not have time to nucleate. The melting point for quartz (SiO_2), the dominant mineral in glass sand or sandstone, is very high (1713°C/3115°F), so limestone and borax is added to reduce the melting temperature. Good deposits of high silica sandstone occur in many locations in North America.

Mineral Resources

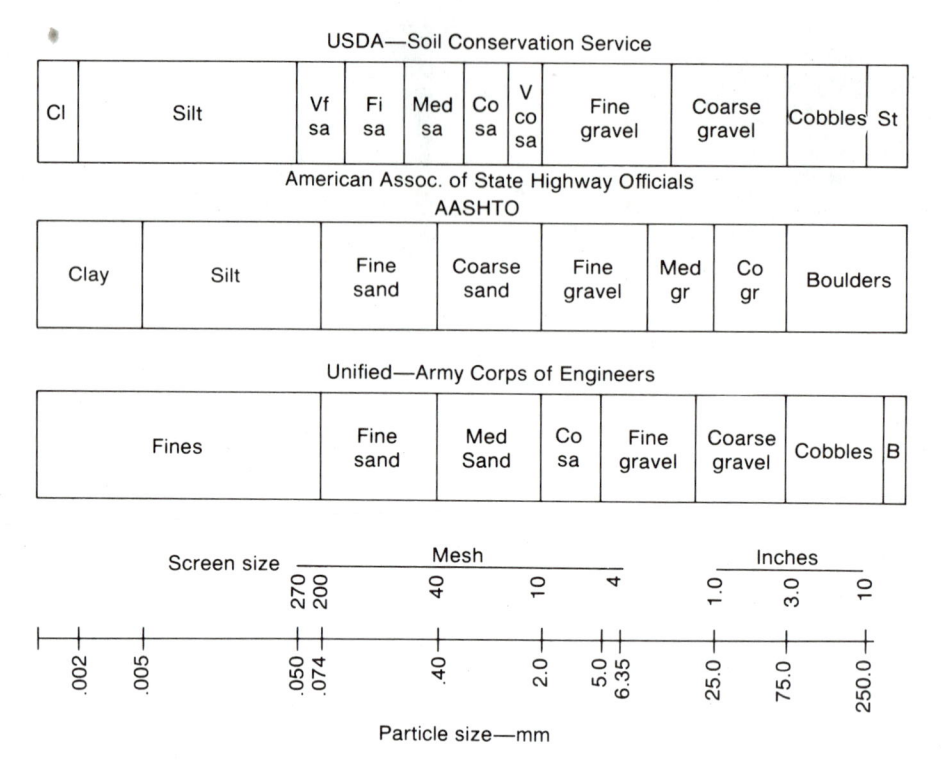

Figure 14.17 The relationship between particle size and textural terms, as defined by various testing agencies. (Scale is logarithmic.)
From R. L. Hausenbuiller, *Soil Science*, 3d ed. Copyright © 1985 Wm. C. Brown Publishers, Dubuque, Iowa. All Rights Reserved. Reprinted by permission.

Cement

As a structural building material, concrete exceeds all other building materials in use by a margin of more than two to one. The word *cement* means to bind together. For the building industry, the word cement should be *portland cement*, a required ingredient in concrete. Portland cement is made by combining proper proportions of $CaCO_3$ (calcite), $MgCO_3$ (dolomite), SiO_2 (quartz), Al_2O_3 (aluminum oxides), and Fe_2O_3 (iron oxides) in a cement kiln and driving off carbon dioxide (CO_2) and water (H_2O) as gases. Concrete is then produced by mixing cement (about 15%) as the bonding agent to an aggregate mix of sand and crushed rock or gravel. Sand used in cement should not contain any organic materials because the organics will weaken the cement. Tremendous amounts of energy are required to produce cement because kiln temperatures must reach nearly 1480°C (2696°F) (figure 14.18).

Plaster

The mineral *gypsum* ($CaSO_4 \cdot 2H_2O$) is the natural resource needed to make plaster. Gypsum is quarried or mined from natural deposits in California, Utah, and Texas in the United States and in Nova Scotia, Canada. Gypsum is also recovered as a by-product in the manufacture of phosphate for fertilizer or phosphoric acid for chemical use. Gypsum is pulverized and then calcined in rotary kilns at temperatures of 177°C (351°F) to drive off 75% of the water of crystallization. The new compound $2CaSO_4 \cdot H_2O$ is called *plaster of Paris*. Adding water to plaster triggers the recrystallization of gypsum into a tightly interlocked mass. In the United States, more than 90% of the plaster produced is used for wallboard by the construction industry. A small but important use for gypsum agriculturally is for reducing soil alkalinity.

Management of the natural resources required for the manufacturing of cement and plaster create few if any environmental problems. Energy use in the production of cement is a concern, but technology could develop more efficient methods to save energy. The products and by-products of both industries do not appear to create environmental or health problems that cannot be solved with present-day technology. The natural resource reserve and potential resource supply for both seem more than adequate for sustainability through the 21st century.

Fertilizer and Chemical Minerals

The fertilizer formula and necessary ingredients for intensive agriculture include certain nonmetallic minerals as raw materials. These are lime ($CaCO_3$) to adjust the pH of acidic soils, and gypsum ($CaSO_4 \cdot 2H_2O$) to adjust

Figure 14.18A A cement plant in Michigan.
(*Photo:* David A. Castillon)

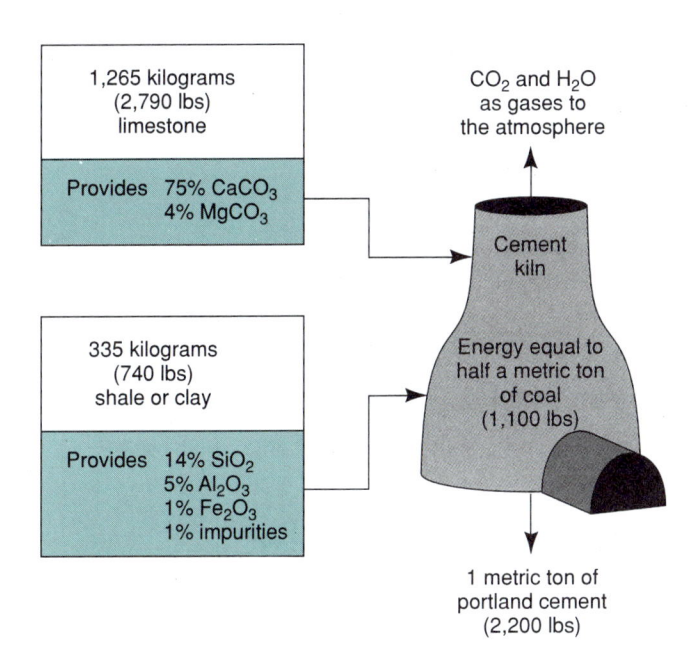

Figure 14.18B Portland cement process to convert limestone to cement.

the pH of alkaline soils. Soil pH must be in the correct range for each crop for fertilizers to work effectively. Nitrogen, phosphorous, and potash (potassium) are vital to world agriculture.

Nitrogen

Nitrogen fertilizer is synthesized from the atmosphere by the Haber-Bosch process (see chapter 9) and as such is not a solid earth mineral resource. Small amounts of nitrogen salts can be mined from the Atacama Desert in Chile but are not important today because of synthetic nitrogen. The rotation planting of legumes can supply all of the nitrogen needed by the soil for sustainable agriculture. Synthetic nitrogen fertilizer would not be needed if agriculture would return to organic farming methods.

Phosphorus

Phosphorus is a natural mineral resource of great importance to agriculture and the chemical industry. Although plant and animal cycles in the biosphere are usually very good at recycling nutrients, the phosphorus cycle is an exception to this general rule. Phosphorus is a vital element for many cellular processes in plants and the skeletal parts of animals. Normal life and decay processes do not return this material to the soil in quantities necessary for healthy regrowth. Therefore, fertilizers must supply this necessary nutrient to the soil.

Apatite $[Ca_5(PO_4)_3(F,OH)]$ is the mineral name for phosphate rock. Apatite occurs in trace amounts in all rocks, but is comparatively rare in igneous and sedimentary deposits. Major marine phosphate deposits are located in the Baja in Mexico and in Florida, North Carolina, and in the phosphoric formation in Idaho, Wyoming, Utah, and Montana. These deposits were laid down in former bays and estuaries during periods of ancient continental flooding. Phosphate-rich igneous rocks are mined in Canada at Cargill (figure 14.19).

To free the phosphate from its crystal structure in apatite requires treatment with dilute sulfuric acid (H_2SO_4), because apatite is relatively insoluble. Complex chemical reactions convert apatite to a superphosphate $Ca(H_2PO_4)_2$, which is water soluble. Superphosphate can be added directly to the soil as a fertilizer.

Mineral Resources

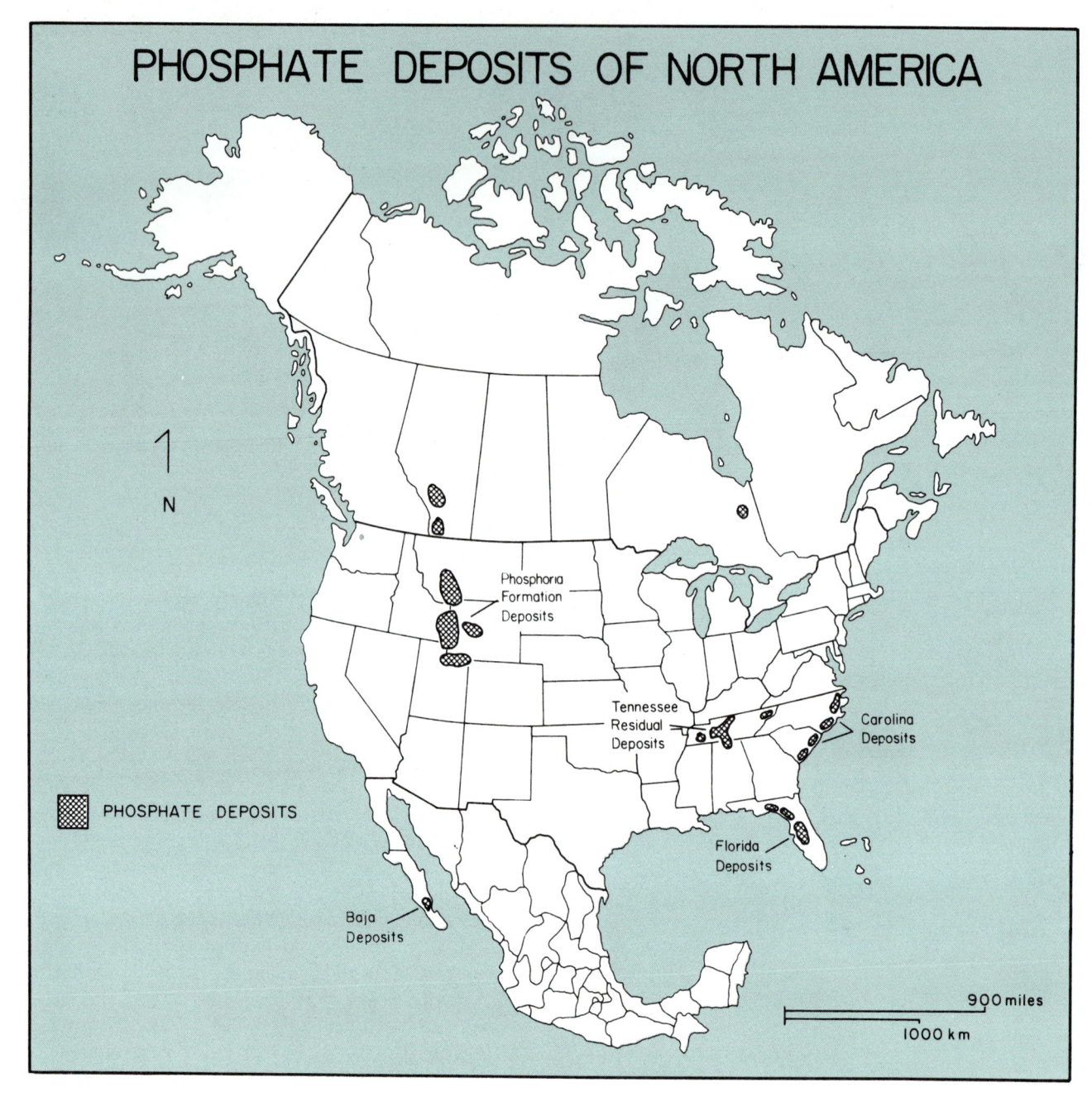

Figure 14.19 Phosphate deposits of North America.
Source: U.S. Geological Survey.
(*Cartographer:* Douglas Hemsath)

Potash (Potassium)

Potassium is also an important natural mineral resource to the agricultural and chemical industries. *Potash* is the common name for potassium compounds. Potassium is widely distributed in insoluble silicate minerals but in its soluble form is confined to marine evaporite deposits. Major North American deposits are mapped on Figure 14.20 and seem adequate for many years.

The deep deposits of potassium-rich salts in the Paradox Basin in Utah and Colorado are being mined by injection. Water to dissolve the salts is injected through drill holes into the deposit. The salty solution is pumped to the surface and the salts are recovered by evaporation. Additional new mining technologies will continue to expand our reserves of necessary agricultural mineral resources. However, care must be taken not to damage or pollute our deep groundwater resources as we use these new techniques.

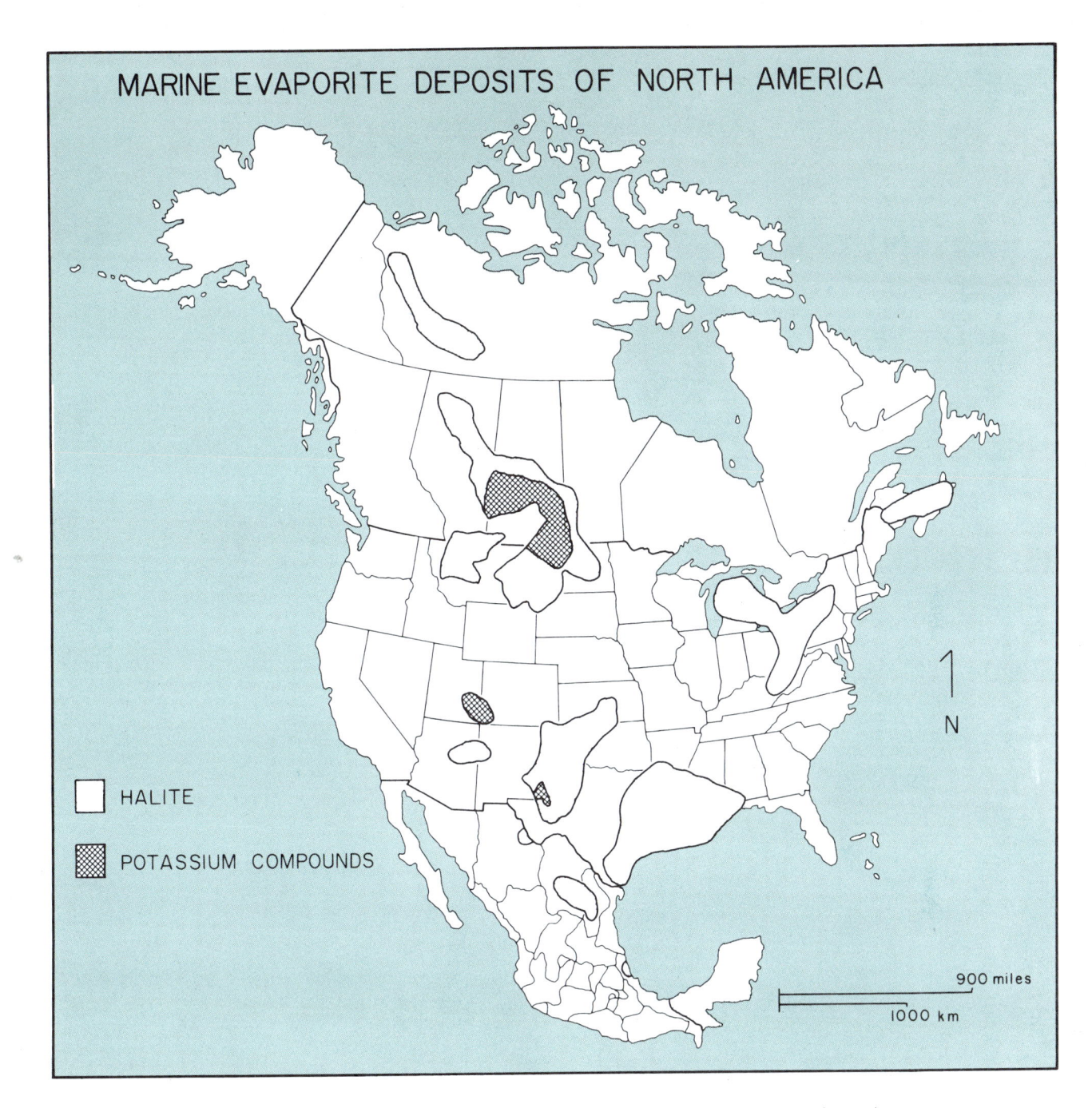

Figure 14.20 Marine evaporite deposits of North America. Both halite (table salt) and potassium compounds are shown.
Source: U.S. Geological Survey.
(Cartographer: Douglas Hemsath).

Halite

Halite (NaCl) is the mineral name for table salt, an important mineral for the chemical industry. Chlorine, caustic soda, and soda ash are the intermediate chemical by-products processed from sodium chloride. Chlorine and caustic soda are necessary chemicals for wood pulp production and paper manufacturing. Soda ash is used in the manufacture of glass. Soaps, detergents, nylon, and foodstuff all require salt or salt by-products in their production.

Figure 14.20 shows halite locations. Halite evaporates out before potassium salts and in greater quantity. The reserve deposits of halite are almost limitless. If desalinization of seawater ever becomes a necessity to supply fresh water for drinking, so much halite will accumulate that disposal or storage will be a major environmental problem. Figure 14.21 contains a map of salt domes around the Gulf of Mexico. Salt domes can also contain geologic structures suitable to trap gas and oil deposits.

Halite or any other soluble mineral can be extracted by the *injection mining* technique (figure 14.22). Water

Mineral Resources 331

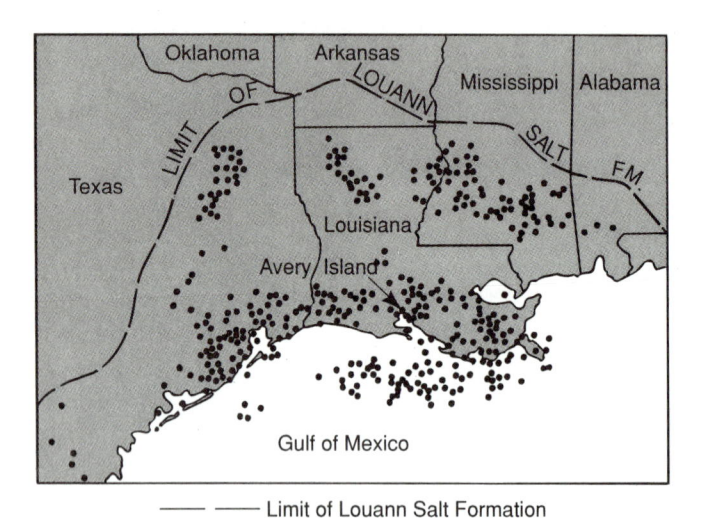

Figure 14.21A Distribution of salt domes in the Gulf of Mexico region.
Source: Data from D. H. Kupfer, 1970.
(*Cartographer:* Douglas Hemsath)

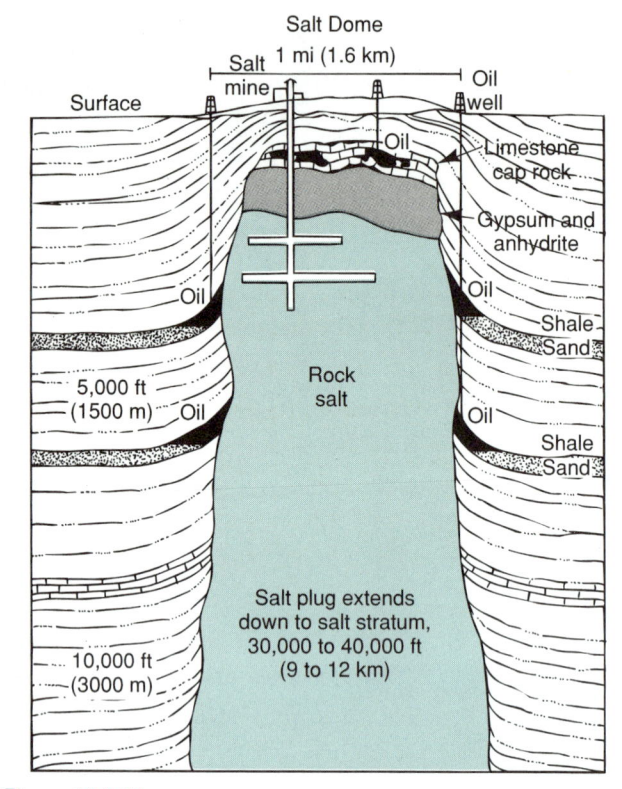

Figure 14.21B A salt plug rises because of density differences, forming a dome.
From A. N. Strahler and A. H. Strahler, *Modern Physical Geography.* Copyright © John Wiley & Sons, Inc., New York, N.Y. Reprinted by permission of John Wiley & Sons, Inc.

Figure 14.21C Avery Island salt dome.
(*Photo:* David A. Castillon)

Figure 14.21D Salt mine in Avery Island, Louisiana.
(*Photo:* David A. Castillon)

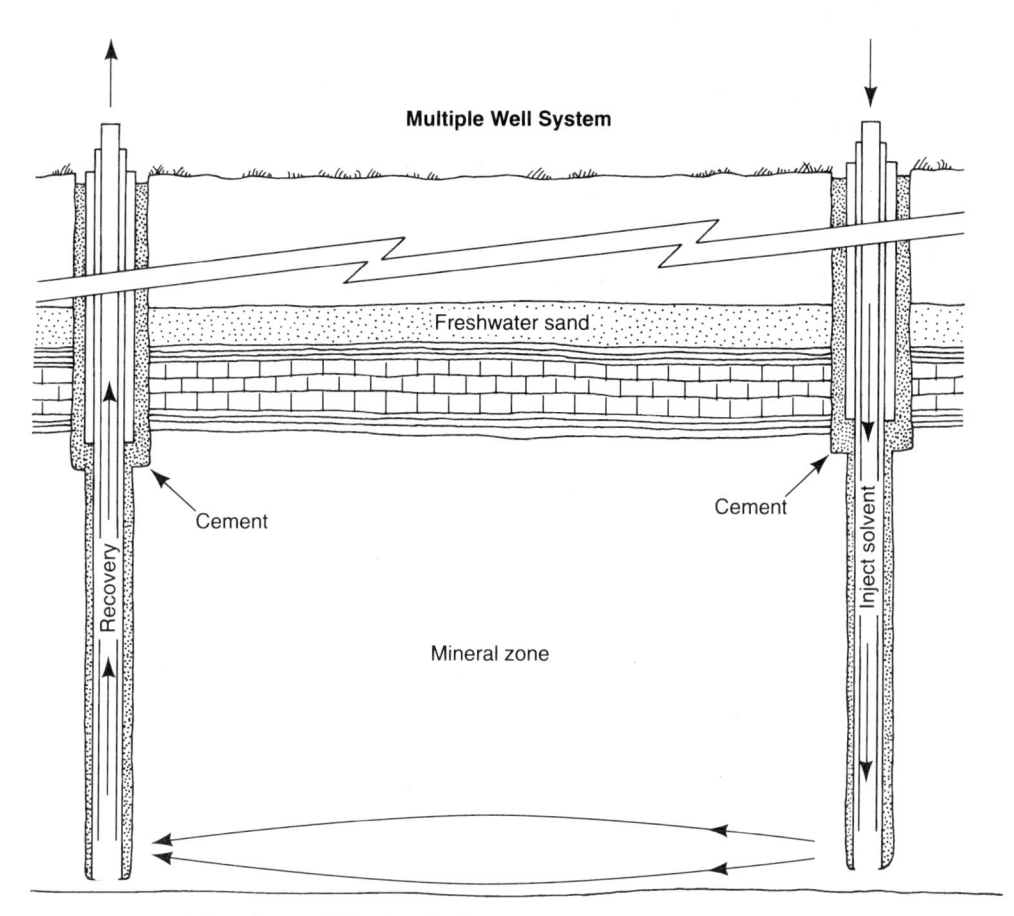

Figure 14.22 Injection mining technique for a soluble mineral using a multiple well system.
The Society for Mining, Metallurgy, and Exploration, Inc. Reprinted by permission.

or any other liquid solvent can be injected into the subsurface and, if injected with enough pressure, can cause hydraulic fracturing of the mineral deposit. Fracturing will enhance the solution process and the mineral in solution can then be extracted from the recovery well. Injection of steam is often used to liquefy heavy oils for extraction. The major detrimental environmental side effect of injection mining is the potential contamination of groundwater supplies from wells in the mined area.

Sulfur

Sulfur is an important elemental mineral of the chemical and agricultural industries. Sulfur is not considered a fertilizer, but is used in the manufacture of both superphosphates and ammonium sulfate. Most insecticides and fungicides require sulfur for their production.

Both halite and elemental sulfur are mined from salt domes (figure 14.21). The petroleum and metal sulfide industries both produce sulfur as a salable by-product. Clean air standards set by the EPA require that high-sulfur coal be scrubbed before use or that filters on stacks for coal-fired plants remove sulfur dioxide before it enters the atmosphere. Both of these industries are selling sulfur or sulfuric acid as a by-product. Environmental laws, and the technology to comply with these laws, will help to keep sulfur out of the environment as a pollutant and in the chemistry lab where it belongs for the foreseeable future.

Minerals Imported By The United States

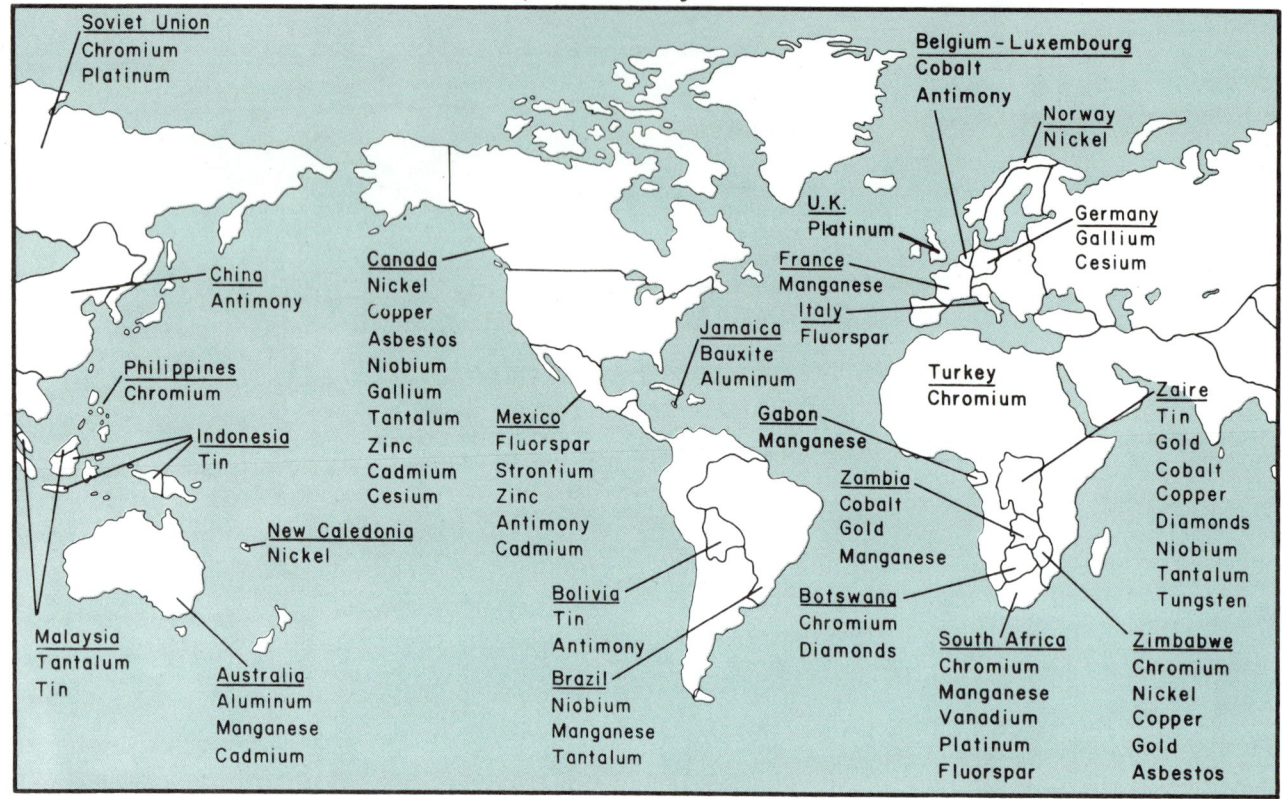

Figure 14.23 Critical and strategic minerals imported by the United States. The United States is dependent on 25 other nations for more than 50% of its supply of 24 strategic materials.
Reprinted with permission from *Chemical and Engineering News*, May 11, 1981, 59 (19):21.
Copyright © 1981 American Chemical Society.
(Cartographer: Douglas Hemsath)

Summary

There are 92 naturally occurring elements on the earth and these elements form thousands of compounds. We have examined in detail a few of these metallic and nonmetallic mineral resources of North America. Citizens and industry must rely on their world neighbors for the mineral resources not found on this continent.

The United States and the Soviet Union are the world's largest producers and consumers of metallic mineral resources. The United States is heavily dependent on imports of critical metallic minerals. For example, there are deposits of manganese ore in Missouri, but recovery of these reserves is currently more costly than imports. Therefore, all of the U.S. manganese supply is imported from South Africa and Brazil. Figure 14.23 is a world map that shows the location of imports to the United States from 25 foreign countries. These countries supply more than 50% of our metallic and nonmetallic minerals. If the political or economic situation of the world changes, some of the minerals that are imported today will change port of origin or shift to the domestic category. Substitutions of metals from technological advancements are also a possibility for industrial sustainability in the United States.

Key Words and Phrases

- Aluminum
- Bauxite
- Boom-and-bust cycles
- Boulders
- Cement
- Copper
- Gold
- Gravel
- Gypsum
- Halite
- Injection mining
- Iron
- Lead
- Lime
- Magnesium
- Manganese
- Mineral
- Nickel
- Phosphorus
- Plaster of Paris
- Platinoid metals
- Portland cement
- Potash
- Potassium
- Sand
- Scarce metals
- Silver
- Stone
- Sulfur
- Titanium
- Zinc

Questions for Discussion Topics

1. What determines if a mineral is in a resource or a reserve category?
2. How abundant are abundant metals and how scarce are scarce metals? Can you find aluminum, the most abundant metal, in your home state? Where would diamonds fit into this categorization?
3. In what ways can the management strategies of industry be used to conserve energy? To conserve mineral resources?
4. What are the hazards of underground mining?
5. What are some uses of underground mine space after a mineral resource has been extracted?
6. More and more office buildings appear to be completely made of glass on the outside. Do you think glass is a durable building material? Are glass buildings energy efficient?
7. Why is so little cut stone used by the building industry today?

References for Further Study

Blunden, J. 1985. *Mineral Resources and Their Management.* New York: Longman. An excellent text on minerals and their management.

Brookins, D. G. 1981. *Earth Resources, Energy and the Environment.* Columbus, Ohio: Charles E. Merrill Publishing Company. A short readable text on earth and energy resources.

Eiseley, L. 1977. *Another Kind of Autumn.* New York: Charles Scribner's Sons. A collection of poems. Quote is from a poem entitled "Another Kind of Autumn."

Frosch, R. A. and N. E. Gallopoulos. Sept., 1989. Strategies for Manufacturing. *Scientific American* 261: No. 3. A good article on industrial ecosystems in a special issue on managing planet earth.

Gordon, R. B., et.al. 1988. *World Mineral Exploration: Trends and Issues.* Washington, D.C.: Resources for the Future. The world minerals situation.

Miller, G. T. Jr. 1990. *Resource Conservation and Management.* Belmont, Calif.: Wadsworth Publishing Company. Excellent text for resources management.

Skinner, B. J. 1986. *Earth Resources.* 3rd ed. Englewood Cliffs, N.J.: Prentice-Hall Inc. A compact introductory source for solid earth resources.

Whitfield, J. W. 1981. *Underground Space Resources in Missouri.* Rolla, Mo.: Missouri Department of Natural Resources, Division of Geology and Land Survey. Report of Inv. No. 65. Underground mining space as a resource in Missouri.

Chapter 15

Waste Management

- Introduction
- Source Reduction
- Waste-to-Energy Plants
- Landfills
- Hazardous Waste Management
    - Household Hazardous Waste
    - Industrial Waste Management
        - Superfund
    - RCRAs Rules
- Wastewater Treatment
    - Sludge as a Resource
- Recycling
    - Paper
        - Paper Recycling at WCB Publishers
    - Plastic
- Summary

*Why should things of like
kind gather together
on a public dump?
Broken clocks, for instance
toys?
Is it because one is thrown
down and furtively
someone brings another and
quietly drops it also
in the same place thinking
two will be less lonely, . . .*

Loren Eiseley, 1977.

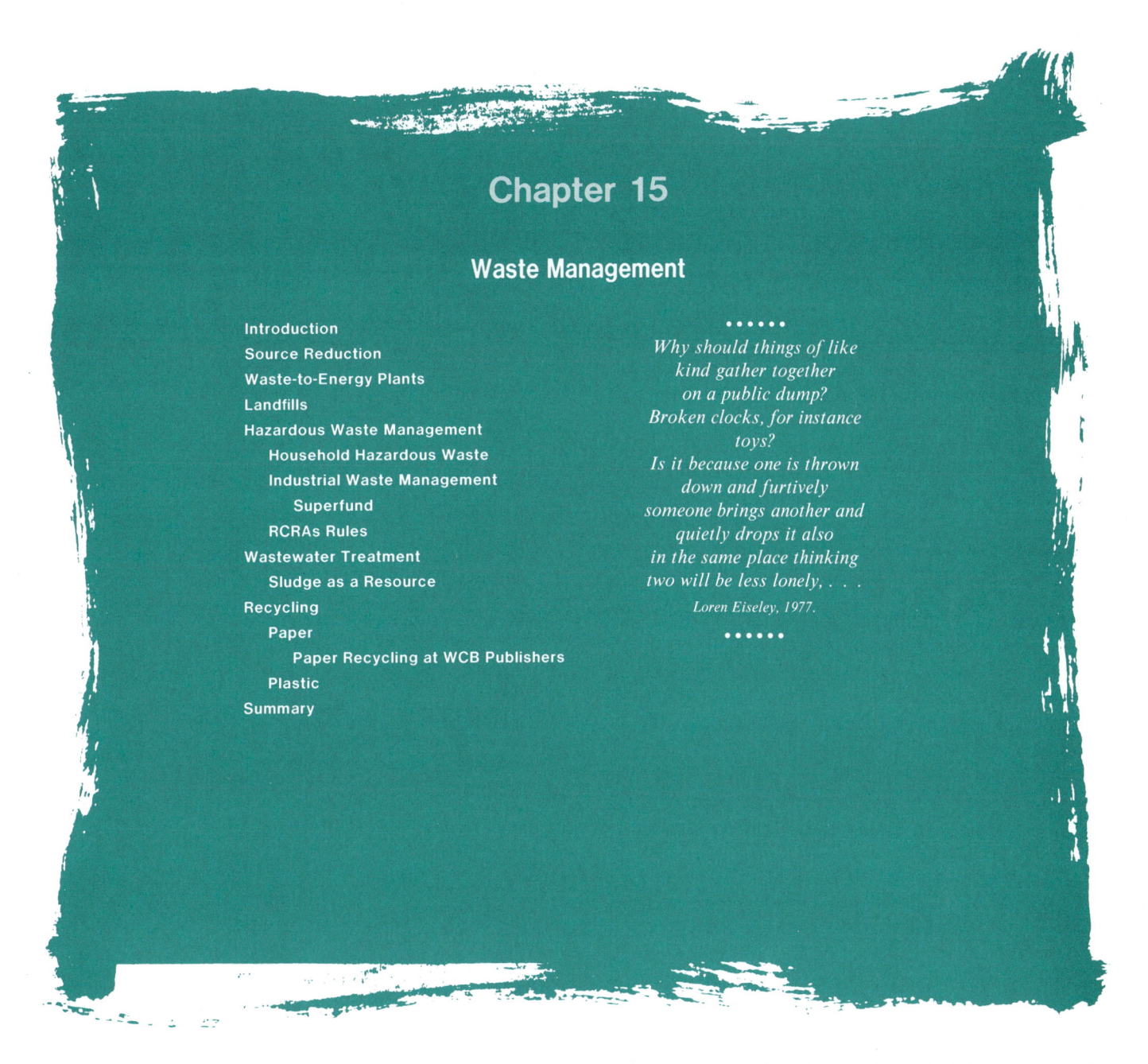

Introduction

The **Resource Conservation and Recovery Act** of 1976 was the modern-day beginning for federal policies concerning waste management. This law, with its reauthorization and amendments in 1984, has established policy for waste management in the United States. Designed to prevent future waste-site problems, this law has made disposing of wastes in landfills increasingly more difficult and more expensive. The law is also responsible for accelerating a trend toward more environmentally sound methods of waste treatment.

The number of landfills in the United States dropped from 18,500 in 1981 to 6,500 in 1988, and the predictions are that this trend will continue. Americans are generating more than half a ton (1,300 pounds-590 kg) of municipal solid waste per person per year and there's no place to put it. The Environmental Protection Agency (EPA) has published "The Solid Waste Dilemma: An Agenda for Action" that recommends a waste-management strategy for the 1990s. The Agency recommends an integrated approach that includes the use of four basic strategies: 1) source reduction; 2) recycling; 3) waste-to-energy plants; and 4) landfilling. Each community or region should custom-tailor a waste management strategy suitable for local conditions.

Americans now generate enough municipal garbage each year to fill a convoy of trucks reaching halfway to the moon (160 MT—145 MMT) (MT-million tons—MMT-million metric tons). Eighty percent of our refuse is sent to landfills, 10% is incinerated, and the remaining 10% is recycled. EPA's goal for the 1990s is to reduce the amount sent to landfills to 55%. Twenty-five percent would be recycled or accounted for by source reduction, and 20% would be incinerated to produce energy (figure 15.1).

Garbage is something we throw away because we don't want to deal with it any longer. We want it to disappear. The problem is that the places to make it disappear are also disappearing. To reduce the 80% of our garbage that is currently landfilled to the 55% proposed by the EPA, we need to examine the makeup of our trash and then devise a strategy that includes **source reduction, recycling, waste incineration,** and **landfilling.** Japan has been in the business of waste management for many years and its models indicate that at least 50% must be disposed of by landfilling.

A close examination of American garbage reveals that most of our trash is paper (table 15.1), which is largely recyclable and easily burned. Yard wastes such as grass clippings, tree trimmings, and leaves are compostable or burnable. Most metals are recyclable, and Americans already recycle more than half of all aluminum cans produced and used. Metal trash containing toxic materials such as cadmium or lead should not be landfilled or incinerated. They must be recycled.

Recycling the bulk of our metal trash would keep many toxins out of the environment and improve environmental quality. Glass is readily recyclable but not as valuable as aluminum, and therefore, it is sent to the landfill. However, finely ground glass can be used in asphalt mixes for road paving. Plastics are petroleum products that are being increasingly recycled. They are also good fuels for waste-to-energy plants. The remaining 17% of the garbage we send to landfills, listed under "other" in table 15.1, is not easily recyclable, but some of these materials could be composted or incinerated for energy.

Source Reduction

EPA defines *source reduction* as the design, manufacture, and use of products so as to reduce the quantity and toxicity of waste produced when products reach the end of their useful lives. Source reduction is not a technology or process to be applied to the solid waste stream, but rather a concept where the ultimate destiny of a product is fully considered when making decisions on how the products are made and which products or materials one uses.

The Office of Technology Assessment Congressional Report entitled "Serious Reduction of Hazardous Waste"

How We Manage Our Waste Now

Landfilled 80 percent

Recycled 10 percent

Incinerated 10 percent

EPA's Agenda-for-Action Goal for the 1990s

Landfilled 55 percent

Recycled 25 percent

Incinerated 20 percent

Figure 15.1 EPAs waste management agenda-for-action goal for the 1990s.

Table 15.1
American Garbage Composition

Material	Percent	Time Required to Decompose
Paper	41	2 to 5 months
Yard Wastes	18	Most less than a year
Metals	9	Aluminum - 90 to 100 years
Glass	8	More than 100 years
Plastics	7	5 to 80 years
Other; Food, Leather, Wood, Textiles, Rubber	17	Leather - 25 to 40 years Nylon cloth - 30 to 40 years

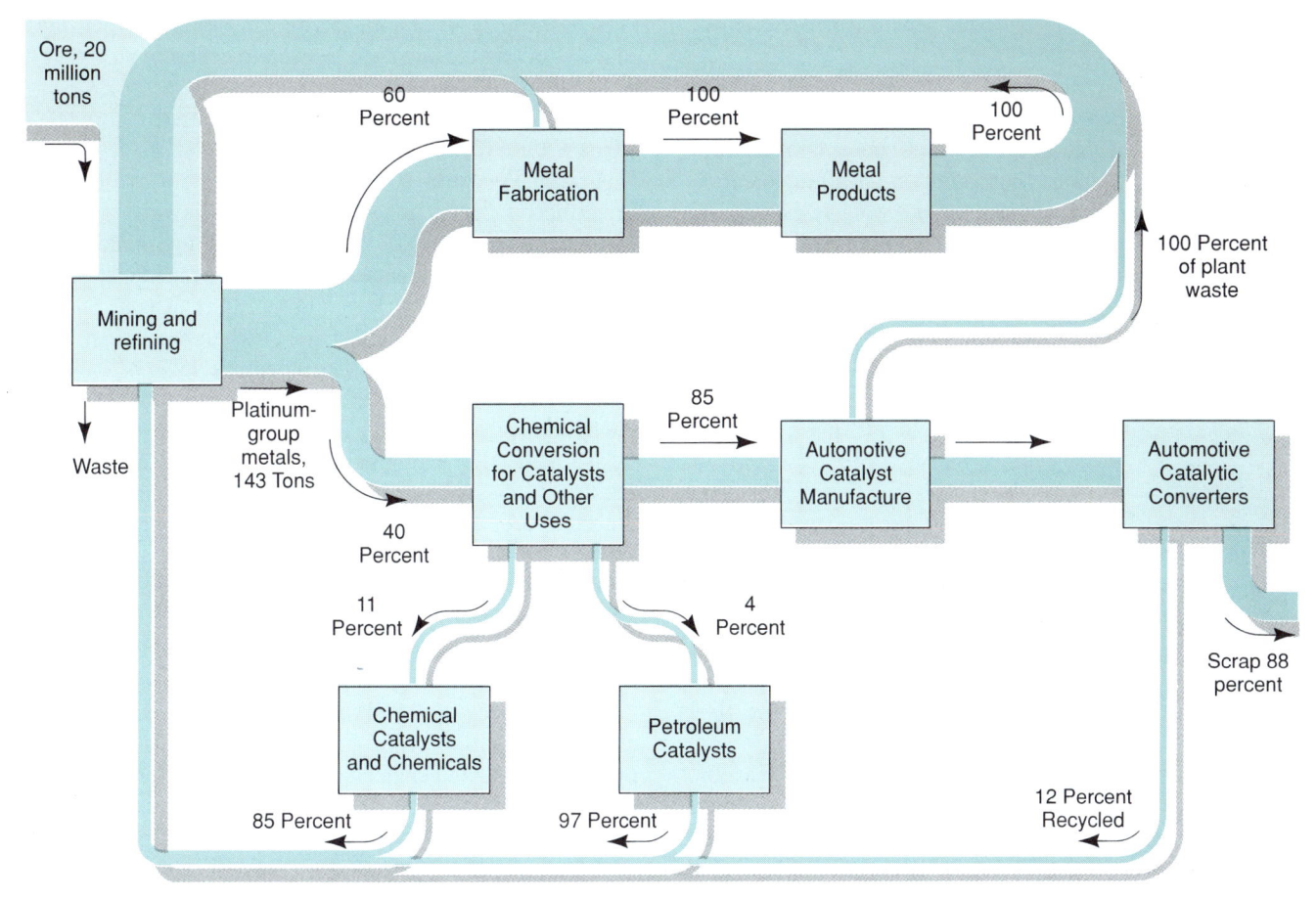

Figure 15.2 Because they are valuable, platinum-group metals can serve as an industrial example of how complete a recycling program can be. Platinum-group metals are recovered efficiently from jewelry and other fabricated objects, two uses that constitute about 60% of consumption. Industrial catalysts and chemicals, also efficiently recycled, account for another 6%. The fastest-growing use for the metals is in automotive catalytic converters, an application marked by low recycling rates. The infrastructure is only now being set up to collect the millions of converters that enter automotive scrapyards each year and to recover the approximately two grams of platinum (worth about $32 in mid-1989) in each converter.
From "Strategies for Manufacturing" by Robert A. Frosch and Nicholas E. Gallopoulos. Copyright © 1989 by Scientific American, Inc. All Rights Reserved.

proposes a four-stage waste reduction program for industry. Stage one includes the common-sense waste reduction measures that can be implemented immediately by good housekeeping procedures. Stage two is an information-driven waste reduction phase. Information on programs that have been successful elsewhere in reducing waste are given to supervisors and these trigger changes in waste handling without changing technology or without equipment purchase. The third stage is audit-dependent. Companies would invest time, money, and people to investigate the source and disposal of the waste generated. Policy changes would be recommended to reduce waste. The fourth and final stage for waste reduction is the research and development phase. Companies would commit resources for research and development to find new, more efficient, and less waste-generating technologies for their manufactured products.

Platinoid minerals are very valuable metals. Every ounce of waste is worth more than $500. Therefore, maximum waste reduction is required. Figure 15.2 illustrates the efficiency of this industry's waste reduction program. Other industries interested in waste reduction could learn some valuable lessons from the platinoid industry.

Implementing source reduction must begin with the consumer. Each individual must recognize that a "throw-away society," in which convenience and easy disposability are the norm, does not make environmental or ecological sense. On the average, each household's garbage contains 41% paper and 18% yard wastes. Most paper is recyclable. Every year Americans throw away 16 billion disposable diapers. Why not use cloth diapers? A cost comparison would show that cloth diapers are less expensive to use and young couples looking for a way to cut the family budget could benefit from the savings. Grass clippings, tree trimmings, and leaves represent organic material that can be composted and reused in your yard. Remember the law of fertility of biological systems. Your yard is a biological system that cannot afford to have nutrients removed on a regular basis without degrading the system. The alternative is to apply expensive fertilizers.

These are just two ways each household can participate in source reduction.

A source reduction ethic is not dominant in today's consumption habits, but waste minimization is an idea whose time has come. The goals and concepts of source reduction are so obvious that adoption and implementation should be an immediate housekeeping response for every individual. Consumers should demand products that are not only degradable but less toxic, recyclable or have a longer life span, and a better potential for reuse. For example, 40% of the 50 billion pounds (2.3 billion kg) of plastic consumed each year in the United States is used to make disposable one-use items. This situation has got to change because there is nowhere to put this trash.

Waste-to-Energy Plants

Solid waste *incineration* has been a part of waste management for many years. Almost every household burned their paper and leaves before communities placed restrictions on these practices (Clean Air Act requirements). Today more than one hundred incinerators reduce the volume of solid waste generated by our "throw-away" society. The Oxford Energy Incinerator will be used as an example later in this section. The Clean Air Act regulations have made incineration less attractive economically because combustion gases and particles must be cleaned or removed before the exhaust can enter the atmosphere. But the technology exists and incineration will become an integral part of the waste management strategy of the 1990s.

Unprocessed solid waste contains from 40% to 75% of the energy contained in coal and can be used as fuel in an incinerator to generate steam for electrical energy. Depending on the type of incinerator, from 140 to 2000 MT (154 to 2200 tons) of solid waste can be burned per day. The steam created can then be used to generate electricity or to heat buildings.

The Oxford Energy Company in Westley, California, burns worn-out tires and converts the energy to electricity (figure 15.3). Up to 700 whole tires an hour are burned (5 million a year), generating 14.4 megawatts of electricity (enough for 15,000 houses). A plant similar to the California plant, but twice the size, burns tires in Sterling, Connecticut. Tires are lower in sulfur than coal but do emit some sulfur dioxide gas (SO_2) when burned. A lime mist scrubbing system is able to capture 95%–97% of the SO_2 emissions. Nitrous oxides are removed at the top of the boiler by spraying the gases with ammonia. The plant's fly ash has a high enough zinc oxide content (the metal in tires contains zinc) to be shipped to zinc smelters as a source of ore. Adherence to strict environmental controls and recycling make the Oxford resource-recovery plant a very safe industry. Every tire converted to electricity is one less for the landfill.

Incineration is not a viable alternative for every community's waste management program. A major capital investment is required and the energy generated must have use. Air pollution from burning garbage is always a problem. Gases and exhaust can contain hydrochloric acid, nitrous oxides, dioxins, and furans. *Furans* are colorless liquid hydrocarbon compounds (C_4H_4O). Land disposal of the ash remaining after incineration is also a problem. Ash can contain high levels of toxins such as lead and cadmium. If this occurs, the Resource Conservation and Recovery Act requires that the ash be handled and disposed of as a hazardous waste (very expensive). In spite of the problems, the EPA is proposing a 100% increase in solid waste-to-energy plants for the 1990s. In solid waste reduction, this would amount to 14.5 MMT (16 MT) of trash each year that would not make its way to the landfills.

Figure 15.3A Modesto energy project in Westley, California, burns worn-out tires and converts the energy to electricity.
(*Photo:* Oxford Energy)

Figure 15.3B Five million tires a year are burned and converted to 14.4 megawatts of electricity.
(*Photo:* Oxford Energy)

Incineration is not the only method of converting wastes to a useful product. In Pompano Beach, Florida, an anaerobic digestion plant uses urban solid waste and sewage sludge to produce methane-rich gas (figure 15.4), which is then burned to produce electricity. The major problem with this process is that the urban garbage must be separated before use in the digester. Discovery of innovative methods of converting waste to useful products await a very receptive American public.

Landfills

Landfills are a necessary part of an integrated waste management program. Prior to the 1970s, most landfills were located on the least expensive land adjacent to waste-producing cities. Disposal sites included quarries, marshes, old mines, sinkholes, gravel pits, and deep gullies or ravines. Waste was dumped and sometimes covered with dirt to keep paper from blowing away and odors from being distributed downwind. Precipitation percolating through waste was dissolving elements and compounds to form a concentrated solution known as *leachate*. The leachate from many landfills was contaminated, and a source of pollution for both surface and groundwater in the area. The geologic setting of many early landfills enhanced the mobility of the leachate through subsurface water systems. Waste dumped in sinkholes provided completely unfiltered leachate to subsurface plumbing. Aquifer contamination made water in many shallow wells undrinkable.

Enforcers of the provisions of the Clean Water Act identified many landfills as point sources of pollution. Thousands of landfills were closed in the 1980s and more are slated to be closed in the 1990s. Waste management engineers are designing new landfills to meet EPA standards. Implementation of the new landfill technologies should take some of the environmental risk out of landfilling.

Figure 15.5 is a diagram of a modern landfill. Major provisions to safeguard the environment include a plastic or impermeable clay liner and a leachate drain. The plastic liner, designed to trap leachate and keep it out of the groundwater, is contoured to effect runoff of the leachate into a collection reservoir for further treatment, usually in the local sewage treatment facility.

Figure 15.4 Anaerobic digestion plant in Pompano Beach, Florida, converts 50 to 100 tons per day of urban solid waste and sewage sludge to methane-rich gas, which can be burned to produce electricity.
(*Photo:* DOE)

Double Liner System for a Landfill

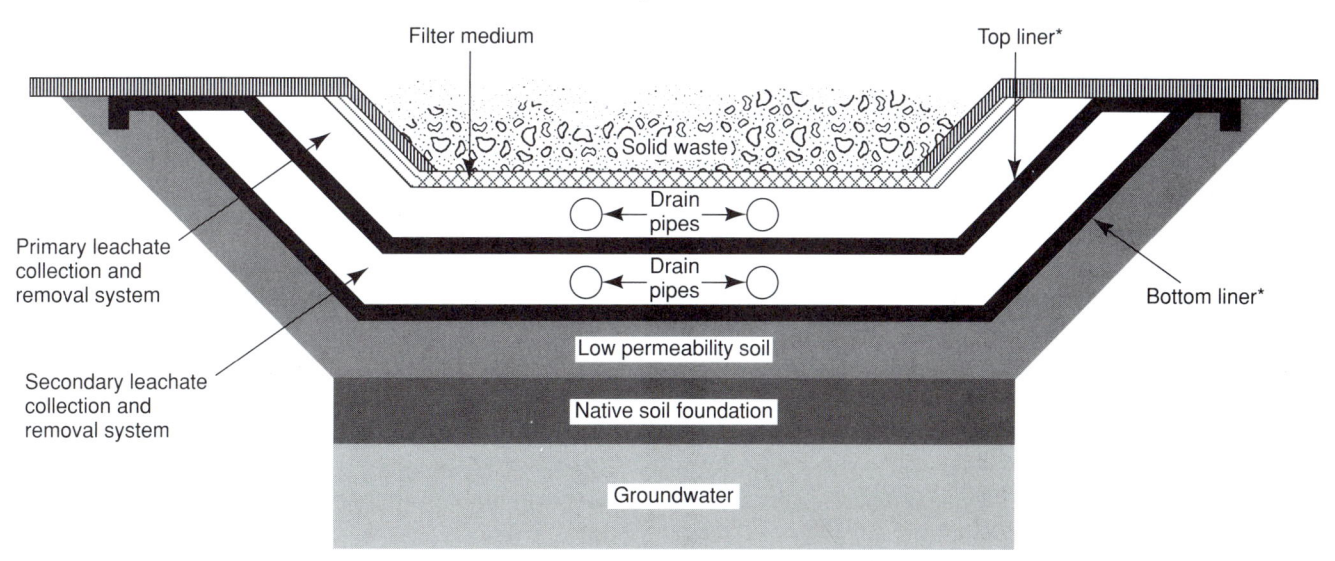

*Flexible Membrane Liner

Figure 15.5 EPA-recommended double liner landfill system. Drain pipes carry leachate to a collection reservoir for removal, usually to a sanitary treatment facility.
Source: Environmental Protection Agency, *Progress in Ground-Water Protection and Restoration.*

Waste Management

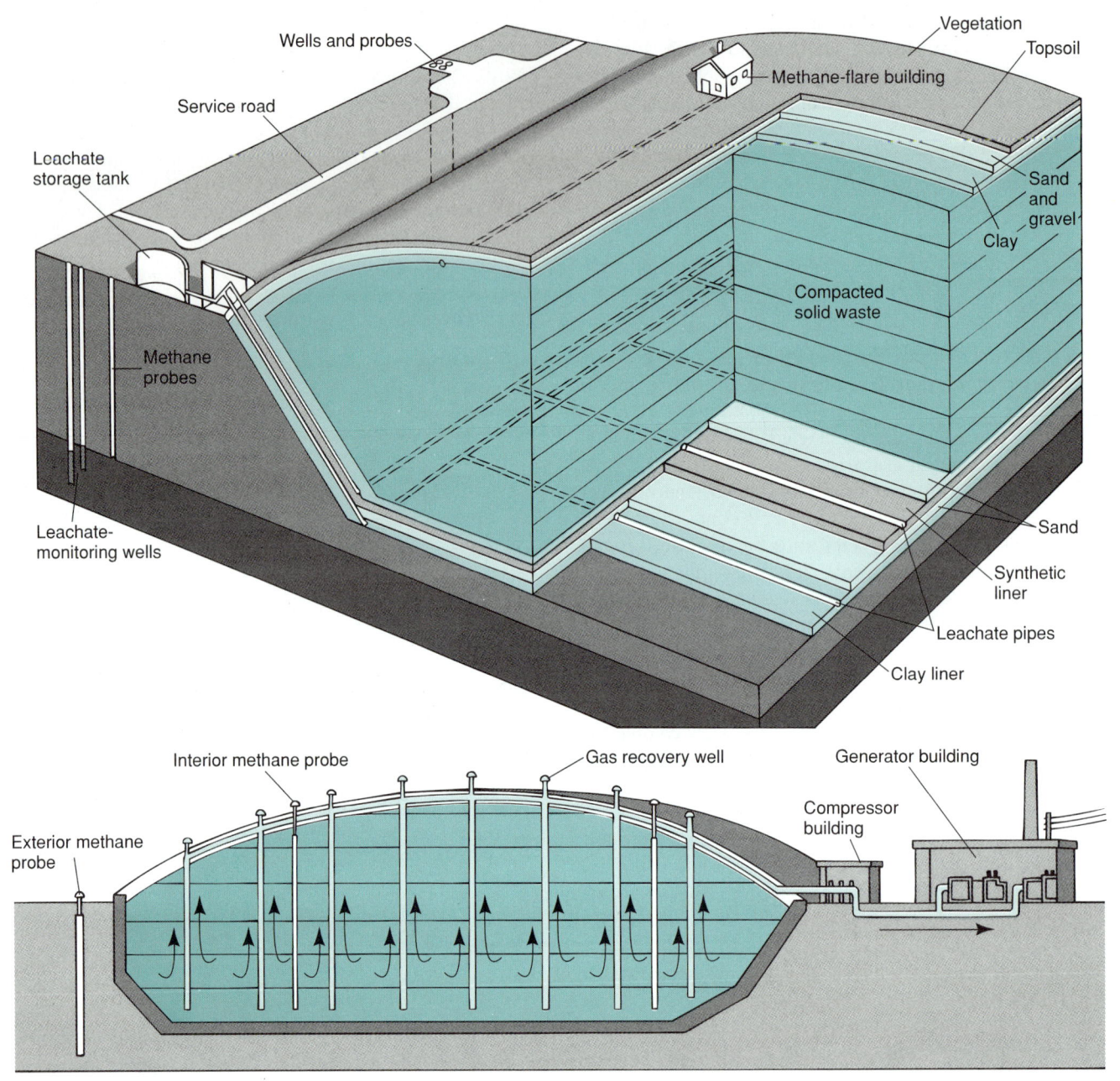

Figure 15.6 Methane-gas-producing landfill design has great potential as a waste-to-energy facility. New landfill technologies (*top*) can protect valuable resources from pollutants. Water from weather and other sources leaches pollutants out of the garbage, forming a solution known as leachate. To protect groundwater from leachate, layers of low-permeability clay and synthetic material line the landfill. The liners contain the leachate, which is pumped out through pipes. Every day layers of waste are dumped, compacted, and covered with soil. When the landfill is full, it is covered with clay, sand, gravel, topsoil, and vegetation to reduce leachate production and minimize erosion. Another landfill pollutant produced by bacteria decomposing waste is the volatile gas methane. Wells and probes are placed at the perimeter of the landfill to detect leakage of leachate or methane. Methane can be burned off by a flare. An alternative to burning methane is to install a recovery system (*bottom*). The system collects the methane and fuels a turbine to generate electricity.
From "Managing Solid Waste" by Philip R. O' Leary, et al. Copyright © 1988 by Scientific American, Inc. All Rights Reserved.

Decomposition of the organic material in the solid waste produces methane gas. Methane gas can be drawn off and pumped to a generating building where it can be burned and converted to steam or electricity. These methane-gas-generating landfills also have leachate protection systems to protect groundwater (figure 15.6).

Hazardous Waste Management

Hazardous waste is defined as any product or material whose use or disposal poses a threat to humans or the environment. A product or material is hazardous if it has one or more of the following properties.

1. Corrosive/Caustic: Any material that can burn or destroy living tissue on contact.
2. Explosive/Reactive: Any material that can explode or detonate from exposure to heat, pressure, or shock.
3. Flammable: Any material that can be ignited or easily set on fire.
4. Toxic/Poison: Any material that can cause injury or death by absorption, ingestion, or inhalation.

Every North American household contains a number of products that can be classified as hazardous. Many industries produce products or by-products that are hazardous. Management procedures for these hazardous waste products must be two-fold. Household hazardous waste should be managed by each household according to established regulations. Industrial hazardous waste should be managed by industry according to the restrictions provided by federal guidelines and legislation. Two federal laws, the **Federal Insecticide, Fungicide, and Rodenticide Act** (FIFRA) and the **Federal Hazardous Substances Act** (FHSA), are hazardous substances labeling laws. FIFRA covers all pesticides, and FHSA covers all toxic, corrosive, irritant, flammable, or radioactive substances. Both laws set minimum standards for information the product label must contain. The EPA is the federal watchdog for hazardous waste management.

Household Hazardous Waste

Look in your bathroom cabinet. Look in your laundry room and under your sink. Look in your workshop. Much of what you see is hazardous material (figure 15.7). Medicines, alcohol, adhesives, cleaning supplies, pesticides, paints, chemicals, batteries, fertilizers, motor oil, antifreeze, and many other products can pose risks to your health and the environment. Consumers going about their daily chores and activities may be placing themselves and their environment at risk by failing to recognize the hazards associated with household hazardous material.

Every household needs a hazardous materials management plan. This plan should include provisions for safely storing and using household hazardous material, and when the product is no longer of use, a waste disposal plan must be followed that conforms to established regulations. Protection of our health and the environment is dependent on being able to recognize the dangers of hazardous products. Each household should have enough information at hand so that an informed decision about where to store and how to use each product can be made. When the time comes, information on how to dispose of household hazardous materials should be available.

The best advice anyone can get or give for the use of hazardous products is READ THE LABEL. After you read the label, FOLLOW THE DIRECTIONS. In our affluent society we have been taught that if "one is good,

Figure 15.7 Household hazardous waste.
(*Photo:* David A. Castillon)

two is better." That's just not true when you're dealing with or using hazardous products. Doubling the amount of fertilizer on a lawn will probably burn the grass or kill the lawn completely. (Why take two aspirins for a headache, when one would get rid of it?)

READ THE LABEL—FOLLOW THE DIRECTIONS.

It goes without saying that hazardous products should be stored out of the reach of children and away from pets. Once again, the label will give directions for storage out of sunlight, in a cool, dry, well-ventilated place, away from the furnace, etc. FOLLOW THE DIRECTIONS! Safe disposal of household hazardous waste is environmental protection and should become a part of each person's environmental ethic. The Water Pollution Control Federation (WPCF) has established a system of hazardous waste disposal that includes four options: 1) Products that can be poured down the drain and flushed through with plenty of water. 2) Products that can be safely sent to the landfill in most regions of the country. 3) Products that should only be taken to a licensed hazardous waste contractor. 4) Products that should be saved for recycling.

Table 15.2 is a Household Hazardous Waste Chart that can be used as a guide for safe waste disposal. There

Table 15.2

Household Hazardous Waste Chart

The following chart prepared by the Water Pollution Control Federation will help you to establish the most effective means of disposing of typical hazardous wastes found around your home.

● Indicates products which can be poured down the drain with plenty of water. If you have a septic tank, additional caution should be exercised when dumping these items down the drain. In fact, there are certain chemical substances that cannot be used with a septic tank. Read the labels to determine if a product could damage the septic tank. Never mix wastes while pouring them down the drain. If amount exceeds one quart call your local wastewater treatment plant before flushing.

■ Indicates materials which cannot be poured down the drain, but can be safely disposed of in the landfill. No other dumping, burning, or burying of hazardous waste is safe or legal. Be certain the material is properly contained before it is put out for collection or taken to the landfill.

☣ Indicates hazardous wastes which should be taken to a licensed hazardous wastes contractor or saved for a community wide collection day. (Even the empty containers should be taken to a licensed contractor if one is available.)

○ In the fourth column indicates recyclable material. Contact your recycling facility for information.

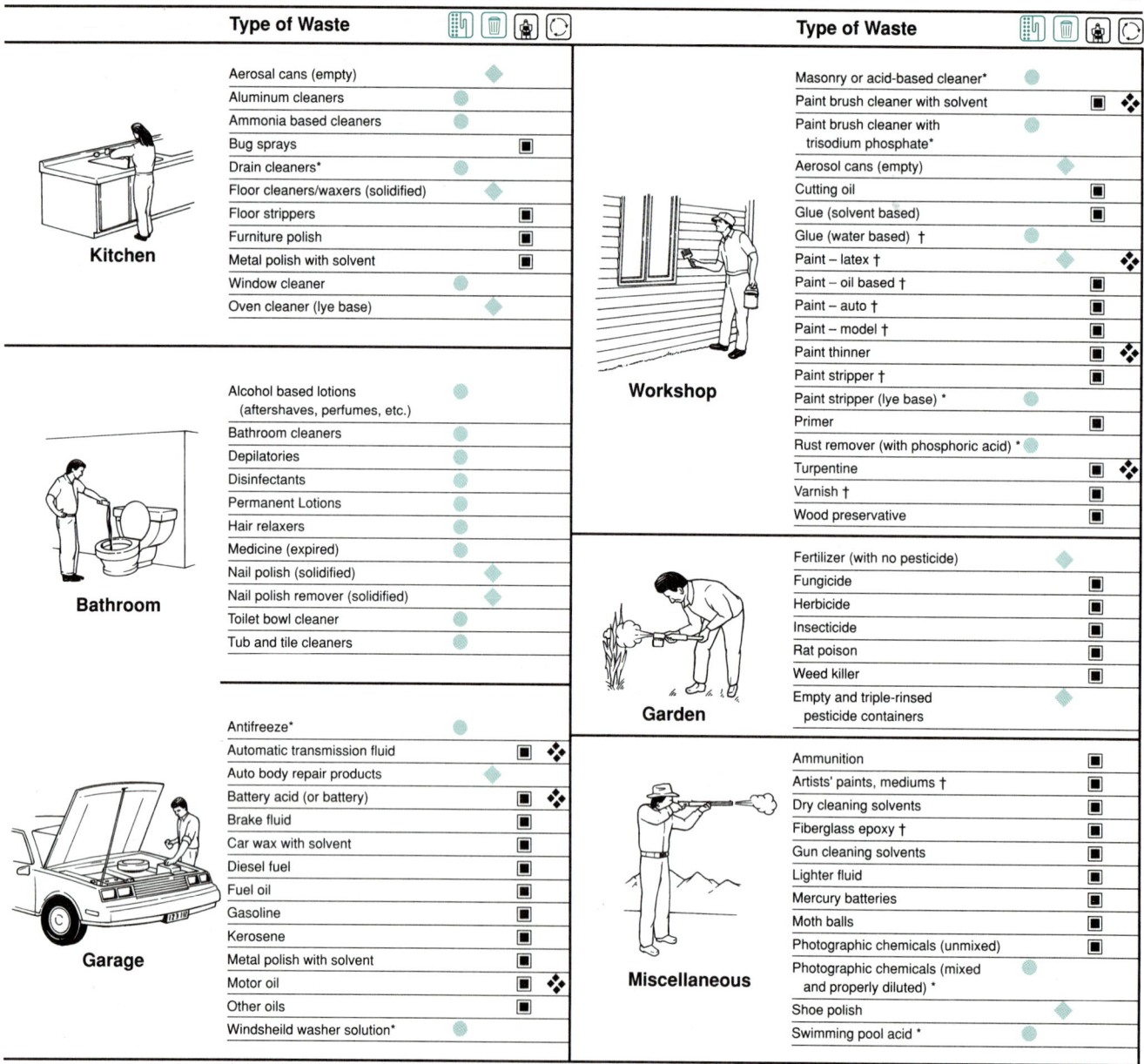

Regional Poison Center .... ☎ (800) 392-9111
Emergency Services .... ☎ _____

Kitchen

Type of Waste	Drain ●	Landfill ■	Hazardous ☣	Recycle ○
Aerosol cans (empty)			◆	
Aluminum cleaners	●			
Ammonia based cleaners	●			
Bug sprays		■		
Drain cleaners*	●			
Floor cleaners/waxers (solidified)		◆		
Floor strippers		■		
Furniture polish		■		
Metal polish with solvent		■		
Window cleaner	●			
Oven cleaner (lye base)	●			

Bathroom

Type of Waste	Drain ●	Landfill ■	Hazardous ☣	Recycle ○
Alcohol based lotions (aftershaves, perfumes, etc.)	●			
Bathroom cleaners	●			
Depilatories	●			
Disinfectants	●			
Permanent Lotions	●			
Hair relaxers	●			
Medicine (expired)	●			
Nail polish (solidified)		◆		
Nail polish remover (solidified)		◆		
Toilet bowl cleaner	●			
Tub and tile cleaners	●			

Garage

Type of Waste	Drain ●	Landfill ■	Hazardous ☣	Recycle ○
Antifreeze*	●			
Automatic transmission fluid		■		◆
Auto body repair products	●			
Battery acid (or battery)		■		◆
Brake fluid		■		
Car wax with solvent		■		
Diesel fuel		■		
Fuel oil		■		
Gasoline		■		
Kerosene		■		
Metal polish with solvent		■		
Motor oil		■		◆
Other oils		■		
Windshield washer solution*	●			

Workshop

Type of Waste	Drain ●	Landfill ■	Hazardous ☣	Recycle ○
Masonry or acid-based cleaner*	●			
Paint brush cleaner with solvent			■	◆
Paint brush cleaner with trisodium phosphate*	●			
Aerosol cans (empty)			◆	
Cutting oil			■	
Glue (solvent based)			■	
Glue (water based) †	●			
Paint – latex †			◆	◆
Paint – oil based †			■	
Paint – auto †			■	
Paint – model †			■	
Paint thinner			■	◆
Paint stripper †			■	
Paint stripper (lye base)*	●			
Primer			■	
Rust remover (with phosphoric acid)*	●			
Turpentine			■	◆
Varnish †			■	
Wood preservative			■	

Garden

Type of Waste	Drain ●	Landfill ■	Hazardous ☣	Recycle ○
Fertilizer (with no pesticide)			◆	
Fungicide			■	
Herbicide			■	
Insecticide			■	
Rat poison			■	
Weed killer			■	
Empty and triple-rinsed pesticide containers				◆

Miscellaneous

Type of Waste	Drain ●	Landfill ■	Hazardous ☣	Recycle ○
Ammunition			■	
Artists' paints, mediums †			■	
Dry cleaning solvents			■	
Fiberglass epoxy †			■	
Gun cleaning solvents			■	
Lighter fluid			■	
Mercury batteries			■	
Moth balls			■	
Photographic chemicals (unmixed)			■	
Photographic chemicals (mixed and properly diluted)*	●			
Shoe polish				◆
Swimming pool acid*	●			

* If using septic tank or lagoon dispose of small quantities over a number of days.
† This product suited to landfill disposal if first solidified.

The preceding chart is based on information from the United States Environmental Protection Agency's Hazardous Waste regulations. W.P.C.F. assume no responsibility and disclaim any liability for any injury or damage resulting from the use or effect of any product or information specified in this publication.

Water Pollution Control Federation • 601 Wythe Street • Alexandria, VA 22314-1994

Copyright © 1989 Water Pollution Control Federation, Alexandria, VA. Reprinted by permission.

Table 15.3
Superfund—State Cleanup Activities and Capabilities

25 states have full fund and enforcement capabilities with active cleanup and oversight program.

Arizona	Kansas	Missouri	Pennsylvania
California	Maine	New Hampshire	Rhode Island
Connecticut	Maryland	New Jersey	South Carolina
Florida	Massachusetts	New York	Tennessee
Illinois	Michigan	Ohio	Texas
Indiana	Minnesota	Oregon	Washington
			Wisconsin

14 states have full fund and enforcement capabilities with limited fund and program activity to date.

Hawaii	Montana	North Dakota	Vermont
Iowa	Nevada	Oklahoma	Virginia
Kentucky	New Mexico	South Dakota	
Mississippi	North Carolina	Utah	

6 states have removal or emergency response programs but limited remedial action authorities or capabilities.

Alabama	Louisiana
Alaska	West Virginia
Arkansas	Wyoming

5 states do not have Superfund programs but deal with waste sites in some manner.

Colorado	Idaho
Delaware	Nebraska
Georgia	

will be nothing to throw away except the container if a product is completely used. Be a wise consumer. Buy only what you need and use all of it. If this is not possible, then follow the advice on the chart. Each person, as guardian of his environment, should follow the recommendations for waste disposal suggested by the chart. Environmental protection is each person's personal responsibility.

Industrial Waste Management

Industrial waste management can be divided into two categories, waste cleanup of past mismanagement and waste disposal for present-day activities. Waste cleanup required because of mismanagement is regulated by the **Comprehensive Environmental Response, Compensation, and Liability Act** of 1980, better known as *Superfund,* and by the **Superfund Amendments and Reauthorization Act** of 1986 (SARA). The 1986 amendments require states to become involved in the Superfund program in a "substantial and meaningful" way. Management of present-day industrial waste is regulated by the **Resource Conservation and Recovery Act** of 1976 (RCRA) and its 1984 amendments. The 1984 **Hazardous and Solid Waste Amendments** (HSWA) to RCRA, when fully implemented, will put Superfund out of business. RCRA and its amendments will ensure that no new superfund sites will be generated.

Superfund

Superfund and its SARA amendments have required that states become actively involved in their own cleanup programs. Figure 15.8 is a map of EPA regions and Super-

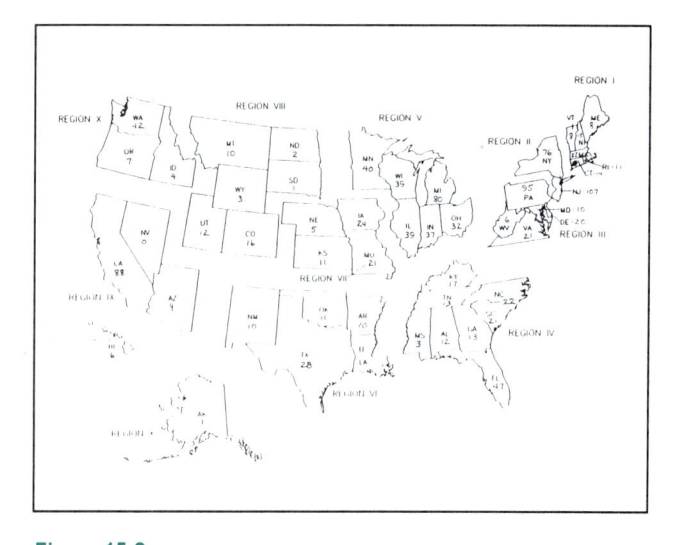

Figure 15.8 EPA regions with the number of Superfund sites on the National Priorities List (NPL)
Source: Environmental Protection Agency.
(*Cartographer:* Douglas Hemsath)

fund sites on the National Priorities List (NPL) as of August 29, 1989. Thirty-nine states have funds and enforcement authorities for cleanup activities. Table 15.3 lists each state's cleanup activities and capabilities. In general, a state Superfund program has some or all of the following characteristics:

1. Procedures for emergency response actions and longer-term remediation of environmental and health risks at hazardous waste sites, including both NPL and non-NPL sites;

Waste Management

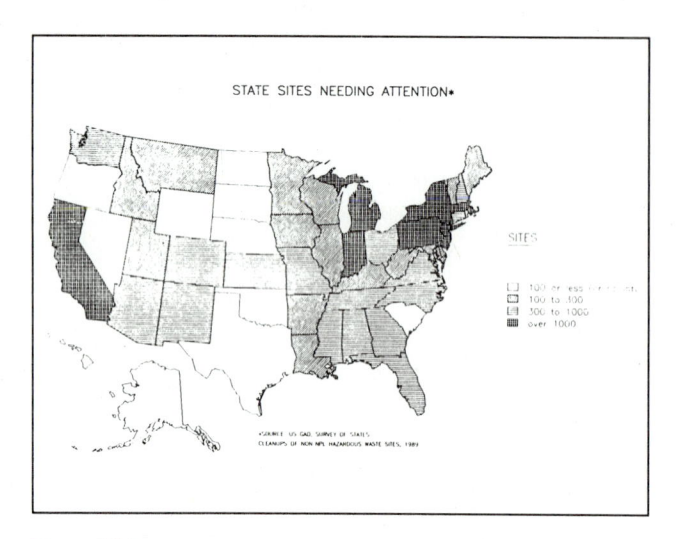

Figure 15.9 The number of hazardous waste sites not on the NPL but needing cleanup attention.
Source: U.S. GAO, *Survey of States: Cleanups of Non-NPL Hazardous Waste Sites*, 1989.
(*Cartographer:* Douglas Hemsath)

Figure 15.10 A concrete barricade blocks the main road into Times Beach, Missouri, EPAs Superfund ghost town.
(*Photo:* David A. Castillon)

2. Provisions for a fund or other financing mechanisms to pay for studies and remediation activities;
3. Enforcement authorities to compel responsible parties (RPs) to conduct or pay for studies and/or remediation;
4. Staff to manage publicly-funded cleanups and oversee RP-led cleanups.

There are a number of emerging state programs that have only recently been authorized or received initial funds, or expect to receive funding in the near future.

In addition to the NPL sites listed by EPA, there are thousands of additional sites needing attention. Figure 15.9 is a map of the states with the number of non-NPL hazardous waste sites in need of cleanup. Industrial hazardous waste cleanup is a tremendous problem facing the United States. If the regulations set down by RCRA and its amendments are rigidly followed and enforced, no new sites will be added to the hazardous waste sites list, but the slow methodical task of cleanup will continue for years to come and cost billions of dollars.

It was discovered in the early 1980s that Times Beach, Missouri, was contaminated with dioxin. A waste oil contractor had spread dioxin-contaminated oil on the dirt and gravel roads to control dust. The entire town was declared a hazardous waste site in 1983 and added to the EPAs priorities list. The State of Missouri bought the entire town for $36 million, using Superfund money, enclosed it with chain-link fences, and posted guards. The ghost town occupies about 400 acres (162 hectares) (figure 15.10) on the floodplain of the Meramac River. The 423 abandoned buildings are a stark reminder of indiscriminate hazardous waste disposal. In 1990, the EPA announced plans to install a hazardous waste incinerator in Times Beach to burn all the dioxin-contaminated soil converting it into noncontaminated material. The incinerator would then stay in Times Beach and accept hazardous waste materials from 26 other sites in Missouri. When the project is completed (5 to 7 years), the Times Beach area would be safe for use and the incinerator removed. The plan is to make Times Beach a riverfront park at an estimated cost of $118 million.

RCRA's Rules

Protection of the environment from hazardous waste is one of EPAs jobs. It has statutory responsibility for ensuring that the rules and regulations of RCRA are met. But, prevention of future environmental damage from hazardous waste is the job of industry. Any industry that generates 100 kg (220 pounds) or more of hazardous waste per month is required to comply with RCRAs rules.

Breaking the land disposal habit won't be easy for industry, but it is a must. Previously discussed options to landfilling are available to industry. Waste reduction, material recovery, energy recovery, and recycling must become a part of the industrial systems pyramid. Another option is waste treatment and destruction.

Biological, chemical, physical, and thermal processes can be used as methods of waste treatment and reduction (figure 15.4). EPA research indicates that incineration can destroy in excess of 99.9999% of the organic constituents in some wastes, and that properly operated incinerators can provide a permanent solution to certain hazardous waste problems with minimal long-term ecological burden. The use of ocean-going incinerator ships has been proposed as a means of destroying hazardous waste away from

Figure 15.11 *Vulcanus*—a Dutch hazardous waste incineration ship. How to control atmospheric and oceanic pollution is an unanswered question that makes burning hazardous waste at sea very controversial.
(Photo: EPA)

people (figure 15.11). However, caution should be used, and research into the effects on marine ecosystems and the ocean atmosphere must be necessary prerequisites to full-scale use of this method.

Chemical waste-reduction processes under study by EPA include precipitation, solid-liquid and liquid-liquid separation, neutralization, and chemical oxidation. Biological processes, including bacteria, yeast, and fungi, are being used in a program to extend the capabilities of biotechnology for hazardous waste treatment. The common white rot in wood, a fungus (*Phanerochaeta chrysasporium*), can destroy DDT and dioxins. Research must continue into safe and effective ways to reduce the hazardous waste of industry.

Wastewater Treatment

More than $60 billion federal, state, and local dollars have been invested in the nation's wastewater treatment infrastructure since the Clean Water Act was passed in 1972. Over $44 billion was in the form of federal grants for construction, operation, and maintenance of municipal wastewater treatment facilities. Federal money was also spent for water quality institutions and programs at every level of government. Assuring adequate operation and maintenance of the infrastructure is an ever increasing challenge in light of population growth and unconventional new pollutants.

The **Water Quality Act** of 1987 amends and reauthorizes the Clean Water Act. The new law provides for a phase-out of federally funded construction grants and a transition to state and local self-sufficiency. Almost $10 billion was spent on direct grants for wastewater treatment facilities to phase out the construction grant program. An additional $8.4 billion is being spent to establish self-sustaining state-revolving loan funds that will continue to provide needed construction assistance to state and local municipalities and to Native American Indian tribes.

The typical wastewater treatment facility depends to a large extent on the size of a community or the dispersion of the population. A widely dispersed population must rely on individual treatment systems such as septic tanks with a lagoon or absorption field. Most communities, however, have a municipal wastewater treatment facility. Figure 15.12 illustrates six different EPA-recognized individual wastewater treatment systems that can be used to treat individual household wastewater. Soil conditions will dictate the best system to use for maximum filtration. An individual home builder should seek advice on the soil conditions and install the proper system to protect the groundwater of the area on which construction is planned.

Figure 15.13 is a diagram of a typical wastewater treatment facility for a municipality. Primary treatment of raw sewage is a mechanical process that first screens and filters out larger debris. Finer solid particles settle out in a sedimentation tank and this material is called sludge. Secondary treatment of fluid sewage is a biological process that uses aerobic bacteria to remove biodegradable organic material. Almost 90% of the oxygen-demanding wastes can be removed by this process. A number of different methods are used to break down the organic wastes. Bacteria and protozoa are used, along with oxygen, to speed up the process. The wastewater discharge, after secondary treatment, goes to a sedimentation chamber where most of the suspended solids and microorganisms settle out as sludge.

Primary and secondary treatment of wastewater cannot remove many of the harmful materials the wastewater contains. Some of the organic material and solids are still in suspension in the water, along with about half of the nitrogen in solution (nitrates). Phosphorus (phosphates), mostly from laundry detergents, are still in solution in the water and so are the toxic metal compounds and pesticides. Additional advanced treatment is necessary before the wastewater can be safely discharged to the surface drainage system.

Methods of advanced treatment for any locale depend mainly on the type of industry-discharged wastewater within the community. Meandering waterways with vegetation to absorb pollutants have been used for advanced treatment. Water hyacinths can absorb some metal compounds and toxic organic chemicals but then disposal of the contaminated plants is a problem.

Chlorination to disinfect wastewater is the final treatment. Disease-carrying bacteria and some viruses are killed by the chlorine. Finally, any water coloration is removed. Then clean, pure water is ready to be released to the surface water system of the area.

Small Wastewater Systems

Alternative Systems for Small Communities and Rural Areas

1 Septic tank and soil absorption field (trench)

Sewage bacteria break up some solids in tank. Heavy solids sink to bottom as sludge. Grease and light particles float to top as scum. Liquid flows from tank through closed pipe and distribution box to perforated pipes in trenches; flows through surrounding crushed rocks or gravel and soil to groundwater (underground water). Bacteria and oxygen in soil help purify liquid. Tank sludge and scum are pumped out periodically. Most common onsite system. Level ground or moderate slope.

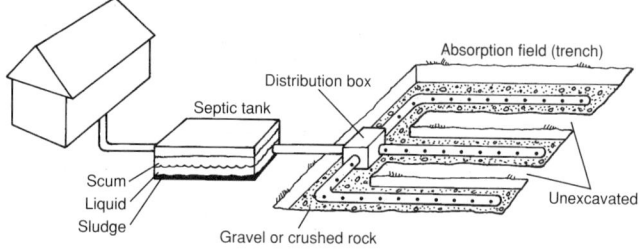

2 Septic system refinements: (A) Dosing (B) Closed loop

(A) Pump or siphon forces liquid to perforated pipes in controlled doses so all pipes discharge liquid almost at same time (dosing). Spreads liquid more evenly and gives field chance to dry out between dosings. (B) Variation of Sketch 1 absorption field. Can be used for dosing and where ground is level or nearly level.

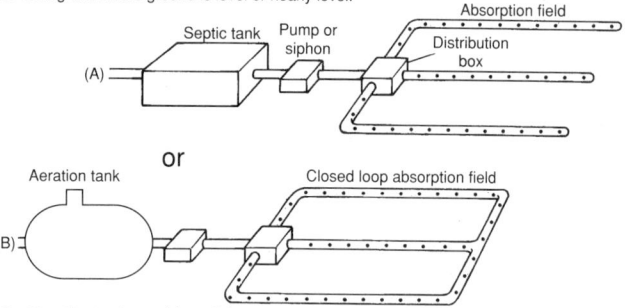

3 Septic tank and leaching chambers

Open-bottom concrete chambers create underground cavern over absorption field. Liquid is piped into cavern and spread over field by troughs, splashplates, or dams. Liquid filters through soil. Chambers replace perforated pipe, trenches and rocks of conventional absorption field. Access holes at top allow maintenance and soil inspection.

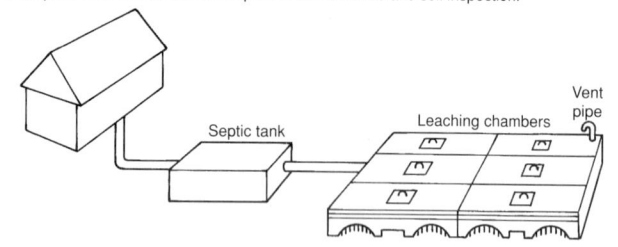

Figure 15.12 Wastewater treatment systems for the individual home not able to connect to a community system. The permeability and slope of the soil will determine the best system to use.
Source: Environmental Protection Agency.

4 Septic tank with sloping field – serial distribution

Pump forces liquid to perforated pipes in contoured absorption field. Drop boxes regulate liquid flow so highest trench fills up first, second fills up next, and lowest fills up last. Plastic fittings can be used instead of drop boxes to regulate flow. Used on slopes.

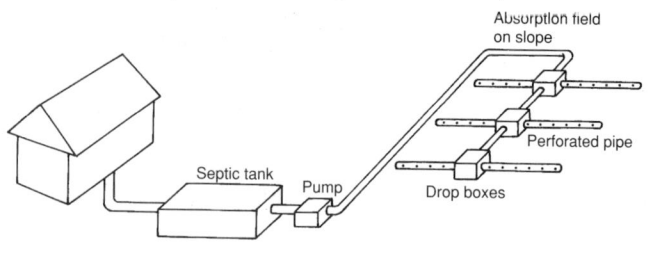

5 Mound system (used with septic or aerobic tank)

Liquid is pumped from storage tank to perforated plastic pipe in sand mound that covers plowed ground. Liquid flows through rocks or gravel, sand and natural soil. Mound vegetation helps evaporate liquid. Rocky or tight soil or high water table.

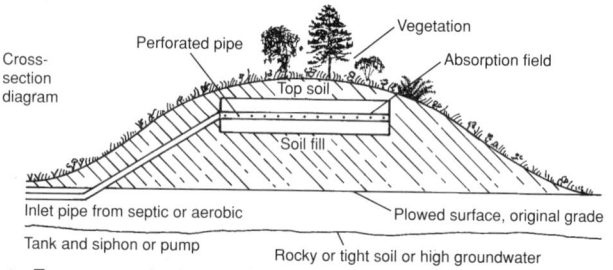

6 Evapotranspiration bed (used with septic or aerobic tank)

Similar to Sketch 5 but sand bed is lined with plastic or other waterproof material. Bed could be mound or level. Liquid evaporates because liner prevents it from filtering through natural soil. Plants speed evaporation by drawing moisture from soil and breathing it into the air. Used where conventional absorption field not possible.

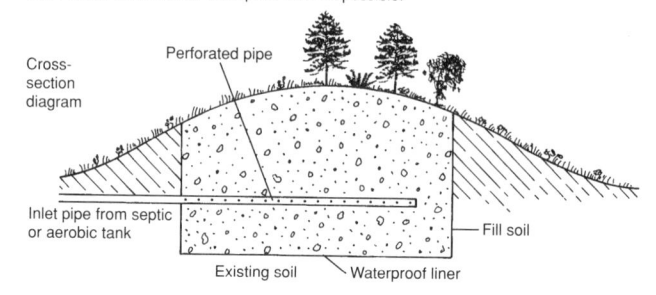

Figure 15.13 (facing page) (a) Primary sewage treatment removes only the biggest solids and suspended sediment. (b) Secondary treatment digests most organic compounds in the effluent and removes many plant nutrients. (c) Advanced sewage treatment produces a cleaner water release and produces some valuable fertilizer for the land. Chlorination kills most pathogens and is the last treatment in the final stage before water is released.
From William P. Cunningham and Barbara Woodworth Saigo, *Environmental Science: A Global Concern*. Copyright © 1990 Wm. C. Brown Publishers, Dubuque, Iowa. All Rights Reserved. Reprinted by permission.

Primary Sewage Treatment

(a) Raw sewage from sewer → Bar grate / Moving screen → Grit chamber → Sludge / Effluent → To secondary treatment

Sludge drying bed → To incineration, landfill, or spread on cropland

(b) Secondary treatment

From primary treatment Effluent + Sludge inoculum → Aeration tank (activated sludge) ← Air pump → Chlorination tank (Chlorine) → Trickling bed evaporation → To advanced treatment

(c) Effluent from secondary treatment → Alum flocculation plus sedimentation → Activated carbon → Desalination (electrodialysis or reverse osmosis) → Nitrate removal → Specialized compound removal (DDT, etc.) → To rivers, lakes, streams, oceans, reservoirs, or industries

- 98% of suspended solids, 90% of phosphates
- 98% of dissolved organics
- Most of dissolved salts

Recycled to land for irrigation and fertilization

Advanced sewage treatment. Shaded areas show recycling of nutrients to land.

Waste Management

Figure 15.13D Components of a typical advanced sewage treatment facility in Springfield, Missouri.
(*Photo:* David A. Castillon)

Sludge as a Resource

Sludge is the solid material removed from wastewater by primary and secondary sewage treatment. Because of its origin and the immense quantities in which it is produced (more than 5.5 MMT-6MT of dry solids per year in the United States), it represents a major solid waste problem for most communities. Sludge is composed of humus, nitrogen, and smaller amounts of phosphorus, potassium, and trace metals, the primary ingredients of fertilizers. This material can be a resource if it is treated properly by heating or composting to remove its harmful bacteria. Toxic metals are more difficult and costly to remove but the technology does exist to remove these contaminants. The EPA estimates that the nutrient content in sludge is worth one billion dollars per year as land fertilizer. Twenty-five percent of the municipal sludge and sewage plant effluent produced in the United States is being used as fertilizer (figure 15.14). The remainder is eliminated by incineration, landfilling, or ocean dumping. This is a terrible waste of a potentially valuable resource. We cannot continue these wasteful practices. Sustainability of agriculture and protection of our waters demands that we make more efficient use of our sludge resource. The oceans or landfills are not places to dump this valuable resource.

Figure 15.14 Dry sludge being applied with a manure spreader on the lawns in Austin, Texas.
(*Photo:* City of Austin)

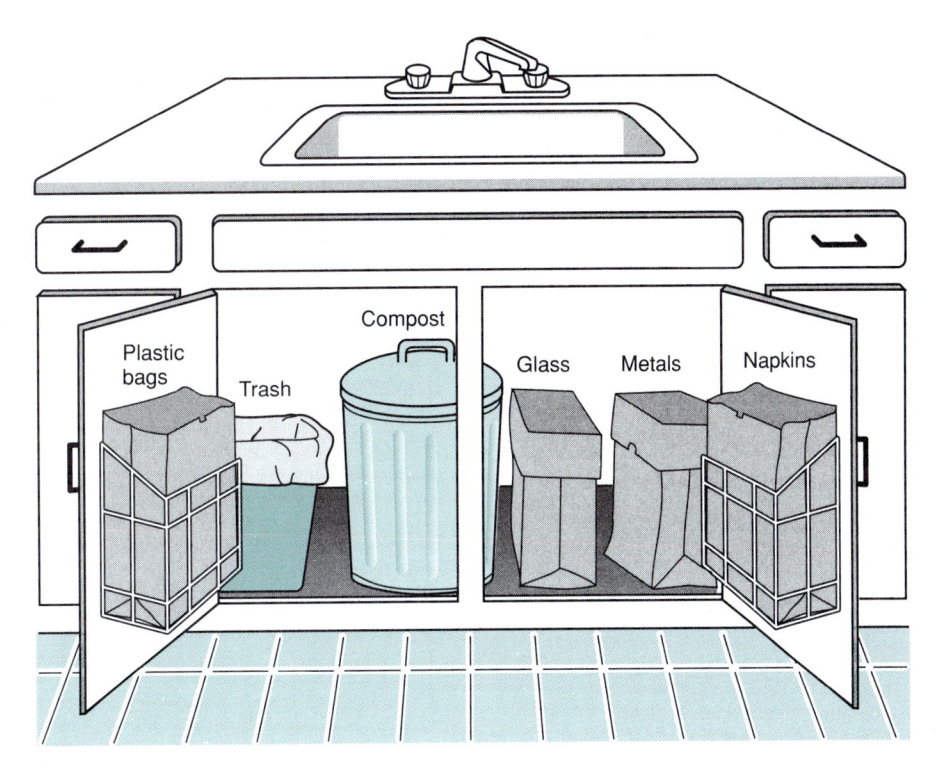

Figure 15.15 Trash separation is the first necessary step in the waste-reduction recycling process. If you don't have room for six containers, use two (landfill trash and recyclables) and separate elsewhere.
From William P. Cunningham and Barbara Woodworth Saigo, *Environmental Science: A Global Concern.* Copyright © 1990 Wm. C. Brown Publishers, Dubuque, Iowa. All Rights Reserved. Reprinted by permission.

Recycling

Recycling represents reuse of only 10% of the solid waste generated in the United States. The potential for recycling shows greater promise than for any other method of solid waste reduction. East Hampton, Long Island, in New York State ran a pilot test on recycling. The Center for the Biology of Natural Systems reported that intensive recycling in East Hampton recovered 84.4% of the residential trash in the form of marketable products. Food garbage and yard wastes were composted. Paper, aluminum and tin cans, and glass were recycled. The EPA has as a goal in their waste management program to increase recyclables to 25%. This figure seems a little low in light of the findings in East Hampton.

What are the problems and what needs to be done to change trash into useable products? Number one is that most Americans simply dislike the inconvenience of separating trash. In most communities there are no economic incentives to separate trash, which is the first necessary step in the recycling process (figure 15.15). Separating trash is no guarantee that the material will be recycled. Industries needed to remanufacture materials must be in place to accept the separated trash and markets must exist for the recycled products. Proponents of recycling contend that the only way the recycling system will work is with economic incentives. These would include tax breaks for businesses using recycled products and materials, and grants and loans to encourage entrepreneurs to build recycling facilities and establish new markets for recycled products. Charging each household by the pound for nonrecyclable trash and picking up separated recyclables free of charge could put an economic incentive in each household budget.

An examination of the solid waste sent to landfills by Americans reveals that most of this material is recyclable. Paper, plastics, glass, aluminum, and steel are readily recyclable. Yard trimmings and food garbage are compostable. The amount of this material is staggering and growing. Paper and paperboard have climbed from 22.3 MMT (24.5 MT) in 1960 to 45.5 MMT (50.1 MT) in 1986 and are expected to increase to 60 MMT (66 MT) by 2000. Plastics have surged from 2.7 MMT (3 MMT) in 1970 to 9.4 MMT (10.3 MT) in 1986 and are expected

Waste Management

to climb to 14.2 MMT (15.6 MT) by the year 2000. Food wastes and glass have remained relatively constant and are expected to continue at present levels. Food wastes represent 11.4 MMT (12.5 MT) and, with population stability, will remain at that level until 2000. Glass has peaked at 11.8 MMT (13 MT) and will probably remain there because of plastic substitutes. Aluminum is the best example of a recyclable material that is being recycled. A record high 42.5 billion aluminum cans were recycled in 1988. This represented more than half (54.7%) of all aluminum cans produced in the United States in 1988.

Metals recycling iron, aluminum, copper, lead, silver, gold, and platinoids are established industries and have been for many years. Paper and plastic recycling, however, are industries of the future and the need to establish recycling facilities to keep these materials out of the landfills are present-day concerns. Metals recycling is discussed in a previous chapter. Therefore, paper and plastic recycling will be discussed in this section.

Paper

Forty-one percent of our solid waste is paper or paper products. Most paper or paperboard products are recyclable back to paper for newsprint, paper towels, toilet paper, and napkins. Other reuse alternatives for paper include cellulose insulation for houses, bedding for animals when shredded, and as a composting material with animal manure for fertilizer. The problem with paper recycling can be illustrated in newsprint recycling.

Newsprint has been collected for many years by Boy Scouts and other community groups as a money-making project. In 1988, 13% of the 12.4 MMT (13.6 MT) of newsprint produced was recycled. But the Boy Scouts income is gone. They were paid $40 per ton for newsprint in 1988. But in 1990 it costs $25 per ton to have it transported to a recycling paper manufacturer.

Collecting old newspapers does not guarantee reuse. Recycled newsprint also has a reuse limit. After being recycled six times, the fiber content is too weak to be run on newspaper presses. Therefore, alternative uses must be found to keep the 41% of our solid waste stream that is paper out of the landfill. The supply of newsprint available for recycling greatly exceeds the demand because there are not enough manufacturing facilities to accept all of the paper collected for recycling. To build a new mill to produce recycled newsprint would cost in excess of $400 million (1990 dollars). However, building the necessary facilities must be a high priority if recycling goals are to be met in the 1990s. Paper, a forest product, is renewable in biologic time. However, our use of paper is so great that forests are being "mined" in many areas to meet this demand. Paper is also a potential resource for energy production.

Table 15.4
Recyclables at WCB Publishers

Uncoated and coated free-sheet wastage from the web presses. WCB produces nearly 1,233 tons of recyclable free-sheet yearly.

Roll wrappers. The protective covering for the web paper yields over 88 tons of recyclable paper yearly.

IGS, a label applied to UV covercoated scraps (plastic coated book covers). WCB sent approximately 502 tons of IGS to Kimberly-Clark, where the UV and hot melt (glue) are eliminated; Kimberly-Clark reprocesses the material into industrial grade paper (paper towels, etc.).

Roll cores. Annually, WCB sends 97 tons of this dense, fibrous product to recycling plants.

Scrap cardboard. Nearly 60 tons are recycled yearly.

Aluminum plates. Yearly, about 54,000 lbs. are saved and shipped to recyclers.

Out-of-print product. About 151 tons are shredded yearly and sent to Kimberly-Clark for reprocessing into industrial grade paper.

Silver. Extracted from Camera Rooms' and Typesetting's film; chemicals are recycled also.

Paper Recycling at WCB Publishers

The paper this text is printed on is recycled paper. WCB has an active program of recycling that includes paper, cardboard, aluminum, and silver. Table 15.4 lists the materials presently being recycled by WCB.

A pilot program to add computer base paper and office-discarded paper to the list is being researched, because each type of paper must be separate. If paper clips or foil wrappers are found in a load of paper, the recycling mill will reject the entire load. Five different waste paper containers in each office to facilitate separation of paper products also creates storage problems. As landfills are closed and waste disposal becomes more expensive, storage of recycling products will not be the problem it seems to be today.

Plastic

The Midwest Research Institute in Kansas City, Missouri, determined that half-gallon polyvinyl chloride (PVC) containers require less than half the energy to produce and transport than do half-gallon glass containers. They also found that PVC containers consume one-twentieth the mass of raw materials and less than one-third as much water in their production. The PVC container generates less than half the solid waste of glass manufacturing. No wonder plastic has replaced glass in the container industry and in the landfill.

How We Recycle

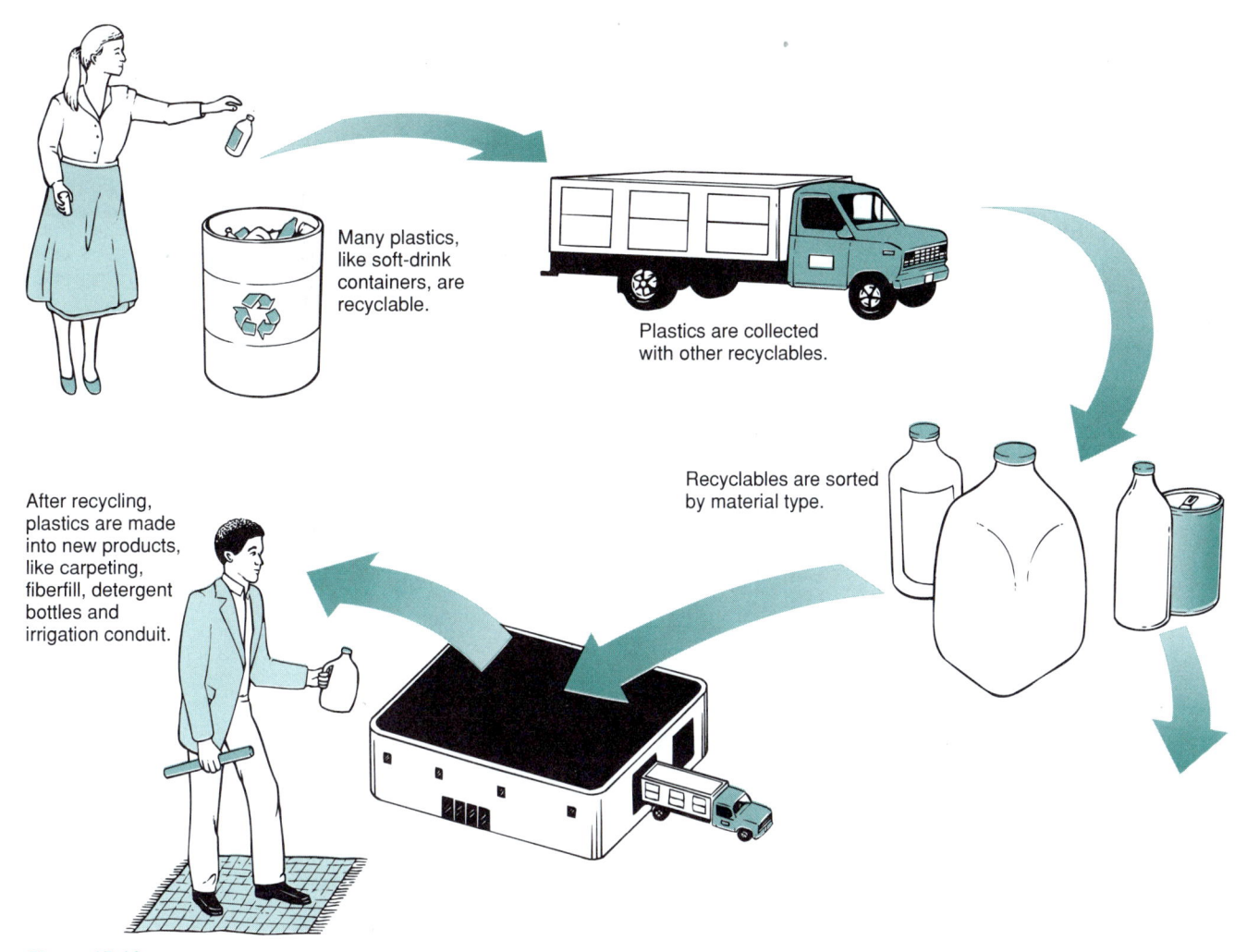

Figure 15.16 The plastic recovery cycle.

Only about 1% of the PVC discarded by the consumer is recycled. The technology exists to recycle PVC (figure 15.16) but there are hazards and liabilities associated with recycled plastics. Food products cannot be put in recycled plastic containers. The chlorine content in PVC does not allow incineration unless the unit has a scrubber to prevent emissions of hydrochloric acid, a contributor to acid rain. As landfills are closed, the only solution to the plastics solid waste problem is recycling.

For recycling of any product to succeed, four phases must be implemented:

1. Collection of the materials
2. Sorting or separating the materials
3. Reclamation of the materials into a usable form, and
4. Reusable products made from the reclaimed materials

A good example of a plastics recycling program that has succeeded is the PET program. PET (polyethylene terephthalate), the material used in carbonated beverage bottles, is recycled in nine states under mandatory deposit laws: California, Connecticut, Delaware, Maine, Massachusetts, Michigan, New York, Oregon, and Vermont (figure 15.17). Bottles collected in these states represent 20% of the 750 million pounds of PET resin produced each year. Recyclers pay up to $140 per ton for PET, making it second in value to aluminum as a recyclable material. The market for recycled PET is limited mostly by lack of collection efficiency.

The DuPont Company, in cooperation with Waste Management Inc., has the first PET recycling facility. Projections are that 50% of all PET containers will be recycled by the mid-1990s. Aggressive recycling programs are planned in the 1990s as industries develop solutions to the solid waste problem.

Waste Management

Plastics Recycling

The Council for Solid Waste Solutions has launched a national program to increase the level of plastics recycling. The council will provide direct assistance to communities seeking to include plastics in their recycling programs. In addition to providing capital assistance and technical expertise to selected communities, the council is sponsoring university research and designing pilot programs to make recycling collection systems more efficient.

The council is a program of the plastics industry, formed under the umbrella organization of The Society of the Plastics Industry Inc.

A

B

Figure 15.17 (a) Plastic recycling must become a major part of the waste reduction process. (b) Milk containers, seen here bound into bales at a recycling center, can be reprocessed into plastic products such as polyester fiber and molded parts. The gap in production versus recycling needs to be closed.
(*Photo:* David A. Castillon)

Figure 15.18 Aluminum can smashers and buyers are available in most communities.
(*Photo:* David A. Castillon)

Building a compost pile

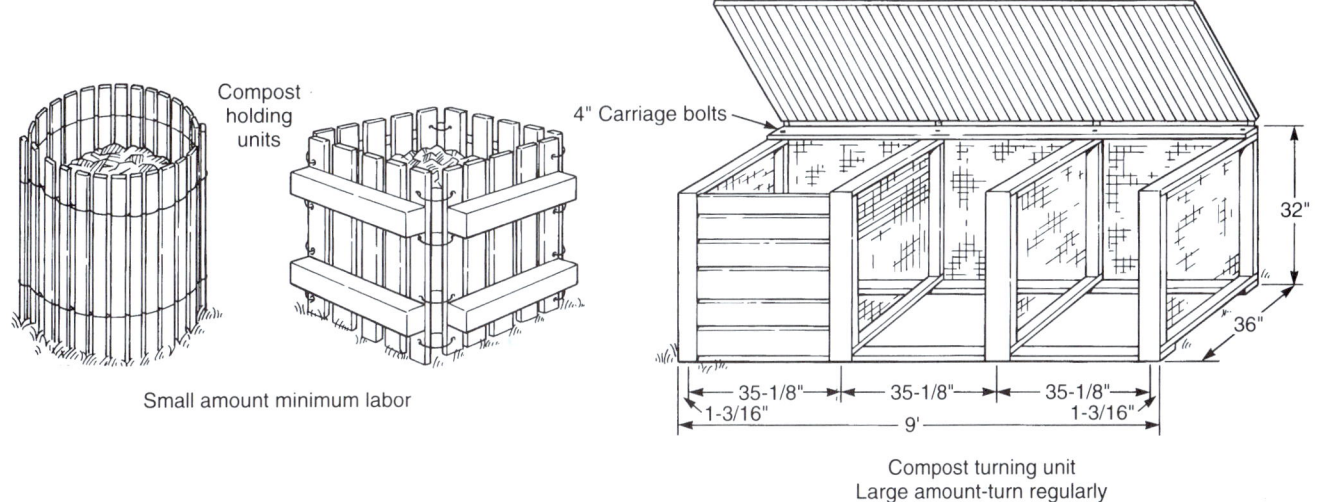

Repeat layering as below
Kitchen scraps
Alfalfa meal (or alfalfa-based cat litter)
2 to 3" layer manure or more grass clippings
Few shovelfuls of soil
6 to 10" layer green plant material and grass clippings

Size of finished pile: 3' square, 4' high

Compost holding units

4" Carriage bolts

32"
36"
35-1/8"
1-3/16"
9'

Small amount minimum labor

Compost turning unit
Large amount-turn regularly

Figure 15.19 Composting your yard trimmings and food garbage can reduce your trash to the landfill by almost 20%.

Summary

The NEPA law charges each individual with the responsibility of environmental protection. Household solid waste management is your responsibility. As a solid waste manager you can do the following to reduce solid waste and environmental degradation:

1. Save all of your aluminum cans and turn them into your local recycling center or give them to a charitable or community group that collects them as a fund-raiser (figure 15.18).

2. Compost your yard trimmings and food garbage (figure 15.19). Your local library or agricultural extension office can help with local specifications or problems.

Waste Management 355

Figure 15.20A We're running out of room and it isn't funny.
Cartoon by Bob Palmer. Copyright © *The News-Leader*, Springfield, MO. Reprinted by permission.

Figure 15.20B Humans dump their sewage in the natural environment (the animal's living room) but wouldn't tolerate the reverse.
THE FAR SIDE copyright 1988 UNIVERSAL PRESS SYNDICATE. Reprinted with permission. All Rights Reserved.

3. Encourage or campaign in your community for curbside separation of trash for recycling. It's a cheaper alternative to the increased costs of landfilling and it's a much better environmental alternative.

4. Follow the disposal method described on the container of any hazardous waste product or material. Seek advice if you're uncertain of a disposal method.

Following these four simple rules of household solid waste management should result in at least a 30% reduction in solid waste sent to the landfill (figure 15.20). Thirty percent is 5% better than EPA's goals for waste reduction in the 1990s.

356 Natural Resources Management

Key Words and Phrases

Furans
Garbage
Hazardous waste
Incineration
Landfills
Leachate
Phanerochaeta chrysasporium
Sludge
Source reduction
Superfund

Questions and Discussion Topics

1. What is included in the concept of source reduction?
2. Is there a "waste-to-energy" plant in your geographic area? What materials do they convert to energy? What other materials might be incinerated for energy?
3. Inventory your kitchen and bathroom for hazardous waste. Select the one item you feel is the most hazardous to the environment. Write down all of the data on the label and bring it to class for discussion.
4. Are there any superfund sites in your locale or state? If yes, what hazardous waste does the site contain? What are the plans to clean up the site?
5. Does your community have a wastewater treatment facility? Does it have primary treatment? Secondary? Tertiary? How does the water look that drains from the facility?
6. If you had a garden, would you spread sludge on it?
7. Do you recycle aluminum cans? Paper? Plastic? If not, why not?
8. What is your personal waste management plan for the 1990s?

References for Further Study

Chemical Manufacturers Association. 1988–89. *Chemecology*. Washington, D.C. Chemecology is published about ten times a year and the following issues are on waste management. 1988–Feb. Vol. 17, No. 1; June Vol. 17, No. 4; 1989–Apr. Vol. 18, No. 3; June Vol. 18, No. 5; Sept. Vol. 18, No. 7.

Conn, W. D. Spring, 1989. Managing Household Hazardous Waste. Chicago, Ill.: *APA Journal*.

Eiseley, L. 1977. *Another Kind of Autumn*. New York: Scribner's. Quote from the poem, *The Time-Keepers*.

Environmental Protection Agency. 1981–1989. *EPA Journal*. Washington, D.C. The following EPA Journal issues were on waste management. 1981–June Vol. 7, No. 6; 1984–Oct. Vol. 10, No. 8; 1986–Apr. Vol. 12, No. 3; and Nov. Vol. 12, No. 9; 1988–Nov/Dec. Vol. 14, No. 7; 1989–Mar/Apr. Vol. 15, No. 2.

Environmental Protection Agency. Jan., 1980. *Small Wastewater Systems for Small Communities and Rural Areas*. No. FRD-10.

Environmental Protection Agency. Oct., 1982. *Sludge: Recycling for Agricultural Use*. No. 430/9–82–008.

Environmental Protection Agency. Sept., 1989. *An Analysis of State Superfund Programs: 50-State Study*. No. EPA/540/8–89/011.

Environmental Protection Agency. Feb., 1990. *Progress in Groundwater Protection and Restoration*. No. EPA 440/6–90–001.

Follmer, L. R. Sept., 1984. *Soil—An Uncertain Medium for Waste Disposal*. Madison, Wisc.: Proceedings of the Seventh Annual Madison Waste Conference. Something to think about.

Goodman, S., K. Morris, and M. Steinwachs. 1988. *Guide to Hazardous Products Around the Home*. Springfield, Mo.: Household Hazardous Waste Project—Greene Co. Missouri.

O'Leary, P. R., P. W. Walsh and R. K. Harn. Dec., 1988. Managing Solid Waste. *Scientific American*. 259: No. 6.

Scientific American. Sept., 1989. *Managing Planet Earth*. A special issue on earth management. A good article on *Strategies for Manufacturing*.

Water Pollution Control Federation. 1987. *Household Hazardous Waste Chart*. Alexandria, Va. A very useful chart for the home.

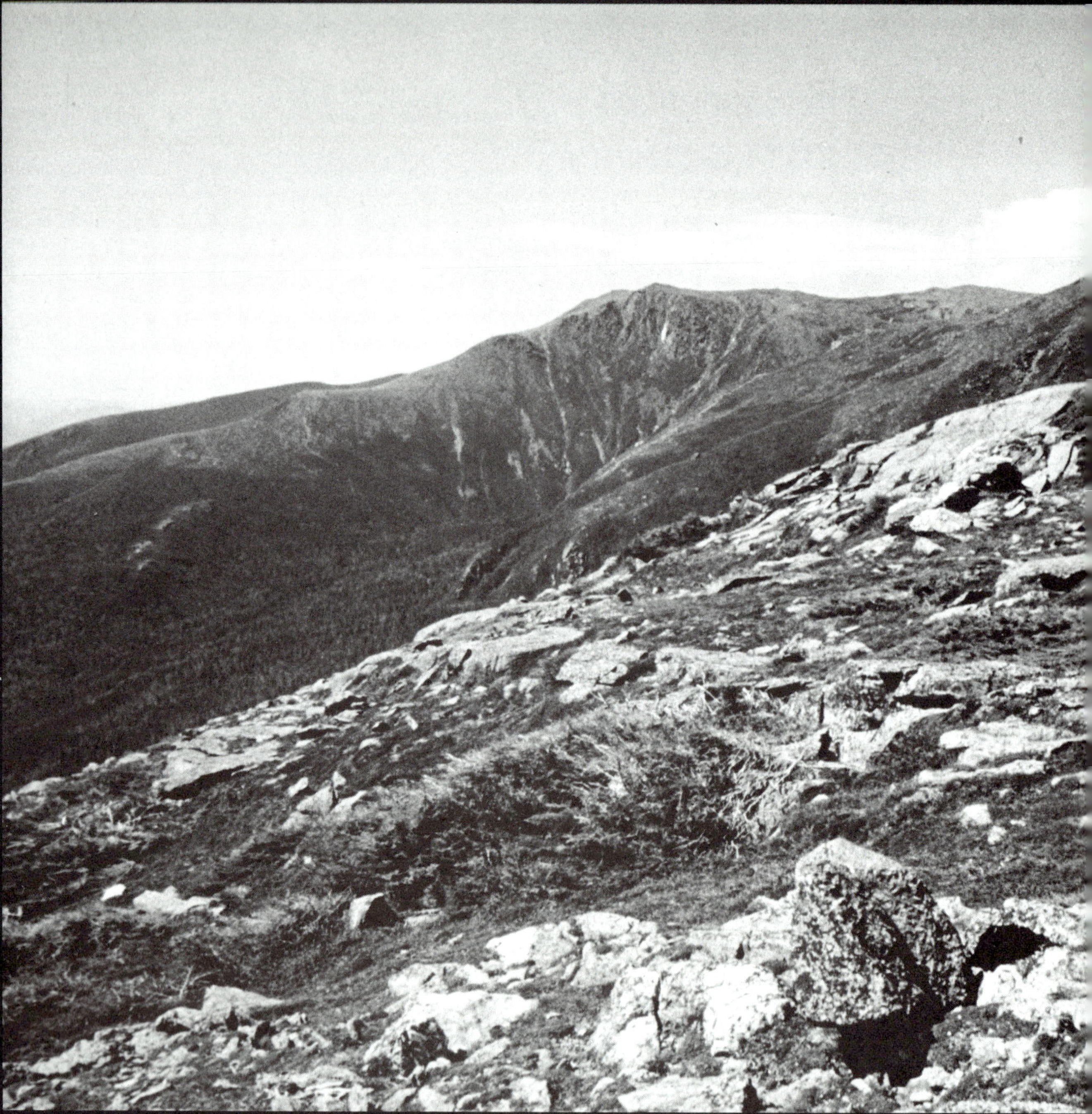

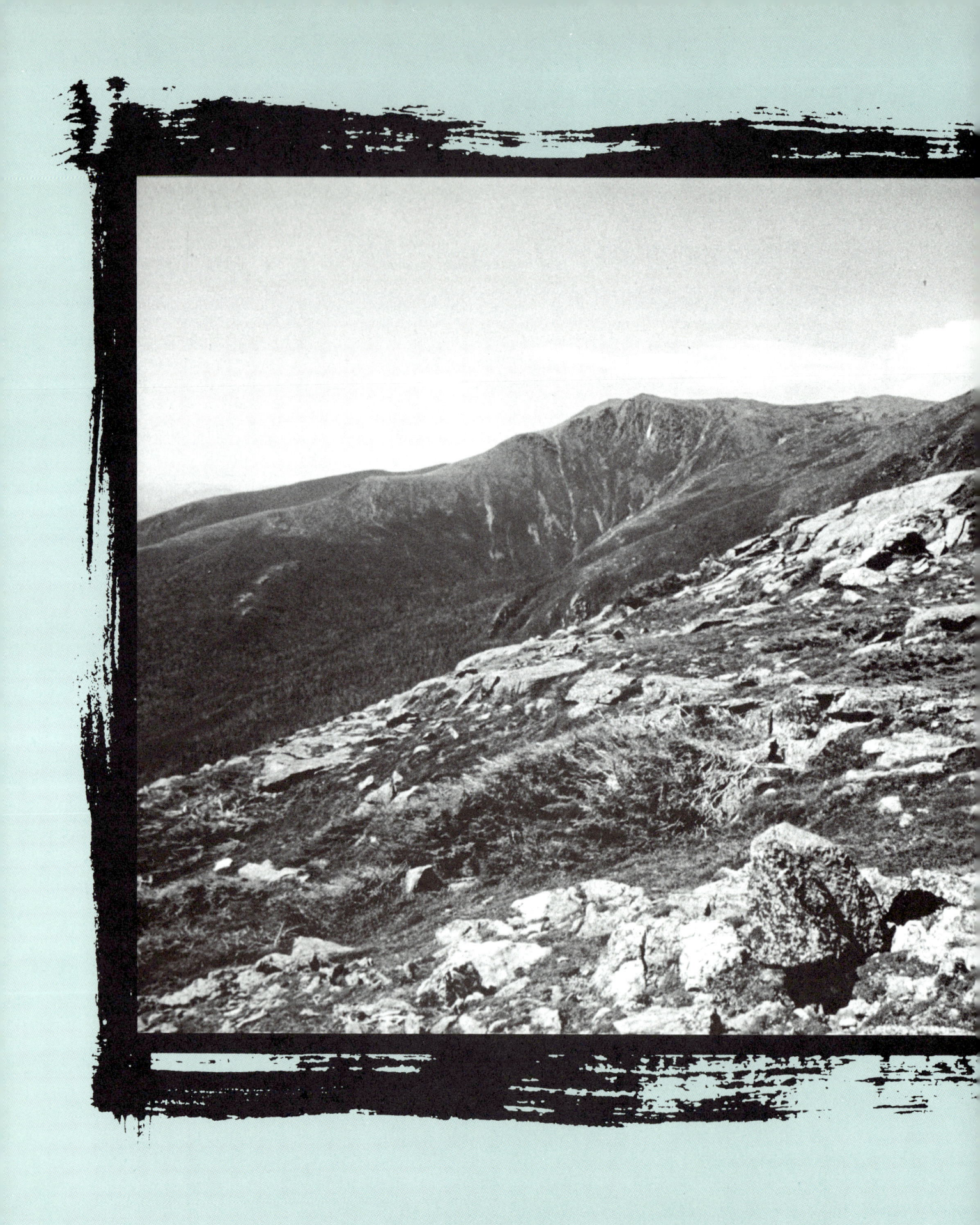

Part Three

People—Land Ethics—Global Sustainability

"This we know: the Earth does not belong to man, man belongs to the Earth. All things are connected like the blood that unites us all. Man did not weave the web of life, he is merely a strand of it. Whatever he does to the web, he does to himself."

Chief Seattle, 1852

Chapter 16

The Human Resource

- Introduction
- The Peopling of North America
- Population Dynamics
- Human Carrying Capacity
- Dealing with Population Increases
  - Birth Control
  - Family Planning
- Urbanization of the Human Population
  - Urban Growth
  - ZPG's Urban Stress Test
    - The Environmental Index of the UST
  - Urban Planning
  - Land Controls
- Sustainability
- A Global View
  - Biodiversity
- Ethics
  - Land Ethics
- Summary

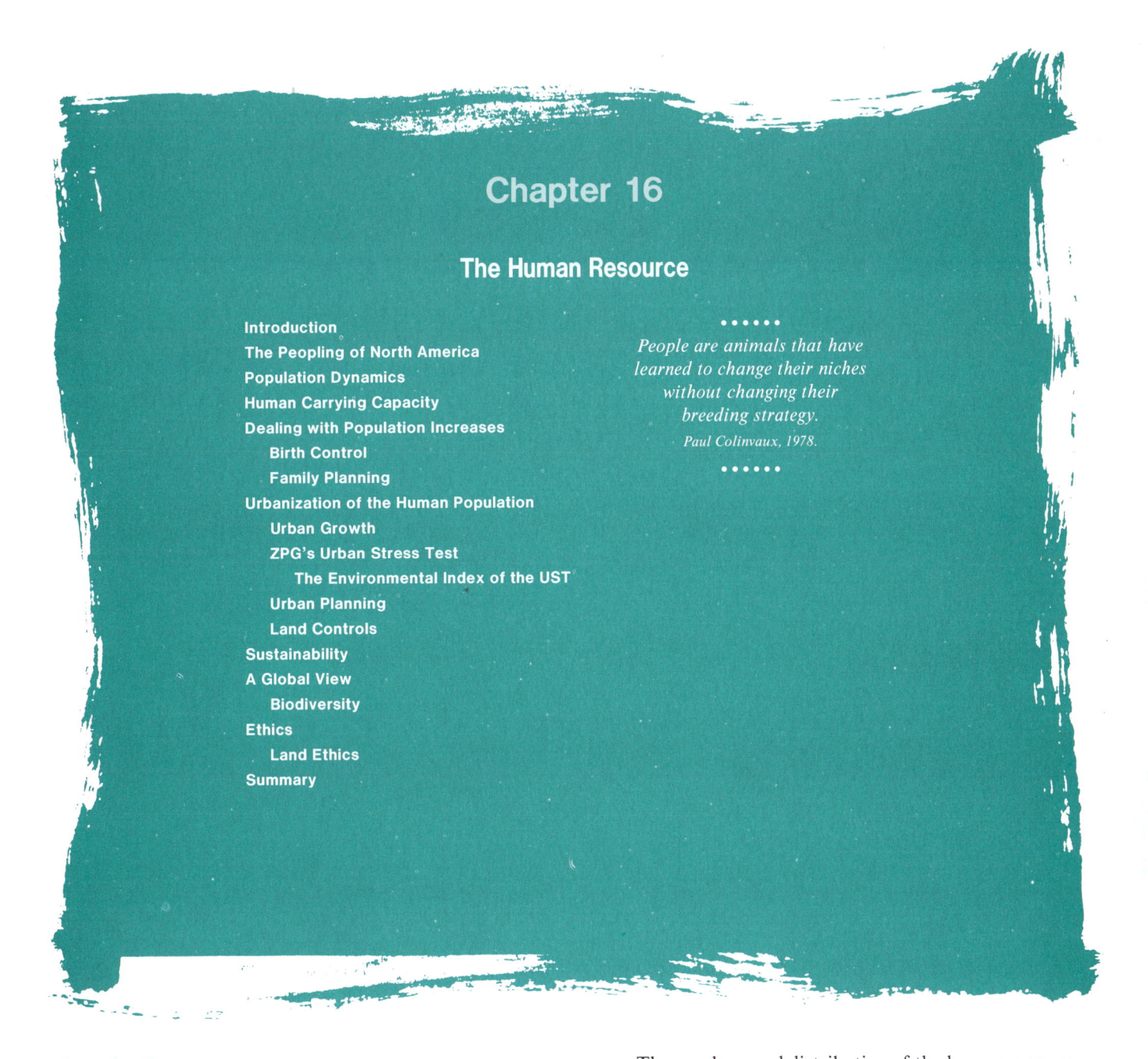

People are animals that have learned to change their niches without changing their breeding strategy.
Paul Colinvaux, 1978.

Introduction

People are a natural resource. In every society, people depend on other people for many things. In highly developed societies, this dependence is significantly greater than it is in more primitive societies. It is this **use** of other people for the acquisition of goods and services that makes people resources. We rely on the ingenuity and wisdom of others for improvement in our living conditions and for the solutions to society's problems.

The numbers and distribution of the human resource has changed drastically over the past 200 years. Figure 16.1 shows the geographic center of population in the United States as it moved westward from 1790 to the present. The trend is south and west, and this trend will continue to follow the old Highway 66 route (presently Interstate 44) through Missouri and on into Oklahoma, crossing the Oklahoma state line about the year 2025. The 1990 census showed the geographic center of population in the United States to be Steelville, Missouri. The pop-

Table 16.1
Population of North America vs. World in Millions

	1790 (est.)	1990 (est.)	2025 projection
Canada	0.34	26.5	33.3
Mexico	7.00	87.0	154.1
United States	3.90	249.6	311.9
World	900.00	5,300.0	8,200.0

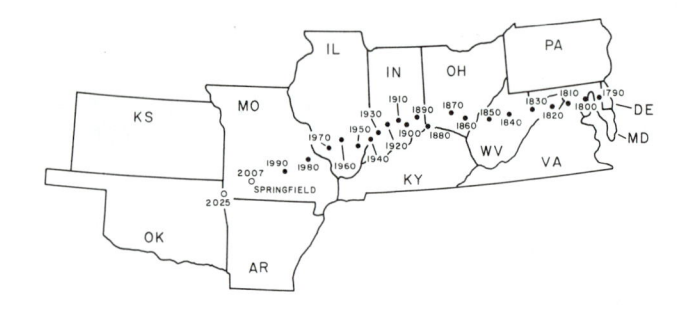

Figure 16.1 The geographic center of population in the United States from 1790 to 1990, with predictions to the year 2025.
Source: Data from the U.S. Bureau of the Census.
(*Cartographer:* Douglas Hemsath)

ulation size has also grown. Table 16.1 gives the population of Canada, Mexico, and the United States as a part of the world total. The population projections for the year 2025 are also given.

To understand the human resource population problem requires an examination of a number of statistical terms used by the demographers that study human populations. Projections of population increases range from pessimistic to optimistic. An examination of both schools of thought will be presented in this chapter.

The Peopling of North America

Exact dates for the peopling of North America are difficult to determine and range as far back as 30,000 years before present (ybp). Most researchers would agree that *Homo sapiens* moved into North America from Siberia across the Bering Sea (ice bridge) prior to 12,000 ybp. The people of Asia that moved down through North America are all believed to have descended from one African "Eve" who lived some 200,000 years ago. Migration of the Asian people southward and eastward are marked by identifiable artifacts called *Clovis points*. Figure 16.2 is a map of Clovis sites in North America. These first North American inhabitants were descended from late Pleistocene hunters who moved south through Canada about 12,000 ybp. This initial native human population has been added to by natural increases and immigration.

The human population has increased irregularly, in response to changing technologies, through time. Figure 16.3 is a graph that shows changes in human population in response to these technological advancements. Stone tools gave way to metal tools, which in turn led to modern agriculture. The present population jump corresponds to the industrial revolution. Population rate decreases are correlated with diseases (e.g., the plague), poor sanitation, and economic depression.

Human population dynamics were discussed in 1798 by the Reverend Thomas Malthus. In his book entitled *An Essay on the Principle of Population as it Affects the Future Improvement of Society,* he stated that population is limited by the means of subsistence, and population increases were the means of subsistence increase unless prevented by powerful preventative checks. Malthus wrote that human populations increase in a geometric ratio (1, 2, 4, 8, 16, 32, 64 . . .) and subsistence increases in an arithmetic ratio (1, 3, 5, 7, 9 . . .). Therefore, populations will eventually outsize their food supply. The most powerful preventative check is *moral restraint*. Celibacy until a couple can support a family, later marriage, and no children were parts of the Malthusian point of view that have been carried over into present-day family planning. But modern medical and chemical methods have taken the place of restraint in our society, which views recreational sex as more important than procreation.

Population Dynamics

Populations would remain stable in a geographic area if the number of persons born were equal to the number that died over the same time period and no one moved into or out of the area. *Zero population growth* (zpg) is the number of births required for a population to continue replacing themselves without increase. In highly developed countries like the United States and Canada, this rate is usually about 2.2 children per couple. It takes more than two to compensate for the couples who choose not to have children and for couples that are infertile.

Demographers use a fertility statistic called the *crude birthrate,* the number of births in a year, divided by the midyear population, and usually expressed as the number of births per thousand persons. The *crude death rate,* likewise, is a measure of the number of deaths per thousand persons. Crude death rate subtracted from crude birthrate gives the *natural increase* of a population. The crude birthrate for the United States is 16 per thousand and the crude death rate is 9 per thousand, giving a natural increase of 0.7%. The natural increase rate in Mexico is 2.5%, which results in a population doubling every 29 years.

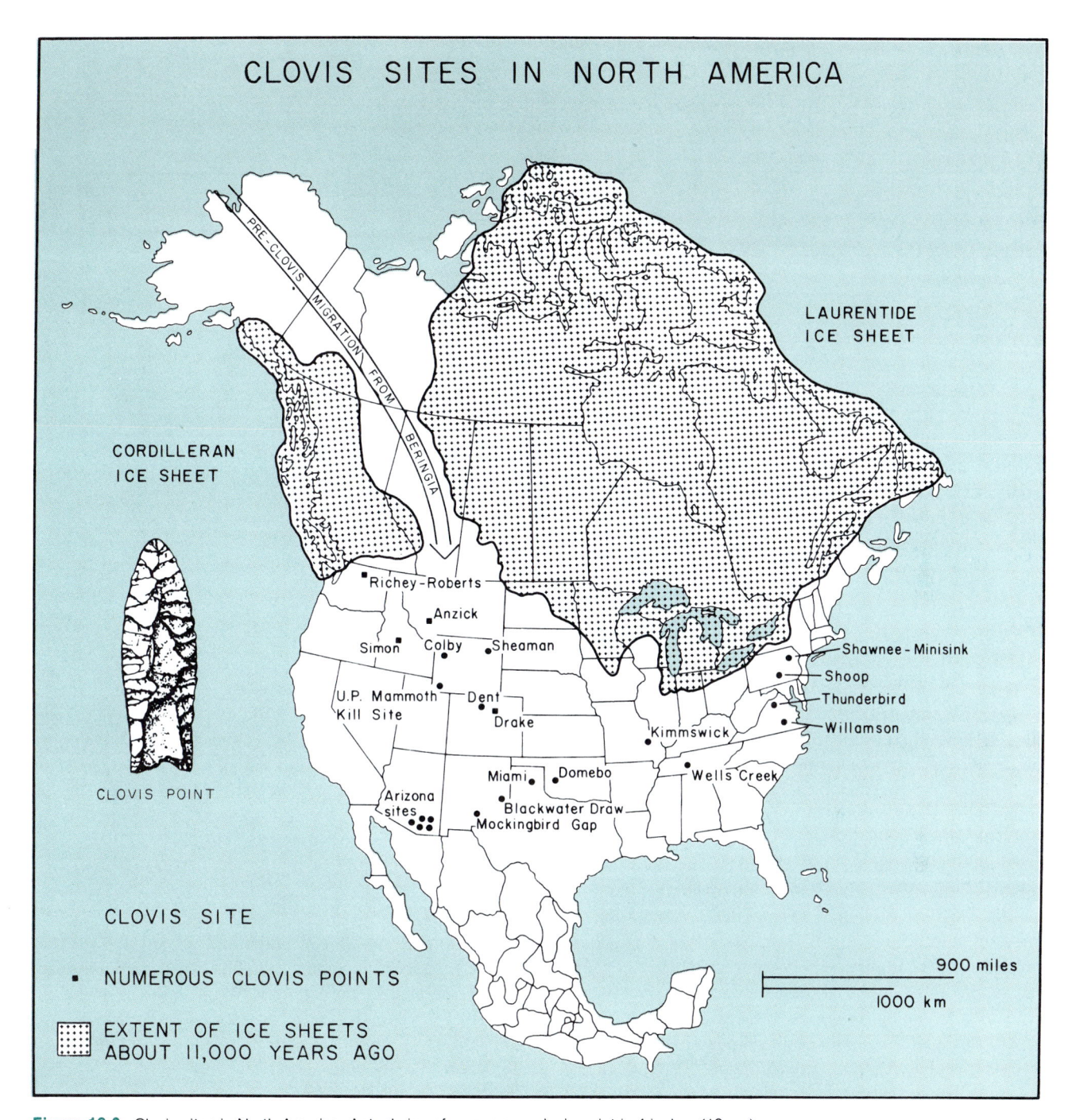

Figure 16.2 Clovis sites in North America. Actual size of an average clovis point is 4 inches (10 cm).
Source: Data from C. Vance Haynes.
(Cartographer: Douglas Hemsath)

The Human Resource

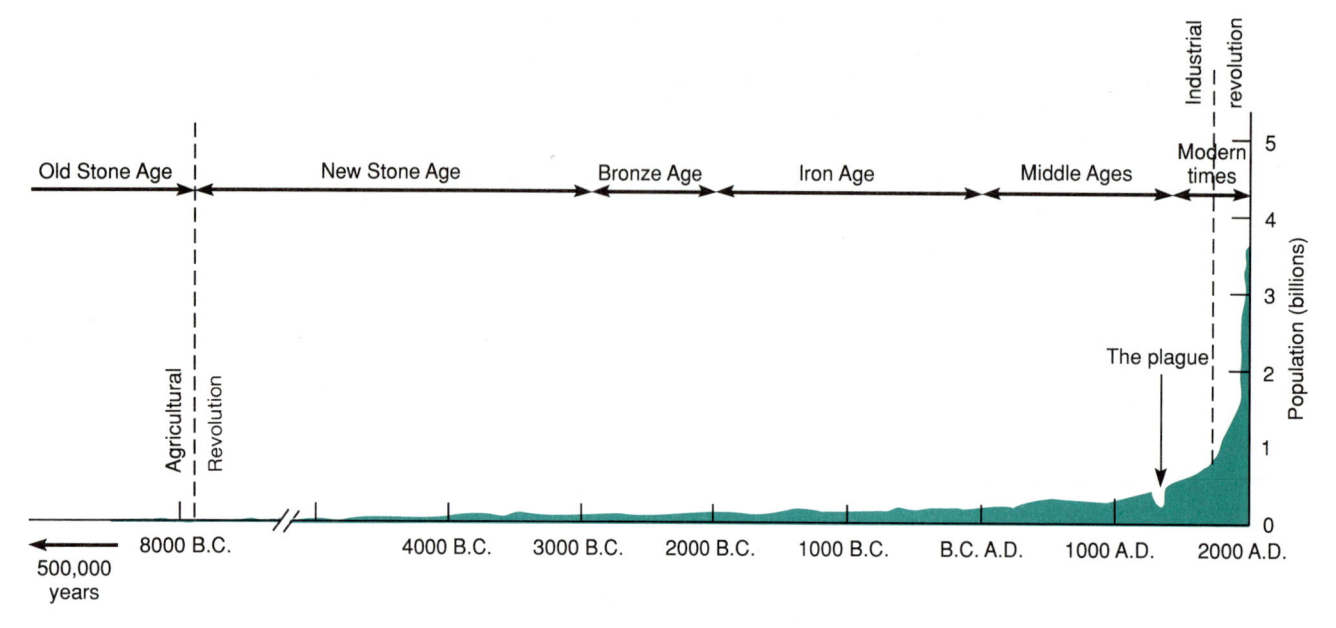

Figure 16.3 Human population increases related to technological advancements.
Source: Jean van der Taak, Carl Haub, and Elaine Murphy, "Our Population Predicament: A New Look," *Population Bulletin,* 34 (5):2. Reprinted by permission.

If natural increase were the only means of population increase in the United States, the population would double in about 100 years. However, immigration into the United States has accounted for 25% of the total population growth since 1820. The largest number of immigrants, both legal and illegal, enter the United States from Mexico. Immigration, along with natural increases, will cause the population of the United States to double in just 50 years.

Population dynamics are a function of age and sex. A woman's fertile years (between 15 and 44) determine the *fecundity* of a population. The total *fertility rate* is the number of children born to an average woman during her reproductive life. Figure 16.4 compares the age and sex distribution of the United States and Mexican populations by means of a population pyramid. Mexico has a natural increase rate of 2.5%, and 42% of its population is below 15 years of age (prereproductive). Even if fertility rates were to go down, the population would increase because of the increased numbers entering their reproductive years. The United States population pyramid shows the bulge of the baby boom (1950s births) entering their mid-life crisis years.

Another factor that affects population numbers is *life expectancy*. It is the average age a newborn infant can expect to attain in a given society, or in other words, average age at death. Declining mortality has been the primary cause of population growth during the past three hundred years. Better sanitation and improved foods are the major factors contributing to longer life expectancy. Even with modern medicine and our increased life expectancy, however, our *life span* (oldest age to which humans live) has not changed. Our bodies just wear out and cannot repair themselves for more than 116 years. The oldest documented human is a 116-year-old woman living in France. What effect would a life expectancy of 100 years have on our population? What effect would it have on society? A person would go to school until he was 20 years old, work for 45 years, and be retired for 35 years. Is that too long to be retired? Would societal changes have to be made? What changes would you suggest?

Human Carrying Capacity

The maximum number of individuals of any species that can be supported on a long-term basis by a particular ecosystem is its *carrying capacity*. What is the carrying capacity of the North American ecosystem for the human species? How many humans represent the equilibrium density of North America?

The United States and Canada represent the optimistic view with regard to population and Mexico represents the pessimistic view.

The United States and Canada represent the optimistic view, because highly industrialized countries utilize modern methods of birth control and/or limit family size by choice. Modern technology has brought growing prosperity to Anglo-America. The need and desire for large families no longer exists. Social reform, economics, and a concern for the environment have played a part in the reduction of family size. A near-zero population growth is an attainable and realistic goal within the next century for the United States and Canada. If the population growth levels off to near zero, and the maximum population reaches 400 million for the United States and Canada by

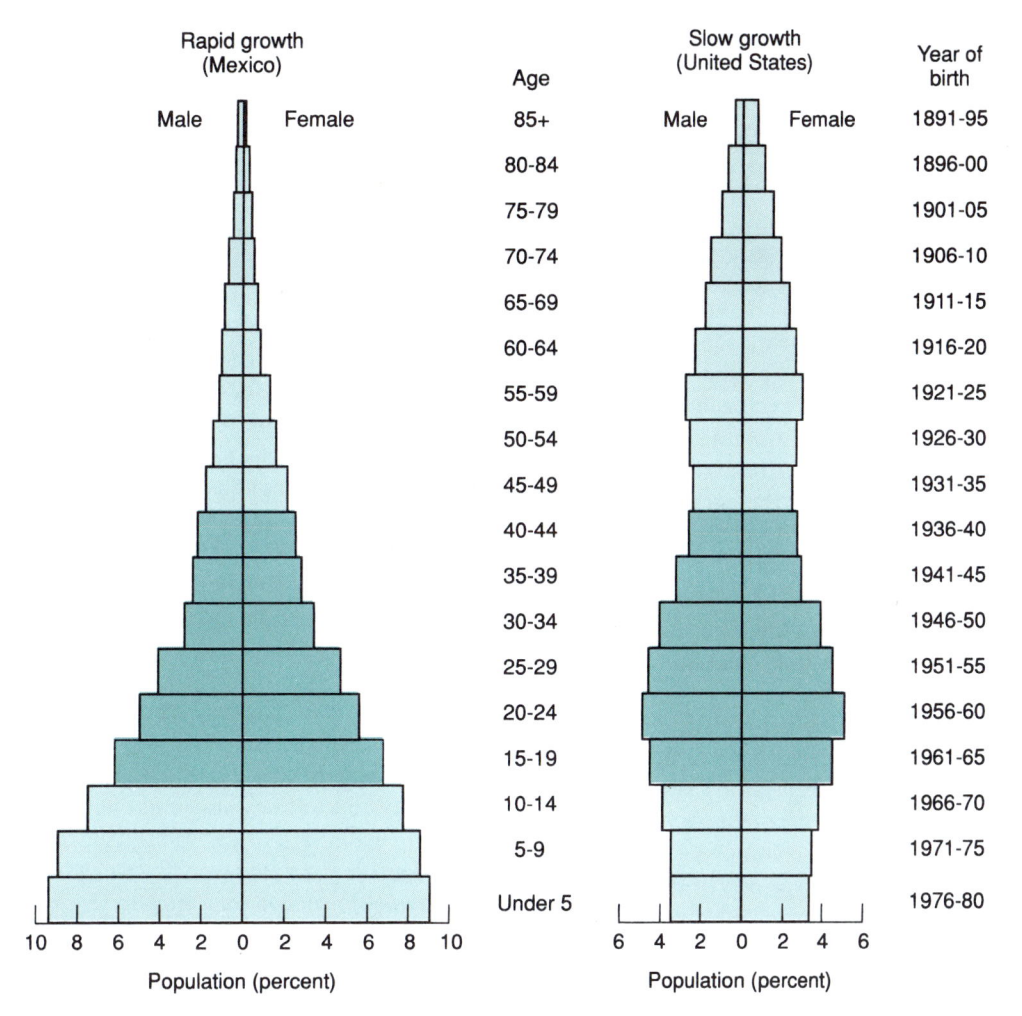

Figure 16.4 Human population by age and sex in Mexico (a rapidly growing country) and in the United States (a slowly growing country). Darker bars represent individuals in the reproductive age range.
Source: Arthur Haupt and Thomas T. Kane, *Population Handbook*, 2nd edition (Washington, DC: Population Reference Bureau, Inc., 1985), p. 14. Reprinted by permission.

2100, the demands for resources from the land will be well below its natural carrying capacity. This scenario also assumes no major climatic or natural disasters. We have no guarantees that catastrophe will not strike.

Mexico represents the pessimistic view because of their status as a *developing nation*. Developing countries have low per capita income, high birth and death rates, low levels of technology, and high natural population growth rates. The Mexico City metropolitan area had a population of approximately 21 million in 1990, the largest urban area in the world, and the urban population continues to grow by 750,000 per year (figure 16.5). Mexico City has been described as an ecological Hiroshima because it has been struck with a population bomb. At present growth rates, the population of Mexico will double in just 29 years. With this doubling, an excessive demand on the limited resources will cause the Malthusian principle to take over and starvation and disease will reduce the population. The original carrying capacity of Mexico

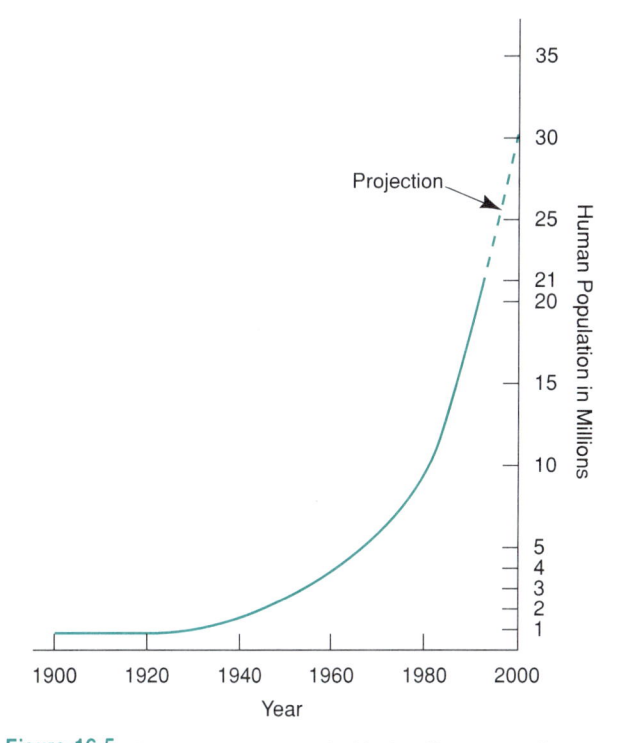

Figure 16.5 Human population in the Mexico City metropolitan area, 1900 to 1990, with projections to the year 2000.

The Human Resource   365

will have been reduced because of environmental degradation. Mexico will exceed the human carrying capacity before the year 2100, and the effects will be felt worldwide. The world will need to come to Mexico's aid to alleviate the problems caused by overpopulation.

Dealing with Population Increases

Because humans are at the top of the biotic pyramid, they control, to a large degree, what is below them in the world environment. They have no natural predators other than microorganisms, many of which have been conquered or controlled by modern medicine. As thinking animals, humans must limit their natural desire to reproduce their species so that they do not exceed the carrying capacity of planet earth. Methods of fertility control and family planning must become an adaptive trait in order to assure survival of the species, *Homo sapiens*. Many animal and bird species have learned, through the laws of adaptation, to limit their population size. Surely humans can do the same.

Family planning and methods of birth control are nothing new. Ancient cultures used abortion, celibacy, infanticide, and polygamy to control family size. Some of these practices are morally unacceptable today. Abortion has divided the United States into two opposing ideological camps, and the issue is a long way from being resolved. WorldWatch calls abortion a reflection of unmet family-planning needs. Religious beliefs and culture both play a big part in deciding what is and is not acceptable as a birth control method. Regardless of culture or religious beliefs, there are acceptable methods of birth control that can limit population growth and keep it within reasonable limits for the earth environment. The human species has the intelligence to solve the population problem. What is needed is the will and determination to do so! How can this determination be channeled to make things happen? Do we plan and work toward established goals, or do we, as individuals and as societies, tend generally to only **react** to crisis situations and tragedies?

Birth Control

Some methods of birth control have been available throughout human history. Avoidance of sex during fertile periods (*rhythm method*) and *celibacy* were proposed by Malthus in 1798. Usually mothers are infertile while breast-feeding their children, so nursing a baby for two or three years is a method of birth control and family planning. Medical science in recent years has developed many new and safe methods for controlling fertility.

Mechanical devices that prevent contact between sperm and egg such as *diaphragms, condoms,* and *cervical caps* are all common methods of birth control. Pharmaceutical compounds such as the *pill, spermicidal jelly,* and *vaginal foam* are also available. Surgical methods that prevent the release of egg or sperm are increasingly being used to control fertility. In males, *vasectomy,* the cutting of the sperm duct (*vas deferens*), is the preferred surgical method. In females, *tubal ligation, sterilization, implanting an intrauterine device* (IUD) and *abortion* are all surgical procedures in common use. New birth-control techniques that show promise include the *morning-after drug,* RU486. (It can be taken up to ten days after a missed period.) Implantation of a slow-release steroid drug called *Norplant,* inserted under the skin in the arm, holds much promise as a birth control method (figure 16.6). The match-stick-sized flexible implant releases progestin for up to five years and prevents embryo implant in the uterus. Studies show that Norplant is as effective as the pill and eliminates the constant awareness needed to remember to take the pill every day.

In 1988, the National Center for Health Statistics in the United States concluded a study showing that 18.5% of the female population of child-bearing age (15–44) used the pill as a birth-control device. They also found that 16.6% of the women had been sterilized, and 7% of the men had had a vasectomy. The majority of the women that had been sterilized were over 30 years old and wanted no more children. Studies have indicated that by age 30 about three-quarters of the women that have been married have had all the children they want. The remaining 10 to 15 years (fertile time past age 30), when it is physically possible to conceive, is a long time to risk pregnancy or take the pill. The highest rate of surgical sterilization, 32.5%, was among women 35 to 44 years of age. Only 1.6% of those 15 to 24 had undergone sterilization.

Family Planning

Economics, social change, and concern for the environment have all played a part in controlling family size and population in the United States and Canada. This, however, is not true in Mexico, where the dominantly Roman Catholic population has religious beliefs that are an obstacle to national family-planning efforts. The Mexican government must take a stand to encourage family planning and fertility control. Education is a key ingredient in any family-planning program. Classes on contraceptive techniques for both women and men, so they can make intelligent decisions in tune with their moral convictions about family size and spacing, are an important starting point for family-planning programs. Public media campaigns to encourage a change in attitude toward birth control and family planning can contribute to social change. Public acceptability of fertility control and smaller family size are important first steps toward population control. Distribution of free birth control materials is another government program that has been tried with success. Financial incentives to limit family size is yet another method governments can use to reduce population growth rates.

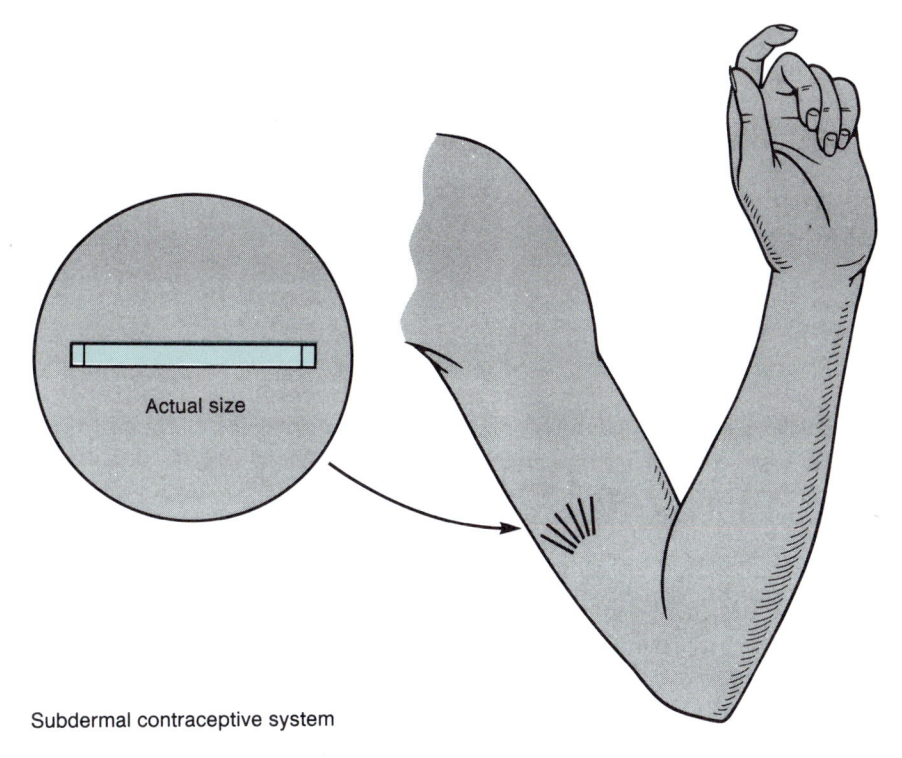

Figure 16.6 Norplant birth control implantation. Six flexible, match-sized capsules are implanted under the skin in the woman's arm. They release a slow but steady supply of birth control hormones over about five years, or they can be removed before then if the woman wants to become pregnant. Some of the contraceptive options available and their first year failure rate include: vasectomy—0.1%; Norplant—0.2%; sterilization—0.2%; oral contraceptive—1–6%; IUD—1–2%; spermicides—10–20%; contraceptive sponges—10–20%; condom—14–16%; diaphragm—14–16%; natural family planning—14–16%.
From William P. Cunningham and Barbara Woodworth Saigo, *Environmental Science: A Global Concern.* Copyright © 1990 Wm. C. Brown Publishers, Dubuque, Iowa. All Rights Reserved. Reprinted by permission.

No other area of conservation or resource management involves a more difficult ethical question than human population control. The right to reproduce oneself is an adaptive trait of every level of the biotic pyramid, including the top. Optimists believe that increases in technology will extend the carrying capacity of the Earth and that rising prosperity will then limit population growth without intervention. This scenario is possible in Mexico only after the Malthusian principle applies itself and takes its toll through starvation, disease, and environmental degradation.

Urbanization of the Human Population

Many of the environmental problems created by the human population are compounded because humans tend to urbanize. Concentrations of people into a restricted geographic space create problems of waste concentration and degradation of natural environmental resources such as air and water. Early humans claimed the amount of space they needed to live off of the land. Humans in hostile environments claimed larger territories and sometimes moved with the seasons to provide a living for their families. Today, most people live in cities or urban areas and by the year 2000 it is predicted that 80% to 90% of the population will live in an urban environment. Cities and the problems of urbanization are also problems for conservation and resource management because cities are point sources of pollution for the surrounding area.

Demographers interested in studying the human resource and population problems turn to the United States Census Bureau (USCB) for data. The USCB collects data on population size and composition in 10-year cycles and publishes these data in a variety of formats. To interpret the data requires an understanding of the definitions of terms that are used to describe urban places. Major concentrations of humans in a restricted geographic space is the subject matter for the urban resources planner.

The United States Census Bureau considers any incorporated community to be a *city,* but a city must have at least 2,500 residents to be classified as *urban.* In most urban areas in North America, the majority of the people are not employed in natural-resource-based jobs. However, many rural residents are employed in agriculture, forestry, or other natural-resource-based activities. The Census Bureau also recognizes urban conglomerations with a central city of at least 50,000 people and a surrounding urban region of at least 100,000 inhabitants as a *Standard Metropolitan Statistical Area* (SMSA) (figure 16.7). The SMSA must have strong economic and social ties to the

Figure 16.7 Four examples of Standard Metropolitan Statistical Areas (SMSAs) in the United States. (a) Seattle, Washington. (b) St. Louis, Missouri. (c) Memphis, Tennessee. (d) New York, New York.
(*Photo:* David A. Castillon)

central city. If two or more population centers merge geographically and have more than 1,000,000 inhabitants, the Census Bureau classifies the area as a *conurbation* and calls it a *Consolidated Metropolitan Statistical Area* (CMSA). When an urban area merges to form an almost continuous chain of cities with a population of more than ten million persons, then it is considered to be a *megalopolis*. The urban area from Boston to Washington D.C. is a megalopolis called Bos-Wash (1990 population about 36 million). Thus, data for the urban resources planner are available in a variety of formats because the USCB organizes its information on the basis of these and other defined statistical areas.

Mexico City is the largest city in the world with a 1990 population estimated at more than 21 million people. The function of a city is to provide people with housing, employment, education, recreation, social interaction, and other cultural services. How can a city of 21 million, that is adding 750,000 new people per year, continue to provide the necessities of life? The answer is they cannot and the results are tragic. The environmental degradation caused by overpopulation is evident in the smog-filled air, in the filthy water, in the accumulation of waste, and in the health of the land. The human degradation is also evident in the substandard housing, lack of jobs, poor or no health care, noise pollution, congestion, and lack of social services (figure 16.8). Things will get worse before they get better

368 People—Land Ethics—Global Sustainability

Figure 16.8A A squatter settlement with 35,000 residents built on a landfill on the edge of Mexico City.
(*Photo:* Russell Gerlach)

Figure 16.8B Squatter settlement built on a highway right-of-way in Mexico City before the highway construction began.
(*Photo:* Russell Gerlach)

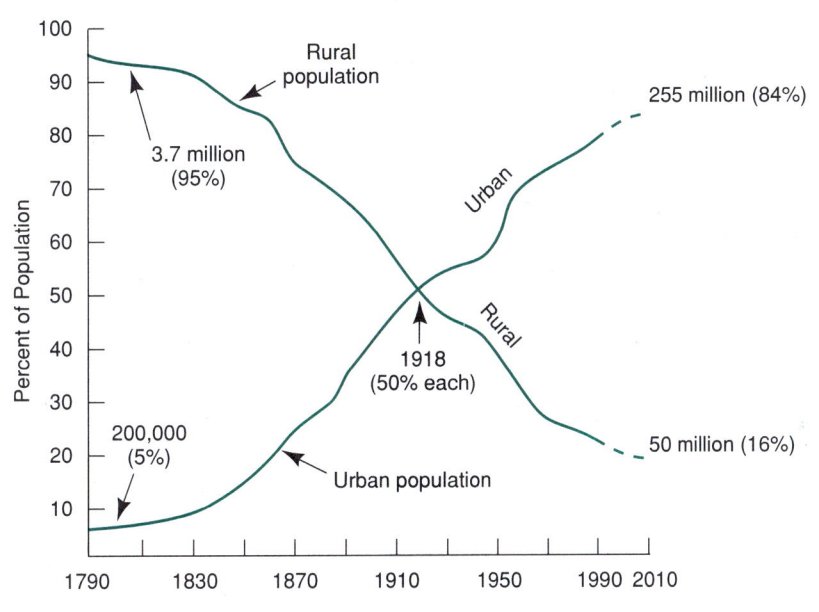

Figure 16.9A Rural-to-urban human population shift in the United States between 1790 and 1990, with projections to 2010.
Source: U.S. Bureau of the Census.

for Mexico City. An examination of the growth of urban areas and their problems may help to keep other cities from experiencing the same problems confronting Mexico City, but the bottom line is an effective population control program.

Urban Growth

Cities grow by natural increase and by immigration. Natural increase occurs when the birthrate exceeds the death rate. Cities have contributed to natural increase because they provide better sanitation, better food supplies, better medical facilities, and, therefore, greater longevity for its people. Immigration to the city occurs when the rural area can no longer provide jobs, because of changes in agriculture, or provide housing or other basic necessities. Figure 16.9 illustrates the rural-to-urban shift that has

Figure 16.9B Urban expansion is claiming more and more rural acres. A subdivision in Iowa expands into the neighboring farmland.
(*Photo:* David A. Castillon)

The Human Resource

Table 16.2
Urban Stress Test Results

The Winners!
Of the 192 cities surveyed, the 22 cities which score the highest marks (2.3 or lower overall) are scattered from California to Connecticut, but the majority are located in the Midwest. Most are relatively small cities, with an average population of 115,881 and an average density of 3,679 people per square mile. The cities are characterized by a lack of crowding, low crime rates, strong community economics and low levels of hazardous waste.

	Population	Overall Score
Cedar Rapids, IA	108,370	1.6
Madison, WI	175,830	1.7
Ann Arbor, MI	107,800	1.8
Lincoln, NE	183,050	1.8
Fargo, ND*	68,020	1.9
Livonia, MI	100,540	1.9
Concord, CA	105,980	2.0
Alexandria, VA	107,800	2.1
Eugene, OR	105,410	2.1
Roanoke, VA	101,900	2.1
Worcester, MA	157,770	2.1
Berkeley, CA	104,110	2.2
Billings, MT*	80,310	2.2
Fremont, Ca	153,580	2.2
Stamford, Ct	101,080	2.2
Topeka, KS	118,580	2.2
Boise, ID	108,390	2.3
Cheyenne, WY*	53,960	2.3
Hampton, VA	126,000	2.3
Manchester, NH*	97,281	2.3
Sioux Falls, SD*	97,550	2.3
Yonkers, NY	186,080	2.3

The Losers!
The 20 cities receiving the worst marks have overall scores of 3.8 and above. Almost one-half of the cities on this list are located in California and Texas. Most of the cities have either large populations or are located near a large metropolitan area. The average population size is 1,154,229 and the average density is 8,228 people per square mile—that's more than twice the density of our winning cities. Many of the cities are characterized by large population changes, overcrowding, high crime rates and unemployment. Their environmental indicators, particularly for hazardous waste levels and water, warn of increased risk.

	Population	Overall Score
Gary, IN	136,790	4.2
Baltimore, MD*	752,800	4.1
Chicago, IL	3,009,530	4.1
Houston, TX	1,728,910	4.1
Jersey City, NJ	219,480	4.1
Pomonoa, CA	115,540	4.1
El Paso, TX	491,800	4.0
Cleveland, OH	535,830	3.9
Fort Worth, TX	429,550	3.9
Inglewood, CA	102,550	3.9
Los Angeles, CA	3,259,340	3.9
St. Louis, MO	426,300	3.9
Detroit, MI	1,086,220	3.8
Miami, FL	373,940	3.8
Newark, NJ	316,240	3.8
New York, NY	7,262,700	3.8
Pasadena, TX	118,050	3.8
Philadelphia, PA	1,642,900	3.8
Phoenix, AZ	894,070	3.8
Stockton, CA	183,430	3.8

*City has a population of less than 100,000, but was included in the survey because it is the largest city in the state.
Zero Population Growth, 1400 16th Street, N.W., #320, Washington, D.C. Reprinted by permission.

taken place in the United States during the past 200 years. Lack of jobs and housing in the rural area are not the only reasons for moving to the city. The chances for upward social and economic mobility are highly attractive attributes for the rural citizen looking for the excitement and glamour that a city can provide. Regardless of reason, cities are the preferred area of habitation for three-fourths of the inhabitants of the United States. Examination of the problems of urban areas could provide some insights for future city development. City and urban planning that attempts to solve the problems of present-day population centers is a necessity for healthful urban habitation.

ZPG's Urban Stress Test

Zero Population Growth, (ZPG) in Washington D.C., is a nonprofit organization founded in 1968 to achieve a sustainable balance of population, environment, and resources. ZPG has designed an Urban Stress Test (UST) to examine how cities are coping with the environmental, economic, and social stresses that result from population growth. The test used eleven interrelated criteria to survey 192 cities in the United States. The criteria include population change, crowding, education, violent crime, births, community economics, individual economics, hazardous wastes, sewage, and water and air quality. All of these criteria can be considered major urban problems. An examination of the results of this test can shed some light on urban planning for the future. Table 16.2 lists the winners and the losers in the second UST.

The data from the second **Urban Stress Test** (1988) definitely indicate that bigger isn't necessarily better. ZPG's 22 best cities all have populations less than 200,000. Smaller size cities have less crowding, lower crime rates, and a generally healthier, better educated, and more stable population. The data indicate that a very strong correlation exists between city population size and urban stress (figure 16.10 and table 16.3).

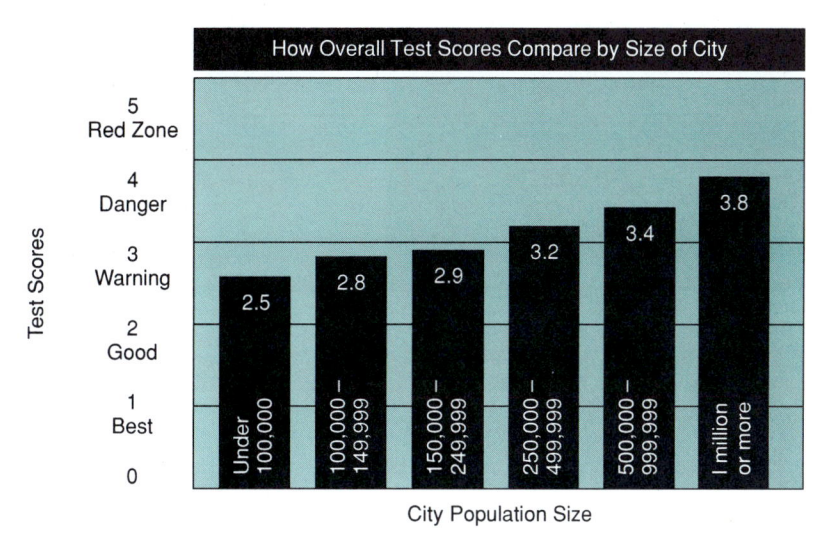

Figure 16.10 Urban human population size versus average test score in the second UST.
Zero Population Growth, 1400 16th Street, N.W., #320, Washington, DC. Reprinted by permission.

Table 16.3

Best Five Cities in Each Population Category on the Second UST

Best Cities (Population over 500,000)

	Overall Score
Columbus, OH	2.6
San Francisco, CA	2.8
Indianapolis, IN	3.0
Boston, MA	3.1
Denver, CO	3.1

(Worst = Baltimore, Chicago, and Houston with scores of 4.1)

Best Cities (Population 250,000–500,000)

	Overall Score
Virginia Beach, VA	2.4
Colorado Springs, CO	2.5
Nashville/Davidson, TN	2.5
Omaha, NE	2.5
Wichita, KS	2.5

(Worst = El Paso, TX with a score of 4.0)

Best Cities (Population 150,000–249,999)

	Overall Score
Madison, WI	1.7
Lincoln, NE	1.8
Worcester, MA	2.1
Fremont, CA	2.2
Yonkers, NY	2.3

(Worst = Jersey City, NJ with a score of 4.1)

Best Cities (Population under 150,000)

	Overall Score
Cedar Rapids, IA	1.6
Ann Arbor, MI	1.8
Fargo, ND	1.9
Livonia, MI	1.9
Concord, CA	2.0

(Worst = Gary, IN with a score of 4.2)

Zero Population Growth, 1400 16th Street, N.W., #320, Washington, D.C. Reprinted by permission.

The Environmental Index of the UST

Air quality, hazardous waste, water, and sewage are the criteria used to establish an environmental index for cities rated by the second UST. Table 16.4 lists the 19 cities who scored best on the environmental index and the 13 cities that received the poorest rating. The best cities environmentally have an average population of 121,123, whereas the poorest have an average population of 785,725. Figure 16.11 illustrates the correlation between the UST environmental index and the population size of the city. The data indicate that the larger the population of the urban area, the poorer the environmental index. Population size and density are key variables to consider in urban planning.

Data from the second UST are valuable information for the urban planners as they plan for the future of an ever-increasing urban population. Cities with comfortable, healthful, environmentally safe human habitats are a requirement for 21st century sustainable living.

Urban Planning

Ian McHarg (1969) wrote a book entitled *Design With Nature*. In this book he developed the theme that humans could live in harmony with the natural environment, even in an urban setting. By carefully planning the location, distribution, and density of housing and services, a person could live as harmoniously in an altered natural setting as a deer could live in an Oak-Hickory forest. One of his model planned communities was the Valleys region northwest of Baltimore, Maryland (figure 16.12). The inevitable development of this beautiful natural area led

Table 16.4
The Environmental Index

The Urban Stress Test includes four environmental indicators: air quality, hazardous waste, water, and sewage. Environmental damage often has far-reaching, long-term, and irreversible impacts. The following is a list of the cities that did best and worst overall on the environmental portion of the test.

Environmental Best Cities	Density pop/sq mi	Environmental Index	Worst Cities	Density pop/sq mi	Environmental Index
Abilene, TX	1,170	1.8	Phoenix, AZ	2,310	5.0
Roanoke, VA	2,360	1.8	Salt Lake City, UT	1,730	4.8
Winston-Salem, NC	2,120	1.8	Houston, TX	2,990	4.5
Berkeley, CA	9,550	2.0	Jersey City, NJ	16,630	4.5
Billings, MT	2,640	2.0	Philadelphia, PA	12,080	4.5
Brownsville, TX	3,530	2.0	Baltimore, MD	9,370	4.3
Chesapeake, VA	400	2.0	Honolulu, HI	4,280	4.3
Colo. Springs, CO	2,010	2.0	Los Angeles, CA	7,000	4.3
Concord, CA	3,620	2.0	Louisville, KY	4,690	4.3
Eugene, OR	3,000	2.0	Pasadena, TX	3,080	4.3
Evansville, IN	3,460	2.0	Seattle, WA	5,820	4.3
Fargo, ND	2,550	2.0	Tacoma, WA	3,330	4.3
Hampton, VA	2,460	2.0	Tempe, AZ	3,540	4.3
Macon, GA	2,380	2.0			
Peoria, IL	2,620	2.0			
Pueblo, CO	3,040	2.0			
Springfield, IL	2,460	2.0			
Syracuse, NY	6,750	2.0			
Tallahassee, FL	2,040	2.0			

Zero Population Growth, 1400 16th Street, N.W., #320, Washington, D.C. Reprinted by permission.

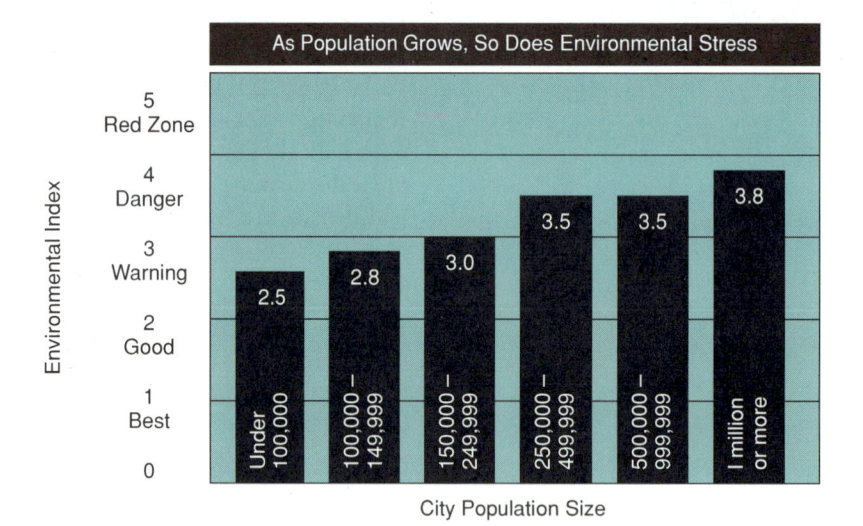

Figure 16.11 Urban human population size versus environmental index in the second UST.
Zero Population Growth, 1400 16th Street, N.W., #320, Washington, DC. Reprinted by permission.

As Population Grows, So Does Environmental Stress

City Population Size	Environmental Index
Under 100,000	2.5
100,000–149,999	2.8
150,000–249,999	3.0
250,000–499,999	3.5
500,000–999,999	3.5
1 million or more	3.8

(Index scale: 5 Red Zone, 4 Danger, 3 Warning, 2 Good, 1 Best)

McHarg and his associates to develop a plan for controlled growth. The proposition for the "Plan for the Valleys" included the following:

- The area is beautiful and vulnerable;
- Development is inevitable and must be accommodated;
- Uncontrolled growth is inevitably destructive;
- Development must conform to regional goals;
- Observance of conservation principles can avert destruction and ensure enhancement;
- The area can absorb all prospective growth without despoliation;
- Planned growth is more desirable than uncontrolled growth, and more profitable;
- Public and private powers can be joined in partnership in a process to realize the plan.

Unforested Plateau Development

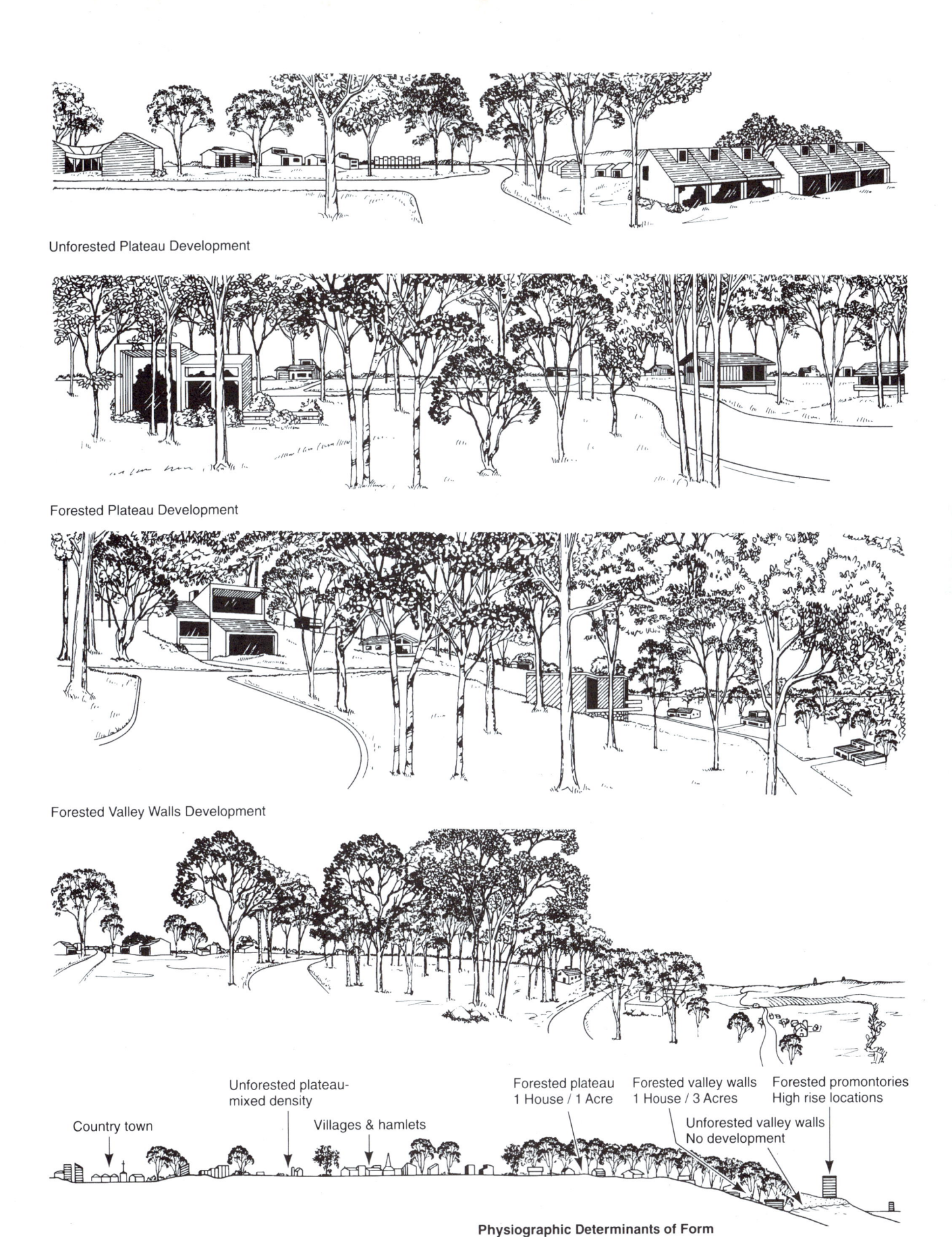

Forested Plateau Development

Forested Valley Walls Development

| Country town | Unforested plateau–mixed density | Villages & hamlets | Forested plateau 1 House / 1 Acre | Forested valley walls 1 House / 3 Acres | Unforested valley walls No development | Forested promontories High rise locations |

Physiographic Determinants of Form

Figure 16.12 Plan for the Valleys incorporated physical variables into the development design.
Source: Ian L. McHarg, *Plan for the Valleys.* Copyright © Wallace-McHarg Associates, Philadelphia, PA.

The Valley's area today is proof that designing with nature is possible and profitable.

Urban planners know that they can build new cities with fewer problems than the old cities. People that can afford to move to these new cities find them the answer to a pleasant urban habitation. The problem facing city planners is what to do with the old cities such as Chicago, Illinois, or Jersey City, New Jersey, that rate as two of the worst urban areas in the United States on the second UST. Population density seems to be a key variable. Jersey City has 16,630 persons per square mile and Chicago has 13,190. Cedar Rapids, Iowa, the city that rated best on the second UST, has a density of 1,970. Low density is no guarantee for a less stressful urban environment, but reducing density could be a starting point for improving quality of life in the urban centers. Reductions in density would also improve many of the remaining categories considered to be urban problems.

There are no quick fixes for our cities' problems, but overall test scores on the second UST strongly correlated with city size (figures 16.10 and 16.11). Population control is the key variable. Every ecosystem has a carrying capacity for individual members of the community; every city also has a carrying capacity for humans. When that capacity is exceeded, the system is no longer in equilibrium. It's unfortunate that humans can't be like the Snowy Owl and reduce clutch size during low lemming years, or like the Jaeger who does not breed when the food supply is low (chapter 1). Establishing a carrying capacity for each city could be a starting point for urban planners. Working toward reducing city size by migration out of or improving conditions within a city to increase carrying capacity would help reduce urban stress and also improve quality of life for urban dwellers.

Land Controls

City and county planning and land-use controls must become a part of every government's design for the future. As Mark Twain once said, "God's not making any new land these days." What is here is all we're going to get. Best use, dictated by the physical variables of the natural environment, should prevail. *Zoning* and *comprehensive long-range planning* are the most important tools of the city planner and resource manager (figure 16.13). *Zoning* is the practice of setting aside an area for a particular use. Table 16.5 is a list of zoning designations in common use today by communities that have planning and zoning ordinances. Zoning will improve and protect urban and suburban areas by preventing conflicting land uses from being adjacent to one another and also by reserving open space for the whole community.

Many people feel that zoning takes away the freedom to do with their land what they want. But these same people would be the ones to scream first and loudest if a decision were made to place a hazardous waste disposal site adjacent to their land. The biggest single problem for Oxford Energy, when they decided to build a tire-burning resource/recovery facility in the New England area, was getting permission to use the land for that purpose (chapter 15). Zoning can be too restrictive or too lenient. Neither case promotes the common good. Zoning ordinances that are too strict can stifle imagination and creativity. An attractive city needs both attributes. Zoning ordinances that are not restrictive will not protect the community from disadvantageous land uses. Zoning can and should protect **environmental values** and **property values.**

Table 16.5
Common Zoning Districts

Category	Use Allowed
Residential	
R-1	One-family houses
R-2	One- and two-family houses
R-3	Low-density multiple family townhouses
R-4	Medium-density multiple-family apartment buildings
R-5	High-density multiple-family apartment buildings
Business— Commercial	
C-1	Limited business and office buildings
C-2	Retail business
Industry— Manufacturing	
M-1	Light industry and manufacturing
M-2	Heavy industry
Special Purpose	
P-1	Public land, schools, parks
P-1/R-1	Present public, if reused R-1
P-1/C-1	Present public, if reused C-1
PUD	Planned Unit Development (multiple categories)
Agriculture	
A-1	Cropland
A-2	Pasture
A-3	Forest
A-4	Open Space Recreation

Land-use controls can be used to regulate urban growth. City utilities, such as water and sewer service, street development, and electric and gas service, can be used to dictate direction of growth and development. Boulder, Colorado, protected itself from the Denver sprawl by establishing a greenbelt between itself and Denver. This greenbelt zone cannot have water or sewer service and, therefore, development is restricted. Cities can require builders to leave a percentage of their subdivision as open space. In this way, open land is left for the entire community to enjoy.

Not a year goes by without a report on the evening news of flooding and the millions of dollars of property damage caused by flooding. Land-use controls could help to prevent this waste and destruction. The taxpayer foots

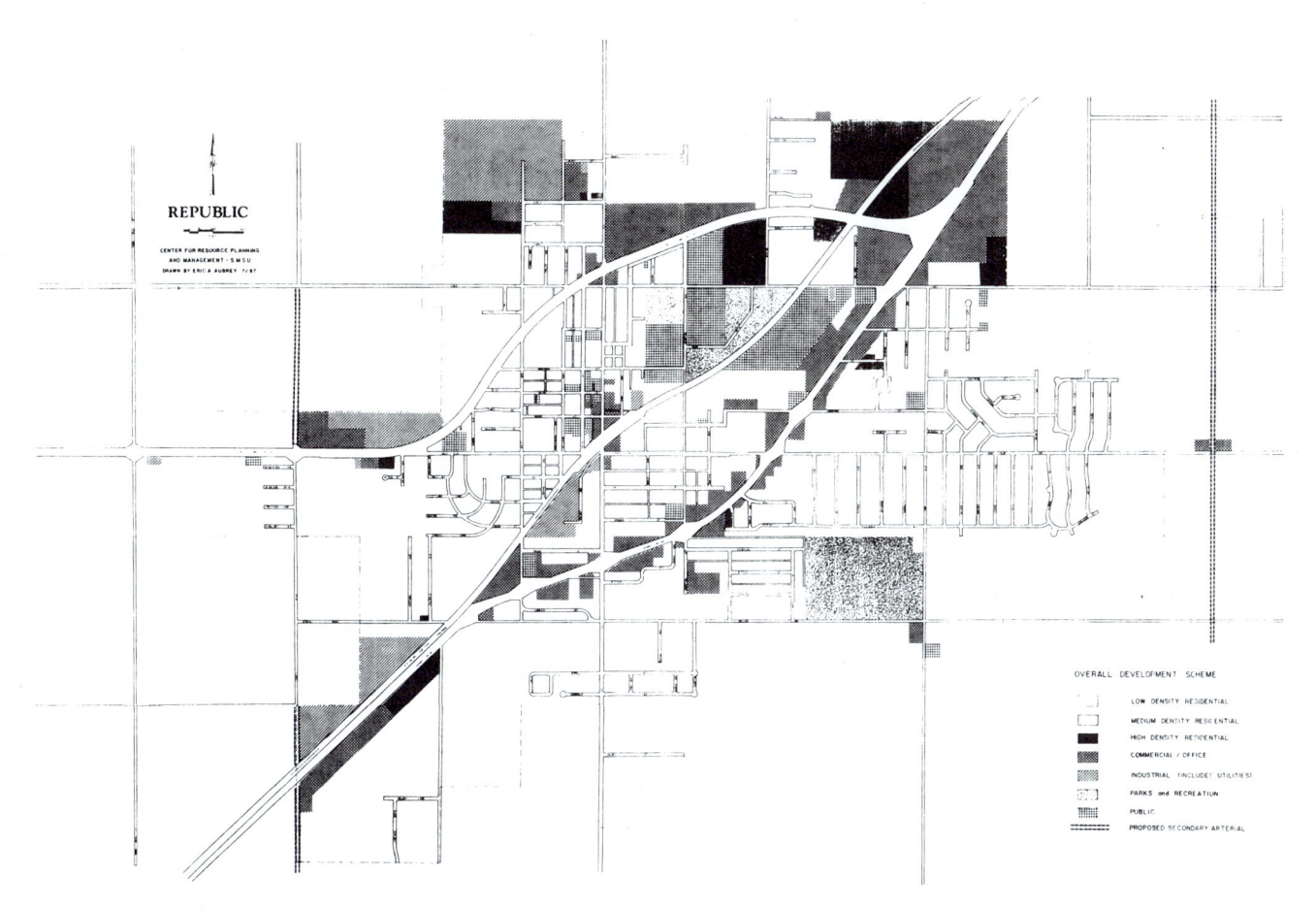

Figure 16.13 Comprehensive development plan for Republic, Missouri, 1988.
Source: Center for Resource Planning and Management, Southwest Missouri State University.

the bill in low-cost loans and disaster relief. Land-use controls should restrict development in flood-prone areas. The hundred-year floodplain of every river should not be used for building. If a person choose to do so, they should be made aware that no insurance or government assistance will be provided if they are flooded out. Banks would be less likely to loan money for building projects in flood-prone areas if there's a chance they may not get their money back after a flood. The same is true for coastal areas where flooding caused by winds, waves, and hurricanes is possible.

Steeply sloping and highly erodable land not only should not be built on, it shouldn't be plowed and farmed. The Farm Bill wants this land put in the Conservation Reserve Program (CRP), and planted in grasses to prevent erosion. Prime agricultural land as classified by the Soil Conservation Service (SCS) should be zoned for agricultural uses. Regional planners suggest that development on any land zoned as agriculture would be restricted to one house per 25 acres (10 hectares).

Marshes, wetland, and aquifer recharge zones should have land-use controls that limit development to open space uses. The Swampbuster provision of the Farm Bill does not want any existing wetlands drained for agricultural uses. Wetlands should be left for wildlife and waterfowl. Aquifer recharge areas should be restricted from use for septic tanks, pesticides, fertilizers, dumping, and any other activity that could contaminate the groundwater supply. Some marshes are being re-created in urban areas to control flooding, improve water quality and drainage, and provide a space for wildlife in the urban environment.

Land-use controls are a necessity in our urban, suburban, and rural landscapes. The loss of freedom created by restrictions on land use is no longer a valid argument for no land-use control. Chaplin B. Barnes gives a list of ten **Land-Use Ethic** prescriptions that are appropriate to consider. If every landowner would subscribe to these *you oughts,* the health of the land would be assured.

1. *You ought* to consider land as a resource that may be yours for a time but is also held in trust for the future. Land is not a commodity that any of us can own in the ordinary sense of the word.
2. You may be a trustee of the land and that will often confer private benefits on you, but *you ought* not to seek benefits that incur disbenefits on the community or other individuals.

3. If you're presently trusted with the management of a piece of land, *you ought* to use it in a manner that benefits the land and does not damage it. Some land uses are abuses that have irreversible consequences, and *you ought* to avoid such abuses.
4. *You ought* to accept that the use of land should be subject to public scrutiny and control and to exercise your responsibility, with others, in ensuring that no use is permitted that is damaging to society as a whole.
5. *You ought* to ensure that the land-use controls developed in your area prevent irreversible damage, avoid waste, protect your natural and cultural heritage, stimulate visual order, regulate and control the unsightly, and safeguard individual liberties (such as mobility and a choice in housing and schooling, so long as those liberties do not impede the liberties of others).
6. *You ought* to recognize that the exercise of land-use controls in the interest of the community can result in costs and benefits to individuals, and be willing to see those costs and benefits equitably adjusted.
7. *You ought* to recognize that these controls can only be exercised democratically through governmental operations. Hence, *you ought* to expect an extension of government to give proper expression to this new land-use ethic.
8. *You ought* to accept that the administration of the ethic must reflect local circumstances and needs, so it will vary from place to place.
9. *You ought* to be ready to give time and talents to fight for this land-use control that is vital for your continued freedom.
10. *You ought* to recognize that you may have to make some sacrifices, along with everyone else, for this control to be effective.*

All of these are *you oughts,* not *you have tos.* Deep down, we know the right thing to do environmentally, but many times economics and greed cause us to act contrary to our convictions. These **land-use ethics** set the stage for an even deeper conviction and commitment to the earth—the establishment of an individual **land ethic.**

Sustainability

Conservation of natural resources in North America is affected by the world community. We cannot lock ourselves in our continental closet and disregard the remainder of the planet. Sustainability requires a global view because of the interconnectedness of the workings of the biosphere. Management of natural resources in North America requires that we consider the ramifications of global biodiversity and sustainability.

William D. Ruchelaus, former administrator for EPA, defines *sustainability* as the nascent doctrine that economic growth and development must take place and be maintained over time, within the limits set by ecology in the broadest sense—by the interrelations of human beings and their works, the biosphere, and the physical and chemical laws that govern it. The doctrine of sustainability holds too that the spread of a reasonable level of prosperity and security to the less-developed nations is essential to protecting ecological balance and, hence, essential to the continued prosperity of the wealthy nations. It follows that environmental protection and economic development are complementary rather than antagonistic processes.

It is inherent in this definition of sustainability that both government and the private citizen must work together. The individual must adjust his life-style to implement the government policy. Government policy must recognize that science does not have all of the information at hand to determine sustainability. Scientific research is a prerequisite to sound policy. Individuals will change if it is in their interest to change, either because they derive some benefit from changing or because they will incur sanctions or penalties if they do not change. The definition also recognizes that sustainability is a global problem and the cost to maintain a reasonable level of prosperity in developing nations must be paid for by wealthy nations.

Government policy must begin by establishing a clear set of values for sustainability that is consistent with current scientific information. Leopold contended that "the ordinary citizen today (1949) assumes that science knows what makes the community clock tick; the scientist is equally sure that he does not. He knows that the biotic mechanism is so complex that its workings may never be fully understood." This statement is equally true today, but we know more than we knew in 1949 and our understanding of the biotic mechanism continues to grow. Money to continue scientific research must be a part of government policy for sustainability. An international program to collect, analyze, and report on environmental trends and risks must be supported by government policy. Earth-Watch, a program of the United Nations Environment Program (UNEP), is an initial move in the right direction.

The environmental laws that have been passed in the United States during the 1970s and 80s provide the beginnings of a set of values for sustainability. The American people want it that way, according to a New York Times/CBS News poll. When asked if they agree, disagree, or don't know to the statement, "Protecting the en-

---

From Chaplin B. Barnes, "A New Land Use Ethic" in *Journal of Soil and Water Conservation,* March/April, Vol. 35, No. 2. Copyright © 1980. The Soil and Water Society. Reprinted by permission.

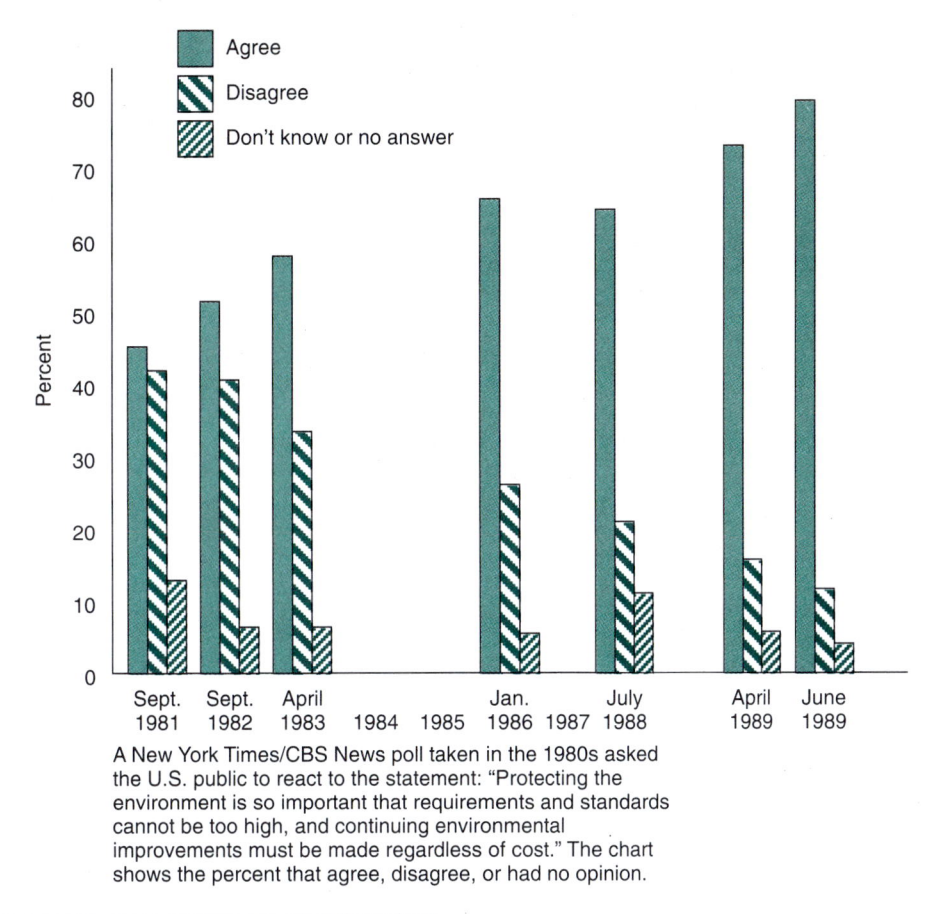

Figure 16.14 Environmental values continued to climb throughout the decade of the 1980s.
Source: Data from William D. Ruckelshaus, "Toward a Sustainable World" in *Scientific American*, September 1989.

A New York Times/CBS News poll taken in the 1980s asked the U.S. public to react to the statement: "Protecting the environment is so important that requirements and standards cannot be too high, and continuing environmental improvements must be made regardless of cost." The chart shows the percent that agree, disagree, or had no opinion.

vironment is so important that requirements and standards cannot be too high, and continuing environmental improvements must be made regardless of cost," 80% said they agree (figure 16.14). The poll indicates that the American people are willing to pay for environmental protection, but the government institutions are not in place to provide protection.

For North America to become a sustainable continent, the following must occur:

1. Every citizen of the continent must accept their position at the top of the biotic pyramid. Acceptance of this position is an admission of dependency on the finite resources of the lower levels of the pyramid. Working within the system to maintain the natural environments that regenerate the ecosystems of the continent is also required.
2. Each citizen must recognize that the North American ecosystem is a part of the planet earth system. Health of the North American environment is dependent on a healthy global environment and vice versa. Cutting down the tropical rain forests in the Amazon basin will eventually affect our North American ecosystem and our sustainability.
3. Environmental economics must become a required part of government policy for sustainability. Environmental resources must be thought of as national capital. The environmental cost of producing goods and/or services, must be added to the price of the commodity to develop a sustainable world. Pricing policy for government-owned resources should reflect the true cost of the product, including environmental costs. The market will adjust to the price increase as it does to true scarcity by product substitution or conservation.

Sustainability requires cooperation between the individual citizen and the government. Both must pay a price. WorldWatch Institute has estimated the cost of sustainable development through the year 2000. Six categories of environmental concerns were listed by

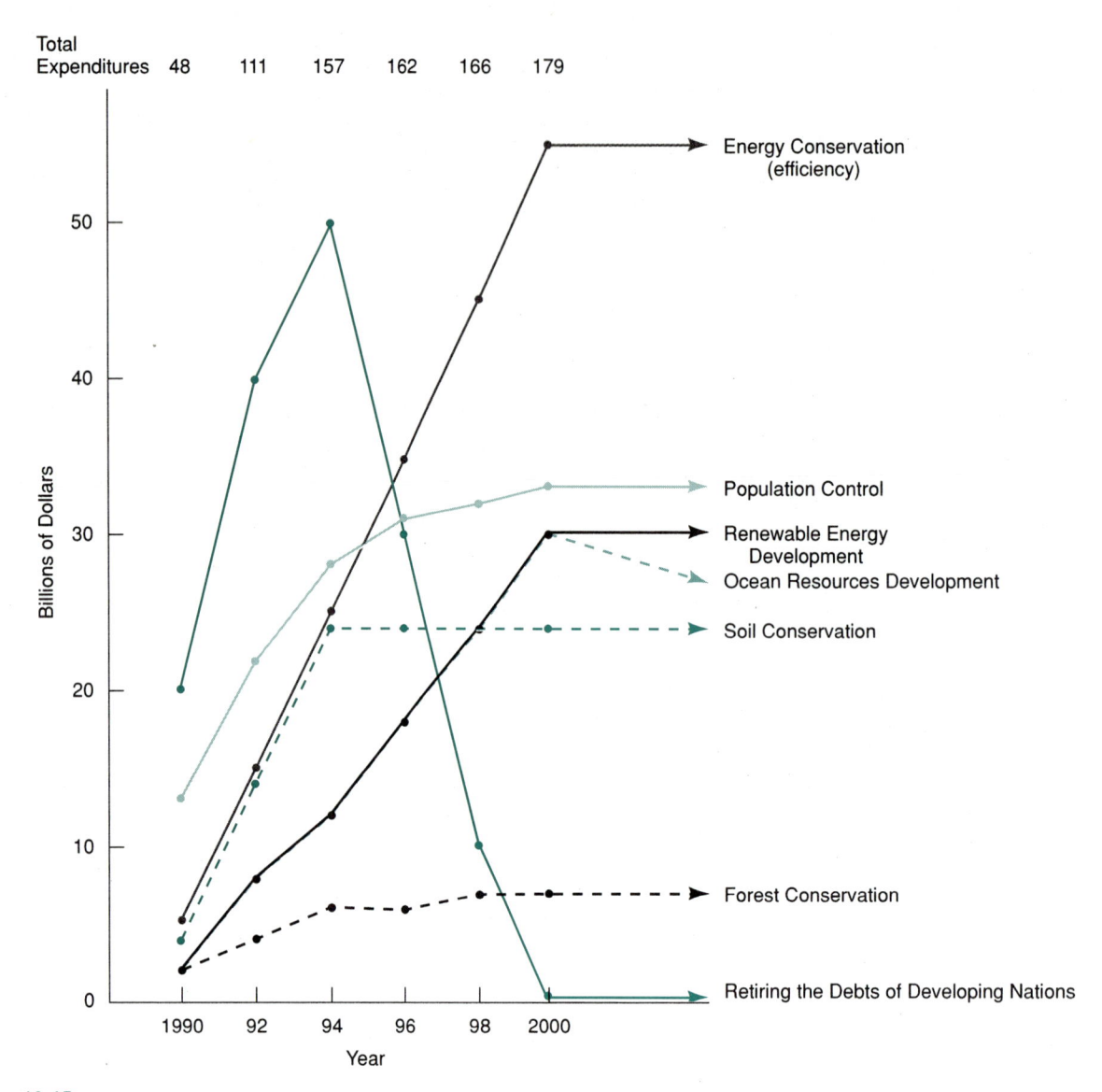

Figure 16.15 Projected costs to achieve sustainable development in the world by the year 2000.
Source: Data from WorldWatch Institute.

WorldWatch. These major line-item concerns with their costs include protecting topsoil, reforestation, reducing population growth rates, improved energy efficiency, developing renewable energy resources, and retiring the debts of developing countries. Developing the ocean resources was added to their list, along with projected costs (figure 16.15). It's interesting to note that the cost per year to achieve sustainable development with this program is less than 18% of the world's military expenditures ($1 trillion per year).

Of the seven major line items identified for sustainable development, one is a relatively new, but critical, concept. Sustainable development of the ocean resource was added to the WorldWatch list because it is a necessity for global sustainability. With world population projected to be 8 billion in the 2020s, and 70% of the earth's surface covered with oceans, the ocean resource must be utilized effectively. Climatic fluctuations that affect the terrestrial ecosystems, especially agriculture, do not alter ocean ecosystems as drastically or as rapidly. Temperature and precipitation variations that change productive agricultural environments to dust bowls are only ripples on the ocean waves. Sustainability requires that we farm the oceans.

A Global View

North America cannot become a sustainable ecosystem without the rest of the world and its oceans. Throughout this discourse on North American resources, our attention has been focused on managing resources in a particular geographic, geologic, and climatic setting. Each of these physical environmental settings is similar to an environment elsewhere in the world. Extrapolating the management strategies that have been successful in North America to the global environment (with site-specific adjustments) is a necessity for a sustainable world.

Since 1900, the world economy has expanded 20 times at great environmental costs. Most countries, including both developed and developing nations, are depleting their stocks of ecological capital faster than they can be replenished. Soils are eroding away, forests are being cut down, energy is being wasted, populations are increasing, and national debts are astronomical. Global warming, acid rain, and the depletion of the ozone layer are warning signals from the ecological systems that something is wrong. Most developing countries have resource-based economies. Their economic capital consists of their soils, forest, fish, wildlife, and parks. Their long-term economic development depends on maintaining and/or increasing these natural resources. Massive transfer of natural resources capital from developing nations to the wealthy must be reduced if the developing nations are to have a chance at sustainability.

Soil loss and land degradation (*desertification*) are global environmental problems that must be addressed. WorldWatch Institute estimates topsoil loss at 25 billion tons (23 BMT) per year. Deserts grow by 6 million hectares (15 million acres) per year. Lack of water in geographic areas where 40% of the world's population resides, is a serious constraint to future development. Soil-management practices that have reversed some of the soil erosion problems in the United States could have application in world regions where climate and physical constraints are comparable (chapter 9). Extrapolation of successful management techniques to the global environment is projected to cost $24 billion per year by the year 2000 to achieve sustainable development (figure 16.15).

The tropical forests of Brazil are being depleted at a rate of 8 million hectares (20 million acres) annually. In Africa, for every 29 trees being cut down, one is planted. Ethiopia had 30% forest cover in 1950. In 1975, it was down to about 5%, and in 1990 it was 1%. India had 50% forest cover in 1900; in 1990, it was reduced to 14%. These natural resources are ecological capital. Some developing countries are on the verge of environmental bankruptcy. The U.S. Forest Service is not managing the forest it is in charge of for sustainability (chapter 8). Canada and its programs of forest management would be better models for the world community than those of the United States.

Reforestation efforts and reduced cutting in the tropical forests are estimated to cost $7 billion per year by the year 2000 (figure 16.15). These efforts should help to reverse the trend in reduction of biodiversity. Maintaining biodiversity at its present level is vital for a sustainable world.

Many countries are selling their capital resource base to foreign countries as primary products. The United States is no exception to this because many wood, agricultural, and petroleum products are exported in an attempt to maintain a balance of trade. A nation's basic stock of natural resource capital should never decrease through time. A constant or sustainable supply of ecological capital is necessary to meet the needs of present and future generations. Countries exporting more than can be produced sustainably are headed for financial and ecological disaster.

A child born in the United States or Canada creates a much greater environmental burden on the world community than does a child born in a developing country. Per capita consumption of natural resources such as energy, forest products, use of water, and other commodities is greatest in the United States. Therefore, ecological costs are higher because resource use and depletion are greater. Slowing the rates of population growth is a major expenditure for developable world sustainability. Estimates are that $33 billion per year will be required by the year 2000 (figure 16.15).

Sustainability requires a continued growth in production, especially for the developing countries. How do you reduce energy consumption while, at the same time, increase production? A significant reduction in energy and raw-material content per unit of production is the answer. Technological advances in many industrialized nations have resulted in a leveling off to absolute reduction in energy cost per unit of product since the 1970s energy crisis. The transition to use of recycled material has not only resulted in a reduction in raw-material content of products, but the recycled materials represent an energy savings as well (chapters 14 and 15). Japan (a forest-poor country) recycles newsprint at a rate that could save Canada (a forest-rich country) 80 million trees a year if they recycled at the same rate. The forest resource capital of Canada would be preserved, and the resulting reduction in energy would be a plus for the global environment. WorldWatch recommends that $55 billion per year be spent on raising energy efficiency by the year 2000. About one third of the total budget for sustainability would be spent to conserve energy. Reduced energy consumption would have the very positive global effect of slowing greenhouse warming.

Developing energy efficiency in appliances, automobiles, air conditioners, furnaces, buildings, and industries would work hand in hand with the development of alternate sources of energy. Solar energy, windpower, geothermal power, biomass digestors for gas production, and minihydroturbines are only a few of the alternate sources of energy that would be environmentally less damaging than burning fossil fuels or nuclear energy (chapter 13). Expenditures of $30 billion per year by the year 2000 are projected for developing renewable energy sources (figure 16.15).

Retiring the debts of developing countries would require expenditures of up to $50 billion per year by 1995, but would reduce to zero by the year 2000 as the debts are retired. The most urgent problem facing Africa and Latin American countries is their debt. It must be solved before these countries can consider their environmental problems. Mass poverty in developing countries is an environmental problem that must be slowed before natural resource protection has any significance. Reducing the debt while at the same time creating greater equity in incomes for the poor in developing countries is the most difficult problem facing the global environment.

Where will the approximately $48 to $179 billion per year come from to finance the budget proposed by WorldWatch for developable world sustainability. The United Nations Environment Program (UNEP) Environment Fund is attempting to increase its budget to $100 million per year with marginal success. It has been as high as $30 million in its best year. That's a long way from the moneys needed for global sustainability. The only budget large enough to fund the sustainable development proposal is military security, which is estimated to be $2.7 billion per day. At that rate, sustainability could be paid for in less than about 65 days of the year, and the other 300 days could fund defense.

Political and economic security have always taken precedence over environment. In the past, military security has been maintained at a very high level to guard against the enemy. In today's world, environmental degradation is the enemy and a greater threat to national security than any political adversary. Since protection of the environment for sustainability is the goal, and the military has the money, a Defense Department that includes environmental defense is proposed. The Army Corps of Engineers, which has created so much environmental havoc, would become the Corps of Environmental Engineers. They would be assigned the task of environmental protection in the United States. Each country's military or defense department would include environmental protection and an equal expenditure of funds would be budgeted for political, economic, and environmental protection. The expenditure of the funds for environmental protection would come from a reduction in funds for political and economic protection. Read my lips: NO NEW TAXES.

If the program for sustainable development were implemented today, by the year 2000 there would be nothing to fight about. The debts of developing countries would be paid off. Poverty would have been decreased and a more equitable level of income for the poor would have been established. The natural-resource base capital for many countries would be improving with reduced soil erosion and forest regrowth. Reductions in biodiversity would be halted. Population growth would be reduced to a level for long-term sustainability. Global warming would have been curtailed because of reduced carbon dioxide emissions. Renewable sources of energy would be replacing fossil fuels as the preferred source of power. Improved environmental conditions would beckon the world tourist to spend increased free time visiting the natural wonders of a sustainable globe.

Biodiversity

Leopold said: "Science has given us many doubts, but it has given us at least one certainty: the trend of evolution is to elaborate and diversify the biota." It has been estimated that 1.4 million species of plants and animals have been named and described. Conservative guesses place the actual number of species at 4 million. Some say it could be as high as 30 million species. Biologic diversity (*biodiversity*) on earth was greater when the human species evolved than at any time in earth's geological history. Biodiversity was lowest at the end of the Mesozoic (65 million ybp), when evolution began elaborating and diversifying the biota to its present state of complexity. Humans and their machines are attempting to reduce biologic biodiversity to its lowest level since the Mesozoic ended.

No matter how many species exist, more than half live in the moist tropical rain forests of the world. Six percent of the terrestrial environments of the earth are tropical rain forests. These areas are warm regions, with an average annual temperature of 26.6C (80° F), and they receive more than 200 cm (79 in) of precipitation per year. Diverse populations of insects and flowering plants thrive in these forests. More than 100,000 sq km (247,000 acres) are cleared per year, or about 1% of the total cover. Only 55% of the original cover remains. This is a serious threat to global biodiversity.

Edward D. Wilson, Professor of Science (Entomology) at Harvard has conservatively estimated that rainforest clearing alone has resulted in the reduction of 4000 to 6000 species of plants and animals per year. This rate of loss is 10,000 times greater than the naturally occurring extinction rate that existed prior to the emergence of humans on earth.

In the United States, 24,300 hectares (60,000 acres) of ancient forests in the Pacific Northwest and the Tongass National Forest in Alaska are being cut each year (figure 16.16). Most of the lumber is exported to Japan and other Pacific Ocean countries as logs. Almost 50% of the most productive forestland of the Tongass has been cut. And, along with the timber goes the original biodiversity. The rule of thumb used to calculate the number of species is: the number of species usually increases with the size of the island (forest) by the fourth root of the area. What this means is that a forest of 100,000 acres will have approximately twice as many species as a forest of 10,000 acres. Reducing the size of a forest has a tremendous effect on reducing numbers of species that can occupy the area.

Every species extinction diminishes humanity. Species diversity is the world's available gene pool and an irreplaceable resource. Every organism has a genetic code etched into its existence that represents from 1 million to 10 million bits of evolutionary information. How do we preserve this storehouse of information for future generations?

Every country needs to expand their taxonomic inventories. Biogeographic mapping of the world's species would identify sensitive areas for priority in conservation. Conservation must team up with economic development, especially in countries where poverty and population density put a strain on natural resources. A reserve cannot be set aside to preserve biodiversity in a country that needs food. Poachers still kill elephants on African reserves set aside to protect that species because ivory still demands a high price on the world market.

Studies indicate that even with a limited knowledge of the forest environment, more economic return can be extracted from natural forest products than from clear-cutting the forest for timber. To clear-cut a tropical forest for agriculture is self-defeating. After a few years (usually less than 5), the forest is gone, the soil is depleted of its poor nutrient supply, and agriculture is no longer sustainable.

Chemical prospecting in a tropical forest has more economic potential than agricultural endeavors. Wild plants of the tropical forests, as yet unnamed or undiscovered, could become the cure for cancer or AIDS, a source of fuel oil, or a new source of food. We know too little about the value of species diversity to take a chance on reducing the number by habitat destruction. Reversing the trend in species extinctions is an important goal for the global community. Maintaining biodiversity is a necessary part of a sustainable world.

Ethics

Conservation of natural resources depends on the human species. Humans, with their ability to think, can manage the natural environment for sustainability indefinitely if natural- or human-caused catastrophes do not abruptly alter the order of natural processes. The natural processes are sometimes slow, sometimes abrupt, in altering the natural order of things (volcanic eruptions, earthquakes, climate change). Managing earth's natural resources involves people working with nature to establish a comfortable standard of living, while at the same time, conserving the natural resources for sustainability. Resource planners and managers must think and plan as a member of the land community. Economic gain without a healthy environment in which to spend the money is no gain at all. Development of a land ethic in each individual is a necessary prerequisite to sustainability, and, ultimately, survival of the human species.

Figure 16.16 Patches of clearcut in the Willamette NF will not regenerate to a forest similar to that which was cut until after the year 2200. Most of us can't wait that long.
(*Photo:* USFS)

Etymologically, *ethics* is derived from the Latin word *ethicus*, which comes from the Greek *etikos*, rooted in the Greek word *ethos*. The primitive meaning of the latter is a stall or a stable where animals are kept. It would appear that ethics has something to do with keeping things in their proper place or the setting up of parameters to assist proper growth and development. With that concept in mind, ethics has become the discipline that seeks to determine the constitutive elements of being human. The popular definition of ethics describes it as "a systematic study of the behavioral implications of being human;" that is, which forms of behavior are humanizing and which are not.

An ethic is *philosophically* a differentiation of social from anti-social conduct. *Ecologically*, an ethic is a limitation on freedom of action in the struggle for existence. According to Aldo Leopold, these are two definitions of one thing. The thing has its origin in the tendency of interdependent individuals or groups to evolve modes of cooperation. The complexity of cooperative mechanisms has increased with population density. The Ten Commandments, which dealt with the relationships between individuals, were the first ethics (figure 16.17). As the social structure evolved, ethics such as the Golden Rule linked the individual to society. Demography is an attempt to integrate the individual into the social organization. The extension of ethics to the human–land relationship is an

Figure 16.17 The Ten Commandments were the first written ethic.
(top and bottom) Reprinted by permission of NEA, Inc.

evolutionary possibility and an ecological necessity. Being humane toward the land that feeds us seems so reasonable. Why then have we mistreated the land the way we have?

The Judeo-Christian culture has viewed humans as having dominion over the earth. The earth was something to be conquered. Leopold took issue with this concept and suggested a community concept to take its place. Humans occupy the position at the top of the biotic pyramid and from that position they must manage each level of its interdependent parts in such a way that an equilibrium is established. Equilibrium is necessary for a long-term sustainability. Keeping things in balance is a difficult task because the base of the pyramid is naturally unpredictable. Human nature and the laws of adaptation suggest that humans must compete for their place on the pyramid. A land ethic implies that cooperation is more appropriate so there will be a place for which they might compete. Leopold's ideas for a land ethic were ahead of their time because humans had not learned to think like a tree. But the time has come for humans to accept their responsibility as members of the ecological community of which they are a part, and extend that responsibility to the entire earth community. Survival of humans depends on the development of a land ethic by each member of the human species.

Land Ethics

On the first Earth Day, April 22, 1970, many Americans expressed their concern for the earth. Finally, there was widespread recognition that we had a problem, which is the first step in solving any problem. By bits and pieces, one small environmental problem after another was solved. Individuals and government were spending money, giving time, and developing programs to stop environmental degradation. Legislation was passed by federal, state, and local governments to stop pollution and improve environmental quality. But governments can't legislate ethics. Ethics are an outgrowth of a social and moral conscience—a feeling of responsibility for something you love. Love of the land is a necessary prerequisite for a land ethic. But to love the land requires an understanding of the land process, knowing how the land works, and recognizing that humans are a part of the mechanism. From love of land follows respect and concern for its health—the beginnings of a land ethic.

Figure 16.18 A land ethic requires that environmental protection take precedence over self-interest.
RUBES by Leigh Rubin. By permission of Leigh Rubin and Creators Syndicate.

Two decades of Earth Days have matured into a genuine concern for the environment. Eighty percent of the American people want strong environmental controls, and they say they are willing to pay for it. There seems to be a willingness to stop environmental degradation. An individual land ethic for each North American citizen would reverse the downward environmental trend and create a sustainable continent.

A land ethic requires that each person recognizes how the biotic system works and his or her place in the biotic community. They must recognize that natural resources are manageable for sustainability within this biotic community. Armed with an understanding and recognition of a human's place in the environment, love of land is possible. A desire to protect the land follows from this love. And placing land protection above self-interest is the highest form of land ethic (figure 16.18).

Summary

Every citizen has a responsibility for the health of the land. To exercise that responsibility, each person can take three actions that will promote conservation of natural resources and global sustainability.

1. Each person should develop for themselves and pass on to their offspring a land ethic, which exhibits a harmony between that person and the land. Recognizing that they are part of the biotic pyramid, occupying a position at the top carries with it great responsibility for stewardship of the land community.
2. Each person should keep informed of legislative issues with environmental significance that are being considered by their elected officials. On a regular basis, write to those officials at the local, state, or national level and express your opinion (see Appendix F). Let your officials know that they are entrusted with protecting your land community, and you expect them to take care of it for you, your children, and your grandchildren.
3. Each person should become a part of an organization that philosophically and ideologically models your land ethic. A list of national and international organizations is given in the Appendix G. Many local and state organizations also exist that promote conservation and sustainability. (Check with your local conservation department or library.) Most national organizations have a paid lobbyist to help promote their philosophical viewpoint. Many also challenge government decisions by taking court action with their legal staff. An organization with 500,000 members carries a great deal of political clout. Become a member of an environmental organization and increase your clout. You'll even get a free magazine with your membership that will keep you up-to-date on environmental issues.

A sustainable world depends on you. Accept your position of responsibility at the top of the biotic pyramid and do your part to be a respected member of the ecosystem. Leave the world to your children and grandchildren better than you found it. Pass on your land ethic so that the younger generation can do the same.

Key Words and Phrases

Abortion
Biodiversity
Carrying capacity
Celibacy
Cervical caps
City
Clovis points
Comprehensive long-range planning
Condoms
Consolidated Metropolitan Statistical Area
Conurbation
Crude birthrate
Crude death rate
Developing nation
Diaphragms
Ecological ethic
Ethics
Ethicus
Ethos
Etikos
Fecundity
Fertility rate
Intrauterine device (IUD)
Life expectancy
Life span
Megalopolis
Moral restraint
Morning-after drug (RU 486)
Natural increase
Norplant
Philosophical ethic
Pill
Rhythm method
Soil loss
Spermicidal jelly
Standard Metropolitan Statistical Area
Sterilization
Sustainability
Tubal ligation
Urban
Vaginal foam
Vas deferens
Vasectomy
Zero population growth (ZPG)
Zoning

Questions and Discussion Topics

1. What do you feel is the human carrying capacity of North America? How about Mexcio?
2. What do you think is the best way of dealing with the problem of population increases? Would your method be acceptable in Mexico?
3. Urban geographers working in the field of city planning must use zoning to control land use. Do you feel that zoning is an infringement on your rights as a citizen of a free country?
4. What are the pros and cons of the WorldWatch program for global sustainability? Do you think money should be added to their program for the development of the ocean resource?
5. Do you think humans will be able to reverse the trend in the reduction of global biodiversity? What needs to be done?
6. Do you have a land ethic? What is it? Did the information in this text help you to establish a land ethic or modify a land ethic you already had?

References for Further Reading

Barnes, C. B. Mar./Apr., 1980. A New Land Use Ethic. Ankeny, IA: The Soil Conservation Society of America. *Journal of Soil and Water Conservation.* 35: No. 2. Land-use ethics defined.

Colinvaux, P. 1978. *Why Big Fierce Animals Are Rare.* Princeton, NJ: Princeton University Press. The endangered list is full of big fierce animals.

DeBlij, H. J. ed. 1988. *Earth '88 Changing Geographic Perspectives.* Washington, D.C.: National Geographic. Proceedings of the centennial symposium for NGS.

Environmental Protection Agency. May, 1988. Cities and the Environment. Washington, D.C.: *EPA Journal.* 14: No. 4. An issue on cities.

Environmental Protection Agency. July/Aug. 1988. An Environmental Ethic: Has It Taken Hold? Washington, D.C.: *EPA Journal.* 14: No. 6. A good issue on ethics.

Leopold, A. 1949. *A Sand County Almanac.* New York: Ballantine Books. Excellent section on land ethics.

MacNeill, J. 1989. *Strategies for Sustainable Economic Development.* New York: W.H. Freeman and Co. Readings from *Scientific American.* "Managing Planet Earth."

McHarg, I. 1969. *Design With Nature.* Garden City, N.Y.: Natural History Press. A classic on urban planning with nature.

National Geographic. Oct., 1988. *The Peopling of the Earth.* Washington, D.C.: 174: No. 4. A special issue on the human population.

Wallace-McHarg Assoc. 1980. *Plan For the Valleys.* Philadelphia, PA: Wallace-McHarg Assoc. Revised plan for the valley area near Baltimore, Maryland.

World Resources Institute. 1990. *World Resources 1990–91.* New York: Oxford University Press. World Resources for 1990.

Zero Population Growth. 1988. *Urban Stress Test.* Washington, D.C.: The results of the second UST.

Appendix A1

Periodic Chart of the Elements

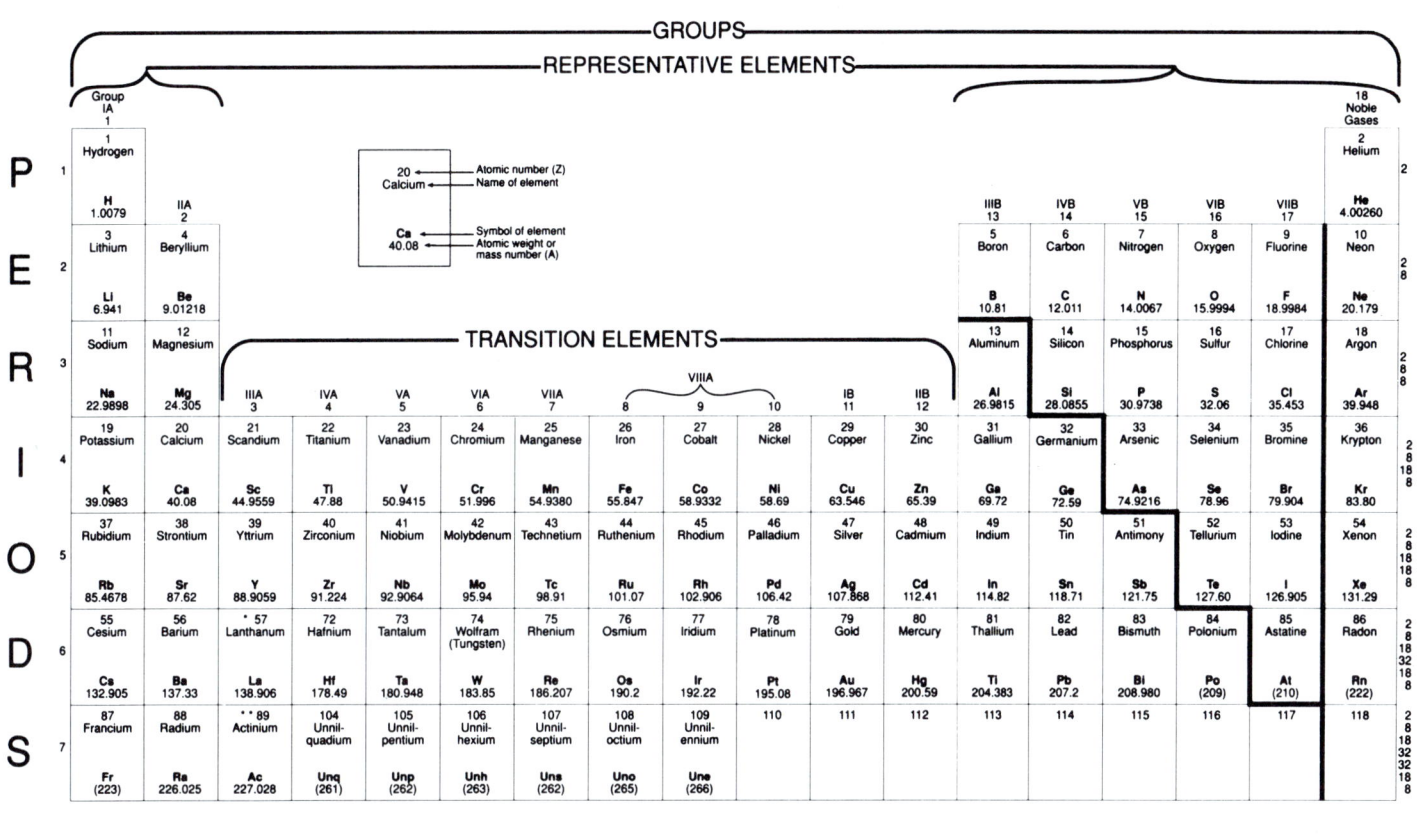

Group IA 1																	18 Noble Gases
1 Hydrogen **H** 1.0079	IIA 2											IIIB 13	IVB 14	VB 15	VIB 16	VIIB 17	2 Helium **He** 4.00260
3 Lithium **Li** 6.941	4 Beryllium **Be** 9.01218											5 Boron **B** 10.81	6 Carbon **C** 12.011	7 Nitrogen **N** 14.0067	8 Oxygen **O** 15.9994	9 Fluorine **F** 18.9984	10 Neon **Ne** 20.179
11 Sodium **Na** 22.9898	12 Magnesium **Mg** 24.305	IIIA 3	IVA 4	VA 5	VIA 6	VIIA 7	VIIIA 8	9	10	IB 11	IIB 12	13 Aluminum **Al** 26.9815	14 Silicon **Si** 28.0855	15 Phosphorus **P** 30.9738	16 Sulfur **S** 32.06	17 Chlorine **Cl** 35.453	18 Argon **Ar** 39.948
19 Potassium **K** 39.0983	20 Calcium **Ca** 40.08	21 Scandium **Sc** 44.9559	22 Titanium **Ti** 47.88	23 Vanadium **V** 50.9415	24 Chromium **Cr** 51.996	25 Manganese **Mn** 54.9380	26 Iron **Fe** 55.847	27 Cobalt **Co** 58.9332	28 Nickel **Ni** 58.69	29 Copper **Cu** 63.546	30 Zinc **Zn** 65.39	31 Gallium **Ga** 69.72	32 Germanium **Ge** 72.59	33 Arsenic **As** 74.9216	34 Selenium **Se** 78.96	35 Bromine **Br** 79.904	36 Krypton **Kr** 83.80
37 Rubidium **Rb** 85.4678	38 Strontium **Sr** 87.62	39 Yttrium **Y** 88.9059	40 Zirconium **Zr** 91.224	41 Niobium **Nb** 92.9064	42 Molybdenum **Mo** 95.94	43 Technetium **Tc** 98.91	44 Ruthenium **Ru** 101.07	45 Rhodium **Rh** 102.906	46 Palladium **Pd** 106.42	47 Silver **Ag** 107.868	48 Cadmium **Cd** 112.41	49 Indium **In** 114.82	50 Tin **Sn** 118.71	51 Antimony **Sb** 121.75	52 Tellurium **Te** 127.60	53 Iodine **I** 126.905	54 Xenon **Xe** 131.29
55 Cesium **Cs** 132.905	56 Barium **Ba** 137.33	*57 Lanthanum **La** 138.906	72 Hafnium **Hf** 178.49	73 Tantalum **Ta** 180.948	74 Wolfram (Tungsten) **W** 183.85	75 Rhenium **Re** 186.207	76 Osmium **Os** 190.2	77 Iridium **Ir** 192.22	78 Platinum **Pt** 195.08	79 Gold **Au** 196.967	80 Mercury **Hg** 200.59	81 Thallium **Tl** 204.383	82 Lead **Pb** 207.2	83 Bismuth **Bi** 208.980	84 Polonium **Po** (209)	85 Astatine **At** (210)	86 Radon **Rn** (222)
87 Francium **Fr** (223)	88 Radium **Ra** 226.025	**89 Actinium **Ac** 227.028	104 Unnilquadium **Unq** (261)	105 Unnilpentium **Unp** (262)	106 Unnilhexium **Unh** (263)	107 Unnilseptium **Uns** (262)	108 Unniloctium **Uno** (265)	109 Unnilennium **Une** (266)	110	111	112	113	114	115	116	117	118

Lanthanide Series 6*

58 Cerium **Ce** 140.12	59 Praseodymium **Pr** 140.908	60 Neodymium **Nd** 144.24	61 Promethium **Pm** (145)	62 Samarium **Sm** 150.36	63 Europium **Eu** 151.96	64 Gadolinium **Gd** 157.25	65 Terbium **Tb** 158.925	66 Dysprosium **Dy** 162.50	67 Holmium **Ho** 164.930	68 Erbium **Er** 167.26	69 Thulium **Tm** 168.934	70 Ytterbium **Yb** 173.04	71 Lutetium **Lu** 174.967

Actinide Series 7**

90 Thorium **Th** 232.038	91 Protactinium **Pa** 231.03	92 Uranium **U** 238.029	93 Neptunium **Np** 237.048	94 Plutonium **Pu** 239	95 Americium **Am** (243)	96 Curium **Cm** (247)	97 Berkelium **Bk** (247)	98 Californium **Cf** (252)	99 Einsteinium **Es** (252)	100 Fermium **Fm** (257)	101 Mendelevium **Md** (256)	102 Nobelium **No** (259)	103 Lawrencium **Lr** (260)

Key: 20 Calcium **Ca** 40.08 — Atomic number (Z), Name of element, Symbol of element, Atomic weight or mass number (A)

Appendix A2

Relative Percentages of Elements in the Earth's Spheres

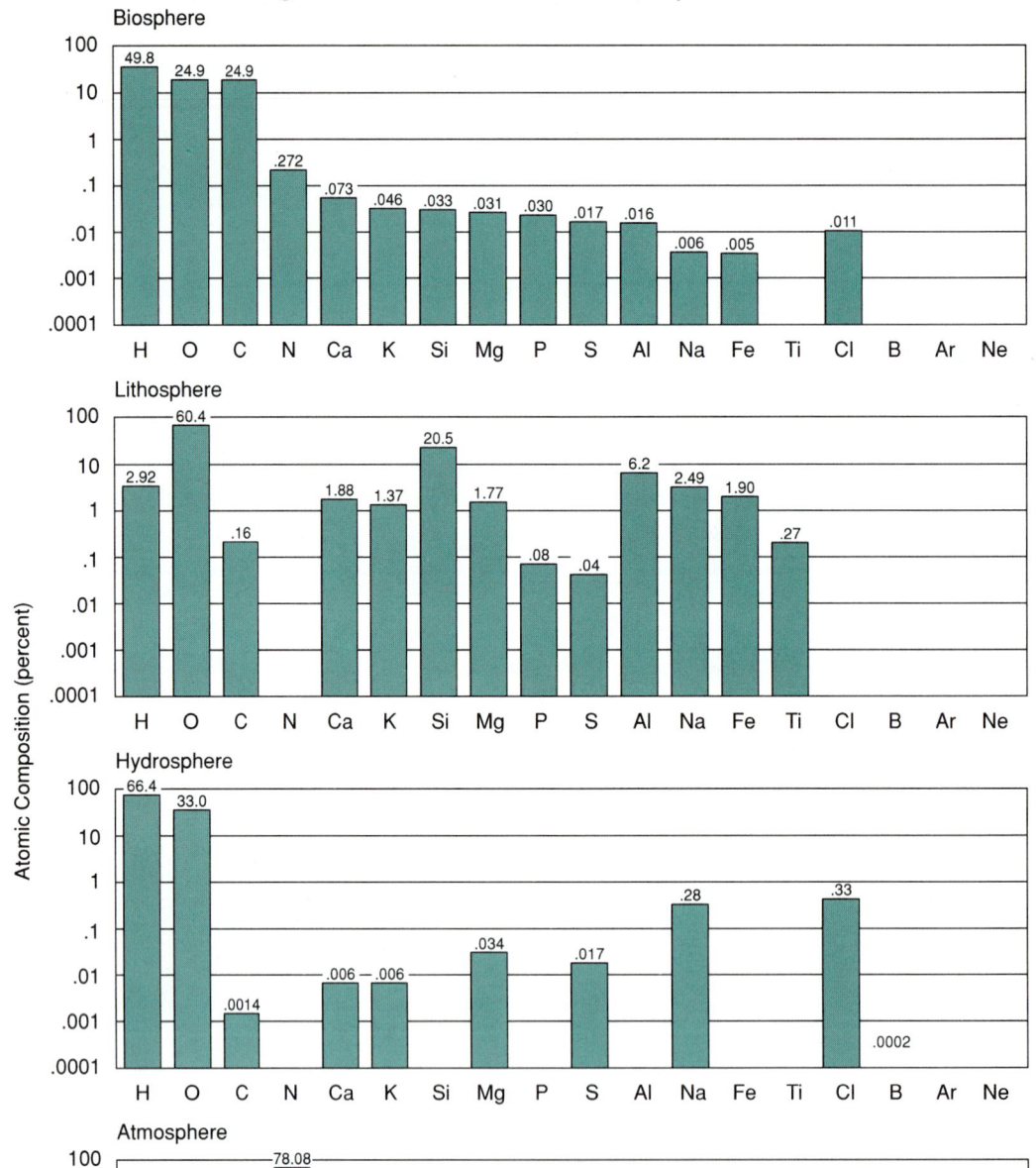

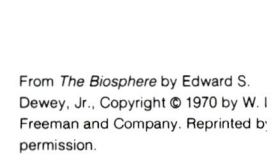

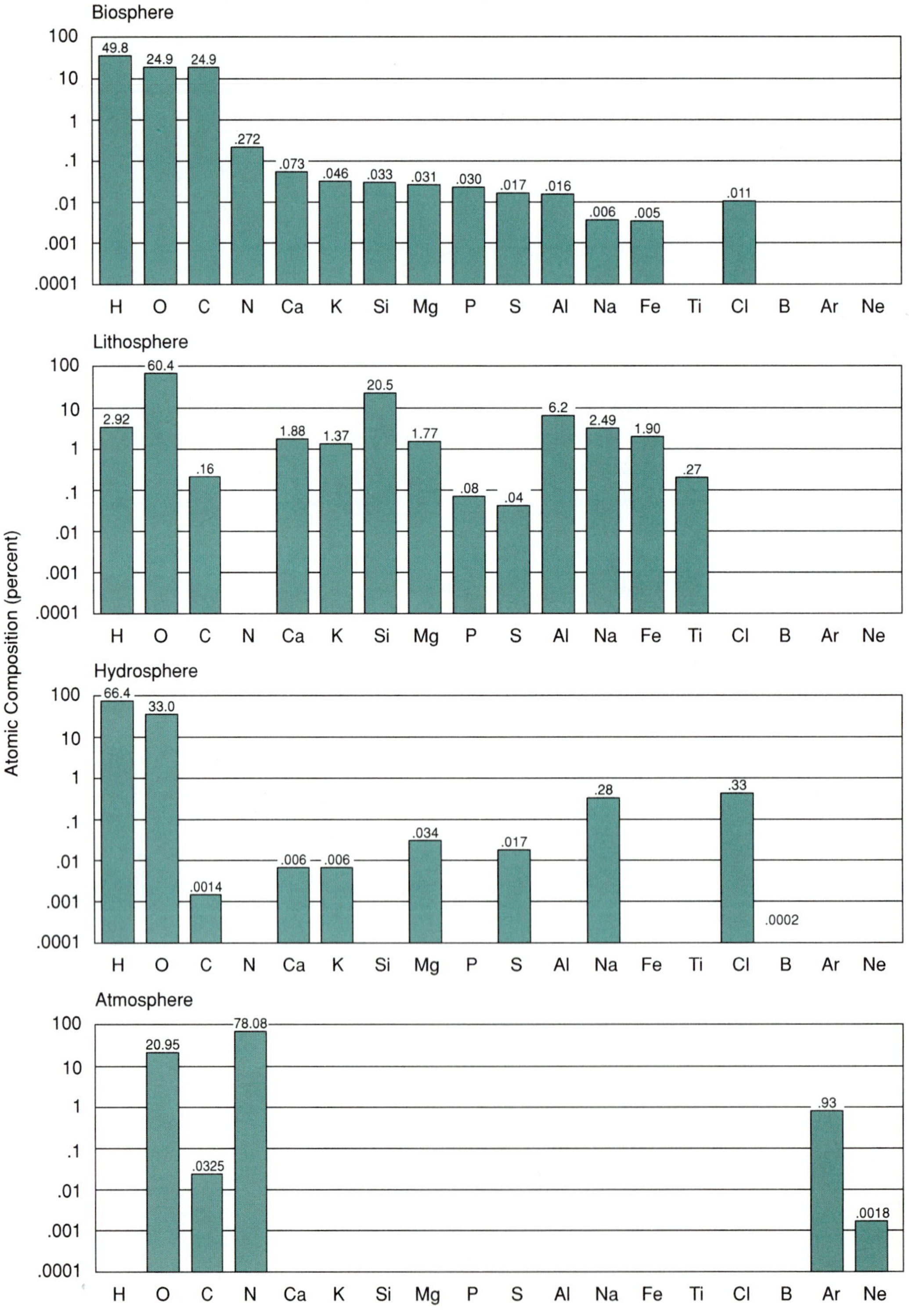

Biosphere

Element	H	O	C	N	Ca	K	Si	Mg	P	S	Al	Na	Fe	Ti	Cl	B	Ar	Ne
%	49.8	24.9	24.9	.272	.073	.046	.033	.031	.030	.017	.016	.006	.005		.011			

Lithosphere

Element	H	O	C	N	Ca	K	Si	Mg	P	S	Al	Na	Fe	Ti	Cl	B	Ar	Ne
%	2.92	60.4	.16		1.88	1.37	20.5	1.77	.08	.04	6.2	2.49	1.90	.27				

Hydrosphere

Element	H	O	C	N	Ca	K	Si	Mg	P	S	Al	Na	Fe	Ti	Cl	B	Ar	Ne
%	66.4	33.0	.0014		.006	.006		.034		.017		.28			.33		.0002	

Atmosphere

Element	H	O	C	N	Ca	K	Si	Mg	P	S	Al	Na	Fe	Ti	Cl	B	Ar	Ne
%		20.95	.0325	78.08													.93	.0018

Atomic Composition (percent)

KEY

- Al Aluminum
- Ar Argon
- B   Boron
- C   Carbon
- Ca Calcium
- Cl Chlorine
- Fe Iron
- H   Hydrogen
- K   Potassium
- Mg Magnesium
- N   Nitrogen
- Na Sodium
- Ne Neon
- O   Oxygen
- P   Phosphorus
- S   Sulfur
- Si Silicon
- Ti Titanium

From *The Biosphere* by Edward S. Dewey, Jr., Copyright © 1970 by W. H. Freeman and Company. Reprinted by permission.

Appendix B

Geologic Time and Formations

Time-rock Units of the Geologic Column	TIME UNITS OF THE GEOLOGIC TIME SCALE Numbers are absolute dates in millions of years before present.			MILESTONES IN THE HISTORY OF LIFE	Relative Lengths of Major Time Divisions In True Scale	
	Eras	Periods	Epochs			
	CENOZOIC	Quaternary	Holocene — 0.01	Expansion of hominids	66.4	Cenozoic
			Pleistocene — 1.8			
		Tertiary	Pliocene — 5.3	Dominance of elephants, horses, large carnivores	245	Mesozoic
			Miocene — 23.7	Development of whales, bats, monkeys, horses Coevolution of insects and flowering plants		Paleozoic
			Oligocene — 36.6	Grazing animals widespread, grasses abundant	570	
			Eocene — 57.8	Primitive horses		
			Paleocene — 66.4	Rapid development of mammals		
	MESOZOIC	Cretaceous — 144		Extinction of dinosaurs and ammonites Development of flowering plants		
		Jurassic — 208		Climax of dinosaurs, cycads abundant Earliest record of birds		
		Triassic — 245		First primitive mammals; conifers and cycads abundant; appearance of dinosaurs; rapid development in reptiles		
	PALEOZOIC	Permian — 286		Development of conifers, extinction of trilobites Spread of reptiles, including mammal-like reptiles		Precambrian
		Pennsylvanian (Upper Carboniferous) — 320		Earliest primitive reptiles Abundant insects Coal-forming forests widespread		
		Mississippian (Lower Carboniferous) — 360		Echinoderms and bryozoa abundant Spreading of fish faunas		
		Devonian — 408		Appearance of amphibians Earliest forests		
		Sulurian — 438		Earliest record of land plants and animals First jawed fish		
		Ordovician — 505		Primitive fishes, the first known vertebrates Diverse communities of marine shelled invertebrates		
		Cambrian — 570		Marine invertebrate faunas abundant; trilobites predominant		
	PRECAMBRIAN TIME			Development of first multicellular animals Expansion of simple marine plants Origin of life	4600	Origin of earth

From James C. Brice, et al., *Laboratory Studies in Earth History*, 4th ed. Copyright © 1989 Wm. C. Brown Publishers, Dubuque, Iowa. All Rights Reserved. Reprinted by permission.

Appendix C

Units of Measurement
Metric/English Conversions

Reference Points	Celsius (°C)	Fahrenheit (°F)
absolute zero	−273.2	−459.7
seawater freezes (depends on salinity)	−2.0 to −3.0	28.4 to 26.6
fresh water freezes	0.0	32.0
human body	37.0	98.6
fresh water boils	100.0	212.0

Common Prefixes

deci-: one-tenth	1 deciliter (dl)	=	0.1 liter
centi-: one-hundredth	1 centimeter (cm)	=	0.01 meter
milli-: one-thousandth	1 milliliter (ml)	=	0.001 liter
kilo-: one thousand	1 kilogram (kg)	=	1,000 grams

Length
- 1 meter = 39.4 inches = 3.28 feet = 1.09 yard
- 1 foot = 0.305 meters = 12 inches = 0.33 yard
- 1 inch = 2.54 centimeters
- 1 centimeter = 10 millimeter = 0.394 inch
- 1 millimeter = 0.001 meter = 0.01 centimeter = 0.039 inch
- 1 micrometer (μm) = 0.000001 meter = 0.0001 centimeter
- 1 fathom = 6 feet = 1.83 meters
- 1 rod = 16.5 feet = 5 meters
- 1 chain = 4 rods = 66 feet = 20 meters
- 1 furlong = 10 chains = 40 rods = 660 feet = 200 meters
- 1 kilometer = 1,000 meters = 0.621 miles = 0.54 nautical miles (nm)
- 1 mile = 5,280 feet = 8 furlongs = 1.61 kilometers
- 1 nautical mile = 1.15 mile

Area
- 1 square centimeter = 0.155 square inch
- 1 square foot = 144 square inches = 929 square centimeters
- 1 square yard = 9 square feet = 0.836 square meters
- 1 square meter = 10.76 square feet = 1.196 square yards = 1 million square millimeters
- 1 hectare = 10,000 square meters = 0.01 square kilometers = 2.47 acres
- 1 acre = 43,560 square feet = 0.405 hectares
- 1 square kilometer = 100 hectares = 1 million square meters = 0.386 square miles = 247 acres
- 1 square mile = 640 acres = 2.59 square kilometers

Volume
- 1 cubic centimeter = 1 milliliter = 0.001 liter
- 1 cubic meter = 1 million cubic centimeters = 1,000 liters
- 1 cubic meter = 35.3 cubic feet = 1.307 cubic yards = 264 US gallons
- 1 cubic yard = 27 cubic feet = 0.765 cubic meters = 202 US gallons
- 1 cubic kilometer = 1 million cubic meters = 0.24 cubic mile = 264 billion gallons
- 1 cubic mile = 4.166 cubic kilometers
- 1 liter = 1,000 milliliters = 1.06 quarts = 0.265 US gallons = 0.035 cubic feet
- 1 US gallon = 4 quarts = 3.79 liters = 231 cubic inches = 0.83 imperial (British) gallons
- 1 quart = 2 pints = 4 cups = 0.94 liters
- 1 acre foot = 325,851 US gallons = 1,234,975 liters = 1,234 cubic meters
- 1 barrel (of oil) = 42 US gallons = 159 liters
- 1 fluid ounce = 29.6 milliliters
- 1 bushel = 8 gallons

Mass
- 1 microgram = 0.001 milligram = 0.000001 gram
- 1 gram = 1,000 milligrams = 0.035 ounce
- 1 kilogram = 1,000 grams = 2.205 pound
- 1 pound = 16 ounces = 454 grams
- 1 short ton = 2,000 pounds = 909 kilograms = 1 ton
- 1 metric ton = 1,000 kilograms = 2,200 pounds
- 1 troy ounce = 31.2 grams
- 1 ounce = 28.4 grams

Temperature
- Celsius to Kelvin °K = °C + 273.2
- Celsius to Fahrenheit °F = (°C × 1.8) + 32
- Fahrenheit to Celsius °C = (°F − 32) ÷ 1.8
- 1° F/1000 ft = 0.2° C/100 m

Energy and Power
- 1 erg = 1 dyne per square centimeter
- 1 joule = 10 million ergs
- 1 calorie = 4.184 joules
- 1 kilojoule = 1,000 joules = 0.949 British Thermal Units (BTU)
- 1 kilocalorie = 1,000 calories = 3.97 BTU = 0.00116 kilowatt-hour
- 1 BTU = 0.293 watt-hour
- 1 kilowatt-hour = 1,000 watt-hour = 860 kilocalories = 3,400 BTU
- 1 horsepower = 640 kilocalories
- 1 quad = 1 quadrillion kilojoules = 2.93 trillion kilowatt-hours
- 1 megawatt = 1000 kilowatts
- 1 atmosphere = 14.7 pounds of pressure per square inch = 1013.2 millibars = 29.92 inches of Hg

Unit	(Metric and English equivalents)
minute	60 seconds
hour	60 minutes; 3600 seconds
day	86,400 seconds ⎫
	24 hours ⎬ mean solar day
year	31,556,880 seconds ⎫
	8765.8 hours ⎬ mean solar year
	365.25 solar days ⎭

Average Energy Contents of Various Fossil Fuels

Fuel	Calories	BTU
1 barrel crude oil	1,460,000,000	5,800,000
1 ton coal	5,650,000,000	22,400,000
1 cubic foot natural gas	257,000	1,020

Speed

centimeter per second (cm s^{-1})
foot per second (ft/sec)
meter per second (m s^{-1})
mile per hour (mph)
nautical mile per hour = kt
1 cm s^{-1} = 0.0328 ft/sec = 1.97 ft/min
1 ft/sec = 30.48 cm s^{-1} = 0.592 kt
1 m s^{-1} = 2.24 mph = 1.94 kt
1 mph = 0.447 m s^{-1} = 0.868 kt
1 kt = 0.515 m s^{-1} = 1.15 mph

Appendix D

Köppen Climate Classification Chart

Legend
(all temperatures °F—
precipitation inches)
TMAX Highest monthly average temperature
TMIN Lowest monthly average temperature
TAVG Average (mean) yearly temperature
NMOF Number of months average temperature over fifty
PMAXS Highest monthly average precipitation for summer*
PMINS Lowest monthly average precipitation for summer*
PMAXW Highest monthly average precipitation for winter*
PMINW Lowest monthly average precipitation for winter*
PTOT Mean total yearly precipitation

* Northern hemisphere
  summer (Apr–Sept)
  winter (Oct–Mar)
* Southern hemisphere
  summer (Oct–Mar)
  winter (Apr–Sept)

R_1 and R_2 define the limits of the BS climate

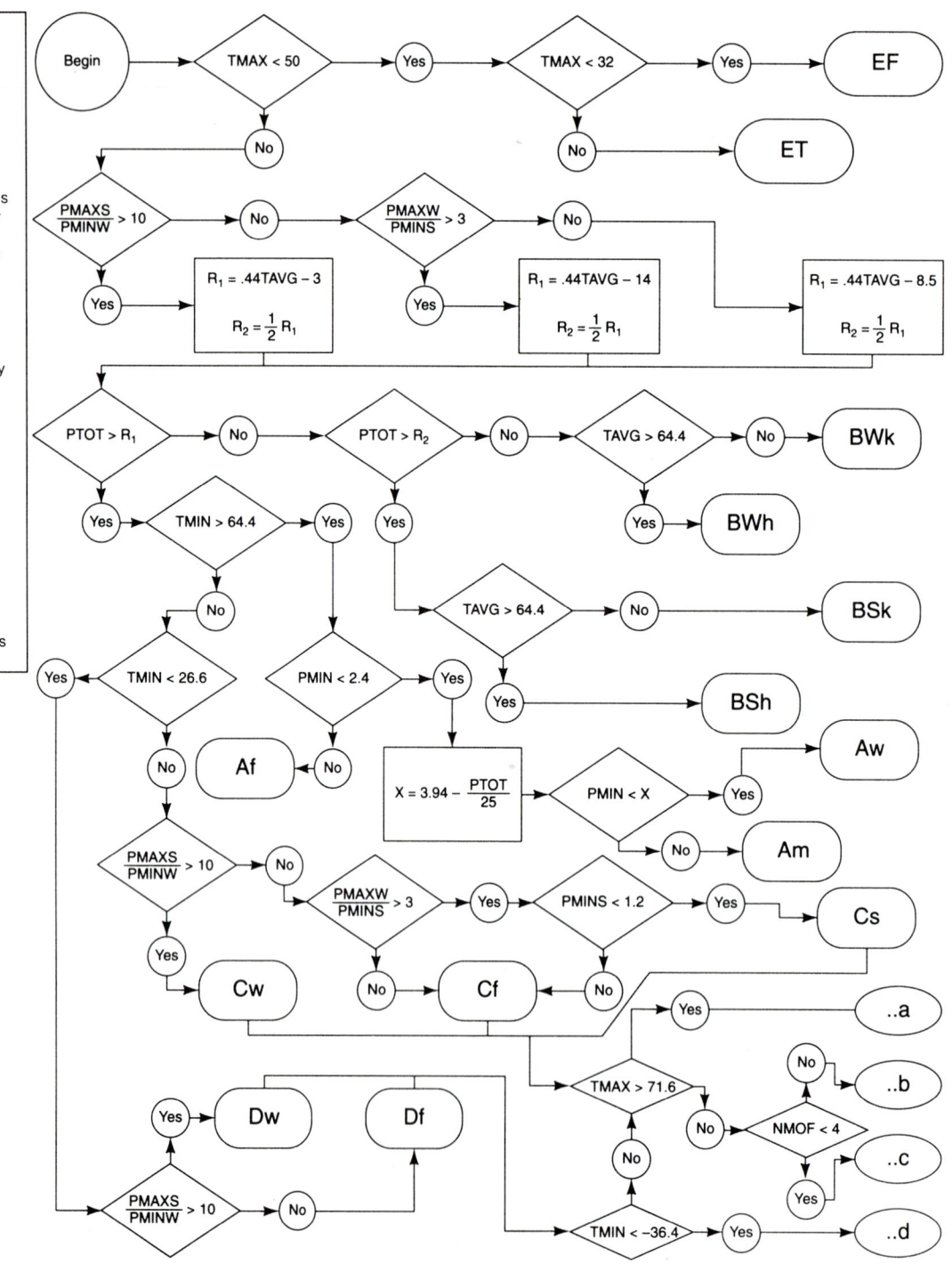

Begin → TMAX < 50 — Yes → TMAX < 32 — Yes → EF
                                      No → ET
            No ↓
$\frac{PMAXS}{PMINW} > 10$ — No → $\frac{PMAXW}{PMINS} > 3$ — No →
  Yes ↓   Yes ↓
  $R_1 = .44\,TAVG - 3$ $R_1 = .44\,TAVG - 14$ $R_1 = .44\,TAVG - 8.5$
  $R_2 = \frac{1}{2} R_1$ $R_2 = \frac{1}{2} R_1$ $R_2 = \frac{1}{2} R_1$

PTOT > R_1 — No → PTOT > R_2 — No → TAVG > 64.4 — No → BWk
                                                     Yes → BWh
  Yes ↓   Yes ↓
TMIN > 64.4 — Yes →   TAVG > 64.4 — No → BSk
  No ↓   Yes → BSh
TMIN < 26.6 — Yes ← PMIN < 2.4 — Yes →
  No ↓   No ↓
  Af $X = 3.94 - \frac{PTOT}{25}$ PMIN < X — Yes → Aw
                                                      No → Am

$\frac{PMAXS}{PMINW} > 10$ — No → $\frac{PMAXW}{PMINS} > 3$ — Yes → PMINS < 1.2 — Yes → Cs
  Yes ↓   No ↓   No ↓
  Cw   Cf

Dw ← Yes — $\frac{PMAXS}{PMINW} > 10$ — No → Df

TMAX > 71.6 — Yes → ..a
  No ↓
NMOF < 4 — No → ..b
  Yes ↓
..c
TMIN < −36.4 — Yes → ..d

Donald H. McInnis, Köppen Climate Classification Chart. Diagram modified after original flow chart by James McQuigg, formerly University of Missouri at Columbia, now deceased. Reprinted by permission.

Appendix E

The National Wilderness Preservation System, 1964–1989.
(See Figure 8.9 in the text for Wilderness Areas Map)

Wilderness Area	Acres	Year Designated	Agency	Public Land Unit
ALABAMA				
Cheaha	7,490	1983, 1988	USFS	Talladega NF
Sipsey	25,906	1975, 1988	USFS	Bankhead NF
State Total: 33,396				
ALASKA				
Admiralty Island National Monument	937,396	1980	USFS	Tongass NF
Aleutian Islands	1,300,000	1980	FWS	Alaska Maritime NWR
Andreafsky	1,300,000	1980	FWS	Yukon Delta NWR
Arctic	8,000,000	1980	FWS	Arctic NWR
Becharof	400,000	1980	FWS	Becharof NWR
Bering Sea	81,340	1970	FWS	Alaska Maritime NWR
Bogoslof	175	1970	FWS	Alaska Maritime NWR
Chamisso	455	1975	FWS	Alaska Maritime NWR
Coronation Island	19,232	1980	USFS	Tongass NF
Denali	1,900,000	1980	NPS	Denali NP
Endicott River	98,729	1980	USFS	Tongass NF
Forrester Island	2,832	1970	FWS	Alaska Maritime NWR
Gates of the Arctic	7,052,000	1980	NPS	Gates of the Arctic NP
Glacier Bay	2,770,000	1980	NPS	Glacier Bay NP
Hazy Islands	32	1970	FWS	Hazy Islands NWR
Innoko	1,240,000	1980	FWS	Innoko NWR
Izembek	300,000	1980	FWS	Izembek NWR
Katmai	3,473,000	1980	NPS	Katmai NP
Kenai	1,350,000	1980	FWS	Kenai NWR
Kobuk Valley	190,000	1980	NPS	Kobuk Valley NP
Koyukuk	400,000	1980	FWS	Koyukuk NWR
Lake Clark	2,470,000	1980	NPS	Lake Clark NP
Maurelle Islands	4,937	1980	USFS	Tongass NF
Misty Fjords National Monument	2,142,243	1980	USFS	Tongass NF
Noatak	5,800,000	1980	NPS	Noatak N Preserve
Nunivak	600,000	1980	FWS	Yukon Delta NWR
Petersburg Creek-Duncan Salt Chuck	46,777	1980	USFS	Tongass NF
Russell Fjord	348,701	1980	USFS	Tongass NF
Selawik	240,000	1980	FWS	Selawik NWR
Semidi	250,000	1980	FWS	Alaska Maritime NWR
Simeonof	25,855	1976	FWS	Alaska Maritime NWR
South Baranof	319,568	1980	USFS	Tongass NF
South Prince of Wales	90,996	1980	USFS	Tongass NF
St. Lazaria	65	1970	FWS	Alaska Maritime NWR
Stikine-LeConte	448,841	1980	USFS	Tongass NF
Tebenkof Bay	66,839	1980	USFS	Tongass NF
Togiak	2,270,000	1980	FWS	Togiak NWR
Tracy Arm-Fords Terror	653,179	1980	USFS	Tongass NF
Tuxedni	5,566	1970	FWS	Alaska Maritime NWR
Unimak	910,000	1980	FWS	Alaska Maritime NWR
Warren Island	11,181	1980	USFS	Tongass NF
West Chichagof-Yakobi	264,747	1980	USFS	Tongass NF
Wrangell-St. Elias	8,700,000	1980	NPS	Wrangell-St. Elias NP
State Total: 56,484,686				

Wilderness Area	Acres	Year Designated	Agency	Public Land Unit
ARIZONA				
Apache Creek	5,420	1984	USFS	Prescott NF
Aravaipa Canyon	6,670	1984	BLM	Safford District
Bear Wallow	11,080	1984	USFS	Apache-Sitgreaves NF
Beaver Dam Mountains	17,003	1984	BLM	Arizona Strip District
Castle Creek	26,030	1984	USFS	Prescott NF
Cedar Bench	14,950	1984	USFS	Prescott NF
Chiricahua	87,700	1964, 1984	USFS	Coronado NF
Chiricahua National Monument	10,290	1976, 1984	NPS	Chiricahua NM
Cottonwood Point	6,500	1984	BLM	Arizona Strip District
Escudilla	5,200	1984	USFS	Apache-Sitgreaves NF
Fossil Springs	11,550	1984	USFS	Coconino NF
Four Peaks	53,500	1984	USFS	Tonto NF
Galiuro	76,317	1964, 1984	USFS	Coronado NF
Grand Wash Cliffs	36,300	1984	BLM	Arizona Strip District
Granite Mountain	9,800	1984	USFS	Prescott NF
Hellsgate	36,780	1984	USFS	Tonto NF
Juniper Mesa	7,600	1984	USFS	Prescott NF
Kachina Peaks	18,200	1984	USFS	Coconino NF
Kanab Creek	68,250	1984	USFS	Kaibab NF
Kanab Creek	8,850	1984	BLM	Arizona Strip District
Kendrick Mountain	6,510	1984	USFS	Coconino, Kaibab NFs
Mazatzal	251,912	1964, 1984	USFS	Tonto NF
Miller Peak	20,190	1984	USFS	Coronado NF
Mount Baldy	7,079	1970	USFS	Apache-Sitgreaves NF
Mount Logan	14,600	1984	BLM	Arizona Strip District
Mount Trumbull	7,900	1984	BLM	Arizona Strip District
Mount Wrightson	25,260	1984	USFS	Coronado NF
Munds Mountain	18,150	1984	USFS	Coconino NF
Organ Pipe Cactus	312,600	1978	NPS	Organ Pipe NM
Paiute	84,700	1984	BLM	Arizona Strip District
Pajarita	7,420	1984	USFS	Coronado NF
Paria Canyon-Vermilion Cliffs	90,046	1984	BLM	Arizona Strip District
Petrified Forest	50,260	1970	NPS	Petrified Forest NP
Pine Mountain	20,061	1972	USFS	Prescott, Tonto NFs
Pusch Ridge	56,933	1978	USFS	Coronado NF
Red Rock-Secret Mountain	43,950	1984	USFS	Coconino NF
Rincon Mountain	38,590	1984	USFS	Coronado NF
Saddle Mountain	40,600	1984	USFS	Kaibab NF
Saguaro	71,400	1976	NPS	Saguaro NM
Salome	18,950	1984	USFS	Tonto NF
Salt River Canyon	32,800	1984	USFS	Tonto NF
Santa Teresa	26,780	1984	USFS	Coronado NF
Sierra Ancha	20,850	1964	USFS	Tonto NF
Strawberry Crater	10,140	1984	USFS	Coconino NF
Superstition	159,757	1964, 1984	USFS	Tonto NF
Sycamore Canyon	55,937	1972, 1984	USFS	Coconino, Kaibab, Prescott NFs
West Clear Creek	13,600	1984	USFS	Coconino NF
Wet Beaver	6,700	1984	USFS	Coconino NF
Woodchute	5,600	1984	USFS	Prescott NF
State Total: 2,037,265				
ARKANSAS				
Big Lake	2,144	1976	FWS	Big Lake NWR
Black Fork Mountain	7,568	1984	USFS	Ouachita NF
Buffalo National River	10,529	1978	NPS	Buffalo National River
Caney Creek	14,344	1975	USFS	Ouachita NF
Dry Creek	6,310	1984	USFS	Ouachita NF
East Fork	10,777	1984	USFS	Ozark-Saint Francis NF
Flatside	10,105	1984	USFS	Ouachita NF
Hurricane Creek	15,177	1984	USFS	Ozark-Saint Francis NF
Leatherwood	16,956	1984	USFS	Ozark-Saint Francis NF
Poteau Mountain	10,884	1984	USFS	Ouachita NF
Richland Creek	11,822	1984	USFS	Ozark-Saint Francis NF
Upper Buffalo	11,746	1975, 1984	USFS	Ozark-Saint Francis NF
State Total: 128,362				

Wilderness Area	Acres	Year Designated	Agency	Public Land Unit
CALIFORNIA				
Agua Tibia	15,933	1975	USFS	Cleveland NF
Ansel Adams	228,669	1964	USFS	Inyo Sierra NF
Ansel Adams	665	1984	NPS	Yosemite NP
Bucks Lake	21,000	1984	USFS	Plumas NF
Caribou	20,625	1964, 1984	USFS	Lassen NF
Carson-Iceberg	160,000	1984	USFS	Stanislaus, Toiyabe NFs
Castle Crags	7,300	1984	USFS	Shasta-Trinity NF
Chanchelulla	8,200	1984	USFS	Shasta-Trinity NF
Cucamonga	12,981	1964, 1984	USFS	San Bernardino, Angeles NFs
Desolation	63,475	1969	USFS	Eldorado NF
Dick Smith	65,130	1984	USFS	Los Padres NF
Dinkey Lakes	30,000	1984	USFS	Sierra NF
Dome Land	94,686	1964, 1984	USFS	Sequoia NF
Emigrant	112,191	1975, 1984	USFS	Stanislaus NF
Farallon	141	1974	FWS	Farallon NWR
Golden Trout	303,287	1978	USFS	Inyo, Sequoia NFs
Granite Chief	25,000	1984	USFS	Tahoe NF
Hauser	8,000	1984	USFS	Cleveland NF
Hoover	48,601	1964	USFS	Inyo, Toiyabe NFs
Ishi	41,600	1984	USFS	Lassen NF
Ishi	240	1984	BLM	Ukiah District
Jennie Lakes	10,500	1984	USFS	Sequoia NF
John Muir	580,675	1964, 1984	USFS	Inyo, Sierra NFs
Joshua Tree	429,690	1976	NPS	Joshua Tree NM
Kaiser	22,700	1976	USFS	Sierra NF
Lassen Volcanic	78,982	1972	NPS	Lassen Volcanic NP
Lava Beds	28,460	1972	NPS	Lava Beds NM
Machesna Mountain	19,880	1984	USFS	Los Padres NF
Machesna Mountain	120	1984	BLM	Bakersfield District
Marble Mountain	241,744	1964, 1984	USFS	Klamath NF
Mokelumne	104,461	1964, 1984	USFS	Eldorado, Stanislaus, Toiyabe NFs
Monarch	45,000	1984	USFS	Sierra, Sequoia NFs
Mount Shasta	37,000	1984	USFS	Shasta-Trinity NF
North Fork	8,100	1984	USFS	Six Rivers NF
Phillip Burton	25,370	1976, 1985	NPS	Point Reyes National Seashore
Pine Creek	13,100	1984	USFS	Cleveland NF
Pinnacles	12,952	1976	NPS	Pinnacles NM
Red Buttes	16,150	1984	USFS	Rogue River NF
Russian	12,000	1984	USFS	Klamath NF
San Gabriel	36,118	1968	USFS	Angeles NF
San Gorgonio	56,722	1964, 1984	USFS	San Bernardino NF
San Jacinto	32,040	1964, 1984	USFS	San Bernardino NF
San Mateo Canyon	39,540	1984	USFS	Cleveland NF
San Rafael	150,610	1968, 1984	USFS	Los Padres NF
Santa Lucia	18,679	1978	USFS	Los Padres NF
Santa Lucia	1,733	1978	BLM	Bakersfield District
Santa Rosa	20,160	1984	USFS	San Bernardino NF
Sequoia-Kings Canyon	736,980	1984	NPS	Sequoia-Kings Canyon NP
Sheep Mountain	43,600	1984	USFS	Angeles, San Bernardino NFs
Siskiyou	153,000	1984	USFS	Six Rivers, Klamath, Siskiyou NFs
Snow Mountain	37,000	1984	USFS	Mendocino NF
South Sierra	63,000	1984	USFS	Sequoia, Inyo NFs
South Warner	70,385	1964, 1984	USFS	Modoc NF
Thousand Lakes	16,335	1964	USFS	Lassen NF
Trinity Alps	495,377	1984	USFS	Klamath, Six Rivers, Shasta Trinity NFs
Trinity Alps	4,623	1984	BLM	Ukiah District
Ventana	164,144	1969, 1978, 1984	USFS	Los Padres NF
Yolla Bolly-Middle Eel	145,404	1964, 1984	USFS	Mendocino, Six Rivers, Shasta-Trinity NFs
Yolla Bolly-Middle Eel	8,500	1984	BLM	Ukiah District
Yosemite	677,600	1984	NPS	Yosemite NP

State Total: 5,926,158

Wilderness Area	Acres	Year Designated	Agency	Public Land Unit
COLORADO				
Big Blue	98,320	1980	USFS	Uncompahgre NF
Black Canyon of the Gunnison	11,180	1976	NPS	Black Canyon of the Gunnison NM
Cache La Poudre	9,238	1980	USFS	Roosevelt NF
Collegiate Peaks	166,654	1980	USFS	Gunnison, San Isabel, White River NFs
Comanche Peak	66,791	1980	USFS	Roosevelt NF
Eagles Nest	133,325	1976	USFS	Arapaho, White River NFs
Flat Tops	235,035	1975	USFS	Routt, White River NFs
Great Sand Dunes	33,450	1976	NPS	Great Sand Dunes NM
Holy Cross	122,037	1980	USFS	San Isabel, White River NFs
Hunter-Fryingpan	74,250	1978	USFS	White River NFs
Indian Peaks	70,374	1978	USFS	Arapaho, Roosevelt NFs
Indian Peaks	2,922	1980	NPS	Rocky Mountain NP
La Garita	103,986	1964, 1980	USFS	Gunnison, Rio Grande NFs
Lizard Head	41,189	1980	USFS	San Juan, Uncompahgre NFs
Lost Creek	105,090	1980	USFS	Pike NF
Maroon Bells-Snowmass	181,138	1980	USFS	Gunnison, White River NFs
Mesa Verde	8,100	1976	NPS	Mesa Verde NP
Mount Evans	74,401	1980	USFS	Arapaho, Pike NFs
Mount Massive	27,980	1980	USFS	San Isabel NF
Mount Massive	2,560	1980	FWS	Leadvill Fish Hatchery
Mount Sneffels	16,505	1980	USFS	Uncompahgre NF
Mount Zirkel	139,818	1964, 1980	USFS	Routt, Roosevelt NFs
Neota	9,924	1980	USFS	Roosevelt, Routt NFs
Never Summer	13,702	1980	USFS	Arapaho, Routt NFs
Platte River	770	1984	USFS	Routt NF
Raggeds	59,519	1980	USFS	Gunnison, White River NFs
Rawah	73,020	1964	USFS	Roosevelt, Routt NFs
South San Juan	127,690	1980	USFS	Rio Grande, San Juan NFs
Weminuche	459,804	1975, 1980	USFS	Rio Grande, San Juan NFs
West Elk	176,092	1964, 1980	USFS	Gunnison NF
	State Total: 2,644,864			
FLORIDA				
Alexander Springs	7,700	1984	USFS	Ocala NF
Big Gum Swamp	13,600	1984	USFS	Osceola NF
Billies Bay	3,120	1984	USFS	Ocala NF
Bradwell Bay	24,602	1975, 1984	USFS	Apalachicola NF
Cedar Keys	379	1972	FWS	Cedar Keys NWR
Chassahowitzka	23,617	1976	FWS	Chassahowitzka NWR
Everglades	1,296,500	1978	NPS	Everglades NP
Florida Keys	6,245	1975, 1982	FWS	Florida Keys NWR
Island Bay	20	1970	FWS	Island Bay NWR
J.N. "Ding" Darling	2,619	1976	FWS	J.N. "Ding" Darling NWR
Juniper Prairie	13,260	1984	USFS	Ocala NF
Lake Woodruff	1,066	1976	FWS	Lake Woodruff NWR
Little Lake George	2,500	1984	USFS	Ocala NF
Mud Swamp/New River	7,800	1984	USFS	Apalachicola NF
Passage Key	36	1970	FWS	Passage Key NWR
Pelican Island	6	1970	FWS	Pelican Island NWR
St. Marks	17,350	1975	FWS	St. Marks NWR
	State Total: 1,420,420			
GEORGIA				
Big Frog	83	1984	USFS	Cherokee NF
Blackbeard Island	3,000	1975	FWS	Blackbeard Island NWR
Brasstown	11,405	1986	USFS	Chattahoochee NF
Cohutta	35,247	1975, 1986	USFS	Chattahoochee NF
Cumberland Island	8,840	1982	NPS	Cumberland Island National Seashore
Ellicott Rock	2,181	1975, 1984	USFS	Chattahoochee NF
Okefenokee	353,981	1974	FWS	Okefenokee NWR
Raven Cliffs	8,562	1986	USFS	Chattahoochee NF

Wilderness Area	Acres	Year Designated	Agency	Public Land Unit
Rich Mountain	9,649	1986	USFS	Chattahoochee NF
Southern Nantahala	12,439	1984	USFS	Chattahoochee NF
Tray Mountain	9,702	1986	USFS	Chattahoochee NF
Wolf Island	5,126	1975	FWS	Wolf Island NWR
State Total: 460,215				
HAWAII				
Haleakala	19,270	1976	NPS	Haleakala NP
Hawaii Volcanoes	123,100	1978	NPS	Hawaii Volcanoes NP
State Total: 142,370				
IDAHO				
Craters of the Moon	43,243	1970	NPS	Craters of the Moon NM
Frank Church—River of No Return	2,361,767	1980	USFS	Bitterroot, Boise, Challis, Nezperce, Payette, Salmon NFs
Frank Church—River of No Return	720	1980	BLM	Coeur d'Alene District
Gospel Hump	205,900	1978	USFS	Nezperce NF
Hells Canyon	83,800	1975	USFS	Nezperce, Payette NFs
Sawtooth	217,088	1972	USFS	Boise, Challis, Sawtooth NFs
Selway-Bitterroot	1,089,017	1964, 1980	USFS	Bitterroot, Clearwater, Nezperce NFs
State Total: 4,001,535				
ILLINOIS				
Crab Orchard	4,050	1976	FWS	Crab Orchard NWR
State Total: 4,050				
INDIANA				
Charles C. Deam	12,935	1982	USFS	Wayne-Hoosier NF
State Total: 12,935				
KENTUCKY				
Beaver Creek	4,756	1975	USFS	Daniel Boone NF
Clifty	13,300	1985	USFS	Daniel Boone NF
State Total: 18,056				
LOUISIANA				
Breton	5,000	1975	FWS	Breton NWR
Kisatchie	8,700	1980	USFS	Kisatchie NF
Lacassine	3,346	1976	FWS	Lacassine NWR
State Total: 17,046				
MAINE				
Moosehorn	7,386	1970, 1975	FWS	Moosehorn NWR
State Total: 7,386				
MASSACHUSETTS				
Monomoy	2,420	1970	FWS	Monomoy NWR
State Total: 2,420				
MICHIGAN				
Big Island Lake	5,500	1987	USFS	Hiawatha NF
Delirium	11,870	1987	USFS	Hiawatha NF
Horseshoe Bay	3,790	1987	USFS	Hiawatha NF
Huron Islands	147	1970	FWS	Huron Islands NWR
Isle Royale	131,880	1976	NPS	Isle Royale NP
Mackinac	12,230	1987	USFS	Hiawatha NF
McCormick	16,850	1987	USFS	Ottawa NF
Michigan Islands	12	1970	FWS	Michigan Islands NWR
Nordhouse Dunes	3,450	1987	USFS	Manistee NF
Rock River Canyon	4,640	1987	USFS	Hiawatha NF
Round Island	378	1987	USFS	Hiawatha NF
Seney	25,150	1970	FWS	Seney NWR
Sturgeon River Gorge	14,500	1987	USFS	Ottawa NF
Sylvania	18,327	1987	USFS	Ottawa NF
State Total: 248,724				

Wilderness Area	Acres	Year Designated	Agency	Public Land Unit
MINNESOTA				
Agassiz	4,000	1976	FWS	Agassiz NWR
Boundary Waters Canoe Area	798,309	1964, 1978	USFS	Superior NF
Tamarac	2,180	1976	FWS	Tamarac NWR
	State Total: 804,489			
MISSISSIPPI				
Black Creek	4,560	1984	USFS	DeSoto NF
Gulf Islands	1,800	1978	NPS	Gulf Islands National Seashore
Leaf	940	1984	USFS	DeSoto NF
	State Total: 7,300			
MISSOURI				
Bell Mountain	8,817	1980	USFS	Mark Twain NF
Devil's Backbone	6,595	1980	USFS	Mark Twain NF
Hercules Glades	12,314	1976	USFS	Mark Twain NF
Irish	16,500	1984	USFS	Mark Twain NF
Mingo	7,730	1976	FWS	Mingo NWR
Paddy Creek	6,728	1983	USFS	Mark Twain NF
Piney Creek	8,087	1980	USFS	Mark Twain NF
Rockpile Mountain	4,089	1980	USFS	Mark Twain NF
	State Total: 70,860			
MONTANA				
Absaroka-Beartooth	920,310	1978, 1983	USFS	Custer, Gallatin NFs
Anaconda-Pintlar	157,874	1964	USFS	Beaverhead, Bitterroot, Deerlodge NFs
Bob Marshall	1,009,356	1964, 1978	USFS	Flathead, Lewis & Clark NFs
Cabinet Mountains	94,272	1964	USFS	Kaniksu, Kootenai NFs
Gates of the Mountains	28,562	1964	USFS	Helena NF
Great Bear	286,700	1978	USFS	Flathead NF
Lee Metcalf	248,944	1983	USFS	Gallatin, Beaverhead NFs
Lee Metcalf	6,000	1983	BLM	Bear Trap Canyon, Butte District
Medicine Lake	11,366	1976	FWS	Medicine Lake NWR
Mission Mountains	73,877	1975	USFS	Flathead NF
Rattlesnake	29,824	1980	USFS	Lolo NF
Red Rock Lakes	32,350	1976	FWS	Red Rock Lakes NWR
Scapegoat	239,296	1972	USFS	Helena, Lolo, Lewis & Clark NFs
Selway-Bitterroot	248,893	1964	USFS	Bitterroot, Lolo NFs
UL Bend	20,819	1976, 1983	FWS	UL Bend NWR
Welcome Creek	28,135	1978	USFS	Lolo NF
	State Total: 3,436,578			
NEBRASKA				
Fort Niobrara	4,635	1976	FWS	Fort Niobrara NWR
Soldier Creek	8,100	1986	USFS	Nebraska NF
	State Total: 12,735			
NEVADA				
Jarbidge	64,667	1964	USFS	Humboldt NF
	State Total: 64,667			
NEW HAMPSHIRE				
Great Gulf	5,552	1964	USFS	White Mountain NF
Pemigewasset	45,000	1984	USFS	White Mountain NF
Presidential Range—Dry River	27,380	1975, 1984	USFS	White Mountain NF
Sandwich Range	25,000	1984	USFS	White Mountain NF
	State Total: 102,932			
NEW JERSEY				
Brigantine	6,681	1975	FWS	Brigantine NWR
Great Swamp	3,660	1968	FWS	Great Swamp NWR
	State Total: 10,341			

Wilderness Area	Acres	Year Designated	Agency	Public Land Unit
NEW MEXICO				
Aldo Leopold	201,966	1980	USFS	Gila NF
Apache Kid	44,650	1980	USFS	Cibola NF
Bandelier	23,267	1976	NPS	Bandelier NM
Bisti	3,968	1984	BLM	Albuquerque District
Blue Range	30,000	1980	USFS	Apache, Gila NFs
Bosque del Apache	30,287	1975	FWS	Bosque del Apache NWR
Capitan Mountains	34,513	1980	USFS	Lincoln NF
Carlsbad Caverns	33,125	1978	NPS	Carlsbad Caverns NP
Cebolla	60,000	1987	BLM	Albuquerque District
Chama River Canyon	50,260	1978	USFS	Carson, Santa Fe NFs
Cruces Basin	18,000	1980	USFS	Carson NF
De-na-zin	23,872	1984	BLM	Albuquerque District
Dome	5,200	1980	USFS	Santa Fe NF
Gila	557,819	1964, 1980	USFS	Gila NF
Latir Peak	20,000	1980	USFS	Carson NF
Manzano Mountain	36,650	1978	USFS	Cibola NF
Pecos	223,333	1964, 1980	USFS	Carson, Santa Fe NFs
Salt Creek	9,621	1970	FWS	Bitterlake NWR
San Pedro Parks	41,132	1964	USFS	Santa Fe NF
Sandia Mountain	37,028	1978, 1980 1984	USFS	Cibola NF
West Malpais	38,210	1987	BLM	Albuquerque District
Wheeler Peak	19,661	1964, 1980	USFS	Carson NF
White Mountain	48,366	1964, 1980	USFS	Lincoln NF
Withington	18,869	1980	USFS	Cibola NF
State Total: 1,609,797				
NEW YORK				
Fire Island	1,363	1980	NPS	Fire Island National Seashore
State Total: 1,363				
NORTH CAROLINA				
Birkhead Mountains	4,790	1984	USFS	Uwharrie NF
Catfish Lake South	7,600	1984	USFS	Croatan NF
Ellicott Rock	4,022	1975, 1984	USFS	Nantahala NF
Joyce Kilmer—Slickrock	13,181	1975, 1984	USFS	Nantahala NF
Linville Gorge	10,975	1964, 1984	USFS	Pisgah NF
Middle Prong	7,900	1984	USFS	Pisgah NF
Pocosin	11,000	1984	USFS	Croatan NF
Pond Pine	1,860	1984	USFS	Croatan NF
Sheep Ridge	9,540	1984	USFS	Croatan NF
Shining Rock	18,450	1964, 1984	USFS	Pisgah NF
Southern Nantahala	10,900	1984	USFS	Nantahala NF
Swanquarter	8,785	1976	FWS	Swanquarter NWR
State Total: 109,003				
NORTH DAKOTA				
Chase Lake	4,155	1975	FWS	Chase Lake NWR
Lostwood	5,577	1975	FWS	Lostwood NWR
Theodore Roosevelt	29,920	1978	NPS	Theodore Roosevelt NP
State Total: 39,652				
OHIO				
West Sister Island	77	1975	FWS	West Sister Island NWR
State Total: 77				
OKLAHOMA				
Black Fork Mountain	4,583	1988	USFS	Ouachita NF
Upper Kiamichi River	9,371	1988	USFS	Ouachita NF
Wichita Mountains	8,570	1970	FWS	Wichita Mountains NWR
State Total: 22,524				

Wilderness Area	Acres	Year Designated	Agency	Public Land Unit
OREGON				
Badger Creek	24,000	1984	USFS	Mount Hood NF
Black Canyon	13,400	1984	USFS	Ochoco NF
Boulder Creek	19,100	1984	USFS	Umpqua NF
Bridge Creek	5,400	1984	USFS	Ochoco NF
Bull of the Woods	34,900	1984	USFS	Mount Hood, Willamette NFs
Columbia	39,000	1984	USFS	Mount Hood NF
Cummins Creek	9,300	1984	USFS	Siuslaw NF
Diamond Peak	52,337	1964, 1984	USFS	Deschutes, Willamette NFs
Drift Creek	5,800	1984	USFS	Siuslaw NF
Eagle Cap	358,461	1964, 1972 1984	USFS	Wallowa-Whitman NF
Gearhart Mountain	22,809	1964, 1984	USFS	Fremont NF
Grassy Knob	17,200	1984	USFS	Siskiyou NF
Hells Canyon	130,095	1975, 1984	USFS	Wallowa-Whitman NF
Hells Canyon	1,038	1984	BLM	Vale District
Kalmiopsis	179,700	1964, 1978	USFS	Siskiyou NF
Menagerie	4,725	1984	USFS	Willamette NF
Middle Santiam	7,500	1984	USFS	Willamette NF
Mill Creek	17,400	1984	USFS	Ochoco NF
Monument Rock	19,800	1984	USFS	Malheur, Wallowa-Whitman NF
Mount Hood	46,520	1964, 1978	USFS	Mt. Hood NF
Mount Jefferson	107,008	1968, 1984	USFS	Deschutes, Mt. Hood, Willamette NFs
Mount Thielsen	55,100	1984	USFS	Umpqua, Winema, Willamette NFs
Mount Washington	52,516	1964, 1984	USFS	Deschutes, Willamette NFs
Mountain Lake	23,071	1964	USFS	Winema NF
North Fork John Day	121,400	1984	USFS	Wallowa-Whitman, Umatilla NFs
North Fork Umatilla	20,200	1984	USFS	Umatilla NF
Oregon Islands	5	1978	BLM	Coos Bay District
Oregon Islands	480	1970, 1978	FWS	Oregon Islands NWR
Red Buttes	3,750	1984	USFS	Siskiyou NF
Rock Creek	7,400	1984	USFS	Siuslaw NF
Rogue-Umpqua Divide	33,200	1984	USFS	Umpqua, Rogue River NFs
Salmon-Huckleberry	44,560	1984	USFS	Mount Hood NF
Sky Lakes	116,300	1984	USFS	Rogue River, Winema NF
Strawberry Mountain	68,303	1964, 1984	USFS	Malheur NF
Table Rock	5,500	1984	BLM	Salem District
Three Arch Rocks	15	1970	FWS	Three Arch Rocks NWR
Three Sisters	285,202	1964, 1978 1984	USFS	Deschutes, Willamette NFs
Waldo Lake	39,200	1984	USFS	Willamette NF
Wenaha-Tucannon	66,375	1978	USFS	Umatilla NF
Wild Rogue	25,658	1978	USFS	Siskiyou NF
Wild Rogue	10,160	1978	BLM	Medford District
	State Total: 2,093,888			
PENNSYLVANIA				
Allegheny Islands	368	1984	USFS	Allegheny NF
Hickory Creek	9,337	1984	USFS	Allegheny NF
	State Total: 9,705			
SOUTH CAROLINA				
Cape Romain	29,000	1975	FWS	Cape Romain NWR
Congaree Swamp National Monument	15,010	1988	NPS	
Ellicott Rock	2,809	1975	USFS	Sumter NF
Hell Hole Bay	1,980	1980	USFS	Francis Marion NF
Little Wambaw Swamp	5,000	1980	USFS	Francis Marion NF
Wambaw Creek	1,640	1980	USFS	Francis Marion NF
Wambaw Swamp	5,100	1980	USFS	Francis Marion NF
	State Total: 60,539			

Wilderness Area	Acres	Year Designated	Agency	Public Land Unit
SOUTH DAKOTA				
Badlands	64,250	1976	NPS	Badlands NP
Black Elk	9,824	1980	USFS	Black Hills NF
State Total: 74,074				
TENNESSEE				
Bald River Gorge	3,887	1984	USFS	Cherokee NF
Big Frog	7,972	1984, 1986	USFS	Cherokee NF
Big Laurel Branch	6,251	1986	USFS	Cherokee NF
Citico Creek	16,000	1984	USFS	Cherokee NF
Cohutta	1,795	1975	USFS	Cherokee NF
Gee Creek	2,493	1975	USFS	Cherokee NF
Joyce Kilmer—Slickrock	3,832	1975	USFS	Cherokee NF
Little Frog Mountain	4,800	1986	USFS	Cherokee NF
Pond Mountain	6,665	1986	USFS	Cherokee NF
Sampson Mountain	8,319	1986	USFS	Cherokee NF
Unaka Mountain	4,700	1986	USFS	Cherokee NF
State Total: 66,714				
TEXAS				
Big Slough	3,000	1984	USFS	Davy Crockett NF
Guadalupe Mountains	46,850	1978	NPS	Guadalupe Mountains NP
Indian Mounds	9,946	1984	USFS	Sabine NF
Little Lake Creek	4,000	1984	USFS	Sam Houston NF
Turkey Hill	5,400	1984	USFS	Angelina NF
Upland Island	12,000	1984	USFS	Angelina NF
State Total: 81,196				
UTAH				
Ashdown Gorge	7,000	1984	USFS	Dixie NF
Beaver Dam Mountains	2,597	1984	BLM	Cedar City District
Box-Death Hollow	26,000	1984	USFS	Dixie NF
Dark Canyon	45,000	1984	USFS	Manti-Lasal NF
Deseret Peak	25,500	1984	USFS	Wasatch-Cache NF
High Uintas	460,000	1984	USFS	Ashley, Wasatch-Cache NFs
Lone Peak	30,088	1978	USFS	Uinta, Wasatch NFs
Mount Naomi	44,350	1984	USFS	Wasatch-Cache NF
Mount Nebo	28,000	1984	USFS	Uinta NF
Mount Olympus	16,000	1984	USFS	Wasatch-Cache NF
Mount Timpanogos	10,750	1984	USFS	Uinta NF
Paria Canyon—Vermilion Cliffs	19,954	1984	BLM	Cedar City District
Pine Valley Mountain	50,000	1984	USFS	Dixie NF
Twin Peaks	13,100	1984	USFS	Wasatch-Cache NF
Wellsville Mountain	23,850	1984	USFS	Wasatch-Cache NF
State Total: 802,189				
VERMONT				
Big Branch	6,720	1984	USFS	Green Mountain NF
Breadloaf	21,480	1984	USFS	Green Mountain NF
Bristol Cliffs	3,738	1975, 1976	USFS	Green Mountain NF
George D. Aiken	5,060	1984	USFS	Green Mountain NF
Lye Brook	14,621	1975, 1984	USFS	Green Mountain NF
Peru Peak	6,920	1984	USFS	Green Mountain NF
State Total: 58,539				

Wilderness Area	Acres	Year Designated	Agency	Public Land Unit
VIRGINIA				
Barbours Creek	5,700	1988	USFS	Jefferson, George Washington NFs
Beartown	6,375	1984	USFS	Jefferson NF
James River Face	8,903	1975, 1984	USFS	Jefferson NF
Kimberling Creek	5,580	1984	USFS	Jefferson NF
Lewis Fork	5,802	1984, 1988	USFS	Jefferson NF
Little Dry Run	3,400	1984	USFS	Jefferson NF
Little Wilson Creek	3,855	1984	USFS	Jefferson NF
Mountain Lake	8,253	1984	USFS	Jefferson NF
Peters Mountain	3,326	1984	USFS	Jefferson NF
Ramseys Draft	6,725	1984	USFS	George Washington NF
Rich Hole	6,450	1988	USFS	George Washington NF
Rough Mountain	9,300	1988	USFS	George Washington NF
Saint Mary's	10,090	1984	USFS	George Washington NF
Shawvers Run	3,665	1988	USFS	Jefferson, George Washington NFs
Shenandoah	79,579	1976	NPS	Shenandoah NP
Thunder Ridge	2,450	1984	USFS	Jefferson NF
	State Total: 169,453			
WASHINGTON				
Alpine Lakes	305,407	1976	USFS	Mt. Baker-Snoqualmie, Wenatchee NFs
Boulder River	49,000	1984	USFS	Mount Baker-Snoqualmie NF
Buckhorn	44,474	1984, 1986	USFS	Olympic NF
Clearwater	14,300	1984	USFS	Mount Baker-Snoqualmie NF
Colonel Bob	12,120	1984	USFS	Olympic NF
Glacier Peak	576,648	1964, 1968 1984	USFS	Mt. Baker-Snoqualmie, Wenatchee NFs
Glacier View	3,050	1984	USFS	Gifford Pinchot NF
Goat Rocks	105,023	1964, 1984	USFS	Gifford Pinchot, Mt. Baker-Snoqualmie NFs
Henry M. Jackson	102,671	1984	USFS	Wenatchee, Mt. Baker-Snoqualmie NFs
Indian Heaven	20,650	1984	USFS	Gifford Pinchot NF
Juniper Dunes	7,140	1984	BLM	Spokane District
Lake Chelan-Sawtooth	150,704	1984	USFS	Okanogan, Wenatchee NFs
Mount Adams	46,776	1964, 1984	USFS	Gifford Pinchot NF
Mount Baker	117,580	1984	USFS	Mount Baker-Snoqualmie NF
Mount Rainier	216,855	1988	NPS	Mount Rainier NP
Mount Skokomish	13,015	1984, 1986	USFS	Olympic NF
Noisy-Diobsud	14,300	1984	USFS	Mount Baker-Snoqualmie NF
Norse Peak	50,902	1984	USFS	Wenatchee, Mt. Baker-Snoqualmie NFs
Olympic	876,669	1988	NPS	Olympic NP
Pasayten	529,850	1968, 1984	USFS	Mount Baker-Snoqualmie, Okanogan NFs
Salmo-Priest	41,335	1984	USFS	Kaniksu Colville NF
San Juan Islands	353	1976	FWS	San Juan Islands NWR
Stephen Mather	634,614	1988	NPS	North Cascades NP
Tatoosh	15,720	1984	USFS	Gifford Pinchot NF
The Brothers	16,682	1984, 1986	USFS	Olympic NF
Trapper Creek	6,050	1984	USFS	Gifford Pinchot NF
Washington Islands	485	1970	FWS	Washington Islands NWR
Wenaha-Tucannon	111,048	1978	USFS	Umatilla NF
William O. Douglas	166,603	1984	USFS	Wenatchee, Gifford Pinchot NFs
Wonder Mountain	2,320	1984	USFS	Olympic NF
	State Total: 4,252,344			
WEST VIRGINIA				
Cranberry	35,864	1983	USFS	Monongahela NF
Dolly Sods	10,215	1975	USFS	Monongahela NF
Laurel Fork North	6,055	1983	USFS	Monongahela NF
Laurel Fork South	5,997	1983	USFS	Monongahela NF
Mountain Lake	2,500	1988	USFS	Jefferson NF
Otter Creek	20,000	1975	USFS	Monongahela NF
	State Total: 80,631			

Wilderness Area	Acres	Year Designated	Agency	Public Land Unit
WISCONSIN				
Blackjack Springs	5,886	1978	USFS	Nicolet NF
Headwaters	19,950	1984	USFS	Nicolet NF
Porcupine Lake	4,195	1984	USFS	Chequamegon NF
Rainbow Lake	6,583	1975	USFS	Chequamegon NF
Whisker Lake	7,345	1978	USFS	Nicolet NF
Wisconsin Islands	29	1970	FWS	Wisconsin Islands NWR
State Total: 43,988				
WYOMING				
Absaroka-Beartooth	23,750	1984	USFS	Shoshone NF
Bridger	428,169	1964, 1984	USFS	Bridger-Teton NF
Cloud Peak	195,500	1984	USFS	Big Horn NF
Encampment River	10,400	1984	USFS	Medicine Bow NF
Fitzpatrick	198,838	1976, 1984	USFS	Shoshone NF
Gros Ventre	287,000	1984	USFS	Bridger-Teton NF
Huston Park	31,300	1984	USFS	Medicine Bow NF
Jedediah Smith	116,535	1984	USFS	Targhee NF
North Absaroka	350,538	1964	USFS	Shoshone NF
Platte River	22,230	1984	USFS	Medicine Bow, Routt NFs
Popo Agie	101,991	1984	USFS	Shoshone NF
Savage Run	14,940	1978	USFS	Medicine Bow NF
Teton	585,468	1964, 1984	USFS	Bridger-Teton NF
Washakie	703,981	1964, 1968 1984	USFS	Shoshone NF
Winegar Hole	14,000	1984	USFS	Bridger-Teton NF
State Total: 3,084,640				
U.S. Total: 90,760,106				

ABBREVIATIONS:

USFS—U.S. Forest Service
NPS—National Park Service
FWS—Fish & Wildlife Service
BLM—Bureau of Land Management
NF—National Forest
NP—National Park
NWR—National Wildlife Refuge
NM—National Monument

NATIONAL WILDERNESS PRESERVATION SYSTEM
Summary Data

Agency	No. of Units	Acreage
U.S. Forest Service	354	32,457,616
National Park Service	43	38,502,565
Fish and Wildlife Service	66	19,332,976
Bureau of Land Management	25	466,949
TOTAL	488	90,760,106

TOTAL UNITS IN NWPS: 474—of the 488 units noted, 14 are managed by more than one agency.

Fourteen wilderness areas lie in more than one state—13 areas are in two states and one area in three.

AREAS IN MULTIPLE STATES:
- Absaroka-Beartooth (MT,WY)–USFS
- Beaver Dam Mountains (AZ,UT)—BLM
- Big Frog (GA,TN)—USFS
- Cohutta (GA,TN)—USFS
- Ellicott Rock (GA,NC,TN)—USFS
- Hells Canyon (ID,OR)—USFS
- Joyce Kilmer-Slickrock (NC,TN)—USFS
- Mountain Lake (VA,WV)—USFS
- Paria Canyon-Vermilion Cliffs (AZ,UT)—BLM
- Platte River (CO,WY)—USFS
- Red Buttes (CA,OR)—USFS
- Selway–Bitterroot (ID,MT)—USFS
- Southern Nantahala (GA,NC)—USFS
- Wenaha-Tucannon (OR,WA)—USFS

AREAS MANAGED BY MORE THAN ONE AGENCY:
- Arizona: Kanab Creek (USFS,BLM)
- California: Ansel Adams (USFS,NPS)
  - Ishi (USFS,BLM)
  - Machesna Mountain (USFS,BLM)
  - Santa Lucia (USFS,BLM)
  - Trinity Alps (USFS,BLM)
  - Yolla Bolla-Middle Eel (USFS,BLM)
- Colorado: Indian Peaks (USFS,NPS)
  - Mount Massive (USFS,FWS)
- Idaho: Frank Church—River of No Return (USFS,BLM)
- Montana: Lee Metcalf (USFS,BLM)
- Oregon: Hells Canyon (USFS,BLM)
  - Oregon Islands (FWS,BLM)

Appendix F

How to Write Your Elected Officials

1. Address your letter properly:
   a. *Your representative:*
      The Honorable _____
      House Office Building
      Washington, D.C. 20515
      Dear Representative _____ ,
   b. *Your senators:*
      The Honorable _____
      Senate Office Building
      Washington, D.C. 20510
      Dear Senator _____ ,
   c. *The president:*
      The President
      The White House
      1600 Pennsylvania Avenue, N.W.
      Washington, D.C. 20500
      Dear Mr. President,
2. Tell who you are and why you are interested in this subject. Be sure to give your return address.
3. Always be courteous and reasonable. You can disagree with a particular position, but be respectful in doing so. You will gain little by being hostile or abusive.
4. Be brief. Keep letters to one page or less. Cover only one subject, and come to the point quickly. Trying to cover several issues confuses the subject and dilutes your impact.
5. Write in your own words. It is more important to be authentic than polished. Don't use form letters or stock phrases provided by others. Speak or write from your own personal experiences and interests. Try to show how the issue affects the legislator's own district and constituents.
6. If you are writing about a specific bill, identify it by number (for instance, H.R. 321 or S.123). You can get a free copy of any bill or committee report by writing to the House Document Room, U.S. House of Representatives, Washington, D.C. 20515 or the Senate Document Room, U.S. Senate, Washington, D.C. 20510.
7. Ask your legislator to vote a specific way, support a specific amendment, or take a specific action. Otherwise you will get a form response that says: "Thank you for your concern. Of course I support clean air, pure water, apple pie, and motherhood."
8. If you have expert knowledge or specifically relevant experience, share it. But don't try to intimidate, threaten, or dazzle your representative. Don't pretend to have vast political influence or power. Legislators quickly see through artifice and posturing; they are professionals in this field.
9. If possible, include some reference to the legislator's past action on this or related issues. Show that you are aware of his or her past record and are following the issue closely.
10. Follow up with a short note of thanks after a vote on an issue that you support. Show your appreciation by making campaign contributions or working for candidates who support issues important to you.
11. Try to meet your senators and representatives when they come home to campaign, or visit their office in Washington if you are able. If they know who you are personally, you will have more influence when you call or write.
12. Join with others to exert your combined influence. An organization is usually more effective than isolated individuals.

Appendix G

List of Environmental Organizations

This is a sampling of nongovernmental national and international environmental organizations. For the more complete, annually updated Conservation Directory, send $15 to the National Wildlife Federation, 1400 Sixteenth Street NW, Washington, D.C., 20036. The directory includes many professional associations and state or local organizations not listed here. Your local library may have a copy. Most of the organizations publish a magazine or newsletter.

African Wildlife Foundation, 1717 Massachusetts Avenue NW, Washington, D.C. 20036 (202-265-8393). Finances and operates wildlife conservation projects in Africa.

American Committee for International Conservation, c/o Mike McCloskey, Sierra Club, 330 Pennsylvania Avenue SE, Washington, D.C. 20003 (202-547-1144). An association of nongovernmental organizations concerned with international conservation.

American Farmland Trust, 1920 N Street NW, Suite 400, Washington, D.C. 20036 (202-659-5170). Works for preservation of family farms and for soil conservation.

American Museum of Natural History, Central Park West at 79th Street, New York, NY 10024 (212-769-5000). Conducts natural history research and publishes educational material.

Center for Environmental Education, 1725 DeSales Street NW, Suite 500, Washington, D.C. 20036 (202-429-5609). A nongovernmental, nonprofit organization that sponsors programs for protection of endangered species.

Center for Science in the Public Interest, 1501 16th Street NW, Washington, D.C. 20036 (202-332-9110). National consumer advocacy organization that focuses on health and nutrition.

Clean Water Action Project, 317 Pennsylvania Avenue SE, Washington, D.C. 20003 (202-547-1196). Works for clean water and for protection of natural resources. Conducts voter education and public awareness projects.

Conservation International, 1015 18th Street NW, Suite 1000, Washington, D.C. 20036 (202-429-5660). Buys land or trades foreign debt for land set aside for nature preserves in developing countries.

Cousteau Society, Inc., 930 W. 21st Street, Norfolk, VA 23517 (804-627-1144). Produces television films, lectures, books, and research on ocean quality and other resource issues.

Defenders of Wildlife Inc., 1244 19th St. N.W., Washington, D.C. 20036 (202-659-9510). Their goal is to preserve, enhance, and protect the natural abundance and diversity of wildlife and their habitats.

Ducks Unlimited, Inc., One Waterfowl Way, Long Grove, IL 60047 (312-438-4300). Perpetuates waterfowl by purchasing and protecting wetland habitat.

Earth First!, P.O. Box 5871, Tucson, AZ 85703. A loose-knit association of radical environmental activists who engage in varying degrees of street theater, civil disobedience, and destruction of property.

Earth Island Institute, 300 Broadway, Suite 28, San Francisco, CA 94133. A clearinghouse for international information on environmental and resource issues. Founded by David Brower to bring together sources of conservation action and news.

Environmental Action Foundation, 1525 New Hampshire Ave. N.W., Washington, D.C. 20036 (202-745-4870). Formed to develop research and conduct broad educational programs on complex environmental issues.

Environmental Defense Fund, Inc., 257 Park Avenue South, New York, NY 10010 (212-505-2100). Protects environmental quality and public health through litigation and administrative appeals.

Environmental Law Institute, 1616 P Street NW, Suite 200, Washington, D.C. 20036 (202-328-5150). Sponsors research and education on environmental law and policy.

Friends of the Earth, 530 Seventh Street SE, Washington, D.C. 20003 (202-543-4312). Affiliated with groups in thirty-two countries around the world. Works to form public opinion and to influence government policies to protect nature.

Fund for Animals, Inc., 200 West 57th Street, New York, NY 10019 (212-246-2096). Advocacy group for humane treatment of all animals.

Greenpeace USA, 1436 U Street NW, Washington, D.C. 20009 (202-462-1177). Worldwide organization that works to halt nuclear weapons testing, to protect marine animals, and to stop pollution and environmental degradation.

Humane Society of the United States, 2100 L Street NW, Washington, D.C. 20037 (202-452-1100). Dedicated to the protection of both domestic and wild animals.

International Alliance for Sustainable Agriculture, 1701 University Avenue SE, Minneapolis, MN 55414. An alliance of organic farmers, researchers, consumers, and international organizations dedicated to sustainable agriculture.

International Union for Conservation of Nature and Natural Resources (IUCN), Avenue du Nont-Blanc CH-1196 Gland, Switzerland (022-64-71-81). Promotes scientifically based action for the conservation of wild plants, animals, and resources.

Izaak Walton League of America, Inc., 1401 Wilson Boulevard, Level B, Arlington, VA 22209 (703-528-1818). Educates the public on land, water, air, wildlife, and other conservation issues.

Land Institute, Route 3, Salina, KS 67401 (913-823-5376). Carries out research on perennial species, prairie polycultures, and sustainable agriculture. Has training programs and conferences.

League of Conservation Voters, 2000 L Street NW, Suite 804, Washington, D.C. 20036 (202-785-8683). A nonpartisan national political campaign committee that strives to elect environmentally responsible public officials. Publishes an annual evaluation of voting records of Congress.

National Audubon Society, 950 Third Avenue, New York, NY 10022 (212-832-3200). One of the oldest and largest conservation organizations, Audubon has many educational and recreational programs as well as an active lobbying and litigation staff.

National Clean Air Coalition, 1400 16th St. N.W., Washington, D.C. 20036 (202-797-5436). An umbrella organization made up of 35 other groups.

National Parks and Conservation Association, 1015 31st Street NW, Washington, D.C. 20007 (202-944-8530). A private nonprofit organization dedicated to preservation, promotion, and improvement of our national parks.

National Wildlife Federation, 1400 Sixteenth Street NW, Washington, D.C. 20036 (202-797-6800). Specializes in wildlife conservation but recognizes the importance of habitat and other resources to all living things. More than 5 million members.

National Wild Turkey Federation, Inc., Wild Turkey Building, P.O. Box 530, Edgefield, SC 29824 (803-637-3106). Dedicated to the wise conservation and management of the American wild turkey.

Natural Resources Defense Council, Inc., 122 East 42nd Street, New York, NY 10168 (212-949-0049). An environmental organization that monitors government agencies and brings legal action to protect the environment.

(The) Nature Conservancy, 1815 North Lynn Street, Arlington, VA 22209 (703-841-5300). Works with state and federal agencies to identify ecologically significant natural areas. Manages a system of over 1000 nature sanctuaries nationwide.

New Alchemy Institute, Box 432, Woods Hole, MA 02543 (617-563-2655). Conducts research and provides education on sustainable agriculture, aquaculture, and bioshelters.

Population Reference Bureau, 777 14th Street NW, Suite 800, Washington, D.C. (202-639-8040). Gathers, interprets, and publishes information on social, economic, and environmental implications of world population dynamics. Excellent data source.

Project Lighthawk, P.O. Box 8136, Santa Fe, NM 87504 (505-9982-9656). Uses light aircraft for aerial surveys of forest condition, range management, and other conservation issues. Offers a unique vantage point to environmentalists.

Quail Unlimited, Inc., P.O. Box 10041, Augusta, GA 30906 (404-724-6647). Dedicated to improving quail and upland game bird populations through habitat management and research.

Rain Forest Action Network, 300 Broadway, Suite 28, San Francisco, CA 94133 (415-398-4404). Shares offices with Earth Island Institute and focuses on actions designed to save rain forests around the world.

Resources for the Future, 1616 P Street NW, Washington, D.C. 20036 (202-328-5000). Conducts research and provides education about natural resource conservation issues.

Rodale Institute, 222 Main Street, Emmaus, PA 18049 (215-967-5171). A leading research institute for organic farming and alternative crops. Publishes magazines, books, and reports on regenerative farming.

The Ruffed Grouse Society, 1400 Lee Dr., Coraopolis, PA 15108 (412-262-4044). Dedicated to improving the environment for ruffled grouse, woodcock, and other forest wild life through habitat management.

Save-the-Redwoods League, 114 Sansome Street, Room 605, San Francisco, CA 94104 (415-362-2352). Buys land, plants trees, and works with state and federal agencies to save redwood trees.

Scientists' Institute for Public Information, 355 Lexington Avenue, New York, NY 10017 (212-661-9110). Enlists scientists and other experts in public information programs and public policy forums on a variety of environmental issues.

Sea Shepherd Conservation Society, P.O. Box 7000-S, Redondo Beach, CA 90277 (213-373-6979). An international marine conservation action program. Carries out field campaigns to call attention to and stop wildlife destruction and resource misuse.

Sierra Club, 730 Polk Street, San Francisco, CA 94109 (415-776-2211). Founded in 1892 by John Muir and others to explore, enjoy, and protect the wild places of the earth. Conducts outings, educational programs, volunteer work projects, litigation, political action, and administrative appeals. Has one of the most comprehensive programs of any conservation organization.

Student Conservation Association, Inc. Box 550, Charlestown, NH 03603 (603-826-5206). Coordinates environmental internships and volunteer jobs with state and federal agencies and private organizations for students and adults.

Trout Unlimited, National Headquarters, 501 Church St., NE, Vienna, VA 22180 (703-281-1100). Dedicated to the protection of clean water and the enhancement of trout and salmon fishery resources.

United Nations Environment Programme, P.O. Box 30552, Nairobi Kenya; and United Nations, Rm. DC2-0803, New York, NY 10017 (212-963-8138). Coordinates global environmental efforts with United Nations agencies, national governments, and nongovernmental organizations.

Waldebridge Ecological Centre, Worthyvale Manor Farm, Camelford, Cornwall P132 9TT England (Tele: 0840 212711). Conducts research and education on a variety of environmental issues. Publishes *The Ecologist*, an excellent global environmental journal.

Wilderness Society, 1400 I Street NW, 10th Floor, Washington, D.C. 20005 (202-842-3400). Dedicated to preserving wilderness and wildlife in America.

World Resources Institute, 1735 New York Avenue NW, Washington D.C. 20006 (202-638-6300). A policy research center that publishes excellent annual reports on world resources.

WorldWatch Institute, 1776 Massachusetts Avenue NW, Washington, D.C. 20036 (202-452-1999). A nonprofit research organization concerned with global trends and problems. Publishes excellent periodic reports and annual summaries.

World Wildlife Fund, 1250 Twenty-Fourth Street NW, Washington, DC 20037 (202-293-4800). Works worldwide to protect endangered wildlife and wildlands, especially in the tropics. Affiliated with the Conservation Foundation.

Zero Population Growth, Inc., 1601 Connecticut Avenue NW, Washington, D.C. 20009 (202-332-2200). Advocates of worldwide population stabilization.

Appendix H

United States Government Agencies

Army Corps of Engineers
Department of the Army
The Pentagon
Washington, D.C. 20310
(202) 272-0001
(Oversees the waterways of the United States)

Bureau of Land Management
C and 18th Street NW
Washington, D.C. 20240
(202) 343-9435
(Administers about half of all public lands, mainly in the western United States. Follows policy of multiple use for maximum public benefit.)

Bureau of Mines
2401 E Street NW
Washington, D.C. 20241
(202) 634-1004
(Oversees mineral production, mine safety, and mine reclamation.)

Bureau of Reclamation
Department of the Interior
Washington, D.C. 20241-0001
(202) 343-4662
(Builds and operates federal water projects, mostly in the western states, together with the Army Corps of Engineers.)

Council on Environmental Quality
722 Jackson Place NW
Washington, D.C. 20503
(202) 395-5750
(Advises the president on environmental matters.)

Department of Agriculture
14th Street and Independence Avenue SW
Washington, D.C. 20250
(202) 447-2791
(Manages national forests and grasslands and oversees farm prices, farm policies, and soil conservation.)

Department of Energy
1000 Independence Avenue SW
Washington, D.C. 20585
(202) 586-5000
(Administers energy programs in the United States.)

Department of Health and Human Services: Food and Drug Administration
5600 Fishers Lane
Rockville, MD 20857
(301) 443-1544
(Enforces laws requiring that foods and drugs be pure, safe, and wholesome.)

Department of the Interior
1800 C Street NW
Washington, D.C. 20240
(202) 343-3171
(Administers national parks, monuments, wildlife refuges, and public lands.)

Environmental Protection Agency
401 M Street SW
Washington, D.C. 20460
(202) 382-2090
(Enforces clean air and clean water laws. Identifies, regulates, and purifies toxic and hazardous materials.)

The Forest Service
P.O. Box 96090
Washington, D.C. 20090-6090
(202) 447-3760
(Administers national forests and grasslands.)

National Park Service
Interior Building
P.O. Box 37127
Washington, D.C. 20013-7127
(202) 343-7394
(Administers the national park system.)

NOAA/NESOIS
U.S. Department of Commerce
Washington, D.C. 20230
(202) 377-2985
(Administers satellite data and other weather and severe storm information.)

Soil Conservation Service
P.O. Box 2890
Washington, D.C. 20013
(202) 447-4543
(Provides technical and educational assistance for soil conservation and watershed protection.)

United States Coast Guard
2100 2nd St. SW
Washington, D.C. 20593
(202) 267-1587
(In charge of environmental cleanup after an oil spill on water.)

United States Fish and Wildlife Service
Washington, D.C. 20240
(202) 343-5634
(Carries out wildlife research and management. Enforces game, fish, and endangered species laws. Administers the national wildlife refuges.)

United States Geologic Survey
119 National Center
12201 Sunrise Valley Drive
Reston, VA 22092
(703) 648-4460
(Oversees the geologic resources of the United States.)

Appendix I

Environmental Publications

The following publications will help you keep informed and up to date on resource and environmental problems. Subscription prices, which tend to change, are not given. National, state, and local resource and environmental organizations are listed in the *Conservation Directory*, published annually by the National Wildlife Foundation, 1400 16th St. N.W., Washington, DC 20036.

American Forests, American Forestry Association, 1516 P St. N.W., Washington, DC 20005. Popular treatment of forest and conservation issues.

Annual Review of Energy, Department of Energy, Forrestal Building, 1000 Independence Ave. S.W., Washington, DC 20585. Basic data.

Audubon, National Audubon Society, 950 Third Ave., New York, NY 10022. Popular summaries of conservation and wildlife issues.

Audubon Wildlife Report, National Audubon Society, 950 Third Ave., New York, NY 10022. Annual summary of wildlife agencies, problems, and species; published since 1985; excellent source of data.

BioScience, American Institute of Biological Sciences, 730 11th St. N.W., Washington, DC 20001. Popular and technical coverage of biological aspects of conservation and environmental issues.

CoEvolution Quarterly, P.O. Box 428, Sausalito, CA 94965. Covers a wide range of environmental and self-sufficiency topics.

Conservation Biology, Blackwell Scientific Publications, Inc., 52 Beacon St., Boston, MA 02108. Semitechnical coverage of wildlife conservation.

Conservation Foundation Letter, Conservation Foundation, 1250 24th St. N.W., Washington, DC 20037. Good summaries of key issues.

Conservation News, National Wildlife Foundation, 1400 16th St. N.W., Washington, DC 20036. Popular coverage of wildlife issues.

Demographic Yearbook, Department of International Economic and Social Affairs, Statistical Office, United Nations Publishing Service, United Nations, NY 10017. Basic population data.

Earth Island Journal, Earth Island Institute, 300 Broadway, Suite 28, San Francisco, CA 94133. Nontechnical summaries of national and global conservation and environmental issues.

The Ecologist, Ecosystems Ltd., 73 Molesworth St., Wadebridge, Cornway PL27 7DS, United Kingdom. Wide range of articles on conservation and environmental issues from an international viewpoint.

Ecology, Ecological Society of America, Dr. Duncan T. Patten, Center for Environmental Studies, Arizona State University, Tempe, AR 85281. Professional journal.

Endangered Species UPDATE, School of Natural Resources, The University of Michigan, Ann Arbor, MI 48109. Monthly reprint of the latest U.S. Fish and Wildlife endangered species technical bulletin, a feature article, and technical notes.

Environment, Heldref Publications, 4000 Albemarle St. N.W., Washington, DC 20016. Nontechnical articles on environmental and resource issues.

Environmental Abstracts, Bowker A & I Publishing, 245 West 17th St., New York, NY 10011. Basic bibliographic tool; in most libraries.

Environmental Action, 1525 New Hampshire Ave. N.W., Washington, DC 20036. Popular coverage of environmental and resource issues; emphasis on political and social action.

Environmental Ethics, Department of Philosophy, University of Georgia, Athens, GA 30602. Major journal in the field.

The Environmental Professional, Editorial Office, Department of Geography, University of Iowa, Iowa City, IA 52242. Semitechnical discussion of environmental and resource issues.

Environmental Quality, Council on Environmental Quality, 722 Jackson Place N.W., Washington, DC 20006. Annual report on environmental problems and progress in environmental protection in the United States.

EPA Journal, Environmental Protection Agency. Order from Government Printing Office, Washington, DC 20402. Nontechnical coverage of environmental issues and updates on EPA activities.

Fisheries, American Fisheries Society, 5410 Grosvenor Lane, Bethesda, MD 20814. Professional journal.

The Futurist, World Future Society, P.O. Box 19285, Twentieth Street Station, Washington, DC 20036. Popular coverage of environmental, resource, and social issues with emphasis on the future.

Geotimes, American Geological Institute, 4220 King St., Alexandria, VA. 22302-1507. Many environmental geology articles.

International Wildlife, National Wildlife Federation, 1400 16th St. N.W., Washington, DC 20036. Popular coverage of global wildlife and other resource conservation issues.

Issues in Science and Technology, National Academy of Sciences, 2101 Constitution Ave. N.W., Washington, DC 20077-5576. Covers a range of issues, including environment and resources.

Journal of Environmental Education, Heldref Publications, 4000 Albemarle St. N.W., Suite 504, Washington, DC 20016. Useful information for teachers.

Journal of Forestry, Society of American Foresters, 5400 Grosvenor Lane, Bethesda, MD 20814. Professional journal.

Journal of Range Management, Society for Range Management, 1839 York St., Denver, CO 80206. Professional journal.

Journal of Soil and Water Conservation, Soil and Water Conservation Society, 7515 NE Ankeny Rd., Ankeny, Iowa 50021. Professional journal.

Journal of Wildlife Management, Wildlife Society, 5410 Grosvenor Lane, Bethesda, MD 20814. Covers basic issues and information.

National Geographic, National Geographic Society, P.O. Box 2895, Washington, DC 20077-9960. Popular coverage of wildlife and environmental issues; beautiful photographs.

National Parks and Conservation Magazine, National Parks and Conservation Association, 1015 31st St. N.W., Washington, DC 20007. Popular coverage of parks and wildlife issues.

National Wildlife, National Wildlife Federation, 1400 16th St. N.W., Washington, DC 20036. Popular coverage of wildlife and other resource conservation issues in the United States.

Natural History, American Museum of Natural History, Central Park West at 79th St., New York, NY 10024. Popular coverage of a broad range of topics, including environmental and resource issues.

Nature, 711 National Press Building, Washington, DC 20045. Summaries of latest research in a range of scientific fields.

New Scientist, 128 Long Acre, London, WC 2, England. Nontechnical coverage of environmental and other issues related to science.

Not Man Apart, Friends of the Earth, 530 Seventh St. SE, Washington, DC 20003. Nontechnical summaries and articles on national and international conservation and environmental issues.

Organic Gardening & Farming Magazine, Rodale Press, 33 E. Minor St., Emmaus, PA 18049. The best guide to organic gardening.

Pollution Abstracts, Cambridge Scientific Abstracts, 7200 Wisconsin Ave., Bethesda, MD 20814. Basic bibliographic tool; in many libraries.

Population and Vital Statistics Report, UN Publications Sales Section, New York, NY 10017. Basic population data.

Population Bulletin, Population Reference Bureau, 777 Fourteenth St. N.W., Suite 800, Washington, DC 20005. In-depth nontechnical articles on population issues.

Science, American Association for the Advancement of Science, 1333 H St. N.W., Washington, DC 20005. Technical articles and popular summaries of scientific issues; in recent years has decreased coverage of environmental and resource issues.

Science News, Science Service, Inc., 1719 N St. N.W., Washington, DC 20036. Popular weekly summaries of scientific developments, including environmental topics.

Scientific American, 415 Madison Ave., New York, NY 10017. Semitechnical articles on science with some coverage of environmental and resource issues.

Sierra, 730 Polk St., San Francisco, CA 94108. Popular coverage of conservation and environmental issues with emphasis on political action.

State of the World, WorldWatch Institute, 1776 Massachusetts Ave. N.W., Washington, DC 20036. Annual summary of environment and resource issues.

Statistical Yearbook, Department of International Economic and Social Affairs, Statistical Office, United Nations Publishing Service, United Nations, NY 10017. Annual summary of data on population, food production, resource production and consumption, energy, housing, and forestry.

Technology Review, Massachusetts Institute of Technology, Room E219-430, Cambridge, MA 02139. Popular discussion of scientific and engineering issues, with about half its pages on environment and resource issues.

Transition, Laurence G. Wolf, ed., Department of Geography, University of Cincinnati, Cincinnati, OH 45221. Quarterly journal of the Socially and Ecologically Responsible Geographers.

Wilderness, Wilderness Society, 1400 I St. N.W., 10th Floor, Washington, DC 20005. Nontechnical articles on wilderness and wildlife conservation.

World Development Report, World Bank, Publications Department, 1818 H Street N.W., Washington, DC 20433. Annual summary of economic development.

World Rain Forest Report, Rain forest Action Network, 300 Broadway, Suite 28, San Francisco, CA 94133. Summary of problems and progress in protecting rain forests.

World Resources, World Resources Institute, 1735 New York Ave. N.W., Washington, DC 20006. Summary of environment and resource problems; useful source of data; published every two years.

WorldWatch, WorldWatch Institute, 1776 Massachusetts Ave. N.W., Washington, DC 20036. Bimonthly magazine giving nontechnical summaries of key environmental and resource issues.

WorldWatch Papers, WorldWatch Institute, 1776 Massachusetts Ave. N.W., Washington, DC 20036. Series of nontechnical reports designed to serve as an early warning system on major environmental and resource problems.

Yearbook of World Energy Statistics, Department of International Economic and Social Affairs, Statistical Office, United Nations Publishing Service, United Nations, NY 10017. Annual summary of data on worldwide energy production.

Appendix J

Important United States Environmental Legislation

General
- National Environmental Policy Act of 1969 (NEPA)
- International Environmental Protection Act of 1983

Energy
- National Energy Act of 1978, 1980

Water Quality
- Water Quality Act of 1965
- Water Resources Planning Act of 1965
- Federal Water Pollution Control Acts of 1965, 1972
- Ocean Dumping Act of 1972
- Safe Drinking Water Act of 1974, 1984
- Clean Water Act of 1977, 1987
- Agricultural Chemicals in Ground Water Strategy of 1985

Air Quality
- Clean Air Act of 1963, 1965, 1970, 1977, 1990

Noise Control
- Noise Control Act of 1965
- Quiet Communities Act of 1978

Resources and Solid Waste Management
- Rivers and Harbors Act/Refuse Act of 1899
- Solid Waste Disposal Act of 1965, 1984
- Resources Recovery Act of 1970
- Resource Conservation and Recovery Act of 1976

Toxic Substances
- Price-Anderson Act of 1957
- Toxic Substances Control Act of 1976
- Resource Conservation and Recovery Act of 1976
- Comprehensive Environmental Response, Compensation, and Liability (Superfund) Act of 1980, 1986
- Nuclear Waste Policy Act of 1982
- Federal Hazardous Substances Act (FHSA) 1960, 1988

Pesticides
- Federal Insecticide, Fungicide, and Rodenticide Act (FIFRA) 1947
- Federal Insecticide, Fungicide, and Rodenticide Control Act of 1972, 1988
- Food, Drug, and Cosmetic Act and Its Amendments from 1954 to 1988

Wildlife Conservation
- Migrating Bird Treaty Act of 1918
- Migrating Bird Conservation Act of 1929
- Migrating Bird Hunting Stamp of 1934
- Fish and Wildlife Coordination Act of 1934
- Pittman Robertson Act of 1936
- Wildlife Restoration Act of 1937
- Anadromous Fish Conservation Act of 1965
- Fur Seal Act of 1966
- National Wildlife Refuge System Act of 1966, 1976, 1978
- Species Conservation Act of 1966, 1969
- Wild Horse and Burro Act of 1971
- Marine Mammal Protection Act of 1972
- Marine Protection, Research, and Sanctuaries Act of 1972, 1981
- Endangered Species Act of 1973, 1982, 1985, 1988
- Fishery Conservation and Management Act of 1976, 1978, 1982
- Whale Conservation and Protection Study Act of 1976
- Adopt-a-Horse (or Burro) Program of 1976
- Fish and Wildlife Improvement Act of 1978
- Fish and Wildlife Conservation Act of 1980 (Nongame Act)

Land Use and Conservation
- Mineral Leasing Act of 1920
- Taylor Grazing Act of 1934
- Multiple Use-Sustained Yield Act of 1960
- Wilderness Act of 1964
- Multiple Use Sustained Yield Act of 1968
- Wild and Scenic Rivers Act of 1968
- National Trails System Act of 1968
- Coastal Zone Management Act of 1972, 1977
- National Coastal Zone Management Act of 1972, 1980
- Forest Reserves Management Act of 1974, 1976
- Forest and Rangeland Renewable Resources Act of 1974, 1978
- Federal Land Policy and Management Act of 1976
- National Forest Management Act of 1976
- Soil and Water Conservation Act of 1977
- Surface Mining Control and Reclamation Act of 1977
- Antarctic Conservation Act of 1978
- Endangered American Wilderness Act of 1978
- Alaskan National Interests Lands Conservation Act of 1980
- Arctic National Interest Lands Conservation Act of 1980
- Coastal Barrier Resources Act of 1982
- Food Security Act (Farm Bill) of 1985, 1990

Appendix K

Environmental Literacy Test with Answers

Public opinion poll data indicate that Americans are, generally speaking, highly concerned about environmental problems, and certainly public opinion plays a key role in the process of determining environmental priorities and policies. Clearly, then, it is important for the public to be adequately informed on environmental issues.

To assist readers in assessing their own understanding of current environmental issues, the following 20 questions are offered as a kind of "environmental literacy test." Readers are invited to take the test by simply circling the proper answer for each question. Answers are given following the test.

(Questions and answers prepared by Arthur Koines, Regulatory Integration Division, in EPA's Office of Policy, Planning, and Evaluation.)

1. Which of the following phenomena is believed to be associated with the greenhouse effect?
    a. global warming
    b. melting of the polar ice caps
    c. sea-level rise
    d. all of the above

2. Which of the following gases is believed to cause the greenhouse effect?
    a. oxygen
    b. carbon monoxide
    c. carbon dioxide
    d. all of the above

3. Today, 18 years after the passage of the Clean Air Act, nearly all major cities in the United States are in compliance with national air quality standards.
    ☐ True ☐ False

4. Which of the following environmental problems has EPA found to be the most threatening to public health?
    a. hazardous waste sites
    b. radon in homes
    c. toxic chemicals in drinking water
    d. leaking underground storage tanks

5. Which of the following environmental problems is the American public most concerned about?
    a. hazardous waste sites
    b. radon in homes
    c. contaminants in drinking water
    d. leaking underground storage tanks

6. Which of these is a major source of air pollution in homes?
    a. building materials and furnishings
    b. electrical heating and cooking appliances
    c. tobacco smoke
    d. none of the above

7. Ozone is beneficial to our environment at high altitudes, yet harmful at low altitudes.
    ☐ True ☐ False

8. If dioxin is such a serious public health threat, why doesn't EPA just ban it?
    a. It is a key material in the production of vital consumer products.
    b. Industries that use dioxin are able to exert a powerful political influence on Congress.
    c. EPA is unable to ban dioxin because it is an unwanted by-product of many industrial activities.
    d. None of the above.

9. The federal government provides the majority of funding for implementing environmental programs.
    ☐ True ☐ False

10. In what way can people be exposed to lead in the environment?
    a. in their drinking water
    b. in dust from lead paint in their homes
    c. in lead-contaminated soils
    d. all of the above

11. What adverse health effects have been associated with human exposure to lead?
    a. anemia
    b. learning disabilities in children
    c. hypertension in adult males
    d. all of the above

12. Nationally, which of the following is the biggest polluter of our air?
    a. the chemical industry
    b. automobiles
    c. hazardous waste incinerators
    d. none are big polluters

13. Which of the following is the source of radon in homes?
    a. ultraviolet radiation
    b. defective home heating systems
    c. uranium in naturally occurring rock formations
    d. none of the above

14. Which of these answers comes close to the amount of garbage created annually by the average American?
    a. 10 pounds
    b. 100 pounds
    c. 1,000 pounds
    d. none of the above

15. What do we do with all the garbage we create?
    a. dispose of it in landfills
    b. burn it in incinerators
    c. recycle it
    d. all of the above

16. A groundwater aquifer is most like:
    a. an underground lake
    b. an underground river
    c. an underground sponge
    d. none of the above

17. Which of the following best describes an estuary?
    a. a large inland water body
    b. an ancient river bed
    c. the confluence of freshwater and saltwater bodies
    d. none of the above
18. Estuaries are important because they:
    a. are major sources of drinking water
    b. are vital marine habitats
    c. normally occur near large population centers
    d. all of the above
19. Although the pollutants causing acid rain are generated mainly in the Midwest, what region of the United States has experienced the worst *effects* from acid rain?
    a. the Northwest
    b. the Northeast
    c. the Southeast
    d. the Southwest
20. In the past, which of these groups has enjoyed cost savings from inadequate pollution controls?
    a. industry
    b. the American consumer
    c. federal, state, and local governments
    d. all of the above

Answers to Environmental Literacy Test

1. The answer is *d*. These phenomena are believed to be causally related. The greenhouse effect causes global warming. Gradually rising temperatures may be expected to cause some melting of the polar ice caps, which, in turn, causes sea-level rise.

2. The answer is *c*. Of the choices given, only carbon dioxide is a greenhouse gas.

3. This statement is *false*. In fact, just the opposite is true: today, most major cities are *not* in compliance with national air quality standards.

4. The answer is *b*. In the study "Unfinished Business: A Comparative Assessment of Environmental Problems," EPA staff and managers identified radon in homes as the most threatening public health problem of the choices given for this question.

5. The answer is *a*. According to a recent Roper Poll, 65 percent of the American public felt that active hazardous waste sites were a "very serious" environmental problem. None of the other choices for this question was rated as very serious by as large a percentage. Radon in homes was rated very serious by only 21 percent.

6. The answer is *c*. Tobacco smoke is acknowledged to be a major source of air pollution in homes where at least one smoker lives and smokes.

7. The statement is *true*. At high altitudes ozone acts as a shield against harmful ultraviolet radiation from the sun. At ground level, ozone can cause respiratory ailments in people and adverse effects on plant life.

8. The answer is *c*. Dioxin is an unwanted by-product of industrial activities. The best known examples are its chemical formation in paper manufacturing and in the incineration of municipal waste.

9. This statement is *false*. Federal funds now account for less than half of most state environmental program budgets. The federal share is decreasing as state programs grow while federal grants to state governments remain constant or are reduced.

10. The answer is *d*. All of the choices are known routes of human exposure to lead.

Source: Environmental Protection Agency Journal, July/August 1988.

11. The answer is *d*. All of the choices represent adverse human health effects that have been associated with lead exposure through epidemiological studies.

12. The answer is *b*. Nationally, of the choices given, automobiles are acknowledged to be the biggest polluter of our air.

13. The answer is *c*. Radon is formed by the radioactive decay of uranium in naturally occurring rock formations.

14. The answer is *c*. The United States has a population of about 240 million people and generates about 140 million tons of garbage annually. The average is 1,167 pounds (or roughly 1,000 pounds) per person.

15. The answer is *d*. While landfilling is still by far the most common waste management practice, both incineration and recycling are used by some communities.

16. The answer is *c*. An aquifer is a soil formation capable of absorbing and storing water. It therefore functions like a sponge.

17. The answer is *c*. An estuary is the confluence of a river and a saltwater body. Some well-known examples of estuaries are the Chesapeake Bay, the Puget Sound, and San Francisco Bay.

18. The answer is *b*. Estuaries result when a river disgorges into a saltwater body. The river supplies nutrients from the land to marine life. The estuary thus creates a vital habitat for marine animals in need of those nutrients.

19. The answer is *b*. The most serious effects of acid rain have thus far been observed in the Northeast United States.

20. The answer is *d*. In a narrow sense, all have enjoyed cost savings from inadequate pollution controls. Industry has saved as a consequence of lower production costs; some of these savings have been passed on to consumers in the form of lower prices on goods and services. Governments have saved from lower costs in the production of public goods and services, such as municipal garbage and sewage disposal. In a broader sense, however, all of these cost savings came at the expense of a clean environment—a cost that our society as a whole must now bear.

Appendix L

Basic Geographic Data on Canada, Mexico, and the United States

Canada

GEOGRAPHY

Total area: 9,976,140 km²; land area: 9,220,970 km²
Comparative area: slightly larger than US
Land boundaries: 8,893 km with US (includes 2,477 km with Alaska)
Coastline: 243,791 km
Maritime claims:
 Continental shelf: 200 meters or to depth of exploitation
 Exclusive fishing zone: 200 nm
 Territorial sea: 12 nm
Disputes: maritime boundary disputes with France (St. Pierre and Miquelon) and US
Climate: varies from temperate in south to subarctic and arctic in north
Terrain: mostly plains with mountains in west and lowlands in southeast
Natural resources: nickel, zinc, copper, gold, lead, molybdenum, potash, silver, fish, timber, wildlife, coal, crude oil, natural gas
Land use: 5% arable land; NEGL% permanent crops; 3% meadows and pastures; 35% forest and woodland; 57% other; includes NEGL% irrigated
Environment: 80% of population concentrated within 160 km of US border; continuous permafrost in north a serious obstacle to development
Note: second-largest country in world (after USSR); strategic location between USSR and US via north polar route

PEOPLE

Population: 26,538,229 (July 1990), growth rate 1.1% (1990)
Birthrate: 14 births/1,000 population (1990)
Death rate: 7 deaths/1,000 population (1990)
Net migration rate: 5 migrants/1,000 population (1990)
Infant mortality rate: 7 deaths/1,000 live births (1990)
Life expectancy at birth: 74 years male, 81 years female (1990)
Total fertility rate: 1.7 children born/woman (1990)
Nationality: noun—Canadian(s); adjective—Canadian
Ethnic divisions: 40% British Isles origin, 27% French origin, 20% other European, 1.5% indigenous Indian and Eskimo
Religion: 46% Roman Catholic, 16% United Church, 10% Anglican
Language: English and French (both official)
Literacy: 99%
Labor force: 13,380,000; services 75%, manufacturing 14%, agriculture 4%, construction 3%, other 4% (1988)
Organized labor: 30.6% of labor force; 39.6% of nonagricultural paid workers

GOVERNMENT

Long-form name: none
Type: confederation with parliamentary democracy
Capital: Ottawa
Administrative divisions: 10 provinces and 2 territories*; Alberta, British Columbia, Manitoba, New Brunswick, Newfoundland, Northwest Territories*, Nova Scotia, Ontario, Prince Edward Island, Quebec, Saskatchewan, Yukon Territory*
Independence: 1 July 1867 (from UK)
Constitution: amended British North America Act 1867 patriated to Canada 17 April 1982; charter of rights and unwritten customs
Legal system: based on English common law, except in Quebec, where civil law system based on French law prevails; accepts compulsory ICJ jurisdiction, with reservations
National holiday: Canada Day, 1 July (1867)
Executive branch: British monarch, governor general, prime minister, deputy prime minister, Cabinet

(Source: Data from Central Intelligence Agency.)

Legislative branch: bicameral Parliament consists of an upper house or Senate and a lower house or House of Commons

Judicial branch: Supreme Court

Leaders: *Chief of State*—Queen ELIZABETH II (since 6 February 1952), represented by Governor General Raymond John HNATSHYN (since 29 January 1990);

Head of Government—Prime Minister (Martin) Brian MULRONEY (since 4 September 1984); Deputy Prime Minister Donald Frank MAZANKOWSKI (since NA June 1986)

Political parties and leaders: Progressive Conservative, Brian Mulroney; Liberal, John Turner; New Democratic, Audrey McLaughlin

Suffrage: universal at age 18

Elections: *House of Commons*—last held 21 November 1988 (next to be held by November 1993); results—Progressive Conservative 43.0%, Liberal 32%, New Democratic Party 20%, other 5%; seats—(295 total) Progressive Conservative 170, Liberal 82, New Democratic Party 43

Communists: 3,000

Member of: ADB, CCC, Colombo Plan, Commonwealth, DAC, FAO, GATT, IAEA, IBRD, ICAO, ICES, ICO, IDA, IDB—Inter-American Development Bank, IEA, IFAD, IFC, IHO, ILO, ILZSG, IMF, IMO, INTELSAT, INTERPOL, IPU, ISO, ITC, ITU, IWC—International Whaling Commission, IWC—International Wheat Council, NATO, OAS, OECD, PAHO, UN, UNCTAD, UNESCO, UPU, WHO, WIPO, WMO, WSG

Diplomatic representation: Ambassador Derek BURNEY; Chancery at 1746 Massachusetts Avenue NW, Washington DC 20036; telephone (202) 785-1400; there are Canadian Consulates General in Atlanta, Boston, Buffalo, Chicago, Cleveland, Dallas, Detroit, Los Angeles, Minneapolis, New York, Philadelphia, San Francisco, and Seattle; *US*—Ambassador Edward N. NEY; Embassy at 100 Wellington Street, K1P 5T1, Ottawa (mailing address is P. O. Box 5000, Ogdensburg, NY 13669); telephone (613) 238-5335; there are US Consulates General in Calgary, Halifax, Montreal, Quebec, Toronto, and Vancouver

Flag: three vertical bands of red (hoist side), white (double width, square), and red with a red maple leaf centered in the white band

ECONOMY

Overview: As an affluent, high-tech industrial society, Canada today closely resembles the US in per capita output, market-oriented economic system, and pattern of production. Since World War II the impressive growth of the manufacturing, mining, and service sectors has transformed the nation from a largely rural economy into one primarily industrial and urban. In the 1980s Canada registered one of the highest rates of growth among the OECD nations, averaging about 4%. With its great natural resources, skilled labor force, and modern capital plant, Canada has excellent economic prospects.

GDP: $513.6 billion, per capita $19,600; real growth rate 2.9% (1989 est.)

Inflation rate (consumer prices): 5.0% (1989)

Unemployment rate: 7.5% (1989)

Budget: revenues $79.2 billion; expenditures $102.0 billion, including capital expenditures of $1.8 billion (FY88 est.)

Exports: $127.2 billion (f.o.b., 1989); *commodities*—newsprint, wood pulp, timber, grain, crude petroleum, natural gas, ferrous and nonferrous ores, motor vehicles; *partners*—US, Japan, UK, FRG, other EC, USSR

Imports: $116.5 billion (c.i.f., 1989); *commodities*—processed foods, beverages, crude petroleum, chemicals, industrial machinery, motor vehicles, durable consumer goods, electronic computers; *partners*—US, Japan, UK, FRG, other EC, Taiwan, South Korea, Mexico

External debt: $247 billion (1987)

Industrial production: growth rate 2.3% (1989)

Electricity: 103,746,000 kW capacity; 472,580 million kWh produced, 17,960 kWh per capita (1989)

Industries: processed and unprocessed minerals, food products, wood and paper products, transportation equipment, chemicals, fish products, petroleum and natural gas

Agriculture: accounts for 3% GDP; one of the world's major producers and exporters of grain (wheat and barley); key source of US agricultural imports; large forest resources cover 35% of total land area; commercial fisheries provide annual catch of 1.5 million metric tons, of which 75% is exported

Illicit drugs: illicit producer of cannabis for the domestic drug market

Aid: donor—ODA and OOF commitments (1970-87), $2.2 billion

Currency: Canadian dollar (plural—dollars); 1 Canadian dollar (Can$) = 100 cents

Exchange rates: Canadian dollars (Can$) per US$1—1.1714 (January 1990), 1.1840 (1989), 1.2307 (1988), 1.3260 (1987), 1.3895 (1986), 1.3655 (1985)

Fiscal year: 1 April-31 March

COMMUNICATIONS

Railroads: 80,095 km total; 79,917 km 1.435-meter standard gauge (includes 129 km electrified); 178 km 0.915-meter narrow gauge (mostly unused); two major transcontinental freight railway systems—Canadian National (government owned) and Canadian Pacific Railway; passenger service—VIA (government operated)

Highways: 884,272 km total; 712,936 km surfaced (250,023 km paved), 171,336 km earth

Inland waterways: 3,000 km, including St. Lawrence Seaway

Pipelines: oil, 23,564 km total crude and refined; natural gas, 74,980 km

Ports: Halifax, Montreal, Quebec, Saint John (New Brunswick), St. John's (Newfoundland), Toronto, Vancouver

Merchant marine: 78 ships (1,000 GRT or over) totaling 555,749 GRT/774,914 DWT; includes 1 passenger, 5 short-sea passenger, 2 passenger-cargo, 12 cargo, 2 railcar carrier, 1 refrigerated cargo, 8 roll-on/roll-off, 1 container, 29 petroleum, oils, and lubricants (POL) tanker, 6 chemical tanker, 1 specialized tanker, 10 bulk; note—does not include ships used exclusively in the Great Lakes ships

Civil air: 636 major transport aircraft; Air Canada is the major carrier

Airports: 1,359 total, 1,117 usable; 442 with permanent-surface runways; 4 with runways over 3,659 m; 30 with runways 2,440-3,659 m; 322 with runways 1,220-2,439 m

Telecommunications: excellent service provided by modern media; 18.0 million telephones; stations—900 AM, 29 FM, 53 (1,400 repeaters) TV; 5 coaxial submarine cables; over 300 satellite earth stations operating in INTELSAT (including 4 Atlantic Ocean and 1 Pacific Ocean) and domestic systems

DEFENSE FORCES

Branches: Mobile Command, Maritime Command, Air Command, Communications Command, Canadian Forces Europe, Training Commands

Military manpower: males 15-49, 7,174,119; 6,251,492 fit for military service; 187,894 reach military age (17) annually

Defense expenditures: 2.0% of GDP, or $10 billion (1989 est.)

Mexico

GEOGRAPHY

Total area: 1,972,550 km²; land area: 1,923,040 km²
Comparative area: slightly less than three times the size of Texas
Land boundaries: 4,538 km total; Belize 250 km, Guatemala 962 km, US 3,326 km
Coastline: 9,330 km
Maritime claims:
  Contiguous zone: 24 nm
  Continental shelf: natural prolongation of continental margin or 200 nm
  Extended economic zone: 200 nm
  Territorial sea: 12 nm
Climate: varies from tropical to desert
Terrain: high, rugged mountains, low coastal plains, high plateaus, and desert
Natural resources: crude oil, silver, copper, gold, lead, zinc, natural gas, timber
Land use: 12% arable land; 1% permanent crops; 39% meadows and pastures; 24% forest and woodland; 24% other; includes 3% irrigated
Environment: subject to tsunamis along the Pacific coast and destructive earthquakes in the center and south; natural water resources scarce and polluted in north, inaccessible and poor quality in center and extreme southeast; deforestation; erosion widespread; desertification; serious air pollution in Mexico City and urban centers along US–Mexico border
Note: strategic location on southern border of US

PEOPLE

Population: 87,870,154 (July 1990), growth rate 2.2% (1990)
Birthrate: 29 births/1,000 population (1990)
Death rate: 5 deaths/1,000 population (1990)
Net migration rate: −2 migrants/1,000 population (1990)
Infant mortality rate: 33 deaths/1,000 live births (1990)
Life expectancy at birth: 68 years male, 76 years female (1990)
Total fertility rate: 3.4 children born/woman (1990)
Nationality: noun—Mexican(s); adjective—Mexican
Ethnic divisions: 60% mestizo (Indian-Spanish), 30% Amerindian or predominantly Amerindian, 9% white or predominantly white, 1% other
Religion: 97% nominally Roman Catholic, 3% Protestant
Language: Spanish
Literacy: 88%
Labor force: 26,100,000 (1988); 31.4% services, 26% agriculture, forestry, hunting, and fishing, 13.9% commerce, 12.8% manufacturing, 9.5% construction, 4.8% transportation, 1.3% mining and quarrying, 0.3% electricity, (1986)
Organized labor: 35% of the labor force

GOVERNMENT

Long-form name: United Mexican States
Type: federal republic operating under a centralized government
Capital: Mexico
Administrative divisions: 31 states (estados, singular—estado) and 1 federal district* (distrito federal); Aguascalientes, Baja California Norte, Baja California Sur, Campeche, Chiapas, Chihuahua, Coahuila, Colima, Distrito Federal*, Durango, Guanajuato, Guerrero, Hidalgo, Jalisco, México, Michoacán, Morelos, Nayarit, Nuevo León, Oaxaca, Puebla, Querétaro, Quintana Roo, San Luis Potosí, Sinaloa, Sonora, Tabasco, Tamaulipas, Tlaxcala, Veracruz, Yucatán, Zacaetecas
Independence: 16 September 1810 (from Spain)
Constitution: 5 February 1917
Legal system: mixture of US constitutional theory and civil law system; judicial review of legislative acts; accepts compulsory ICJ jurisdiction, with reservations
National holiday: Independence Day, 16 September (1810)
Executive branch: president, Cabinet
Legislative branch: bicameral National Congress (Congreso de la Unión) consists of an upper chamber or Senate (Cámara de Senadores) and a lower chamber or Chamber of Deputies (Cámara de Diputados)
Judicial branch: Supreme Court of Justice (Suprema Corte de Justicia)
Leaders: *Chief of State and Head of Government*—President Carlos SALINAS de Gortari (since 1 December 1988)
Political parties and leaders: (recognized parties) Institutional Revolutionary Party (PRI), Luís Donaldo Colosio Murrieta; National Action Party (PAN), Luis Alvarez; Popular Socialist Party (PPS), Indalecio Sayago Herrera; Democratic Revolutionary Party (PRD), Cuauhtemoc Cardenas; Cardenist Front for the National Reconstruction Party (PFCRN), Rafael Aguilar Talamantes; Authentic Party of the Mexican Revolution (PARM), Carlos Enrique Cantu Rosas
Suffrage: universal and compulsory (but not enforced) at age 18
Elections: *President*—last held on 6 July 1988 (next to be held September 1994); results—Carlos Salinas de Gortari (PRI) 50.74%, Cuauhtémoc Cárdenas Solórzano (FDN) 31.06%, Manuel Clouthier (PAN) 16.81%; others 1.39%; note—several of the smaller parties ran a common candidate under a coalition called the National Democratic Front (FDN)
Senate—last held on 6 July 1988 (next to be held September 1991); results—PRI 94%, FDN (now PRD) 6%; seats—(64 total) number of seats by party NA;
Chamber of Deputies—last held on 6 July 1988 (next to be held September 1991); results—PRI 53%, PAN 20%, PFCRN 10%, PPS 6%, PARM 7%, PMS (now part of PRD) 4%; seats—(500 total) number of seats by party NA

Other political or pressure groups: Roman Catholic Church, Confederation of Mexican Workers (CTM), Confederation of Industrial Chambers (CONCAMIN), Confederation of National Chambers of Commerce (CONCANACO), National Peasant Confederation (CNC), National Confederation of Popular Organizations (CNOP), Revolutionary Workers Party (PRT), Mexican Democratic Party (PDM), Revolutionary Confederation of Workers and Peasants (CROC), Regional Confederation of Mexican Workers (CROM), Confederation of Employers of the Mexican Republic (COPARMEX), National Chamber of Transformation Industries (CANACINTRA), Business Coordination Council (CCE)

Member of: FAO, G–77, GATT, Group of Eight, IADB, IAEA, IBRD, ICAC, ICAO, ICO, IDA, IDB—Inter-American Development Bank, IFAD, IFC, ILO, ILZSG, IMF, IMO INTELSAT, INTERPOL, IRC, ISO, ITU, IWC—International Whaling Commission, LAIA, OAS, PAHO, SELA, UN, UNESCO, UPU, WHO, WIPO, WMO, WSG, WTO

Diplomatic representation: Ambassador Gustavo PETRICIOLI Iturbide; Chancery at 1911 Pennsylvania Avenue NW, Washington DC 20006; telephone (202) 728–1600; there are Mexican Consulates General in Chicago, Dallas, Denver, El Paso, Houston, Los Angeles, New Orleans, New York, San Francisco, San Antonio, San Diego, and Consulates in Albuquerque, Atlanta, Austin, Boston, Brownsville (Texas), Calexico (California), Corpus Christi, Del Rio (Texas), Detroit, Douglas (Arizona), Eagle Pass (Texas), Fresno (California), Kansas City (Missouri), Laredo, McAllen (Texas), Miami, Nogales (Arizona), Oxnard (California), Philadelphia, Phoenix, Presidio (Texas), Sacramento, St. Louis, St. Paul (Minneapolis), Salt Lake City, San Bernardino, San Jose, San Juan (Puerto Rico), and Seattle; US—Ambassador John D. NEGROPONTE, Jr.; Embassy at Paseo de la Reforma 305, Mexico 5, D.F. (mailing address is P. O. Box 3087, Laredo, TX 78044); telephone [52] (5) 211–0042; there are US Consulates General in Ciudad Juarez, Guadalajara, Monterrey, and Tijuana, and Consulates in Hermosillo, Matamoros, Mazatlan, Merida, and Nuevo Laredo

Flag: three equal vertical bands of green (hoist side), white, and red; the coat of arms (an eagle perched on a cactus with a snake in its beak) is centered in the white band

ECONOMY

Overview: Mexico's economy is a mixture of state-owned industrial plants (notably oil), private manufacturing and services, and both large-scale and traditional agriculture. In the 1980s Mexico experienced severe economic difficulties: the nation accumulated large external debts as world petroleum prices fell; rapid population growth outstripped the domestic food supply; and inflation, unemployment, and pressures to emigrate became more acute. Growth in national output dropped from 8% in 1980 to 1.1% in 1988 and 2.5% in 1989. The US is Mexico's major trading partner, accounting for two-thirds of its exports and imports. After petroleum, border assembly plants and tourism are the largest earners of foreign exchange. The government, in consultation with international economic agencies, is implementing programs to stabilize the economy and foster growth.

GDP: $187.0 billion, per capita $2,165; real growth rate 2.5% (1989)

Inflation rate (consumer prices): 20% (1989)

Unemployment rate: 20% (1989 est.)

Budget: revenues $36.1 billion; expenditures $56.1 billion, including capital expenditures of $7.7 billion (1988)

Exports: $23.1 billion (f.o.b., 1989); commodities—crude oil, oil products, coffee, shrimp, engines, cotton; partners—US 66%, EC 16%, Japan 11%

Imports: $23.3 billion (c.i.f., 1989); commodities—grain, metal manufactures, agricultural machinery, electrical equipment; partners—US 62%, EC 18%, Japan 10%

External debt: $95.1 billion (1989)

Industrial production: growth rate 1.3% (1988)

Electricity: 26,900,000 kW capacity; 103,670 million kWh produced, 1,200 kWh per capita (1989)

Industries: food and beverages, tobacco, chemicals, iron and steel, petroleum, mining, textiles, clothing, transportation equipment, tourism

Agriculture: accounts for 9% of GDP and over 25% of work force; large number of small farms at subsistence level; major food crops—corn, wheat, rice, beans; cash crops—cotton, coffee, fruit, tomatoes; fish catch of 1.4 million metric tons among top 20 nations (1987)

Illicit drugs: illicit cultivation of opium poppy and cannabis continues in spite of government eradication efforts; major link in chain of countries used to smuggle cocaine from South American dealers to US markets

Aid: US commitments, including Ex-Im (FY70–88), $3.0 billion; Western (non-US) countries, ODA and OOF bilateral commitments (1970–87), $6.8 billion; Communist countries (1970–88), $110 million

Currency: Mexican peso (plural—pesos); 1 Mexican peso (Mex$) = 100 centavos

Exchange rates: market rate of Mexican pesos (Mex$) per US$1—2,660.3 (January 1990), 2,461.3 (1989), 2,273.1 (1988), 1,378.2 (1987), 611.8 (1986), 256.9 (1985)

Fiscal year: calendar year

COMMUNICATIONS

Railroads: 20,680 km total; 19,950 km 1.435-meter standard gauge; 730 km 0.914-meter narrow gauge

Highways: 210,000 km total; 65,000 km paved, 30,000 km semipaved or cobblestone, 60,000 km rural roads (improved earth) or roads under construction, 55,000 km unimproved earth roads

Inland waterways: 2,900 km navigable rivers and coastal canals

Pipelines: crude oil, 4,381 km; refined products, 8,345 km; natural gas, 13,254 km

Ports: Acapulco, Coatzacoalcos, Ensenada, Guaymas, Manzanillo, Mazatlan, Progreso, Puerto Vallarta, Salina Cruz, Tampico, Veracruz

Merchant marine: 68 ships (1,000 GRT or over) totaling 1,041,229 GRT/1,552,478 DWT; includes 5 short-sea passenger, 10 cargo, 2 refrigerated cargo, 2 roll-on/roll-off cargo, 31 petroleum, oils, and lubricants (POL) tanker, 3 chemical tanker, 7 liquefied gas, 4 bulk, 4 combination bulk

Civil air: 174 major transport aircraft

Airports: 1,785 total, 1,484 usable; 190 with permanent-surface runways; 2 with runways over 3,659 m; 31 with runways 2,440–3,659 m; 259 with runways 1,220–2,439 m

Telecommunications: highly developed system with extensive radio relay links, connection into Central American Microwave System; 6.41 million telephones; stations—679 AM, no FM, 238 TV, 22 shortwave; 120 domestic satellite terminals; satellite earth stations—4 Atlantic Ocean INTELSAT and 1 Pacific Ocean INTELSAT

DEFENSE FORCES

Branches: Army, Air Force, Navy, Marine Corps

Military manpower: males 15–49, 21,575,525; 15,803,322 fit for military service; 1,118,046 reach military age (18) annually

Defense expenditures: 0.5% of GDP

United States

GEOGRAPHY

Total area: 9,372,610 km²; land area: 9,166,600 km²; includes only the 50 states and District of Columbia

Comparative area: about four-tenths the size of USSR; about one-third the size of Africa; about one-half the size of South America (or slightly larger than Brazil); slightly smaller than China; about two and one-half times the size of Western Europe

Land boundaries: 12,248.1 km total; Canada 8,893 km (including 2,477 km with Alaska), Mexico 3,326 km, Cuba (US naval base at Guantánamo) 29.1 km

Coastline: 19,924 km

Maritime claims:
Contiguous zone: 12 nm
Continental shelf: not specified
Extended economic zone: 200 nm
Territorial sea: 12 nm

Disputes: maritime boundary disputes with Canada; US Naval Base at Guantánamo is leased from Cuba and only mutual agreement or US abandonment of the area can terminate the lease; Haiti claims Navassa Island; has made no territorial claim in Antarctica (but has reserved the right to do so) and does not recognize the claims of any other nation

Climate: mostly temperate, but varies from tropical (Hawaii) to arctic (Alaska); arid to semiarid in west with occasionally warm, dry chinook wind

Terrain: vast central plain, mountains in west, hills and low mountains in east; rugged mountains and broad river valleys in Alaska; rugged, volcanic topography in Hawaii

Natural resources: coal, copper, lead, molybdenum, phosphates, uranium, bauxite, gold, iron, mercury, nickel, potash, silver, tungsten, zinc, crude oil, natural gas, timber

Land use: 20% arable land; NEGL% permanent crops; 26% meadows and pastures; 29% forest and woodland; 25% other; includes 2% irrigated

Environment: pollution control measures improving air and water quality; acid rain; agricultural fertilizer and pesticide pollution; management of sparse natural water resources in west; desertification; tsunamis, volcanoes, and earthquake activity around Pacific Basin; continuous permafrost in northern Alaska is a major impediment to development

Note: world's fourth-largest country (after USSR, Canada, and China)

PEOPLE

Population: 250,410,000 (July 1990), growth rate 0.9% (1990)
Birthrate: 15 births/1,000 population (1990)
Death rate: 9 deaths/1,000 population (1990)
Net migration rate: 2 migrants/1,000 population (1990)
Infant mortality rate: 10 deaths/1,000 live births (1990)
Life expectancy at birth: 73 years male, 80 years female (1990)
Total fertility rate: 1.9 children born/woman (1990)
Nationality: noun—American(s); adjective—American
Ethnic divisions: 85% white, 12% black, 3% other (1985)
Religion: Protestant 61% (Baptist 21%, Methodist 12%, Lutheran 8%, Presbyterian 4%, Episcopalian 3%, other Protestant 13%), Roman Catholic 25%, Jewish 2%, other 5%; none 7%
Language: predominantly English; sizable Spanish-speaking minority
Literacy: 99%
Labor force: 125,557,000 (includes armed forces and unemployed); civilian labor force 123,869,000 (1989)
Organized labor: 16,960,000 members; 16.4% of labor force (1989)

GOVERNMENT

Long-form name: United States of America; abbreviated US or USA
Type: federal republic; strong democratic tradition
Capital: Washington, DC
Administrative divisions: 50 states and 1 district*; Alabama, Alaska, Arizona, Arkansas, California, Colorado, Connecticut, Delaware, District of Columbia*, Florida, Georgia, Hawaii, Idaho, Illinois, Indiana, Iowa, Kansas, Kentucky, Louisiana, Maine, Maryland, Massachusetts, Michigan, Minnesota, Mississippi, Missouri, Montana, Nebraska, Nevada, New Hampshire, New Jersey, New Mexico, New York, North Carolina, North Dakota, Ohio, Oklahoma, Oregon, Pennsylvania, Rhode Island, South Carolina, South Dakota, Tennessee, Texas, Utah, Vermont, Virginia, Washington, West Virginia, Wisconsin, Wyoming
Independence: 4 July 1776 (from England)
Constitution: 17 September 1787, effective 4 June 1789
Dependent areas: American Samoa, Baker Island, Guam, Howland Island; Jarvis Island, Johnston Atoll, Kingman Reef, Midway Islands, Navassa Island, Palmyra Atoll, Puerto Rico, Virgin Islands, Wake Island. Since 18 July 1947, the US has administered the Trust Territory of the Pacific Islands, but recently entered into a new political relationship with three of the four political units. The Northern Mariana Islands is a Commonwealth associated with the US (effective 3 November 1986). Palau concluded a Compact of Free Association with the US that was approved by the US Congress but to date the Compact process has not been completed in Palau, which continues to be administered by the US as the Trust Territory of the Pacific Islands. The Federated States of Micronesia signed a Compact of Free Association with the US (effective 3 November 1986). The Republic of the Marshall Islands signed a Compact of Free Association with the US (effective 21 October 1986).
Legal system: based on English common law; judicial review of legislative acts; accepts compulsory ICJ jurisdiction, with reservations
National holiday: Independence Day, 4 July (1776)
Executive branch: president, vice president, Cabinet
Legislative branch: bicameral Congress consists of an upper house or Senate and a lower house or House of Representatives
Judicial branch: Supreme Court

Leaders: *Chief of State and Head of Government*—President George BUSH (since 20 January 1989); Vice President Dan QUAYLE (since 20 January 1989)

Political parties and leaders: Republican Party, Lee Atwater, national committee chairman and Jeanie Austin, co-chairman; Democratic Party, Ronald H. Brown, national committee chairman; several other groups or parties of minor political significance

Suffrage: universal at age 18

Elections: *President*—last held 8 November 1988 (next to be held 3 November 1992); results—George Bush (Republican Party) 53.37%, Michael Dukakis (Democratic Party) 45.67%, others 0.96%;
Senate—last held 8 November 1988 (next to be held 6 November 1990); results—Democratic Party 52.1%, Republican Party 46.2%, others 1.7%; seats—(100 total) Democratic Party 55, Republican Party 45;
House of Representatives—last held 8 November 1988 (next to be held 6 November 1990); results—Democratic Party 53.2%, Republican Party 45.3%, others 1.5%; seats—(435 total) Democratic Party 259, Republican Party 174, vacant 2

Communists: Communist Party (claimed 15,000–20,000 members), Gus Hall, general secretary; Socialist Workers Party (claimed 1,800 members), Jack Barnes, national secretary

Member of: ADB, ANZUS, CCC, Colombo Plan, DAC, FAO, ESCAP, GATT, IADB, IAEA, IBRD, ICAC, ICAO, ICEM, ICES, ICO, IDA, IDB—Inter-American Development Bank, IEA, IFAD, IFC, IHO, ILO, ILZSG, IMF, IMO, INTELSAT, INTERPOL, IPU, IRC, ITC, ITU, IWC—International Whaling Commission, IWC—International Wheat Council, NATO, OAS, OECD, PAHO, SPC, UN, UPU, WHO, WIPO, WMO, WSG, WTO

Diplomatic representation: US Representative to the UN, Ambassador Thomas R. PICKERING; Mission at 799 United Nations Plaza, New York, NY 10017; telephone (212) 415-4444

Flag: thirteen equal horizontal stripes of red (top and bottom) alternating with white; there is a blue rectangle in the upper hoist-side corner bearing 50 small white five-pointed stars arranged in nine offset horizontal rows of six stars (top and bottom) alternating with rows of five stars; the 50 stars represent the 50 states, the 13 stripes represent the 13 original colonies; known as Old Glory; the design and colors have been the basis for a number of other flags including Chile, Liberia, Malaysia, and Puerto Rico

ECONOMY

Overview: The US has the most powerful and diversified economy in the world, with a per capita GNP of over $21,000, the largest among the major industrial nations. In 1989 the economy entered its eighth successive year of growth, the longest in peacetime history. The expansion has featured continued moderation in wage and consumer price increases, an unemployment rate of 5.2%, (the lowest in 10 years), and an inflation rate of 4.8%. On the negative side, the US enters the 1990s with massive budget and trade deficits, huge and rapidly rising medical costs, and inadequate investment in industrial capacity and economic infrastructure.

GNP: $5,233.3 billion, per capita $21,082; real growth rate 2.9% (1989)

Inflation rate (consumer prices): 4.8% (1989)

Unemployment rate: 5.2% (1989)

Budget: revenues $976 billion; expenditures $1,137 billion, including capital expenditures of NA (FY89 est.)

Exports: $322.3 billion (f.o.b., 1988); *commodities*—capital goods, automobiles, industrial supplies and raw materials, consumer goods, agricultural products; *partners*—Canada 22.9%, Japan 11.8% (1988)

Imports: $440.9 billion (c.i.f., 1988); *commodities*—crude and partly refined petroleum, machinery, automobiles, consumer goods, industrial raw materials, food and beverages; *partners*—Japan 19.6%, Canada 19.1% (1988)

External debt: $532 billion (December 1988)

Industrial production: growth rate 3.3% (1989)

Electricity: 776,550,000 kW capacity; 2,958,300 billion kWh produced, 11,920 kWh per capita (1989)

Industries: leading industrial power in the world, highly diversified; petroleum, steel, motor vehicles, aerospace, telecommunications, chemicals, electronics, food processing, consumer goods, fishing, lumber, mining

Agriculture: accounts for 2% of GNP and 2.8% of labor force; favorable climate and soils support a wide variety of crops and livestock production; worlds' second-largest producer and number-one exporter of grain; surplus food producer; fish catch of 5.7 million metric tons (1987)

Illicit drugs: illicit producer of cannabis for domestic consumption with 1987 production estimated at 3,500 metric tons or about 25% of the available marijuana; ongoing eradication program aimed at small plots and greenhouses has not reduced production

Aid: donor—commitments, including Ex-Im (FY80–88), $90.5 billion

Currency: United States dollar (plural—dollars); 1 United States dollar (US$) = 100 cents

Exchange rates: *British pounds* (£) per US$—0.6055 (January 1990), 0.6099 (1989), 0.5614 (1988), 0.6102 (1987), 0.6817 (1986), 0.7714 (1985); *Canadian dollars* (Can$) per US$—1.1885 (February 1990), 1.2307 (1988), 1.3260 (1987), 1.3895 (1986); *French francs* (F) per US$—5.695 (February 1990), 5.9569 (1988), 6.0107 (1987), 6.9261 (1986), 8.9852 (1985); *Italian lire* (Lit) per US$—1,244.8 (February 1990), 1,301.6 (1988), 1,296.1 (1987), 1,490.8 (1986), 1,909.4 (1985); *Japanese yen* ( ) per US$—145.55 (February 1990), 128.15 (1988), 144.64 (1987), 168.52 (1986), 238.54 (1985); *FRG deutsche marks* (DM) per US$—1.6775 (February 1990), 1.7562 (1988), 1.7974 (1987), 2.1715 (1986), 2.9440 (1985)

Fiscal year: 1 October–30 September

COMMUNICATIONS

Railroads: 270,312 km

Highways: 6,365,590 km, including 88,641 km expressways

Inland waterways: 41,009 km of navigable inland channels, exclusive of the Great Lakes (est.)

Pipelines: 275,800 km petroleum, 305,300 km natural gas (1985)

Ports: Anchorage, Baltimore, Beaumont, Boston, Charleston, Cleveland, Duluth, Freeport, Galveston, Hampton Roads, Honolulu, Houston, Jacksonville, Long Beach, Los Angeles, Milwaukee, Mobile, New Orleans, New York, Philadelphia, Portland (Oregon), Richmond (California), San Francisco, Savannah, Seattle, Tampa, Wilmington

Merchant marine: 373 ships (1,000 GRT or over) totaling GRT/NA DWT; includes 2 passenger-cargo, 37 cargo, 22 bulk, 165 tanker, 13 tanker tug-barge, 10 liquefied gas, 124 intermodal; in addition there are 248 government-owned vessels

Civil air: 3,297 commercial multiengine transport aircraft, including 2,989 jet, 231 turboprop, 77 piston (1985)

Airports: 15,422 in operation (1981)

Telecommunications: 182,558,000 telephones; stations—4,892 AM, 5,200 FM (including 3,915 commercial and 1,285 public broadcasting), 7,296 TV (including 796 commercial, 300 public broadcasting, and 6,200 commercial cable); 495,000,000 radio receivers (1982); 150,000,000 TV sets (1982); satellite earth stations—45 Atlantic Ocean INTELSAT and 16 Pacific Ocean INTELSAT

DEFENSE FORCES

Branches: Department of the Army, Department of the Navy (including Marine Corps), Department of the Air Force

Military manpower: 2,247,000 total; 781,000 Army; 599,000 Air Force; 793,000 Navy (includes 200,000 Marine Corps) (1988)

Defense expenditures: 5.8% of GNP, or $302.8 billion (1989)

Appendix M

Acronyms Used in This Text

ACE	Army Corps of Engineers		MSS	Multispectral Scanners
ANWR	Arctic National Wildlife Refuge		MT	metric ton
ASCS	Agricultural Stabilization and Conservation Service		NASA	National Aeronautics and Space Administration
BLM	Bureau of Land Management		NEPA	National Environmental Policy Act
BNE	belt of no erosion		NFMA	National Forest Management Act
CCC	Civilian Conservation Corps		NOAA	National Oceanic and Atmospheric Administration
CEQ	Council on Environmental Quality		NPL	National Priorities List
CFCs	chlorofluorocarbons		NPS	National Park Service
CMSA	Consolidated Metropolitan Statistical Area		PET	polyethylene terephthalate
CRP	Conservation Reserve Program		PPBV	parts per billion in volume (ppbv)
DO	dissolved oxygen		PPM	parts per million (ppm)
DOE	Department of Energy		PVC	polyvinyl chloride
EIS	Environmental Impact Statement		RCRA	Resource Conservation and Recovery Act of 1976
EOSAT	Earth Observation Satellite Company		RES	Radio-echo-sounding
EPA	Environmental Protection Agency		RPA	Forest and Rangeland Renewable Resources Planning Act
ERTS	Earth Resources Technology Satellite		SARA	Superfund Amendments and Reauthorization Act of 1986
FDA	Food and Drug Administration		SMSA	Standard Metropolitan Statistical Area
FFDCA	The Federal Food, Drug, and Cosmetic Act		SSPS	Satellite Solar Power Stations
FHSA	Federal Hazardous Substances Act		TAPS	Trans-Alaska Pipeline Systems
FIFRA	Federal Insecticide, Fungicide, and Rodenticide Act		TM	Thematic Mapper
GIGO	garbage in—garbage out		TSI	Timber stand improvement
GIS	Geographic Information Systems		TVA	Tennessee Valley Authority
GNP	Gross National Product		UNEP	United Nations Environment Program
HSWA	Hazardous and Solid Waste Amendments		USCB	United States Census Bureau
ILCC	Industrial location constraint criteria		USDA	U.S. Department of Agriculture
IPM	Integrated Pest Management		USFS	U.S. Forest Service
IR	Infrared		USFWS	U.S. Fish and Wildlife Service
IUD	Intrauterine Device		UST	Urban Stress Test
LFC	Large-Format Camera		WCB	William C. Brown Publisher
LNG	liquid natural gas		WCRT	Whooping Crane Recovery Team
LWR	light water reactors		WPCF	Water Pollution Control Federation
MDC	Missouri Department of Conservation		YBP	years before present (ybp)
MDNR	Missouri Department of Natural Resources		ZPG	Zero population growth (zpg)
MMT	million metric tons			

Appendix N

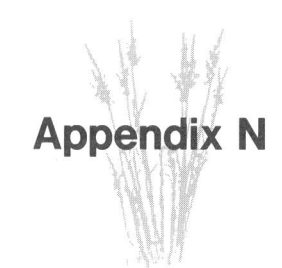

Threatened and Endangered Species List for the United States

This list contains the names of 526 species protected under the provisions of the Endangered Species Preservation Act of 1966 and its later amendments.

Threatened (T) Endangered (E)

State abbreviations indicate where the species are known or suspected to exist (e.g. WY).

*Indicates no common name.

MAMMALS
- Alabama beach mouse E (AL)
- Amargosa vole E (CA)
- Anastasia Is. beach mouse E (FL)
- Black-footed ferret E (CO, MT, ND, SD, UT, WY)
- Carolina northern flying squirrel E (NC, TN)
- Choctawhatchee beach mouse E (FL)
- Columbian white-tailed deer E (OR, WA)
- Delmarva Peninsula fox squirrel E (DE, MA, VA)
- Dismal Swamp southeastern shrew T (NC, VA)
- Florida manatee E (FL, GA, LA, MS, NC, SC, TX)
- Florida panther E (FL)
- Fresno kangaroo rat E (CA)
- Giant kangaroo rat E (CA)
- Gray bat E (central, southeastern US)
- Gray wolf E (ID, MT, NM, WA, WI, WY; T—MN)
- Grizzly bear T (ID, MT, WA, WY)
- Guadalupe fur seal T (CA)
- Hawaiian hoary bat E (HI)
- Hawaiian monk seal E (HI)
- Hualapai Mexican vole E (AZ)
- Indiana bat E (eastern, midwestern US)
- Jaguarundi E (AZ, TX)
- Key deer E (FL)
- Key Largo woodrat E (FL)
- Key Largo cotton mouse E (FL)
- Lower Keys rabbit E (FL)
- Mexican long-nosed bat E (NM, TX)
- Morro Bay kangaroo rat E (CA)
- Mount Graham red squirrel E (AZ)
- Ocelot E (AZ, TX)
- Ozark big-eared bat E (MO, OK, AR)
- Perdido Key beach mouse E (AL, FL)
- Red wolf E (NC)
- Salt marsh harvest mouse E (CA)
- San Joaquin kit fox E (CA)
- Sanborn's long-nosed bat E (AZ, NM)
- Sonoran pronghorn E (AZ)
- Southeastern beach mouse T (FL)
- Southern sea otter T (CA)
- Steller sea-lion T (AK, CA, OR, WA)
- Stephen's kangaroo rat E (CA)
- Tipton kangaroo rat E (CA)
- Utah prairie dog T (UT)
- Virginia big-eared bat E (KY, NC, VA, WV)
- Virginia northern flying squirrel E (VA, WV)
- Woodland caribou E (ID, WA)

BIRDS
- Akiapola'au E (HI)
- Aleutian Canada goose E (AK, CA, OR, WA)
- American peregrine falcon E (all except HI)
- Arctic peregrine falcon T (all except HI)
- Attwater's greater prairie-chicken E (TX)
- Audubon's crested caracara T (FL)
- Bald eagle T (MI, MN, OR, WA, WI; E—remaining coterminous US)
- Black-capped vireo E (KS, OK, TX)
- Brown pelican E (NC/SC to TX/CA; OR, WA)
- California clapper rail E (CA)
- California condor E (CA)
- California least tern E (CA)
- Cape Sable seaside sparrow E (FL)
- Crested honeycreeper E (HI)
- Eskimo curlew E (AK, KS, NE, OK, SD, TX)
- Everglade snail kite E (FL)
- Florida grasshopper sparrow E (FL)
- Florida scrub jay E (FL)
- Golden-cheeked (wood) warbler E (TX)
- Hawaii akepa E (HI)
- Hawaii creeper E (HI)
- Hawaiian common moorhen E (HI)
- Hawaiian coot E (HI)
- Hawaiian crow E (HI)
- Hawaiian dark-rumped petrel E (HI)
- Hawaiian duck E (HI)
- Hawaiian goose E (HI)
- Hawaiian hawk E (HI)
- Hawaiian stilt E (HI)
- Inyo brown towhee T (CA)
- Kauai akialoa E (HI)
- Kauai 'O'o E (HI)
- Kirtland's (wood) warbler E (MI, WI)
- Large Kauai thrush E (HI)
- Laysan duck E (HI)
- Laysan finch E (HI)
- Least Bell's vireo E (CA)
- Least tern E (Mississippi River basin)
- Light-footed clapper rail E (CA)

Source: Data from Liz Boussard, *Wilderness* (Summer 1991).

Masked bobwhite E (AZ)
Maui akepa E (HI)
Maui parrotbill E (HI)
Mississippi sandhill crane E (MS)
Molokai creeper E (HI)
Molokai thrush E (HI)
Newell's Townsend's shearwater E (HI)
Nihoa finch E (HI)
Nihoa millerbird E (HI)
Northern aplomado falcon E (TX)
Northern spotted owl T (CA, OR, WA)
Nukupu'u E (HI)
Oahu creeper E (HI)
'O'u E (HI)
Palila E (HI)
Piping plover E (Great Lakes and Northern Plains states) T (Atlantic and Gulf Coast states)
Po'ouli E (HI)
Red-cockaded woodpecker E (Southeast)
Roseate tern E/T (CT, FL, ME, MA, NY, RI)
San Clemente loggerhead shrike E (CA)
San Clemente sage sparrow T (CA)
Small Kauai thrush E (HI)
Whooping crane E (MT/ND to NM, TX)
Wood stork E (AL, FL, GA, SC)
Yuma clapper rail E (AZ, CA)

AMPHIBIANS
Cheat Mountain salamander T (WV)
Desert slender salamander E (CA)
Houston toad E (TX)
Red Hills salamander T (AL)
San Marcos salamander T (TX)
Santa Cruz long-toed salamander E (CA)
Shenandoah salamander E (VA)
Texas blind salamander E (TX)
Wyoming toad E (WY)

REPTILES
Alabama red-bellied turtle E (AL)
American crocodile E (FL)
Atlantic salt marsh snake E (FL)
Blue-tailed mole skink T (FL)
Blunt-nosed leopard lizard E (CA)
Coachella Valley fringe-toed lizard T (CA)
Concho water snake T (TX)
Desert tortoise T (AZ, CA, NV, UT)
Eastern indigo snake T (AL, FL, GA, MS, SC)
Flattened musk turtle T (AL)
Gopher tortoise T (AL, MS, LA)
Green sea turtle E/T (west coast; east coast TX–VA)
Hawksbill sea turtle E (HI; east coast TX–MA)
Island night lizard T (CA)
Kemp's ridley sea turtle E (east coast TX–VA)
Leatherback sea turtle E (west coast; east coast TX–MA)
Loggerhead sea turtle T (HI; east coast TX–MA)
New Mexican ridge-nosed rattlesnake T (NM)
Olive (Pacific) ridley sea turtle E/T (west coast)
Plymouth red-bellied turtle E (MA)
Ringed sawback turtle T (LA, MS)
San Francisco garter snake E (CA)
Sand skink T (FL)

FISHES
Alabama cavefish E (AL)
Amber darter E (AL, GA)
Apache trout T (AZ)

Ash Meadows Amargosa pupfish E (NV)
Ash Meadows speckled dace E (NV)
Bayou darter T (MS)
Beautiful shiner T (AZ, NM)
Big Bend gambusia E (TX)
Big Spring spinedace T (NV)
Blackside dace T (TN, KY)
Bonytail chub E (AZ, CA, CO, NV, UT)
Borax Lake chub E (OR)
Boulder darter E (AL, TN)
Cape Fear shiner E (NC)
Chihuahua chub T (NM)
Clear Creek gambusia E (TX)
Clover Valley speckled dace E (NV)
Colorado squawfish E (AZ, CA, CO, UT, WY)
Comanche Springs pupfish E (TX)
Conasauga logperch E (GA, TN)
Cui-ui E (NV)
Desert dace T (NV)
Desert pupfish E (AZ, CA)
Devils Hole pupfish E (NV)
Foskett speckled dace T (OR)
Fountain darter E (TX)
Gila trout E (AZ, NM)
Greenback cutthroat trout T (CO)
Hiko White River springfish E (NV)
Humpback chub E (AZ, CO, UT)
Hutton tui chub T (OR)
Independence Valley speckled dace E (NV)
June sucker E (UT)
Kendall Warm Springs dace E (WY)
Lahontan cutthroat trout T (CA, NV, OR, UT)
Leon Springs pupfish E (TX)
Leopard darter T (AR, OK)
Little Colorado spinedace T (AZ)
Little Kern golden trout T (CA)
Loach minnow T (AZ, NM)
Lost River sucker E (CA, OR)
Maryland darter E (MD)
Moapa dace E (NV)
Modoc sucker E (CA)
Mohave tui chub E (CA)
Neusho madtom T (KS, MO, OK)
Niangua darter T (MO)
Okaloosa darter E (FL)
Owens pupfish E (CA)
Owens tui chub E (CA)
Ozark cavefish T (AR, MO, OK)
Pahranagat roundtail chub E (NV)
Pahrump killifish E (NV)
Paiute cutthroat trout T (CA)
Pallid sturgeon E (Miss. R. system)
Pecos bluntnose shiner T (NM)
Pecos gambusia E (NM, TX)
Pygmy sculpin T (AL)
Railroad Valley springfish T (NV)
Roanoke logperch E (VA)
San Marcos gambusia E (TX)
Scioto madtom E (OH)
Short-nose sucker E (CA, OR)
Slackwater darter T (AL, TN)
Slender chub T (TN, VA)
Smoky madtom E (TN)
Snail darter T (AL, GA, TN)
Sonora chub T (AZ)
Spikedace T (AZ, NM)

Spotfin chub T (NC, TN, VA)
Unarmored threespine stickleback E (CA)
Virgin River chub E (AZ, NV, UT)
Waccamaw silverside T (NC)
Warm Springs pupfish E (NV)
Warner sucker T (OR)
Watercress darter E (AL)
White River spinedace E (NV)
White River springfish E (NV)
Woundfin E (AZ, NM, NV; T—UT)
Yaqui catfish T (AZ)
Yaqui chub E (AZ)
Yaqui topminnow E (AZ, NM)
Yellowfin madtom T (TN, VA)

INSECTS
American burying beetle E (AR, KY, MA, NE, OK, RI)
Ash Meadows naucorid T (NV)
Bay checkerspot butterfly T (CA)
Delta green ground beetle T (CA)
El Segundo blue butterfly E (CA)
Kern primrose sphinx moth T (CA)
Kretschmarr Cave mold beetle E (TX)
Lange's metalmark butterfly E (CA)
Lotis blue butterfly E (CA)
Mission blue butterfly E (CA)
Northeastern beach tiger beetle T (Northeast)
Oregon Silverspot butterfly T (CA, OR, WA)
Palos Verde blue butterfly E (CA)
Pawnee montane skipper T (CO)
Puritan tiger beetle T (CT, MA, MD, NH, VT)
San Bruno elfin butterfly E (CA)
Schaus swallowtail butterfly E (FL)
Smith's blue butterfly E (CA)
Tooth Cave ground beetle E (TX)
Valley elderberry longhorn beetle T (CA)

ARACHNIDS
Bee Creek Cave harvestman E (TX)
Tooth Cave pseudoscorpion E (TX)
Tooth Cave spider E (TX)

CRUSTACEANS
Alabama cave shrimp E (AL)
California freshwater shrimp E (CA)
Cave crayfish E (AR)
Hay's Spring amphipod E (DC)
Kentucky cave shrimp E (KY)
Madison Cave isopod T (VA)
Nashville crayfish E (TN)
Shasta crayfish E (CA)
Socorro isopod E (NM)
Squirrel Chimney cave shrimp T (FL)

SNAILS
Chittenango ovate amber snail T (NY)
Flat-spired three-toothed snail T (WV)
Iowa Pleistocene snail E (IA, IL)
Magazine Mountain shagreen T (AR)
Noonday snail T (NC)
Oahu tree snail E (HI)
Painted snake coiled forest snail T (TN)
Stock Island snail T (FL)
Virginia fringed mountain snail E (VA)

CLAMS
Alabama lamp pearly mussel E (AL, TN)
Appalachian monkeyface pearly mussel E (TN, VA)
Arkansas fatmucket T (AR)
Birdwing pearly mussel E (TN, VA)
Cracking pearly mussel E (AL, KY, TN, VA)
Cumberland monkeyface pearly mussel E (AL, TN, VA)
Cumberland bean pearly mussel E (KY, TN, VA)
Curtis' pearly mussel E (MO)
Curtus' mussel E (AL, MS)
Dromedary pearly mussel E (TN, KY, VA)
Dwarf wedge mussel E (MA, MD, NC, NH, NY, VA, VT)
Fanshell E (AL, IL, IN, KY, OH, PA, TN, VA, WV)
Fat pocketbook E (AR, IA, IL, IN, KY, MO)
Fine-rayed pigtoe E (AL, TN, VA)
Green-blossom pearly mussel E (TN, VA)
Higgins' eye pearly mussel E (IA, IL, MN, MO, NE, WI)
Inflated heelsplitter T (AL, LA, MS)
James River spiny mussel E (VA, WV)
Judge Tait's mussel E (AL, MS)
Little-wing pearly mussel E (AL, KY, NC, TN, VA)
Louisiana pearlshell E (LA)
Marshall's mussel E (AL, MS)
Orange-footed pearly mussel E (AL, IA, IL, KY, TN)
Pale lilliput pearly mussel E (AL, TN)
Penitent mussel E (AL, MS)
Pink mucket pearly mussel E (AL, IL, IN, KY, MO, OH, TN, VA, WV)
Purple cats paw pearly mussel E (AL, KY, TN)
Ring pink mussel E (AL, KY, PA, TN, WV)
Rough pigtoe E (KY, TN, VA)
Shiny pigtoe E (AL, TN, VA)
Speckled pocketbook E (AR)
Stirrup shell E (AL, MS)
Tan riffle shell E (KY, TN, VA)
Tar River spiny mussel E (NC)
Tubercled-blossom pearly mussel E (IL, IN, KY, TN, WV)
Turgid-blossom pearly mussel E (AL, TN)
White cat's paw pearly mussel E (IN, OH)
White wartyback pearly mussel E (AL, IN, IL, KY, TN)
Yellow-blossom pearly mussel E (AL, TN)

PLANTS
Alabama canebrake pitcher-plant E (AL)
Alabama leather flower E (AL)
Aleutian shield-fern E (AK)
Amargosa niterwort E (CA, NV)
American hart's-tongue fern T (AL, MI, NY, TN)
Antioch Dunes evening-primrose E (CA)
Arizona agave E (AZ)
Arizona cliffrose E (AZ)
Arizona hedgehog cactus E (AZ)
Ash Meadows blazing-star T (NV)
Ash Meadows gumplant T (CA, NV)
Ash Meadows ivesia T (NV)
Ash Meadows milk-vetch T (NV)
Ash Meadows sunray T (NV)
Ashy dogweed E (TX)
Autumn buttercup E (UT)
Bakersfield cactus T (CA)
Barneby ridge-cress E (UT)
Beautiful pawpaw E (FL)
Black lace cactus E (TX)
Black-spored quillwort E (GA, SC)
Blowout penstemon E (NE)
Blue Ridge goldenrod E (NC, TN)
Bradshaw's lomatium E (OR)
Brady pincushion cactus E (AZ)
Brooksville bellflower E (FL)
Bunched arrowhead E (NC, SC)
Bunched cory cactus T (TX)

California jewelflower E (CA)
Canby's dropwort E (DE, GA, MD, NC, SC)
Carter's mustard E (FL)
Carter's panicgrass E (HI)
Chapman rhododendron E (FL)
Chisos Mountain hedgehog cactus T (TX)
Clay phacelia E (UT)
Clay-loving wild-buckwheat E (CO)
Cochise pincushion cactus T (AZ)
Contra Costa wallflower E (CA)
Cooke's koki'o E (HI)
Cooley's water-willow E (FL)
Cooley's meadowrue E (FL, NC)
Crenulate lead-plant E (FL)
Cumberland sandwort E (KY, TN)
Cuneate bidens E (HI)
Davis' green pitaya E (TX)
Decurrent false aster T (IL, MO)
Deltoid spurge E (FL)
Diamond Head schiedea E (HI)
Dudley Bluffs bladderpod T (CO)
Dudley Bluffs twinpod T (CO)
Dwarf bear-poppy E (UT)
Dwarf lake iris T (MI, WI)
Dwarf naupaka E (HI)
Dwarf-flowered heartleaf T (NC, SC)
Eastern prairie fringed orchid T (IA, IL, ME, MI, OH, VA)
Eureka Valley evening-primrose E (CA)
Eureka Dune grass E (CA)
Ewa Plains 'akoko E (HI)
Fassett's locoweed T (WI)
Florida bonamia T (FL)
Florida golden aster E (FL)
Florida torreya E (FL, GA)
Florida ziziphus E (FL)
Four-petal pawpaw E (FL)
Fragrant prickly-apple E (FL)
Furbish lousewort E (ME)
Garber's spurge T (FL)
Garrett's mint E (FL)
Geocarpon minimum* T (AR, MO)
Green pitcher-plant E (AL, GA, NC, TN)
Gypsum wild-buckwheat T (NM)
Hairy rattleweed E (GA)
Harper's beauty E (FL)
Harperella E (AL, GA, MD, NC, SC, WV)
Hawaiian vetch E (HI)
Heliotrope milk-vetch T (UT)
Heller's blazingstar T (NC)
Highlands scrub hypericum E (FL)
Hillebrand's gouania E (HI)
Hinckley's oak T (TX)
Hoover's woolly-star T (CA)
Houghton's goldenrod T (MI)
Jesup's milk-vetch E (NH, VT)
Johnston's frankenia E (TX)
Jones cycladenia T (AZ, UT)
Kauai hau kuahiwi E (HI)
Kearney's blue-star E (AZ)
Kern mallow E (CA)
Key tree-cactus E (FL)
Knowlton cactus E (CO, NM)
Ko'oloa'ula E (HI)
Koki'o E (HI)
Kral's water-plantain T (AL)

Kuenzler hedgehog cactus E (NM)
Lakela's mint E (FL)
Lakeside daisy T (OH, IL)
Lanai sandalwood E (HI)
Large-flowered fiddleneck E (CA)
Large-flowered skullcap E (GA, TN)
Large-fruited sand verbena E (TX)
Last Chance townsendia T (UT)
Lee pincushion cactus T (NM)
Little amphianthus T (AL, GA, SC)
Lloyd's hedgehog cactus E (NM, TX)
Lloyd's Mariposa cactus T (TX)
Loch Lomond coyote-thistle E (CA)
Longspurred mint E (FL)
Lyrate bladderpod T (AL)
MacFarlane's four-o'clock E (ID, OR)
Maguire daisy E (UT)
Maguire primrose T (UT)
Malheur wire-lettuce E (OR)
Mancos milk-vetch E (CO, NM)
Mat-forming quillwort E (GA)
Mauna Kea silversword E (HI)
McDonald's rock-cress E (CA)
McKittrick pennyroyal T (TX, NM)
Mead's milkweed T (IA, IN, KS, MO)
Mesa Verde cactus T (CO, NM)
Miccosukee gooseberry T (FL, SC)
Michaux's sumac E (GA, NC, SC)
Michigan monkey-flower E (MI)
Minnesota trout lily E (MN)
Missouri bladderpod E (MO)
Mohr's Barbara's buttons E (AL, GA)
Mountain golden heather T (NC)
Mountain sweet pitcher-plant E (NC, SC)
Na'u E (HI)
Narrow-leaved haplostachya E (HI)
Narrow-leaved stenogyne E (HI)
Navajo sedge T (AZ)
Navasota ladies'-tresses E (TX)
Nehe E (HI)
Nellie cory cactus E (TX)
Nichol's Turk's head cactus E (AZ)
North Park phacelia E (CO)
Northern wild monkshood T (IA, NY, OH, WI)
Osterhout milk-vetch E (CO)
Palmate-bracted bird's beak E (CA)
Papery whitlow-wort T (FL)
Pedate checker-mallow E (CA)
Peebles Navajo cactus E (AZ)
Penland beardtongue E (CO)
Persistent trillium E (GA, SC)
Peter's Mountain mallow E (VA)
Pitcher's thistle T (IL, IN, MI, WI)
Pondberry E (South)
Prairie bush-clover T (IA, IL, MN, WI)
Presidio manzanita E (CA)
Price's Potato-bean T (AL, KY, MS, TN)
Pygmy fringe-tree E (FL)
Relict trillium E (AL, GA, SC)
Rhizome fleabane T (NM)
Roan Mountain bluet E (NC, TN)
Robbins' cinquefoil E (NH, VT)
Rough-leaved loosestrife E (NC, SC)
Round-leaved chaff-flower E (HI)
Rugel's pawpaw E (FL)

Running buffalo clover E (IN, KS, KY, OH, WV)
Ruth's golden aster E (TN)
Sacramento Mountains thistle T (NM)
Sacramento prickly-poppy E (NM)
Salt Marsh bird's-beak E (CA)
San Benito evening-primrose T (CA)
San Clemente Island broom E (CA)
San Clemente Island bush-mallow E (CA)
San Clemente Island Indian paintbrush E (CA)
San Clemente Island larkspur E (CA)
San Diego mesa mint E (CA)
San Francisco Peaks groundsel T (AZ)
San Joaquin wooly-threads E (CA)
San Mateo thornmint E (CA)
San Rafael cactus E (UT)
Sandplain gerardia E (CT, MA, MD, NY, RI)
Santa Ana River woolly-star E (CA)
Santa Barbara Island liveforever E (CA)
Santa Cruz Cypress E (CA)
Scrub blazingstar E (FL)
Scrub lupine E (FL)
Scrub mint E (FL)
Scrub plum E (FL)
Shale barren rock-cress E (VA, WV)
Short's goldenrod E (KY)
Siler pincushion cactus E (AZ, UT)
Slender rush-pea E (TX)
Slender-horned spineflower E (CA)
Slender-petaled mustard E (CA)
Small whorled pogonia E (New England, Mid-Atlantic, IL)
Small's milkpea E (FL)

Small-anthered bittercress E (NC)
Snakeroot E (FL)
Sneed pincushion cactus E (TX, NM)
Solano grass E (CA)
Spineless hedgehog cactus E (CO, UT)
Spreading avens E (NC, TN)
Spring-loving centaury T (CA, NV)
Steamboat buckwheat E (NV)
Swamp pink T (DE, GA, MD, NC, NJ, NY, SC, VA)
Tennessee purple coneflower E (TN)
Texas poppy-mallow E (TX)
Texas prairie dawn-flower E (TX)
Texas snowbells E (TX)
Texas wild-rice E (TX)
Tiny polygala E (FL)
Toad-flax cress E (UT)
Tobusch fishhook cactus E (TX)
Todsen's pennyroyal E (NM)
Truckee barberry E (CA)
Tumamoc globe-berry E (AZ)
Uhiuhi E (HI)
Uinta Basin hookless cactus T (CO, UT)
Virginia round-leaf birch E (VA)
Virginia spiraea T (GA, KY, NC, PA, TN, VA, WV)
Welsh's milkweed T (AZ, UT)
Western prairie fringed orchid T (Midwest)
White bladderpod E (TX)
White-haired goldenrod T (KY)
Wide-leaf warea E (FL)
Wireweed E (FL)
Wright fishhook cactus E (UT)

Index

A

Abyssal zone, ocean, 80
Acid rain
  causes of, 72–73
  defined, 72
  effects of, 73–74
Adaptation, law of, 18
Adiabatic rate, dry and wet rate, 65
Adopt-a-Horse (or Burro) Program, 228
Adsorption, solar energy, 45, 47
Aerial photography, 164
Agricultural management
  Agricultural Chemicals in Groundwater Strategy, 204
  alternative pest controls, 204
  and climate, 210–211
  Farm Bill provisions, 209–210
  farming without chemicals, 205–208
  Integrated Pest Management, 204–205
  for soil erosion, 201
  soil fertility factors, 211–213
Agricultural Stabilization and Conservation Service, 209
Agriculture, North American regions for, 200
Agroecosystem, defined, 204
Air and Rain: The Beginnings of a Chemical Climatology (Smith), 71
Air plant, 122
Air pollution, from incineration, 340
Alaskan current, 66
Albedo, of surface, 49
Albinos, 18
Alfisols, 98
Algae, 122
Alluvial deposits, 77
Alternative farming, 206
Aluminum, 315–316
American Trader, consequences of spill, 284
Anaerobic digestion plant, 341
An Essay on the Principle of Population as it Affects the Future Improvements of Society (Malthus), 362
Animals, cold-blooded and warm-blooded, 121. *See also* Wildlife; Wildlife management
Animal units, 221
Anoxic environment, 38
Apatite, 329
Aphotic zone, ocean, 80
Appalachian Mountains, 25
Aquaculture. *See* Fish farming

Aquatic environments, 68–87
　freshwater environments, 68, 69–77
　groundwater, 85–87
　saltwater environments, 68, 77–80, 83–85
Aquatic resource management
　lake management, 264–270
　legislation related to, 250–252
　pond management, 261–264
　states and fisheries management, 252
　stream management, 252–261
　waterfowl management, 270–275
Aquifers, 66
　largest, 85
　nature of, 85
　recharge zones of sole aquifers, 176
Arctic National Interest Conservation Act, 283
Arctic National Wildlife Refuge, 280, 283
Arctic zone, 123, 127
Area of encroachment, 127, 130
Argon, atmospheric, 47
Aridisols, 100
Arroyo, 225
Ash, toxins in, 340
Aspect, defined, 38, 127
Asthenosphere, 27
Atlantic Ocean, 29, 32
Atmosphere
　circulation of, 49–50
　composition of, 47
　and remote sensing, 168–171
Atmospheric circulation system, 33
Atmospheric pressure, standard, 47
Atomic energy, 12. *See also* Nuclear energy
Audubon Society, 189

B

Backslope, 38
Bacteria, 32
　nitrogen-fixing organisms, 116
　and soil, 102
Barbed wire, and grazing, 218
Barnes, Chaplin B., 375
Bass, 76, 253
Bathyal zone, ocean, 80
Bauxite, 315
Belt of no erosion, 38
Benthic zone, lakes, 71
Big sagebrush, 223
Bioaccumulation, 266
Bioclimactic, soil formation, 95
Biodiversity, 380–381
Biogeochemical weathering, types of, 95
Biogeography
　and climate, 119, 121–122
　of region, defined, 6
Biographic communities, types of, 117–118
Biologic productivity, plants, 130–131
Biologic time, 15–16
Biologic weathering, 95
Bioremediation, process of, 284
Biosphere
　carbon cycle, 114–115
　chemical composition of, 113–114
　defined, 18
　detrital cycle, 114

energy flow in, 112–113
laws of
　adaptation, 18
　control, 20–21
　fertility, 18, 20
　production, 18
　succession, 20
nitrogen cycle, 116–117
number of organisms of, 39
oxygen cycle, 115–116
and remote sensing, 172, 175
sedimentary cycle, 117
through geologic time, 38–39
Biotic pyramid, 16–18
Birth control, methods of, 366
Blowouts, 127
Bogs, 106
Bottomland hardwood forests, 106
Bryoids, plants, 122
Bureau of Land Management, 186, 220–221
Bureau of Reclamation, 250, 252, 274
Burros, feral, problem of, 227–229
Bush administration, environmental actions of, 11

C

Calcification, soil formation, 96–97
Calcium, 117
California condor, 235
California current, 66
Canadian Shield, 25
Canadian zone, 123
Canopy, forests, 121
Carbon
　atmospheric, 115
　storehouses of, 114
Carbon cycle, 114–115
Carbon dioxide
　atmospheric, 47, 114
　and greenhouse effect, 57–59
　and photosynthesis, 67
Carnivores, 112
Carp, 76
Carrying capacity, 18, 21
　factors in, 221
　North America, 364–366
Cars, solar automobile, 302
Carson, Rachel, 202, 203
Catfish, 76, 253
　farming, 263–264
Cement, 328
Cenozoic Era, 26
Channelization, stream management, 256
Chemical prospecting, 381
Chemical weathering
　rock, 27
　types of, 95
Chert, 38–39
Chlordane, 203
Chlorination, wastewater treatment, 347
Chlorine, 117
Chlorine components, and ozone, 59
Chloroflurocarbons
　alternatives to, 60–61
　and ozone depletion, 59–61
Chloroplasts, 130

Civilian Conservation Corps, 9
Clams, 80
Clay, 93
Clean Air Act, 10, 73, 177, 340
Clean air standards, 177
Clean Water Act, 251, 252, 270, 341
Clearcutting, forest management, 186
Climate
　as biogeographic control, 119, 121–122
　climactic extremes, 54–55
　climate change, 56–57
　defined, 50
　effects on wildlife, 232, 239
　and environment, 59
　greenhouse effect, 57–59
　Köppen system, 51–54
　ozone depletion, 59–61
　and vegetation, 112
Climax communities, 117–118
Climax vegetation, 20
Closed forests, 183
Coal, 287–291
　emissions from, 287
　end of reserves, 289
　as environmental hazard, 287, 289
　formation of, 287
　as nonrenewable resource, 12
　Surface Mining Control and Reclamation Act, 289, 291
　synfuel, 289
　types and heat values, 287
Coastal Zone Management Act, 10, 178
Coastlines, primary and secondary, 35
Coho salmon, 259
Cold-blooded animals, 121
Colloids, 65–66
Community, 17
　biographic communities, 117–118
　natural climax communities, 117–118
Compensation depth, lakes, 71
Concave-up longitudinal profile, of river, 76
Condensation nuclei, 117
Condor, California, 235
Conservation Compliance, 209
Conservation, historical view, 7–11
Conservation Reserve Program, 209, 210, 375
Conservation tillage program, 104, 201
Consolidated Metropolitan Statistical Area, 367
Consumers, 17
　environmental decisions by, 177
　primary and secondary, 112
Continental drift, 31–32
Continental shelves, 29
Control, law of, 20–21
Controlled burning, forest fires, 185
Copper, 320–321
Coral, 54
Coriolis effect, 49
Corrasion, 76
Corrosion, 76
Council on Environmental Quality, 177
Crabs, 80
Crown fires, forests, 185
Crude birth and death rates, 362

Index　425

D

Dams, advantages/disadvantages to, 268–269
Darwin, Charles, 15, 18
DDT, 203
Decomposers, 112, 114
Decreasers, 222
Deep ocean basins, 29
Deibler Dam, 253
Denitrification, nitrogen, 116
Density factors, rocks, 37
Department of Energy, 11, 306–307
Department of Interior, 11, 164
Desertification, 379
    and grazing, 225
Desert region, characteristics of, 152–153
Design With Nature (McHarg), 371
Detrital cycle, 114
Developing countries
    debts of, 380
    population, 366–367
Diatoms, 80
Diffuse reflection, solar energy, 45
Dimictic lakes, 69
Dinoflagellates, 80
Dioxin, 346
Disinfectants, 201
Dissolved oxygen, 253, 264
Dolostone, 114
Drainage basins, 252
Drinking water, groundwater, 85
Drought
    cycles of, 210–211
    effects of, 211
    of 1988, 210
    and resource management, 211
Dry-steam deposits, geothermal energy, 297
Duck Stamps, 273
Ducks Unlimited, 273

E

Earth, motors for geologic systems, 25
Earth Days, 382
Earth Observation Satellite Company, 164
Earthquakes, 39
Earth Resources Technology Satellite, 164
Earth-Watch, 376
Ecoregions (North American)
    desert region, 152–153
    hot continental region, 140–141
    marine region, 154–155
    mediterranean region, 156–157
    prairie region, 148–149
    steppe region, 150–151
    subarctic region, 144–145
    subtropical region, 138–139
    tropical region, 134–135
    tropical savanna region, 136–137
    tundra region, 146–147
    warm continental region, 142–143
Ecosystems, 17–18
Eelpouts, 32
Eiseley, Loren, 13

Elevation
    defined, 38
    measurement of, 37
Endangered species
    Endangered Species Act, 234–235, 236
    endangered species habitats, 176
    in the United States, 419
Endogenic processes, 25
    litologic circulation, 31–32
    sea level, 29–31
Energy management, 307–308
    future view, 307–308
    home heating choices, 307
Energy sources
    coal, 287–291
    fossil fuels, 278–286
    geothermal energy, 297–298
    hydropower, 305–306
    natural gas, 286–287
    nuclear energy, 291–297
    solar energy, 298–305
    wind power, 306–307
Entisols, 100
Environmental impact statement, 10, 279
Environmental monitoring, 176–177
Environmental movement, 5
Environmental problems
    acid rain, 72–74
    decline of wetlands, 107
    global warming, 57–59
    greenhouse effect, 57–59
    ocean dumping, 83, 85
    ozone depletion, 59–61
    resource depletion, 12
Environmental Protection Agency, 204
    role of, 177
    waste management strategies, 337–338
Environmental Quality Report, 177
Epilimnion, 69
Epiphytes, 122
EROS Data Center, 165
Erosion
    agents of, 33
    control in stream management, 254
    effects on landforms, 35
    soil, 102–104
Estuaries, 77, 80, 106
    organisms of, 80
Ethics
    defined, 381–382
    land ethics, 6
    philosophically and ecologically, 6
Eutrophic lakes, 71
Eutrophication, 117
Evaporation, water, 64–65
Evapotranspiration, water, 65–66
Even-aged management program, 186
Exogenic processes, 25
    circulation systems, 33
    continental glaciation, 35, 37
    and erosion, 33, 35
    topography, 37–38
Exxon Valdez, 11, 177, 283–284
    consequences of, 284

F

Family planning, 366–367
    aspects of, 366
Farm Bill, 375
    provisions of
        Conservation Compliance, 209
        Conservation Reserve Program, 209, 210
        funds for vegetative cover, 209–210
        1990 Farm Bill, 210
        Sodbuster provision, 209
        Swampbuster program, 209
Federal environment-related agencies, 11
Federal Food, Drug and Cosmetic Act, 201, 202
Federal Hazardous Substances Act, 343
Federal Insecticide, Fungicide, and Rodenticide Act, 201, 202, 343
Federal Water Pollution Control Act, 10
Feral horses and burros, problem of, 227–229
Fertility, law of, 18, 20, 66
Fertility rate, 364
Fertilizer and chemical minerals
    halite, 331
    nitrogen, 329
    phosphorus, 329
    potassium, 330
    sulfur, 333
Field data, for environmental monitoring, 176–177
50-year plans, U. S. Forest Service, 188–190
First law of thermodynamics, 113
Fish
    of lakes, 69
    of oceans, 83
Fish and Wildlife Coordination Act, 234
Fisheries, states protection of, 252
Fish farming, 263–264
    catfish farming, 263–264
    requirements of, 264
Fish stocking, 256, 258–259, 261, 263
Flood control
    goal of, 270
    and zone of no development, 268
Floodplain, 38
Fluoro-carbon-134a, 61
Flyways, 270
Food chain
    as energy flow system, 112–113
    organisms of, 112
Food Security Act, 178. *See also* Farm Bill
Footslope, 38
Forest and Rangeland Renewable Resources Planning Act, 219–220
Forest dieback, 74
Forest fires, 184–185
    controlled burning, 185
    statistical information, 184–185
    types of, 185
Forest lake sterility, 74
Forest management, 194–196. *See also* U. S. Forest Service, forest management
    components of, 194
    forest management cycle, 194–195
    and logging industry, 194
    timber stand improvement, 195

Forest Resource Management Act, 178
Forests
    and acid rain, 74
    canopy, 121
    closed forests, 183
    importance of, 181–182
    open forests, 183
    reforestation, 183
    size of North American forests, 182
    understory, 121–122
    wood products from, 183
Fossil fuels, 12, 278–286
    oil, 278–285
Freeze-thaw, 95
Freshwater environments, 68, 69–77
    acid-rain problem, 71–74
    impoundments, 68
    lakes, 69–74
    Missouri River, 74–77
    moving water systems, 68
    streams, 74
Frugivores, 231
Fuelwood, 183
Fungi, 122
Fungicides, 201
Furans, 340

G

Garbage, recycling, 13
Gas. *See* Natural gas
Genetic engineering, for pest control, 204
Geographic Information System, 172, 175–176
    applications for, 175–176
    defined, 175
Geologic hazards, 39
Geologic time, 13–15
    biosphere through, 38–39
Geothermal energy, 11, 297–298
    benefits and problems of, 298
    sources of, 297–298
Giant tube worms, 32
GIGO concept, 176
Glaciation, ages of, 35, 37
Gleization, soil formation, 98
Global heat balance latitude, 45
Global warming, greenhouse effect, 57–59
Gold, 322
Grasses, annual and perennial, 225
Gravel, 326–327
Gravel bars, 76
Grazing
    benefits of, 222
    and desertification, 225
    grazing vegetation, 222, 225
    legal control of, 220–221
    overgrazing, effects of, 221–222, 225
Great Lakes, 268–270
    monitoring of, 267
    polluted fish, 267
    toxic chemicals in, 266–267
    and zebra mussels, 267–268
Greenhouse effect, 57–59
    effects of, 57–59
    process of, 57
Ground cover, 122

Ground fires, forests, 185
Groundwater, 85–87
    aquifers, 85
    nature of, 85
Groundwater zone, 66, 69
Group selection, forest management, 186
Gulf Stream, 66

H

Haber process, 211
Habitats
    means of destruction of, 238
    requirements for wildlife, 231
Hadal zone, ocean, 80
Halite, 331
Halophytes, 121
Hard mast, 195
Hazardous waste
    characteristics of, 343
    definition, 342
    household hazardous waste, 343–345
    industrial waste, 345–347
    laws related to, 343
    management of, 342–345
Health effects, acid rain, 74
Heat, internal heat of earth, 25
Herbicides, 201
Herbs, 122
Hessler, Robert R., 32
Hibernation, 121
Hickel, Walter, 279
Histosols, 100
Holocene Epoch, 15, 37, 56, 118
Homestead Act, 218
Horizons, soil, 93–95
Horses, feral, problem of, 227–229
Hot continental region, characteristics of, 140–141
Household hazardous waste, 343–345
    guide for disposal of, 344
How Flowers Changed the World (Eiseley), 13
Hubble Space telescope, 175
Hudsonian zone, 123, 127
Human-altered environments, 118
Human waste
    recycling, 13
    sewage sludge, 83
Humphrey, Hubert, 185, 190
Humus, 93, 102
Hunting. *See also* Wildlife management
    market hunting, 238
    reduction in, 242
Hydroclimatic, soil formation, 95
Hydrologic circulation system, 33
Hydrologic cycle, 64–66
Hydrophytes, 121
Hydropower, 305–306
    advantages and disadvantages of, 306
    hydroelectric power generation, 270
    past uses of, 305
Hydrosphere
    composition of, 67–68
    and remote sensing, 171–172
Hygrophytes, 121
Hypolimnion, 69
Hyporheic zone, 77

I

Ice Ages, 37
Igneous intrusive rocks, 26, 27
Igneous rock, 25
Ilmenite, 317
Impoundments, 68
Inceptisols, 100–101
Incineration, air pollution from, 340
Increasers, 222, 223
Individual tree selection, forest management, 186
Industrial waste management, 345–347
    Resource Conservation and Recovery Act, 345, 346–347
    site selection for dumping, 175–176
    Superfund, 345–346
Inexhaustible resources, types of, 11–12
Infrared scanners, 164
Injection mining, 331, 333
Insecticides, 201
Insectivores, 231
Integrated Pest Management, 204–205
Interior and Atlantic Coastal plains, 26
Interior Highlands, 25
Interpretation service, national parks, 193
Invaders, 222, 223
Invertization, soil formation, 98
Iron, 117, 314–315
Irrigation
    problems related to, 104, 106
    soil, 104–106

J

Juvenile water, 32

K

Kennedy, John F., 9
Koch, Edward, 83
Köppen system, climate classification, 51–54

L

Labrador current, 66
Lake Erie, 266, 267–268
Lake management, 264–270. *See also* Great Lakes
    control of water pollution, 270
    flood control, 270
    goals of, 266
    hydroelectric power generation, 270
    multiple-use philosophy, 269–270
    recreational management, 270
    and U.S. Army Corps of Engineers, 268–270
Lakes, 69–74, 106
    and acid rain, 74
    classification of, 69, 71
    lake zones, 71
    layers of, 69
    nature of, 69
Lake Superior, 266
Laminar water flow, 74
Land degradation, 225
Land ethics, 376
    nature of, 6–7
    requirements of, 382

Landfills, 83, 341–342
    and leachate, 341
        safeguards to environment, 341–342
        sites of, 341
Landsat program, 164–166
Land use controls, 374–376
Land Use Ethic, scope of, 375–376
Large Format Camera, 172
Latent heat, 49
Lateral erosion, 76
Laterization, soil formation, 96
Leachate, and landfills, 341
Lead, 321
Leopold, Aldo, 6, 16, 270, 381, 382
Lichens, 122
Life expectancy, 364
Life span, 364
Light water reactors, 291–292
Limestone, 114
Limnetic zone, lakes, 71
Liquid natural gas, 287
Lithologic circulation system, 27
Lithosphere
    composition of, 26–27
    defined, 26
    endogenic processes, 27–33
    exogenic processes, 33–38
    lithologic circulation system, 27, 31–32
    lithology, 27
    and remote sensing, 166
Littoral zone
    lakes, 71
    ocean, 80
Lobsters, 80
Lower Austral zone, 123, 127
Low-input farming, 206
Loxahatchee National Wildlife Refuge, 172
Lutz, Richard A., 32

M

McHarg, Ian, 371
Macronutrients, types of, 117
Magma, 25
Magnesium, 117, 316–317
Malthusian view, population, 362
Man, and land ethics, 6
Manganese, 317–318
Marine Protection, Research, and Sanctuaries Act, 83
Marine region, characteristics of, 154–155
Market hunting, and wild turkey population, 238
Marshes, 106
Mather, Stephen, 8, 193
Mediterranean region, characteristics of, 156–157
Mega Borg, 284
    and bioremediation, 284
Megalopolis, 368
Mesozoic Era, 26, 39
Mesquite, 223
Metallic minerals, recycling, 13
Metamorphic rocks, 27
Micrometer, 164

Migratory Bird Conservation Act, 234
Migratory Bird Hunting Stamp Act, 234
Migratory Bird Treaty Act, 232
Migratory birds, legal protection, 232, 234
Mineral Leasing Act, 279, 280
Minerals
    abundant metals, 312
    aluminum, 315–316
    boom-and-bust cycles of mineral industry, 313–314
    copper, 320–321
    defined, 311
    gold, 322
    investigative methods for exploration, 312
    iron, 314–315
    lead, 321
    magnesium, 316–317
    manganese, 317–318
    nickel, 321
    platinoids, 323
    scarce metals, 318–323
    silver, 322–323
    titanium, 317
    zinc, 321
Minerals management. *See also* Fertilizer and chemical minerals; Nonmetallic minerals
    new strategies for industry, 323–324
    underground mining, 324
Mining
    injection mining, 331, 333
    underground mining, 324
Missouri River, 74–77
    natural profile of, 76–77
Mollisols, 100
Monomictic lakes, 69
Montreal Protocol, 61
Mount St. Helens, 170–171
    environmental consequences of, 32–33
Mudflats, 106
Multiple-use philosophy, U.S. Army Corps of Engineers, 269–270
Multiple Use-Sustained Yield Act, 185
Multispectral scanners, 164
Muskellunge, 69

N

Nanometer, 164
National Aeronautics and Space Administration, 164
National Bison Range, 232
National Environmental Policy Act, 5, 10, 11
National Forest Management Act, 185, 188
National Oceanic and Atmospheric Administration, 165
National Park Service, 186, 190
    creation of, 192
National Park Service Director, first, 8
National parks, 192–194
    crowding problem, 193–194
    historical view, 192
    interpretation service, 193
    management of, 192, 193
    of North America, 193
National Space Council, 165

National Wildlife Refuge system, 232
Natural gas, 286–287
    end of reserves, 286
    formation of, 286–287
    home heating choice, 307
    as nonrenewable resource, 12
    transportation of, 287
    unconventional sources of, 287
Natural resource management
    forest management, 194–196
    national parks, 192–194
    planning process in, 177–178
    public and private decisions, 177
    questions in planning for, 177–178
    technology of
        environmental monitoring, 176–177
        Geographic Information System (GIS), 175–176
        remote sensing, 164–175
    U.S. Forest Service, forest management, 185–190
    wilderness preservation, 190–191
Natural resources
    defined, 11
    inexhaustible resources, 11–12
    nonrenewable resources, 12
    potential resources, 12
    renewable resources, 12
Neihardt, John G., 74
Nematicides, 201
Nene goose, 235
Neritic zone, ocean, 80, 83
Nickel, 321
Nitrogen
    artificial nitrogen, 211
    atmospheric, 47, 116
    denitrification, 116
    as mineral, 329
    nitrogen-fixing organisms, 116
    soil fertility, 211
Nitrogen cycle, 116–117
Nitrogen oxides, 73
Nonmetallic minerals
    cement, 328
    plaster, 328
    sand and gravel, 326–327
    stone, 325–326
Nonrenewable resources, 277
    types of, 12
Noodling, 252
North America
    ecoregions of, 131–157
    natural biotic regions, 118–119
    physiographic regions of, 25–26
    zonation of vegetation, 123–130
North Atlantic Drift, 66
Northeast trade winds, 50
North Equatorial Current, 66
North Slope Alaskan Oil Field, 279–281
No-till agricultural system, 104, 201
Nuclear energy, 291–297
    light water reactors, 291–292
    and Price-Anderson Act, 291
    Shippingport Nuclear Reactor, 295–297
    waste disposal, 292–295
Nuclear Waste Policy, 293

O

Ocean dumping
  nuclear waste, 295
  of waste, 83, 85
Oceans, 80–83
  basis for life in, 32
  currents, types of, 66–67
  oceanic circulation system, 33
  organisms of, 80, 83
  zones of, 80
Ogallala aquifer, 85, 104, 106
Oil, 278–285
  Arctic National Wildlife Refuge, 283
  crude oil, 279
  end of reserves, 279
  formation of, 279
  as nonrenewable resource, 12
  North American reserves, 279
  North Slope Alaskan Oil Field, 279–281
Oil-eating bacteria, 284
Oil spills
  American Trader, 284
  Exxon Valdez, 283–284
  Mega Borg, 284
Oligotrophic lakes, 69
Omnivores, 112
100-year floodplains, 176
Open forests, 183
Organic enrichment, soil zone, 95
Organic farming, 205–206
  seven-year grain rotation, 205–206
  terms for, 206
  yields from, 205
Organic matter, soil fertility, 211
Our Margin of Life (Poirot), 211
Overgrazing problem, rangeland, 221–222, 225
Overturn, lakes, 69
Oxford Energy Incinerator, 340
Oxidation, 95, 96
Oxisols, 100
Oxygen
  atmospheric, 47, 114
  oxygen cycle, 115–116
  oxygenation of atmosphere over time, 38–39
  and photosynthesis, 115–116
Oysters, 80
Ozone, atmospheric, 59
Ozone depletion, 59–61
  and chloroflurocarbons, 59–61
  effects of, 60

P

Pacific Coastal ranges, 26
Pacific Ocean, 29, 32
Paleomicrobiota, 38
Paleozoic Era, 25
Paper, recycling, 352
Pelagic plankton, 80
Pelagic zone, ocean, 80
Pelican Island, 232
Permafrost, 54, 97, 176

Pesticide management
  Agricultural Chemicals in Groundwater Strategy, 204
  alternatives to, 204
  farming without chemicals, 205–206
  Integrated Pest Management, 204–205
  laws related to use, 201–202, 204
Pesticides
  defined, 201
  effects of, 203
  types of, 201
PET program, 353
Phosphorus, 117, 329
  soil fertility, 211, 213
Photic zone, ocean, 80
Photons, 130
Photoperiod, 130
Photosynthesis, 16–17, 39
  biogeography, defined, 112
  and carbon dioxide, 67
  formula for process of, 111
  and oxygen, 115–116
  and phytoplankton, 67–68, 131
  process of, 130
Photovoltaic cells, 299, 302
Phreatophytes, 121
Physical weathering, rock, 27
Physiographic regions, 25
Phytoplankton
  and carbon cycle, 115
  and photosynthesis, 67–68, 131
Pike, 69
Pinchot, Gifford, 8, 185
Pitman-Robertson Act. *See also* Wildlife Restoration Act
Plane of the ecliptic, 44
Plankton
  of lakes, 69
  of ocean, 80
Plants
  biologic productivity, 130–131
  bryoids, 122
  classification by water needs, 121
  epiphytes, 122
  layers in forests, 121–122
  thallophytes, 122
  zonation of vegetation, 123–130
Plaster, 328
Plastic, recycling, 352–353
Plate tectonics, defined, 29, 31
Platinoids, 323
Pleistocene Epoch, 35, 37
Plow zone, soil, 95
Podzolization, soil formation, 96
Poirot, Gene, 211
Polar easterlies, 50
Polar front jet, 50
Polyvinyl chloride containers, recycling of, 352–353
Pond management, 261–264
  fish farming, creation of, 263–264
  and multiple-use of pond, 262–263
  pond-building program, 261
  stocking of pond, 263
Pools, and stream management, 253

Population
  birth control, 366
  carrying capacity, 364–366
  community, 17
  crude birth and death rates, 362
  developing countries, 366–367
  dynamics of, 362, 364
  family planning, 366–367
  fertility rate, 364
  life expectancy, 364
  Malthusian view, 362
  size and carrying capacity, 21
  urbanization of, 367–376
  zero population growth, 362
Potassium, 117, 330
  soil fertility, 213
Potential evapotranspiration, 54
Potential natural vegetation, 118
Potential resources
  recyclable resources as, 13
  types of, 12
Potholes, 106
Prairie region, characteristics of, 148–149
Prairie States Forest Project, 8
Precambrian Era, 26
Price-Anderson Act, 291
Producers, 17, 112
Production, law of, 18
Profundal zone, lakes, 71
Prudhoe Bay oil deposit, 279, 283
Put-and-take trout fishing, 258
Pyrethrin, pest control, 204

Q

Quaternary, 37

R

Radiation balance, 44
Radioactive decay, 25
Radio-echo-sounding, 171
Rain forest depletion, 379
Rangeland. *See also* Grazing
  biogeography of, 222–225
  defined, 215
  historical view, 217–221
  overgrazing problem, 221–222, 225
  public lands, use of, 218–219
Rangeland management
  aspects of, 226–227
  and Bureau of Land Management, 220–221
  Forest and Rangeland Renewable Resources Planning Act, 219–220
  Taylor Grazing Act, 220–221
  Wild Horse and Burro Act, 227–229
Rare and Endangered Species Act, 11
Reagan administration, negative environmental impacts, 10–11
Real vegetation, 118
Recharge zones of sole aquifers, 176
Recycling, 338, 351–353
  paper, 352
  PET program, 353
  phases of, 353
  plastic, 352–353

problems related to, 351
recyclable materials, 13, 351–352
Reforestation, 183
rain forest, 379
Refuse Act. *See also* Rivers and Harbors Act
Remote sensing, 164–175
and atmosphere, 168–171
and biosphere, 172, 175
defined, 164
future of, 172, 175
and hydrosphere, 171–172
Landsat program, 164–166
land use/land cover classification system, 172
and lithosphere, 166
process of, 164
watershed inventory, 252–253
Renewable resources, types of, 12
Resource Conservation and Recovery Act, 10, 337, 345, 346–347
rules of, 346–347
Respiration, defined, 112
Revolution, of earth, 44
Rhizobium bacteria, 116
Riffles, and stream management, 253
Ring-necked pheasant management, 244–245
Riprap, 253
Rises, 29
River and I, The (Neihardt), 74
Rivers and Harbors Act, 250, 266, 268
Road-building program, U.S. Forest Service, 189–190
Rocks
density factors, 37
metamorphic rocks, 27
sedimentary rocks, 27
silicate rocks, 26–27
weathering of, 27
Rodenticides, 201
Roosevelt, Franklin D., 8
Roosevelt, Theodore, 8, 185, 232
Root expansion, 95
Rotation of earth, 44
Roundwood, 183
Ruchelaus, William D., 376

Safe Drinking Water Act, 204, 251
Safe failure, plan for, 177
Sagebrush, 223
Sageland Rebels, 221
Salinization, and calcification, 97
Salmon, coho salmon, 259
Saltwater environments, 68, 77–80, 83–85
estuaries, 77, 80
ocean basins, 80–83
Sand, 326–327
Sand County Almanac (Leopold), 270
Sand dunes, 127
Sandstone, 66
Satellite Solar Power Stations, 302
Sawnwood, 183
Scattering, solar energy, 45
Sea-floor spreading zone, 29, 31

Sea level, 29–31
effects of changes, 29–31
elevation, 37
formation of, 29
Second law of thermodynamics, 113
Sedimentary cycle, 117
Sedimentary rocks, 27
Seed tree cutting, forest management, 186
Sensible heat, 49
Seven-year grain rotation, 205–206
Sewage sludge, 83
Shale, 66
Shelterwood cutting, forest management, 186
Shippingport Nuclear Reactor, 295–297
Shrubs, defined, 122
Sierra Club, 189
Silent Spring (Carson), 202–203
Silicate rocks, 26–27
Silver, 322–323
Slope, 29
defined, 38
Sludge
as fertilizer, 83, 85
nature of, 83
as resource, 350
Smith, Robert Angus, 71
Sodbuster provision, Farm Bill, 209
Sodium, 117
Soil: The Miracle We Take For Granted (Steinhart), 91
Soil
classification of, 98–101
conservation practices, 104
defined, 93
erosion, 102–104
erosion prevention programs, 201
formation of, 27, 95–98
calcification, 96–97
gleization, 98
invertization, 98
laterization, 96
podzolization, 96
functions of organisms in, 102
horizons, 93–95
irrigation, 104–106
soil biota, 101–102
wetlands, 106–107
Soil Conservation Service, 8–9, 38, 375
Soil fertility
importance of, 211
nitrogen, 211
organic matter, 211
phosphorus, 211, 213
potassium, 213
Soil sediment, and stream pollution, 252
Soil water zone, 69
Solar constant, 44
Solar energy, 11, 298–305
future view, 305
greatest potential for use, 298
photovoltaic cells, 299, 302
Satellite Solar Power Stations, 302
solar automobile, 302

Solution, 95
Source reduction, 338–340
implementation of, 339–340
stages of, 339
Southeast trade winds, 50
Species, 18
Spermivores, 231
Spodosols, 98
Sports equipment, tax on manufacture of, 234
SPOT images, 172
Spotted owl, 235
Springs, 85
Standard Metropolitan Statistical Area, 367
Steel, 314
Steinhart, Peter, 91
Steppe region, characteristics of, 150–151
Sterilization of animals, 246
Stone, 325–326
Stream management, 252–261
channelization, 256
erosion control, 254
fish stocking, 256, 258–259, 261
habitat improvement, 253–254
and species of fish, 253
watershed inventory, 252–253
Streams, 74
rate of flow, 74
soil sediment as pollution, 252
Stromatolites, 38
Subarctic region, characteristics of, 144–145
Sublittoral zone, ocean, 80
Subtropical high pressure belt, 49
Subtropical jet, 50
Subtropical region, characteristics of, 138–139
Succession, Law of, 20
primary and secondary, 20
Sulfur, 117
as mineral, 333
Sulfur dioxide, 73
Summit of hill, 38
Sun, 25
energy of, 44–47
and photosynthesis, 130
radiation and surface of earth, 49
Sunless ecosystems, 32
Superfund, 345–346
characteristics of program, 345–346
Surface fires, forests, 185
Surface Mining Control and Reclamation Act, 289, 291
Sustainability, 376–381
defined, 376
and environmental laws, 376–377
global view, 378–381
and government policy, 376
and production, 379
program for future, 379–380
requirements for North America, 377
Sustained yield, 186
Swampbuster program, 209
Synfuel, 289

T

Taylor Grazing Act, 220–221
Tennessee Valley Authority, 9, 250, 252
Thallophytes, 122
Thematic mapper, 164, 165
Thermal expansion, 95
Thermal regulator, water as, 64
Thermocline, 69
Thermodynamics, first and second laws of, 113
Thompson, Francis, 15
Timber stand improvement, 195
Time
    biologic time, 15–16
    future time, 16
    geologic time, 13–15
Times Beach, Missouri, 348
Titanium, 317
Toeslope, 38
Topography
    and acid rain, 74
    aspects of, 37–38
Toxic Substances Control Act, 10
Trans-Alaska Pipeline System, 280–281
    environmental concerns, 280–281
Transition zone, 123
Tree line, 54
Trees, defined, 122
Trenches, 29
Trenching zone, 32
Tropical life zone, 123
Tropical region, characteristics of, 134–135
Tropical savanna region, characteristics of, 136–137
Tropophytes, 121
Trout, 69, 76, 253
    brown trout, 259, 261
    increasing population of, 258–259
    put-and-take trout fishing, 258
Tundra region, 97
    characteristics of, 146–147
Turbulent water flow, 74

U

Udall, Stewart, 9
Ultisols, 98, 100
Understory, forests, 121–122
Uneven-aged management program, 186, 188
United Nations Environment Program, 225, 376, 380
Upper Austral zone, 123, 127
Urbanization, 367–376
    classification of city as urban area, 367–368
    land use controls, 374–376
    megalopolis as, 368
    urban growth, 369–370
    urban planning, 371–374
    Urban Stress Test, 370–371
    zoning, 374
U.S. Army Corps of Engineers, 250, 252, 274, 380
    dam building, 268
    multiple-use philosophy, 269–270
U.S.–Canadian Joint Commission, 267
U.S. Census Bureau, 367
U.S. Fish and Wildlife Service, 172, 273
U.S. Forest Service, 8
    forest management, 185–190
        even-aged management program, 186
        50-year plans, 188–190
        road-building program, 189–190
        sustained yield, 186
        uneven-aged management program, 186, 188

V

Vegetation
    real vegetation, 118
    zonation of, 123–130
Vertisols, 100
Vibert Box, 258–259
Volcanism, 25

W

Walleye pike, 259
Warm-blooded animals, 121
Warm continental region, characteristics of, 142–143
Waste disposal
    environmentally sensitive areas, 176
    industrial waste site selection, 175–176
    nuclear waste, 292–295
    and ocean dumping, 83, 85
    sludge, 83, 85
Waste management
    hazardous waste management, 342–345
    industrial waste management, 345–347
    landfills, 341–342
    recycling, 351–353
    source reduction, 338–340
    waste-to-energy plants, 340–341
    wastewater treatment, 347–350
Waste-to-energy plants, 340–341
    anaerobic digestion plant, 341
    Oxford Energy Incinerator, 340
    problems of incineration, 341
Wastewater treatment, 347–350
    aspects of treatment facility, 347
    chlorination, 347
    sludge, as resource, 350
Water
    aquatic environments, 68–87
    evaporation, 64–65
    evapotranspiration, 65–66
    forms of, 63–64
    hydrologic cycle, 64–66
    and law of fertility, 66
    soil water zone, 66
    as thermal regulator, 64
Waterfowl
    migration of, 270
    observations of, 270–272
Waterfowl management, 270–275
    and duck stamps, 273
    and loss of habitat, 272–273
    nesting site development, 274–275
    preservation of habitat, 273–274
Water pollution, and nitrogen, 117
Water Pollution Control Act, 250, 250–251
Water power, 11
Water Quality Act, 250, 347
Water Quality Improvement Act, 250
Watershed, defined, 252
Watershed management. *See* Stream management
Water table, 66
Weather, defined, 50
Weather radar, 168
Weather satellites, 170
Weathering
    biogeochemical weathering, 95
    biologic weathering, 95
    chemical weathering, 95
    of rock, 27
Wells, 85
Westerlies, 50
Wetlands, 106–107, 176
    decline of, 107
    Swampbuster program, 209
    types of, 106
Wet-steam deposits, geothermal energy, 297–298
White Amur, control of aquatic vegetation, 259
White-tailed deer management, 242–244
Whooping crane recovery team, 236, 238
Wild Horse and Burro Act, 227–229
Wild and Scenic Rivers Act, 193, 266
Wild turkey restoration program, 238–242
Wilderness
    defined, 191
    designated areas, 191
Wilderness Act, 9, 266
Wilderness preservation, 190–191
    bill for, 190
    goal of, 191
Wilderness Society, 189, 190
Wildlife
    and climatic extremes, 232
    food preferences, 231
    habitat requirements, 231
Wildlife management
    history of, 232
    legal efforts, 232–235
    migratory bird protection, 234
    protection of endangered species, 234–235
    ring-necked pheasant management, 244–245
    sterilization of animals, 246
    white-tailed deer management, 242–244
    whooping crane recovery team, 236, 238
    wild turkey restoration program, 238–242
Wildlife Restoration Act, 234
Wilson, Edward D., 380

Wind
- importance of wind systems, 50
- nature of, 50
- types of wind systems, 50

Wind power, 11, 306–307
- disadvantages of, 307
- experimental windmill, 307
- past uses of, 306

Windows, 164, 176
Windthrow, 186
Wisconsian period, 35, 37, 119
- influences of, 56

Wood products, of forests, 183
WorldWatch Institute, 377–378
Worst-case scenario, plan for, 177

X

Xerophytes, 121

Y

Yellowstone Park, 8, 192
- forest fires, 185

Yucca Mountains, radioactive waste, 293–294

Z

Zahniser, Howard, 190
Zebra mussels, 267–268
Zero population growth, 362
Zero Population Growth organization, 370
Zinc, 321
Zone of aeration, 66
Zonation of vegetation, 123–130
Zoning, 374